THE SHADOW OF GOD AND THE HIDDEN IMAM

Publications of the Center for Middle Eastern Studies
Number 17
Richard L. Chambers, General Editor

1. Beginnings of Modernization in the Middle East: The Nineteenth Century
   Edited by William R. Polk and Richard L. Chambers
2. The Mosque in Early Ottoman Architecture
   By Aptullah Kuran
3. Economic Development and Regional Cooperation: Kuwait
   By Ragaei El Mallakh
4. Studies in the Social History of Modern Egypt
   By Gabriel Baer
5. Conflicts and Tensions in Islamic Jurisprudence
   By Noel J. Coulson
6. The Modern Arabic Literary Language
   By Jaroslav Stetkevych
7. Iran: Economic Development under Dualistic Conditions
   By Jahangir Amuzegar and M. Ali Fekrat
8. The Economic History of Iran, 1800–1914
   By Charles Issawi
9. The Sense of Unity: The Sufi Tradition in Persian Architecture
   By Nader Ardalan and Laleh Bakhtiar
10. The Forgotten Frontier: A History of the Sixteenth-Century Ibero-African Frontier
    By Andrew C. Hess
11. Muslim National Communism in the Soviet Union:
    A Revolutionary Strategy for the Colonial World
    By Alexandre A. Bennigsen and S. Enders Wimbush
12. Karim Khan Zand: A History of Iran, 1747–1779
    By John R. Perry
13. The Economic History of Turkey, 1800–1914
    By Charles Issawi
14. Tribe and State in Bahrain
    By Fuad I. Khuri
15. Islam and Modernity
    Transformation of an Intellectual Tradition
    By Fazlur Rahman
16. Wisdom of Royal Glory (Kutadgu Bilig):
    A Turko–Islamic Mirror for Princes by Yūsuf Khāṣṣ Ḥājib
    Translated with an Introduction and Notes, by Robert Dankoff
17. The Shadow of God and the Hidden Imam:
    Religion, Political Order, and Societal Change in Shiʿite Iran from the Beginning to 1890
    By Said Amir Arjomand

SAID AMIR ARJOMAND

The Shadow of God and the Hidden Imam

Religion, Political Order, and Societal Change in Shiᶜite Iran from the Beginning to 1890

The University of Chicago Press
Chicago and London

The University of Chicago Press, Chicago 60637
The University of Chicago Press, Ltd., London

Paperback edition 1987
Printed in the United States of America

96 95 94 93 92 91 90 89 88 87   5 4 3 2

LIBRARY OF CONGRESS CATALOGING IN PUBLICATION DATA

Arjomand, Said Amir.
The shadow of God and the hidden imam.

(Publications of the Center for Middle Eastern Studies: no. 17)
Bibliography: p.
Includes index.
1. Iran—Politics and government. 2. Shī ah—Iran—History. 3. Islam and politics—Iran. I. Title. II. Series.
DS292.A75 1984   955   83-27196
ISBN 0-226-02782-1 (cloth)
ISBN 0-226-02784-8 (paper)

To the Happy Few

The declaration of Shiʿism as the state religion of Iran in 1501. The caption reads: "On Friday, the exalted king went to the congregational mosque of Tabriz and ordered its preacher, who was one of the Shiʿite dignitaries, to mount the pulpit. The king himself proceeded to the front of the pulpit, unsheathed the sword of the Lord of Time, may peace be upon him, and stood there like the shining sun."

From the *History of Shāh Ismāʿīl*, British Library MS. Or 3248 (*Ross Anonymous*), fol. 74a. Photograph courtesy of the British Library.

Contents

Acknowledgments

The original version of the present work was defended as a doctoral thesis at the University of Chicago in August 1978, that is, before the Shadow of God on Earth as the King of Kings took flight from Iran and disappeared, and the Hidden Imam all but reappeared in the form of an omnipotent deputy, the Sovereign Jurist. It is most fortunate that the bulk of the research had been undertaken and completed before the onset of the Islamic revolution. This has meant, I hope, that the work is unaffected by the type of present-oriented and anachronistic interpretation of the development of Shiʿism that mars most of the publications on Shiʿite Islam and politics appearing since the revolution.

In the intervening years, a research grant from the Joint Committee on the Middle East of the Social Science Research Council and the American Council of Learned Societies in 1979–80 and a Visiting Fellowship to St. Antony's College, Oxford, in 1981–82, offered me the necessary leisure and opportunity to carry out two extensive revisions, and to incorporate new materials.

Of the teachers, colleagues, and friends who have given me kind and invaluable intellectual guidance and scholarly advice in connection with this book, I am especially grateful to Professor Edward Shils, and to Professors Joseph Ben-David, Morris Janowitz, Donald Levine, Fazlur Rahman, John Woods, and Marvin Zonis of the University of Chicago, Professor Wilfred Madelung of Oxford University, Professor Ernest Gellner of the London School of Economics, and Dr. Husayn Modarresi Tabatabaʾi of the Hawza-ye ʿIlmiyya of Qum. I am also indebted to Professors ʿAbdulhusayn Zarrinkoob and Ismaʿil Rizvani of the University of Tehran for drawing my attention to important sources. Many thanks are due to Kathryn Arjomand for inspiring me to write chapters 1 and 3 and for her editorial help with the entire manuscript. Needless to say, errors and shortcomings are entirely mine.

Finally, I am most grateful to the editors of the *Archives européennes de sociologie* and of the *Journal of Asian History* for their kind permission to use materials previously published in the following articles:

"Religion, Political Action and Legitimate Domination in Shiʿite Iran: 14th to 18th Centuries A.D.," *Archives européennes de sociologie* 20 (1979): 59–109.

"The Shiʿite Hierocracy and the State in Pre-Modern Iran: 1785–1890," *Archives européennes de sociologie* 22 (1981): 40–78.

"Religious Extremism (*Ghuluww*), Sufism and Sunnism in Safavid Iran: 1501–1722," *Journal of Asian History* 15 (1981): 1–35.

S. A. A.

General Introduction

I.1 An Interpretive Perspective on Religion, Politics, and Societal Change

The purpose of this study is twofold. Drawing on the sociology of Max Weber, it purports to offer a new interpretive perspective for the analysis of the role of religion in political action and societal change in premodern societies. At the same time, it aims at a comprehensive examination of the Safavid and early Qājār sources pertaining to the establishment and consolidation of Shiʿite Islam as the state religion of Iran. It is conceived both as a foray into neglected areas of sociological enquiry and an attempt to throw light on a most important era in Iran's social and cultural history.

Contemporary views on social change are overwhelmingly influenced by two phenomena: the industrial revolution and the impact of the West on non-Western forms of social and political organization. Important as these phenomena undoubtedly are in world history, they do not by any means exhaust the variety of societal change amenable to sociological analysis. As my subject matter, I have deliberately chosen a different type of societal change, one in which religion acts as the primary motive force and which focuses on political action and political organization. The historical period under consideration is accordingly circumscribed so as to exclude the complicating intermingling of the consequences of industrialization and of Western-inspired modernization of the state.

The analytical framework of the present study derives from Max Weber's fundamental precepts on the formative role of world religions in societal transformation, my basic premise being that Twelver Shiʿism, as a branch of Islam, can be fruitfully considered a "world religion" as conceptualized by Weber—that is, as an autonomous intellectual pattern or belief system, which is embodied in meaningful social action and enfolded in sentiments.

Beyond the adoption of Weber's sociological conceptualization of world religions, a considerable number of Weberian concepts have been employed in this study. These fall into two groups: basic sociological concepts that classify varieties of social action, social groups, and organizational forms; and the epistemologically more ambitious typologies of cultural orientations and historical forms of sociopolitical organization. It should become apparent that the primary utility of the second group of concepts consists in their suggestiveness: they have enabled me to pose and answer crucial questions, and to uncover important interconnections. It is true that their application has inevitably exacted a price—namely, the omission of details enriching the specificity of concrete historical and sociocultural phenomena under consideration. However, the price exacted has, in my judgment, been minimal. On the other hand, the pregnant suggestiveness of Weberian concepts—as opposed to rigid extensional implications of those pertaining to alternative theoretical systems—has enabled me to avoid many of the pitfalls of "grand theorizing" in the social sciences.

The absence of grand theorizing will in no way imply lack of methodological consistency—that is, of systematic application of sociological method based on interpretive understanding. It may be noted at the outset that the systematic integration of this study's subject matter within a consistent framework called for an extension of Weber's interpretive sociological analysis to areas neglected by Weber himself. As is well known, Weber regarded the understanding of "meaningful social action" as the basic task of the social sciences. From this point of view, of his four types of social action, "instrumentally rational" and "value-rational" action are meaningful and therefore are said to lend themselves readily to understanding. "Affectual" and "traditional" action, on the other hand, are considered to be on the borderline of meaningful social action and are by implication opaque and obdurate subjects for interpretive sociology.[1] This assessment follows from the overly individualistic bias of Weber's sociology. Since his time, historical ethnography and social anthropology have demonstrated the utility of understanding meaningful symbolic products of the collective mind which provide normative governance for much traditional action and for recurrent patterns of affectual action. We shall later have occasion to examine the (meaningful) normative order governing unconsciously or half-consciously pursued traditional action and habitually held traditional attitudes in the political sphere. We shall also examine the lasting moods and dispositions induced by the Shiᶜite theodicy of suffering through recurrent affectual action. At this point, however, a more general observation on the type of social change under consideration seems in order.

Weber contrasts charisma and reason or rationalism as the most fundamental forces of social change, emphasizing the particular importance of charisma as the revolutionary force in traditional periods.[2] The history of the replacement of Sunnism by Shiᶜism in Iran and its consequences supports this view. However, it also suggests the theoretical necessity of closer attention than that paid by Weber to the belief systems conducive to the emergence of charismatic authority. Furthermore, it confronts us with a type of process of "rationalization" different from that associated with the evolution of the modern forms of economic, social, and political organization.[3] In Weberian terms, social change, when consisting in industrialization and bureaucratization, increases the preeminence of instrumentally rational action in social life. The process of rationalization set in motion by the imposition of a new belief system is different. It consists in value rationalization and entails the gradual modification of the pattern of traditional and affectual action in the light of new norms and values. As will become evident presently, the phrase "value-rationalization," though deceptively simple, denotes a complex social process that profoundly affects the social structure and the political order. This process of value rationalization offers us a good opportunity to apply interpretive normative and cultural analysis to the interaction—to clashes, adoptions, compromises, and an eventual synthesis—between two normative orders, the one emanating from a prophetic world religion, the other from the cosmology predating it. We shall use this opportunity, first, to apply the interpretive method to the political implications of the preworld-religion cosmologies that were by and large neglected by Weber.[4] Second—and this is much more central—we shall apply the interpretive sociological method to illuminate societal change in traditional societies. Our story begins and ends in a society where the importance of the traditional type of social action remains unaltered despite the considerable transformation of the social and political order. It would be absurd to abdicate the task of arriving at a sociological understanding of the process involved. This would be so even if the recent Islamic revolution had not, almost a century after our period, demonstrated the continued vitality of the Shiᶜite tradition and its political relevance in the modern world.

I.1.1 Religion, Sociopolitical Action, and Social Change

According to the conception we have adopted, the world image and ethos of Shiᶜism as a world religion constitute a *source of motivation* to social action. They constitute a source of motivation in that they shape the believers' attitudes, and in that they differentially affect the believers' propensities to action in various spheres of life. What is at issue is the positive or negative evaluation of different types of social action. This evaluation is implied in the world image and ethos of a religion, *by omission as much as by commission*, in the differential relevance of various social pursuits to salvation as the foremost religious goal. In other words, the differential soteriological significance of different types of social action, or their respective relevance to service to God in theistic religions, amounts to their respective religious evaluation. This religious evaluation, ranging from sacralization to radical devaluation, in turn affects the believers' propensities to engage in them. In this manner, a world religion can induce or inhibit propensities to different kinds of activity. Thus, according to Weber, otherworldly and mystical religiosity tend to induce a negative valuation of economic activity and lessen the propensity of the believer to engage in it. Protestantism, by contrast, through the investment of economic activity with soteriological significance and the consequent sacralization of the usually profane economic sphere, results in the intensification of men's propensity to economic action. Political activity is analogously susceptible to religious influence, and one may expect attitudes in the political sphere and propensities to political action to be similarly affected by religious beliefs. Thus, through the motivation implied in its world image, a world religion affects political attitudes and political action.

The world image and ethos of a world religion rest on a doctrine, consisting of explicit beliefs, which include ethical rules purporting to direct the action of the believer along prescribed paths. Again—and this time entirely by commission—*through the application of its ethics* as embodied in the concrete provisions of the sacred law, a world religion can be expected to have an impact on social action and on institutional norms, and, as such, to constitute a potential force in societal dynamics. In his substantive work, Weber's attention was largely devoted to the "economic ethics" of world religions and to their bearing on social action. But, as Troeltsch's classic study eloquently demonstrates,[5] world religions can also contain "political ethics" whose analogous bearing on social action and on attitudes toward the political order can be subjected to sociological analysis.

In fact, the choice of Shi^cism as the world religion to be studied here shifts the nexus of significant interrelationships from the economic to the political sphere. While the establishment of Shiᶜism in Iran was not found to have any demonstrable effect on economic action and on the transformation of the economy, it did have a notable impact on political action, and did, in the course of time, significantly transform Iran's polity. We are therefore obliged to turn to the religious motivation of *political* action and to "*political* ethics," topics that were by and large neglected by Weber. This entails an examination of those specific elements of the Shiᶜite sacred law which can be classified as its political ethics, as well as of the effect of the Shiᶜite religious beliefs on the ethics of kingly patrimonialism that prevailed in Iran prior to the advent of Shiᶜism.

World religions as autonomous belief systems can be expected to impinge not only on social action but also on the social *structure*. What concerns us here is the relation between religious norms and the principles of social and political organization. In this relation, the drive for consistency between the former and the latter constitutes a potential "rationalizing" force that can be activated under favorable conditions. In this impersonal process, constrained if not fully determined by the logical structures of the religious doctrine and of the rival traditional belief systems, men, as bearers of distinct ideas around which vested interests are or can become clustered, enter into relations with one another that are largely independent of their will. The sociological dimension of the process of rationalization is all important. "Not ideas," declares Weber in a well-known though not entirely unambiguous passage, "but material and ideal interests, directly govern men's conduct. Yet very frequently the 'world-images' that have been created by 'ideas' have, like switchmen, determined the tracks along which action has been pushed by the dynamics of interest."[6]

Our task here is to investigate how, amid their interplay with men's pursuit of material interests and their struggle for power, the normative ideals of Shiᶜism as embodied in its life-regulating belief system came to act as switchmen and to determine the tracks into which political action was directed. In this connection, the incompatibilities between the inherited institutions and religious norms, and the necessarily imperfect translation of religious ideas and beliefs into concrete institutional arrangements, emerge as important factors in the dynamics of social change.

As regards the political sphere, the institutional pattern of the relations of authority, or the societal structure of domination, may be changed under the impact of religious norms, an impact that is transmitted through the principles of legitimacy of various types of authority and the determination of their respective scopes. In particular, one would expect this kind of impact in the case of Twelver Shiᶜism, whose doctrines were fully systematized by the time of its importation from the Arab lands into Iran by the Safavids (1501–1722). This expectation is borne out by historical evidence regarding the impact of Shiᶜism on the norms governing the legitimacy of the component parts of the traditional societal structure of domination in Iran.

I.1.2 Kingship, Religion, and the Legitimacy of the Societal Structure of Domination

Among human institutions, sacral kingship is both older and more universal than the world religions of salvation. It is often the cornerstone of ancient cosmologies of world order. The prescriptive implications of these cosmologies amount to powerful political ethics which the later world religions have invariably confronted but rarely, if ever, totally subjugated to a religious ethic of ultimate salvational ends.

Troeltsch was fully appreciative of the significance of the confrontation between Christianity and the imperial state and its political ethos. By contrast, Weber's treatment of the relation between religion and kingly authority ignores the normative foundation of kingship.[7]

In the chapters of *Economy and Society* dealing with the institutionalization of charisma—though not in his systematic formulations—Weber mentions two fundamental sources of charismatic authority: the charisma of the divinely inspired and the charisma of the warlord.[8] In institutionalized forms, too, religious (hieratic) and political (temporal) charisma appear as equally fundamental, in the sense that one cannot be reduced to the other. This is reflected in Weber's parallel definition of "ruling organization" and "hierocratic organization" (or, when compulsory, "state" and "church"),[9] and in his parallel treatment of political and hierocratic domination. And it is this dichotomy of the ultimate sources of legitimacy that underlies Weber's rough schema for typifying the varying role of religion in the charismatic legitimation of domination, namely, theocracy, hierocracy, and caesaropapism.[10] This tripartite typology is informed by the notion of the relative preponderance of one of the two autonomously charismatic types of domination: the religious or the political.

The autonomous legitimacy of the prince derives from political charisma, engendered by the possession and exercise of power: "ultimately every charisma is akin to religious powers in that it claims at least some remnant of supernatural derivation; in one way or another, legitimate political power therefore always claims the 'grace of God.'"[11] But this is not going far enough. We must bear in mind that the earthly ruler's claim to the grace of God is normatively rationalized by theories of kingship and cosmic order. These invoke principles of legitimacy that are not only independent of religious doctrine but in fact predate the advent of the world religions of salvation.

The fact that, quintessentially, power engenders charisma and that the continuous effective exercise of power is self-legitimatory in no way implies the absence of a normative order or the analytical redundancy of such an order. In Soghdian, the Middle Iranian dialect of the northeast, we encounter a highly significant term for king that bears precisely on the above-mentioned fact. The term is $x^{v}t'^{v}$, which is $x^{v}at\bar{a}^{v}$ representing an ancient $x^{v}a\text{-}t\bar{a}^{v}\text{-}(ya)$ (he who is powerful by himself, who holds power only from himself). The term is the exact counterpart of the Greek *autokratōr*. What is even more remarkable is that $x^{v}t'^{v}$ passes into Middle Persian, where it assumes the form of *khudā*, which in modern Persian means God, thus conceived as the holder of absolute sovereignty.[12] These primeval concepts, while encapsulating the potential of power in the generation of charisma, are also of great normative potency and generate normative order which lives on independently of individual warlords and heroes. In fact, once such an order is generated, the war hero as *autokratōr* has to be fitted into a cosmic order and thus tends to cede its primacy to the idea of king as the imitation of the universe and the source of law. As Hocart shows, the cardinal attributes of kingship render not one but two prototypes: the law king and the executive or war king.[13] The latter may well be the repository of Weber's heroic charisma, but it is primarily the former who is endowed with sacrality as a pillar of the cosmic order. To use the imagery of sun and moon, which is found in frequent respective association with these prototypes, as a rule the moon king is destined to be overshadowed by the sun king as the moon receives its light from the sun.[14]

After the advent of Islam, the ruler could no longer be a god but before long assumed the exalted title of the Shadow of God on Earth. Much of the political ethos of sacral kingship was retained. Nevertheless, political power was fairly drastically desacralized, making room for the emergence of religious or hierocratic authority deriving directly from the transcendent God. What is crucial to note here is that the normative considerations pertaining to the interaction between the two world images and their implications play a major role in the mutual articulation within the polity of political and hierocratic or clerical authority, and in determining the extent of differentiation or partial overlap of their respective scopes.

It is true that Weber's political sociology begins with a discussion of legitimacy, and that his famous three types of domination—charismatic, traditional, and rational-legal—are characterized not only by their administrative organization but also by the nature of the beliefs or principles legitimating them. Nevertheless, Weber's exposition of the types of domination is too formalistic, and his attention to the normative content of these principles of legitimacy too cursory, especially as regards the traditional type of domination. In other words, Weber does not specify the variable normative content of the grounds of legitimation of authority in traditional polities despite his recognition of the importance of this normative content.

Writing of the crucial significance of the "ultimate grounds of the validity of a domination" as a determinant of its organizational structure, Weber remarks: "For a domination, . . . [the] justification of its legitimacy is much more than a matter of theoretical or philosophical speculation; *it rather constitutes the basis of very real differences in the empirical structure of domination*."[15]

Weber then comes close to the discussion of specific norms that legitimate domination, such as what he describes as the myths of highly privileged groups, but quickly backs off and reverts to the formalism characteristic of his typology of domination. When Weber does pay attention to the content of the principles of legitimacy of domination, as in his discussion of feudal legitimation,[16] he is able to deduce consequences for the concrete structure of domination. More specifically, the content of the principles of legitimacy of domination in the form of the rules of fealty and subinfeudation had consequences that were not deducible from Weber's characterization of that type of domination—i.e., "traditional." Weber wrongly equates the "ultimate grounds" of validity with "ultimate principles" and arrives at the above-mentioned three types of domination which are said to correspond to "these possible types of legitimation."[17] But types of legitimation are not categories of the same order as the "ultimate grounds" of validity of a domination, the former being analytical categories of the sociologist, the latter, ideas in the minds of the people, the historical actors. As a result of this confusion, despite his acknowledgment of the consequences of (specific) justification of legitimacy indicated in the passage cited above, and contrary to the tenets of his interpretive sociology, Weber has little to say about the normative content of the principles underlying legitimate domination in his political sociology.

In our analysis of the historical development of Shi^cism in Iran, we shall attempt to assess the impingement of the principles of legitimacy of political and hierocratic authority upon the "empirical structure of domination" over the course of some three centuries. The assumption will be that the institutions inherited from the past as well as the necessarily imperfect institutionalization of beliefs and norms in social arrangements and social organization can constitute a source of tension which, under suitable conditions, may set in motion a trend in the direction of *greater congruence* between cultural logic and historically contingent institutional arrangements. As a result of both shifts in the balance of social and institutional power, and of propitious historical contingencies, normative principles can be shown to impinge upon various components of the societal structure of domination and bring them into congruence with the cultural logic of Shi^cism.

This progressive impingement, tending to modify the "empirical structure of domination" in the direction of increasing congruence with the Shi^cite doctrine, may be viewed as a process of "rationalization" of the societal structure of domination. It will be seen, in fact, to have constituted a major force in societal dynamics. But to analyze this process of rationalization, we need to go beyond Weber's own analysis of legitimacy, along the lines indicated above, and to pay close attention to the *principles* in accordance with which the relations of domination were rationalized. This requires the extension of the framework of Weberian political sociology in accordance with the basic methodological precepts of his interpretive sociology.

In Weber's substantive analysis of political charisma, too, the normative foundations of kingship are by and large ignored. This introduces an inadvertent reductionism to aggravate Weber's individualistic methodological bias. Kingly charisma is derived from the heroic charisma of the warlord and normative considerations are bypassed. In one passage, the institution of kingship is merely presented as the routinization of the charisma of the warlord into the *charisma of office* of the king. It is seen as a solution to the problem of succession by ritual transmission of charisma through coronation, supplemented, in dynastic cases, by the *hereditary charisma* of kingship inhering in the successor.[18] This analysis is sociologically richer than Montesquieu's picture of Oriental despotism, sustained only by fear, in *The Spirit of Laws*, or Wittfogel's model of total power and total fear in *Oriental Despotism*.[19] Nevertheless, it is equally deficient in interpretive understanding of the normative order that endows kingship with its charisma and authority. Since Weber, a considerable amount of ethnological and historical work on the normative foundations of kingship has been produced. This body of work provides us with a guideline for correcting the deficiency of Weber's analysis of political charisma and domination.

The omission of interpretive understanding of the norms operative in the political sphere, among other factors, precludes any substantive analysis of the intricate situations in which the simultaneous prevalence of distinct sets of principles of legitimacy could produce a plurality of normative orders bearing on domination. This possibility, which Weber concedes only in the abstract,[20] is brought to the foreground by our subject matter. As has been pointed out, confrontation and some eventual form of compromise between sacral kingship and the world religions of salvation is typical. It is therefore not surprising that our consideration of the grounds of legitimacy of "traditional" domination in Shiᶜite Iran reveals the coexistence, at times uneasy, of two distinct sets of principles of legitimacy of authority. It thus reveals a composite—a dual—normative order whose components are of different provenience (the one from the Shiᶜite religion, the other from the pre-Islamic ethos of patrimonialism) and which possess different structural properties.

I.1.3 Law, Ethics, and Legitimate Political Order

For sociology, interpretive or otherwise, empirical uniformities in social action and social relations constitute the indispensable starting point. When these empirical uniformities can be accounted for in terms of the orientation of the actors toward determinable norms or maxims, one may speak of the prevalence of an "order." Insofar as social action is normatively governed by the terms of the order in question, one may speak of its "validity" from the viewpoint of sociology. As we shall see in the next section, in this sociological sense, the validity of the order may result from the belief in its legitimacy but may equally result from custom, self-interest, sheer expediency, or coercion. Thus, as Weber points out, "for sociological purposes there does not exist, as there does for the law, a rigid alternative between the validity and lack of validity of a given order."[21] A system of order may thus be upheld by a variety of subjective motives and external sanctions. In this perspective, law, convention, and ethics form a continuum of categories of order. Thus,

> the relations of law, convention and "ethics" do not constitute a problem for sociology. From a sociological point of view an "ethical" standard is one to which men attribute a certain type of value and which, by virtue of this belief, they treat as a valid norm governing their action.[22]

In view of our concern with the extension of the interpretive method in sociology, let us focus on the relevance of law and ethics to the relationship between traditional and value-rational action. Weber defines traditional action as "determined by ingrained habituation."[23] However, he is aware that "the transition from the merely unreflective formation of a habit to the conscious acceptance of the maxim that action should be in accordance with a norm is always fluid."[24] Furthermore, he explains that "whenever the regularities of action have become conventionalized, i.e., whenever a statistically frequent action has become a consensually oriented action . . . we shall speak of 'tradition.'"[25] It should be pointed out that the transition from regularities of action resting on unreflective habit to consensually oriented action involving the understanding and following of a norm corresponds exactly to the transition from traditional to value-rational action. (In this context, one is speaking of analytical or logical transition and not usually of any transition in the chronological sense.) One may conceive of a value-rational act corresponding to many a habitual and unconsciously performed act in traditional as well as in modern societies. In such cases the actors engaged in traditional action could be said to behave *as if* they were engaged in value-rational action, and their action would thus be normatively governed from the sociological point of view. Therefore norms governing both types of action may be arrived at through the interpretive analysis of the systems of legal and ethical order. It may be added that systems of legal and ethical order are therefore of utmost importance for the understanding of rule-governed value-rational and traditional action. But they are not the only cultural sources available to the observer. Poetry and literature, too, can on occasion encapsulate norms that are of sociological significance insofar as they may reveal ends toward which social action is directed.

For comparative and historical sociology, it would be as unprofitable to equate law with the legislation of the modern nation state as it would be misleading to speak of the absence of law in the manner of the writers on Oriental despotism. In the modern situation, "constitutional theory" can be said to contain norms of legitimacy of the political order. In the premodern situation, the total body of the ruler's edicts and reglementation, which can be justifiably regarded as "public law,"[26] omits the discussion of the norms of legitimacy or rather takes them for granted. For very different and complicated reasons to be discussed below,[27] the sacred law of Islam, having developed as the "personal law" of the adherents of various rites (singular *madhhab*) rather than a law of the land (*lex terrae*), is overwhelmingly concerned with the minute articulation of private law. Although, as we shall see, Shiʿite sacred law does contain a few important provisions on the relations with the ruler, these do not add up to systematic public law and are interspersed in sections on various ethical duties of the believers in the legal handbooks. It is therefore to the works on ethics that we must turn as our most important source for the systematic description of the legitimate political order, the rights and duties of ruler and subject, and other norms of political behavior. It may be noted that these tracts on social and political ethics are often written by the jurists themselves, who must be presumed to have considered them the more appropriate medium for the discussion of political matters than the manuals of applied religious jurisprudence.

I.1.4 Religion, Legitimation of Political Domination, and Political Attitudes

In addition to his tripartite typology of domination, the analytical section at the beginning of *Economy and Society* also contains Weber's discussion of the "bases of legitimacy,"[28] which deals with the motivation to uphold the normative order bearing on legitimate domination. In it Weber points out that the principles of legitimacy of an order—i.e., the system of ideas and norms that presents an order as legitimate—should be distinguished from the motives of individuals and groups for upholding that order. In addition to the belief in the legitimacy of an order—the acceptance of its principles of legitimacy—an order may be upheld in specific instances because of habit, self-interest, expediency, or coercion. This distinction between normative principles and the motives for upholding them has two merits. It enables us to accommodate the possibility of both habitual and utilitarian motivation for upholding normative principles. Furthermore, by reminding us that normative ideals may be upheld for a variety of reasons, it alerts us to the fact that norms are not only often honored in breach but can also be perpetuated by being hypocritically held for personal and utilitarian motives. In doing so, the distinction points to an important factor making for the autonomy of the normative principle legitimating an order, and thus strengthens the argument in section I.1.2 above for considering the drive for consistency to be an important factor in the process of rationalization of the autonomous body of norms bearing on the legitimacy of the political order.

In his substantive work, however, Weber does not carry the analysis of the motivation to comply with authority very far. Our subject matter requires that we do so. To this end, we could find a guideline in Weber's sociology of religion, or, more specifically, in his analysis of religious motivation of social action. When considering the influence of the Shiʿite religion on political attitudes, we could focus on three types of religious beliefs: beliefs affecting the motivation to comply with authority; those affecting the propensity to political action in opposition to the established structure of domination and aiming at the abrogation of the normative order legitimating it; and, finally, those inducing political indifference and withdrawal from political activity.

What was said about the attempt here to extend Weber's analysis of traditional domination to include the normative content of its principles of legitimacy also applies to the attempt to amplify Weber's analysis of the motivation to submit to established authority, or, conversely, to refuse to uphold the prevalent normative order. Here, too, Weber's paradigmatic analysis needs to be elaborated in accordance with the basic premises of his "interpretive" sociology, which he best observed in his sociology of religion.

As factors accounting for the upholding or rejection of a legitimate order, habit, self-interest, expediency, utilitarian motivation, and, to a lesser extent, coercion have continuous random incidence among individuals and groups, which is hard for the investigator to trace. The task of tracing the effectiveness of the motivation to uphold an order—i.e., the assessment of its validity—is helped greatly by the existence of three forms of intellectual and social institutionalization. Stated more simply, the cultivation of widespread belief in legitimacy of political domination depends, to a large extent, on (1) the availability of political and ethical theories expounding the norms of legitimacy and (2) their propagation and continuous reinforcement through ritual statement and ceremonial and symbolic reiteration. Last but not least, the validity of a legitimate political order depends on (3) the consolidation of an organization with vested interest in the enforcement of these norms by spiritual and coercive sanctions. The first factor directs our attention to the role of theorists and their juristic, social, and ethical writings; the second to the role of the legitimators, the extent of their subservience to the ruler or conversely the extent of their independence and organizational assets, which might enable them to exact a price for their legitimatory service; and the third factor to the vested interest of the state in maintaining a convenient legitimate order and its ability to secure compliance with authority by nonnormative means, be they economic or coercive.

I.1.5 Social Organization of Religion

What has been said above applies equally to the factors underlying the motivation to uphold religion as a normative order. In addition to genuine belief in its truth, the profession of religion may rest on habit, self-interest, expediency, or coercion. Similarly, the cultivation of widespread belief in the truth of a religion depends on the availability of religious ideas and doctrines, and their propagation and continuous reinforcement through practice and ritual. Above all, the emergence and consolidation of an institution with vested interest in the enforcement of religious beliefs and norms by spiritual and coercive sanctions—i.e., the emergence of a hierocracy—greatly enhances the sociological validity of the religious order in question.

World religions institute a system of authority which, in principle, is derived from God. The desacralization of kingship entailed by the world religions of salvation assures the theoretical autonomy of religious—or, when organized, hierocratic—authority from the earthly powers. Furthermore, as the exponents of the foremost goal of life, the holders of religious authority can in principle claim to determine the ideals and norms governing all spheres of life, including the political. In practice, however, their ability to enforce such a claim and to engage effectively in social action in pursuit of religious norms and ideals depends crucially on the institutionalization and social organization of religious authority.

In this context, we have an opportunity to explore the comparative possibilities with regard to Troeltsch's valuable but exclusively Christian-oriented trichotomy of church, sect, and mysticism. Troeltsch's trichotomous typology may be accepted as the most economical conceptual tool for capturing the range of variance in sociological and organizational implications of the Christian religion—or, from our point of view, its implications for the structure of religious authority. However, its potential for *direct* application to the case of Shiᶜite Islam is strictly limited. The "Church" as the living extension of Incarnation and the mystical body of Christ is too specifically Christian to be useful in comparative sociology. I have therefore adopted the weaker and doctrinally more neutral term "hierocracy."[29] "Sect," too, as the "second classic form of the social doctrine of Christianity,"[30] is conceived and characterized by Troeltsch in exclusively Christian terms and cannot be borrowed as such. Nevertheless, "sect" in its broader general sense is a most useful term for referring to Shiᶜism before the sixteenth century. From the eighth century (the second century of Islam) onwards, the Imāmī Shiᶜites were organized as a sect, in the usual sense of the word, and came to consider themselves as constituting the *dār al-īmān* (realm of faith) within the Islamic body politic. Shiᶜism assumed specific "sectarian" features that, as we shall see, contrast with the Shiᶜite "orthodoxy" as it emerged after the establishment of Shiᶜism as the state religion by the Safavids. Finally, Troeltsch's third type, "mysticism," with its implication of minimal social institution of religious authority, finds an interesting parallel in "gnostic Shiᶜism" (*ᶜirfān*), which constituted a significant mode of religiosity in seventeenth-century Iran.

On the other hand, the *idea* of the normative governance of the social organization of religious authority, which underlies Troeltsch's typology, is most suggestive. Norms of authority in religion contain crucial implications for religious ranking and sociopolitical stratification within the community of believers, and thus can have a profound impact on the societal structure of domination. Shiᶜism contains several norms of authority—all ultimately deducible from the theory of imamate (infallible leadership of the community of believers)—which have the potential for such an impact. As we shall see in detail below, the Akhbārī (Traditionalist) conception of imamate, which was dominant before the eleventh/fifth century and was revived in the seventeenth/eleventh century, was hostile to all extension of the authority of the Imams after the concealment of the Twelfth Imam in the ninth/third century, and conceded de facto religious authority only to the compilers of their traditions (*akhbār*). Indirectly, however, it enhanced the stratification of the Shiᶜite community into ordinary believers and the *sayyids*, descendants of the Prophet, who could claim to partake of the charisma of the Imams through descent. As we shall see, their charisma of descent from the Prophet and the Imams thus became a source of legitimacy for their privileges under the Safavids, and enhanced their sociopolitical domination. The Akhbārī orientation thus encouraged the fusion of religious and political domination and militated against the consolidation of differentiated religious authority.

A second historically important norm of authority in Shiʿism is the mahdistic tenet—the belief in the return of the Twelfth Imam as the Mahdi at the end of time. This chiliastic norm of authority, when successfully activated by a claimant to mahdihood—as it was in the fifteenth and nineteenth centuries—immediately instituted a charismatic structure of domination in which religious and political authority were fused in the person of the supreme leader.

Last and most important, we have the Shiʿite norm of the juristic authority of the specialists in religious learning. In contradistinction to the two previous norms, the juristic principle enhances differentiated religious authority and creates a basis on which hierocratic authority can be accommodated into the societal structure of domination alongside political authority and independently of it. As we shall see, this last norm of religious authority emerges with the rise of the Shiʿite science of jurisprudence (*Uṣūl al-fiqh*) in the eleventh century and assumes its final form in the division of the Shiʿite community into *mujtahid* (jurist) and *muqallid* (follower) in the nineteenth century.

The normative principles of authority mentioned above cannot be fruitfully examined in isolation from the social groups or organizations that constitute their bearers. This is especially the case with respect to the juristic principle of religiopolitical authority. The full development of this principle of legitimate religious authority spans over eight centuries and its final triumph over mahdism and Akhbarism goes hand in hand with the final consolidation of an autonomous hierocracy as the unrivaled guardian of Shiʿism in the nineteenth century. The evolution of the normative principles of religious authority should therefore be viewed in the context of the interests of their bearers and the latter's sociopolitical power and organizational autonomy and strength in relation to the champions of alternative norms. In this connection, the extent of the social cohesion and professional organization of men of religion assumes crucial significance.

In the sectarian phase, the Shiʿite *ʿulamāʾ* (theologians and jurists) were a distinct social group but did not constitute a recognized institution, a hierocracy. Any attempt to find an appropriate sociological term to describe them meets with difficulty. If "sodality," suggested by Roth and Wittich, were not such an uncommon term, it would be appropriate, standing both for Weber's *Einverständnisgemeinschaft* (translated as "consensual status group") as regards the social aspect, and for his *Rechtsgenossenschaft* (legally privileged sodality) in its politico-legal aspect.[31] However, it is an awkward term, and we shall make do with the *ʿulamāʾ* itself.

The Safavid period marks the transition of the Shiʿite *ʿulamāʾ* from a privileged sodality to a hierocracy.[32] A decree by the Safavid ruler Ṭahmāsp in the second quarter of the sixteenth century considers the *ʿulamāʾ* a crucially important consensual status group and *Rechtsgenossenschaft*, and entrusts the eminent Shiʿite theologician al-Karakī with its hierocratic organization.[33] As we shall see, a century and a half was needed before a hierocracy of religious professionals distinguished itself from the *sayyids* and the representatives of "gnostic" Shiᶜism and firmly consolidated its exclusive religious authority.

Once a world religion creates a hierocratic component in the societal structure of domination, religion inevitably becomes a factor in the dynamics of the polity. It is then necessary to examine the relationship between political domination and religion *qua* religion, i.e., irrespective of doctrinal content and outlook, and merely as the basis of domination. This implies that, even when the political sphere is considered amoral and devoid of soteriological significance, religion is still inevitably involved in politics. However otherworldly a religion, religious dignitaries are still drawn into political processes because of their institutional power and institutional interests. The nature of this involvement is determined by factors that are largely extraneous to the religious dogma: notably, the structure and organizational character of the religious institution and of the state, and the constellation of political and hierocratic power. In other words, one must inevitably deal with the "church-state problem" or its equivalent.

1.1.6 Social and Political Determinants of Religious Evolution

As might be expected, the organizational characteristics of both the charismatic leadership of the Mahdis and of the hierocratic authority of the Shiᶜite doctors have been among the crucial factors determining the impact of religion on the political sphere. The Safavid Empire was established by the military feat of a claimant to mahdihood in the early years of the sixteenth century, and the emergence of an independent Shiᶜite hierocracy constituted the precondition for the momentous impact of Shiᶜism on Iran's premodern polity in the early nineteenth century.

On the other hand, it goes without saying that religion is not the only factor in societal change, and that religious beliefs are not the sole determinants of social action. It follows that the impact of religious norms on political organization are to be put in the total context of the mutually interpenetrating religious and sociopolitical forces. Furthermore, religious developments themselves are affected by their social and political environment. The extent and nature of the impingement of its social and political environment on religion is closely related to the social organization of religion. Broadly speaking, in the absence of a hierocracy with a monopoly on spiritual sanction and access to the means of coercion through the state, the development of religious ethics is likely to bear the imprint of the interests, life-style, and elective affinities of the lay adherents to the creed. When a hierocracy representing the religion of the state comes into being, the political interests of the state first and foremost in the domestication of the masses, and second in the legitimation of political power, have important consequences for the evolution of religious beliefs and practices.

In order to take the influence of the social factors upon religion into account systematically, an analytical framework consistent with the conceptual considerations raised in the sections above is needed. Such a framework has been constructed in light of a reconsideration of Weber's basic conception of a world religion as a system of life regulation with the help of a set of subsidiary analytical concepts dealing with the relationship between religion and politics. Before I describe this framework, however, one remaining crucial property of the world religions of salvation needs to be examined.

I.1.7 World-embracing and World-rejecting Tendencies in Religion

Weber's substantive work in interpretive sociology begins with an analysis of the impact of religion on social action in the case of Protestantism. It is true that from this very beginning he was aware of the tension between religion and this-worldly action. But *The Protestant Ethic and the Spirit of Capitalism* was concerned with a case in which the resolution of the tension between religion and "the world" resulted in the intensification of this-worldly action aiming at the mastery over the world and thus at its transformation. Later, in *Economy and Society*, alongside with "inner-worldly asceticism" characteristic of the Puritans, Weber contrasts the ideal-types of "world-rejecting asceticism" and "world-fleeing mysticism"[34] as the other salient modes of religious orientation toward the world and social action. With the extension of his interest to other major world religions, Weber's attention was increasingly directed to instances where the tension between religion and "the world" could *not* be resolved and would result in *withdrawal* from certain spheres of life and in aversion to certain types of social action. The majority of the instances of tension between religion and the world mentioned in *Economy and Society*[35] are in fact of this latter type, which inhibits varieties of this-worldly social action rather than stimulating them or bringing them within the reach of religiously based normative governance.

However, it was only in one of his last articles that Weber came to address the issue systematically.[36] What is of great theoretical significance in this article is Weber's change of emphasis. Rather than focusing on the differences between "world-rejecting asceticism" and "world-fleeing mysticism" as contrasting ideal types, Weber considers them as instances of the "religious rejections of the world" whose varying directions are determined by the corresponding type of religious *rationalism*.[37] The novelty of emphasis, in contrast to Weber's analysis of the regulative influence of "economic ethics" and sacred laws of the world religions on social action is brought into sharp relief at the outset with Weber's declaration of intent to clarify the "motives from which religious *ethics* of world abnegation have originated, and the directions they have taken."[38] Weber was thus finally turning to a major concern presaged in the following statement in *Economy and Society*: "The more a religion of salvation has been systematized in the direction of an ethic of ultimate ends [*Gesinnungsethik*], the greater becomes its tension in relation to the world."[39]

The focus of the article is on the tension created by the inevitable incompatibilities between the rationalization of life in view of the attainment of salvation as the ultimate religious end, and the instrumental and formal rationalization of social action in the light of economic, political, aesthetic, and other interests. This tension between religious rationalism and social action in other spheres of life can ultimately lead to the total rejection of the world, as in the Indian religions of salvation, but can also produce various "compromises" and result in varying degrees of indifference to action in other spheres of life. The tension of the religious ethic of ultimate ends in relation to the world thus generates a spectrum of positions ranging from various forms of compromise with the logic of economic and political activity to the complete withdrawal from the economic and political spheres and radical economic and political indifferentism.[40]

The implications of Weber's position are more momentous than they may appear at the first sight. The tenor of much of Weber's substantive work on the major religions of the world had underscored the importance of the religiously motivated sociopolitical transformations, and of the ethical regulation of economic and political action. In "Religious Rejections of the World," by contrast, he highlights the self-limiting potential of the world religions—and, it should be emphasized, of *all* the world religions—for inhibiting the impact of religious beliefs, especially ethical beliefs, on social action and societal transformation. This implication is not only left implicit and unexplored, but is actually obscured by Weber's method of applying his ideal-types of religious orientation such as "asceticism" and "mysticism" to entire religious traditions rather than to modes to be found, albeit with varying salience, within each of them. On various occasions, Weber himself seems to be aware of the problem and feel uneasy about it. In the essay under discussion, for instance, Weber concedes the possibility that the "contemplative mystic" too, "like the inner-worldly ascetic, [may] remain in the orders of the world (inner-worldly mysticism),"[41] but without drawing out the implications of this concession. Nor can one recall any instances of explicit application of "inner-worldly mysticism" to which Weber apparently does not find a world religion to correspond in its entirety.

Rather than follow Weber in classifying the world religions in their entirety as "world-rejecting" (e.g., Buddhism) and "this-worldly" (e.g., Islam),[42] it seems much more fruitful to consider the world-rejecting *and* world-embracing tendencies within each religion systematically. This, after all, was the procedure followed by Troeltsch as regards Christianity, and more narrowly, by Niebuhr as regards Protestantism.[43] With respect to the "world-rejecting" religions, Weber himself had noted the this-worldly political ethic of Hinduism for the Ksatriya caste,[44] while Tambiah, adopting a Weberian perspective, has dealt with the world-embracing aspects of the most otherworldly of religions, Buddhism, with regard to the political order.[45] Only by considering the world-rejecting alongside the world-embracing tendencies within a world religion can we understand, without prejudice, not only the extent of the religious motivation and ethical regulation of sociopolitical action but also the degree of religious inhibition of social action: the inhibition of commitment to nonreligious sociopolitical action generally, and the inhibition of the tendency to "rationalize" sociopolitical action in terms of nonreligious values in particular. More concretely, while Weber's characterization of Islam as "this-worldly" provisionally leads us to expect some impingement of Shiᶜite Islam on political action and political organization, we shall at the same time remain alert to the factor of Shiᶜite ethical value rationalism that fosters world-rejecting tendencies and thus militates against such impingement.

I.1.8 Political Action and Religion

The social and political consequences of the world-rejecting tendencies in a religion are, as a rule, fairly clear. They lead to a sharp differentiation of the religious and the secular sphere of life and make for their mutual independence, accompanied by religious indifference to nonreligious social action. The consequences of the world-embracing tendencies of a religion are more ambiguous. They comprise two sets of contrary and entangled components, the first reflecting the impact of religion on the world, the second the impact of the world on religion. Here, therefore, what is needed is an analytical schema for determining, without prejudice, the respective contribution of the requirements of the religious doctrine and the exigencies and pressures of worldly social action to the shaping of the final "compromises," which are embodied in the officially sanctioned normative regulation of social and political life.

As regards the ethical and social teachings of Shiᶜism during the period under consideration, our analysis of religious orientation to the political sphere seems unproblematic. When and to the extent that the world-rejecting tendencies in Shiᶜism have the upper hand, we may expect a negative valuation of the political sphere, and indifference to politics, to be reflected in the religious literature. This results in the maximum mutual independence of the religious and the political spheres. When and to the extent that the world-embracing tendencies of Shiᶜism prevail, we encounter two ideal-typical situations: (1) where the ethical tenets of the Shiᶜite doctrine have a political content that impinges upon practice—and here one is considering the influence of religion in the political sphere —and (2) where the Shiᶜite ethical tenets are modified or extended under the pressure of political interests and political practice—and here one may speak of the impingement of politics upon the religious sphere.

At the level of action, the same basic assumptions may be used to disentangle the respective contribution of religious and political factors, but a more elaborate analytical schema is needed. I propose the following: to take the impingement of religion upon the political sphere into account, when religion influences political attitudes and political action, I shall speak either of (a) *politically relevant religious attitude or action*, referring to the group of attitudes and actions that are primarily oriented to religious ends but which have political consequences, or of (b) *religiously conditioned political attitude or action*, referring to the group of attitudes and actions that are primarily oriented to political ends but which are influenced by religious dispositions or take religious factors into account.

Similarly, to allow for the impingement of politics upon the religious sphere, when politics influence religion, I shall conceive of two types of action: (c) *religiously relevant political action*, that is, action that is primarily oriented to political ends but which has consequences for religion, and (d) *politically conditioned religious action*, that is, action that is primarily oriented to religious ends but which is influenced by political interests or takes political factors into account.[46]

Finally, there is the possibility of virtual *disjunction* of the religious and the political spheres. When religion does not impinge upon the political sphere, I shall simply speak of (e) *political action*, unaffected by any qualifying religious influence. Conversely, when politics does not impinge upon the religious sphere, we are dealing with (f) *religious action* independent of political factors. Political action will mean politically motivated action, that is, action motivated by the desire to acquire or consolidate (religious, political, economic) power. Religious action will mean religiously motivated action, that is, action motivated by religious beliefs. It should be clear that types e and f represent the extremes of our continuum, and that our interest chiefly lies in the types a, b, c, and d, which indicate the variety of overlap between the religious and the political spheres. Furthermore, it should be evident that the relationship between the hierocracy and the state constitutes the matrix within which the most important instances of politically and religiously relevant and politically and religiously conditioned action occur.

We may now relate this schema to the previous remarks on the properties of world religions as belief systems. The central component of the world image put forward by a world religion is the notion of salvation. The pursuit of salvation—in theistic religions, through obedience to or intercession with God—may therefore be considered the ultimate goal of religious action. Pursuit of salvation may or may not generate politically relevant religious action or religiously conditioned political action. If it does, action thus generated may or may not be governed by the *ethics* of the sacred law. If it does not, religious action results in pious detachment from political activity reflected in doctrinal indifference to the regulation of political life.

Actions of type a, b, c, d, e, and f will, whenever necessary, be further characterized as "societal" or "communal" action. "Societal action" will refer to action carried out within the framework of the state (when the hierocracy is heteronomous) or the state and the hierocracy (when the hierocracy is autonomous). It implicitly upholds the legitimacy of prevalent normative order, and its byproduct is the perpetuation of the political and hierocratic institutions within whose framework they are conducted—namely, the status quo. "Communal action" refers to action carried out outside the framework of the state. Its aims may be justified in terms of the prevalent normative order or they may imply the rejection of the legitimacy of the prevalent normative order, thus posing a revolutionary threat to the status quo.[47]

1.1.9 Outline of the Analytical Perspective

I. A world religion impinges on (1) the societal structure of domination
   (a) through institution of religious authority;
   (b) through the modification of principles of legitimacy of political domination.
   The *degree* of this impingement depends on
   (c) the normative conception of religious authority and the direction of religious rationalization;
   (d) the tenacity of the inherited institutions.
   A world religion also impinges on (2) political attitudes and action
   (a) through the motivation to differentially evaluated types of activity implied in its image of the world;
   (b) through explicit prescriptions: political ethics.
   The *degree* of this impingement depends on
   (c) the vigor of charismatic leadership or the strength and autonomy of the hierocracy, the foremost institutions enforcing the religious system of life regulation;
   (d) the social and institutional forces impeding the embodiment of religious precepts in political action.

II. A world religion is in turn impinged upon by its social context
   (a) through the interests and elective affinities of the individuals and social classes that adhere to it (most relevant to the sectarian phase);
   (b) through the material interests of the state and the hierocracy (most relevant to the period of the "establishment" of a religion).
   The *degree* of this impingement depends on
   (c) the hegemony of the state and the weakness and heteronomy of the hierocracy;
   (d) the susceptibility of the religious authorities to the influence of the laity (especially relevant during the sectarian phase) or, conversely, the ability of the hierocracy to pursue its own institutional interests (in the period of establishment).

III. A world religion does not affect the types of political activity and forms of political organization toward which it displays pious indifference. Indirectly, however, such pious indifference facilitates the predominance of political power in the societal structure of domination.

With this analytical scheme, we can now turn to Shiᶜite Islam in order to study its impact on Iran's polity after its establishment as the state religion in the second year of the sixteenth century, an impact that transformed the polity in stages but which did not imprint its indelible mark until three centuries later. This study, therefore, begins in part 1 with the formation and growth of the Imāmī (subsequently "Twelver" Shiᶜite) sect from the eighth/second to the fifteenth/ninth centuries, a period during which much of Shiᶜite theology and ethics became definitely systematized. It proceeds to the period beginning with the proclamation of Twelver Shiᶜism as the religion of the Safavid state (1501–1722) and examines the consequences of the establishment of Shiᶜism in Iran in part 2. Part 3 concludes the study with an analysis of the final consolidation, in the first decades of the nineteenth century, of a dual Shiᶜite polity with the state and the hierocracy as its two organs. Collaboration and discord between the hierocracy and the state down to the last decade of the century, and the ability of this dual structure of domination to withstand various challenges, are also considered. The nationwide protests of 1891 marks the end of the period under consideration and the beginning of the era of modern politics in Iran.

I.2 Criticism of Some Current Views on the Political Implications of Shiᶜism

In addition to the desire to bring a largely neglected type of societal change within the ambit of substantive sociological analysis, the choice of subject matter for this study was determined by its intrinsic significance in the social history of Iran as reflected in the scholarly literature. Even before their sudden reemergence in politics as the leaders of the Islamic revolution of 1979, the power and prestige of the Shiᶜite doctors, the *ᶜulamāᵓ*, during the Qājār period (1795–1925), and their political importance, in contrast to the relative political feebleness of the *ᶜulamāᵓ* of Sunni Islam in modern times, had attracted the attention of students of Persian history and politics; moreso, probably, than any other topic in the social history of Iran in the second half of the nineteenth century. However, current scholarly views on the political implications of Shiᶜism have been formulated in the context of the history of this latter half of the nineteenth century. Consequently, they are unduly colored by the situation in that period. The period, however, is not of particular significance in the evolution of Shiᶜism in Iran, and therefore of no great relevance to our understanding of the political orientations of Shiᶜite Islam.

Sir John Malcolm was struck by the power and prestige of the Shiᶜite doctors (sing. *mujtahid*) in the early years of the nineteenth century,[48] but, quite rightly, he did not correlate this fact with any presumed lack of legitimacy of temporal rule. In a letter to Tocqueville from Tehran in 1857, Gobineau, mindful of the conflict between the Shiᶜite doctors and Muhammad Shāh (1834–48) and of the recent rising of the Bāb, who claimed to be the Mahdi and the reappearing Shiᶜite Twelfth Imam, remarked that the existence of elements from various past epochs in the Persian government resulted in "the strangest constitutional theory" he had ever known. While administrative laws and reglementations were a continuation of the pre-Islamic theory and practice, the shah possessed no legitimacy, as the Shiᶜites considered all dynasties of the Islamic period including the reigning dynasty as usurpers. This was so because the Shiᶜites believed that rightful rule, imamate, belonged to ᶜAlī and his descendents, the last of whom was believed to be in concealment until his reappearance at the end of time.[49]

It is interesting to note in passing that Weber makes several incidental remarks on the legitimacy of the shah and his relationship with the Shiᶜite hierocracy. Regarding the political charisma of the office of the king in Iran, he observes that the function of the grand vizier is to deflect blames from the person of the shah and thus protect his kingly charisma.[50] Commenting on the strength of political power in relation to the hierocracy in Islam, Weber correctly takes note of certain caesaropapist prerogatives enjoyed by the monarch:

> Even though the Persian Shiᶜites reject [the religious] role of the caliph and place their eschatological hope in the *parousia* of the prophet's legitimate successor, in Persia, the Shah's position is predominant; this is not changed by the fact that the mood of the local population is considered in the appointment of priests [presumably the *imām jumᶜa*].[51]

These prerogatives, however, are not too impressive on a comparative scale. Elsewhere, Weber contrasts the stronger caesaropapistic claims of the Byzantine emperors with the weaker ones of the Ottoman sultans "to say nothing of the precarious legitimacy of the Persian Shahs vis-a-vis their Shiᶜite subjects."[52] In another passage, the shah is referred to as a "religiously illegitimate ruler."[53]

The views expressed by Gobineau and Weber on the shah's lack of legitimacy[54] are similar to those formulated by a number of contemporary scholars who, writing on the nineteenth century, have argued that Twelver Shiᶜism makes the legitimacy of the ruler precarious while enhancing the political authority of the Shiᶜite doctors.[55] The argument rests on the alleged implications of the Shiᶜite doctrine of imamate, and of the occultation (*Ghaybat*) of the Twelfth Imam, for the (il)legitimacy of the government, and for the political authority of the religious elite. It purports to explain the alleged denial of the legitimacy of political domination as deducible from the doctrinal foundations of clerical (hierocratic) authority. According to this view, the occultation of the Twelfth Imam, and the expectation of his *parousia* (*ẓuhūr*), render all government illegitimate.

This thesis makes sweeping assumptions in an overly deductive manner and has been challenged by a number of scholars, including the present author.[56] The evidence presented in the following pages makes it untenable.[57] It is regrettable that contemporary Shiᶜite propagandist writings and the Islamic revolution in Iran have induced more than one scholar to reaffirm this simplistic argument and even to project it back to the earlier periods covered in the present study.[58]

Another noteworthy thesis that should be mentioned, especially as it is not likely to be reiterated in the near future because of the recent politicization of Shiᶜism, is the one put forward by Corbin and supported by Nasr. This latter view is phenomenological and philosophical, and does not directly deal with political matters; nevertheless it has clear implications regarding political attitudes. The inherent esoteric quality of Shiᶜism in this view induces a drastic devaluation of the exoteric world, thus reducing the propensity to engage in this-worldly political action and nurturing an attitude of radical political indifferentism. Shiᶜism, writes Corbin emphatically in his *Histoire de la philosophie islamique*, is, in its essence, "l'ésoterisme de l'Islam." As such, it is identical with Sufism.[59] Corbin, drawing heavily on the work of the fourteenth-century Shiᶜite philosopher Ḥaydar Āmulī, is referring to the deduced phenomenological identity of Shiᶜite and Sufi esoteric spirituality, and is not interested in their respective social forms. Nasr, though in substantial agreement with Corbin at the phenomenological level, is careful to put forward a more nuanced account of the historical connection between Sufism and Twelver Shiᶜism that nevertheless highlights their close affinity and relatedness.[60]

As we shall see, the historical picture is a good deal more complicated than Corbin's and Nasr's accounts would lead us to believe, and contains, among other things, a good deal of antagonism between Shiᶜism and Sufism during the period under consideration.[61] Furthermore, as we shall see, the final consolidation of Twelver Shiᶜism in Iran in fact went hand in hand with the persecution of Sufism. Nevertheless, Corbin does offer us great insights into the political orientations of gnostic Shiᶜism (*ᶜirfān*), which represented the blending of Twelver Shiᶜism and "high" Sufism. What the philosophers Corbin and Nasr leave out is the specification of temporal and social—or historical and sociological—incidence of gnostic Shiᶜism and of the political attitudes deriving from it. Needless to say, it is this all-important specification of the incidence in historical time and social space of gnostic Shiᶜism and its derivative political attitudes that is imperative from the viewpoint of historical sociology and is carried out in the ensuing pages.

PART ONE

The Historical and Cultural Background of the Emergence of a Shiʿite Polity in Iran

Introduction to Part One

The origin of Shiᶜism lies in the nucleus of "partisans of ᶜAlī" (*Shiᶜat ᶜAlī*) who supported the Prophet's cousin and son-in-law ᶜAlī ibn Abī Ṭālib (d. 661), the last of the "rightly-guided caliphs" (*al-Khulafāʾ al-Rāshidūn*) and the first Shiᶜite Imam. ᶜAlī's supporters, the proto-Shiᶜites, were particularly strong in Kufa. It was the Kufan who invited ᶜAlī's son, Husayn, to Kufa and were implicated in his tragic death in 680. The movement of the "penitents" (*tawwābūn*) was the spontaneous reaction of the people of Kufa to the horrifying killing of Ḥusayn and his family in Karbalā.[1] This movement enhanced the solidarity of the proto-Shiᶜites and constituted the prelude to a series of Shiᶜite revolts against the Umayyads (661–750).

The definitive formation of the Imāmī (subsequently Ithnā ᶜAsharī or Twelver) Shiᶜite sect took place in the eighth/second century under the leadership of Ḥusayn's grandson and great-grandson, Muḥammad al-Bāqir (d. 733) and Jaᶜfar al-Ṣādiq (d. 765), the fifth and sixth Imams. Imāmī Shiᶜism developed a distinct doctrine and a distinct system of jurisprudence, while the diverse proto-Shiᶜite and early Shiᶜite elements were organized into a sect. Though the imams resided in Medina, Kufa remained the important center of Imāmī Shiᶜism in the eighth/second century.

The ninth/third century was a period of political decline. Nevertheless, it was also a period of intellectual consolidation and growth of religious scholarship. The center of Imāmī Shiᶜism was moved from Kufa, which was too near the new ᶜAbbasid capital, Baghdad, to the remote city of Qum, where its sacred lore was kept alive by the Imāmī traditionalist school before reappearing in Baghdad a century later. The basic features of the sectarian Imāmī religiosity of this period are best depicted by Kulaynī (d. 940/329), the "Renovator" of the tenth/fourth century, in his monumental *Uṣūl al-Kāfī*. In it, *īmān* (faith), primarily, ᶜ*aql* (reason), and ᶜ*ilm* (knowledge) emerge as linked with salvation. *Īmān* (faith) in particular, assumes fundamental importance in Imāmī inner-worldly piety, and is equated with true religion—Shiᶜism—and is said to include and surpass Islam—i.e., formal religion—as the highest form of religious consciousness and the most conducive to salvation.[2] Observance of the ethic of brotherly love within the Imāmī community, conceived as *dār al-īmān* (realm/house of faith), assistance to the members of the community of the faithful (*muʾminīn*), and devotional piety are also manifestations of *īmān* and the means of attaining salvation.

When, at the close of the ninth century, Kulaynī moved to Baghdad, the seat of the representative (*wakīl, safīr*) of the Hidden Imam, dusk was already setting in at Qum, and the owl of Minerva was taking its flight with *Uṣul al-Kāfī*, the consummate fruit of Qum traditionalism. Though the traditionalist school of Qum was to produce yet another great theologian, Ibn Bābūya (d. 991/381), the center of Imāmī learning had decidedly shifted to Baghdad.

The conquest of northern Syria by the Hamdanids, who were Twelver Shiᶜites in 944/333 led to the spread of Imāmī Shiᶜism in Syria—a region that was to supply the Safavid period with most of its religious scholars some six or seven centuries later. But far more momentous for the future of the Imāmī doctrine was the rise of the Buyid rulers in central Iran in the tenth/fourth century, and their seizure of power in the ᶜAbbasid capital, Baghdad (945/334), which gave considerable impetus to the proselytizing activity of the Imāmī sect and the growth of Imāmī Shiᶜism. The period of Buyid domination also witnessed the birth of a brilliant school of Imāmī learning in Baghdad which produced an impressive corpus of polemical, theological, and legal literature. Its major representatives, al-Mufīd (d. 1022), al-Murtadā (d. 1044), and al-Ṭūsī (d. 1067) progressively laid the foundations of the Imāmī rational theology (*kalām*)[3] and of the principles of jurisprudence.[4] The traditionalist outlook of the Imāmīs was considerably modified: while al-Mufīd had to concede to his polemicist opponent that thinking believers were few in the Shiᶜite community,[5] the author of the *Kitāb al-Naqḍ* (written some two centuries later, ca. 1170) boasted in martial terms of the "subjugation and suppression" (*qamᶜ va qahr*) of traditionalism by the rationalist doctors,[6] and could tirelessly refer to the *Madhhab-e Shīᶜa-ye* or *Imāmiyya-ye Uṣūliyya*, stressing the importance of deduction of beliefs from the principles (*Uṣūl*) and thus the rational character of Imāmī religiosity.

The religious situation under the Saljūqs (eleventh and twelfth centuries) is marked by the spread of Maturidite Ḥanafism of the school of Samarqand, championed by the Saljūq sultans and brought about by a sustained migration of highly esteemed eastern scholars to other parts of the empire.[7] In Baghdad, the Shiᶜites lost the protection of the Buyids and consequently suffered reversals in the second half of the eleventh century. However, the Saljūq attempt to establish Ḥanafism as the official religion disturbed the balance among the Sunni schools, giving rise to factional antagonism among them.[8] Sunni factionalism, erupting at times of weakened control of central government into recurrent and destructive violence, can be presumed to have created a leeway for the spread of Imāmī Shiʿism, especially as the Imāmīs appear to have been close to the Ḥanafīs. In fact, we do have evidence of the growth of Imāmī Shiʿism in Iran in the twelfth/sixth century, and important Shiʿite communities, among which the Imāmīs were the strongest, existed in Persian and Arab Iraq, the Caspian coast, and Khurasan.[9]

The disintegration of the Saljūq Empire was followed by a period of reassertion of the power of the ʿAbbasid Caliphate under al-Nāṣir (1180–1225/575–622). But the caliph al-Nāṣir already came to witness the beginning of the Mongol invasion which was to culminate in the conquest of Baghdad and the overthrow of the ʿAbbasid Caliphate. The Mongol invasion, which began in 1220, profoundly altered the conditions of religious life in the Islamic East. During the Mongol and Il-Khanid periods (the thirteenth/seventh and the first part of the fourteenth/eighth century), Imāmī theology became stabilized into its canonical forms.[10] Thanks to their forwardness and the presence of the great Shiʿite philosopher and theologian Naṣīr al-Dīn Ṭūsī (d. 1274/672) in the Mongol camps as an influential counsellor to the conquering Hülegü, the Imāmī center of Ḥilla was spared from Mongol depredation. The clerical aristocracy of Ḥilla established lasting connection with the Il-Khanid court. Ghāzān (1295–1304) had a definite Shiʿite leaning, and his successor Öljeitū (Muḥammad Khudā-Bandeh; 1304–16), after previous conversions to several religions, converted to Shiʿism in 1309–10/709 through the influence and efforts of the prominent Shiʿite statesman Sayyid Tāj al-Dīn Muḥammad Āvajī. The great theologian, the ʿAllāma Ibn al-Muṭahhar al-Ḥillī (d. 1326/726) and his son were invited to the court and remained there in Öljeitü's company.[11] Nevertheless, Twelver Shiʿism did not spread in this period. This was due in part to strong Sunni resistance, which forced Öljeitü to abandon Shiʿism,[12] but more fundamentally to a novel religious phenomenon: the spread of Sufism among the masses.

Until the conversion of Ghāzān to Islam in 1295, the Mongol rulers were non-Muslims; shamanism, Buddhism, and Christianity spread in their domains. The link between political power and the custodians of orthodox Islam was thus severed. Regulation of much of religious life was taken over by the Sufi shaykhs of the locally organized orders, over whom the *ʿulamāʾ* as the custodians of dogma had no influence. Thus, at the grass roots, the spread of Sufism, which had started during the Saljūq period, gathered phenomenal momentum. Murtazavi underlines one of the unique features of the Īl-Khānid period: the religious tolerance of the rulers. This tolerance insured complete religious freedom and gave rise to lively disputations among the representatives of various religious viewpoints in the presence of the Īl-Khān.[13] But at the popular level, the spread of Sufism went hand in hand with the decline of all formal, dogmatic religion, including Imāmī Shiʿism. Murtazavi also emphasizes the support of the Īl-Khān rulers and their great viziers, Rashīd al-Dīn and Ghīyāth al-Dīn, for Sufi shaykhs and their munificence toward Sufi orders. Numerous *khāniqāhs* (Sufi convents) were built and generously endowed.[14]

The caliph al-Nāṣir li-Dīn Allāh had pursued a daring and novel religious policy of simultaneously joining the *futuwwa* organization of the urban guilds and artisans, and the Sufi order of his spiritual mentor ᶜUmar Suhrawardī (d. 1234/632). The policy established a firm link between Sufism and urban popular organization, and cultivated widespread devotion to ᶜAlī as the patron of the *futuwwa*, and to ᶜAlī's descendants.[15] As this policy was oriented toward popular religion and bypassed the official custodians of the sacred law, its lasting effects continued throughout the Mongol period, aided by the severance of the link between the state and the *ᶜulamā*ʾ.

The penchant for Shiᶜism on the part of Ghāzān and Öljeitü had been entirely due to their attachment to the house of the Prophet.[16] Shiᶜite notions regarding the virtues of the house of the Prophet had wide popular appeal, and were selectively adopted and incorporated into Sufism during the Īl-Khānid and subsequent periods. The history of the Kubravī Sufi order is instructive as an example of the gradual penetration of Shiᶜite notions into Sufism. Saᶜd al-Dīn Ḥamūya, the shaykh of the Kubravī order, adopted the doctrine of the twelve Imams, identifying them with the Sufis' *awlīyā*ʾ ("friends of God"), whose number he determined to be twelve, the twelfth being the Lord of Time (*Ṣāḥib al-zamān*—the Shiᶜite designation for the Hidden Imam), who will return to bring justice to the world. A later Kubravī shaykh and philosopher, the eminent ᶜAlāʾ al-Dawla Simnānī, exalted the rank of ᶜAlī far above the other rightly guided caliphs.[17] Finally, the formal transition to Shiᶜism for the Kubraviyya occurred under Nūrbakhsh.[18] However, Sufi thought retained its distinct mystical framework, and the penetration of Shiᶜite ideas into it was random and unsystematic. Sufism with a Shiᶜite tinge may well be the most important religious feature of the period.[19] But it should be emphasized that there is no evidence of the spread of the "rationalized" (*Uṣūlī*) Shiᶜism of the kind Qāḍī ᶜAbd al-Jalīl spoke of in the preceding period.

The fourteenth/eighth and fifteenth/ninth centuries thus witnessed the spread of Shiᶜite notions, and of popular devotion to the house of the Prophet, as manifested in the manuals of the guilds and, more spectacularly, in the building of the Gawharshād mosque on the site of the tomb of the Eighth Imam in Mashhad by the Timurid queen.[20] These notions fell upon the fertile soil of undisciplined religiosity cultivated by Sufism, giving rise to a number of millenarian movements all of which formally professed Shiᶜism. Furthermore, there were Sunnis who accepted the legitimacy of some or all of the twelve Imams after the first three rightly guided caliphs.[21] But there was no growth of the Imāmī sect once the ᶜAllāma al-Ḥillī's attempt to propagate Twelver Shiᶜism through Öljeitü was foiled.

The pre-Safavid development of Shiᶜism thus shows two distinct trajectories. On the one hand, we have the intellectual development of Imāmī Shiᶜism from the late tenth and early eleventh to the early fourteenth century. Imāmī Shiᶜites remained an urban sect throughout this period, with first Baghdad and then Ḥilla as their most important centers of learning. Then from the thirteenth century onwards, we witness an independent religious phenomenon, popular Sufism, some branches of which selectively adopted a number of Shiᶜite notions. This second trend produced both dogmatically undisciplined "extremist" Shiᶜite movements and increasing general devotionalism toward the Imams—the house of the Prophet—on the part of the rest of the population. The first trend represents the internal development of sectarian Imāmī Shiᶜism, the second, the elective affinity of the Sufi masses for ideas and stories about the lives and miracles of the holy Imams. The two trends did not meet until the beginning of the sixteenth century.

Chapter 1 undertakes the indispensable task of analyzing the formative period of the development of the Shiᶜite religion with close attention to its political orientation. Chapter 2 confronts the problem of the chiliastic potential inherent in the Shiᶜite doctrine, a potential that was activated during periods when religious discipline was absent but which was abhorred by the sober doctors of post-Buyid Shiᶜism, as it was to be by the later Shiᶜite hierocracy, which was equally bent on its perpetual containment. In chapter 3, we finally turn to the crucial nonreligious factor in the political ethos of medieval Iran.

CHAPTER ONE

Sectarian Shiʿism within the Islamic Body Politic

Eighth/Second to the Thirteenth/Seventh Century

1.1 The Differentiation of Religion from Government in Islam and in Early Imāmī Shiʿism

The widely held view that any Islamic polity is, in theory, a theocracy is not only inadequate but also misleading. Although an Islamic theocracy, like a Christian theocracy, is a legitimate concept and can have normative or descriptive validity in specific instances, there is no inherent dogmatic connection between God and political authority in Islam.[1] In the Qurʾan the terms *mulk* and *malakūt* occur and are said to belong to God.[2] However, these terms signify the universe and its lordship and *not* specifically political sovereignty. In contrast to the this-worldly and political Yahweh of the Israelites,[3] Allāh is the creator of the universe and the lord of this and of the other world, but he is not directly involved in mundane political events, nor does he intervene in worldly matters on behalf of a chosen people.

From the viewpoint of soteriology, Allāh is a god of otherworldly salvation: he promises and threatens to mete out justice upon Resurrection, and holds out rewards and punishments in the other world for possession or lack of faith—*īmān* and *kufr*—and for the observance or infringement of its ethics of salvation in the deeds committed in this world.[4] The Qurʾan does not adumbrate a distinct political sphere. In contrast to pre-Islamic Persian cosmologies, the constitution of the polity is not endowed with sacrality as a replica of the cosmos; and political relations per se are devoid of intrinsic soteriological significance. What is directly invested with soteriological import, and normatively governed by religiously induced motivation, is the devotional or ethically commendable deed. What soteriological significance pertains to particular political deeds does so indirectly—that is, insofar as they are enjoined by the "political ethic" of Islam and rewarded in the other world. The "political ethic" of Islam can be conceived as having two sets of constituents. Of the explicitly stated principal ethical duties, at least three have implications for political action: *jihād* (holy war) and the more general ethical duties of *amr bi'l-maʾrūf* (enjoining the good) and *nahy ʿan al-munkar* (forbidding the evil). In addition to these principal ethical duties, there is the Qurʾanic verse enjoining obedience to "those in authority":

> O believers, obey God, and obey the Messenger and those in authority among you. . . .
> [4.59]

Finally, there are the more specific details of the sacred law with political implications.

Nevertheless, for the first Muslim communities, the polity was defined in terms of religious allegiance. Religious commitment, at least in theory, comprised the total life of the adherents of the new faith. The leadership of the community of believers was entrusted to the *amīr al-muʾminīn* (the commander of the faithful). Although recent scholarship has tended to underscore the rather limited scope of the authority of the first "commanders of the faithful," especially as regards matters pertaining to religion,[5] in the later periods the memory of the fusion of religion and the state under Muhammad, which was presumed to have continued under the four rightly guided caliphs, could be idealized into a "golden age" of pristine theocracy.

Faced with the problem of administering a vast conquered empire, the Umayyads (661–750) increasingly concentrated their efforts on the political aspects of leadership at the expense of the religious ones, and were accused of "secularizing" the hitherto theocratic Islamic government, of turning the caliphate into kingship (*mulk*). At the same time, the Umayyad period also witnessed the emergence of a body of learned Muslims, separated from and independent of the caliphate, who gradually consolidated their position in Muslim communities as private religious advisors and jurists and thus formed a religious elite guarding and developing Muhammad's heritage.

As Lapidus shows, with the growth of religious activities independent of the state and the emergence of the schools of jurisprudence (sing. *madhhab*), the caliphate was no longer the sole identifying symbol of Islam.[6] In fact, the emergence of the *ʿulamāʾ* as a distinctly religious elite marked the disjunction between the caliphate and the institution embodying the Islamic revelation.

The differentiation of religion from the state opened the way for a number of alternative developments. One such alternative is the transformation of the theocratic ideal into a *political ideology*. This was done by the Khurasanians, whose movement overthrew the worldly Umayyads and transferred Islamic rulership to the house of ʿAbbās in 750. For these militants, the rightly guided caliphate had become a model of presumed pristine theocracy to be restored by armed rebellion, and as such the cornerstone of their ideology. Under the ʿAbbasid caliph al-Maʾmūn (813–33), this tradition of militancy for religious principles as embodied in the pristine Islamic community was taken up by Ibn Ḥanbal (d. 855) and the Ḥanbalī preachers in Baghdad, and has left its imprint upon Ḥanbalism every since.[7] In contrast to Ḥanbalism, the development of Imāmī Shiʿism represents the opposite alternative of the renunciation of militancy in pursuit of the theocratic ideal, and a marked separation of the spiritual (religious) domain from politics.

In the first two centuries of Islam, we witness the radical divergence of Shiʿism from the main Sunni currents. With the organization of the early Shiʿites into a sect, the divergence of the Shiʿite outlook was reflected in an evolving theory of imamate that was at marked variance with the Sunni notions of political leadership. For the Imāmīs, there was no *explicit* recognition of the separation of temporal and religious authority, and, *de jure*, the Imam was considered the supreme political and religious leader of the community. However, de facto, the conception of imamate was drastically depoliticized. As Hodgson shows, the de facto depoliticization of imamate was concomitant with the sectarian reorientation of the early Shiʿites in the eighth/second century.[8]

Both Muḥammad al-Bāqir and Jaʿfar al-Ṣādiq explicitly rejected the idea of armed rebellion.[9] The religio-political movement that overthrew the Umayyads espoused the restoration of theocratic caliphate under any branch of the house of the Prophet. After the death of the ʿAbassid Ibrāhīm and on the eve of the final takeover, Abū Salama, the leading figure of the movement, offered the imamate to Jaʿfar al-Ṣādiq. Jaʿfar refused it.[10] The ʿAbbasids were then installed as caliphs. Consonantly with the aims and character of the movement which brought them to power, the early ʿAbbasids assumed the designations first of *mahdī* and then of *imām*, seeking to emphasize the Islamic character of their political regime, thereby implying the political, theocratic conception of imamate (= the caliphate).[11] By contrast, Jaʿfar al-Ṣādiq, the author of an influential mystical commentary on the Qurʾan,[12] made a sustained effort to discipline religio-political "extremism" (*ghuluww*).[13] At the same time, he transformed the early political Shiʿism into an introverted and quietistic religious movement. The Imams ceased to be anticaliphs (as they were in the Shiʿite revolts of the Umayyad period), and became the spiritual guides of the Shiʿite (Imāmī) sectarians.

The earliest Islamic usage of the term *imām* connotes divine authority whose end is the guidance of mankind. It was therefore drawn upon to designate authority in divine law, whether personal or impersonal. The Qurʾan refers to the book of Moses as *imām*; and the Qurʾan itself and the Sunna (normative tradition) are referred to as *imām* in the earliest legal literature.[14] In accord with this religio-legal conception, the founders of the Sunni schools of jurisprudence, who also came to be designated *imām*, were seen by their followers as authoritative teachers in religious dogma and ethics, and not as pretenders to political rule.

Their contemporary Muḥammad al-Bāqir similarly performed the function of the teacher of legal doctrine and laid down many of the basic concepts and rules of Shiʿite jurisprudence for his substantial body of followers.[15] His son Jaʿfar al-Ṣādiq organized the Shiʿites into a sect whose principles of leadership were elaborated as the theory of imamate.[16]

Jaʿfar al-Ṣādiq went much further than the contemporary founders of the legal schools. He developed the notion of authority stemming from the divine guidance of mankind into a principle of absolute and infallible authority. It is to the imams that "God has ordained obedience" (Qurʾan, 4.59; the "authority verse"); "God delegated to the Imams spiritual rulership over the whole world, which must always have such a leader and guide." The Imam of the time, in Jafri's close paraphrase,

> is a pillar of God's unity [*tawḥīd*]. The Imam is immune from sin [*khaṭā*] and error [*ḍalāl*]. The Imams are those from whom "God has removed all impurity and made them absolutely pure" [Qurʾan, 33:33]; they are possessed of the power of miracles and of irrefutable arguments [*dalāʾil*]; and they are for the protection of the people of the earth just as the stars are for the inhabitants of the heavens. They may be likened, in this community, to the ark of Noah: he who boards it obtains salvation and reaches the gate of repentance.[17]

Hishām ibn al-Ḥakam, a prominent follower of al-Ṣādiq, was chiefly responsible for the systematic formulation of the Imāmī conception of imamate in accordance with al-Ṣadiq's instructions. The theory of imamate, as elaborated by Hishām in this formative early stage, remained definitive for Twelver Shiʿism. The theory

> rests on the idea of the permanent need for a divinely guided Imam who could act as the authoritative teacher of mankind in all religious matters. The Imam thus was the legatee [*waṣī*] of the Prophet. He was infallible [*maʿṣūm*] in all his acts and words. . . . Whoever obeyed the Imam was a true believer, and whoever opposed or rejected him, an infidel [*kāfir*].[18]

There appears to have been some reluctance on the part of a number of Imāmīs to accept the claim to infallibility made on behalf of the Imams in this period. Some of their companions would concede the Imams' legal authority and consider them pious men of learning (*ʿulamāʾ abrār*), but would dispute their infallibility.[19] The issue gave rise to a crisis at the time of succession of the Ninth Imam, whose competence as a young child to interpret the divine law authoritatively was seriously questioned.[20] Isolated instances of resistance to the belief in the infallibility of the Imams are recorded as late as the tenth/fourth century; but it became a cardinal tenet of the Imāmī belief system and was not disputed in later periods. Other elements of the theory of imamate were categorically accepted from the earliest period onwards.

The tenet that the Imam was the legatee (*waṣī*) of the Prophet points to the strong sentiment of legitimism that sustained the cause of the ᶜAlids (descendants of ᶜAlī) in general. Jaᶜfar al-Ṣādiq also preserved the legitimist contention on behalf of the descendants of ᶜAlī by insisting upon *naṣṣ* (designation)—modeled after the explicit designation of ᶜAlī by Muḥammad—as the indispensable condition of imamate. In the context of the newly elaborated theory, the notion of *naṣṣ* implied "that the imamate is located in a given individual, *whether he claims rule or not*; and is to be transferred from one to another by explicit designation, *naṣṣ*."[21]

Against the background of an emerging institution of sacred learning and instruction, the de facto disjunction between imamate and political rule was facilitated by resting the former upon the possession of divinely inspired *ᶜilm* (knowledge). The Imam was the repository of God's knowledge and interpreter of His revelation. By implication, the responsibilities of the Imam were differentiated from those of the ruler, making the former the final authority in matters of salvation, conscience, and sacred law: "The idea of an imamate by *naṣṣ*, restricted to a definite individual out of all the ᶜAlids, continuing through all *political circumstances*, was complemented by that of an imamate *based not primarily on a political claim, but on special knowledge*, *ᶜilm*."[22]

The death of the Eleventh Imam, who apparently had no son, produced a serious crisis which was eventually solved by the doctrine of *Ghaybat* (occultation). The Twelfth Imam was said to be alive and to fulfill the functions of imamate in concealment. Although, as we shall see in section 1.2, other motives also underlay the elaboration of the doctrine of occultation, the doctrine was, at least in part, an attempt to explain the fact that political power was not in the hands of the Shiᶜites. As such, it was premised on the divorce of imamate from actual political rulership. The doctrine of occultation, by postulating the necessary absence of the Imam, accentuated the divorce between imamate and political rule. Thus, the soteriological and eschatological transposition of the initially political notion of imamate was complete. Imamate was destined to become a topic in sacred history and an abstract principle of Shiᶜite theology but not the basis for public law or political theory.

One of the first manifestations of the new sectarian spirit was the preoccupation with spiritual ranking.[23] At the same time, political quietism became characteristic of the Shiᶜite sectarians. Jaᶜfar al-Sādiq made it permissible for them to engage in normal intercourse with the larger community, and to acquire property and possessions that has passed through impure hands.[24] The Shiᶜites were also permitted to serve the illegitimate government. The famous Shiᶜite practice of *taqiyya* (dissimulating one's faith to assure survival) bore al-Ṣādiq's emphatic sanction and became current among the Imāmīs.[25] It made for political quietism by removing the motivation for assertiveness and conspicuous fulfillment of religious obligation under inconvenient circumstances. Two centuries later, Ibn Bābūya (d. 990) was to affirm the *obligatoriness* (not mere permissibility) of *taqiyya*: *taqiyya* is as obligatory as the daily prayer, and he who ceases to practice it before the return of the Mahdi has ceased to subscribe to the Imāmī religion.[26] Meanwhile, piety and spiritual zeal continued to characterize the Imāmiyya.

The pietistic inner-worldliness of the Shiʿism of the ninth/third century could only enhance the differentiation of the religious from the political sphere, which accompanied the progressively enhanced disjunction between imamate and actual political rule and the doctrinal neglect of the latter. With the works of al-Mufīd, al-Murtaḍā, and al-Ṭūsī, we witness the development and systematization of the Shiʿite legal theory and jurisprudence—*fiqh*. It is true that imamate remained the most distinctive and the most salient of Imāmī tenets,[27] but only at the cost of losing its political connotation and becoming, like prophecy, a topic pertaining to philosophical theology on the one hand and to sacred history on the other. With the development of jurisprudence as a new branch of religious learning, which did not include a systematic theory of authority or temporal rule, the import of imamate as a topic in public law was drastically reduced, while it increasingly appeared as a purely theological topic, its practical implications becoming less and less clear. Imamate became a real theological doctrine but only a utopian substitute for positive political theory. The subsequent course of events did not modify this situation, though the philosophical treatment of the topic of imamate became more rigorous and more elaborate.

The way in which the elevation of the conception of imamate into a basic principle of the cosmic constitution rescinded its connection with daily realities of political life becomes evident in Kulaynī's treatment of imamate in the *Uṣūl al-Kāfī*, written less than two centuries after the death of Jaʿfar al-Ṣādiq. The Imams are said to be the *ḥujja* (evidence, proof) of God, of which this world cannot be devoid in any moment. As the evidence of God, the Imams are the light (*nūr*) of God, his witnesses (*shuhadāʾ*), gates (*abwāb*), and signs (*ʿalāmāt*). They have intimate connections with the angels, are endowed with the Holy Spirit (*Rūḥ al-qudus*), and, above all, are "those firm in knowledge" (*rāsikhun* [*fiʾl-ʿIlm*]:[28] not only do they know the "apparent" and "real" meaning (*ẓāhir* and *bāṭin*) of the Qurʾan, but they are also in possession of other allegedly revealed books, and know the Hundredth or Greatest Name of God.[29] Given the onset of the period of occultation, which around the time of the death of Kulaynī was to be declared to last until the end of time, the above-mentioned qualities of imamate could only be attributed to ʿAlī and his eleven descendants as figures in sacred history who were receding fast into the increasingly remote past. Concurrently, imamate was acquiring, in the minds of the believers, an order of reality and relevance distinct from that of mundane politics. The belief in imamate as conceptualized by Kulaynī could, and no doubt did, give rise to the metahistorical utopia of direct divine guidance through the Imams. But the properties of this spiritual utopia—in contrast to the utopia of the golden age of the rightly-guided caliphs drawn upon by the Ḥanbalites in their pursuit of theocracy—were such as to make it unsuitable as a basis for sacralization of the political sphere and of political action.

Endowing imamate, in addition to prophecy, with cosmic significance as the mechanism of mediation between God and men required that a great deal of emphasis be put on the ᶜ*iṣma* (infallibility, sinlessness) of the Imam.[30] The Imam's infallibility is conjoined with the principle of the grace (*luṭf*) of God. In a typical polemic against the Sunnis, the shaykh al-Ṭūsī claims that this divine grace, by making it incumbent upon God to have an infallible guide among mankind, proves "the necessity of supreme (religious) leadership." Consequently, al-Ṭūsī rejects the Sunni doctrine of imamate (= caliphate) by "election" (*ikhtīyār*) in favor of imamate by "divine appointment" (*naṣb*),[31] the last such divine appointment, to last until the end of time, having already been made. In similar polemics, Imāmī jurists endlessly criticized the grounds for the election of the rightly guided caliphs and therefore the legitimacy of their rule. In doing so, they attacked and ruled out every variant of a positivistic political theory of imamate.[32] In these debates, centering on the first centuries of Islam and devoid of any consideration of the contemporary situation, they gave the doctrine of imamate the quality of a utopian substitute for political theory. De jure, the Imam remained the supreme authority in all matters pertaining to this and the other world. Centuries after the disappearance of the last Imam, the ᶜAllāma, Ibn al-Muṭahhar al-Ḥillī would still state formulaically, "The imamate is a universal authority (*rīyāsa*) in the things of religion and of the world belonging to some person and derived from (*nīyāba*) of the Prophet."[33] But the unbridged gap between dogma and political reality made idealistic theological abstractness rather than legal positivism the distinctive mark of the Shiᶜite doctrine of imamate.

The notion of imamate acquired a wholly different significance. Al-Ḥillī, whose dogmatic statements have remained highly authoritative to this day, underscored the cosmic theological significance of (historical) imamate. Imamate as a pillar of his system of rational theology became, like prophecy, the channel of divine guidance of mankind and the manifestation of God's grace. As prophecy referred to the historical prophets, imamate, pending the appearance of the Hidden Imam, could only refer to the twelve Imams of sacred history. Al-Ḥillī thus delineated imamate as an ᶜ*Aṣl al-Dīn* (principle of religion), thus firmly integrating it into the Shiᶜite *theological* system, and *not* into Shiᶜite *jurisprudence* (which might have led to the development of a political theory). It is highly significant that in his treatise on imamate, the *Minhāj al-Karāma*, al-Ḥillī reproached the ᶜAbbasids with the reprehensible introduction of the name of the caliph in the Friday sermon (*khuṭba*) in order to underline the separation of religion and rulership. The practice was considered an abuse of religion for political ends.[34] Like prophecy in the absence of a prophet, imamate in the absence of an Imam was devoid of direct implications for political rule. Its indirect implications remained latent and were not deduced by the authoritative interpreters of the Shiᶜite doctrine until centuries later, until the topic finally did appear in Shiᶜite jurisprudence.

After the thirteenth/seventh century, the notion of imamate became even more apolitical under Ismāᶜīlī and Sufi influences. According to Madelung,

> The eternal reality of the imamate, now commonly termed *walāya* (quality of a *walī*, "friend of god"), was defined as the esoteric aspect of prophecy. The Imam was thus viewed as the initiator into mystical truth by virtue of the theophanic quality of his essential nature as well as by his teaching as expressed in the transmitted logia of the Imams.[35]

I have tried to show how the formative sectarian differentiation of Twelver Shiᶜism from the caliphal body politic left its permanent imprint on the delineation, in doctrine, of the religiously significant and the profane spheres of life, relegating political authority to the latter sphere. Doctrinal indifference to political theory amounted to granting autonomy to the norms of legitimacy of political rulership. Political rule was thus "secularized." I therefore fully concur with Scarcia, who considers the distinctiveness of Twelver Shiᶜism to consist in the basic "separation and reciprocal independence of the theological and the political spheres."[36]

1.2 The Cessation of Historical Imamate and the Formulation of the Doctrine of Occultation (*Ghaybat*)

The eighth/second and early ninth/third centuries were a period of intense chiliastic yearning both among various Shiᶜite groups, and even more generally in the Islamic body politic.[37] *Rajᶜa* (return of the dead before the day of Resurrection) was a distinctly Shiᶜite belief of the period. The death of each Shiᶜite leader invariably created an acute problem of succession, with splinter groups either denying his death of believing in his imminent return. In these cases, the deceased leader was believed to return as the *Qāʾim* (redresser of wrongs, especially the usurpation of the sovereign right of the house of ᶜAlī) to lead the chiliastic uprising (*khurūj*). He was typically conceived of as the *Qāʾim bi'l-sayf* (redresser through the sword). The redresser was also referred to as the Mahdi ([apocalyptic] leader).

A Shiᶜite tradition quotes al-Bāqir as follows: "When the *Qāʾim* from the family of the Prophet will rise, he will distribute equally among the people and will establish justice among his subjects." In another tradition, al-Ṣādiq is reported to have explained that the *Qāʾim* is known as such "because he will rise [*qāma*] after his death for an important task, and will rise by the command of God." Al-Ṣādiq is also reported to have affirmed in response to another questioner that the

Qā'im and the Mahdi are one and the same person who is named Mahdi "because he guides to the secret things; and he is named *Qā'im* because he will rise after death. He will rise for an important task." [38]

As has been pointed out, al-Bāqir and al-Ṣādiq sought to curb "extremism" by insisting that the redresser is not to be expected in the present. Nevertheless, chiliastic yearning recurrently intensified at the time of succession. Expectation of the imminent return of the deceased Imam on the part of many of the followers of the Sixth, Seventh, and Eleventh Imams [39] created serious problems for the inner circle of disciples who sought to maintain the sectarian discipline inherited from Jaᶜfar al-Ṣādiq. The death of the Eleventh Imam, apparently without a son and heir, produced what appears to have been the worst of the crises of succession. The Imāmī community splintered into some fourteen or fifteen sects; this number increased to twenty over the seven decades prior to the formulation of the doctrine of occultation. Of these, at first only three or four believed that the Imam had left behind a son.[40] One such group, which maintained that there was a son in hiding from fear of the tyrannical ᶜAbbasid ruler, was to survive as the Imāmī sect. Their despondency and unwillingness to discuss the thorny and not easily defensible question of the concealment of the Imam is evident in Nawbakhtī's statement a quarter of a century later (ca. 900):

> The twelfth group, who are the Imamites, maintain that the case is not as all other factions having upheld. There is a *ḥujja* [proof] for God on earth among the descendants of al-Ḥasan b. ᶜAlī [al-ᶜAskarī]. God's decree is in effect and he is the legatee [*waṣī*] of his father. . . . The earth cannot be void of a *ḥujja*. . . .
>
> It is also unlawful to mention his [al-ᶜAskarī's] successor's name or ask his whereabouts until such time as God decides. This is so because if he (peace be on him) is protected, fearful and in concealment, it is by God's protection. *It is not up to us to seek for reasons for what God does*.[41]

But before long, reasons for what God does had to be sought by the leading Imāmīs in order to preserve the integrity of their religious community.

Since the sectarian organization of Shiᶜites by Jaᶜfar al-Ṣādiq, the Imams had had plenipotentiaries or deputies (sing. *wakīl*) who acted as their agents in the collection of religious tax (*khums*) and discharge of day-to-day functions. After the death of Ḥasan al-ᶜAskarī, the routine management of the affairs of the Imāmī faction appears to have devolved upon a father and son who had acted as his agents. They claimed to be acting as the deputies of an Imam in hiding. The father, ᶜUthmān ibn Saᶜīd al-ᶜAmrī, died in the same year as al-ᶜAskarī (874–75/260). His son, Abū Jaᶜfar Muḥammad ibn ᶜUthmān al-ᶜAmrī (d. 916 or 917/304 or 305) must then have taken over. He managed the affairs of the Imāmī community for over forty very difficult years.

The situation of the Imāmiyya began to improve markedly with the political fortune of the Imāmī houses of Furāt and Nawbakhtī in the tenth century. To consolidate the position of the Imāmīs and win over sympathetic Shiᶜites from other factions, Abū Jaᶜfar al-ᶜAmrī was crucially assisted by Abū Sahl Ismāᶜīl ibn ᶜAlī al-Nawbakhtī (d. 922–23/310), a very wealthy functionary of the ᶜAbbasid caliph, theologian, man of letters, and the political head and representative of the Imāmī community in Baghdad. Abū Sahl, who survived al-ᶜAmrī by a few years, resolved the question of succession to deputyship in favor of a member of his own family, Abu'l-Qāsim Ḥusayn ibn al-Rūḥ Nawbakhtī (d. 939/326). We may presume the considerable initial resistance to the acceptance of Ibn al-Rūḥ[42] was connected to the shift in the Imāmī community from a somewhat plebian outlook[43] to the predominance of the aristocratic orientation of the politically prominent Shiᶜite families. While the first deputy, ᶜUthmān al-ᶜAmrī, had been a seller of cooking fat (*sammān*), the man who became the representative—deputy or mediator (*safīr*)—of the Hidden Imam half a century later belonged to the Nawbakhtī family, one of the foremost among the nobility of Baghdad. The presumably plebian opposition to Ibn Rūḥ Nawbakhtī was overcome, and the aristocratic outlook of the prominent Shiᶜite families prevailed in the Shiᶜism of the ensuing three centuries.

The first deputies, when challenged about the existence of the Hidden Imam, would merely confirm that "the *Ṣāḥib al-Amr* [Lord of Command] is present during the *ḥajj* [pilgrimage to Mecca] every year, and he sees the people and knows them, although they fail to see him or know him." Alternatively, they would present ordinances (sing. *tawqīᶜ*) in the Imam's handwriting.[44] But in the long run, such ad hoc assertions and claims could not resolve the difficulties of the Imāmī leadership. Not long after his kinsman, the author of *Firaq al-Shīᶜa*, had forbidden the Imāmīs to ask about the reason for the current state of the imamate, Abū Sahl was obliged to elaborate a *theological* statement on the concealment of the Imam, and put forward what was to become the Imāmī doctrine of occultation (*Ghaybat*).

The second ᶜAmrī in his last years, and Ibn Rūḥ Nawbakhtī in particular, controlled considerable revenues consisting of contributions of prosperous Imāmīs. The latter became highly influential in Baghdad.[45] Though Ibn Rūḥ was more cautious and less outspoken than Abū Sahl, and is said to have practiced *taqiyya*, he eventually became widely recognized as the deputy (*wakīl*) of the Hidden Imam.[46] Ibn Rūḥ appears to have been greatly respected by the elite of Baghdad. Under him, the Shiᶜite feast of *Ghadīr Khumm*, commemorating the designation of ᶜAlī by the Prophet as his successor, was for the first time publicly celebrated.

To consolidate its position, the nascent nucleus of religious leadership was in need both of dogmatic promulgation of the Imāmī creed, and suppression of heretical and "extremist" dissidence. While seeking a definitive solution to the problem posed by the chronic crisis of succession, Abū Sahl was thus at the same time reacting to the problem of religious "extremism" (*ghuluww*), which was present and serious. Among the various post-ᶜAskarī Shiᶜite factions, one chiliastic group had maintained a doctrinal position dangerously close to that of the Imāmīs. This group (the neo-Wāqifīyya, as they may be called[47])

> maintained that al-ʿAskarī had died and would live again after his death as al-Qāʾim al-Mahdī, because, they contended, al-Qāʾim was a person who rose after death and in consequence had no successor. . . . They added, he was living after death and was hidden because of fear, since. . . . they too believed in the necessity of the *ḥujja* on earth, whether alive, manifest, or hidden.[48]

Against the neo-Wāqifī group, Abū Sahl reaffirmed the death of the Eleventh Imam while proclaiming the concealment of his son who was the *Ḥujja* (proof) of God on earth.[49] The fact that the son was alive would rule out his chiliastic return from the dead as the redresser by the sword. Furthermore, Abū Sahl was at the same time reacting to the serious threat posed by the Imāmī mystic Manṣūr al-Ḥallāj, who was succeeding in converting many Imāmīs at the ʿAbbasid court. To Abū Sahl, Ḥallāj issued forth the challenge: "I am the Deputy (*wakīl*) of the Lord of the Age (*Ṣāḥib al-Zamān*)," while proceeding further with his followers to claim incarnation of God (*ḥulūl*) in accordance with his doctrine derived from the tradition of monistic mysticism. Abū Sahl denounced him to the government as a "claimant to divinity" (*mudda ʿī al-rubūbiyya*). Massignon also speculates that the prominent Shiʿites must have used their network of ties with Ẓāhirite school to influence the Ẓāhirite qadi, Ibn Dāwūd, whose famous *fatwā* (ruling) set in motion the process leading eventually to Ḥallāj's trial for heresy and execution.[50]

To thwart present and future challenges to the authority of the deputy as the head of the religious institution and the sole representative of the Imam, all rival claims to imamate and mahdihood had to be discredited. Abū Sahl therefore adopted elements of the doctrine of occultation and presented it as a rationally established dogma, asserting the necessary existence and the (necessary) absence of the Hidden Imam. The Hidden Imam was said to be alive and in concealment, and to communicate with his followers solely through his deputy, the head of the Imāmī religious community.[51]

Abū Sahl's theorizing, however, did not solve the problem in the short run. The third deputy, Ibn Rūḥ Nawbakhtī, had to deal with the problem of extremism *within* the inner circles of Imāmī religious leadership. Shalmaghānī, his assistant and lieutenant (*nāʾib*) during his imprisonment for nonpayment of taxes, claimed to be the vice-gerent and *bāb* (gateway) of the Expected Imam,[52] and preached divine incarnation and other extremist ideas. In 924–25/312, Ibn Rūḥ produced from the prison a decree (*tawqīʿ*) dictated by the Hidden Imam, excommunicating Shalmaghānī and his followers. Shalmaghānī's challenge demonstrated the weakness of the institution of deputyship. He had written to a friend that both he and Ibn Rūḥ knew exactly what they were doing in the matter of claiming the deputyship: "We were wrangling over this matter just as dogs would do over a corpse." [53]

The definitive step to suppress all claims to mahdihood came with the fourth and last deputy, ʿAlī ibn Muḥammad al-Samarrī, who, according to testimony of the great tenth/fourth century theologian, Ibn Bābūya, in 940/329, six days before his death, produced another ordinance by the Hidden Imam stating that his occultation was to last until the end of time. Anticipating the appearance of claimants to direct contact with the Imam, the ordinance declares: "whoever claims seeing [me] before the rising of Sufyānī and the [cosmic] battle-cry [*Ṣaiḥa*—signs of the end of time] is deceitful and calumnious." [54] All possible future wrangling over the matter of deputyship was thus avoided, and the period to be termed the complete occultation a century later was inaugurated.

Despite Abū Sahl Nawbakhtī's efforts, the period of "confusion" (*ḥayra*) for the Imāmiyya continued into the second half of the tenth/fourth century. This is reflected in three important works written on occultation in the middle or latter half of the tenth/fourth century. All three authors attest to the perplexity of the Shiʿites about the occultation of the Imam, in response to which they had undertaken to write their respective tracts.[55] To allay the confusion of the Shiʿites who had asked him to explain the occultation of the Imam to them, the most eminent of these authors, Ibn Bābūya, produced his *Book of Perfection of Religion and Completion of Benefaction in Proof of Occultation and Removal of Confusion* in order to demonstrate that occultation did not mean nonexistence (*ʿadam*).[56]

As Kohlberg points out, these tracts amassed a set of traditions to demonstrate that there could only be *twelve* Imams, and the belief in the occultation of the last Imam was presented as a direct corollary of the belief in the twelve Imams. The Imāmī Shiʿites thus became the Twelvers.[57]

It remained for the rationalist doctors of the subsequent century to supplement this traditionalist doctrine of occultation with theological arguments. In doing so, the rationalists sought to overcome the chiliastic elements of the doctrine or rather to sublimate them into an eschatology. The Shaykh al-Mufīd (d. 1022/413) adopted the antichiliastic position alluded to in connection with Nawbakhtī. The link between the notion of the Qāʾim and return from death (*rajʿa*) was broken, and the latter was placed at the end of time. Al-Mufīd wrote with sobriety and objectivity and avoided the accounts of the miraculous birth of the Hidden Imam. The Hidden Imam was presented as the "Mahdi of the people" (*al-mahdī al-anām*) who will reappear at the end of time, rather than as the redresser whose parousia (*ẓuhūr*) and uprising (*khurūj*) could be expected imminently.[58] Nor did he pay any attention to what was likely to happen when the Mahdi returned. According to al-Mufīd, the Shiʿites believed the Hidden Imam to be "the Seal of the Proofs of God [*khātam al-ḥujaj*], the legatee and the Qāʾim of the Age. They justify such a possibility on rational grounds inasmuch as its impossibility is removed [i.e., it cannot be rationally ruled out]." [59]

As Sourdel points out, except for the confirmation of *rajᶜa*, of the return of the dead at the end of time, al-Mufīd's attitude is highly intellectualist.[60] Two generations later, Muḥammad ibn Ḥasan al-Ṭūsī, while retaining much of the traditionalist apocalyptic and miraculous materials, nevertheless provides us with a systematic theological exposition of the doctrine of occultation. The antichiliastic position of the Shiᶜite theology was enhanced by al-Ṭūsī's introduction of the notion of complete occultation (*al-ghayba al-tāmma*) to modify the less satisfactory position of the tenth/fourth century traditionalists who merely maintained that there were two forms of occultation.[61] As distinct from the earlier period of concealment in which the Imam communicated with the believer through the mediators (*sufarāʾ*)—significantly, al-Ṭūsī did not restrict this group to the four deputies—the period begun in 940, which was to last until the end of time, was one of complete occultation. All privileged channels of communication with the Hidden Imam were blocked.

Doctrinal assertions regarding the occultation of the Twelfth Imam came under heavy polemical attack during the heated theological debates of the tenth/fourth and eleventh/fifth centuries, but were retained, rationalized as far as possible, and made an integral part of the doctrine of imamate. As such, they were incorporated into the evolving Imāmī theological system at its formative period, and acquired dogmatic status. Thus, from the tenth/fourth century onwards, the development and systematization of the Shiᶜite sacred literature rested on the premise of the absence of the Imam, with little provision being made for his return.

An authoritative formulation of the doctrine of occultation can be found in al-Ṭūsī's *Kitāb al-Ghayba*. Al-Ṭūsī attempts to establish occultation on rational grounds by deducing it from two principles: the necessity of the existence of a leader, Imam (as the instrument of divine guidance, itself deducible from the principle of *luṭf* or grace of God), and the necessity of certainty of the Imam's *ᶜiṣma* (sinlessness/infallibility).[62] The sinfulness and fallibility of political leaders—those commonly considered imams by the (Sunni) people—is taken to establish, with certainty, "that the Infallible Imam is absent and hidden from [men's] views."[63] Al-Ṭūsī proceeds to affirm that the grace of God obtains during the state of occultation, and enumerates the benefits accruing to the Shiᶜite community as a result of the concealment of the Imam of the Age.[64] A later work, written in the fourteenth/seventh century, the *Muᶜtaqad al-Imāmiyya*, a Persian adaptation of Ibn Zuhra's (d. 1192) *Ghunyat-al-Nuzūᶜ ila ᶜIlm al-Uṣūl wa'l-Furūᶜ*, also contains a clear statement of the doctrine of occultation:

> While ethical obligations remain incumbent upon men, and men are not infallible, it is necessary [*wājib*] that there be amongst them an infallible and explicitly designated Imam, through whom they may avoid sinfulness and approach obedience. It was explained that this is grace [*luṭf*], and that kindness toward His worshippers is incumbent upon God. . . . As today, there is no Imam apparent who meets this qualification, it is necessary that he should

be absent [*ghāʾib*], so that there be no contradiction in the [stated] proofs, as the necessity of imamate has been made evident by rational and transmitted proofs.[65]

Thus, while extremism mainly consisted in the divinization of the imam as the intermediary between God and men, often accompanied by the belief in his presence, the Imāmī or Twelver Shiʿite dogma came to insist on the theological mediation of the Imam, and on his *absence*.[66]

1.3 The Value-Rationalism of Islamic Jurisprudence and Its Axiological Bases

In contrast to the markedly varying patterns of differentiation of the religious from the political sphere in Shiʿism and in Sunni Islam, Shiʿite and Sunni law differ only in minute matters of detail.[67] Therefore we must begin with a few remarks about the characteristics and institutional features of Islamic law in general, and of the legal science that gave definitive form to the *sharīʿa* (divinely ordained way), thus producing the sacred law.

In his sociology of law, Weber noted that hierocratic rationalization of law is substantive in character, as there is no interest in the separation of law and ethics. Therefore the theocratic influence produces legal systems that are combinations of legal rules and ethical demands, and leads to the creation of a specifically nonformal type of legal system.[68] In another passage, Weber again states that the hierocratic approach to law aims at material rather than formal rationalization of the law. Though formalistic, in a special sense, its predilection is for the construction of a purely theoretical casuistry, maintaining, through reinterpretation, "practical applicability of . . . unchangeable norms to changing needs."[69]

The essential features of Islamic law bear the permanent imprint of its formative period. Islamic law assumed the character of a *sacred* law because of the orientation of the pious legal scholars who undertook its rationalization and systematization in the eighth/second century. During the latter Umayyad period, when, as Goldziher puts it, "religious people were pushed into the background by the rulers, they, like the Jewish rabbis under Roman rule, occupied themselves with research into the law, which had no validity for the real circumstances of life but represented for themselves the law of their ideal society."[70] The fact that these pious scholars were men of religion and not of law meant that the systematization and islamicization of law took place as an intertwined process.[71] These scholars "impregnated the sphere of law with religious and ethical ideas . . . and incorporated it into the body of duties incumbent on every Muslim. . . . [Thus,] the popular and administrative practice of the late Umayyad period was transformed into the *religious* law of Islam."[72]

The twin process of islamicization and systematization of law created the *sa-*

cred law of Islam. I shall refer to this process as "rationalization," while attempting to explicate its nature and direction. Though many of the first jurists were also judges, the significant strides in systematic reasoning were taken not by judges, but by pious religious scholars such as Jaʿfar al-Ṣādiq (d. 765), Abū Ḥanīfa (d. 767),[73] Mālik ibn Anas (d. 795), and al-Shāfiʿī (d. 820), who is commonly regarded as the founder of the science of *Uṣūl al-fiqh* (principles of jurisprudence).

Although the eighth/second century founders of the schools of law were uniformly intent on islamicizing the law by making it consistent with, and in theory derivative of, the moral norms and values of Islam, they differed in their axiology—i.e., in the determination of the relative importance of the *sources* of law as the embodiment Islamic moral values and ideals. As one would expect, the Qurʾan, as the Word of God, and the sayings and deeds attributed to the Prophet were endowed with normative status by all as sources of law. Beyond that, however, there were differences. The principle of infallibility of the Imams as teachers in religion meant that the saying and injunctions of Jaʿfar al-Ṣādiq had normative force as a foremost source of law for his Shiʿites. Mālik, by contrast, in seeking to supplement positive law with historical, documentary foundations, gave predominant weight to the practice (*ʿamal*) and consensus (*ijmāʿ*) of Medina, the city of the Prophet and center of pious learning in Umayyad times. Abū Ḥanīfa, relied on legal reasoning and opinions (*raʾy*), also occasionally proffered by Mālik, to a greater extent than the others. As Goldziher emphasizes, Mālik was "not a mere collector of traditions [of the Prophet] but first and foremost an interpreter of them from the point of view of praxis"; and his legal compendium, the *Muwaṭṭā*, was a *corpus juris* and not a *corpus traditionum*.[74] Abū Ḥanīfa had similarly cited a number of prophetic traditions (sing. *ḥadīth*) in his legal arguments but without formalizing their normative status into the principal source of law overriding all others. It was al-Shāfiʿī who brought about the decisive grounding of the sacred law of Islam in the prophetic traditions.

Al-Shāfʿī's principles of jurisprudence consisted of a conservative synthesis of the methods of the founding fathers of Islamic law in which the traditions were given axiological priority over consensus (*ijmāʿ*) and legal reasoning (*qīyās*) as a source of law. The latter two retained their validity as sources of law in descending order, but were restricted to matters not covered by the Qurʾan and traditions. The eventual acceptance of al-Shāfiʿī's principles of jurisprudence by the followers of Mālik and Abū Ḥanīfa, who increasingly viewed themselves as a school (sing. *madhhab*) on the model of the one instituted by the *Aṣḥāb al-Shāfiʿī*, represented the victory of the party of tradition—*aṣḥāb al-ḥadīth*—against the party of opinion—*aṣḥāb al-raʾy*—of whom Abū Ḥanīfa came to be regarded as the foremost representative, and who had advocated less rigid restrictions on legal reasoning.[75]

It is true that the distinction between ethical and legal considerations were not completely obliterated, and that the tension between *formal* legal reasoning and the overriding concern with the *value*-rationality of jurisprudence did from time to time make itself felt.[76] Yet, al-Shāfiʿī's emphatic and categorical assertion that in cases of such conflict he would abide by a well-authenticated tradition of the Prophet (as the embodiment of supreme values), however contrary to legal reasoning, set what was in the long run very strict limits to formal rationalization of Islamic law. Instead, al-Shāfiʿī harnessed systematic reasoning to the construction of a consistent system of law rationalized in terms of divinely ordained values. These values were assumed to be embodied in God's commandments in the Qurʾan, and in the Sunna or tradition of the Prophet. Al-Shāfiʿī's great systematic innovation consisted in the assertion of the overriding authority of traditions of the Prophet as authentic reports of his normative, model behavior (Sunna). The divinely ordained values were revealed in the Qurʾan in the first place, but the Sunna of the Prophet was equally sacred as "God has made obedience to the Prophet obligatory." In fact, the Qurʾan was to be interpreted in the light of the Sunna of the Prophet, which therefore prevails upon it. Staunch traditionalism thus became the hallmark of value-rationalism in Islamic jurisprudence. The normative basis of sacred law came to be more rigorously restricted to the Sunna of the Prophet, as embodied in well-authenticated traditions, over the opinions of the companions and their established practices, and over the "living traditions" of the schools of jurisprudence.[77]

Consistency and systematization are the characteristic features of al-Shāfiʿī's jurisprudence.[78] As Weber noted, although formal justice was repugnant to both theocratic and patrimonial power—a repugnance reflected in the informality of qadi justice—the exact opposite of this indifference and aversion to practical formalism occurs in the explicit formulation of norms of the sacred law, and an extremely formalistic casuistry develops.[79] This casuistry is characterized by an "analogical, as opposed to an analytical, way of thinking."[80]

There is a tendency in the Weberian sociological literature to couple substantive rationality with value-rationality.[81] Formal and substantive rationality of law have also been accordingly contrasted.[82] At the procedural level, such a contrast holds for our subject matter and I shall therefore use the terms "substantive justice" and "substantive rationalism" to describe the summary *administration* of theocratic justice ("qadi justice") as well as secular justice in the ruler's court on the basis of the ad hoc consideration of norms of fairness (patrimonial justice).[83] The contrast, however, is no longer valid when we consider Islamic law in general and turn to the nature of *law finding*, which is *both* formal and value-rational. Al-Shāfiʿī's jurisprudence will therefore be characterized as a formal but *value-rational* systematization of law. However, it should be borne in mind that rigid limits are set for this value-rational formalism by its immutable axiological basis: by the *formally* irrational character of sporadic Qurʾanic legislation and the varying and at times contradictory traditions of the Prophet.[84]

The place of reason in al-Shāfiʿī's value-rational jurisprudence was determined by its restrictive axiological role: *if* and *only if* the legal norm for a specific act is not known from the Qurʾan, the traditions, or through consensus, the Muslims are to exert themselves in systematic reasoning—*ijtihād*—and undertake a fresh and independent study of the Qurʾan and the traditions in order to find indications regarding the appropriate legal norm.[85] This determination of the subordinate role of reason to the elicitation of norms *from the authenticated prophetic logia* remained definitive for Islamic jurisprudential rationalism, including Twelver Shiʿite jurisprudence, which is in fact distinguished from the Sunni schools by the continued vitality of value-rationalism down to the nineteenth century.

The jurisprudence of Abū Ḥanīfa, Mālik, and even al-Shāfiʿī antedated the full development of the movement for the study of the traditions. Without the latter movement, al-Shāfiʿī's theoretical elevation of the traditions would remain untranslated into a legal corpus. The actual union of practical legal formulas and the study of the traditions was the achievement of the pious scholars of the subsequent generations, and found embodiment in the great compendiums of the ninth/third century, the *muṣannafāt* collections of classified traditions. Al-Bukhārī (d. 870/256), perhaps the greatest of the collectors of traditions, still had to give occasional paragraph headings without an appropriate tradition. This was in part due to al-Bukhārī's rigorous criterion for the acceptance of the authenticity of a tradition. Within a generation after al-Bukhārī, if not earlier, the urge to create a corpus of law based on the prophetic traditions resulted in the complete relaxation of his rigorous criterion, and in the consequent incorporation of many dubious traditions relating to the minutest points in the four later "canonical" compendiums known as the *sunann* traditions.[86]

In the tenth/fourth century, ʿAbd al-Raḥmān ibn Idrīs al-Rāzī (d. 938–39/327) wrote a treatise in the new branch of religious sciences concerned with the evaluation of critical objections to the authenticity and relative reliability of the traditions, a massive number of which attributed to the Prophet were in circulation. As Goldziher reports in his classic chapter on the Hadith Literature, during one of al-Rāzī's lectures, a student reproached him for his audacity in casting doubt on the integrity and trustworthiness of the revered dead transmitters of the traditions:

> The book fell from his hands and he was in such a state of excitement that he could not continue the lecture. These were feelings of even critical minds when reverence for traditions overcame them. . . . From such motives later Traditionists re-established what former stricter research had thrown out from the material of tradition.[87]

Thus, in the ninth/third century, compendiums of classified traditions, traditionalism as theoretically justified by al-Shāfiʿī prevailed. The jurisprudence (*fiqh*) of the *aṣḥāb al-ḥadīth*, those who best understood the sense of the prophetic traditions, decisively triumphed over that of the *aṣḥāb al-raʾy*, the party of legal opinion.[88] In short, al-Shāfiʿī's highly conservative but unambiguous identification of divinely ordained values provided a firm axiological basis for the construction, some two generations later, of a consistent system of law which was both rigorously value-rational and emphatically traditionalist. To the few dozen Qurʾanic legal commandments were added a massive number of traditions. The acceptance of the traditions—words and deeds of the Prophet—as the embodiment of divinely ordained values led to stereotypification of Islamic law. A satisfactory formalistic assessment of the chain of authorities relating a tradition—*isnād*—would make its content—*matn*—a stereotypical legal norm immune from substantive criticism. The crudest anachronisms would have to be accepted if the *isnād* proved correct, and reason could be employed only to harmonize contradictory traditions.[89]

It is instructive to compare the development of Roman and Islamic law. Of *ius* and *fas*, secular and religious law respectively, it was *ius* that was destined to develop into the rationalized practical system of Roman law, while *fas* became practically innocuous and completely ineffective "through its own inherent means of refined rationalization of magical casuistry."[90] The development of Islamic law presents the opposite extreme. It was secular customary law (*ʿurf*) that was left in its unsystematized primitive form, while all juristic efforts at rationalization and systematization were devoted to sacred law, the *sharīʿa*.

As has been pointed out, the eighth/second century witnessed the development of various legal schools around pious scholars. In the 750s/ca. 140, the secretary of the ʿAbbasid state, Ibn Muqaffaʿ, proposed to the caliph al-Manṣūr a project for reform of the legal administration in the Islamic empire:

> He pointed out the wide divergencies in jurisprudence and in administration of justice existing between the several great cities and between the schools of law. . . . These divergencies, he said, either perpetuated different local precedents or came from systematic reasoning which was sometimes faulty or pushed too far. The Caliph should review the different doctrines with their reasons and codify and enact his own decisions in the interest of uniformity.

Ibn Muqaffaʿ insisted that the caliph could *not* interfere with the major duties of religion. He did, however, possess supreme authority to give binding orders in the light of the Qurʾan and the Sunna in all matters on which there was no precedent.[91] According to Schacht, when Ibn Muqaffaʿ was active in the service of the state, first under the last Umayyads and then under the first ʿAbbasids, the identification of Sunna with the Sunna of the Prophet as reflected in the prophetic logia was by no means complete, and it was to a great extent the administrative practices and regulations of the Umayyad government that determined the content of the "living traditions." Ibn Muqaffaʿ suggested that the caliph was free to fix and codify this Sunna, which would then be promulgated as a code of law and be uniformly enforced by the qadis.

However, Ibn Muqaffaᶜ's suggestion for the incorporation of Islamic law into the state was *not* implemented, and religious law became largely theoretical while the state developed a secular jurisdiction of its own. Consequently, as Weber emphasized, "the sacred law of Islam is throughout specifically a 'jurists' law.'" It is a "jurists' law" rather than a "judges' law," which it might have become had Ibn Muqaffaᶜ's suggestion been taken up. As Schacht puts it, Islamic law is an extreme case of "jurists' law" where "scholarly handbooks have the force of law"; there being "not a corpus of legislation but the living result of legal science."[92] With Ibn Muqaffaᶜ's failure and the subsequent triumph of al-Shāfiᶜi's value-rational jurisprudence, there remained no possibility of "any notion of an authority attaching to the activities of legal tribunals as a source of law. . . . Jurisprudence divorced from actual legal practice, had become an introspective science. . . ."[93] The judgments of the qadis thus came to have no influence on Islamic law comparable to the "cautelary" advice of the jurists or *muftī*s.[94]

One momentous consequence of the failure to create legal systems along the lines suggested by Ibn Muqaffaᶜ was the subsequent prevalence of the principle of "personal law" and of legal particularism in Islam. Law was not a law of the land (*lex terrae*) but rather the privilege of the person as a member of a *madhhab* (school of law, rite). The individual thus carried his *professio juris* with him wherever he went. Different rites coexisted and cases are known of qadis ruling according to more than one rite.

Another consequence to be noted was the possibility of invidious contrasts between sacred law and customs. Once the Qurʾan and the tradition of the Prophet were firmly established as the axiological basis of the sacred law, analogously to Pope Gregory VII's (d. 1085) significant dictum "the Lord did not say 'I am custom' but 'I am truth,'"[95] custom and by extension the ruler's tribunals could, under certain circumstances, be pejoratively depicted as ungodly command (*ḥukm al-ṭāghūt*).[96] This would reinforce the attitude of pious antipathy toward the law of the state and tend to inhibit the world-embracing tendency of the *sharīᶜa* regarding public law.

The emergence of Islamic sacred law as a jurists' law in turn greatly reinforced its infusion with ethical consideration.[97] Furthermore, Islamic sacred law became inherently idealistic and indifferent to the administration of justice. The legal literature abounds with expressions of distaste on the part of the jurists for the office of judge.[98] The moralistic antipathy of the pious jurists to the administration of justice, best reflected in the rules of evidence,[99] amounted to the self-imposition of severe limits upon the scope of the jurisdiction of the sacred law in practice, and a fortiori, on any *procedural* rationalization of the legal system.[100] Thus, in contrast to the value-rational systematization of the legal norms in the eighth/second and ninth/third centuries, we have a complete absence of procedural formalism, which was to remain characteristic of Islamic sacred law. Because of the jurists' self-imposed terms of reference, public law and most instances of criminal justice were left in the hands of the ruler and his representatives at the temporal tribunals—the *maẓālim*.[101]

As has been pointed out, the foundations of the Shiʿite legal system were laid in the eighth/second century. The traditions compiled by the companions and students of the Fifth and Sixth Imams—the so-called four hundred principles—formed the basis of the later compilations of Imāmī *ḥadīth*.[102] However, the tenet of the infallibility (*ʿiṣma*) of the Imam as the interpreter of divine law meant that there was no need for the adoption of al-Shāfiʿī's principles of jurisprudence. It was long after the occultation of the last Imam and in the Buyid period that these principles were adopted and value-rationalism became the characteristic feature of Shiʿite jurisprudence. As was the case with the Sunni school of law, the Qurʾan and tradition form the axiological bases of the Shiʿite jurisprudential value-rationalism, with the traditions of the Imams supplementing those of the Prophet as the source of sacred law. However, certain additional sectarian features were to remain characteristic of the Shiʿite legal system.

By way of comparison, it is worth referring to Pauline Christianity at this point. Christians were not to make use of state authorities, and Paul referred Christians who disagreed among themselves to the judgment of the community or of arbitrators. This constituted the beginning of an independent system of law.[103] With its sectarian organizations by Jaʿfar al-Ṣādiq, we witness a parallel development in Imāmī Shiʿism. In a few well known traditions, notably in two related by Abū Khadīja, al-Ṣādiq enjoins the Imāmīs to "look to a man among you who knows something of our rulings and put him [an arbitrator] between you. [Consider that] I have appointed him judge." The period of traditionalist retrenchment in Qum is marked by a persistent sectarian endeavor to preserve the independent Imāmī legal system by forbidding resort to the official courts of law. Kulaynī thus forbids seeking the judgment of ungodly powers (*ṭāghūt*), and emphasizes the "reprehensibility of having resort to the judges of oppression [*quḍāt al-jawr*]."[104] The judiciary authority of the Shiʿite *ʿulamāʾ* during the occultation of the Imam was reaffirmed by al-Ṭūsī in the subsequent century:

> As for giving judgment among people and judging between litigants, it is not permissible except for him to whom the True Sovereign [i.e., the Imam] has given permission in that regard. And they [the Imams] have entrusted this [function] to the jurists of their sect [*shīʿa*] during such time as they are not able to exercise it in person.[105]

On the basis of these safeguards for its independence, a Shiʿite legal system could be constructed through the elaboration of rules for *law making* and for the *implementation* of the law. A set of rules aiming at the preservation and articulation of the sacred law was energetically put forward by the Shiʿite learned doctors from the late tenth and early eleventh centuries onwards. However, because of the sectarian conditions of Shiᶜism, the formulation of rules envisioning the institutional implementation of the sacred law made little headway. What the shaykh al-Ṭūsī termed the *sharīᶜat al-īman*—the sacred law of faith (i.e., of the Shiᶜite sect)—became impressively elaborate but with few provisions for its routine execution. Consequently, it was reflected in judiciary practice even more dimly than its Sunni counterpart.[106]

The sectarian condition of Shiᶜism in the Sunni body politic resulted in a high degree of informality of judiciary procedure. In the light of the above-mentioned traditions of al-Ṣādiq, which formed the basis of what Binder has aptly described as *ex ante* delegation,[107] no appointment to the office of the judge was necessary. According to the Muḥaqqiq al-Ḥillī, qadiship fell upon the jurist (*faqīh*) possessing the quality of competence to issue *fatwā* (ruling according to the sacred law). The ᶜAllāma al-Ḥillī ruled that if more than one qualified jurist was available in a locality, the litigant could choose among jurists. This implied, among other things, that no definitive end was set to the process of litigation. As for the judge, because his authority derived from the competence to construe the presumed command of the Imam, he was not bound by the rulings of other judges. What is more, the ᶜAllāma in fact stated that correspondence between judges was not permissible.[108] Finally, the issue of enforcement of the qadi's ruling was not treated by our jurists. Needless to say, all this made for very considerable judiciary instability and ran counter to any formal rationalization of the judiciary process.

Calder points to a crucial sociological factor that hindered the formal rationalization of the judiciary process: the vested interest of the jurists as a privileged sodality. Weber noted that the vested interests of the legal *honoratiores* could curb the formal rationalization of law, as they did in the case of the guild of English solicitors.[109] The legal particularism of Islam generally, and the sectarian condition of Shiᶜism in particular, meant that the Shiᶜite jurists had to forge their professional authority without reference to the coercive force of the state or its judiciary branch. They did so by sanctioning and generous acknowledgment of *ikhtilāf* (differences of opinion) among the prominent jurists. In the absence of coercive means or hierarchical organizational discipline, the acceptance of *ikhtilāf* was essential to enable the clerical class to remain the exponents of the (theoretically) unchanging sacred law and the depositories of the institutionalized charisma of revelation. The principle of *ikhtilāf* in interpretation thus acted as a means of giving the sacred law the appearance of fixity and permanence as the continuation of revelation.[110] At the same time, it perpetuated judiciary instability and prevented the rationalization of legal administration.

While the problem of institutionalization of judiciary procedure received little attention and remained largely unresolved, the learned rationalist doctors of the eleventh/fifth century took impressive strides toward the articulation and elaboration of the sacred law. These were continued by the subsequent generations of jurists. In the *Means to the Foundations of the Sacred Law*, al-Murtaḍā (d. 1044) separates the "principles of jurisprudence" (*uṣūl al-fiqh*) from the "principles of religion" (*uṣūl al-dīn*), instituting the former as an autonomous science distinct from theology.[111] Al-Murtaḍā confirms the mooring of the sacred law to the traditions. Furthermore, at the formal level, he greatly enhances the axiological importance of the traditions as a source of law for two reasons. First, al-Murtaḍā obviates the autonomous normative validity of consensus and makes it derivative. The validity of consensus is said to be the consequence of the fact that it is indicative of the saying of the Infallible Imam. Second, to safeguard the strict value-rationalism of the sacred law, al-Murtaḍā denies the general validity of *ijtihād*, legal reasoning by analogy which al-Shāfiʿī considered the fourth source of law.[112] However, the substantive scope of the sacred law thus based on the traditions is drastically circumscribed by two other jurisprudential principles of this most rationalist of the Shiʿite doctors.

Al-Murtaḍā refused to allow normative validity (*ḥujiyyat*) to the "singly related" (*āḥād*) traditions.[113] Consequently, a large number of traditions that were not multiply corroborated were discarded and the legal domain covered them in detail released from the normative governance of the sacred law. At the same time, al-Murtaḍā advanced the principle of permissibility (*ibāḥa*) of acting in accordance the dictates of reason (*ʿaql*):

> What we have said makes clear that there has to be, in all kinds of rules for acts, a necessary principle in reason [*ʿaql*]: what is seen indeed to have the quality of injustice [*ẓulm*] is necessarily vile according to reason, and that which has the quality of justice [*inṣāf*] and of gratitude for divine benefactions [*niʿma*] is necessarily incumbent. Thus it is necessary that there be in reason [*fi' l-ʿaql*] the principle of permissibility. . . .[114]

Concrete examples are also given by al-Murtaḍā: property is regulated by a rational principle and "is not conditional upon tradition [*samʿ*]," whereas inheritance and booty are undoubtedly regulated by "principles found in the sacred law [*asbāb sharʿiyya*] outside of reason."[115] This principle recognizes a secular sphere of life in which the sacred law permits autonomous rational guidance of action without any encumbrance of the weaker, singly related traditions. Thus, al-Murtaḍā's value-rationalism, though entailing considerable traditionalism, also allows a large scope for both instrumental and substantive legal rationalism on the basis of expediency and general utility.

However, al-Murtaḍā's moderate traditionalism, coupled with the advocacy of unrestricted employment of reason for the normative regulation of the secular spheres of life, was to give way to a traditionalism as staunch as that of the jurisprudence of the Sunni *aṣḥāb al-ḥadīth*. Traditionalism already set in with al-Murtaḍā's pupil al-Ṭūsī, the shaykh al-Ṭāʾifa (d. 1067). Al-Ṭūsī took the contrary view to that of his teacher on the relative axiological salience of the traditions. He accepted the validity of the singly related traditions as a source of law, thereby enormously expanding the corpus of the Shiʿite sacred law and consequently the substantive scope of its value-rational *and* traditionalistic normative regulation of social life. For reasons put forward in section 1.5 below, al-Ṭūsī responded to the pressure to embrace the world emanating from the sociopolitical condition of the Shiʿites, and to the constant debates with the Sunni scholars resulting from this condition, by opening up much new grounds in Shiʿite law. Having written the *Nihāya* in the tradition of Shiʿite legal thought, al-Ṭūsī had to counter the Sunni criticisms of the restricted substantive scope of the Shiʿite sacred law. To do so, he decided to expand the substantive scope of the sacred law instead of insisting, as al-Murtaḍā had done, that where firmly authenticated traditions for the normative regulation of action were not available, reason was the valid guide. In his *Kitāb al-Mabsūṭ* and *Kitāb al-Khilāf*, modeled after Sunni legal works, many substantive cases previously not dealt with by the Shiʿite jurists were discussed. The results of much Sunni legal scholarship thus passed into the Shiʿite sacred law. The latter's value-rationalism took on a markedly traditionalist character similar to that of the Shāfiʿite law. This was so because, although al-Ṭūsī retained the validity of legal reasoning, its importance diminished as a result of the acceptance of the normative authority of singly related traditions. The comparison with al-Shāfiʿī as the founder of value-rational traditionalism in Islamic law seems especially apt in light of the fact that for a century after his death, the shaykh al-Ṭāʾifa was considered the definitive legal authority and his followers called themselves "the Followers," *muqallida*.

In the second half of the twelfth/sixth century, we witness a sharp reaction to the shaykh in the form of a sustained effort to revive the rationalist method of al-Murtaḍā and to reject the normative validity of the singly related traditions. Muḥammad ibn Idrīs al-Ḥillī (d. 1202/598), the leading figure of this period, was the first Shiʿite jurist to give reason (*ʿaql*) the explicit status of the fourth source of normative validity in law.[116] This critical reaction to the shaykh al-Ṭāʾifa was not destined to triumph and eventually faded. The attempt to restrict the scope of traditionalism and to couple it with utilitarian rationalism in the legal regulation of the secular spheres of life, as advocated by al-Murtaḍā, thus ended in failure. The towering authorities of the thirteenth and early fourteenth centuries, the Mụaqqiq al-Ḥillī and his nephew the ʿAllāma, retracted, reaffirmed, and refined the traditionalism of al-Ṭūsī.

The failure, however, was by no means total, and al-Murtaḍā's rationalism had a permanent impact on Shiʿite jurisprudence, especially on the analytical classification of legal subjects. Another prominent pupil of his, Sallār [Sālār] al-Daylamī (d. 1056–57/448), divided legal and ethical norms into two categories: *ʿibādāt* (devotional duties) and *muʿāmilāt* (transactions), with the latter subdivided into *ʿuqūd* (contracts) and *aḥkām* (commandments) and *aḥkām* subdivided again in turn. This schema for the analytical classification of the legal domains, which, as Schacht remarks, has no counterpart in Sunni jurisprudence,[117] was refined by the Muḥaqqiq into the four domains of *ʿibādāt*, *ʿuqūd*, *īqāʿāt* (one-sided contractual obligations), and *aḥkām*.

The expansion of the substantive content of the Shiʿite sacred law by the shaykh al-Ṭūsī entailed confusion and inconsistencies that were refined and resolved by the Muhaaqqiq al-Ḥillī (d. 1277). Furthermore, the acceptance of the singly related (*āḥād*) traditions by the shaykh meant a massive increase in the number of normative legal stereotypes to be considered and reconciled (and a continuing increase as the traditions continued to be fabricated and then duly collected). It was left to the ʿAllāma al-Ḥillī (d. 1325) to adopt the classificatory system of one of his teachers, Abu'l-Faḍāʾil Aḥmad ibn Ṭāwūs,[118] and to make the greatest contributions to the assessment of traditions and the classification of the degree of their normative authority through the assessment of the reliability of their transmitters.[119] The beginning of the fourteenth/eighth century thus marked the maturity of al-Ṭūsī's value-rational traditionalism, which has remained definitive for the Shiʿite sacred law.

It is well known that in Sunnism, with the "closure of the gates of *ijtihād*" (law finding by legal reasoning), the value-rational systematization of Islamic law came to an end, and the third principle of the validity of legal norms—consensus (*ijmāʿ*)—came to rigidify the sacred law. Thanks to al-Murtaḍā's virtual negation of consensus as an independent principle,[120] this did not happen in Shiʿism, which Scarcia has aptly characterized as an "Islam without *ijmāʿ*." [121] As we have seen, the value-rational science of *Uṣūl al-Fiqh* gathered momentum with al-Murtaḍā long before the formal adoption of the principle of *ijtihād*. It is fascinating to note that, even though centuries later reason (*ʿaql*) came to be adopted as the fourth source of validity of legal norms, as Ibn Idrīs had suggested, and even though its application, *ijtihād*, became the distinctive feature of Shiʿite jurisprudence, the concern with value-rationality and the restriction of *ijtihād* to cases of absence of explicit or easily extractable norms remained unchanged. By the latter part of the thirteenth/seventh century, the Muḥaqqiq al-Ḥillī already admitted that the Shiʿite jurists had in effect been practicing *ijtihād*. The final step to sanction *ijtihād* formally was taken by the ʿAllāma early in the subsequent century.[122] *Ijtihād*, as advocated by the ʿAllāma, Ibn al-Muṭahhar al-Ḥillī, in the Il-khanid period, and following him by al-Karakī, Ḥasan ibn Zayn al-Dīn, and Bahāʾ al-Dīn al-ʿAmilī in the Safavid period, consisted in the application of grammatical and linguistic rules, and rules of valid logical inference to the transmitted traditions of the Imams, with the aim of extracting valid legal norms. The value-rational formalism was harnessed to the task of inferring single legal norms case by case. It had a definite antisystematic bias, as the lawfulness of each single norm had to be meticulously established, ultimately with reference to an explicit text (*naṣṣ*). This inevitable reference to the text of a tradition, paradoxical as it may seem, shackled the Shiʿite sacred law ever more firmly to the accumulating mass of traditions as its value-rational methodology became more developed. Reason was retained but emasculated; it became the maid-servant of legal traditionalism, with its task defined as the maximal extraction of legal meaning and implications from the traditions as normative stereotypes.

1.4 The Social Position and Cultural Outlook of the Imāmiyya and Their Relations with the Rulers

Let us recall the division of the epoch under consideration into two periods: the period of retrenchment (most of the ninth/third century) and the period of expansion (the tenth/fourth to the twelfth/sixth century). Little can be said about the socioeconomic activities of the Shiᶜite community when Qum constituted the only important Imāmī center, except to remark the prodigious religious activity of the scholars. The small Imāmī community of Qum was evidently able to sustain a number of outstanding scholars. But it could not have been nearly large enough for the socioeconomic needs of its lay members to create any demand for practical jurisprudence to be satisfied by the *ᶜulamā*ᵓ. Larger political concerns appear to have been equally remote from the preoccupations of the isolated Shiᶜite community of Qum.

In the period of expansion, we find the situations of the Shiᶜites greatly changed. As was pointed out in section 1.2, the aristocratic outlook of the prominent Imāmī families of Baghdad became predominant in the tenth century even before the Buyid seizure of power. The Buyids supported the Imāmī community. The great theologian al-Mufīd enjoyed their favor, as did their distant relatives, the prominent Mūsawī family of the aldermen (sing. *naqīb*) of the ᶜAlids, whose most prominent representatives were the brothers Sharīf al-Murtaḍā and Sharīf al-Raḍī. Sharīf al-Murtaḍā (d. 1044/436), the towering Imāmī intellectual figure of the first half of the eleventh century, was one of the wealthiest and politically most prominent notables of Baghdad and was befriended by the Buyids, the caliph, and a number of viziers.[123]

In the twelfth century, we find the Imāmīs forming cohesive urban communities with considerable emphasis on mutual assistance among their members.[124] These communities included different occupational groups and were dominated by an aristocracy consisting of families of local notables. In a study based on the *Kitāb al-Naqḍ*, Calmard draws our attention to the following sociological facts about Imāmī Shiᶜism during the Saljūq period. The Shiᶜite communities, constituting sizable minorities in a number of cities in central and northern Iran, included men from the lower occupations such as cobblers, hatters, and weavers, and the poor who constituted its lower stratum. Above this stratum, we find a middle stratum of men in the military occupations consisting of a large proportion of the Imāmīs, either in the armed retinues of the potentates or at the service of the state. Finally, we have the Shiᶜite aristocracy, families of notables (*sayyids*), many of whom acquired great prominence in government service. This wealthy urban aristocracy was the dominant stratum of the Shiᶜite community and can be considered the bearers of its culture.

In fact, the Maecenas-like munificence of the Shiᶜite notables who occupied important positions in the Saljūq administration, as recorded by Qāḍī ᶜAbd al-Jalīl, created many mosques and centers of learning where Imāmī culture flourished and was propagated. Propaganda techniques of the Buyid period were revived. The practice of *manāqib-khwānī* flourished and appears to have enjoyed enough popularity to have brought a Sunni counterpart into existence. The *manāqib-khwān*s were singers who recited songs extolling the "virtues" (*manāqib*) of ᶜAlī and the other Imams in streets and bazaars; the Sunnis, in reaction, began to have *faḍāʾil-khwāns* who extolled the virtues of the rightly guided caliphs. The Shiᶜite ceremonies marking the martyrdom of the third Imam also gained popularity, even among the Sunnis.

As the reference to the *Kitāb al-Naqḍ* has already indicated, Imāmī Shiᶜism—the *Madhhab-e Shīᶜa-ye Uṣuliyya*—appears as a religious movement with a fairly pronounced rationalistic character. It is interesting to note further that the *qaṣīda*s recited in praise of the Imams contained doctrinal and theological elements such as the concepts of *tanzīh* (the absolute transcendence of God), *ᶜadl* (justice of God), and *ᶜiṣma* (infallibility [of the Imams]). Imāmī Shiᶜism was as much opposed to extremist movements—the *Ghulāt* and the Imāᶜīlīs—as Sunnism.[125] Similarly, most Imāmīs in this period appear to have been even more anti-Sufi than were the Sunnis; they seem to have objected to Sufism from the standpoint of strict monotheistic "rationalism," condemning the Sufis for their pantheism, orgiasticism, antinomianism, and for their denial of the transcendence of God.

If the sources enable us to draw only a tentative picture of the social and economic position of the Imāmīs, they leave us in no doubt about the close ties between the Shiᶜite notables and the Sunni rulers. Many Imāmīs entered the service not only of the ᶜAbbasid and the Saljūq Sunni rulers but also of the pagan Mongols, and achieved great prominence. The Banū Yaqṭīya (the eighth/second century), the Nawbakhtīs, and some of the members of the Furāt family (late ninth/third and early tenth/fourth centuries) are notable examples of Imāmīs who served the ᶜAbbasid caliphate and attained vizierates and other high governmental positions.[126] Yaqṭīn ibn Mūsā served the ᶜAbbasid caliph al-Mahdī (775–85), as did ᶜAlī ibn Yaqṭīn (d. 798–99/182), who also was a close associate of al-Mahdī's successors. The Shiᶜite vizier of the Buyid Bahāʾ al-Dawla, Abū Naṣr Sābūr [Shāpūr] ibn Ardashīr (d. 1025–26/416), was a notable patron of Shiᶜite learning, and founded an important library in the Shiᶜite quarter of Baghdad, the Karkh.[127] Al-Nāṣir (1178–1225/575–622), the most important ᶜAbbasid caliph of the post-Saljūq period, had a number of Imāmī viziers;[128] the Shiᶜite vizier Ibn al-ᶜAlqamī played an important role in the events of the reign of the last universally recognized ᶜAbbasid caliph, al-Mustaᶜṣim, and is generally believed to have cooperated with the Mongols in bringing about his downfall.[129]

In the Saljūq domains, the opening of government careers to Imāmī talent began under Malik Shāh (1072–92) and continued under Sanjar (1118–57) and his successors. Malik Shāh had at least one Shiᶜite grand vizier, and his son Muḥammad had one. Two of Sanjar's six grand viziers were Imāmīs. Of the latter, Mukhtaṣṣ al-Mulk Kāshī was the head of a family of Shiᶜite notables that supplied Suleymān Shāh (1160–61) and Tughril III (1176–94) with their viziers. Like the last ᶜAbbasid, the last Saljūq of Iran had an Imāmī vizier: Fakhr al-Dīn Varāmīnī.[130] The Imāmīs (or *Rāfiḍīs*, to use the pejorative term) became highly conspicuous in the chanceries of the Saljūq rulers—so much so that the resentful Sunni historian Rāvandī could attribute the decline of the kingdom to the "tyranny of the *Rāfiḍī* generals and scribes" ("ẓulm-e sarhangān va dabīrān-e rāfiḍī").[131]

The political prominence of the Shiᶜite dignitaries continued throughout the Mongol and Il-Khanid periods. The learned notable families of Ḥilla had close ties with Ibn al-ᶜAlqamī (d. 1258/656), the Shiᶜite vizier of the last ᶜAbbasid caliph, who was confirmed in that position after the Mongol conquest of Baghdad by Hülegü. Al-ᶜAlqamī's son, a subsequent vizier, was a student of the great jurist al-Muḥaqqiq al-Ḥillī.[132] A delegation of Shiᶜite *ᶜulamā*ʾ from Ḥilla came to Hülegü during the seige of Baghdad to express their submission and ask for the appointment of a police chief for that city.[133] Raḍī al-Dīn ibn al-Ṭāwūs, the leading member of another prominent dynasty of Ḥillī scholars, was appointed alderman (*naqīb*) of the ᶜAlids in Baghdad.[134] As we have already pointed out, the ᶜAllāma, Ibn al-Muṭahhar al-Ḥillī, and his son Fakhr al-Muḥaqqiqīn (d. 1369–70/771) enjoyed the favors of Öljeitü. Favorable disposition toward the Mongol government was not confined to the Ḥillī clerical dynasties. The Shiᶜite philosopher and theologian Naṣīr al-Dīn al-Ṭūsī had been one of Hülegü's closest counsellors, and the famous Shiᶜite scholars of Bahrain, Maytham ibn ᶜAlī al-Baḥrānī, had dedicated to his commentary on the *Nahj al-Balāgha* to the historian and Mongol governor of Baghdad, ᶜAṭā-Malik Juvainī.[135]

1.5 The World-embracing Tendency in Imāmī Shiᶜism and the Political Ethic of the Sectarian Phase

The Shiᶜite political ethic during the period of historical imamate has been alluded to in section 1.1 of this chapter. It was pointed out that armed rebellion was forbidden by the Fifth and Sixth Imams. For al-Ṣādiq, "the Imam was not expected to revolt against the existing illegal government, and rebellion without his authorization was unlawful." [136] This position was confirmed by their successors. The Eighth Imam, ᶜAlī al-Riḍā, for example; is reported to have made the following statement:

> Only that believer who accepts admonishment is capable of being commanded to the good and forbidden from the evil. But not the wielder of the sword and the whip. Verily he who stands up against a tyrannical ruler, and a calamity thereby befalls him, shall have no reward for it. . . .[137]

At the same time, the Imams encouraged the service of illegitimate rulers when it could improve the plight of the brethren within the Shiʿite sect. The Seventh Imam, Mūsā al-Kāẓim, whose disciple ʿAlī ibn Yaqṭīn was a high official of the caliphs,[138] had this to say: "Verily the group of men who associated with the ruler and whom the believers take as their refuge are secure on the Day of Resurrection."[139]

Needless to say, this quietism and political pragmatism went hand in hand with an attitude of inner detachment necessitated by the primacy of loyalty to the spiritual authority of the Imam and the primacy of preoccupation with spiritual excellence and piety as enjoined by Jaʿfar al-Ṣādiq and his successors.

The conditions of the ensuing period of retrenchment influenced the direction in which the traditionalist scholars of Qum steered the Shiʿite religious rationalism of the period: away from worldly concerns and toward the systematic compilation of the reported sayings and deeds of the Imams for the spiritual and moral guidance of the pious. This religious rationalism, whose axiological basis consisted of the traditions of the Imams, in turn fostered a corresponding religious attitude of inner-worldly piety, many of whose features, immortalized in Kulaynī's compendiums, were passed on to the Shiʿism of the later periods.[140]

Troeltsch's characterization of the apolitical and quietistic attitude of Pauline Christians suggests a parallelism with that of the sectarian Shiʿites of the eighth, ninth, and tenth centuries. It was "not founded on love and esteem for the existing institutions but upon a mixture of contempt, submission and relative recognition." It tolerated the existing political order while inwardly undermining it.[141] A similar attitude among the Shiʿite sectarians may be presumed to have fostered a spirit of inner detachment and independence which is reflected in the inner-worldly pietistic writings of the traditionalists of Qum. This negative evaluation of the political sphere and inner antipathy toward it was greatly attenuated in the subsequent period, and the tendency toward a positive evaluation of the political sphere and of political activity took the upper hand.

The increased worldly activities and political/administrative engagement of the Shiʿites in the period of expansion channeled the development of religious rationalism in a world-embracing direction. Madelung has dealt with the receptivity of eleventh-century Shiʿism to the rationalism of the Muʿtazila at the doctrinal level, that is, with regard to Shiʿite theology.[142] In the preceding section, we surveyed the impact of rationalism on Shiʿite jurisprudence. Now, it is with regard to the social, economic, and political ethic of Shiʿism that we shall trace the influence of the social position and outlook of the Shiʿites on the direction in which the Shiʿite religious rationalism unfolded.

In assessing the impact of the social position and cultural outlook of the dominant stratum of the Shiʿite community on the direction of religious rationalism of the period of expansion, first and foremost the sectarian condition of Shiʿism should be borne in mind. The lack of functional differentiation in the authority of the *ᶜulamāᵓ* is indeed typical in the Buyid period, irrespective of doctrinal and sectarian affiliation.[143] Not unlike the rabbis, who were in principle unpaid until the fourteenth century, both the Sunni and the Shiᶜite *ᶜulamāᵓ* held a variety of other occupations.[144] The sectarian condition of Shiᶜism perpetuated this and precluded the establishment of an institutionally differentiated hierocracy. Many of the Shiᶜite theologians and jurists such as the Nawbakhtīs, the Mūsavī brothers in Baghdad, and the scholars of the family of the Muḥaqqiq and those of the house of Ṭāwūs in Ḥilla, belonged to the politically dominant families of the Shiᶜite community and often took active leading roles in politics. The members of this politically dominant stratum, who also constituted the bearers of the Shiᶜite religious culture and ethos, could therefore directly remold certain features of Shiᶜism in accordance with their elective affinities. They did so by embracing the world: by evaluating worldly concerns more positively and through a sustained effort to bring much socioeconomic and political activity under the normative governance of religious ethics.

Second, one should also bear in mind the atmosphere of competition among schools of theology and law that was prevalent prior to the gradual definition and formation of a Sunni orthodoxy in Saljūq times. The Imāmī doctors of the Buyid period took part in the general intellectual and doctrinal debates and competition. In doing so, they could and did avail themselves of the intellectual armory of their Sunni rivals, be they Muᶜtazilī theologians or Shāfiᶜī jurists.

The theoretical means for the embracing of the world and regulation of activity was the science of jurisprudence (*uṣūl al-fiqh*). The reader may recall that al-Murtaḍā rejected the normative validity of the singly related traditions and at the same time held the permissibility of dealing with necessities of life not covered by a well-authenticated tradition in accordance with the dictates of reason. In the Islamic tradition, where the Christian distinction between nature and grace does not exist, al-Murtaḍā's "shiᶜitization" of the normative regulation of the necessities of life in accordance with reason roughly amounted to the Thomist acceptance of natural law in areas not covered by the smaller corpus of well-authenticated traditions.[145] As was pointed out, however, such formal shiᶜitization of social and economic ethics did not prove lasting, and, from the time of al-Ṭūsī onwards, the world-embracing tendency of Shiᶜism acquired a definitively traditionalistic direction and manifested itself in the extension of the sacred law, based on the larger and growing mass of dubious traditions in addition to authentic ones. In response to the criticism of his Sunni rivals that his *Nihāya* was too brief and inadequate, leaving many areas of life unregulated, al-Ṭūsī proceeded to write the much bulkier *al-Mabsūṭ*. For similar reasons, he endowed singly related traditions with normative validity. Furthermore, he freely borrowed from Sunni works, especially with regard to substantive details on transactions. What the shaykh had hurriedly borrowed was digested and incorporated into the Shiᶜite sacred law by the Muḥaqqiq in his masterpiece of legal harmonization, the

Sharāyiᶜ al-Islām. This enabled the ᶜAllāma after him to take a further step in substantive borrowing from the Sunni law. The latter completed the world-embracing extension of the sacred law by thus greatly enlarging its section on transactions.[146]

In section 1.1 of this chapter, I tried to depict the differentiation of the religious and the political authority in the Imāmī world view, and the life conditions and activities of the Imāmīs. We can now turn to an examination of the political ethic of Imāmī Shiᶜism as the agency of the normative regulation of the political sphere, which developed as a part of the world-embracing rationalization of life in accordance with religious principles by the exponents of Shiᶜism in the eleventh century.

The fundamentally quietistic feature of the Shiᶜism of the earlier period was reaffirmed by the rejection of armed rebellion and by the emphasis on the lawfulness of *taqiyya* (dissimulation). Al-Mufīd stressed this continuity, pointing out that the situation cannot change before the reappearance of the Hidden Imam as the Mahdi, whose ancestors

> far from holding it a religious duty to rise in armed revolt against their enemies, . . . disapproved of any incitement to such action, and . . . the religion by which they approach God consisted of dissimulation [*taqiyya*], restraining the hand and guarding the tongue, carrying out the prescribed worship, and serving God exclusively by good works.[147]

In practice, a usual way of extending the sacred law in a system formally professing rationalism with regard to the values embodied in the traditions was simply to fabricate a tradition containing a customary norm or set of norms and attribute it to an Imam. In this manner, a customary usage could become a normative stereotype resting on the authority of an Imam, and thus "islamicized" and incorporated into the sacred law. An interesting illustration of this means of extending the sacred law with regard to the political ethic occurs in the Buyid period. In his famous compilation of the sayings of the First Imam, *Nahj al-Balāgha*, Sharīf al-Raḍī, al-Murtaḍā's brother, included a document not found where one would expect it in earlier sources. It was in the form of a letter by ᶜAlī to Mālik al-Ashtar, whom he appointed governor of Egypt in 658–59/38, and reproduces the substance of the political ethic of pre-Islamic Iran (to be discussed in chapter 3). The appointed governor is urged to rule with justice. To do so, an army is needed, which in turn depends on the revenue of the state. The collection of this revenue depends on the tax collectors, secretaries, and qadis, whose material substance depends on peasants, craftsmen, and merchants. Each of these classes of subjects should be treated with justice and propriety.[148]

In Imāmī Shiᶜism, *jihād* had tended to be transposed to the spiritual plane ever since the Fifth Imam, al-Bāqir, declared it to be in abeyance.[149] In Kulaynī's compendium, the "Greater *Jihād*"—in contrast to the "Lesser *Jihād*"—was presented as the spiritual struggle against one's instinctive nature (*nafs*). Ibn Bābūya asserted that the true *jihād* consisted in striving for knowledge (*ʿilm*). As for the *jihād* involving actual warfare, the obligation to undertake it became narrowly circumscribed in the time of occultation. Al-Mufīd, following Kulaynī, added the *dār al-īmān* (the realm of faith) to the traditional dichotomy of the *dār al-Islām* (house/realm of Islam) and the *dār al-kufr* (realm of infidelity), and presented *jihād* as the (nonviolent) struggle to convert the realm of Islam to the realm of faith (i.e., Shiʿism), postponing the onslaught on the infidels.[150] A generation later, al-Ṭūsī considered holy war in the absence of the Imam an error (*khaṭā'*);[151] and over two centuries later, the Muḥaqqiq al-Ḥillī similarly ruled that *jihād* was not obligatory unless the believer was summoned by the Imam. Except for a passage in which *jihād* was considered "commendable" (*mustaḥabb*) but not obligatory on the frontier in the absence of the Imam, the possibility of holy war during the occultation was not envisaged. Therefore, the Muḥaqqiq in effect limited *jihād* to defensive war.[152]

Thus the importance of holy war was very much played down in the Imāmī jurisprudence. By contrast, the incumbency of other main ethical duties mentioned earlier, *amr bi'l-maʿrūf* (enjoining the good) and *nahy ʿan al-munkar* (forbidding the evil) was asserted as rigorously as in Sunni jurisprudence. The obligatoriness of these ethical duties, however, was in effect restructed to nonviolent action. The Sharīf al-Murtaḍā considered these ethical categories *kifāʿī* (collectively dischargeable) obligatory duties—i.e., duties not incumbent on believers individually so long as they are adequately fulfilled by an adequate number of the members of the community.[153] His disciple al-Ṭūsī considered these duties individually incumbent (*ʿaynī*). Al-Ṭūsī distinguished three ways in which they could be carried out: through the heart, the tongue, and the hand. When "enjoining the good" through the last two means are dangerous to the individual or to others, "the belief in the necessity of enjoining the good through the heart [*bi'l-qalb*] suffices, and nothing more is incumbent upon him."[154] The same holds for "forbidding the evil."[155] According to al-Ṭūsī, "enjoining the good by using one's hand [*bi'l-yad*]"—i.e., involving coercion and violence—requires the permission of the ruler of the time (*sulṭān al-waqt*).[156] The Muḥaqqiq al-Ḥillī considered it preferable to regard these categories of ethical duty as individually incumbent ethical obligations. He took over al-Ṭūsī's classification, but restricted the incumbency of the variety involving coercion even further by making it dependent on the permission of the Imam, who, in contrast to the ruler of the time, had been and was to remain absent for centuries.[157]

The eleventh/fifth century also witnessed a more general attempt to bring the political sphere into the ambit of ethical regulation, and to encourage ethically correct activity in politics. This bold attempt amounted to an emphatic affirmation that the differentiation of imamate from political rulership need not impede the normative, ethical regulation of political life.

Al-Murtaḍā, the leading theologian of the Buyid period—the period in which the rapprochement between the Imāmī doctors and political powers was at a height—set out to provide a systematic ethical guideline for action in the political sphere and for the regulation of the Imāmīs' relationships with political authorities. This attempt resulted in a much more positive religious evaluation of political activity and produced a political ethic enjoining active involvement in government and judiciary services. Al-Murtaḍā himself accepted the office of the judge of the ruler's court (*maẓālim*).[158] Both the legitimist revolutionary ethic of the proto-Imāmī Shiᶜism and the pietistic withdrawal of Qum traditionalism were discarded for political pragmatism within the existing structure of domination.

We already find the basic elements of this pragmatic political ethic in al-Mufīd.[159] These elements are systematically elaborated in a treatise by al-Murtaḍā, where responsible political involvement in government receives a positive evaluation. In his treatise on working for the government, written in view of a discussion held in the presence of the vizier Abu'l-Qāsim al-Ḥusayn ibn ᶜAlī al-Maghribī in 1025/415, al-Murtaḍā states:

> Know that the ruler may be of two kinds: legitimate [*muḥiqq*] and just, or illegitimate [*mubṭil*], unjust and usurpatory. There is no question in regard to holding office on behalf of the legitimate, just ruler since *it is permissible and may even be obligatory*, if the ruler commands it as a duty and makes its acceptance incumbent. The discussion thus concerns only the tenure of office on behalf of the usurper. This may be of several kinds: obligatory (and it may exceed obligatoriness toward compulsion), licit, and evil and forbidden. It is obligatory if the one accepting office knows, or considers it likely on the basis of clear indications, that he will through the tenure of the office be enabled to support a right and to reject a false claim or to order what is proper and to forbid what is reprehensible, and if it were not for this tenure, nothing of this would be accomplished. In this case, the acceptance of the office is *obligatory* for him because of the obligatoriness of that for which it is a means and an expedient for its accomplishment.[160]

The Sharīf then enumerates the remaining cases: when the acceptance of assignments from a tyrannical ruler and entry into his service are necessary, indifferent, reprehensible, or forbidden respectively. Al-Murtaḍā proceeds to deny the categorical reprehensibility of wielding authority delegated by an unjust ruler. He maintains that this reprehensibility is obviated in case of coercion, and when the appointee is able to further the cause of the morally good: to redress rights (of men) and to fulfill ethical obligations (to mankind). This is so because, if the appointee exercises his authority in the affairs of the community in accordance with the sacred law and with the dictates of the Prophet and his house, he exercises authority only apparently on behalf of the unjust ruler but in reality on behalf of the rightful Imams, may peace be upon them. Depending on the circumstances, such exercise of delegated authority becomes "commendable" or "incumbent," as it is in reality on behalf of the rightful Imam and the Lord of the Age (*Ṣāḥib al-Amr*). After dealing briefly with cases of reprehensibility and indifference, al-Murtaḍā concludes by reaffirming the ethical commendability of entering into the service of an unjust ruler in order to fulfill the needs of the believing brethren, to uphold their rights, and to eliminate the evil.[161]

The shaykh al-Ṭāʾifa subscribed to al-Murtaḍā's view on political authority, and commended the acceptance of authority delegated by an unjust ruler when it could be exercised to enforce the sacred law—that is, when it could be viewed as being exercised on behalf of the true Imam.

At one point such tenure of office on behalf of the tyrannical ruler is even referred to as being "among the greater *jihād*":

> He who undertakes authority on behalf of an oppressor to execute a *ḥadd* [penalty] or enforce a commandment [of the sacred law], believing that he undertakes this on behalf of the True Sovereign [i.e., the Hidden Imam] and in order to carry it out as required by the sacred law of faith [*sharīʿat al-īmān*] . . . verily [what he does] is among the greater *jihād*.[162]

Al-Ṭūsī then turns to the clear and unproblematic case of the tenure office on behalf of a just ruler:

> Undertaking office on behalf of the ruler who commands the good and forbids the reprehensible and who puts things in their [proper] place is permissible, being a desirable act, and perhaps borders on being incumbent because it makes possible to command the good and forbid the reprehensible and to put things in their [proper] place.[163]

Finally, al-Ṭūsī returns to the necessity of working with oppressors, this time to emphasize the commendability of assistance to the Shiʿite sectarians community made possible by the acceptance of office. He states that the acceptance of political and judiciary office is commended because it makes possible (1) the upholding of the Shiʿite sacred law on behalf of the Hidden Imam, and (2) the promotion of the good of the Shiʿite community on behalf of the sectarian brethren.[164]

Some two centuries later, the Muḥaqqiq al-Ḥillī addressed the topic in the narrower and more specific context of administration of justice. He took a cautious view about the acceptance of judgeship from a tyrannical ruler.[165] However, as regards a just ruler, the Muḥaqqiq is much more affirmative: "The acceptance of judgeship from a just ruler is commendable and perhaps 'obligatory' upon him who is confident [of his ability]."[166]

For Shiʿism, the existence of the doctrine of imamate barred legitimation of the ruler similar to that of the sultan in Sunni Islam, thus secularizing political rulership. It also entailed doctrinal indifference to legitimation of political power. This doctrinal indifference to the principles of legitimacy of political power prevailed all the more easily because, their constituency being a minority sect within the Islamic body politic, legitimation of rulership was not a service demanded from the Shiᶜite jurists by the rulers. Al-Murtaḍā advocated a consistently Shiᶜite political ethic despite the secularity of rulership. In our terminology, a sharp bifurcation was instituted between the ethically regulated *motivation to political action*, which is a matter of great interest to al-Murtaḍā, and the normative *principles legitimating political domination*, which are of no interest to our jurist. From this lack of interest in principles of legitimacy of political domination, it follows that the motivation either to reject or comply with the authority of the ruler is not categorical but pragmatic, guided by the considerations of expediency and possibility of assistance to the Shiᶜite community.

The freeing of the attitude toward the supreme political authority from religious consideration and the permissibility of compliance with the authority of the ruler—irrespective of the latter's moral qualities or performance in office—allowed the Shiᶜites to adopt a totally practical and pragmatic attitude toward their rulers. Consequently, it was made possible for the Shiᶜites to base their relationship with the rulers completely on pragmatism even to the extent of flattery. Thus, though refraining from legitimating his personal rulership in their legal writing, Sharīf al-Raḍī and Sharīf al-Murtaḍā would address their *qaṣīda*s to the caliph al-Qādir with whom they were on friendly terms; and Qāḍī ᶜAbd al-Jalīl, having accused his (neo-) Sunni adversary of considering government to be in the hand of "usurpers and tyrants" (*ghāṣibān va ẓālimān*),[167] goes so far as to state that the princes (sing., *amīr*) and the Turks—i.e., the rulers—who have risen to extirpate irreligion [of the Ismāᶜīlīs] are all deputies (*nāʾibān*) of the Mahdi, the Imam of the Age, who, thanks to their effort, does not need (*mustaghnīʾst*) to take action.[168] Other statements also demonstrate a positively deferential and subservient attitude toward the Saljūq rulers.[169]

To conclude, the "political ethic" elaborated in al-Murtaḍā's treatise and adopted by the subsequent Imāmī theologians enjoins positive and ethically responsible involvement in administrative and judiciary activity within the existing political framework. At the same time, the elimination of the justice of the ruler as a condition for obedience and service to him allows for a largely pragmatic and utilitarian assessment of "ethical responsibility" in light of such concerns as general probity and furtherance of the common good of the brethren within the Shiᶜite community.

CHAPTER TWO

Millenarian Religio-Political Movements in the Fourteenth/Eighth and Fifteenth/Ninth Centuries

The towering intellectual figure of fourteenth/eighth century, the ᶜAllāma Ibn al-Muṭahhar al-Ḥillī, died in 1326. In the ensuing period, the moving force in the social history of the Shiᶜite religion ceased to be the unfolding of *ratio*—the world-embracing rationalization of the Shiᶜite world view and ethos by the great theologians and jurists, and came to reside in the charisma of a number of individuals who claimed the supreme personal authority of the Mahdi. The decisive force in social change stemmed not from the Shiᶜite doctors' attempt to improve the consistency of doctrine and to increase the impact of the religious creed on the world through the ethical disciplining of economic and political action, but rather from the harnessing of the ethically undisciplined millenarian yearning of the masses to religio-political action by a number of charismatic leaders who drew on the Shiᶜite doctrine of the return of the Hidden Imam. Our attention will accordingly shift from the *ᶜulamāʾ*s control of lay religiosity through the advocacy and enforcement of the Shiᶜite ethics of salvation to the charismatic domination of the masses by leaders claiming absolute authority as the savior incarnate, the Mahdi, or on behalf of the Mahdi whose *parousia* was said to be imminent.

2.1 Sufism and the Elective Affinity of the Masses for Certain "Extremist" Shiᶜite Beliefs

The phenomenal growth of Sufism in Iran after the Mongol invasion has been noted. Unlike Imāmī Shiᶜism, which was an urban movement dominated by patrician strata, Sufism was distinctly plebeian.[1] It spread among the masses and was much more susceptible to the influences and demands of the laity to which, as a rule, it succumbed. Sincere mystics, like the great poet Awḥadī, severely criticized deceitful shaykhs for deviating from the goal of spiritual perfection and exploiting the gullibility of the masses, making the *khāniqāhs* houses of superstition, trickery, and snake-charming.[2] In the eyes of Awḥadī, the "Sufism of the *khāniqh*" was disreputable and thaumaturgic shaykhs were charlatans. The masses, however, greatly venerated the famous shaykhs and attributed numerous miracles (*karāmāt*) to them.

Sufism, by admitting the possibility of immediate contact with God, provided a fertile ground for the growth of undisciplined religiosity, and heightened the receptivity to apocalyptic and "exaggerated" claims to mahdihood and *ḥulūl* (incarnation), similar to those found in the history of Shiᶜism but anathematized as *ghuluww* ("extremism") by its guardians, the *ᶜulamāʾ*. Aberrant religious groups manifesting religious extremism[3] especially concentrated in a region comprising northwestern Iran and Anatolia which had experienced a massive influx of Turkman nomadic tribes as a result of the displacement caused by the Mongol invasion and the earlier Saljūq tribal policy. The islamization of these Turkman tribes was most superficial, and Central Asiatic shamanistic elements remained prominent in their religion. Sufism and certain notions associated with extremism penetrated into their folk religion. The veneration of ᶜAlī as a godhead became widespread, and Shiᶜite elements were superimposed on the veneer of Sunni Islam. Cahen aptly speaks of a "shiᶜitization of Sunnism" in this period as opposed to spread of conscious Shiᶜism.[4]

2.2 The Politicization of Sufism: The Case of the Marᶜashī Shiᶜite Order

With the "shiᶜitization of Sunnism" against the background of the constant expansion of the Sufism, a number of Sufi orders came to profess Shiᶜism formally. In these cases, their Shiᶜism was at best a secondary characteristic, while their primary defining features were those of popular Sufism.

In Sufism, salvation is attained by following the exemplary life of the spiritual guide (*pīr*), and not through adherence to an ethical code of conduct. One of the important consequences of the spread of Sufism was the emergence of a number of prominent shaykhs who enjoyed enormous hieratic influence as holy saviors and not as the proponents of any normative creed. They dispensed blessings for rule over specific domains, and granted legitimacy to rulers in exchange for tax exemptions and material support. Some of them amassed great fortunes.[5] Asking for the *duᶜā-ye khayr* (prayer/blessing) of an eminent shaykh became a regular practice with rulers and governors.[6] One such Sufi shaykh, Mīr Qavām al-Dīn Marᶜashī (d. 1379/781), who was a Shiᶜite, even became the formal head of a small local state, and the founder of a dynasty in Ṭabaristān.[7]

The episode of Qavām al-Dīn illustrates an interesting feature of popular

Shiᶜite Sufism of the period: the tension between the requirements for spiritual salvation, as specified by Sufi mystical philosophy, enjoining both avoidance and transcendence of this world, and the vociferous demands of the mass of the lay members of Sufi congregations for this-worldly action. Because of these demands, any religious movement was likely to become "politically conditioned" to a significant degree.

In the mid-fourteenth/eighteenth century, Sayyid Qavām al-Dīn, a disciple of Shaykh Ḥasan Jūrī (see section 2.3 below) established a dervish order of Shiᶜite affiliation in Ṭabaristān, and began his missionary activity. The local ruler of Āmul, Kiyā Afrāsiyāb, joined his order, and attempted to exploit it to further his political aims. He soon fell out with Qavām al-Dīn, and their struggle eventually ended in a battle in which Kiyā Afrāsiyāb was killed (1358/760). Qavām al-Dīn was carried to Āmul by his excited followers, and assumed rule. As a result of the campaigns of his sons, his domain expanded to include most of Ṭabaristān. Sayyid Qavām al-Dīn directed the religious life of his adherents and concerned himself with the guidance of the converts who flocked to his dervish order, repenting their sins, while his sons, formally appointed by him, ruled in his name and dealt with political and military matters.

According to the history of the dynasty written by one of his descendants, Mīr Ẓahīr al-Dīn (d. 1486/892), when addressing his sons upon his triumphant entry to Āmul, Qavām al-Dīn affirmed that he had never sought worldly domination, and would continue to remain a recluse, but commanded them to fight the enemies of religion and rule with justice, assuring them of his *duᶜā-ye khayr* (blessing). Under the direction of his sons, however, the enthusiasm of formal conversion and joining the order became linked with the taking up of arms and readiness for military action. In 1361/763 his son Kamāl al-Dīn pleaded with him to take part in the military campaign against the governor of Sārī. Qavām al-Dīn agreed, which greatly heightened the morale of the fighting dervishes. In a later expedition to the fortress of Fīrūz-kūh, he was not only persuaded to accompany the dervishes, but also prevailed upon to wear a weapon: a "simple sword" was fastened onto his belt.[8]

In terms of our schema, the creation of the Marᶜashī local state out of a Sufi religious movement can be analyzed as follows: the absence of a centralized state in northern Iran created a political environment in which religion emerged as a highly effective weapon for mobilizing masses for political action. This "political conditioning" militated against the disjunction of political and religious action and made it very likely that the religious movement would become politicized.

However, the political conditioning of the Marᶜashī movement, despite the movement's profession of Shiᶜism, did not induce the adoption of a basic tenet of "extremist" Shiᶜism: the mahdistic tenet. In other words, the influence of the political environment did not result in the activation of the mahdistic tenet and initiation of chiliastic action. For this reason, the Marᶜashī movement, though Shiᶜite, is best viewed as a politically conditioned Sufi religious movement.

By contrast, the five selected movements to be considered below, though also bearing the strong imprint of Sufism, have as their distinctive feature the unfolding of the mahdistic potential of extremist Shiᶜism. In these cases, the pressure of the political environment *was* translated into religious terms by the activation of the mahdistic tenet.

2.3 Militant Messianism in the Shiᶜite "Republic" of the Sarbidārs, 1338–81

2.3.1 The Historical Development of the Sarbidār State: An Analysis of Its Religious Motivation

In the early fourteenth century, Shaykh Khalīfa, a dervish and preacher (*vāᶜiẓ*) from Mazandaran, appeared in Sabzavār, Khurasan, and acquired a following. His "worldly" (*dunyavī*) propaganda—according to Petrushevsky, in favor of general equality and resistance to oppression—alarmed the Sunni *ᶜulamāʾ*, who accused him of "innovation" and ruled that he be killed. He was found strangled in the mosque where he taught. One of his disciples, Ḥasan Jūrī, set out to unify the shaykh's followers and spread his teachings. According to Ḥāfiẓ-e Abrū, he registered the names of the adherents, telling them "now is the time of concealment" and promising to signal the time of appearance.[9] The mahdistic tenet contained in the Shiᶜite doctrine of occultation was thus adopted as a tool for the mobilization of the masses for political action.

By an uneasy alliance in 1338 with the rebellious ruler of Sabzavār, Amīr Masᶜūd, Ḥasan became a second head of the Shiᶜite Sarbidār state. He was soon assassinated by Amīr Masᶜūd during a campaign in which he and his dervish militia took part.

After a turbulent interval, Shams al-Dīn ᶜAlī, a shaykh of the order founded by Shaykh Khalīfa and Ḥasan Jūrī, accepted the position of head of state and ruled effectively, with the support of the dervish and the local (*futuwwa*) militia, from 1347 to 1353. One of his coins from 1349–50/750 bears the inscription "the victory is near."[10] He ruled Sabzavār as an egalitarian Islamic theocracy, rigorously observing rules of morality and justice in anticipation of the appearance of the Hidden Imam, the Lord of Time. In matters of law he deferred to the "*ᶜulamāʾ* of the true religion." Shams al-Dīn ᶜAlī "was insistent upon 'enjoining the good' and 'forbidding the evil'":[11] he banned prostitution, smoking, and drinking, and apparently fell victim to his severity in the enforcement of morality.[12]

The last Sarbidār ruler, ᶜAlī Muᵓayyad, came to power through an alliance with a certain Darvīsh ᶜAzīz Majdī, who had rebelled in Ṭūs.[13] In Ṭūs, Darvīsh ᶜAzīz had struck a coin (1357–58/759) bearing the inscription "Sulṭān Muḥammad, the Mahdi"—i.e., the Hidden Imam. After the alliance, ᶜAlī Muᵓayyad became the ruler of the Sarbidār state.

ᶜAlī Muᵓayyad immediately had to contend with dervish power, and, like Amīr Masᶜūd before him, ordered his troops to kill his dervish partner and some seventy of his followers (1364–65/766). He disbanded the Shaykhiyya-Jūriyya order. (Years later, the exiled dervishes were to bring about ᶜAlī Muᵓayyad's downfall.[14]) On the other hand, ᶜAlī Muᵓayyad confirmed his adherence to Shiᶜism and struck coins in the name of the twelve Imams. Mahdistic expectations persisted and a caparisoned horse was brought out to the gates of the city of Sabzavār twice a day in expectation of the appearance of the Hidden Imam.[15] Presumably to prevent the recurrence of dervish chiliasm, ᶜAlī Muᵓayyad, upon the advice of a councillor, commissioned the jurist Muḥammad ibn Makkī al-ᶜĀmilī, known as the Shahīd al-Awwal (first martyr; d. 1384/786), to write a book on Shiᶜite law and come to Sabzavār to assist in the establishment of Twelver Shiᶜism as taught by the Imāmi scholars. However, shortly after the manual was completed, Tīmūr (Tamerlane) conquered Sabzavār and put an end to the Sarbidār state (1381/783).

2.3.2 Sarbidār Impetus to the Development of Shiᶜite Sacred Law

In the episode of the Sarbidārs, we encounter the phenomenon of Shiᶜite Sufi militancy, which was to occur a century later with the Safavid order under Junayd, Ḥaydar, Sulṭān ᶜAlī, and Ismāᶜīl. However, in contrast to the Qizilbāsh, the Shaykhiyya-Jūriyya Sufis did not go beyond the *expectancy* of the advent of the Mahdi, and did not attribute Mahdihood to any leader. This had important consequences. Their zest in political and military action in anticipation of the *parousia* did not render the sacred law inoperative. On the contrary, the expectation of the imminent appearance of the Hidden Imam tended to promote, as it did during the rule of Shams al-Dīn ᶜAlī, the strict observance of ethical and moral rules of the sacred law and the creation of a just kingdom pleasing to the expected Lord of the Age.

In the last years of the Sarbidārs we also encounter an attempt—again foreshadowing that of the Safavids—to substitute the legalistically and theologically rationalized Shiᶜism of the Imāmī sect for the Shiᶜite-tinged Sufi extremism. Such an attempt was likely to be made once the chiliasm of the dervishes lost its political utility and became more of a liability than an asset to the ruler. Although the Sarbidār state collapsed before this plan could be implemented, the attempt had important consequences for the future development of Shiᶜism. ᶜAlī Muᵓayyad had commissioned the Shahīd al-Awwal to write a legal treatise with a view to institutionalizing the implementation of the Shiᶜite sacred law in the Sarbidār realm. The Shahīd produced the *Lumᶜat al-Dimashqiyya*, a work characterized by the author's concern for practical implementation of the sacred law and thus marking an important step toward further regulative embracement of the world.[16]

In his practically oriented legal work, the Shahīd categorically states that the authority (*wilāya*) of a qadi is established on the basis of common report (*shiyāᶜ*) or the witness of two just men.[17] This statement constitutes an important positive legal norm for the institutionalization of judiciary authority. It is, furthermore, pregnant with implication. The same is true of an incidental remark the Shahīd makes in a different context: "The congregational Friday prayer does not take place except with the Imam or his deputy [*nāʾib*], *even if he be a jurist* [*wa law kāna faqīhan*], given the possibility of assembling during the occultation."[18]

The primary objective of the statement is to enhance the social aspect of the Shiᶜite religion by ruling in favor of the controversial issue of the permissibility of congregational prayer. However, while doing so, the Shahīd takes the opportunity to increase the social commitment *and authority* of the jurist by recognizing him as a kind of deputy of the Hidden Imam.

All this was destined to stimulate future development of Shiᶜism, but much later—that is, after the Safavids successfully carried out in their empire what ᶜAlī Muʾayyad had intended for his small dominion. As for the historical actualities, we may conclude by saying that the Sarbidār "republic" was the creation of a religiously conditioned *political* movement whose strong religious orientation was due to the use of the mahdistic tenet as a tool to motivate a political action. The crucial and continued importance of the Shaykhiyya-Jūriyya order in the Sarbidār polity assured the continued reliance on the mahdistic tenet, and hence the continued religious conditioning of the Sarbidār movement. As the mahdistic tenet was used to motivate political and military action *without*, however, any person claiming mahdihood, the religious conditioning of the Sarbidār political movement took the form of emphasis on the observance of the sacred law.

2.4 The Ḥurūfiyya

The foundation of the Shiᶜite Marᶜashī state by the sons of the shaykh of a Sufi order has been presented here as a politically conditioned religious movement in which distinctly Shiᶜite beliefs played no demonstrable role. The Sarbidār "republic" has been presented as a political movement that was religiously conditioned by the emphatic use of a distinctly Shiᶜite belief—the belief in the return of the Hidden Imam as the Mahdi. However, the millenarian potential of the mahdistic tenet has been unfolded only in part. The full unfolding of this tenet, which was able to shift the source of motivation of religio-political action from the *ratio* contained in the sacred law to the revolutionary charisma of a self-legitimating claimant to mahdihood, is encountered only in the remaining movements. The Sarbidār movement was not a religious revolution because the unfolding of the mahdistic tenet was only partial. By contrast, the chiliastic potential of the mahdistic tenet was fully activated in the movements to be discussed next, which, for this reason, fully belong to the category of Shiᶜite extremism and constitute religious or religio-political revolutions.

2.4.1 The Epiphany of Faḍl Allāh of Astarābād and His Alphabetistic Dispensation

The Ḥurūfiyya were a heterodox sect founded by Faḍl Allāh Astarābādī (d. 1394/794) in northwestern Iran, in the milieu of Sufism and Shiᶜite extremism, at the end of the fourteenth/eighth century.

At the age of forty, after three days of ecstasy, Faḍl Allāh heard a voice referring to him as the "Lord of Time [*Ṣāḥib al-zamān*], the Sultan of all Prophets: others attain faith by imitation and learning, whereas he attains it by inner and clear revelation [*kashf va ᶜiyān*]."[19] He retired to seclusion in Isfahan until a dying dervish announced to him that the time of revelation of divine glory (*Ẓuhūr-i Kibriyāʾi*) had come (ca. 1386/788). He then made his public proclamations, began writing the *Jāvīdān-nāmeh* (Book of Eternity), and formed the Ḥurūfī sect. "This is the new Ordinance"; thus Faḍl Allāh refers to his teaching in his testament.[20]

Faḍl Allāh's doctrine, clearly showing the influence of Ismāᶜīlī esoteric tradition,[21] is briefly as follows: Divine revelation takes the form of manifestation (*Ẓuhūr*) of God in men, and moves in cycles. His formula for the *Adhān* (call to prayer) placed the phrase "I bear witness that Adam [= man] is the vicar of God" before the phrase attesting to Muḥammad's prophecy. Words emanate from God. Man, the vicar of God, can gain knowledge of Him through a science based on the interpretation of the (gnostic) significance of the letters of the alphabet in their diverse combinations (hence the name of the sect, which derives from *ḥurūf*, i.e., letters of the alphabet). Letters of determinate significance combined to form words that were conceived "realistically" as identical with their embodiments in objects and in the human body, especially the face, on which the actual name of God was written in clear letters. Man could know God through the cabalistic/gnostic interpretation of the incidence of words in accordance with the significance of the letters of the alphabet and their numerical values as determined by the widely known *abjad* system.[22]

2.4.2 The Social Position of the Ḥurūfīs

This esoteric "mystery" religion was actively missionary. The sources allow us to form a fairly clear impression of the social position of its adherents. Ḥurūfism was a literate urban movement and gained widespread following above all among artisans and intellectuals. The Ḥurūfīs were active in the cities of Azerbaijan and Anatolia, Iran and Syria, where they gave birth to a religious and literary movement of some momentum.[23] The verses of Nasīmī illustrate the exuberant confidence of those fortified and exalted by initiation to the unitive knowledge of God through the teachings of the "Master of Interpretation" (*Ṣāḥib-e taʾvīl*), i.e., the founder.[24]

2.4.3 The Politicization of the Ḥurūfī Movement

Two sets of factors working in the same direction explain the subsequent politicization of the Ḥurūfī religious movement: persecution and the proclivities of its adherents.

The conversion of a ruler is no small boon to a missionary religion. This political consideration determined the modest extent of the initial political conditioning of Ḥurūfism. Faḍl Allāh himself tried to convert the great Tatar conqueror, Tīmūr, but perished by the order of Tīmūr's apprehensive son, Mirānshāh, in 1394/796. Not surprisingly, Mirānshāh became the Dajjal (the Antichrist, counterpart of the Mahdi) of the new religion. (Nevertheless, abortive attempts were subsequently made by his successor to convert a number of rulers.) It is quite possible that after the failure to convert Mirānshāh, the founder contemplated the propagation of Ḥurūfism by violent means.

Recurrent persecution forced the Ḥurūfiyya to become clandestine. They drew upon the Twelver Shiʿite theodicy of suffering—the tragedy of Karbalā and the martyrdom of Imām Ḥusayn—to make sense of the experience of persecution. On the eve of his execution in Shīrvān, Faḍl Allāh wrote:

> The Ḥusayn of the Age am I, and each worthless foe a
> Shimr and a Yazīd.
>
> My life is a day of mourning, and Shīrwān my Karbalā.[25]

The Ḥurūfīs' theodicy of suffering also extols deliverance through martyrdom:

> He who remembreth me, loveth me; and he who loveth me passionately desireth me; and him who passionately desireth me I passionately desire; and whom I passionately desire I slay; and of him whom I slay, I am the Blood-wit.[26]

This theodicy of suffering was accompanied by the reappearance of messianic hope and the reactivation of the mahdistic tenet. The belief in the second coming (*rajʿa*) of Faḍl Allāh spread.[27] The Ḥurūfī tract, *Maḥram-nāmeh*, written over three decades after the martyrdom of Faḍl Allāh in 1424–25/828, talks of the supremacy of the Hidden Imam, the Mahdi, the "Lord of the Sword" (*Ṣāḥib-e sayf*), who will appear to deliver the Ḥurūfīs from tyranny and persecution.[28]

Persecution of Ḥurūfīs occurred not only because of the apprehensiveness of the powers regarding the possible political ambitions of the movement, but also at the instigation of the guardians of Islamic orthodoxy, the *ʿulamāʾ*, who considered Ḥurūfism an abominable heresy. At least one injunction (*fatwā*) was issued for the execution of Faḍl Allāh by a jurist, and there was probably a conference of ᶜ*ulamā*ᵓ to condemn him to death.[29] A generation later, at the insistence of a local ᶜ*ālim*, Mawlānā Muḥammad, who considered their heresy a threat to Islam, and on the basis of an injunction begrudgingly issued by Mawlānā Najm al-Din Uskūᵓī, the Qaraquyūnlū monarch, Jahānshāh (1436–76), was prevailed upon to order a massacre in which some 500 Ḥurūfīs perished.[30] The massacred Ḥurūfīs included the founder's revered daughter, Kalimāt al-ᶜulyā ("the highest word," standing for Kalimāt Allāh hiya'l-ᶜulyā ["the word of God which is the highest"]) also known as the Qurrat al-ᶜayn ("delight to the eye").[31]

With the reappearance of mahdism, there are also firm indications of clandestine political activity among the Ḥurūfiyya. In 1426–27/830, the poet Qāsim al-Anvār was implicated in an attempt to assassinate the Timurid king, Shāhrukh, and was accused of collusion with the Ḥurūfīs. The conspirators were found to be a group of Ḥurūfī artisans in the city of Herat who had adopted the Niẓarī Ismāᶜīlī techniques of terrorism.[32]

The episode brings to our attention the second cause of the politicization of the Ḥurūfī movement: the propensity of its urban adherents to political action, especially of the clandestine and millenarian type. We may safely infer from the cabalistic emphasis on the power of literacy that there was no basis for any hierocracy that could mold the political attitudes of the Ḥurūfī sectarians and discipline their extremist religiosity and chiliastic yearning. We also know from comparative evidence that mystery religions akin to Ḥurūfism, such as Ismāᶜīlism in the preceding and Nuqṭavism in the succeeding periods, appealed to urban artisans and intellectuals who were the social group most prone to clandestine millenarian political activism.[33]

2.4.4 Ḥurūfism and the Transcendence of Shiᶜism

Through the actualization of epiphany (*Ẓuhūr*), Faḍl Allāh created a religious revolution. He transformed Shiᶜism into a new religion, which, in marked contrast to Twelver Shiᶜism, rested upon knowledge and mystery as opposed to piety and faith. With him, the latent religious substratum of the doctrine of the Hidden Imam engendered a gnostic prophecy, a new dispensation, and finally an intellectual movement. The messianic potential of Shiᶜism was thus consummated in epiphany and prophecy. However, repression by jealous political powers and the orientation of its literate urban adherents caused the politicization of the Ḥurūfī movement—mahdism reappeared and attempts to proselytize the rulers gave place to clandestine millenarian activism.

2.5 The Mystical Mahdism of Nūrbakhsh

I have already mentioned the works of two shaykhs of the Kubravi order, Saᶜd al-Dīn Ḥamūya and ᶜAlā al-Dawla Simnānī, to illustrate the unsystematic penetration of Shiᶜite ideas into (Sunni) Sufism. Steps in the same direction were taken by Sayyid ᶜAlī b. Shihāb al-Dīn Hamadānī, who also was a Sunni, and by Sayyid Muḥammad Nūrbakhsh (d. 1463). Only the latter, who came from the Shiᶜite region of Qaṭīf and Bahrain,[34] openly professed Shiᶜism. Besides professing Shiᶜism, Nūrbakhsh came to claim mahdihood, and it is the nature of this claim that is of primary interest to us.

Non-Kibravī influences on Nūrbakhsh were also quite strong.[35] His father and grandfather came from the Twelver Shiᶜite region of Aḥsāʾ and he studied with the famous Imāmī scholar of Ḥilla, Aḥmad ibn Fahd al-Ḥillī (d. 1437/841). In a *risāla* attributed to his teacher Aḥmad ibn Fahd, we can read, "the Greater *Jihād* [the inner holy war against the instinctual nature] necessitates that there be an imam, a *valī* [friend of God] perfect in the stage of *vilāya*."[36]

In 1425/828, the Timurid monarch Shāhrukh was informed of a rebellion in northeastern Iran in which a renowned Sufi shaykh, Khwāja Isḥāq Khatlānī, called a "young *sayyid*" (*sayyid-zādeh*) the Mahdi, and it was said that he was the Imam. The rebellion was suppressed, and Khwāja Isḥāq and eighty Sufis were killed, but the life of the young *sayyid* (descendant of the Prophet) was spared on the grounds that his guilt was not so great "as his Shaykh told him: you are the Mahdi—and made him rise."[37]

After his release by Shāhrukh, the young *sayyid*, Muḥammad Nūrbakhsh, succeeded Khwāja Isḥāq as the shaykh of the Kubravī order. It appears that for a long time he was reluctant to declare his mahdihood publicly. His followers, on the other hand, were firmly convinced that he was the expected Imam, and had visions of him.[38] It is reasonable to assume that Nūrbakhsh's primary preoccupation was with spiritual guidance of his followers and in his writings he explicitly emphasized the importance of world renunciation in the form of poverty (*faqr*) on the part of the "perfect guide."[39]

Even so, given the inevitability of some "politically conditioned" action on the part of any religious movement in dealing with the forces of its political environment, the possibility of using the absolute mahdistic authority in worldly political action remained a real one. This was so especially in view of the thirst that the as-yet-unenlightened followers had for it. Nūrbakhsh does appear to have had such followers, some of whom struck coins and delivered the *khuṭba* (sermon) in his name in Kurdistan. As one would expect, jealous political powers were keenly appreciative of this possibility and worried about it. Thus the Timurid monarch, Shāhrukh, had Nūrbakhsh arrested again and sent to Herat, and made him mount the pulpit during a Friday congregation in the year 1436/840 to repudiate and deny all "claim to caliphate" (*daᶜvī-ye khilāfat*).[40]

Some years later, Nūrbakhsh made it clear that this disclaimer did not regard his spiritual authority. In a letter to Shāhrukh, he arrogantly stated that it was evident to the wise that he and only he was the "Deputy of the Lord of the Age," and the "Deputy of the Imam of the Age and the promised Mahdi." He called upon Shāhrukh to cease molesting him, to apologize for having imprisoned him three times, and to ask for his forgiveness while there was still time so as not to be ashamed in front of the Prophet in the hereafter.[41] In a letter to another contemporary ruler, Nūrbakhsh based his supreme spiritual authority on unparalleled excellence in all sciences, including literature, religious jurisprudence, and the rational sciences, and, above all, on gnostic insight to the constitution of the universe. These qualities, he claimed, made him the supreme spiritual guide of the age.[42]

Finally, in the *Risālat al-Hudā* (Treatise on Guidance; ca. 1451/856), Nūrbakhsh explained the nature of his claim to mahdihood more systematically. After pointing out the difficulties of knowing a *valī* (friend of God) and especially a perfect *valī*, he adduces the traditions on the Mahdi, and argues that they refer to him. The proofs of his mahdihood are, on the one hand, numerous visions, and, on the other hand, "rational proofs" (*dalāʾil ʿaqliyya*)—notably that he has guided more students over the past forty years than anyone else. However, mystical experience is the ultimate basis of his claim to mahdihood and indicative of its nature. According to Nūrbakhsh, the Mahdi is like a light and is not incarnate. The Mahdi was seized by and infused in him as the celestial spirit coexistent with the terrestrial body of Nūrbakhsh.[43]

For Nūrbakhsh, true Islam was Sufism, embracing all aspects of religion: the *sharīʿat* (Law), the *ṭarīqat* (Way), and *ḥaqīqat* (Truth).[44] The *sharīʿat* comprehends only a third of religion: the exoteric religion. It is clear from his writings that Nūrbakhsh had a very low opinion of exoteric religious sciences and of the *ʿulamāʾ*.[45] As for esoteric religion, initiation by imperfect persons leads the believer astray, hence the importance of the perfect spiritual guide for salvation.

In its final version, the mahdism of Nūrbakhsh replaces millenarian eschatology by an eschatology of the soul. In the teeth of his followers clamoring for chiliastic action, which had more than once tempted him to seek worldly domination in vain, he appears to have made an effort to depoliticize his mahdistic authority. Despite the pressure from the political environment, in his later years Nūrbakhsh used his mahdistic authority to guide the followers along the path of spiritual perfection. Nūrbakhsh's son and successor, Shāh Qāsim, continued this tradition of spiritual guidance, and even chided whomever reminded him of his father's claim to mahdihood.[46]

2.6 The Thaumaturgical Mahdism of Mushaʿshaʿ

Sayyid Muḥammad ibn Falāḥ (d. 1461 or 1465/866 or 870) was also a student of Aḥmad ibn Fahd al-Ḥillī. Claiming descent from the Seventh Imam, he succeeded in gaining power among the Arab tribes of Khuzistan and assumed the title of Mushaᶜshaᶜ—"the radiant."[47] Relying on a military force that, according to the historian Jaᶜfarī, consisted of ten thousand "ignoramuses, bandits and thieves" who had gathered under his banner, Sayyid Muḥammad established an obscurantist religious tyranny.[48]

Mushaᶜshaᶜ varied his claim according to the audience he was addressing, from being the "introduction to," the "veil of," and the "locus of" the Mahdi, to being the Mahdi himself. His son, Mawlā ᶜAlī, advanced even more exaggerated claims to being the reincarnation of the First Imam, ᶜAlī, and of the divinity. In a letter to a certain religious scholar from Baghdad, Sayyid Muḥammad attributes the exaggerated exaltation of himself and his son to the gullibility of the ignorant masses he is leading away from extremism and into the right path. In reality, however, Mushaᶜshaᶜ did his best to perpetuate the extremist adulation of himself by his followers. In his *Kalām al-Mahdī*, he asserts the essential identity of the prophets, the imams, and the *awliyā*ᵓ (friends of God) who appear in different human forms in different period, the last instance of the appearance being that of himself, the Mahdi of the age. Mushaᶜshaᶜ also composed *Sūra*s in imitation of the Qurᵓan.[49] Furthermore, he put forward his own code of law in which his obsession with ritualistic detail and with pollution found expression in minute ritualistic regulations and in ferocious punishments decreed for ritualistic tort.

We know that extremism prevailed under Mushaᶜshaᶜ's descendant, Mīr Fayyāḍ, who also claimed divinity and was killed in a ferocious battle by Ismāᶜīl I in 1508/914,[50] and was revived from time to time until Mushaᶜshaᶜ's doctrines were finally revoked by his descendant, Mubārak (ruled 1589–1616/998–1025), who invited the learned ᶜAbd al-Laṭīf Jāmī to Khuzistan, and, with the latter's help, introduced Twelver Shiᶜism in his dominion.[51]

Mushaᶜshaᶜ's rule can be characterized as a case of thaumaturgical domination in which social life is subjected to ritualistic legislation conceived in the light of the presumed magical properties of things and acts and promulgated on the basis of Mahdistic authority. Mushaᶜshaᶜ too exploited the millenarian potential of extremist Shiᶜism for creating what was in effect a new religious system based on new sacred texts and a new legal code.

2.7 The Rise of the Safavids: Theophanic Domination and Militant Chiliasm

The Safavid theocracy arose in the milieu of Sufism and of extremism. It involved the transformation of the Sufi order founded by Shaykh Ṣafī al-Dīn Ardabīlī into a warrior theocracy of Turkman tribesmen: the Qizilbāsh order.

Ṣafī al-Dīn Ardabīlī (1252–1334/650–735) was one of the most influential and highly favored shaykhs of the Il-Khanid period. A Sunni, he acquired great eminence and his convent totally dominated the life of the city of Ardabīl.[52] Like the Kubraviyya, the Safavid order underwent the transition from Sunnism to Shiᶜism. However, unlike the Kubraviyya, the transition was not gradual but sudden. The intellectual and ideational considerations in this transition were minimal, and the political considerations maximal.

2.7.1 The Geopolitical Factor and the Influence of the Turkman Adherents

A decisive factor in this transition was the geographical location of the order in Ardabīl, near the frontiers of Islam. Once the worldly ambitions of the descendants of Shaykh Ṣafī had been kindled, this location facilitated the transformation of the Sufi order into a basis for *ghazā* (holy war, a specific type of *jihād*) against the neighboring Christian unbelievers (*kuffār*). For centuries, *ghazā* had been the dominant feature of political organization in the frontier region of Anatolia, and consisted of raids into Byzantine territories and Christian enclaves to capture booty and enslave the population. The strong material interest in booty, coupled and rationalized by the emphatic ethical injunction to extend the frontiers of Islam, formed the effective basis for political and military organization of small *ghāzī* principalities.[53] With the political segmentation following the fall of the Īl-Khānid and Timūrid empires, small-scale *ghazā* spread to northwestern Iran.

According to Mazzaoui, up to the middle of the fifteenth/ninth century, the Safavid order continued to be an important center of Sufism, engaged in missionary dissemination of its doctrines and practices under the leadership of the descendants of Shaykh Ṣafī. In later sources we read of a group of Turkman prisoners of war, released by Tīmūr at the request of the Safavid shaykh, Khwāja ᶜAlī (d. 1429/832), who joined the order in the early years of the fifteenth century. Even though these were probably settled in Ardabīl, the composition of the order remained predominantly Persian and urban. The Safavids resisted being drawn into holy warfare despite the depredation of Ardabīl by the Georgians. The pattern of involvement of the Safavid shaykhs in politics was typical, consisting of the benediction of the rulers in exchange for material and political privileges. Furthermore, even though Khwāja ᶜAlī did expand the missionary activities of the order into the areas affected by the Shiᶜite extremism of Mushaᶜshaᶜ, no signs of Shiᶜism, either of the Twelver or of the extremist variety, are discernible in the life of the Safavid Sufi order.

The missionary activities of the Safavid order in the first half of the fifteenth century became increasingly directed toward Anatolia, where some of the chiliastic followers of Qāḍī Badr al-Dīn joined the order after the collapse of their extensive rebellion of 1416 against the Ottomans. Nevertheless, the outlook of the Safavid movement, determined by Ardabīl, remained unchanged until the death of Khwāja ᶜAlī's successor, Shaykh Ibrāhīm, in 1447.[54]

In 1447, a split occurred in the Safavid order. Shaykh Jaᶜfar, "the most cultivated and the most learned of the Safavid Shaykhs,"[55] continued the Sufi missionary tradition of the order in Ardabīl.[56] He resisted the pressure toward the militarization of the Safavid order and its ivolvement in warfare against the Christians, and accepted an appointment as the Shaykh al-Islām of Ardabīl from the Qaraqūyūnlū monarch, Jahānshāh. Shaykh Ja'far appears as a religious dignitary with no political ambitions. A document dated 1453/857 refers to him as the "Rectifier of Truth and the Sacred Law and Religion."[57] Under his leadership, which lasted until the 1470s, the Ardabīl branch of the Safavid movement resisted the pressure of its geopolitical environment and did not change its religious character.

This was not so with the Anatolian branch, the Safavid order in exile under Ja'far's nephew, Junayd (1447–60). There, under the leadership of Junayd, the Safavid order was suddenly transformed into a militant *ghāzī* movement. The teaching of Sufism and cultivation of religious grace suddenly gave place to intense millenarian religio-political activity.

Junayd was the first descendant of Ṣafī al-Dīn to add "worldly sovereignty" to spiritual sovereignty,[58] and set out to transform the Safavid order into a militant *ghāzī* movement. The hostile Sunni jurist and contemporary historian, Faḍl Allāh Rūzbihān Khunjī, ponders on the way Junayd changed his ancestors' tradition of spiritual guidance: "What a pity that, while Ṣafī al-Dīn preserved his being from a doubtful repast [*luqma-yi shubha*], he did not restrain his children from the vanities of this world [*ḥuṭām*]. As a result his progeny forsook poverty and humility [*khāksāri*] for the throne of a kingdom."[59]

Junayd was exiled from Ardabīl by his uncle's patron, Jahānshāh. While in exile in Diyār Bakr, Junayd tied himself by marriage to the rival Aqqūyūnlū dynasty, and acquired new followers whose way of life and religious outlook were very different from the urban members of the order in the city of Ardabīl. Shaykh Junayd's adherents were Turkman nomads, whose conversion to Islam was recent and most superficial, and who retained many of their Central Asiatic beliefs and customs. Junayd responded to their demands for military action and booty and organized them into the *ghuzāt-e ṣūfiyya*, later to become known as the Qizilbāsh (on account of the red headgear devised for them by Junayd's son, Ḥaydar). They engaged in irregular raids in Georgia and the Christian enclave in Trabzon. This transformation was completed under Junayd's son, Ḥaydar (1460–88), who succeeded his father in his early teens, having read, according to Khunjī, the unedifying *Epic of Kings* instead of taking religious instructions, and "instead of exercising his pen upon the Sacred Book, [having] exercised his sword upon the dogs of Ardabīl."[60]

Ḥaydar reconquered Ardabīl, which was flooded and overwhelmed by the Turkman followers and became the seat of his *ghāzī* principality. With Ḥaydar, and briefly with his son, Sulṭān-'Alī, the entire Safavid movement came under the sway of warrior millenarianism. Before falling in battle in 1493/898, the youthful

Sulṭān-ᶜAlī transferred the Qizilbāsh crown, together with the secret of the order, to his six-year-old brother, Ismāᶜīl, thus setting the stage for the final culmination of warrior millenarianism of the Qizilbāsh in the creation of the Safavid empire.

2.7.2 Adoption of the Shiᶜite Mahdistic Tenet

It is clear that from an early impressionable age, Ḥaydar came under the tempting influence of the adulatory religious beliefs of his fanatical Turkman followers: "The deputies [*khulafā*] of his father turned to him from ever direction, and expressed—as a testimony to their shameless stupidity—the claim to his divinity. The excess of obedience of the people of Rum caused the son of the Shaykh to acquire reprehensible habits and calamitous manners."[61]

Khunjī accuses Ḥaydar of all manner of tyrannical cruelty toward those inhabitants of Ardabīl suspected of disloyalty. He is also accused of charlatanry, including snake-charming (*mār-bāzī*). Of the Turkman followers of the Safavids he writes:

> The fools of Rūm, who are a crowd of error and a host of devilish imagination, struck the bell of the inane claims of Christians on the roof of the monastery of the world . . . they openly called Shaykh Junayd "God [*ilāh*]" and his son "Son of God [*ibn-Allāh*]". . . . In his praise they said: "He is the Living one, there is no God but he." Their folly and ignorance were such that, if someone spoke of Shaykh Junayd as dead, he was no more to enjoy the sweet beverage of life.[62]

The ideational and theological elements of the shiᶜitized Sufism of the Qizilbāsh appear to have been extremely crude, covering a substratum of shamanistic and anthropolatric folk religiosity. They believed in a line of twelve Imams, the twelfth being the Mahdi. Notions current among the Shiᶜite extremists, veneration of the Imams, and the elevation of ᶜAlī to the level of godhead were adopted by them. The element of extremism was most notable in Safavid leaders' claim to be the descendants and reincarnations of the Imams, and hence of God. This claim was fully acceptable to the Turkmans, in whose religion the belief in metempsychosis had an important place.[63] This is shown in a poem by Ismāᶜīl on the coming of the kingdom of the Mahdi:

> The heroic *ghāzī*s have come forth with "crowns of happiness" on their heads. The Mahdi's period has begun. The light of eternal life has dawned [upon] the world.
>
> With all your heart, accept the scion of Imām Shāh Ḥaydar. My Imams Jaᶜfar al-Ṣādiq and ᶜAlī-[ibn] Mūsā al'Riḍā have come.[64]

When Ismāᶜīl I, Ḥaydar's son and the founder of the Safavid empire, rose in his teens in 1499/905, to gather his supporters and sympathizers in Anatolia, "Leaflets announcing to those expecting the appearance of that Majesty [i.e., Ismāᶜīl] who is the prelude to [the appearance of] the Lord of the Age were disseminated in every direction."[65]

The earliest chronicle of Shāh Ismāʿīl's reign relates the testimony of a holy Sufi to the consecration of Shah Ismāʿīl by the person of the Lord of the Age. Dada Muḥammad Rūmlū, a Sufi of "vision and charismata," testified to having been an eyewitness to a ceremony taking place near Mecca in which the Lord of the Age bestowed his blessing upon Ismāʿīl and gave him his sword. On the momentous day of the proclamation of Shiʿism as the state religion in Tabriz in 1501/907, while the Twelver Shiʿite *khuṭba* (sermon) was being delivered, Ismāʿīl stood in front of the *minbar* (pulpit) holding the unsheathed sword of the Lord of the Age. In *Ross Anonymous*, Ismāʿīl's reign is said to be the prelude to the reign of the Lord of the Age, and Ismāʿīl the wielder of the sword.[66]

Like Mushaʿshaʿ before him, Ismāʿīl varied his claim to mahdistic authority according to the audience. With the more enthusiastic and less islamicized Turkman tribesmen, Ismāʿīl does not appear to have been content with being merely the "introduction" to the Mahdi, and put forward more elevated claims.

In this regard, the poetry of Shāh Ismāʿīl is of great documentary value. Written under his nom de plume, Khatāʾī, and collected in his *dīvān*, the poems are in the Turkish of the Turkmans, in preference to Persian, the literary language. As Minorsky has pointed out, this clearly indicates that he was addressing his Qizilbāsh adherents. Furthermore, as Melikoff has more recently shown, the recitation of Ismāʿīl's poems was a part of the initiation process.[67]

The themes of deification, first of ʿAlī, and then of Ismāʿīl himself, are striking. ʿAlī is exalted above the Prophet as the demiurge (*kirdigār*) and the creator of heaven and earth. Then we come to Ismāʿīl himself:

> He had already appeared in this world by order of ʿAlī. He is of the same essence as ʿAlī and is composed of the latter's Mystery. A man can be a manifestation of Godhead; Ismāʿīl is the Adam having put on new clothes. He has come as God's light, as the Seal of the Prophets, as a Perfect Guide, as the guiding Imam. He is Agens Absolutus, Oculus Dei (or even Deus ipse!), his body is God's house, he commands the Sun and the Moon.[68]

Ismāʿīl insisted on being worshiped through the act of *sajda* (prostration). In another poem Ismāʿīl sets forth his claim to divinity as the perfect guide and the incarnation of God's light:

> By the Lord! Come and behold: God's light has appeared; Muḥamad Muṣṭafā, the Seal of the Prophets has come!
> The Perfect Guide has arrived. Faith has been [brought] to all. All the *ghāzī*s are full of joy at the coming of the Seal of the Prophets.
> A man [has become] a manifestation of Truth. Prostrate thyself! Pander not to Satan! Adam has put on new clothes God has come, God has come.[69]

2.7.3 Mahdism and the Abeyance of Sacred Law

The emergence of a military Sufi order engaged in *ghazā* under the leaders claiming divine military and religious authority was a unique phenomenon. In contrast to Sunni *ghāzīs*,[70] the nature of the charismatic authority of the Safavid leaders was such as to make the Islamic normative order inoperative. Not only did they claim the charisma of the warlord, drawing on the (nonreligious) epic tradition of pre-Islamic Iran, they also arrogated to themselves the incarnation of the omnipotent God, demanding worship. The divinity of the commander entailed the abeyance of the sacred law.

This stance implied the suspension of all Islamic normative influences, which, for their efficacy, depended critically on the transcendence of God and mediation of the sacred law between God and man. It amounted to the abolition of all normative order independent of the personal will of the supreme leader, who was, at one and the same time, the Sufi *murshid*, the Shiᶜite Imam, and the primordial godhead. Correspondingly, for the Qizilbāsh followers, what mattered was the worship of the incarnation of God, and immediate infusion by his spirit in military chiliastic action. Action governed by ethical norms was devoid of significance for salvation.

Even the thaumaturgical Mushaᶜshaᶜ had claimed privileged contact with the *transcendent* God, and presented his tabooistic legislation as *divine law*. Only in the Safavid case was the transcendence of God not respected. The claim of the Safavids to incarnation of God left no room for the rule of divine law. No wonder the prime accusation leveled against the early Safavids from Junayd onwards was *ibāḥa*: disregard of the sacred law.

2.8 The Mahdism of the Extremist Shiᶜite Movements in Analytical Perspective

I have sought to identify the doctrinal basis of religiously motivated social action in the fourteenth and fifteenth centuries: the belief in the appearance of the Hidden Imam as the Mahdi. The Mahdistic tenet, when fully activated, has been shown to render the ethically rationalized normative order inoperative. Pending possible affirmation by the claimant to mahdistic authority, ethical tenets are suspended, and ethically undisciplined extremist religiosity is channeled into chiliastic action under charismatic leadership.

Two important factors account for the spread of the aberrant Shiᶜite movements organized on the basis of the mahdistic tenet: the elective affinity of the masses, nurtured by popular Sufism, for this-worldly salvation through millenarian political action, and political decentralization, which made mass movements on the basis of such millenarian aspirations possible.

The Shiᶜite belief in the advent of the Mahdi, when activated under the influence of the factors discussed above, creates a millenarian movement resting on a structure of domination characterized by the attribution of intense personal charisma to an acclaimed leader. Salvation is believed to be attainable through submission to the acclaimed leader thus invested with mahdistic authority. The claimant of supreme mahdistic authority determines its nature concurrently with the nature of soteriologically significant social action. Thus, through the extent of fusion or differentiation of the political and the religious spheres, he initially determines the degree of politicization of the ensuing movement.

From the outset, Mushaᶜshaᶜ gave his thaumaturgical authority as the Mahdi a political as well as a religious character. Beginning with Junayd, the Safavid movement was characterized by millenarian militarism. Military action under the leadership of the incarnate savior was endowed with immediate soteriological significance, thus motivating the Qizilbāsh to chiliastic action on the battlefield.

By contrast, Faḍl Allāh Astarābādī and the later Nūrbakhsh defined their authority primarily as guides to inner-worldly gnostic and mystical salvation respectively. However, even in these cases, two sets of factors made the politicization of the religious movements an ever-present possibility. The first set derived from the political environment of these movements. These religious movements were always politically conditioned by the yearning of their adherents for this-worldly action, which was often stimulated by the absence of a centralized political power. The case of the Marᶜashī movement was included in the analysis to demonstrate the existence of this yearning for this-worldly political action even when mahdism was absent. Another source of pressure toward politicization was the anticipation of its possibility by the jealously watchful political authorities, who would resort to violent repression. Such impingements of political power on the religious sphere in the form of religiously relevant repressive action would in turn tend to accentuate the movement's political conditioning. Mahdistic millenarianism was a likely reaction to preemptive repression.

The second set of factors had to do with the very structure of charismatic domination brought into existence by the full activation of the mahdistic tenet, a structure of domination that facilitated the transmission of the impact of adherents yearning for this-worldly political action. The mahdistic principle instituted a *personal* relationship between the leader and his followers. He could have a number of deputies (*khalīfa*s) who were (lay) members of the congregation representing him personally, but not a hierocratic staff. The absence of a hierocracy drastically reduced the autonomy of the religious sphere from the political. It did so because the unmediated domination of the Mahdi over his followers increased his susceptibility to their political demands and yearnings, the satisfaction or sublimation of which was of crucial importance to the perpetuation of the charismatic domination.

The Sarbidār case is an exception in that the unfolding of the mahdistic tenet in political action was incomplete. It represents a religiously conditioned *political* movement that stimulated the development of sectarian Shiᶜism in a direction suggested by the requirements of a religion of the state. The chiliastic impulse, deriving from the mahdistic tenet, was used to motivate political action but *without* charismatic acclamation of a supreme leader. Here the rulers were more often than not secular, and the structure of domination mediating the unfolding of the mahdistic tenet in action was hieratic. The great importance of the Sufi order in the power constellation assured the firm religious conditioning of the Sarbidār politics. The authority of the religious leaders was legitimated by its function of preparation of an earthly kingdom pleasing to the expected Imam. The dervishes used their hieratic domination and influence to mobilize and direct religiously conditioned political action. For this reason, the Sarbidār state, when the hieratic leaders had the upper hand, was a true theocracy. The *ethics* of salvation remained fully operative. In anticipation of *parousia*, the sacred law of God was observed. In fact, the last Sarbidār ruler commissioned a legal manual in which important substantive provisions of the Shiᶜite sacred law were clarified and the authority of the *ᶜulamāʾ* was extended to cover important functions they could now perform in a Shiᶜite state.

CHAPTER THREE

The Shadow of God on Earth

The Ethos of Persian Patrimonialism

3.1 World Religions and the Political Ethos of Sacral Kingship

The primitive cosmologies built around the central notion of sacral kingship have a number of essential characteristics in common. The king is equivalent to the cosmos, being typically "identified with the sky, and amid the sky with the sun." "The germ which . . . expands into law is the king's imitation of the universe, and more particularly of the sun which is the life of the universe." Thus the king "is the upholder of ordinances." Justice or order, in the sense of a body politic ordered in harmony with the cosmos—as the antithesis of chaos and disorder—is the central ethico-cognitive notion of these cosmologies. To this central notion of kingship, best reflected in the prototype of the sun king, was added the secondary notion of king as a warlord, usually associated with the prototype of the war king, which tended to recede into the background after the founding of dynasties and establishment of order. Another essential feature of these cosmologies is their materialism: their "all-embracing conception of welfare, the life of the world," which makes the furtherance of prosperity of the land and the subjects, by magical, political, or ethical means, the essential responsibility of the king.[1]

"Whatever was significant was imbedded in the life of the cosmos," Frankfort tells us in his classic study of kingship in ancient Egypt and Mesopotamia, "and it was precisely the king's function to maintain the harmony of that integration." The pharoah's primary obligation is to maintain *maat*—the right order. In Mesopotamia, more relevant to our concern because of the direct influences consequent upon its conquest by Cyrus the Great, the king was not a god but a man. On the other hand, the "Mesopotamian king was, like Pharoah, charged with maintaining harmonious relations between human society and the supernatural powers." Furthermore, "in historical times the Mesopotamian, no more than the Egyptian, could conceive of an ordered society without a king."[2]

The antithesis between the ethical religions of salvation, based as they are on monotheism and on the transcendence of God, and the materialist cosmologies incorporating sacral kingship is fundamental.[3] As we shall see in chapter 8, it inevitably generates some measure of antipathy toward the earthly powers. Nevertheless, what is strikingly demonstrated by the discussions in this chapter is the likelihood of the persistence of these archaic normative orders despite the superimposition of a world religion, and the often negligible impact of the latter upon the former.

In this respect, the case of Judaism is exceptional. The evidence for the prevalence of sacral kingship in ancient Israel is compelling.[4] Yet the transcendence of Yahweh and his uniqueness as a war god entailed some unusual features in Hebrew sacral kingship, making for the preponderance of elements associated with the moon king prototype. According to the Hebrew conception, the most important functions of the king were leadership in war and the administration of justice. The king was also the vicegerent of God. He was the Messiah or the "anointed" of Yahweh, endowed with Yahweh's spirit, and his person was sacrosanct.[5] However, with the termination of historical kingship and continued subjugation of the Jews, sacrality of kingship was completely transposed into messianic hope associated with the house of David.[6] With the absence of dynastic rulers with a vested interest in mirroring the cosmic order and embodying the spirit of Yahweh, the eschatological transposition of sacral kingship could be achieved. Earthly kingship disappeared, and the crown came to put on the Torah. In no other case do we witness such a complete triumph of a world religion over the cosmology of sacral world order and kingship.

H. A. R. Gibb states: "The nemesis of the over-rapid conquests of the Arabs—and the political tragedy of Islam—was that the Islamic ideology never found its proper and articulated expression in the political institutions of the Islamic states."[7] Islam is not alone among the world religions in not having had a notable impact on the constitution of the polity or on the political ethos prevalent in the lands it conquered. The same is true of Eastern Christianity, and of all Christianity down to the latter part of the eleventh century. Writing about the post-Constantine period, Troeltsch considers the influence of Christianity on political institutions to have been "extraordinarily slight":

> The institutions and intellectual culture rooted in the old ideas were too ancient, too independent, too radically remote, to be able to assimilate new impulses, while the Church, on the other hand, was still too much concerned with the next world, . . . still inwardly too detached to be able to weave ideas of that kind into the inner structure of the State. . . .
>
> Thus in the Early Church we can only look for a theoretical adjustment of

> the relationship between the Church and the Kingdom of God on the one hand, and the State and the world on the other, as of two inwardly essentially separate magnitudes which . . . are prevented from mutual interpenetration.[8]

The divergent courses of evolution in Western and Eastern Christianity from that point on, bearing the respective influences of Eusebius Of Caesarea (d. 339?) and Saint Augustine (d. 430), are instructive. Both Christianity and Islam encountered the same political ethos of sacral kingship in the form of Persian and Hellenistic theories of universal monarchy. In Eastern Christianity, the theory of universal monarchy was endorsed by the hierocracy and incorporated into the Orthodox belief system. Eusebius adopted the Hellenistic philosophy of kingship, and presented imperial government as a copy of the rule of God in heaven. The Roman emperor was therefore the vicegerent of the Christian God. For the Hellenistic philosopher Diotegenes, the state had been the mimesis of *kosmos* (which means "order" as much as it means "universe"). Eusebius substituted the kingdom of heaven for cosmos. The Hellenistic theory in which God was the archetype of the true king was adopted virtually in its entirety: "Eusebius had only to drop the Godhead of the king and to put in its place the Vicegerent of God."[9] Diotogenes had stated:

> As God is to the universe, so is the king to the State (*polis*), and as the State is to the universe, so is the king to God. For the State, which is a body joined together in harmony from many different parts, imitates the system and harmony of the universe; and the king, who exercises an authority [which] is not responsible [to any earthly superior], and who is in himself Animate Law, thus becomes the figure of a God among men.[10]

In the *Tricennial Oration*, or *De laudibus Constantini*, Eusebius declares:

> So crowned in the image of heavenly kingship, [the emperor] steers and guides men on earth according to the pattern of his prototype . . . God the Great King . . . is the standard of kingly power; and it is He who determines the establishment of a single authority for all men. . . . So there is one King; and the Word and the law that proceed from Him are one, expressed not in letters and syllables, or in inscriptions and pillars that perish with the passage of time, but living and subsisting as the Word that is God. . . .[11]

A specifically Christian touch was added by the title of Equal of the Apostles, bestowed upon Constantine and retained by his successors,[12] otherwise the theory retained its pre-Christian characteristics. In the fifth century (ca. 428), Cyril of Alexandria would address the emperor as the image of God on earth. Even at the end of the fourteenth century, when the Orthodox patriarchate was far larger than the shrunken empire, Patriarch Antony IV sharply reminded the grand prince of Muscovy, Basil I, that the holy emperor was God's viceroy on earth and the consecrated head of the Oecumene: "The Eusebian conception still endured."[13] It endured to the last, the fall of Constantinople, only to be transplanted, to the anachronistic delight of the grand prince, to the Third Rome to bestow caesaropapist legitimacy on the czars.[14]

Saint Augustine's replacement of a God-ordained oecumene by the dichotomy of the City of God and the *civitas terrena* precluded a consistent legitimation of caesaropapist political monism in Western Christianity: "Far from regarding a Christian empire as a realisation of God's kingdom on earth, [Augustine] doubts whether there is any possibility of realizing the Christian postulates in it."[15] The state, though a consequence of sin, can be legitimated if it is based on justice, as earthly peace and earthly justice are the gifts granted to fallen humanity; but it can be so legitimated as *temporal* rule. For centuries to come, theories of sacral kingship were retained and Germanic elements were added to the idea of universal monarchy; but henceforth, in the eyes of the Christian believers, they could only legitimate kingship as temporal rule. "Two there are, august emperor," would write Pope Gelasius I (d. 496) to the emperor Anastasius, "by which this world is chiefly ruled, the sacred authority [*auctoritas*] of the priesthood and the royal power [*potestas*]."[16] Nevertheless, the christianization of Germanic kingship was a slow process, and centuries had to pass before the institutional development of the papacy and a suitable constellation of political and hierocratic power would allow the "rationalization" of the principles of legitimacy of royal authority in Western Christendom by bringing them into congruence with Augustine's fundamental conceptions. Charlemagne had been "addressed as *Rex and Sacerdos*, and even reverenced as the Vicar of St. Peter, and vested with the 'two swords.'"[17] This conception of the "priest-king" was justified with reference to the biblical figure Melchizedech. Furthermore, in the ninth century, Christ was often identified with David and depicted as a warrior king. In 877, Pope John VIII could accordingly regard Charles the Bald as "the *principem populi* established by God in imitation of Christ, the true king; what Christ possessed by nature Charles could have by grace; he was the *salvator mundi*."[18] Unlike in Byzantium, in the West this early medieval conception of *Rex et Sacerdos* had to give way to *Papa versus Imperator* in the later Middle Ages. Royal consecration lost the character it had in Carolingian times, and was forever excluded from the seven sacraments. The king was granted a place in the ecclesiastical hierarchy—not as the head but only as an arm.[19] The twelfth and thirteenth century emperors no longer claimed priestly authority but only direct endowment with the temporal sword by God. The papacy, on the other hand, conceived of the emperor as a "mere officer who had to draw his sword at the bidding of the papacy." For Innocent III, "the pope as the Vicar of Christ had the right to create the universal protector of Christiandom [i.e., the emperor] . . . [hence] the repeated emphasis on the sun-moon allegory in [Innocent's] text, the moon receiving its light from the sun."[20] A world religion may be forced to a prolonged or permanent compromise with the idea of a sun-king, representing divine order, justice, and peace, but easily accommodates that of a moon-king, the war-king, and can willingly legitimate his temporal authority as a warrior and protector of faith. Thus, although the principle of universal monarchy was retained, it could only legitimate kingship as temporal domination. Thus, in Western Christianity, kingship was *secularized.*[21]

A comparable development had taken place many centuries earlier in ancient India, where kingship had had a pronounced sacral character.[22] As Dumont has shown, the analogous separation of the religious sphere from the political, accompanied by the exclusive appropriation of religious authority by the Brahmans, resulted in the secularization of kingship in Hinduism. Furthermore, with greater consistency than in the case of medieval Western Christianity, kingship was legitimated as *temporal* rule, that is, as authority pertaining to the "politico-economic domain, . . . [a] domain [which] is *relatively* autonomous with regard to absolute values." With this assumption, Kautilya (d. ca. 300 B.C.), the author of the *Artha-śāstra*, uses the notions of *danda* (punishment) and *artha* (material advantage) as cornerstones of his theory of government to legitimate kingship, in Dumont's paraphrase, as "the exercise of force for the pursuit of interest and the maintenance of order."[23]

As we have seen in chapter 1, the definitive separation of religious authority from the political during the formative period of the development of Imāmī Shiᶜism entailed the secularization of kingship. Doctrinal indifference to the principles of legitimacy of temporal rule—which was thus relegated to the realm of the profane, "the world"—amounted to granting autonomy to the pre-Islamic theory of sacral kingship and at the same time restricting its relevance to the temporal sphere. With the replacement by a world religion—Islam and then its Shiᶜite branch—of the cosmology of which the idea of sacral kingship was the central part, the husk of the theory of kingship, emptied of divine attributes, was retained while whatever *religious* motivation had previously contributed to its upholding was dessicated. But the husk was soon filled by earthly majesty, profane and perhaps even pagan, but nevertheless capable of inducing the motivation to submit to its authority. Though like the theories of monarchy in medieval Western Christianity, and unlike Kautilya's theory, the principles legitimating kingship in Persian political theories were not systematically shorn of formal sacralizing elements, the clear differentiation of political and religious authority in Shiᶜism meant that they could consistently legitimate kingship only as *temporal* rule.

3.2 Principles of Legitimacy in the Persian Theories of Kingship

I do not know of any satisfactory account of the transition from the (nomadic) tribal notion of kingship one encounters at the time of the founding of the Persian

Empire by Cyrus the Great[24] to the divine charisma of the Sasanian kings at the time of the Arab conquest—an account, that is, which would show the respective influence of the Mesopotamian and the Aryan theories of kingship.

Pending the appearance of an authoritative study of this transition, we may plausibly assume that the Aryan influence became predominant in the long run because of Zoroastrianism, which originated in northeastern Iran and persisted through the Hellenistic period, to be fully restored by the Sasanians in the third century A.D. The subsequent analysis is therefore exclusively focused on the Aryan, Zoroastrian influence, which, in any event, was decisive in the terminology of kingship eventually to be adopted by medieval Islam.

Christensen places the organization of monarchy among the Aryan tribes of eastern Iran between 900 and 775 B.C., some 150 to 300 years before the appearance of Zoroaster as the reformer of the Mazdist religion. The notion of charismatic kingship that emerged in this first heroic age of political organization is recorded in the pre-Zoroastrian proto-yashts (especially yashts 13 and 19).[25] There we first meet the terms "*x^varenō* [Middle Persian *farrah*] of the Aryans" (*airyanem x^varenō*), and more importantly, "*x^varenō* of the Kavis [kings]" (*kavaēm x^varenō*). Bailey painstakingly establishes the primary meaning of *x^varenō* as "a thing obtained or desired" and suggests "welfare, well-being" or "fortune" or, more concretely, "good things" as equally satisfactory translations. This primary meaning is found in such verses as "O Fortune [*aši*], bestowing good things [*x^varenō*]." *X^varenō* of the Kavis, Royal Fortune, represents the pre-Zoroastrian abstract hypostasis of the notion in the legends of the earliest kings. This kingly Fortune was Yama's until he abandoned *Arta* (Right/Order) for the *Drug* (False). Then, "the *x^varenō* went from Yama . . . in the form of the bird Vāragna."[26] The Turanian Franrasyan forfeited the Fortune of the Kavis by killing the Zainigav and adhering to the false faith. He attempted to recover it by swimming in the lake Vorukaša (Lake Hāmūn), the eternal repository of *x^varenō* of the Kavis and the Aryans. But Royal Fortune escaped from him to be recovered by his vanquisher, Kavi Haosravah. Finally, Kavi Vištāspa, the champion of Zoroastrian faith, offered sacrifice to the goddess Fortune (*Aši*, hypostasis of good things bestowed), and came to possess the Fortune of the Kavis.[27] Ahura Mazdā enjoins every man to seek the "unseized *x^varenō*" of the lake Vorukaša, which he who has not *aša* (*Arta*, Right) cannot hold. Needless to say, *x^varenō*, thus hypostasized as Royal Fortune, maintains its connection with prosperity, order, and the sun as a bestower of good things.

With Zoroastrianism, a third abstract hypostasis makes its appearance in the Avesta: the *x^varenō* of Zoroaster. The emergence of Zoroaster as the religious reformer, *ratu*, and keeper of Right (*aša*) meant that one would in time speak of *x^varrah* (*farrah*) *i dēn* (religion) as a force in the invisible world bestowing fortune; the unseized *x^varenō* could also subsequently be claimed by the priests by virtue of their knowledge of Ahura Mazdā.[28]

While Zoroastrianism was growing but long before it became the established religion of the state, the local rulers of northeastern Iran assumed the etymologically remarkable title of *x*^{v}*atā*^{v} (he who is powerful by himself, *auto-kratōr*) mentioned in the introduction. The notion behind the title later found general acceptance in Iran and produced a conception of lordship, *x*^{v}*atāyīh*, which, as Benveniste points out, was at complete divergence with those of the Latin *rex* and Sanskrit *rāj* at the two extremities of the Indo-European world, both of which gave royalty the character of "rector," the sovereign's role consisting only in "tracing the right way." This Iranian conception of lordship was also indicated by *xšaθra* (Sanskrit *kṣatra*), from which the Old Iranian *xšāyaθiya* (corresponding to the Sanskrit *kṣatriya*) meaning king, and therefore the Achemenid *xšāyaθiya xšāyaθiyānām* (king of kings) and the inverted *shāhān shāh* were derived.[29] However, the apotheosis of the king of kings is not a feature of the Achemenid Empire, and very probably began with the founder of the Parthian dynasty, Arshak, who according to the well-informed Ammianus Marcellinus

> was placed among the stars according to the sacral custom of their country; and—they believe—he was the first of all to be so honored. Hence to this day the over-boastful kings of that race suffer themselves to be called brothers of the Sun and Moon. . . . Hence they venerate and worship Arsak as a god.

Henceforth, in Widengren's words,

> the king is holy, because his descent is from the gods. His person is of a divine character. He is the Brother of Sun and Moon and has his real home among the stars. He is the Aion incarnate. Some kings are regarded more as Sun-kings, other as Moon-kings. His real nature is fire, for he has descended from heaven as lightning in a column of fire.

However, the peaceful sun king aspect predominated over the warlike moon king aspect throughout Iranian history.[30]

The man to capture the Royal Fortune and establish the Sasanian Empire in A.D. 226 was Ardashīr, son of Pāpak. He sought and obtained the aid of "the divine Fortune of Iran [*yazdān x*^{v}*arrah i ērānšahr*]." Shortly before his final victory, the wise vizier of Ardavān, the last king of the Parthian dynasty to be overthrown by him, reportedly interpreted an incident in which Ardavān was chasing the fugitive Ardashīr when a "great ram," after pursuing the latter for a time, mounted behind him on the horse, meaning that "the Royal Fortune [*x*^{v}*arrah i kayān*] has reached Ardashīr and he cannot in any way be taken."[31]

Ardashīr made the restoration of Zoroastrianism the pillar of his newly founded empire. He was the restorer of Right/Order (*Arta*, Old Iranian *ṛta*, Avestan *aša*) and styled himself *Artaxšēr* (*Arta xšaθra*) or the King/Lord of Right/Order. In this he was assisted by the Zoroastrian priesthood. A letter attributed to his great *hērbad*, Tansar, has come down to us in Persian translation. The core of the letter is very probably from the time of Ardashīr, and may well have been written by Tansar.[32] It expounds the foremost principle upon which imperial order was restored:

> Do not wonder at my zeal and ardour for promoting order in the world, so that the foundation of the laws of religion (*dīn*) may be made firm. For religion and kingship were born of the one womb, joined together and never to be sundered. Order (*ṣalāḥ*) and corruption, health and sickness of both has the same constitution.[33]

Religion and kingship were born of one womb and were the equally indispensable constituents of *Arta* (Right/Order).

According to Zaehner, in the Zoroastrian ethos "the King is the center of the universe, and the goal of the universe is happiness." The prosperity of the subjects depends on the quality of the king. Furthermore, "God is absolute lord of both worlds; the King is his representative on earth and, as such, may himself take the title of *bagh*, 'god.'" In the *Dēnkart*, we have the affirmation of the principle, "Religion is royalty, and royalty is the religion." Further, "the symbol of the Holy Spirit surely manifests itself on earth in [the person of] the good and righteous King, one whose will [*akhw*] is bent on increase, whose character is pure, whose desire for his subjects is good."[34]

Thus, over the whole world stands the King of Kings, who, in Zaehner's words, "is the guardian of religion as he is of justice and order. Religion indeed, in the Zoroastrian sense, is almost synonymous with justice and order." What is striking is the materialism of the Zoroastrian cosmology:

> The fruit of the Good Religion is the benefit of the creatures, that of false religion is their harm. . . .
>
> Injustice gives strength to the demons in their ruining of the material world. . . .
>
> From belief in . . . the Good Religion proceeds the formation of character, from the formation of character the Mean: from the Mean is justice born, from justice good thoughts, good words, and good deeds; from [the latters] the welfare of Man. . . . The spiritual world is made straight and the material world brought into order.[35]

It is important to note that this charismatic legitimacy was conditional upon the king's being good and righteous, and was forfeited in case of tyranny: "whereas the good king was the symbol of the divine sovereignty (Light) on earth, the wicked king or tyrant was rather that of Ahriman (The Evil Spirit of Darkness)."[36]

Kingship was associated not only with Royal Fortune but also with light and splendor, as reflected in such phrases as *aβrōčāk x*ᵛ*atāyīh* (splendid lordship). We are thus told in the *Kārnāmak* that "Pāpak one night saw in a dream how the sun shone from the head of Sāsān and made the whole world bright."

According to Bailey, under the influence of Manichaean and Christian writers and translators, the primary meaning of "fortune" was partly forgotten and merged with the idea of splendor of lordship. *Xᵛarr* (*farrah*) thus acquired the vaguer meaning of "glory" and was symbolized by the nimbus of light or fire surrounding the head of the king.[37]

The Sasanian kings had no difficulty in accommodating the apotheosis of kingship they had inherited from the Parthians into this Zoroastrian framework. Shahpur II would thus call himself "King of Kings, partner with the stars, brother of the Sun and Moon."[38] Furthermore, the Sasanian kings not only called themselves gods: they imitated gods in their attire, notably in their crown, the crown being adorned by objects that symbolized the *Farrah* or Royal Fortune/Glory. With the accretion of emblems the crown became so heavy that it could not be worn by the king and hung above the throne. "This usage passed to the court of Byzantium, where it was observed in 1170 by Benjamin of Tudela. As for the shapes of the throne, they were perpetuated at the court of the Baghdad caliphs."[39]

Except for the deification of the king, this picture bears a remarkable similarity to the world view and ethos of imperial China, where

> the impersonal power of Heaven did not 'speak' to man. It revealed itself in the regimen on earth, in the firm order of nature and tradition which were pat of the cosmic order, and, as elsewhere, it revealed itself in what occurred to man. The welfare of the subjects documented heavenly contentment and the correct functioning of the order.[40]

Weber's characterization of Chinese rule as "theocratic patrimonialism"[41] therefore seems also applicable to Sasanian Iran, both with regard to the charismatic position of the monarch and to the centrality of the notion of the "welfare state," with a strong materialistic emphasis on the prosperity of the kingdom and on the economic well-being of the subjects, the *raᶜāyā* or *raᶜiyat* (original meaning "tended livestock").[42] However, Sasanian theocratic patrimonialism, unlike that of the Chinese, had to face the onslaught of a world religion of salvation to which it succumbed.

Like the imperial crown, the influence of the Sasanian ethos of universal monarchy penetrated into Islam as early as the eighth/second century through the work of Ibn Muqaffaᶜ, the chancellor of the ᶜAbbasid caliph al-Manṣūr, both in administrative handbooks and in mirrors for princes. The most important of the Sasanian tracts on kingship and statecraft translated into Arabic in the eighth/second century bore the significant title of the *Covenant of Ardashīr* (*ᶜAhd Ardashīr*). It takes the form of the testament of Ardashīr, Lord of Right/Order, to his successors among the kings of Persia:

> Know that kingship and religion are twin brothers; there is no solidity for one of them except through its companion because religion is the foundation of kingship and kingship the protector of religion. Kingship needs its foundation and religion its protector as whatever lacks a protector perishes and whatever lacks a foundation is destroyed.[43]

Similarly, the Sasanian idea of kingship influenced the ᶜAbbasid idea of caliphate: "The ᶜAbbasid Caliphs themselves at least tolerated the idea that their caliphate was a continuation of Persian royalty."[44] The caliphs' strong claim to Islamic legitimacy as the "heir of the Mantle [of the Prophet], the Staff and the authority [*ḥukm*] of God," was effectively buttressed by their claim to righteous sovereignty as the source of prosperity of the realm as reflected in panegyrics of the court poets: "through you the expanses of land have become fertile. / How can the world be barren when you are its protector?"[45]

The Būyid seizure of power in Baghdad in the mid-tenth/fourth century ushered in a major bifurcation in the Islamic structure of domination. The caliph's position became largely ceremonial, yet it precluded any claim on the part of the actual rulers of the Islamic lands to be the heirs of the Prophet. The Sasanian idea of kingship could then be seen as the most effective means for the legitimation of temporal power. Thus the Būyids revived the full-fledged conception of kingship. In the tenth/fourth century, the Būyid rulers assumed the title of shāhanshāh, which continued to be borne by the Saljūq sultans in the following century.[46] Thus, with the eclipse of the ᶜAbbasid caliphate in the tenth/fourth century, political theory came to center around the de facto ruler—later to be designated "*Sulṭān*"—rather than the caliph, and by the second half of the eleventh/fifth century, the tradition of seeing the ruler as the "Shadow of God on Earth" became firmly established. The Sasanian idea of kingship had been adopted by Islam.

In the last quarter of the eleventh/fifth and the early years of the twelfth/sixth century, when the bifurcation of the Islamic structure of domination into caliphate and rulership had become fully established, some of the most important treatises on rulership, statecraft, and political ethics made their appearance. By then, the eighth/second- and early ninth/third-century Sasanian translations had become fully assimilated into the conventional wisdom. However, the separation of the caliphate, associated with the prophetic tradition and with religion, from temporal rulership necessitated a subtle change of emphasis in political theory. Ibn Muqaffaᶜ had chosen to speak of religion (*dīn*) rather than Islam. As religion, retaining its pre-Islamic connotations, implied a right order based on justice, the explicit role of justice was secondary and the term was used in a general rather than a legal sense.[47] With the eighth/second- and ninth/tenth-century differentiation of religion and the prophetic tradition from the political order, and with the tenth/fourth- and eleventh/fifth-identification of caliphate with Islamic orthodoxy, justice replaced right religion as the twin companion of kingship; and kingship as supreme temporal rule claimed direct and autonomous divine sanction in the form of the *Farr* (*Farrah*)-*e Īzadī*, the *Yazdān xᵛarrah* of the *Kārnāmak-e Ardashīr*, now assuming the meaning of divine effulgence.

As Lambton points out, in one of the famous treatises on government, *Siyāsatnāmeh*, Niẓām al-Mulk tacitly regards the theory of divine effulgence (*Farr-e Īzadī*) as superseding the classical theory of the caliphate. Although Niẓām al-

Mulk emphasized the importance of right religion and stability, justice rather than religion—including religious law—became the basis of his theory of kingship: "The object of temporal rule was to fill the earth with justice." In another famous treatise of the period, al-Ghazālī's *Naṣīḥat al-Mulūk*, the emphasis on justice is predominant. The one qualification he makes for a true sultan is the exercise of justice. This trend was typical throughout the Middle Ages. Sasanian notions were recast in Islamic and Hellenistic terms: the theory of the ruler as the Shadow of God on Earth was taken from Sasanian sources, and the Hellenistic idea of the philosopher king was assimilated to it. Justice rather than the right religion became the foundation of the medieval theory of righteous rule.[48]

The first important impact of Islam—like that of other world religions—on the ethos of universal monarchy was to change the notion of justice, which came to acquire the connotation of enforcement of the sacred law rather than the maintenance of the "right order" in harmony with the cosmos. This impact is unmistakable and the notion of justice becomes firmly connected with the enforcement of the sacred law.[49] Nevertheless, the impact was not strong enough to generate a systematic public law. The political economy of the reconstituted ethos of kingly patrimonialism is clearly expressed in a slightly earlier treatise:

> Make it your constant endeavor to improve cultivation and to govern well, for understand this truth, good government is secured by armed troops, armed troops are maintained with gold, gold is acquired through cultivation and cultivation is sustained through payment of what is due to the peasantry, by just dealing and fairness: be just and equitable therefore.[50]

The overriding fear of anarchy and bloodshed made the Muslim jurists and legal theorists enjoin unconditional obedience to "those in authority" (Qur'an, 4:59), contenting themselves with emphasizing that the latter were held morally accountable to God. Protection of the subjects and just administration of the kingdom was the responsibility of the ruler, for which he was answerable to God. Ghazālī cites the tradition that states: "the harshest torment at the Day of Resurrection will be for the unjust ruler."[51] That the king is also responsible for the action of those to whom he delegates his authority is clearly brought out in a passage in the *Siyāsat-nāmeh*, in which Niẓām al-Mulk urges the land assignees and governors to protect the subjects and treat them as the king treats them—i.e., with justice, "so that the subjects should be content with the justice of the king, and the king be immune from suffering and punishment in the other world."[52] Gibb pointed out that the Sunni doctrine of imamate as effective political rule became divorced, step by step, from the sacred law and moved in the direction of absolutism.[53] With the subsequent substitution of sultanate for imamate in medieval Persian political theory after the eleventh/fifth century, this trend was reinforced. Even so pious a jurist as Ghazālī mentioned the sacred law only in one section of his treatise on government.[54] The attribution to the sultan, as the

Shadow of God on Earth, of autonomous charisma as divine reflection upon the *temporal* world, and the emphasis on the exercise of substantive justice by him, minimized the effects of Islamic tenets on the patrimonial theories of temporal rule. The notion of justice that came to prevail in these theories was the unformalized substantive justice of Sasanian patrimonialism: protection of the weak from the strong, removal of oppression and administration of punishment for wrongdoings and for contraventions of customary norms of fairness.

The emphasis on justice entailed the abhorrence of injustice and tyranny (*ẓulm*). Al-Māwardī had equated injustice with irreligion; and the notion of *ẓulm* as the antithesis of justice assumes an equally central position. Here, too, however, the connection between "tyranny" and the sacred law is slight. *Ẓulm* retains its primeval connotation of darkness (*ẓulma*) as the shadow of death (*ẓill al-maniyya*). Tyranny, connoting disorder and darkness, was opposed to justice, connoting order and light.

The overthrow of the ᶜAbbasid caliphate by the Mongols ended the bifurcation of the structure of domination, and made possible a closer association between rulership, religion, and the sacred law. Two of the most important post-ᶜAbbasid treatises on political ethics, the *Akhlāq-e Nāṣirī* of Naṣīr al-Dīn Ṭūsī (the second half of the thirteenth/seventh century) and the *Akhlāq-e Jalālī* of Jalāl al-Dīn Davvānī (the second half of the fifteenth/ninth century), put forward two contrasting interpretations of the interdependence of the twin-born religion and royalty, which, however, accommodate the rule of the sacred law of Islam to the ethic of kingly patrimonialism with equal theoretical consistency. (Incidentally, as has been pointed out, Naṣīr al-Dīn Ṭūsī was a Shiᶜite thinker and the teacher of ᶜAllāma al-Ḥillī, who was greatly influenced by his philosophy and presumably by his political theory.) Both authors confirm the covenant of Ardashīr: religion and kingship are twin-born. However, they offer contrasting interpretations of the nature of this interdependence in relation to the sacred law.

Justice, equated with the Aristotelian mean, remains central to Ṭūsī's political theory: "Prosperity of the world depends on civic justice, and the ruin of the world on civic injustice." And the preservation of justice among the people depends on three factors: divine law, human ruler, and money (*dīnār*). Ṭūsī equates the divine *nomos* (*nāmūs-e ilāhī*) of the ancients—i.e., the Greeks—with the sacred law (*sharīᶜat*) of the traditionists and presents it as the greatest or first *Nāmūs*. The ruler as the animate law (*nomos empsychos*) of Diotogenes and the Byzantines then takes its place in Ṭūsī's hierarchy as the second *Nāmūs*. Money (*dīnār*), which is said to be a just *nomos*, then follows as the third *Nāmūs*. The health of the body politic, the prevalence of a just order, is determined by these three, and it is necessary for the second *Nāmūs*, the ruler, to follow the first, the sacred law, as it is for the third to follow the second. Ṭūsī's synthesis thus offers us a combination of the Hellenistic and Sasanian notions of order and the Islamic notion of the sacred law in his hierarchy of three differentiated orders: the religio-legal, the political, and the economic. Formally, the supremacy of the sacred law makes this system a divine nomocracy. Substantively, however, Ṭūsī pays only minimal attention to the sacred law, and his conception of justice consists in the proper treatment of the classes of society according to the norms of Sasanian patrimonialism. Once the rules of justice are followed, beneficence and charity (*iḥsān*) are the most important principles of statescraft; however, they should be exercised judiciously so as not to impair the awe (*haybat*) of authority: "Beneficence must be commensurate with awe [*haybat*] [of authority] as the glory [*farr*] and honor of kingship stems from awe . . . and beneficence without awe [of authority] would cause the wantonness of the subjects, embolden them and increase their covetousness and greed."

In the following paragraph, Ṭūsī sums up his conception of the health of the body politic:

> As the rectitude of the body depends on nature and the rectitude of one's nature depends on the soul [*nafs*] and the rectitude of the soul on reason, the rectitude of cities depends on kingship [*mulk*] and the rectitude of kingship on statecraft [*siyāsat*] and that of statecraft on wisdom [*ḥikmat*]. When wisdom prevails and the True *Nomos* [*nāmūs-e ḥaqq*] is followed, order [*niẓām*] is obtained, as is the attention to the perfection of beings. But if wisdom departs, *Nāmūs* is impaired and when *Nāmūs* is impaired the adornment of kingship disappears and disorder [*fitna*] makes its appearance. The customs of chivalrous generosity become delapidated and prosperity [*niᶜmat*] turns into rancor and adversity.[55]

While retaining the hierarchy of the three differentiated orders—the religio-legal, the political, and the economic—and presenting the ruler as the second *Nāmūs*, Jalāl al-Dīn Davvānī pays far greater attention the sacred law and declares that the ruler should consult its interpreters in *ᶜibādāt* (devotional duties). Tyranny is defective government in which the ruler strives to enslave the servants of God. Just rule, on the other hand, means the rule of the sacred law; otherwise the just ruler cannot rule and his subject cannot prosper.[56]

Other motifs of the ethos of kingly patrimonialism and rules of statecraft are also to be found in the treatise. Davvānī extols the typical virtues of the "mirrors for princes," such as sobriety, moderation, and close supervision of administration, and adduces alleged signs of divine favor vouchsafed to his patron, Sulṭān Ūzūn Ḥasan. At the same time, the prominence given to the sacred law in Davvānī's theory enables him to claim a stronger Islamic legitimacy for the ruler observing it, calling the latter the deputy (*khalīfa*) of God:

> The sovereign is a person distinguished by divine support so that he might lead individual men to perfection and order their affairs. . . . The first concern of [the ruler] is the maintenance of the injunctions of the Sacred Law. In specific details, however, he retains the power to act in accordance with the *public interest* of his age as long as his actions fall within the general princi-

ples of the Sacred Law. Such a person is truly the Shadow of God, the Caliph of God, and the Deputy of the Prophet.[57]

Davvānī's return to the ʿAbbasids' stronger claims to Islamic legitimacy was not to have a lasting effect in Iran because of the advent of Shiʿism. As we shall see, the caesaropapist claims of the Safavids had to be stated in terms of the deputyship of the Hidden Imam, and not that of God and the Prophet. However, the conception of the ruler as the shadow of God on earth, together with the substance of Davvānī's political ethic of patrimonialism, was passed down to posterity.

The creation of a distinct religious sphere by Islam as a religion of salvation and the somewhat slight and unformalized connection between the patrimonial conception of justice and the sacred law of Islam tended to restrict the pertinence of the theories of universal monarchy to *temporal* domination even before this restriction was made definitive by the impact of Shiʿism. When Ghazālī interpreted the notion of "divine effulgence" as the "shadow of God on *earth*," he was legitimating rulership as earthly domination within the *temporal* sphere. It is not accidental that, together with the influence of the Sasanian political ethos, the purely secular notion of *Dawla* as the fortunate "turn" (of a dynasty) makes its appearance in the ʿAbbasid annals.

As was pointed out in the introduction, we occasionally come across topics not treated in political ethics and political theory which are nevertheless enormously important in affecting people's political attitudes and motivation to submit to authority. *Dawla*, like its Hellenistic counterpart Fortune, is one such popular belief recorded in Islamic historiography. The primeval notion they embody is perhaps nowhere as systematically elaborated as in the Chinese theory of the mandate of heaven, according to which "heaven sent this ruin [the overthrow]" on the last ruler of the Shang dynasty so that the conquering "Chow merely assisted by carrying out [the Heavenly] Mandate . . ." (twelfth century B.C.).[58] Nevertheless, we do find parallel ideas in a wide variety of historical contexts. The "kin-right" of the Germanic kings in the early Middle Ages, for instance, rested on their being charismatic "repositories of the tribal 'luck.'" It consisted of a claim for the family, whose original foundations were "an unusual power, a fortunate virtue, a special divine vocation, with which legend all times loves to enwrap the figures of the founders of dynasties."[59]

More pertinently to our subject matter, the goddess Fortune (*Tyche*) dominated the third century B.C. to such an extent that even sober historians like Polybius "did not disdain the concession to popular belief implied in the use of her name. She was not blind chance, but some order of affairs which men could not apprehend."[60] By reversing her wheel she would bestow her favor on a new dynasty (or nation), thus endowing it with venerability and legitimacy. In the Hellenistic East, the fortune (*Farrah*) of the king would naturally be rendered in Greek as *Tyche* of the king.[61] That such a deep-rooted popular belief persisted after the establishment of Christianity is reflected in Procopius's (d. 565?) explanation of the submission of the Byzantine senate and people to the upstart imperial couple he detested (Justinian and Theodora): "All of them, I imagine, were subdued by the thought that this was the fate assigned to them, and accordingly lifted no finger to prevent this revolting state of affairs, as though Fortune had given a demonstration of her power. . . ."[62]

In Islamic history, similarly, the notion of *Dawla* (turn [of fortune]), by compelling though unstated implication, endows the ruling dynasty with temporal if not pagan charisma, and legitimates its rule, which is granted it by divine favor. The legends surrounding the founding of a dynasty and the continuation of its fortunate virtue as God's manifest approval of its rule are effectively legitimatory. A new dynasty is given a *Dawla* for reasons best known to God. This conception of *Dawla* as the divinely granted turn in power was supported by a Qur'anic verse: "Say, O God, possessor of sovereignty, you give sovereignty to whomever you choose and take it from whomever you choose" (3:26). The ʿAbbasids had claimed that their *Dawla* was synonymous with the divinely granted turn of power of Islam.[63] The Buyids claimed a new *Dawla*, as did the other dynasties rising in the eastern lands of the Caliphate. Thus, the vizier and historian Bayhaqi in the eleventh/fifth century explains the rule of the dynasty he served as follows:

> If any defamer or jealous person says that this great house has come from humble or unknown origin, the answer is that God, since the creation of Adam, has decreed that kingship be transferred from one religious polity [*ummat*] to another and from one group to another. . . . So it should be realized that God's removal of the shirt of kingship from one group and his placing it on another group is in that sense divine wisdom and for the commonweal of mankind, [wisdom] which surpasses human understanding. . . . [God knows] that in such and such a spot a man will appear through whom men will obtain happiness and good fortune.[64]

From the Mongol conquest until the establishment of Shiʿism by the Safavids, Iran was ruled by Turko-Mongolian dynasties. In the materialist cosmology of these nomadic tribes as reflected in the paleo-Turkic inscriptions of Mongolia and Siberia, the *Kagan* (emperor) was the terrestrial counterpart of the great sky god, Tängri. He came from the sky and possessed a celestial mandate, ruling in harmony with cosmic order as long as his mandate lasted.[65] After their islamization, these grounds of legitimacy of the rule of the great Khans were transformed to a nomadic principle of legitimacy akin to the Germanic kin-right, according to which the right to rule rested with the male members of the family of the Khan. Genealogies claiming the descent of the Turkman dynasties from Changīz Khān and from the legendary Turkish ruler Oghūz were regularly produced to demonstrate and legitimate the fortunate turn in power of the Īl-Khāns, the Timurids, the Jalayirids, the Quaraqūyūnlū, and the Aqqūyūnlū.[66]

Although the conception of *Dawla* has not been a topic in Islamic political theory, its retention singly and in various combinations as the term denoting "government" attests to its continued importance in implicitly legitimating temporal rule as earthly majesty throughout the medieval period and beyond.

If the above analysis is correct, the striking secularity of the Persian "mirrors for princes" is hardly surprising. In these, no less clearly than in Kautilya's *Artha-šāstra*, government pertains to the temporal realm, the realm of material advantage and of "punishment" or the use of force to maintain order. Indeed, the word for "politics," contained in the title of Niẓām al-Mulk's treatise and treated at great length in all the mirrors[67]—*siyāsat*—means "punishment" and is no other than Kautilya's *danda*. And the rule to serve as a mirror for the prince to assure the welfare and prosperity of the subjects is no other than the *Artha-šāstra*, the science of polity.[68]

Conclusion to Part One

Al-Bāqir and al-Ṣadiq's disapproval of armed rebellion signified the subsidence of this-worldly eschatological millenarianism and its replacement by religious legalism (al-Bāqir, al-Ṣadiq) and a quietistic mystical piety (al-Ṣadiq). Al-Ṣadiq's injunction to the Shiʿites to transact with the rest of the Muslims and to enter the service of non-Shiʿite governments signified the acceptance of "the world." The development of Shiʿite jurisprudence during the period of expansion signaled the Imāmī scholars' determination to pursue al-Bāqir's goal: to subject worldly activities to the governance of the ethical precepts deriving from the prophetic teaching and divine inspiration. At the same time, the injunction to ethically responsible worldly activity, including activity in the political sphere, removed the religious inhibition to engagement in political activity and facilitated the attainment of high political office by many Shiʿites.

The great traditionalists of the period of retrenchment, on the other hand, put the accent on the development of the spiritual teaching of al-Ṣādiq. Withdrawn from the world in the isolated city of Qum, the great traditionalist theologians laid open a vast inner space for the cultivation of spiritual life, and gave the Shiʿite inner-worldly piety a solid foundation in their writings. Though traditionalist inner-worldly piety soon gave way to the world-embracing jurisprudential rationalism of the period of expansion as the dominant religious orientation, it remained a possible, albeit uncommon, mode of religiosity, and a dormant potential to be revived in the seventeenth century.

Both the world-embracing rationalism of al-Murtaḍā and the pietistic traditionalism of Kulaynī share one fundamental feature: the differentiation of religious and political authority instituted by the Shiʿite doctrines of imamate and of the greater occultation. The rationalist thelogians sought to perpetuate this differentiation by coupling the doctrine of occultation with the principle of grace (*lutf*), which asserted that the benefits of imamate to mankind obtained *without* the Imam being the actual ruler.

Yet the rationalized Shiᶜite theological/jurisprudential world view containing this separation of religious and political authority was threatened with abeyance from within because of the retention of the eschatological belief in the return of the Hidden Imam as the Mahdi. The adoption of the latter belief by the extremist Shiᶜite movements of the fourteenth and fifteenth centuries resulted in the millenarian fusion of religious and political domination. The legalistic guardians of the *ratio* contained in the Shiᶜite ethics of salvation gave place to the charismatic claimants to mahdihood who, by virtue of their immediate salvational power granted them by the Shiᶜite mahdistic tenet, had total and ethically unconstrained freedom of action.

On the other hand, the mere profession of Shiᶜism, unless accompanied by the swift promulgation of a new divine dispensation—as was the case with Ḥurūfism—would constitute a beginning for a swing of the pendulum in the long run. This was so because Shiᶜism did after all possess an ethics of salvation that could not be declared in abeyance indefinitely and that was bound to be noted in the course of the routinization of mahdistic charisma by rulers interested in stability (the Sarbidār and Safavid cases).

The charismatic force of the mahdistic principle, by engendering the warrior millenarianism of the Qizilbāsh, created the Safavid empire, into which, with the onset of the period of stabilization, the Shiᶜite *ᶜulamāʾ* were invited to bring their rationalized belief system, and to make it prevail. By this time, however, as we shall see, the mahdistic principle had created solidly vested political interests—including, above all, those of the ruling dynasty—that could very effectively resist the complete imposition of the Shiᶜite theological/jurisprudential *ratio*, though without destroying its potential for being realized in some future point under suitable conditions. The pendulum would swing, but its swing would not be unencumbered by the initial fusion of religious and political authority resulting from the historical espousal of mahdism by the early Safavids.

We have examined the tension between two religious elements, the mahdistic principle of extremism and the differentiation of religion from the political authority in Twelver Shiᶜism. We have also considered the extrareligious component completing the picture: the principles of legitimacy of kingship. Once mahdistic millenarianism could be contained, the coexistence of the principle of legitimacy of kingship with Shiᶜism became unproblematic because of the latter's doctrinal indifference to the topic of rulership.

PART TWO

Shiʿism as the Religion of the State under the Safavids, 1501–1722

Introduction to Part Two

The Twelver Shiᶜite doctrine, systematized in a form that was to become definitive by the end of the fourteenth century, was propagated in Iran by Ismāᶜīl the Safavid from 1501 onwards. The doctrine did not enter a cultural and religious vacuum, nor did its non-Persian custodians, the Shiᶜite theologians, who came to Iran at the invitation of the Safavid rulers, enter into a sociopolitical vacuum. On the contrary, Shiᶜism and its authoritative interpreters stepped into a culturally structured and sociopolitically populated realm whose indigenous cultural and sociopolitical order offered resistance to the impact of Shiᶜism, and in turn modified some of its features. On the religious plane, Twelver Shiᶜism entered a domain dominated by extremism, Sufism, and Sunnism; on the plane of political culture, it entered a universe normatively structured by the ethos of Persian patrimonialism, whose principles legitimated kingship as a God-ordained institution. Finally, on the plane of social and political organization, the incoming Shiᶜite doctors encountered an indigenous clerical estate with diffuse but institutionally entrenched religio-administrative authority, and with definite political vested interests.

Let us first turn to the religious plane. It is a well-known fact that pre-Safavid Iran was predominantly Sunni. It is also common knowledge that the fifteenth century was a period marked by the flourishing of a number of millenarian movements, the last of which gave birth to the Safavid empire. However, what is not so commonly realized is that beyond the recognition of the twelve Imams, fifteenth-century Shiᶜite extremism had little in common with Twelver Shiᶜism or the doctrine of the Imāmī sect. Furthermore, though Imāmī scholarship developed freely—notably in Ḥilla—contrary to expectation, there is no evidence of missionary activity on the spread of Imāmī Shiᶜism in Iran in the period preceding the establishment of the Safavid empire.[1] According to the earliest chronicle of his rule, when, despite the trepidation of his entourage, Shah Ismaᶜil proclaimed Twelver Shiᶜism the state religion in Tabriz in 1501/907, that city, like the rest of Iran, was predominantly Sunni. It was only after much searching that a book containing the basic tenets of Imāmī Shiᶜism, the *Qawāʾid al-Islām* by Ibn al-Muṭahhar al-Ḥillī, was found in the library of a qadi, and was made the basis of the new religion.[2] Not even in Kashan, referred to by the sources as the *dār al-muʾminīn* (realm of the faithful; a designation reserved for the old centers of Imāmī Shiᶜism), was a competent Shiᶜite jurist to be found for over a decade.[3]

Scarcia-Amoretti aptly uses the phrase "religiously promiscuous ambiance" to refer to the late fifteenth century. As she points out, for example, the staunch Sunni opponent of the Shiᶜite Safavids, Rūzbihān Khunjī, wrote a poem in praise of the twelve Shiᶜite Imams, and held the martyred Imām Ḥusayn in greatest respect and admiration.[4] In this atmosphere of relative religious eclecticism, devotional attachment to ᶜAlī in particular, and to the house of the Prophet (his daughter Fāṭima and the twelve Imams) in general, was widespread among the population. Because of the persistence of the trend set in motion by the caliph al-Nāṣir, ᶜAlī was often considered the model of the *fatāʾ* or *futuwwa*: the moral quality most highly valued by urban associations and guilds. It was natural for guilds, in view of their characteristic attachment to the house of the Prophet, to adopt ᶜAlī, or another Shiᶜite Imam, as their "patron saint" alongside the prophets and other figures in sacred history.[5]

The cult of the shrines of the putative descendants of ᶜAlī (sing. *imām-zādeh*) is also a feature of popular religion to be encountered in this period. A mosque in the Shiᶜite center of Qum known as Panjeh ᶜAlī (Hand/Five Fingers of ᶜAlī) contains as inscription, dated 1480/886, that is indicative of the eclectic devotional religiosity of the period. The mosque is said to have been built for Imām-zādeh Ḥārith, son of Imām Mūsā al-Kāẓim, who has gone into occultation: "Through the blessing [*barakat*] of the occultation of the infallible [*maᶜṣūm*] prince [i.e., the *imām-zādeh*] it will not be destroyed until the end of time."[6]

The widespread pro-ᶜAlī and pro-house of the Prophet sentiments of the population facilitated the propagation of Shiᶜism after Ismāᶜīl's conquest of Iran. Despite some resistance, especially in eastern Iran and Fars,[7] the *formal* profession of Shiᶜism spread speedily. However, the conversion achieved by Safavid propagandists does not seem to have involved anything beyond publicly cursing (*laʾn*) the first three rightly guided caliphs, and exalting ᶜAlī and his descendants.[8] A number of passages in *Ross Anonymous* clearly show the superficiality of the sudden conversion to Shiᶜism. For instance, we are told that in 1509/915, the inhabitants of Sarakhs (in Khurasan) uttered the "slogan of the Imāmī religion" (*shiʾār-e madhhab-e imāmiyya*), and were immune from depredation by Ismāᶜīl's army.[9] There are indications that even some of *ṣadr*s (see chapter 5 for the description of this office) did not possess adequate knowledge of Twelver Shiᶜism. Thus in the year 1514/920, Amīr Shihāb al-Dīn Lāleh, of the Lāleh-ī Sunni branch of the Kubraviyya in Azarbaijan, was appointed *ṣadr* but was soon removed from office and replaced by Mīr Jamāl al-Dīn Shīrangī Astarābādī, "in whose Shiᶜism," as author of *Takmilat al-Akhbār* tells us revealingly, "there was no doubt."[10]

Shāh Ismāᶜīl invited Shaykh ᶜAlī al-Karakī al-ᶜĀmili (d.1534/940) to his empire to propagate Twelver Shiᶜism. Al-Karakī settled in the Arab Iraq and paid intermittent visits to the court of Ismāᶜīl.[11] He continued to supervise the conversion of Iran to Shiᶜism under Ṭahmāsp.[12] The importation of the Twelver Shiᶜite theologians and jurists, notably from Jabal ᶜĀmil, continued throughout the sixteenth and seventeenth centuries. In addition to the sustained activities of the Shiᶜite theologians, the prolonged task of the conversion of Iran to Twelver Shiᶜism required the persistent adherence of the Safavid state to a vigorous religious policy, which is examined in chapter 4. This religious policy, which was judged politically expedient and pursued for "reasons of the state," constitutes the single most momentous series of "religiously relevant" political acts of the Safavid rulers. It represents the direct impingement of political action upon the religious sphere with the consequence of replacement of Sunnism by Shiᶜism and the transformation of the latter from a sectarian into a national religion.

In chapter 5, we shall move to the domain of social and political organization. In the sixteenth and the most part of the seventeenth century, the structural relationship between the religious and the political institutions in Shiᶜite Iran did not differ appreciably from the "caesaropapist" pattern to be found in the Sunni Ottoman Empire. Until the last decades of the seventeenth century, the religious and judiciary institutions remained under the firm control of a distinct status group of "clerical notables." This group consisted of a landed nobility with strong local roots claiming descent from the Prophet. Its members were incorporated into the Safavid state as administrators with a number of judiciary and quasi-religious functions. In order to establish their exclusive hierocratic authority as religious professionals, the incoming Shiᶜite doctors and the native students they subsequently trained had to contend with the rivalry of this powerful estate of indigenous clerical notables. The struggle for hierocratic domination was prolonged, and the eventual victory of the religious professionals did not come until the end of the seventeenth century.

In chapter 6, we shall examine the transformation of sectarian Shiᶜism into an established orthodoxy and its otherworldly reorientation. Chapter 7 then considers the political implications of the otherworldly soteriology of orthodox Shiᶜism alongside the implications of the inner-worldly soteriology of gnostic Shiᶜism—Shiᶜism as represented mainly by the opponents of the hierocracy, namely, the clerical notables.

Chapter 8 completes the analysis of the Safavid normative order by examining the respective contributions of the Shiᶜite religion and the ethos of patrimonialism. World-rejecting tendencies in the Shiᶜism of the period are analyzed in chapter 9. In contradistinction to the preceding treatment of the interlinkage between the religious and the political spheres, the mode of world rejection in Shiᶜite religiosity can be shown to contribute to the disjunction of these spheres. Chapters 3 and 9, flanking part 2, represent the extreme ends of the spectrum covering the relationship between religion and politics: the former depicts a self-contained political normative order independent of religion, the latter a self-contained religious normative order inducing pious detachment from the political sphere.

CHAPTER FOUR

Safavid Religious Policies and the Establishment of Twelver Shiᶜism in Iran, 1501–1629

> On Friday, the exalted king went to the congregational mosque of Tabriz and ordered its preacher, who was one of the Shiᶜite dignitaries, to mount the pulpit. The king himself proceeded to the front of the pulpit, unsheathed the sword of the Lord of Time, may peace be upon him, and stood there like the shining sun.[1]

Thus, on a Friday in the fall of 1501/907, Ismāᶜīl the Safavid declared Shiᶜism the state religion of his empire in the conquered Aqqūyūnlū capital, Tabriz. Ismāᶜīl's decision to convert Iran to Twelver Shiᶜism was reaffirmed by his successor, Ṭahmāsp. This conversion required the persistent adherence of the Safavid state to a ruthless religious policy carried out on four fronts. The policy consisted in the eradication of millenarian extremism, persecution of popular Sufism, suppression of Sunnism, and, finally, the propagation of Twelver Shiᶜism. The spread of the Shiᶜite doctrine among the population of Iran did not decisively change the religious outlook of the country until after the virtual completion of the first three processes under ᶜAbbās the Great (1587–1629). The conversion of Iran to Shiᶜism—this most important of the religiously relevant political acts of the Safavid rulers—was, for the most part, carried out for "reasons of state" and aimed at stamping out actual or potential centers of power. Only from the last quarter of the seventeenth century onwards did the Shiᶜite hierocracy, born as a result of Safavid religious policy, instigate the state to carry out religious persecutions to purge the Safavid dominions of heterodoxy in the form of "high" Sufism and Sunnism.

4.1 The Suppression of Millenarian Extremism among the Qizilbāsh

Under Ismāᶜīl I (1501–24), the anthropolatric extremism of the Qizilbāsh continued unabated. The missionary activity of the Safavid order of which he was the supreme head (*murshid-e kāmil*: the perfect guide), and which was conducted through a network of his *khalīfa*s (deputies) in Anatolia, remained of crucial importance. It culminated in the serious pro-Safavid rebellion of Bābā Shāh Qulī in Qarāmān against the Ottomans in 1511/917,[2] and eventually provoked the Ottoman Sultan Selim's massive decimation of the Qizilbāsh in Anatolia. Ismāᶜīl continued to use the *khalīfa*s not only to mobilize his worshipful Turkman supporters in Anatolia and Azerbaijan, but also, on occasions, to lead the Qizilbāsh military forces in campaigns in Iran.[3] The prominence of the *khalīfa*s under Ismāᶜīl indicates the thorough permeation of the military pillar of his state with extremist religion in the form of millenarian savior worship.

Nevertheless, once the conquest of Iran was completed, millenarian extremism tended to lose its political utility and became more of a liability than an asset. In any event, the Italian merchant who saw Ismāᶜīl in Tabriz tells us: "But I have heard that Ismael is not pleased with being called a god or a prophet."[4] In fact, Ismāᶜīl put to death several of his disorderly fanatical devotees who came to Iran after Bābā Shāh Qulī's rebellion on charges of highway robbery and murder.[5] But it was above all through the broadening of the social support for his regime—that is, through the incorporation of the Persian notables into the patrimonial bureaucracy of his empire[6]—that Ismāᶜīl paved the way for his successors' suppression of Qizilbāsh extremism.

Despite the continued missionary activity of the *khalīfa*s in Anatolia and the arrival of Turkman adherents to the foot of the new shah's throne,[7] Ṭahmāsp (1524–76), whom they continued to venerate as God,[8] took firm steps to suppress extremism. Later copies of Shāh Ismāᶜīl's *dīvān* omit verses where he proclaims himself to be the Mahdi or his precursor. Shāh Ṭahmāsp ordered the bloody suppression of the presumably extremist Turkman tribe of Sārūlū on account of their "irreligion" (*ilḥād*) (1531–32/938), and put down the heresy of a group of Sufis who proclaimed him the Mahdi (1554–55).[9] Finally, in 1565–66/973, the members of another irreligious (*murtadd*) Turkman clan were put to death or imprisoned in the fortress of Alamūt.[10]

With the adherence of the devout Ṭahmāsp to the Imāmī doctrine and his abandonment of Sufi practices, the religio-ritualistic functions of the order must have devolved increasingly on the *khalīfa*s of the Turkman tribes and especially on their leader, the *khalīfat al-khulafā*ʾ. It is therefore not surprising that, after Ṭahmāsp's death and the succession of his son Ismāᶜīl II, whom the Qizilbāsh were not so wont to invest with divine charisma, the *khalīfat-al-khulafā*ʾ should appear to an Italian diplomat (an admittedly casual observer) as the chief hierophant ("persona principale della fede").[11] The loyalty of the Qizilbāsh to the *khalīfat al-khulafāʾ*, Ḥusayn Qulī Khān, made Ismāʿīl II (1576–77) highly apprehensive.[12] After a series of clashes, Ismāʿīl blinded the *khalīfat al-khulafāʾ*, and massacred a large number of his Sufis in Qazvīn.[13]

During the unstable reign of Sulṭān Muḥammad Khudābandeh (1577–87) and the first years of ʿAbbās the Great (1587–1629), which were marked by internecine Qizilbāsh tribal warfare, appeals were repeatedly made on the shah's behalf to the *ṣūfīgarī* (Sufi probity) of the Turkman (usually coupled with *ikhlās* and *iʿtiqād*) as meaning sincere loyalty and unquestioning obedience to the king as the supreme spiritual leader (*murshid*).[14] But after consolidating his rule, ʿAbbās carried out a series of momentous centralizing reforms which included the introduction of a new slave corps of (largely Georgian) royal *ghulāms*. The composition of the military forces of his empire was thus drastically altered. This enabled ʿAbbās I to "secularize" his military organization by dispensing with the anthropolatic spirit of extremism; the Qizilbāsh military forces were reorganized as *qūrchī*s (pretorians). To assure their loyalty, appeals came to be made to *shāhsevanī* or *shāhī-sevanī* (the quality of those who love the king, with highly secular connotations) instead of the quasi-religious *ṣūfīgarī*.[15]

In 1614–15/1023–24 ʿAbbās ordered the massacre of the Sufis of Qarajadāgh —also known as the "old Sufis of Lāhījān," a designation denoting their priority over other Sufis as the oldest adherents of the Safavid order. They were accused of collaboration with the Ottomans, and of failing to place "acquiescence to the will of the *murshid* before all worldly interests." [16] As for the rest of the hard core of practicing Turkman Sufis, who were distinguished by still wearing the traditional headgear (*tāj*), ʿAbbās had already been ruthlessly exploiting their blind loyalty to the supreme leader, not only in using them as guards and gatekeepers for his palace, but also in giving them even baser types of employment as jailers, executioners, and hangmen.[17] Some of them were even induced to make a profession out of one of the more gruesome elements of their central Asiatic heritage, and formed a small special group of cannibalistic executioners whose function was the "live-eating" (*zindeh-khwārī*) of the disgraced by ʿAbbās's order.[18]

As often happens with traditional relics, and not unlike the shamans and the lamas of the Īl-Khānids after their conversion to Islam, the *khalīfat al-khulafāʾ*, and a number of religiously anomalous ceremonies associated with his office,[19] survived to the very end of the dynasty; and the *khalīfa* is mentioned in the *Tadhkirat al-Mulūk* among the high functionaries of the Safavid court. Nevertheless, the sharp decline in the status and occupational position of the Qizilbāsh and of the Sufis continued. In 1660, Du Mans would find the title of Grand Sophi, attributed to the Safavid monarch by Europeans, truly puzzling, and surmised that the shah would consider it an insult. He points out that the Sufis, still wearing their traditional headgear (*tāj*), are regarded as the riffraff (*bī sar va pā*) and, besides being the royal guards, carry out the most menial functions—such as sweeping—in the royal buildings.[20] Some three decades later, another Christian missionary, Sanson, confirms Du Mans's account.[21] The "society" of the Sufis is now said to "serve for nothing else but Porters, Bailiffs, and Common Executioners of Justice."

The above account of the suppression of extremism and the decline of the Qizilbāsh element in Safavid polity confirms Aubin's conclusion that there was a "parallel development between the elimination of the characteristically Safavid element and the consolidation of Twelver Shiʿism in Iran."[22]

4.2 The Suppression of Sufism

In the words of the author of *Rawḍāt al-Jinān va Jannāt al-Janān* Ismāʿīl I "crushed all the *silsila*s [Sufi orders]; the graves of their ancestors were destroyed, not to mention what befell their successors."[23] He "made despondent and eradicated most of the *silsila*s [orders] of *sayyids* and *shaykh*s."[24] One such was the order of Abū Isḥāq Kāzirūnī in Fars. In 1503/909, only some two years after the conquest of Tabriz, the order was extirpated after the massacre of 4,000 persons and the desecration of the tombs of Sufi shaykhs in that region.[25] Out of political expediency, Ismāʿīl did compromise with some of the Sufi shaykhs—notably those of the Niʿmatullāhī order, but there can be no doubt about his relentless hostility toward the rival Sufi orders, a policy continued by his successors.

While the Safavid order became highly militarized in the last quarter of the fifteenth century, other important orders continued their religious activities in the mystical tradition. Of these, the Naqshbandī, the Khalvatī, the Niʿmatullāhī orders, and the two branches of the Kubraviyya, the Dhahabiyya and the Nūrbakhshiyya, are the most important. Sooner or later each of these was to undergo a sharp decline; and by the end of the Safavid era, they had all disappeared from the Iranian scene, except for the Kubravī branches—Nūrbakhshiyya and Dhahabiyya—which, though greatly enfeebled, persisted. What follows is a brief but, I hope, fairly comprehensive account of this decline.

4.2.1 The Naqshbandiyya

Not surprisingly, the Naqshbandīs, who trace their spiritual descent through Abū Bakr (the first of the rightly guided caliphs, ritualistically cursed by Ismāʿīl's followers), were the first order to be ferociously suppressed. The Naqshbandīs were particularly strong in eastern Iran and Herat,[26] but also important in Azerbaijan.[27] There is also evidence of Naqshbandī presence in Isfahan and Qazvin. After Ismāʿīl's conquest of Herat in 1510, the tombs of the famous Naqshbandī mystics, Kāshgharī and Jāmī, were desecrated. The Naqshbandī shaykh, Mawlānā ʿAlī Kurdī (d. 1519), who had been particularly active in Qazvin, was also killed.[28] Though we hear of one individual, the *sayyid* Amīr ʿAbd al-Ghaffār (d.

1521/927), who was favored by Ismāʿīl despite his Naqshbandī affiliation,[29] there can be little doubt that the Naqshbandiyya were effectively extirpated in western and central Iran. The vehemence of the hostility toward the Naqshbandīs is reflected in a polemical exchange that took place in late sixteenth century. The Sunni polemicist accuses the Shiʿite jurists not only of general hostility to Sufism, but also, more specifically, of considering the shedding of the blood of a Naqshbandī incumbent.[30] This accusation is affirmed and defended by his Shiʿite opponent.[31] The consulted sources of Ṭahmāsp's (1524–16) reign contain no mention of the Naqshbandīs.

4.2.2 The Khalvatiyya

Like the Naqshbandiyya, the Khalvatīs were Sunni, and like the former, they were important in eastern Iran[32] and in Azerbaijan. Dede ʿUmar Rawshanī (d. 1486/891 or 892) and his brother Mawlānā ʿAlāʾ al-Dīn, shaykhs of the Khalvatī order, were highly respected by the Aqqūyūnlū rulers under whose protection their order flourished. Dede ʿUmar's *zāwiya* (convent) in Tabriz was frequently visited by Sulṭān Yaʿqūb (d. 1490). Already by the last decades of the fifteenth century ʿAlāʾ al-Dīn had left Tabriz for Istanbul where the Sufi sultan Bāyazīd (1481–1512) was to shower favors upon the Khalvatīs. Dede ʿUmar's disciple, Ibrāhīm Gulshanī (d. 1534/940), succeeded him after his death. In the Safavids' eyes, Gulshanī was particularly suspect because of his close ties with the Aqqūyūnlū dynasty, and left Tabriz after Ismāʿīl's conquest and "declaration of Shiʿism," proceeding first to Diyārbakr, then to Jerusalem, and finally to Cairo, where he built his famous convent around 1520/926. The Khalvatī order flourished in Egypt and the Ottoman capital. It appears to have become extinct in Safavid Iran after its adherents left for these much more congenial Ottoman domains.[33]

Before proceeding to consider the orders that survived longer, mention should be made of the Ismāʿīlīs, who, by the time of Ismāʿīl I appear in Sufi garb.

4.2.3 The Ismāʿīliyya

Shāh Ṭāhir (d. 1545 or 49/952 or 56) was the Imam of the Muḥammad–Shāhī branch of Ismāʿīlism. According to the historian Firishteh, as the Khwandiyya *sayyids*, the Imams of the Ismāʿīlīs were respected Persian notables engaged in the spiritual guidance of the populace as Sufi shaykhs in the region close to Qazvin. Shāh Ṭāhir was forced to give up his position as a Sufi shaykh, and after remaining in Ismāʿīl's court for some time, was appointed to a professorship in Kashan in 1510–11/916, where many of his followers appeared to have followed him. This made Ismāʿīl apprehensive, and he issued an order for the execution of Shāh Ṭāhir. Informed about this menace ahead of time by another Persian notable, Shāh Ḥusayn Iṣfahānī, who was Ismāʿīl's chancellor at the time,

Shāh Ṭāhir fled to India in 1520/926, and settled in the Deccan.[34] After Ismāʿīl's death, he sent his son Ḥaydar to the court of Shāh Ṭahmāsp.[35] He seems to have intended to return to Iran himself.[36] Evidently, however, his son Ḥaydar received no encouragement from Ṭahmāsp either personally or regarding his father's intention. He returned to India after Shāh Ṭāhir's death to succeed him as the shaykh of his Sufi order (*ṣāḥib-e sajjādeh*) in India,[37] and as the Imam of the Muḥammad-Shāhī Nizārīs.

Another branch of Nizārī Ismāʿīlism, the Qāsim-Shāhī branch, whose Imams resided in Anjūdān near Kashan, survived somewhat longer, that is, to the end of Ṭahmāsp's reign. In 1574–75/982, Ṭahmāsp massacred the Ismāʿīlī community in Anjūdān and imprisoned their thirty-sixth Imam, Murād,[38] who was subsequently executed under Shāh ʿAbbās.

4.2.4 The Dhahabiyya

The order branched off from the Kubraviyya when Shaykh Ḥājī Muḥammad Khabūshānī refused to follow Sayyid Muḥammad Nūrbakhsh, and founded his own order. The *Rawḍat al-Jinān* mentions twenty-eight of his *khalīfa*s, and asserts that some of them or their successors were still active at the time of the writing (ca. 1582/990), but it is clear from his tone that their activities—which are not mentioned in detail—could not have been all that lively. Perhaps the most important of Khabūshānī's *khalīfa*s was the author's great-grandfather, Amīr Sayyid Aḥmad Lāleh (d. 1507/912), who settled in Azerbaijan where he acquired considerable following. The Lālehīs continued to profess Sunnism. Shāh Ismāʿīl appears to have spared this order, and even appointed Sayyid Aḥmad's son, Amīr Shihāb al-Dīn Lāleh (d. 1540/947) to the office of the *ṣadr* for a very brief period. Though the author does not supply us with any specific details, the sharp decline in the activities of Dhahabī Sufis under the leadership of the Lāleh family can be inferred from the fact that no list of *khalīfa*s and disciples are mentioned for Amīr Shihāb al-Dīn and the subsequent generation. Furthermore, Shihāb al-Dīn's brother, Amīr Khalīlullāh is reported to have died in Isfahan in 1548–49/955, indicating (forcible) displacement from the seat of the Lālehī order. We may also note that the author himself was writing the book after many years of exile.[39]

Nevertheless, some of Khabūshānī's thirty-seven *khalīfa*s must have remained active, as Karbalāʾī asserts, and the Dhahabī order subsisted. One of their shaykhs, Shaykh Muḥammad ʿAlī Muʾadhdhin Khurāsānī, even acquired some prominence amongst the literati of the reign of ʿAbbās the Great.[40] Under ʿAbbās II, Muḥammad Taqī Majlisī the Elder (d. 1660/1070) subscribed to the Dhahabī tradition. We also hear of the renowned Shaykh Ganj-ʿAlī Tabrīzī, a disciple of Ḥājj Mīr Muḥammad Lāleh of Tabriz.[41] The Dhahabī order has survived in Fars to this day, but despite its (temporary) vitality under the eminent shaykh Quṭb al-Dīn Sayyid Muḥammad Shīrāzī (d. 1757 or 1771/1170 or 1185),[42] its decline as an organized supralocal order was not reversed. Already in 1832 the author of *Bustān al-Siyāha* would deplore the absence of an illuminated spiritual master among them for generations.[43]

4.2.5 The Nūrbakhshiyya

In 1500, the Shiʿite order founded by Nūrbakhsh was continuing to flourish under his son, Shāh Qāsim (d. 1511/917), the Fayḍ-bakhsh. Ismāʿīl showed no hostility to the aged and highly respected shaykh, and even assigned to him a prosperous estate near Rey.[44] However, his son, Shāh Bahāʾ al-Dīn, joined Ismāʿīl's entourage after the death of his Timurid patron, Sulṭān Ḥusayn Bayqarāʾ, but within two or three years "was, according to the dictates of Fate, interrogated, and died."[45] The eminent Nūrbakhshī shaykh of Shiraz, Shams al-Dīn Muḥammad Lāhījī (d. 1515/921), appointed *khalīfa* by the founder himself, and the author of a very influential commentary on *Gulshan-e Rāz*, appears to have narrowly escaped liquidation by a subtly sycophantic reply to Ismāʿīl's peevish questions about his reason for wearing black clothes.[46] Another Nūrbakhshī shaykh in Shūshtar also tenuously managed to survive Ismāʿīl's conquest of southwestern Iran.[47]

The death of Ismāʿīl and the ascension of his ten-year-old son Ṭahmāsp in 1524 temporarily halted the decline of the Nūrbakhshiyya. Amīr Qavām al-Dīn, the great-great-grandson of Nūrbakhsh, consolidated his power in the region near Rey.[48] But in 1537/944 he was summoned to Ṭahmāsp's camp near Tehran to answer for his "astonishing pride,"[49] for overstepping the boundaries of dervishhood, and for behaving "in the manner of exalted kings."[50] In the presence of Ṭahmāsp, a certain Qāḍī Muḥammad asked him whether he was a king or a dervish. Qavām al-Dīn replied he was a dervish. The Qāḍī then asked him: "What is the reason for fortress building, and for gathering arms and armors?"[51] Failing to produce a satisfactory answer, Qavām al-Dīn was imprisoned, his beard having been burnt on the spot, and put to death.[52] The fate of the subsequent generations of Nūrbakhshī *sayyids* is obscure. Sometime during Ṭahmāsp's reign an eminent Nūrbakhshī *sayyid*, Shāh ʿAbd al-ʿAlī moved from Bam to Yazd to become a qadi.[53] Much later, in the 1650s and 1660s, members of his family reappear as local notables in the city of Yazd.[54] With regard to Shūshtar and southwestern Iran, the emigration of Qāḍī Nūrullāh Shūshtarī (d. 1610/1019) to India can be taken as indicative of the decline of the order's activities.[55]

According to the spiritual genealogy of the order given in *Ṭarāʾiq al-Ḥaqāʾiq*, the leadership of the Nūrbakhshī mystical tradition passed out of the founder's family (even Bahāʾ al-Dīn and Qavām al-Dīn's names are struck from the list of spiritual leaders).[56] It would therefore be safe to take the elimination of Qavām al-Dīn by Ṭahmāsp in 1530–31/937 to mean the liquidation of the Nūrbakhshiyya as an organized supralocal order. The mystical tradition, however, survived. Two highly interesting names appear in the chain of the Nūrbakhshī spiritual geneaology: Bahā᾽ al-Dīn ᶜĀmilī (d. 1621/1030)[57] and Mullā Muḥsin Fayḍ (d. 1680/1091). Bahā᾽ al-Dīn ᶜĀmilī was the most eminent of the *ᶜulamā᾽* of the reign of ᶜAbbās I; Mullā Muḥsin Fayḍ, of the reign of ᶜAbbās II.[58] Both were greatly respected and highly favored by these monarch respectively. Here, as is often the case with the chains of Sufi shaykhs forming *silsila*s, spiritual filiation does not denote any organizational continuity of an order as congregation. In fact, there is no evidence of the emergence of a reorganized Nūrbakhshī order in the eclectic "high" Sufism of the mid-seventeenth century.[59] But the Nūrbakhshī mystical tradition was kept alive, and we hear of the writings of an important exponent of this tradition, ᶜAbd al-Raḥīm Damāvandī, ca. 1747/1160, some two decades after the overthrow of the Safavid dynasty.[60]

4.2.6 The Niᶜmatullāhiyya

Long before the advent of Ismāᶜīl I, India had proved a congenial region for the expansion of the Niᶜmatullāhī order, founded by Shāh Niᶜmatullāh Valī (d. 1431/834), whose successors as the shaykhs of the order had moved to the Deccan in the mid-fifteenth/ninth century. The order remained very active in Kirman, Bam, Yazd, Shiraz, and part of Khurasan throughout the fifteenth century; some of Niᶜmatullāh's numerous great-grandsons settled in Yazd, which became the order's Iranian center.[61] After the advent of Ismāᶜīl, the order declared itself to be Shiᶜite,[62] and made a lasting alliance with the Safavids. A descendant of Shāh Niᶜmatullāh, Mīr Niẓām al-Dīn ᶜAbd al-Bāqī (d. 1514/920), who was the *murshid* of the order in Yazd, was appointed *ṣadr* by Ismāᶜīl I in 1511–12/917,[63] and subsequently became his plenipotentiary deputy with the title *vakīl-e nafs-e humāyūn*.[64] ᶜAbd al-Bāqī's family tied themselves to the Safavids through a number of marriages and rose to great prominence among the Safavid elite.[65] Of these, the most notable is Mīrmīrān Yazdī (d. 1591/999), who emerges as one of the most influential and wealthiest of the provincial notables in the second half of the sixteenth century.[66]

The order does not seem to have fared so well in the seventeenth century. During the first troubled years of ᶜAbbās I's reign, the aged Mīrmīrān suffered considerable indignity at the hands of one of ᶜAbbās's generals, Yaᶜqūb Khān, with whom, however Mīrmīran's son, Shāh Khalīlullāh, allied himself temporarily. But Yaᶜqūb Khān rebelled in Fars, and was suppressed by ᶜAbbās, who then visited Yazd and was entertained lavishly by Shāh Khalīlullāh in 1591/999.[67] This visit marks the height of Niᶜmatullāhī prominence in Safavid national politics. Shāh Khalīlullāh entertained Shāh ᶜAbbās in his capacity as the political head of the Niᶜmatullāhī family, while his brother, Shāh Niᶜmatullāh IV, received him as the spiritual representative of the head of the order.[68] After this year, there seems to be only one other reference to the activities of the Niᶜmatullāhiyya as a Sufi order. Shāh Khalīlullāh moved to Isfahan and remained the most eminent *sayyid* of the realm. But ᶜAbbās I set out to curb his power as soon as he felt secure enough, and in 1593/1001, Khalīlullāh is reported to have become resentful when ᶜAbbās showered favors upon the rival *sayyid*, Mīrzā Muḥammad Amīn of Isfahan. Though ᶜAbbās is said to have "pulled him out of sulking" ("ū rā az kūft bīrūn āvard") on one public occasion,[69] Khalīlullāh received no further appointments, and must be presumed to have continued to sulk to his death in 1607–8/1016. His sons sank into obscurity. Khalīlullāh's younger brother, Shāh Suleymān Mīrzā (d. after 1640–41/1050), who also lived in Isfahan (very probably forcibly), appears to have controlled some of the religious endowments traditionally entrusted to his family and is the last important spiritual leader of the order in Iran.[70] While his sons were allowed to return to Yazd (presumably when they no longer represented a threat) by Shāh Ṣafī (1629–42), there are no indications of their Sufi activity. The offices of *kalāntar* (alderman) and of *naqīb* (leader of the *sayyids*) of Yazd remained in the hands of Shāh Suleymān Mīrzā's descendants, at least down to 1671–72/1082, but in contrast to references to Shāh Suleymān Mīrzā's spiritual guidance (*irshād*) and gnosis (*ᶜirfān*), the author of *Jāmiᶜ Mufīdī* repeatedly mentions his descendants' zeal in the consolidation of the foundations of sacred law (*taqviyat-e arkān-e sharīᶜat, tashyid-e qavāᶜid-e sharᶜ*), and their conscientiousness in looking after the interests of the *sayyids* and the *ᶜulamā*ʾ.[71]

The Persian Niᶜmatullāhīs representing the mystical tradition are mentioned in genteel intellectual occupations in India, whither they migrated. One Mīr Hāshim Shāh, son of the calligrapher Mīr ᶜAbdullāh (1662–23/1073–1738/1151) was to become the founder of the Hāshim-Shāhī branch of the order in Delhi.[72] The Niᶜmatullāhī Sufis did not return to Iran until the very end of the eighteenth century.

In the sixteenth century, the Niᶜmatullāhīs were very probably the most highly organized of the Sufi orders, a fact that goes a long way toward explaining why their alliance with the Safavids lasted for over a century. Their *tekke* in Tabriz (in northwestern Iran, far from their center) is one of the two or three supralocal ones (as distinct from the local convents, usually associated with families of *sayyids* with landholdings in the area) mentioned by Karbalāʾī.[73] They had *tekkes* in many other cities too. Circumstantial evidence suggests that ᶜAbbās I turned these *tekkes* increasingly over to the youth and recreational organizations of the city quarters where they were located. Fights between the city quarters were of course an old phenomenon. In Tabriz, where both the Niᶜmatullāhīs and the Ḥaydarīs had *tekkes*, such conflicts appear to have clustered around these respective *tekkes* in the latter part of Ṭahmāsp's reign.[74] There probably was some tendency for the pattern to repeat itself in other cities. Be that as it may, ᶜAbbās is known to have encouraged and manipulated faction fights, and specifically, as early as 1594–95/1003, in Qazvin, he is reported to have watched a fight between the Niᶜmatīs (Niᶜmatullāhīs) and the Ḥaydarīs.[75] With the eclipse of the Niᶜmatullāhiyya as a Sufi order, their *tekkes* were increasingly taken over as the headquarters of neighborhood organizations, and were used especially for the Muḥarram ceremonies of flagellant processions. Interfactional conflicts occurring during the Muḥarram processions, starting from and returning to these *tekkes*, represented an extremely serious problem for the maintenance of law and order in cities in the late Safavid period, one that remained unsolved until the fall of the dynasty and beyond.[76]

Thus, once the cultural activity of the Niᶜmatullāhiyya—the perpetuation of its mystical tradition—had definitely shifted to India as a result of ᶜAbbās's religious policy, its organizational base was taken over by the city-quarter communes and harnessed to a particularly destructive form of communal sport—faction fights—fused with the Muḥarram ceremonies mourning the martyrdom of the third Shiᶜite Imam, Ḥusayn.

4.2.7 Qalandariyya/Malāmatiyya and the Sufism of the Ascetic Virtuosi

The ecstatic and antinomian Sufism of the hirsute Qalandars (roaming dervishes) and the quasi-eremitical Sufism of the ascetic virtuosi are polar opposites from the viewpoint of religious discipline. But what they have in common is the strong capacity for survival under persecution because of the absence of congregational organization and the emphasis on the individualistic mode of activity.

In addition to individual dervishes, Karbalāʾī also mentions the *tekke* of the Ḥaydarīs belonging to the Qalandariyya in Tabriz.[77] Throughout the Safavid era, sporadic references to Qalandars attest to their presence on the religious scene. On a number of occasions, especially in periods of political instability and collapse of central power, we meet them as leaders of local uprisings.[78]

Under the events of the year 1616/1025, Iskandar Munshī cites a *rubāᶜī* from Bābā Sulṭān Qalandar-e Qumī, who is said to be one of the "*tekke*-holding dervishes."[79] In the accounts given of the city of Isfahan of the mid-seventeenth century by European travelers, shaggy, ill-clad dervishes hanging out in the streets and around coffee houses appear as an element of the social scene. Olearius (1637) mentions a "certain type of ecclesiastics who are called *abdāl* for whom the king has built a *tekke*".[80] Du Mans (1660) describes the dervishes, the *duᶜā-gūs* (those who pray for the alms-giver's health and salvation) and the Qalandars together;[81] and Sanson (1695) talks of the "Derviches or Abdals," who preach austerely on street corners and in coffee houses, tell stories, and are not highly regarded.[82]

We have so far concentrated on organized popular Sufism, and have omitted to consider the ascetic Sufi virtuosi. What emerges clearly from the *Rawḍāt al-Jinān*, a book of unusual documentary interest, is the great importance of virtuoso Sufism, even in the pre-Safavid period. Roughly speaking, as many Sufi virtuosi and intellectuals as members of identified orders, with a definite rank or relationship within them, are mentioned. More importantly, even in cases where order affiliations are mentioned, the center of attention is usually the Sufi virtuosi—i.e., individual mystics, their spiritual attainment, their absorption of divinity (*jadhaba*), intuition of revelations (*mukāshafa*), and ascetic, contemplative, or visionary qualities. Their affiliations to orders and the frequenting of specific masters appear only of secondary importance. The Sufi virtuosi could be accommodated by a variety of social niches, ranging from supranational orders to local orders dominated by land-owning notables (*sayyid*s) a single *khāniqāh* (convent), crafts, and finally voluntary support by admiring laymen.[83]

Therefore, the demise of the Sufi orders did not put an end to virtuoso Sufism. Among the persons mentioned in the *Rawḍāt al-Jinān*, virtually all of the fifteen or twenty easily identifiable sixteenth-century Sufis who died during Ṭahmāsp's reign or later (after 1524/930) are either dispossessed *sayyid*s of former local orders, or fall into the virtuoso and literati categories.[84] Ascetic virtuosi and mystic literati figure prominently among the Sufi masters of the period. Shaykh Khiḍr, for instance, was an eminent Sufi to whom ᶜAbbās I wrote a respectful letter. The famous philosopher Mīr Findiriskī (d. 1640–41/1050) was another Sufi who traveled to India to study asceticism and became a recluse for seven years.[85] Among the mystic literati, we may name the royal scribe Āqā Abu'l-Fatḥ Iṣfahānī (d. 1611–12/1020) and his grandson Khwāja ᶜAlī Akbar.[86] In the latter part of the seventeenth century, too, the ascetic virtuosi continued to remain among the important representatives of Sufism. *Jāmiᶜ Mufīdī* devotes a chapter to brief biographies of some six prominent contemporary ascetic and hermitic Sufis of the city of Yazd.[87] The chapter of *Qiṣaṣ al-Khāqānī* on the eminent men of ᶜAbbās II's reign includes a section on the ascetic Sufis that contains bibliographical entries on nineteen nationally renowned ascetic virtuosi.[88]

As has already been pointed out, the bearers of the ascetic and contemplative Sufism share one characteristic with the Qalandars: the absence of any congregational organization. In fact, they are much more radically individualistic, and their eremitical individualism and uncomprising rejection of the world makes them quite tolerable to political powers who perceive no threat from their direction. Despite the demise of the orders, the Sufi virtuosi survived, acting as the transmitters of the mystical tradition, which, after nearly a century and a half of latency, bloomed in the mid-seventeenth century, briefly but with dazzling brilliance and in a highly intellectual form.

4.3 The Persecution of Sunnism under Ṭahmāsp and ᶜAbbās I

It is hardly surprising that Sunnism was eradicated only gradually. Many Persian clerical notables who were not willing to give up their formal profession of Sunnism under the early Safavids migrated from Iran.[89] Under Shah Ṭahmāsp, Sunnism persisted in no less central a city than Qazvin, where those members of the Sunni community who had never cursed the rightly guided caliphs were awarded remuneration from the royal treasury by Ṭahmāsp's pro-Sunni son Ismāʿīl II.[90] In a *qaṣīda* in criticism of the people of Qazvin, the poet Mawlānā Ḥayratī claims to have "found Sunnism among the dignified and the notables" (of Qazvin).[91] Dickson adduces enough evidence to suggest that Qāḍī Jahān, one of the most eminent of Qazvin's notables, who held the grand vizierate under Ṭahmāsp twice (1524–26 and 1535–50) was a crypto-Sunni.[92] Thus there is strong evidence for the persistence of crypto-Sunnism among the Persian clerical notables throughout the sixteenth century. This partial retention of the Sunni outlook interestingly manifests itself in the case of those who migrated to India. It was said of Emperor Akbar's tutor, ʿAbd al-Laṭīf, that "while in Persia, from which country he was a refugee, he was accused of being a Sunni, and in India of being a Shiʿa."[93] There are also indications of political opposition of the Persian notables to Safavid rule. It is also clear that the Safavid rulers on their part reacted ruthlessly whenever they suspected such opposition.[94] The historian Mīr Yaḥyā (author of *Lubb al-Tawārīkh*), who belonged to the notable family of the Sayfī *sayyid*s of Qazvin, was executed by the order of Ṭahmāsp in 1555/962 after being denounced as a Sunni and imprisoned two years earlier.[95] Another Sunni notable, Mīr ʿImād of Qazvin, the calligrapher, was killed on the way to a public bath at the instigation of ʿAbbās I.[96]

Ismāʿīl II attempted to reestablish Sunnism during his brief reign (1576–77)[97] but was forced to give up the project in the face of Qizilbāsh opposition.[98] The failure of Ismāʿīl II's religious policy of course attests to the preponderant strength of Shiʿism in Iran by the third quarter of the sixteenth century. But what is even more instructive, apart from the very fact that such a policy could be undertaken with some expectation of success, is the assessment of this policy by the contemporary of near-contemporary historians. The aim of the policy is stated as the winning-over of the Sunni elements by making possible their peaceful coexistence and cooperation with the Shiʿites. Though they may have considered its execution imprudent or miscalculated, neither the Sunni historian Bidlīsī[99] nor the Shiʿite historians Qāḍī Aḥmad Qumī and Iskandar Munshī considered this policy intrinsically unrealistic.[100] Furthermore, it is noteworthy that Ismāʿīl II could enlist the active support of some of the Persian notables—for instance Mīr Makhdūm Shīrāzī and Shāh ʿInāyatullāh Iṣfāhānī, formerly the *qāḍī muʿaskar* (army judge), whom he appointed *ṣadr*—and presumably rely on the tacit sympathy of many more.[101]

The reign of ʿAbbās the Great, decisive for the establishment of Shiʿism, also witnessed instances of persecution of the Sunnis. At the beginning of his reign, Sunnism was still fairly strong in eastern Iran. Thus, after the Uzbek conquest of Herat in 1588, "many *tāzīks*—Persians, non-Turks—despite the congruence of their religion [with that of the Sunni Uzbeks] were also killed with the Qizilbāsh dignitaries."[102] ʿAbbās's astrologer and historian reports the violent persecution of the Sunnis of Surkheh in northwestern Iran in 1599. The confirmation of a *farmān* by ʿAbbās I, by his successor Shāh Ṣafī in 1630/1039 shows that the persecution of 1599 resulted in the spread of Shiʿism in the area surrounding Surkheh (Simnān) though not so much in Surkheh itself.[103] In 1608/1017, ʿAbbās executed the alderman (*kadkhudā*) of Hamadan (in western Iran), who was also the leader (*raʾīs*) of the Sunni community, for ill-treating the Shiʿites of that town.[104]

ʿAbbās I made a point of excluding the Sunnis from occasional tax exemptions he would grant his other subjects. This is shown by ʿAbbās's *Farmān*s preserved in the congregational mosques of Simnān, Damāvand (dated 1615/1024), and Ardistān.[105]

CHAPTER FIVE

The "Clerical Notables" and the Final Emergence of a Shiᶜite Hierocracy in Iran

A new finding of great importance emerges from the research presented here: in the Safavid period the term *ᶜulamāʾ*, together with the more specific religious titles and designations, refers to two distinct social groups: an "estate" of clerical notables, who were Sunnis prior to the conquest of Iran by Ismāᶜīl I but formally professed Shiᶜism and entered the service of the Safavids as judges and clerical administrators, and a group of religious professionals consisting of the Shiᶜite doctors. The two groups were very distinct during the first half of the sixteenth century because of their different geographical backgrounds and social ties. The fusion of these two groups reached its highest point in the first decades of the seventeenth century. Thereafter, the two groups became increasingly differentiated. The Safavid era begins with the hegemony of a homogeneous mandarin-like clerical estate, with a fairly broad cultural outlook, engaged in a number of judiciary, quasi-political, and quasi-religious functions, and ends with the uneasy coexistence of this estate with a markedly different: a group of religious professionals, with a narrowly dogmatic and juristic outlook, forming the nascent Shiᶜite hierocracy. With the increasing predominance of this latter professional group, the religious institution in Shiᶜite Iran begins its evolution from a position of embeddedness in political organization—that is, the state—toward differentiation and eventual autonomy.

In an important article, Aubin has traced the incorporation of a crucial status group, which may be referred to as an "estate" of the clerical notables, into the Safavid state under Ismāᶜīl I.[1] The local power of the Persian clerical notable families rested on their large landholding (often accompanied by the administration or supervision of endowments and charitable and religious activities associated with local shrines), and, very often, on their charisma of lineage as well-established *sayyid*s or descendants of the Prophet. This status group formed the recruitment basis of pre-Safavid administration, especially religious and judiciary institutions: the offices of the *ṣadr* (in charge of the administration of religious endowments and the distribution of their revenue) and the qadiships. As Aubin demonstrates, the Persian clerical notables were speedily incorporated into Ismāᶜīl's Turkman empire of conquest in the course of its consolidation. The obituary notices of the Safavid chronicles confirm not only the continued social eminence of the *sayyid*s and other established clerical families under Ṭahmāsp and ᶜAbbās I and throughout the seventeenth century, but also their continued dominance over the educational, judiciary, and the religious institutions of the Safavid state.[2]

What is of interest here is the characteristics of the Persian notables as a *clerical* estate, their relationship to the intellectual, religious, and legal institutions, and the reception they granted to the immigrant Shiᶜite theologians from the Arab lands and their students.

5.1 The Institutional Bases and Culture of the "Clerical Notables"

The Safavids inherited from the Timurids and the Aqqūyūnlū the typical Islamic cluster of intellectual institutions consisting of the qadiships, the mosques, the *madrasa*s (colleges), and the religious endowments (*awqāf*). The state controlled these institutions through the office of the *ṣadr*, an office with no exact equivalent in the Ottoman or ᶜAbbasid polities. The Timurid decrees recorded in the *Sharaf-nāmeh* of Morvārīd (d. 1516/922) show two important facts about the office of the *ṣadr*. As regards the social position of its occupants, we can note that the office tended to remain within the same families of notables, a fact indicating a strong hereditary tendency in the appropriation of the office.[3] With regard to the extensive jurisdiction of the office, its twofold functions can be seen to consist in (1) the supervision and administration of the religious endowments and distribution of their revenue to the students and clerics and to charitable undertakings; and (2) the supervision of the administration of the sacred law as the chief judiciary authority of the state.[4]

Because of its financial control over most religious endowments and many religious activities, the office of the *ṣadr* was the most important "religious" office of the realm. In the militarized conquest-oriented state of Ismāᶜīl I, the *ṣadr*, as a rule, simultaneously held the rank of an *amīr* (general).[5] Ismāᶜīl's defeat by the Ottomans at the battle of Chaldirān in 1514/920 marked the end of his military expansionism. Shortly after Chaldirān, with the appointment of Mīr Jamāl al-Dīn Shīrangī, who remained in office until his death in 1525/931, the office of the *ṣadr* became clearly differentiated from Safavid military organization, and exclusively concerned with (financial) religious and judiciary affairs.[6] The Safavid *ṣadr*s thus assumed the functions of the Timurid *ṣadr*s as the foremost clerical administrator of the realm,[7] with certain judiciary responsibilities which became more extensive in the seventeenth century.[8] As we shall see presently, the hereditary tendency in the appropriation of the office also set in at the beginning of the seventeenth century, and soon became very pronounced.

Under the Safavids, the administration of the religious endowments became centralized, and conducted under the supervision of one, or on occasion, two *ṣadr*s, who appointed deputies, with or without the title of *nāʾib al-ṣadāra*, to the regions. It is not clear from the sources whether the *ṣadr* controlled the appointment of the local qadis in the sixteenth century, but in the seventeenth century their centralized control over the religious institutions included the prerogative of appointment of qadis.

However, the centralized control of the *ṣadr* did not extend over the most richly endowed shrines—notably those in Mashhad and Ardabīl—whose administrators (sing. *mutavallī*) were appointed directly by the shah. The administratorship (*tawliyat*) of the independent endowments of these shrines was firmly retained by the clerical notables, who were also often entrusted with other purely administrative functions.[9]

The primacy of this administrative (over the religious) aspect of the office of *ṣadr* is shown by the fact that both its geographical division under Ṭahmāsp and earlier, and much more clearly, its division into *ṣadr-e khāṣṣeh* (*ṣadr* of the royal domains) and the *ṣadr-e mamālik* (*ṣadr* of the [fiscally autonomous] provinces) in the seventeenth century,[10] followed a strictly administrative logic. Furthermore, it is instructive that Ḥazīn's detailed picture of the religious and intellectual circles in the early decades of the eighteenth century makes no references to the *ṣadr*.[11] It is significant that ʿAbbās II (1642–66) appointed his *ṣadr*, Mīrzā Mahdī, to grand vizierate, presaging the post-Safavid transformation of *ṣadārat*. Under the Qājārs (1785–1925), the term *ṣadr* lost all religious connotations, and as *Ṣadr-e Aʿẓam* (Grand Ṣadr) came to designate the highest *administrative* office of the state: that of the prime minister. But neither in the sixteenth century nor at any other time did the *ṣadr* act as the authoritative custodian of the Shiʿite doctrine.

The *shaykh al-Islām* of a city was its chief religious dignitary, and the qadi its religious judge. They were appointed by the state. The qadis, and certainly the *shaykh al-Islām*s, were scholars, and were likely to have students and hold academic classes in their residence or elsewhere. In addition, there were the *madrasa*s under the direction of their respective professors (sing. *mudarris*). Chardin puts the number of the *madrasa*s of Isfahan in the 1660s at fifty-seven. Each of these had dormitories and maintained a number of students indefinitely on the income drawn from its endowments, and subventions from the *ṣadr*.[12] Finally, there were the mosques with appointed prayer leaders (sing. *pīsh-namāz*). We know that in the seventeenth century an administrator (*mutavallī*) with distinctly secular/financial functions was appointed for each endowed mosque, in addition to the *pīsh-namāz* as the director of its religious activities.[13] A qadi was usually also a professor, and it was possible for a qadi to hold the office of *pīsh-namāz* simultaneously.[14]

Given the royal appointment of the *shaykh al-Islāms* and the important qadis and the underlying centralized financial control of the *ṣadr*, this complex of financial, legal, educational, and religious institutions had the potential of being unified into a "religious institution" incorporated into the Safavid state, as were its counterparts in the Ottoman Empire.[15] But it was not. Why?

The answer must be sought, at least in part, in the resistance of the Persian "clerical estate" to the reception of the incoming Arab doctors and their students, who enjoyed the patronage of the Safavid shahs in exchange for the propagation of Shiᶜism. As we shall see presently in detail, the first great immigrant Shiᶜite theologian, Shaykh al-Karakī (d. 1534/940), failed to capture the permanent control of the complex of religious-legal-intellectual institutions for the Shiᶜite hierocracy. A Shiᶜite doctor trained by him did hold the office of the *ṣadr* for twenty years but exclusive control of the office reverted to the clerical notables. The holders of the office of the *ṣadr*, over the subsequent 150 years, were drawn without exception from the clerical estate.

The office(s) of the *ṣadr* remained within the hands of a small number of notable families, with marked hereditary tendencies, even before the reign of Shāh Ṣafī (1629–42). From then onwards—that is, during the last century of Safavid rule—*ṣadārat* became confined, with the possible exception of a single *ṣadr*, to three eminent families who were closely related to the Safavids.[16] Meanwhile, the tenure of the office became very long, usually for life. Shāh Sulṭān-Ḥusayn (1694–1722) had a single *ṣadr* who was his maternal uncle (see table 5.1).[17]

Turning now to the other important offices, we note an important trend that adversely affected the institutional domination of the clerical estate. It consisted of a marked decline in the prominence of the qadis in the polity, especially with the establishment of a powerful centralized government by ᶜAbbās the Great. This decline is reflected in table 5.2.

The lowered status honor of the qadis indicated by the low figure for the reign of ᶜAbbās is paralleled by a drastic decline in the importance of the office of *qāḍī muᶜaskar*—the army judge (which, however, continued to exist until the end of the Safavid era). The decline in the importance of the qadis was not reversed in the seventeenth century.

To complete our picture with regard to the seventeenth century, we must add another important category of the clerical estate: the *sayyids*, who, either because of the lack of vacant post or for other reasons, did not engage in any administrative functions, but whose (undefined) functions were religious. Though they must have possessed some religious learning, this learning was secondary to the basis of their status honor, which rested primarily on their *charisma of lineage* as the descendants of the Prophet and the Imams. According to Du Mans,

TABLE 5.1 Composition of the *Ṣadrs* under the Important Safavid Monarchs[a]

	Total	Immigrant *ṣadrs* or their descendants	Clerical notables	of whom: Sufis	of whom: Jurists	of whom: Adm. Clerics	Other	Fathers, sons, or relatives of other *ṣadrs*
Ismāʿīl I (1501–24)	6	—	5	2	—	3	1	—
Ṭahmāsp (1524–76)	11	1	10	1	2	7	—	5[b]
ʿAbbās I (1587–1629)	8	—	8	—	2	6	—	4[c]
Ṣafī (1629–42) and ʿAbbās II (1647–66)	2	—	2	—	—	2	—	2[d]
Suleymān (1666–94)	3	—	3	—	—	3	—	2[e]
Sulṭān-Ḥusayn (1694–1722)	1	—	1	—	—	1	—	1[f]

a. Based on T. Akh., Ross Anon., Kh. T., Ah. T., T. A. Ab., and V. S. A., additional information regarding the intellectual outlook drawn from R. Ad.

b. Of these, three were the members of the family of Naqīb Iṣfahānī, and two of the notable *sayyids* of Shūshtar. Between them, the two families held the office of the *ṣadr*, either indepenently or as joint *ṣadrs* for over forty years (T. Akh.: years 938, 964, 965, 970–71, 975; Kh. T.: 145a–46, 183a–84, 107).

c. All the four belonged to the Shahristānī *sayyids* of Isfahan, who from the second generation onwards became the closely related kin of Shāh ʿAbbās through marriage (T. A. Ab., 2:1089).

d. Mīrzā Ḥabībullāh and his son Mīrzā Mahdī, descendants of al-Karakī. Although al-Karakī's great-grandson through his daughter, Mīrzā Ḥabibullāh, appointed *ṣadr* by Ṣafī in 1631/1041 (Z.T. A. Ab.: 91), and the latter's son Mīrzā Mahdī, who succeeded him in 1654/1064 (Ab. N.: 143) were descendants of the *mujtahid*, there is every indication that they had by then been assimilated to the clerical estate as the inheritors of the vast landed estates in central Iran accumulated by their fathers. In fact, not only do they not appear as jurists, they also assumed the title of Mīrzā while serving the Safavids as high-ranking clerical administrators.

e. Mīrzā Abū Ṣāliḥ and Mīrzā Abū Ṭālib from the notable family of the Raḍavī *sayyids* of Mashhad.

f. Mīrzā Sayyid Muḥammad Bāqir Ḥusaynī. His son and another close relative of his were appointed *ṣadrs* by Tahmasp II (Modarresi Tabataba'i, pp. 22–23).

TABLE 5.2 Qāḍīs as Percentage of the Prominent Clerical Dignitaries

Period	%	(Absolute numbers)
Ismāᶜīl I (1501–24)	32	(12/38)
Ṭahmāsp (1524–76)	18	(20/113)
Qizilbāsh interregnum (1576–87)	24	(5/21)
ᶜAbbās I (1587–1629)	9	(4/46)

SOURCES: H. S. (written in 1520s/930s), 4:603–18, is used for the reign of Ismāᶜīl I; Shaykh al-Karakī's name is not mentioned on those pages but was added. Kh. T. and T. A. Ab., 1:143–58, are drawn on for Ṭahmāsp's period. Kh. T. (written in 1594–95/1003), especially the obituary notices at the closing section of each year, is used for the interregnum. Kh. T., Nq. A., but mainly T. A. Ab. are used for ᶜAbbās I's period.

The absolute numbers are given in brackets are of course not comparable as the sources are different. (The relatively large number of persons for Ṭahmāsp's reign is due to the fact that T. A. Ab.'s compact picture of the dignitaries of Ṭahmāsp's reign [1:143–58] is drawn with a hindsight different from the viewpoint of the earlier Kh. T.)

they collected the religious taxes (*zakāt*), and, more significantly, *khums*.[18] In addition, they received regular stipends from the *awqāf* through the *ṣadr*'s department, in exchange for praying for the perpetuity of the dynasty (*duᶜā-gūʾī*).[19] Chardin tells us that the Ḥusaynī *sayyids* of Isfahan, belonging to the ancient nobility of the kingdom, even arrogate *ijtihād* to themselves, and often accept penitence (*tawbeh*) as do the *mujtahids*.[20]

The incorporation of the estate of clerical notables into the judiciary and administrative offices of Ismāᶜīl's regime was, as we have seen, accompanied by the violent elimination of those notables who opposed the regime and by the migration of those who were not willing to give up their formal profession of Sunnism. Despite the probable insincerity in their initial outward profession of Shiᶜism and the persistence of Sunni proclivities among them,[21] there can be no doubt that the vast majority of the clerical notables did in fact become Twelver Shiᶜites by the seventeenth century. However, what is of crucial importance is that this change in doctrinal profession affected their cultural outlook very little, if at all. Comparing the descriptions of the intellectual interests and competence of the members of the clerical estate given in *Ḥabīb al-Siyar* (1520s) and *Jāmiᶜ Mufīdī* (1670s), one is struck by the constancy in their cultural outlook.[22] Perhaps it can be said that rhetoric figures somewhat more prominently in the former source, and religious sciences, mathematics, and calligraphy in the latter, but in both cases the same broad range and catholicity of intellectual interests and training is evident. Philosophy, the religious sciences, grammar and logic, calligraphy, mathematics, astronomy, rhetoric, composition and literary style, and, less

TABLE 5.3 Origins of the Prominent Shīʿite *ʿUlamāʾ* of the Safavid Period[a]

Date of death	Place of birth						Total
		Arab lands					
	Iran	Total	Jabal ʿĀmil	Arab Iraq	Bahrain	Other	
I. 907–79	5	8					13
1501–72			5	1	1	1	
II. 980–1050	16	13					29
1573–1640			9	3	1	—	
III. 1051–1100	18	10					28
1641–89			5	—	5[b]	—	
IV. 1101–51[c]	15	12					27
1689–1738			2	2	8	—	
Total							97

a. As reported in the Shiʿite bibliographical compendia, of which R. J. and Q. U. are used as the basis of the tabulation. Six brief entries of minor Baḥrānī *ʿulamāʾ* from Q. U. (pp. 188–89) were excluded. So were thirteen undatable entries in R. J. (of whom six resided in Iran and seven abroad). Had these two sets of persons been included, they would quite probably have given an even stronger representation of the dominant trends shown in this and the following table.

b. Two persons from Ḥuwayza are included in the Bahrain entry because of the great cultural-linguistic similarity of the two areas.

c. The terminal year 1151 was chosen instead of 1150 to assure the inclusion of one single important person, the last *Mullā-bāshī* of Sulṭān-Ḥusayn.

frequently, history and the composition of puzzles (*fann-e muʿammā*), appear as the main subjects of study.[23] Though we may infer from our sources that a few did naturally specialize in the religious sciences,[24] there can be no doubt that the broad and eclectic cultural outlook continued to be typically characteristic of the clerical mandarins under the Safavids.

5.2 The Geographical Background and Culture of the Imāmī Hierocracy

The cultural outlook of the Imāmī *ʿulamāʾ* of the Arab lands was markedly different from that of the Persian clerical estate. They had had no comparable ties with any state and therefore lacked a similarly broad legal, administrative, financial, and political base, having for centuries acted as private jurists and religious advisors to the Shiʿite minorities in the Arab Iraq, Syria, or in the isolated Bahrain. Consonantly with their more narrowly professionalized function as advisors to the Shiʿite communities in matters of dogma, ritual, and sacred law, the cultural outlook of the Shiʿite *ʿulamāʾ* was strictly religious.[25] Though philosophy (usually in conjunction with rational theology [*kalām*]), Arabic grammar, (as a tool of religious jurisprudence), and, to a much lesser extent mathematics were included in the syllabus of learning, the overwhelming preponderance of strictly religious interests is clearly reflected in the publications of the Shiʿite *ʿulamāʾ* of the Safavid period as reported in Shiʿite biographical encyclopedias,[26] and in the Safavid chronicles.[27]

The geographical factor is of crucial importance in understanding the cultural orientation of the Shiʿite hierocracy. To show the importance of the centers of Shiʿite learning in the Arab lands, it seems useful to begin with a preliminary consideration of the origins of the prominent Shiʿite *ʿulamāʾ*.

Table 5.3 is primarily useful in indicating a shift from the clear predominance of Jabal ʿĀmil over the other Arab regions in the first 140 years of our period to an equally clear predominance of Bahrain in the last fifty. But it does not reflect the extent of influence of the Shiʿite traditions of the Arab lands because it does not show the movement of the Shiʿite *ʿulamāʾ* of Iran to the centers of learning abroad. The extent of this cultural influence is better reflected in table 5.4 which shows the main residence of the important Shiʿite *ʿulamāʾ*.

The combination of the total number of *ʿulamāʾ* resident abroad, and the number of first-generation immigrant doctors in Iran for each period (the figures in boldface in table 5.4) give us a good index of the degree of preponderance of the influence of the Arab centers of Shiʿism.[28] The figures in boldface demonstrate that the marked cultural preponderance of these centers continued despite the emergence of a great center of learning in Isfahan under ʿAbbās the Great. This continued cultural dominance is explained by the considerable immigration of Shiʿite *ʿulamāʾ* from Jabal ʿĀmil to Isfahan.[29] But the students of the immigrant

TABLE 5.4 Geographical Distribution of the Prominent Shiʿite *ʿUlamāʾ* of the Safavid Period[a]

	Main residence									
	Iran			Abroad						
		of whom			of whom					
Date of death	Total	from Iran	1st gen. immigr.	Total	Jabal ʿĀmil	Mecca	Arab Iraq	Bahrain	Other	Total[d]
I. 907–79	6			**8**						14 (13)
1501–72		4	**2**		3	—	2	1	2	
II. 980–1050	19			**11**						30 (29)
1573–1640		12	**7**		3	3	3	1	1	
III. 1051–1100	18			**12**						30 (28)
1641–89		16	**2**		2	3	3	3[b]	1	
IV. 1101–51[c]	18			**10**						28 (27)
1689–1738		14	**4**		—	—	2	8	—	
Total										102 (97)

a. SOURCES: Those used for table 5.3 (R. J. and Q. U.).
b. Observations made under table 5.3 apply equally to this table.
c. See the observation on the terminal year under table 5.3.
d. A total of five cases of double entry have had to be made. The figures in parentheses in the totals column show the absolute number of persons involved.

doctors representing this influx were predominantly drawn from the Iranian population. They remained active in Iran (sixteen of them rose to prominence during the subsequent period as compared to a total of fourteen scholars who were either residents abroad or Arab immigrants). The vitality of Isfahan continued into the last decades of the seventeenth and the first decades of the eighteenth century, while its closer proximity to Bahrain, in addition to the flourishing trade in the Persian Gulf, brought a pool of Shiᶜite scholars in Bahrain into the network of erudite religious communication. However, it should be emphasized that even in the latter part of the seventeenth and the first quarter of the eighteenth century, a substantial proportion of the community of Shiᶜite religious scholars resided in the Arab lands. Thus the common cultural outlook of the Shiᶜite *ᶜulamāʾ* did not stem from common bases in the Safavid polity—as did that of the clerical notables—but from the identity of their cultural functions as the teachers of, and advisors in, religious jurisprudence, ritual, and dogma. Unlike the estate of clerical notables, the former constituted a sodality of *religious professionals*.

Most of the immigrant Shiᶜite *ᶜulamāʾ* found an (exalted) institutional niche in Safavid society in the more narrowly religious offices of *shaykh al-Islām* of the important cities, and the *pīsh-namāz* of the royal household, and of the most important mosques. Instances of an eminent theologian's being appointed qadi (not even of the most important cities) have rarely been noticed. Instead, those religious scholars who chose to accept the royal patronage were invariably appointed *shaykh al-Islām*[30] or (less frequently) *pīsh-namāz*.[31] The number of immigrant doctors was not large enough to exclude the Persian clerical notables from the majority of such offices. The appointees to *pīsh-namāzī*, through the nature of the office, tended to be strictly religious professionals.[32] It seems probable that under the influence of the eminent Shiᶜite doctors, the appointments to "shaykh al-Islāmates" also tended to go increasingly to religious professionals, though contrary instances are not lacking.[33] In short, we can say that the Shiᶜite religious professionals came to absorb the offices of *pīsh-nāmāzī* and "shaykh al-Islāmate", and to assimilate the outlook of their holders, who thus came to constitute a decentralized and heteronomous Shiᶜite hierocracy in Iran. In addition, this hierocracy contained members who held no office. A man of learning who had acquired fame and risen to the exalted rank of *mujtahid* could continue to teach and lead a pious life in total independence from the state, and was revered all the more if he chose to do so.

As *mujtahid*s, *shaykh al-Islām*s, scholars, and *pīsh-namāz* of the most important mosques, the members of the Shiᶜite hierocracy became increasingly conspicuous in Safavid society (see table 5.5).

As the term *ᶜulamāʾ* (the learned, scholars) indicates, teaching is and always has been a primary function of the Shiᶜite doctors. As has been pointed out, even those appointed to the office of *shaykh al-Islām* would usually continue to hold their classes. Because of its amorphousness and flexibility (the students could

TABLE 5.5 Members of the Shiᶜite Hierocracy[34] as Percentage of the Prominent Clerical Dignitaries[35]

Period	%	(Absolute numbers)
Ismāᶜīl I (1501–24)	5	$\left(\frac{2}{38}\right)$
Ṭahmāsp (1524–76)	12	$\left(\frac{13}{113}\right)$
Qizilbāsh interregnum (1576–87)	19	$\left(\frac{4}{21}\right)$
ᶜAbbās I (1587–1629)	20	$\left(\frac{9}{46}\right)$

SOURCES: Those used for table 5.4.

take lessons in different subjects from *any* professor within the geographical vicinity and often moved to other cities to join the classes of eminent professors), the educational system proper also absorbed its share of the immigrant *ᶜulamā*ᵓ as professors (sing. *mudarris*) of the "transmitted sciences" and Shiᶜite jurisprudence. Given the declaration of the Imāmī doctrine and jurisprudence as the official and only valid religious tradition, the immigrant Shiᶜite *ᶜulamā*ᵓ had no difficulty in capturing the teaching of the "transmitted" religious sciences (*manqūl*)—as distinct from "rational" theology and philosophy (*maᶜqūl*)—and are repeatedly mentioned as the professors of *manqūl*. However, even within the intellectual institutions, they could not oust the professors of the rational sciences; and their attempt to take over the judiciary and financial branches of the complex of "religious" institutions met with both the firm resistance of the clerical estate and encountered internal obstacles; consequently it came to naught. It is to this undiscovered struggle that we should now turn.

5.3 The Struggle for Hierocratic Domination

5.3.1 Ṭahmāsp's Royal Patronage and the First Steps toward the Institution of a Distinct Shiᶜite Hierocracy in the Sixteenth Century

Though there is no inherent logic in the pattern of change reflected in tables 5.2 and 5.5, a comparison between the two suggests that, roughly speaking, the clerical estate's overall loss of institutional power because of the decline of qadiship corresponded to the Shiᶜite hierocracy's gain in prestige and control over the "shaykh al-Islāmates". In other words, the configuration of the complex of religious-legal-educational institutions changed: a fairly well-differentiated hierocracy of religious professionals was structurally accommodated within it while the salience of the legal components of the complex was reduced. What underlay this change was a tangled struggle for domination between the two groups. The nature and course of the struggle are difficult to detect and chart because one of the two parties involved, the party of religious professionals, was itself undergoing a major internal transformation determined by two contrary factors: the trend toward professionalization on the one hand, and, on the other, a major change in composition owing to the recruitment of its younger members from the opposing camp, namely, the clerical estate. The detection and charting of these trends can therefore be done only with historical hindsight, as the actors involved were themselves at times only dimly conscious of the full repercussions of their action and the ultimate goal they were striving toward.

Glassen has noted the hostility with which the prominent members of the Persian clerical estate encountered the eminent doctor Shaykh ᶜAlī al-Karakī and his party at the time of his arrival in Iran.[36] This hostility persisted throughout the sixteenth century, thus militating against a smooth mutual assimilation between the slowly immigrating Shiᶜite doctors and the Persian clerical notables. In fact, the clerical notables bitterly resented both the intrusion of the Shiᶜite religious professionals under the protection and patronage of the ruler, and their preemption of the term *ᶜulamā*ʾ—the learned. One clerical notable and historian of Ṭahmāsp's reign, Qāḍī Aḥmad Ghaffārī (d. 1567–8/975), even dared to state bluntly:

> But in his [Shāh Ṭahmāsp's] eyes, they were turning the ignorant—*juhalā*ʾ—into the learned—*fuḍalā*ʾ—and were attributing the station of the ignorant to the learned. Therefore most of his domains became devoid of men of excellence and knowledge, and filled with men of ignorance; and only a few men of [true] learning are to be found in the entire realm of Iran.[37]

However, Ṭahmāsp's determined support assured the survival of the Shiᶜite hierocracy and paved the way for its eventual triumph. Soon after the rise of Ismāᶜīl the Safavid, al-Karakī moved from his native Jabal ᶜĀmil in Syria to the closeby Arab Iraq, and is reported to have visited Ismāᶜīl in Isfahan as early as 1504–5/910.[38] He repeated his visits to Ismāᶜīl and saw him in his camps in Harat and just before the battle of Chaldirān. He finally moved to central Iran toward the end of Ismāᶜīl's reign.[39] But his definitive chance to act as the supreme member of the Shiᶜite hierocracy came after the death of Ismāᶜīl I, who after all, was himself the incarnation of God.

Ismāᶜīl's son, the young Ṭahmāsp, was a devout Twelver Shiᶜite who, unlike his father and forefathers, had no pretense to divine incarnation. He greatly respected al-Karakī, who is often referred to as the "Propagator of the [Shiᶜite] Religion" (*muravvij-e madhhab*). In 1532–33/939, a year before al-Karakī's death, in order to put an end to an acrimonious fight between two major factions of the Shiᶜite *ᶜulamā*ʾ, Ṭahmāsp issued a *farmān* which can be regarded as the milestone marking both the creation of a Shiᶜite hierocracy in Iran and the definitive transition from extremism to Twelver Shiᶜism. The *farmān* designated al-Karakī the *nāʾib* (vicegerent/deputy) of the Imam, thus devolving the supreme religious authority upon him as the most qualified or the "seal of the *mujtahids*" (*khātam al-mujtahidīn*) and as the guardian of the heritage of the Seal of the Prophets (Muhammad).[40]

Al-Karakī's self-designation as the deputy of the Imam, however, preceded this explicit royal recognition, having begun with his ambitious political project as the foremost Imāmī jurist. In 1510/916, in a tract on taxation of agricultural land (*kharāj*), he explicitly put forward his views as the deputy of the Imam during his occultation.[41] The reader should recall the positive world-embracing attitude of al-Murtaḍā, who, under the bright political conditions of the Buyid period, moved away from the inner-worldly withdrawal entailed by the pious posture of the traditionalists, and attempted to enjoin world-embracing political attitudes, and to encourage ethically responsible activity within the existing political framework. With the creation of the first Shiᶜite empire in history by Ismāᶜīl, al-Karakī had an even greater incentive than al-Murtaḍā to overcome the ideal of pious antipathy to earthly power. He took up the unprecedented challenge of bringing the Safavid political order within the ambit of the Shiᶜite religious norms, and of securing an important institutional base for its custodians. To assure the involvement of the *ᶜulamā*ʾ in political organization, he not only emphatically ruled in favor of the permissibility of receiving salaries from "tyrannical rulers," paid out of land taxes, but also envisioned some supervision over the distribution of these taxes by the deputy of the Imam.[42] To enhance the world-embracing social aspect of Shiᶜism in the controversial issue of the Friday prayer during the occultation of the Imam, he ruled that it was incumbent, thus assuring the weekly gathering of the believers, and, incidentally, securing for the Shiᶜite *ᶜulamā*ʾ positions as prayer leaders (sing. *pīsh-namāz*) of the mosques.[43] Numerous treatises were written on this question, for and against the permissibility of the Friday congregational prayer during the occultation, but al-Karakī's affirmative, world-embracing view eventually prevailed over the negative, world-rejecting view. The social commitment of Shiᶜism was considerably enhanced by the institution of congregational prayer to be led by the *ᶜulamā*ʾ on behalf of the Hidden Imam.

Having taken the consistent ideological position described above, al-Karakī embarked upon the conquest of the religious institutions for the Shiᶜite hierocracy, beginning with the most important: the office of the *ṣadr*. In 1527–28/934, for the first (and last) time, an immigrant Imāmī doctor, Mīr Niᶜmatullāh Ḥillī (d. 1534/940), a student of al-Karakī's, himself "claiming *ijtihād*," was appointed the joint-*ṣadr*, sharing the office with a clerical notable, Mīr Qavām al-Dīn Ḥusaynī, the *naqīb* of Isfahan. Mīr Qavām died in the following year, and Amīr Ghiyāth al-Dīn Manṣūr (d. 1542/949), a distinguished scholar and the scion of a renowned family of clerical notables from Shiraz, succeeded him as the joint-*ṣadr*. The Shiᶜite hierocracy and the Persian clerical estate clashed in the persons of Shaykh al-Karakī, the *mujtahid*, and Ghiyāth al-Dīn Manṣūr, the scholar-administrator.[44]

Al-Karakī and Ghiyāth al-Dīn Manṣūr were worlds apart in their intellectual outlooks. The writings of the "Seal of the *Mujtahids*" were exclusively religious and jurisprudential.[45] By contrast, Ghiyāth al-Dīn Manṣūr, one of whose various titles was "Seal of the Philosophers" (*khātam al-ḥukamā*), had numerous publications in the "rational sciences" (philosophy and philosophical theology) in the tradition of his father, who had conducted an animated philosophical debate with the famous philosopher Jalāl al-Dīn Davvānī.[46] According to *Takmilat al-Akhbār*, he surpassed the other scholars (*ᶜulamāᵓ*) in philosophy, astronomy, mathematics, and medicine, but "had no accomplishment in religious jurisprudence" ("ū rā az fiqh bakhshī nabūd").[47] Controversy raged between the two men, and the pious young shah exercised his decisive political authority in favor of the "deputy of the Imam." In connection with the events of the year 1529–30/936, Ṭahmāsp writes in his autobiography:

> At this time learned controversy arose between the *Mujtahid* of the Age [*mujtahid al-zamānī*], Shaykh ᶜAlī ᶜAbd al-ᶜĀlī [al-Karakī], and Mīr Ghiyāth al-Dīn Manṣūr, the *ṣadr*. Even though the *mujtahid* of the age was triumphant, *they* [*sic*] did not acknowledge his *ijtihād*, and were bent on hostility. We took note of the side of Truth, and affirmed him in *ijtihād*.[48]

In the above passage, the emphasized "*they*" must refer to the hostile clerical notables whose hostility shows the crucial importance of the royal patronage for al-Karakī's success. Two years later, in 1531–32/938, the Mujtahid of the Age secured the dismissal of Ghiyāth al-Dīn Manṣūr, the *ṣadr* and the "Seal of the Philosophers." Mīr Muᶜizz al-Dīn Muḥammad Iṣfahānī, a clerical notable, but this time also a strict jurist and a student and protégé of al-Karakī, was appointed *ṣadr*.[49] Finally, the *farmān* of 1532–33/938 established al-Karakī as the deputy of the Imam and as such the supreme religious authority of the realm. The influence of al-Karakī lingered on after his death in 1534/940. After the dismissal of Mīr Muᶜizz al-Dīn in 1536/942, Mīr Asadullāh Shūshtarī, a student of al-Karakī's who had also been highly recommended by him to Shāh Ṭahmāsp,[50] was appointed *ṣadr* and held the office for over twenty years.[51] But al-Karakī's success in establishing the Shiᶜite doctors' control over the office of the *ṣadr* was temporary, and the monopolistic control of the office reverted to the clerical notables after the death of Shūshtarī (see table 5.1).

Al-Karakī's attempt to unify all religious institutions within the framework of the state also encountered considerable opposition *from within* the Shiᶜite clerical community. It came under vehement attack by the eminent doctor, Ibrāhīm al-Qaṭīfī, who upheld the ideal of pious antipathy to earthly powers and rejection of all worldly domination. For reasons of expositional convenience, the systematic treatment of the world-rejecting mode reflected in al-Qaṭīfī's attitude is delayed until chapter 9. Here I am simply stating the fact that he staunchly opposed the incorporation of the *ᶜulamāᵓ* into the Safavid political organization. He uncompromisingly rejected any association with the ruler as proof of interest in worldly gains and of lack of piety, adducing a strongly worded *ḥadīth* attributed to the Prophet: "When you see a reader of the Qurʾan seeking shelter with the ruler, know that he is a thief."[52] Al-Qaṭīfī wrote a treatise on the "impermissibility" of the Friday prayer during the great occultation,[53] and ruled on the "reprehensibility" of receiving gifts from the ruler and on the "impermissibility" of accepting land assignments (subject to the land tax, *kharāj*) from him, while enjoining the avoidance of all transactions with him insofar as possible. In short, he opposed al-Karakī on every major ideological point, as well as attacking him personally for his "love of the world (*ḥubb al-dunyā*) as demonstrated in his vast amassed landed fortune.[54]

Mīr Niʿmatullāh Ḥillī (d. 1534/940), though he had been a student of al-Karakī's and had almost certainly been appointed *ṣadr* through his support, took the side of al-Qaṭīfī in the controversy, and made an attempt to organize a clerical party against the Mujtahid of the Age, an attempt that cost him his office and brought about his banishment.[55] The involvement of Qaṭīfī in the political intrigue against al-Karakī gives us reason to doubt the sincerity of his motives in opposing the latter's world-embracing extension of Shiʿite ethics. It is important to bear in mind that al-Karakī and al-Qaṭīfī represented two different Arab centers to Shiʿism, one in Syria, the other in Qaṭīf and the Bahrain area. As the chief rival of al-Karakī, al-Qaṭīfī resented Ismāʿīl's choice of the former as spokesman for Shiʿism. Ismāʿīl's considerable donations to al-Karakī for the maintenance of his students and *madrasas*[56] must have aroused the jealousy of Qaṭīfī and the scholars from his region who felt deprived of such favors. Through Mīr Niʿmatullāh Ḥillī, they unsuccessfully sought to offer their services to the Safavid ruler and thus replace al-Karakī and his party of predominantly ʿĀmilī scholars. It is also important to note that in this instance of intense rivalry between the Shiʿite doctors of different regions for royal favor, the party whose ambitions for material advantage and political power were frustrated found it expedient to make effective, albeit hypocritical, appeal to the ideal of pious aloofness of the men of religion from earthly domination. Although the evidence suggests that Qaṭīfī's denunciation of the evils of association with the earthly powers was insincere, the denunciation nevertheless had a lasting effect in limiting the extension of the normative ambit of the sacred law into important areas of social, economic, and political life. The episode thus illustrates the utility of our distinction between the motives for upholding a normative ideal and the "validity" or efficacy of that ideal, and proves that the latter might obtain even when the ideal is upheld insincerely and from the motive of self-interest.

Furthermore, there were instances of genuine pious antipathy to involvement with earthly powers. More sincerely than al-Qaṭīfī, and more consistently than in the case of Mīr Niʿmatullāh, the *ṣadr* who was himself deeply involved in the state, a few of the prominent *ʿulamāʾ* upheld the attitude of pious antipathy to political involvements and shunned any association with the earthly ruler. These could be put under no authoritative or organizational pressure to acknowledge the claims of al-Karakī, and of his equally political grandson, Mīr Sayyid Ḥusayn after him, to be the "Mujtahid of the Age." As the most eminent member of this group in the second half of the sixteenth century, we may mention the *mujtahid* Mullā Aḥmad Ardabīlī, the Muqaddas (d. 1585/993) who shunned all political associations and who wrote a treatise on land taxation (*kharāj*) upholding al-Qaṭīfī's point of view.[57]

The designation of the deputy of the Imam, accompanying that of the "Seal of the Mujtahids" (*khātam al-mujtahidīn*) in Ṭahmāsp's *farmān* was primarily significant in formally putting an end to the complete fusion of *political* and *religious* leadership; that is, as the ruler's acknowledgment of a differentiated supreme religious authority. But the term "deputy of the Imam" did not come into formal usage. Instead, the designation "Mujtahid of the Age" was used to confer the supreme hierocratic authority. After al-Karakī, it was bestowed upon his not-too-politically-active son, Shaykh ʿAbd al-ʿĀlī (d. 1584–85/992–93)[58] and after the latter upon al-Karakī's grandson through his daughter, Mīr Sayyid Ḥusayn al-Karakī (d. 1592–93/1001),[59] who was very active politically. However, the bestowal of the title of Mujtahid of the Age did not amount to a formal appointment, and its recognition was not binding according to the Imāmī doctrine of *ijtihād*. As other members of the Shiʿite hierocracy came increasingly to claim and/or be accredited with the rank of *mujtahid*, it became possible for religious authorities to exist independent of the state. From the beginning of the seventeenth century onwards, the "shaykh al-Islāmate" of Isfahan emerged as the highest office of the state reserved for the hierocracy.[60] But the primacy of the position of *Shaykh al-Islām* of Isfahan—fully reflected in ceremonial occasions such as the coronations of the kings from 1629 onwards[61]—was tacit and not formal. It was only with the creation of the office of *Mullā-bāshī* for Muḥammad Bāqir Khātūnābādī in 1712/1124 that formal institutionalized recognition was granted to an eminent doctor as the head of the Shiʿite hierocracy.[62]

To recapitulate briefly, the Shiʿite hierocracy failed to capture the religio-administrative office of the *ṣadr* because of the vested interest of the cleric-administrators who continued to hold that office. Despite the favorable disposition of supreme political power in the person of Shāh Ṭahmāsp, the charisma and authority of the "deputy of the Hidden Imam" did not become fused with the authority of the "most learned *mujtahid*" and did not find institutional embodiment in a supreme hierocratic office. This failure was also due, in no small part, to the deep intrahierocracy division, resting on the difference in the local geographical background of the Shiʿite *ʿulamāʾ* and availing itself of two antithetical attitudes, the one world-embracing, the other world-rejecting.

5.3.2 Principles of Differentiated Hierocratic Authority

The failure to control the religio-legal-administrative institutions of the Safavid caesaropapist state did not, however, adversely affect the *religious* authority of the Shiʿite doctors but rather promoted its clearer *differentiation* from political domination.

From a strictly doctrinal viewpoint, the office of the *ʿulamāʾ* is "secular" in very much the same way as the office of the Lutheran ministers is secular.[63] In both cases the absolute transcendence of God obviates the personal charisma of any priestly functionary. As with Lutheranism centuries later, in Islam divine charisma is reified in the Word, and there is no room for any priestly distribution of grace. It can be argued that the same is true of Shiʿite Islam after the occultation of the last divinely inspired Imam. If this strict doctrinal aspect were the only relevant consideration, the very applicability of the term "hierocracy" to the Shiʿite *ʿulamāʾ* would be somewhat questionable. However, it is not. In the eyes of the Shiʿites, something of a charismatic quality had always inhered in the persons of the great theologians by virtue of the great favors bestowed upon them by the Hidden Imam.[64] Numerous "charismatic" or minor miraculous deeds (*karāmāt*), not the least of which consisted of attenuated forms of contact with the Hidden Imam in dreams, visions, and during the *Ḥajj* ceremonies in Mecca,[65] came to be attributed to the *ʿulamāʾ*. With the transition from the rationalism of the sectarian phase to the orthodoxy of the later Safavid period, great emphasis came to be put on the charismatic quality of the *ʿulamāʾ*. They were said to be the means of clinging to the infallible Imams as the "Ark of Salvation"; their pen was superior to the blood of the martyrs; they were doors to heaven, and insulting them would bring the wrath of God upon the offender.[66] The pages of the *Qiṣaṣ al-ʿUlamāʾ* are replete with the lengthy accounts of the *karāmāt* attributed to the eminent Shiʿite divines.[67] In addition, the *ʿulamāʾ* arrogated to themselves the function of *Shafāʿa* or intercession in the hereafter.[68] Consulting the Qurʾan upon demand of the laymen to determine whether or not an act should be undertaken (*istikhāra*) figured prominently among their functions.[69] This attribution of supernatural charisma to the Shiʿite *ʿulamāʾ* enhanced their professional status as advisors on correct ritualistic practice, and gave their authority a distinctly "hierocratic" aspect. With the increasingly universal acceptance of the "incumbency" of the Friday prayer during the occultation of the Imam, the function of leading the Friday prayer—and by extension all the daily prayers—added another dimension to the hierocratic aspect of the *ʿulamāʾ*'s office.

With these introductory considerations in mind, let us turn to the principles on which hierocratic domination rested in the Safavid period. The most influential sixteenth-century commentary on the Qurʾan is the *Zubdat al-Bayān*, written by Mullā Aḥmad Ardabīlī, the Muqaddas. Its "political ethic" dealing with authority contains a novel element of tremendous importance. In the chapter on "Enjoining the Good and Forbidding the Evil," we can read: "And the 'imitation' [*taqlīd*] of the *Mujtahid* is good and permissible or rather incumbent with the existence of proof upon the *ijtihād* of the *Mujtahid*."[70]

Here, as in the two major near-contemporary works on the "principles of jurisprudence"—Bahā᾽ al-Dīn ᶜĀmilī's *Zubdat al-Uṣūl*[71] and Ḥasan ibn Zayn al-Dīn's *Maᶜālim al-Uṣūl*[72]—we find the conjunction of the notions of *taqlīd* (imitation) and *ijtihād* (competence to determine the application of legal norms), both of which were, significantly, firmly *rejected* by the early Imāmīs.

Kulaynī is firm in his rejection of *taqlīd*, as it leads the believer astray.[73] Al-Mufīd similarly rejects *taqlīd* outright.[74] His disciple al-Murtaḍā, however, breaks with the traditional view, and justifies the permissibility and desirability of *taqlīd* in the sense of the recourse of the layman to the jurist (*muftī*) to seek advice. Though at one point he even uses the term *wujūb* (incumbency) of the recourse of the layman to the jurist on grounds that the layman does not himself possess the necessary knowledge of the detailed ethical commandments with regard to (new) occurrences (*ḥawādith*), his aim is clearly to establish the *permissibility* (*jawāz*) of *taqlīd*. Al-Murtaḍā's argument on the permissibility of *taqlīd* as the recourse of the questioning layman (*mustaftī*) to the jurist (*muftī*) is coupled with his much stronger assertion that once such recourse to the jurist has been made, it is *incumbent* upon the layman to follow the jurist's ruling or *fatwā*.[75] The layman should seek advice from the most learned jurist, but should there be a number of qualified jurists equal in learning and piety, he can choose among them.[76] In the above manner, al-Murtaḍā takes the first step in the enhancement of the juristic authority of the *ᶜulamā᾽*. However, it should be pointed out that his justification of *taqlīd* is cautious and qualified. Not only does he reject *taqlīd* in the "principles" of religion or "fundamentals of faith" (on which point he has been followed by the Shiᶜite *ᶜulamā᾽* to this date), he also rejects the permissibility of *taqlīd* for whomever is able to possess the (necessary) knowledge (*ᶜilm*) himself,[77] and has a telling explanation as to why *taqlīd* is permissible for the layman: "And if the *taqlīd* of the *ᶜālim* is permissible for the questioning layman [*mustaftī*] *it is because the latter does not possess the [necessary] knowledge*, and not because of what the former possesses of knowledge."[78]

Some three centuries later,[79] Ibn Muṭahhar al-Ḥillī, the ᶜAllāma, was to follow al-Murtaḍā's argument closely. He justifies *taqlīd* on account of its practical necessity, as laymen do not have the necessary time to devote to acquiring the expert knowledge necessary for determining the ethically and ritually correct behavior in conjunction with new occurrences, and to attempt to do so would prevent them from earning their livelihood. He reaffirms the permissibility of *taqlīd* in *furūᶜ* (the derivatives), and rules that it is incumbent upon the layman if he is unable to acquire the necessary juristic competence himself.[80] Like al-Murtaḍā, the ᶜAllāma is more concerned with establishing the *permissibility* of *taqlīd* than in making an emphatic assertion of its *incumbency* as an ethical obligation.

The acceptance of *ijtihād* by the Imāmīs came much later. Although the Muḥaqqiq had acknowledged that the Shiᶜite jurists had been practicing *ijtihād*, the first major theologian to accept *ijtihād* explicitly was the ᶜAllāma al-Ḥillī. *Ijtihād* had been rejected by al-Mufīd and even by al-Murtaḍā, albeit with some qualification.[81] In fact, the ᶜAllāma himself seems to have accepted the *ijtihād* with something of a dramatic suddenness.[82] It is no accident that the later works on jurisprudence often begin with al-Ḥillī's definition of *ijtihād* as the exertion of capacity on the part of the jurist for the acquisition of "probable opinion" (*ẓann*) as to the commandment of the divine law.[83] Al-Ḥillī's acceptance of *ijtihād* constitutes a crucial step in the enhancement of the juristic authority of the *ᶜulamā*ᵓ; other steps, however, remained to be taken. It is true that the correlation of *ijtihād* and *taqlīd* does in fact occur in the ᶜAllāma's writings, but he still deals with the juristic authority of the *ᶜulamā*ᵓ under the heading: "On the Muftī [jurist] and the Mustaftī [questioning layman]."[84] More importantly, he relates *ijtihād* to *competence with respect to specific problems and fields*, and does not restrict it to *ijtihād muṭlaq*: the general competence of the person of the *mujtahid* in all fields of sacred law.[85]

This last crucial step was taken in the Safavid period by Ardabīlī the Muqaddas and his contemporaries. Al-Karakī, the "*Mujtahid* of the Age," ruled emphatically against the permissibility of following a dead *mujtahid*,[86] thus assuring the continued transitiveness of juristic authority and precluding its exclusive attribution to the eminent jurists of the past as in Sunnism. Though the disagreements that existed on this point continued for some time,[87] al-Karakī's opinion eventually prevailed. The juristic authority of the (living) *ᶜulamā*ᵓ came to be treated in the works on the principles of jurisprudence under a heading formally conjoining the notions of *ijtihād* and *taqlīd*. Of these, by far the most important are *Zubdat al-Usūl* and *Maᶜālim al-Dīn*. In the former, Shaykh-e Bahāᵓī (d. 1620–21/1030) defines *ijtihād* as "the competence through which one is able to deduce the derivative legal [*sharᶜī*] commandment from the fundamental,"[88] and is content to establish the permissibility of *taqlīd* as "acting according to the saying of another without reason[ing]," and is strictly concerned with establishing its permissibility (*jawāz*, *idhn*, *ibāḥa*).[89] As regards *ijtihād*, the Shaykh-e Bahāᵓī follows al-Ḥillī in considering the division of *ijtihād* according to problems and fields (*tajazza*) permissible. Zayn al-Dīn notes the divergence of opinion on this question, argues against specialized competence (*ijtihād mutajazzī*), and stresses the importance of general competence (*ijtihād muṭlaq*) as necessary for the valid deduction of all derivative commandments.[90]

It is clear from these discussions, as well as from Ardabīlī's, that our theologians are still very much in the process of laying the foundations of hierocratic authority in the face of a strong contrary Shiᶜite tradition, whose lingering influence forces them to be cautious in justifying their break with it. Nevertheless, the decisive conjunction of *ijtihād* and *taqlīd*, and the emergence of the notion of *ijtihād muṭlaq*, lodging hierocratic authority clearly in the *person* of the *mujtahid*, were both significant in their own right and indicative of the direction of the subsequent developments. Furthermore, it is of crucial importance that, without waiting for the resolution of various minute problems connected with reconciling the doctrine of *ijtihād* and *taqlīd* with the Shiᶜite traditional heritage, the Muqaddas proceeded with its *incorporation into Shiᶜite ethics* by subsuming it under the ethical duties of "enjoining the good and forbidding the evil." As we have seen, he presented obedience to the hierocratic authority of the *mujtahid* in matters relating to the sacred law as an ethical obligation. Furthermore, the Muqaddas affirmed the layman's duty to act according to the ruling of the *mujtahid*, once such ruling was issued, and asserted the incumbency of "following" (*taqlīd*) the "most learned" of the jurists.[91]

A second, less important development in legal theory should also be considered. It is much vaguer and less important as a Shiᶜite norm of authority for the Safavid period, but one that proved ripe for further development in the nineteenth and twentieth centuries.

The vested interest of the Shiᶜite jurists of the sectarian period in the continued suppression of all mahdistic claims forced them to consider some of the specific functions of the Imam in abeyance (*sāqiṭ*) during the occultation. This was in part necessary to curb mahdism, as the possibility of direct representation of the Hidden Imam through a *bāb* or a *safīr* was not categorically ruled out. It is therefore not surprising that very little attention was paid to the notion of *niyāba* (vicegerency) of the Hidden Imam. In the great legal compendiums of the late twelfth/early thirteenth century, those of al-Muḥaqqiq al-Ḥillī, we find references to "gerency [on behalf] of imamate [*walāʾ al-imāma*]"[92] or to the authority of him "for whom there is a commandment [*ḥukm*] regarding the right to vicegerency"[93] only in highly specific contexts such as the rules for the collection of alms and their distribution, the disposal of the property of the heirless after their death, and the like. But there is no general discussion of "vicegerency" as the foundation of clerical authority.

With the increasing social involvement of Shiᶜism resulting from its "establishment," there was an urge to legitimate hierocratic authority with reference to the authority of the Hidden Imam, and to extend it to some of the functions of the Imam that were earlier declared to be in abeyance. One such function was the leading of the congregational prayer. As we have seen in the treatise written for implementation by the Sarbidār ruler, the first martyr recognized the jurist as a kind of deputy of the Imam who could lead the congregational prayer on his behalf. It is in connection with congregational prayer that al-Karakī goes further than the first martyr, and puts forward the concepts of "general vicegerency" (*niyāba ᶜāmma*) of the Shiᶜite jurists on behalf of the Hidden Imam. In arguing that congregational prayer might and ought to be performed during the occultation, al-Karakī maintains that no specific deputy is necessary for the purpose because there exist the jurists whom the Imams "have appointed deputy in a general manner [*ᶜalā wajh al-ᶜumūm*]" upon the words of al-Sadiq in the tradition related by ᶜUmar ibn Ḥanẓala.[94] This is the earliest instance when the tradition of Ibn Ḥanẓala, very similar to the one by Abū Khadīja which was cited previously,[95] is rather timidly drawn upon to adumbrate the notion of "general vicegerency." Although, as was pointed out, al-Karakī is more categorical in claiming vicegerency of the Imam in his treatise on the land tax, it is unlikely that he intended the notions to extend beyond judging and leadership of the congregational prayer. As Calder points out, al-Karakī does not apply the concept to other spheres such as religious taxes, implementation of *ḥudūd*, and holy war in his comprehensive legal work, *Jāmiᶜ al-Maqāṣid*.[96]

A somewhat more extensive concept of general vicegerency is to be found in the legal works of ᶜAlī ibn Zayn al-Dīn, the second martyr (d. 1557/965).[97] Although the second martyr makes use of the concept in connection with religious taxes in addition to judging and the congregational prayer, there is no general discussion of the concept, nor indeed any employment of the phrase *niyāba ᶜāmma*. Nevertheless, by repeated juxtaposition of specific and general vicegerency, the second martyr establishes a parallelism between the deputies of the Imams in their lifetimes and the Shiᶜite jurists during the occultations.

Thus the scope of the authority vicariously exercised on behalf of the Hidden Imam in the religio-legal sphere came to be vaguely delineated. The well-informed Sunni notable, Mīr Makhdūm (d. 1587/995), delimits this scope, to the exclusion of *jihād* (holy war): "The *mujtahid* is the vicegerent [*nāᵓib*] of the Imam, as regards [legal] commandments, criminal punishments and acts of worship." Elsewhere, his function of eliciting commandments (*aḥkām*) is said to include "resolution of hostilities, ruling on litigations, administration of criminal justice."[98] Mīr Makhdūm's account is corroborated by his Shiᶜite opponent, Qāḍī Nūrullāh Shūshtarī.[99] It is interesting to note that Mīr Makhdūm defines the *nāᵓib ᶜāmm* (general vicegerent) as "he who has reached the stage of *ijtihād* [competence to determine juristic norms],"[100] and restricts it to the single most learned (*aᶜlam*) of the *mujtahids*. His Shiᶜite opponent, though emphasizing that there are learned men in the important cities of Iran competent to practice *ijtihād*, is careful not to describe them as the vicegerents of the Imam. Furthermore, we know from other Safavid sources that in Iran, only Shaykh al-Karakī, and after him his grandson Shaykh Ḥusayn, were officially recognized as the "*Mujtahid* of the Age" (*mujtahid al-zamān*).

In his tract justifying the congregational prayer, al-Karakī's grandson-in-law, Mīr Dāmād (d. 1631–32/1041), endorses the position taken by al-Karakī, and puts forward the strongest recorded claim for hierocratic authority prior to the twentieth century.[101] He remarks in passing that the "Just Ruler is the Infallible Imam, or he who is appointed by Him (Blessing of God be upon Him), or he who deserves to act as a deputy for Him (may Peace of God be upon Him) generally."[102] Mīr Dāmād does not elaborate. Elsewhere, however, he argues in favor of *ijtihād muṭlaq* (absolute) and against specialization in legal competence.[103] The intention is clearly to restrict supreme religious authority as much as possible, to one or at most a few jurists.

In the second half of the seventeenth century, Chardin confirms that the acclaimed *mujtahids* are very few, and at times there may be none alive. Chardin knew only one such doctor.[104]

In the sixteenth century, Mīr Makhdūm could maliciously remark that a general vicegerent was as likely to be absent as the Hidden Imam, thus causing the abeyance of the sacred law.[105] This objection indicates that general vicegerency had not yet been clarified to mean the *collective* responsibility of the *mujtahids*, and tended to be associated with the person of the "*mujtahid* of the age." In the seventeenth century, we find a more general claim put forward for the entire body of jurists on the basis of an ordinance purportedly issued by the Hidden Imam: "And concerning the events which occur, refer to the transmitters of our Traditions: they are my proof unto you, as I am the Proof of God unto you."[106] The *ᶜulamā*ʾ are therefore said to be the proof (*ḥujjat*) of the proof of God [i.e., the Hidden Imam] to all the Shiᶜites, to all the "followers" (*muqallidān*).[107]

However, the logic of "rationalization" of the concept of general vicegerency was not rigorously worked out during the Safavid period. The late sixteenth century, controversy between Mīr Makhdūm and Qāḍī Nūrullah shows that some of the attributes of imamate tended to be transferred to the *mujtahid* as his "deputy," in spite of the logical inconsistencies arising as a result of this transfer. Some Shiᶜites said that the existence of the *mujtahid* was due to grace of God (*luṭf*).[108] Nearly a century later, Chardin similarly points out that some men of religion consider that the vicegerent of the Imam should be a "mouchtehed massoum" (*mujtahid maᶜṣūm*).[109] Here we see the Imams' attribute of *ᶜiṣma* (infallibility, sinlessness) transferred to the *mujtahid*. Now these incongruencies exactly parallel those regarding political domination, and whose removal was impeded by the dynastic interest of the Safavids (see section 7.2.3). It seems that as long as the Safavids resisted the rationalization of a convenient anomaly of the extremist heritage regarding political authority, the hierocracy was not likely to insist too much on the logical consistency in the rationalization of this anomaly at *their* expense—i.e., regarding hierocratic authority solely. As shall be explained at some length, the resolution of the contradictions between doctrine of occultation and the normative order governing political and hierocratic domination came only when *both* sides had to relinquish the anomalous tenet they had inherited from the period of extremism.

Despite these unresolved problems in the Safavid period, the Shiᶜite sacred law which, thanks to the repetition of the doctrine of imamate as a theological substitute for political theory, made no reference to temporal domination, came to contain provisions relating to and legitimating hierocratic authority. To enhance their domination over the masses, the members of the Shiᶜite hierocracy did not rely solely on jurisprudence and legal theory. In line with the otherworldly Shiᶜism they were popularizing among the masses (see chapter 6), they also claimed special heavenly privileges and divine favors:

> It is necessary to know that the *ᶜulamā*ᵓ and the jurists are the heirs to the Prophets, and upon the death of each and every one of them the angels weep. [They are] the permanence of the earth and gates of heaven and the death of each is the cause of weakness in Islam and faith, because they are citadels of Islam, and the angels spread their wings on their ways and pray for forgiveness for them.[110]

5.3.3 The Struggle between the Notable (Sayyid) and the Jurist in the Seventeenth Century

I have compared the clerical notables who joined the Safavid state from the time of Ismāᶜīl I onwards with the Chinese mandarins in their outlook. However, the mandarins who dominated the patrimonial bureaucracy of China were spared the competition of an autonomous hierocracy as the pontifical caesaropapist domination of the emperor was spared the competition of prophecy.[111] Not so with the clerical notables in Shiᶜite Iran.

With the emergence of Isfahan as the foremost metropolitan center of Shiᶜite learning in the seventeenth century, for the first time in history the majority of Shiᶜite religious doctors consisted of Iranians (see table 5.4, rows 3 and 4), many of whom were in fact descendants of the clerical notables. What were the consequences of this shift in the ethnic-cultural composition of the Shiᶜite *ᶜulamā*ᵓ resulting from the infusion of the recruits from the clerical estate for the outlook of hierocracy, and for its institutional entrenchment?

At first, we witness a period of mutual assimilation. As we have seen, toward the end of his life, al-Karakī's influence began to permeate the clerical estate, and two important clerical notables who were students of his were appointed *ṣadr*s. However, the reverse trend also took place, modifying the outlook of the hierocracy under the impact of the influence of the clerical estate. This reverse tendency is nowhere more clearly discernible than in the family of al-Karakī himself. He had a number of students among the Persian clerical notables, to some of whom he also married his daughters. Not counting those descendants of his who became merged with the clerical-administrative estate and held the office of the *ṣadr* for some three decades, two of his descendants through his daughters attained the rank of the *mujtahid*: Mīr Sayyid Ḥusayn in the late sixteenth century, and Mīr Muḥammad Bāqir, Mīr Dāmād (d. 1631–32/1041), who conducted the coronation of Shāh Ṣafī in 1629 as the *Shaykh al-Islām* of Isfahan. Another important figure in this period, Bahāᵓ al-Dīn ᶜĀmilī, more commonly referred to as the Shaykh-e Bahāᵓī, was a friend and contemporary of Mīr Dāmād. Although he came to Iran as a young boy with his learned father from Jabal ᶜĀmil, Shaykh-e Bahāᵓī's education, notably in Qazvin, followed the typical eclectic Persian pattern.[112] Shaykh-e Bahāᵓī and Mīr Dāmād are the towering intellectual figures in Shiᶜism of their time. Through them the culture of the Persian clerical estate as the bearers of the philosophical tradition made its maximum impact on the outlook of the hierocracy.

As I have had occasion to remark, Shaykh-e Bahāʾī was prone to mysticism. In addition to being an authority in religious jurisprudence, he was also an accomplished mathematician.[113] His eminent friend Mīr Dāmād was a student of the "rational sciences," and drew directly on the philosophical heritage of Davvānī, and of al-Karakī's opponent, Ghiyāth al-Dīn Manṣūr, and the latter's student, Fakhr al-Dīn Samākī (another outstanding representative of the "catholic" intellectual outlook of the Persian clerical estate).[114] Drawing on this philosophical tradition, Mīr Dāmād founded the school of gnostic philosophy (*ᶜirfān*), the school of Isfahan. But as we shall see presently, the impact of the culture of the mandarins of the clerical estate, i.e., the philosophical tradition, on the outlook of the Shiᶜite hierocracy did not prove lasting. In the subsequent generations, one was not to find *mujtahid*s who, like Bahāʾī and Mīr Dāmād, were also gnostic philosophers.

The Revival of Akhbārī Traditionalism. It was not until the seventeenth century that the Persian clerical estate countered the Shiᶜite doctors' bid for hierocratic domination with a radically different interpretation of Shiᶜism and a counter-ideology of their own. We may speculate about the causes of this delayed reaction. It seems entirely plausible that as neo-Shiᶜites they lacked the self-confidence necessary to challenge the authority of their religious teachers. It is also plausible to suppose that they did not perceive any serious threat emanating from the Shiᶜite doctors. Be that as it may, once the intellectual representatives of the clerical estate set forth to create their distinct variant of Shiᶜism, they rediscovered the rich heritage of the pietistic traditionalism of Qum and reconciled it with gnostic philosophy. In reviving Akhbārī traditionalism, they discarded the legalistic exoteric rationalism of the *mujtahid*s in favor of a gnostic rationalism that advocated innerworldly salvation through the hermeneutic comprehension of the sacred texts.

Early in the seventeenth century, Mullā Muḥammad Amīn Astarābādī (d. 1626–27/1036), encouraged by his teacher Mīrzā Muḥammad ibn ᶜAlī Astarābādī (d. 1619/1028), who was, like his pupil, resident in Mecca, set out to revive the traditionalism of ninth-century Qum, and in his *Fawāʾid al-Madaniyya* fulminated against the innovations of the three famous Buyid theologians, al-Mufīd, al-Murtaḍā, and al-Ṭūsī, and of the ᶜAllāma al-Ḥillī. Astarābādī attacked the *mujtahid*s for applying reason in jurisprudence like the Sunnis, and sought to reestablish sound traditionalism through exclusive reliance on the statements of the Imams. Al-Ḥurr al-ᶜĀmilī (d. 1708–9), the *Shaykh al-Islām* of Mashhad, adhered to Astarābādī's traditionalism and, in his *Wasāʾil al-Shīᶜa*, collected traditions attributed to the Imams that were not found in the four "canonical" books but that he considered reliable.

The Akhbārī school flourished in the seventeenth and eighteenth centuries. It is significant that both its founder, Mullā Muḥammad Amīn Astarābādī, and his master belonged to the Persian "clerical estate." Akhbārī traditionalism was endorsed by the two eminent representatives of gnostic Shiʿism—Majlisī the Elder and Mullā Muḥsin Fayḍ. Therefore, it should be emphasized that, though with the adhesion of al-Ḥurr al-ʿĀmilī, it gained popularity among the Arab Shiʿite *ʿulamāʾ*, and especially in Bahrain, Akhbārī traditionalism first met with the opposition of the *mujtahid*s of Jabal ʿĀmil, one of whom wrote the *Fawāʾid al-Makkiyya* in refutation of Astarābādī's *Fawāʾid al-Madaniyya*.[115]

Two very important aspects of Akhbārī traditionalism served the vested interests of clerical notables in their effort to meet the challenge of the Shiʿite hierocracy for exclusive hierocratic domination. It explicitly challenged the hierocratic authority of the *mujtahid*s, and, by implication, it greatly enhanced the charisma of lineage of the ruling dynasty and of the *sayyid*s who formed the clerical estate.

The Akhbārīs firmly rejected *ijtihād*, thus wreaking havoc with the newly laid foundations of hierocratic authority. For them

> *Ijtihād*, leading to mere *ẓann* [probable opinion, as opposed to certainty] and *taqlīd*, i.e., following the opinions of a *mujtahid*, are forbidden. Every believer must rather follow the *akhbār* of the Imams for whose proper understanding no more than a knowledge of Arabic and the specific terminology of the Imams is needed. If an apparent conflict between two traditions cannot be resolved by the methods prescribed by the Imams, *tawaqquf*, abstention from a decision is obligatory.[116]

It is interesting to note that Mullā Muḥsin Fayḍ, in his treatise devoted to the refutation of *ijtihād*, the *Safīnat al-Najāt* ("Ark of Salvation"), adduces the "authority verse" of the Qurʾan to condemn all recourse to *mujtahid*s. As obedience is due to God, the Prophet, the Imams, and none else, the norms of the sacred law can be directly obtained from the traditions (*akhbār*) of the infallible Imams.[117] Thus Akhbārī traditionalism posed a serious and direct challenge to the principle of legitimacy of hierocratic authority in jurisprudence and consequently hindered the consolidation of a differentiated hierocracy of religious professionals.

Akhbārī traditionalism bore the imprint of the outlook of the clerical estate, which tended to prefer philosophy and hermeneutics and devotional mysticism, centering around the figures of the Imams, to the syllogistic hairsplitting of the jurists. Furthermore, as we shall see presently, it implied an essentially stratified model of the religious community, separating the happy few, the intellectual virtuosi capable of innerworldly salvation through gnosis, and the mass of ordinary believers whose lot was the devotional piety to the figures of the Imams and the observance of their explicitly transmitted instructions. The devotionalism advocated by the proponents of traditionalism made it attractive to ordinary believers, and it grew into a movement of very considerable importance.

The devotional attachment to the Imams also enhanced the hegemony of the *sayyid*s of the clerical estate by strengthening their charisma of lineage, which can safely be assumed to have been on the wane since the suppression of extremism[118] and the advent of Shiʿite *ʿulamāʾ* as the professional specialists in religion. A statement in a historical romance, the *ʿĀlam-ārā-ye Ṣhāh Ismāʿīl*, written in 1675–76/1086 and therefore bearing the broad cultural impact of Akhbārī traditionalism, neatly illustrates the enhancement of the charisma of lineage, hand in hand with the implicit attenuation of legitimacy of juristic authority of the *mujtahid*s. The author reports how Ismāʿīl I desecrated the tomb of Abū Ḥanīfa, exhumed and burned his bones, and buried a dog instead of him. To justify this deed, the author finds it sufficient to state that Abū Ḥanīfa—the founder of one of the four schools of jurisprudence, and, as such, the prototype of a learned jurist—"was not a *sayyid*, and was not a descendant of an Imam (*imām-zādeh*). He did not have nobility; nor did he possess lineage."[119] The *Faḍāʾil al-Sādāt*, written in 1691–92/1103 by a descendant of Mīr Dāmād, is a treatise on the superiority of the *sayyid*s and the necessity of loving them. The excellence of the clerical notables is established on the basis of a number of verses from the Qurʾan and a number of traditions, followed by stories and commentaries. The author first expounds the special position and privileges of the house of the Prophet, and then extends these to the entirety of the *sayyid*s. The Hāshimites are said to be superior to the non-Hāshimites. Hostility toward the offspring of the Prophet is said to bring punishment in the next world, and to be one of the signs of bastardy.[120]

Thus the important political consequence of Akhbārī traditionalism was the enhancement of the charisma of the (purported) descendants of the Imams. In Weberian terms, the social honor conferred by prophetic descent became a most important basis of domination by the estate of clerical notables.[121]

The Anticlerical Policies of Ṣafī and ʿAbbās II and the Revival of Sufism in the Mid-Seventeenth Century. ʿAbbās the Great, whose religious policy accounts for the eclipse of the Niʿmatullāhiyya, the last of the organized Sufi orders, tolerated the individualistic and apolitical Sufism of the literati and of the mystic virtuosi. These, of course, did often preserve their spiritual affiliation to the Sufi traditions. However, these links no longer corresponded to membership of organized congregations, but rather denoted the variety of mystical traditions brought by individual mystics to a common and remarkably eclectic forum. In this manner, Shaykh Muḥammad ʿAlī Muʾadhdhin Khurāsānī, who dedicated a book to Shāh ʿAbbās, represented the Dhahabī traditions,[122] and one of ʿAbbās's secretaries in the bureau of royal domains (*khāṣṣeh*), Āqā Abu'l-Fatḥ Iṣfahānī, appears as a shaykh of the Dhu'l-Nūnī tradition.[123]

There is strong evidence that the Shiʿite *ʿulamāʾ* were disgruntled by the lack of support from Shāh Ṣafī (1629–42) and his *ṣadr*. They deplored the fact that Ṣafī had abandoned the good example of his fathers in propagating Shiᶜism, ceased association with the doctors of religion, and had become lax and tolerant toward Sunnism.[124] It is also in the reign of Ṣafī that we witness the beginning of a brilliant philosophical renaissance, heavily influenced by the currents in the intellectualized mysticism of the literati and the ascetic shaykhs, which produced the tradition of *ᶜirfān* or gnostic philosophy. The reign of ᶜAbbās II (1642–66) marks the apogee of "high" Sufism and of gnostic philosophy.

A key figure in the rise of *ᶜirfān* was Sayyid Ḥusayn, Sulṭān al-ᶜulamā'. He had intermittently held the office of vizier under ᶜAbbās I and Ṣafī. ᶜAbbās II appointed him grand vizier in 1645/1055. Sulṭān al-ᶜulamā' (d. 1654/1064) was an outstanding student of the mystically inclined Bahā' al-Dīn ᶜĀmilī,[125] and as such belonged to the circle of Persian *ᶜulamā'* who sought to unify Shiᶜite religious lore and gnostic philosophy. His appointment to the grand vizierate was resisted by Mīrzā Qāḍī, the *Shaykh al-Islām* of Isfahan, whom ᶜAbbās II dismissed.[126] The dismissal of Mīrzā Qāḍī signified the onset of the decline of the influence of the dogmatic *ᶜulamā'*. The unmistakable predominance of the philosophically oriented proponents of *ᶜirfān* over the dogmatic religious scholars under ᶜAbbās II can be inferred from the biographies of the twenty-five eminent scholars of his reign in a contemporary chronicle.[127] This circle enjoyed the patronage of Sulṭān al-ᶜulamā', and after his death, that of the monarch, ᶜAbbās II. It included Muḥammad Taqī Majlisī the Elder (d. 1659–60/1070), Mullā ᶜAbd al-Razzāq Lāhījī (d.? 1661–62/1072), Mullā Muḥsin Fayḍ (d. 1679–80/1090), Muḥammad Bāqir Sabzavārī (d. 1679/1090)—a student of Sulṭān al-ᶜulamā' and a close friend of Majlisī the Elder—and Sabzavārī's student and brother-in-law Āqā Ḥusayn Khwānsārī (d. 1689/1099), referred to in one source as the *qibla-ye ᶜurafā'* (Mecca of the gnostics).[128] ᶜAbbās II appointed Muḥammad Bāqir Sabzavārī the *Shaykh al-Islām* of Isfahan, and commissioned Majlisī the Elder to write a commentary in Persian on Ibn Bābūya's *Man la-Yaḥḍuruhu'l-Faqīh* which bore the resoundingly royalist title of *Lavāmiᶜ Ṣāḥibqarānī*. Above all, ᶜAbbās II lavished royal favors on Mullā Muḥsin Fayḍ, for whom he ordered his physician, Saᶜīd Qumī—himself another member of the gnostic philosophers—to build a Sufi *tekke* in Isfahan in 1658/1068.[129] The Sufi virtuosi were also respected and favored by ᶜAbbās II, whom his official historian at one point calls *Shāh-e darvīsh-dūst* (the dervish-loving Shah). In 1660/1070, he visited the recluse Sufi and philosopher Mullā Rajab-ᶜAlī Tabrīzī, and the mystic Darvīsh Muḥammad Ṣāliḥ Lunbānī, for whom he built a *tekke* on a choice cite requisitioned for the purpose. In 1663/1073 he paid another visit to the convent of Darvīsh Muḥammad Ṣāliḥ.[130]

ᶜAbbās II's hostility toward the Shiᶜite jurists was stronger and more systematically a part of his policy of autocratic royal centralization. The royal slaves (sing. *ghulām*) had been the predominant element in Safavid military organization since the time of ᶜAbbās I. ᶜAbbās II used the elite slave corps to strengthen centralized control over the administrative apparatus, appointing twenty-three or possibly twenty-five *ghulāms* as provincial governors (out of the total of thirty-seven gubernatorial positions).[131] Consistently with this policy, ᶜAbbās would not tolerate an independent hierocratic center of power within his state, and displayed open hostility toward Shiᶜite religious dignitaries.[132]

The microscopic picture of the society of the city of Yazd in the second and third quarters of the seventeenth century found in *Jāmiᶜ Mufīdī* allows us to appreciate the incidence of Sufism among the ascetics[133] and among the literati.[134] Consonantly with the outlook of its bearers, Sufism in this period consisted of an intellectualized eclectic blending of various mystical traditions. These merged together into a unified form of "high" Sufism which bore the imprint of its bearers: the ascetic virtuosi and the literati, the most prominent among whom were a group of philosophically oriented *ᶜulamāʾ*. As one would expect, the latter group sought to unify Sufism and Shiᶜism. For instance, Majlisī the Elder, having professed spiritual allegiance to the Dhahabī tradition, cites Ḥaydar Āmulī's dictum regarding the identity of Shiᶜism and Sufism, and Ibn Abī Jumhūr al-Aḥsāʾī's statement that there is no difference between the mosque and the *khāniqāh*, and finally invokes the authority of his renowned teacher Shaykh Bahāʾ al-Dīn ᶜĀmilī to defend Sufism and mystical gnosis against the "formal science" (*ᶜilm-e rasmī*) of the dogmatic *ᶜulamāʾ*.[135]

The Clash of Cultural Outlooks and Norms of Authority. As the preceding pages indicate, the impact of the Persian intellectual tradition upon the cultural outlook of the Shiᶜite hierocracy did not consist in gradual mutual assimilation and uniform osmotic permeation. Rather, it produced a sharp rift. The synthesis represented by Shaykh-e Bahāʾī and Mīr Dāmād did not prove lasting, and the two hostile divisions persisted until the final extinction and expurgation of the proponents of the philosophical tradition from the ranks of the Shiᶜite hierocracy. In the seventeenth century, the clash of the two irreconcilable outlooks first became conspicuous with the hostility of the strict religious professionals and jurists to the great philosopher Mullā Ṣadrā Shīrāzī (d. 1640/1050). Already before the death of his master, Mīr Dāmād, Mullā Ṣadrā came under the fierce attack of some of the members of the Shiᶜite hierocracy for his heretical—because gnostic/philosophical—views.[136] He was excommunicated and countered by a vehement attack on the literalist or "official" (*rasmī*) *ᶜulamāʾ* in the only one of his treatises written in Persian.

Mullā Ṣadrā's conception of *ᶜilm* (knowledge) ultimately as pure existence, informed as it was by a fundamental premise of his philosophical system, the identity of the intellect and the intelligible,[137] diverged radically from the dogmatic notion of *ᶜilm* as the religious and jurisprudential sciences taught and studied by the literalist *ᶜulamāʾ*. As regards religion specifically, he considered the object of studying the revealed and transmitted texts—the Qurʾan and the *ḥadīth*—to arrive at their inner meaning through *hermeneutic interpretation*, and not through the pedestrian syllogistic logic of the literalist theologians and jurists.[138] This objective could be undertaken only after the acquisition of insight through the "science of the self" (*ᶜilm-e nafs*), of which the orthodox "official" (*rasmī*) *ᶜulamāᵓ* are devoid.[139] But above all, the head-on collision with orthodox dogmatism comes with Mullā Ṣadrā's much highlighted conception of *maᶜād* (resurrection; return to origin; afterlife), which is intimately connected with the "knowledge of the (real) self" (*maᶜrifat-e nafs*).[140] Mullā Ṣadrā sets his innerworldly notion of *maᶜād* as the intellect's (mystical) cognition of origin and destination—beginning and end[141]—against the dogmatic conception of *maᶜād* as otherworldly physical resurrection, which constituted one of the five pillars or principles of the Shiᶜite creed. A generation later Qāḍī Saᶜīd Qumī devoted his *Kilīd-e Bihisht* ("The Key of Paradise") to a systematic exposition of *mabdaᵓ* (origin) and *maᶜād* (destination, end, salvation) within the framework of the philosophy of the school of Isfahan, totally bypassing the Shiᶜite dogma.[142]

As an anecdote reporting a conversation between Mīr Dāmād and Mullā Ṣadrā indicates,[143] not all the members of the philosophical group were as blunt and unbending in stating their views. In fact, Mullā ᶜAbd al-Razzāq Lāhījī, one of Mullā Ṣadrā's most eminent students, took a much more conciliating attitude; his *Gawhar-e Murād* is a systematic statement of the principles of the Shiᶜite creed within a philosophical framework comprising the "knowledge of the self" and the "knowledge of God" or "psychology" and theology.[144] Substantively, however, with Lāhījī, as Madelung points out, we reach the culmination of the development in which rational theology (*kalām*) is entirely replaced by philosophy, and the doctrines of the philosophers are invariably preferred to those of the theologians.[145]

In his short polemical tract *Rafᶜ al-Fitna*, Mullā Muḥsin Fayḍ, having stated "I am the follower [*muqallid*] of the Qurᵓan and the Prophet," distinguishes between two sciences: the exoteric science of *ᶜilm-e ẓāhir*, consisting of the science of the sacred law and of the path (*tarīqat*), and the esoteric science (*ᶜilm-e bāṭin*), consisting of the science of truth. The latter is the true science, and is also interpreted as *ḥikmat*, from which the "knowledge of origin and destination" can be obtained. Fayḍ then attacks the jurists whose objective is said to be the attainment of fame and worldly dominion over the masses, and who are "in reality ignoramuses but in the eyes of the ignorants and the masses, the learned [*ᶜulamāᵓ*]."[146]

In a perceptive passage written some twenty years after Mullā Ṣadrā's death, Du Mans mentions two antagonistic groups of clerics: the *fuqahāᵓ* (jurists) and the *ᶜulamāᵓ*. It is significant that Du Mans reserves the term *ᶜulamāᵓ* for the gnostic/philosophical group, a fact reflecting their predominance under ᶜAbbās II (more exactly, in 1660). The *fuqahāᵓ* are presented as literalist explainers of ceremonies, rituals, and obligations and the expounders of a paradise with *ḥūrīs*, while the *ᶜulamā͗* are those who say the Qur͗an has seven layers of veils (*haft pardeh*), and who lay their emphasis on generalities (*kullīyyāt*): "ils veulent partout des démonstrations géometriques pour l'unité d'un Dieu. . . ." The *ᶜulamā͗* consider the *fuqahā͗* "bipedal animals" (*ḥeyvān-e dō-pā*); the *fuqahā͗* consider the *ᶜulamā͗* "heretics" (*mulḥid*).[147]

A decade later we find revealing evidence concerning the directly political dimension of the struggle. The clash between hierocratic authority, deriving from religious learning, and the charismatic domination of the clerical notables, resting on holy descent, is brought to light:

> The learned scholar wants to be confirmed at the head of the gathering as the leader, and the *sayyid* [clerical notable] claims to be more eager than all for the attainment of that position. The scholar would submit that the chain of filiation to the House of Prophecy and Imamate lacked solidity without association with knowledge and practice, and that the Lord of the Sacred Law would not include descent without merit in the circle of validity. . . . The *sayyid* would proffer that the comprehension of truth by means of *ijtihād* is possible for everyone but belonging to the fruitful tree of Imamate and Caliphate is never possible for a creature through effort and endeavor.

Having thus described a typical scene of confrontation between a Shiᶜite jurist and a clerical notable in the early 1670s, the author severely criticizes Majlisī the Younger for taking the side of the *ᶜulamā͗* and being hostile to the *sayyid*s, for whom love and friendship is an incumbent religious duty.[148] His own view as a spokesman for the clerical notables is stated clearly:

> I believe that the *sayyid*s are offspring of the masters [*khwājeh-zādehgān*], and others are offsprings of slaves [*bandeh-zādehgān*] and if a notable [*khwajeh-zādeh*] be, hypothetically speaking, bereft of religious sciences, [even then] how could the son of a slave with utmost learning boast of equality with him? This is a bounty from God. . . . If the *sayyid* is adorned by the ornament of science . . . his superiority is a matter of consensus [*ijmāᶜ*], and no one can dispute it.[149]

5.3.4 The Final Onslaught and Triumph of the Hierocracy under the Leadership of Majlisī

Suleymān (1666–94) disowned ᶜAbbās II's secularism and showed an interest in religious affairs.[150] He maintained reasonable relations with the proponents of the philosophical outlook for the most part of his reign, favoring Aqā Ḥusayn Khwānsārī (d. 1688/1099) and entrusting him with various assignments.[151] Khwānsārī's son, Āqā Jamāl (d. 1710/1125), also acquired great fame, and his student, Shaykh Jaᶜfar Kamareh-ī (d. 1703/1105), became the *Shaykh al-Islām* of Isfahan under Shāh Sulṭān-Ḥusayn.[152] These two men were perhaps the last important representatives of the gnostic/philosophical outlook within the Shiᶜite hierocracy not to suffer persecution.

However, Suleymān did imprison the gnostic philosopher Qāḍī Saᶜīd Qumī for a period in the fortress of Alamūt.[153] Furthermore, his relationship with the dogmatic party was very good. He allowed himself to be courted by them and is known to have invited Shiᶜite doctors to take up residence in Isfahan.[154] He invited a relative of Majlisī, Mawlānā Mīrzā Shīrvānī (d. 1687–88/1099), from Najaf to Isfahan and purchased a house for him.[155] Above all, Suleymān supported Muḥammad Bāqir Majlisī. In fact, under Suleymān, the dogmatic party was already gaining the upper hand, even though its decisive triumph came only with the succession of Shāh Sulṭān-Ḥusayn in 1694.

Briefly, Du Mans's *fuqahā*ʾ can be characterized as dogmatic reactionaries who violently opposed mysticism and who firmly rejected philosophy as the "innovation" (*bidᶜa*, a highly pejorative term) of the Greek infidels. Intellectually, they advocated retrenchment into strictly religious learning. Their attack on the gnostic philosophers in the hierocracy had already begun under ᶜAbbās II. Mullā Muḥammad Ṭāhir Qumī, the *Shaykh al-Islām* of Qum, who lived to be 100, was "extremely bigoted against the Sufis and against whomever did not take part in the Friday prayer." He attacked Muḥammad Taqī Majlisī and Mullạ Khalīl Qazvīnī, both of whom were favored by Abbās II.[156] His intolerant attacks redoubled under Suleymān. Under Suleymān, dogmatic reaction found a number of powerful adherents who gathered under the leadership of Muḥammad Bāqir Majlisī (d. 1699/1111), the son of the eminent representative of gnostic Shiᶜism who dramatically changed his allegiance to the opposing camp and wrested the "Shaykh al-Islāmate" of Isfahan out of the philosophical party's hands for himself. The dramatic *volte-face* by Majlisī the Younger signified that the imprint of the doctors of the hierocracy upon the mind of the Persian recruits from the clerical estate was to prevail. And it was to prevail with a vengeance.

Having changed sides, Majlisī was too well aware of his opponents' most valuable moral asset, and too intelligent to leave them in possession of their entire ideological armory. He realized that there were two distinct components to the outlook of the clerical notables and their intellectual spokesmen: Akhbārī traditionalism, which resonated strongly with popular devotion to the figures of the Imams; and high Sufism and gnostic philosophy, which were inevitably elitist and could only appeal to the literate. Majlisī set out to detach these two components, to absorb the popular Akhbārī-inspired devotional component, and to isolate the gnostic mystical/philosophical outlook and single it out for fatal attack. With the spread of Akhbārī traditionalism, the twelve Imams as historical figures and their lives and sayings had come to the foreground of religious discussion and practice. Legends had grown around the figures of the Imams who had become objects of intense devotional attachment. Majlisī, who, as we know, was ready to exploit all religious trends, could be expected to attempt to wrest this one from the possession of his opponents. He in fact indicated his sympathy for and capitalized on this Akhbārī-inspired popular sentiment, and devoted many books to the lives of the Prophet, his daughter, Fāṭima, and the Imams: the "Fourteen Immaculates."[157]

Other members of the dogmatic party adopted the same strategy. Mullā Muḥammad Ṭāhir Qumī, for instance, confirmed his adherence to traditionalism while detaching it from both Sufi mysticism and gnostic philosophy, and giving it a new antirational bias. To attack the philosophical and Sufi orientation of gnostic Shiᶜism, Mullā Muḥammad Ṭāhir also found it convenient to attack rationalism in jurisprudence[158] and to consider commentaries on the Qurᵓan so impious as to earn their authors a place in the fire of hell. This was so because "repeated Traditions have expounded that the commentators on the Book of God are the House of the Prophet, Peace be upon Them, and that their followers are the saved."[159]

Like so much else associated with Majlisī's achievement, this development had far-reaching consequences. It meant that Akhbārī traditionalism could be largely purged of its seventeenth-century association with gnostic philosophy, and appropriated by orthodox Shiᶜism. It is true that such association could be revived, as it was by Shaykh Aḥmad Aḥsāᵓī in the early nineteenth century. But it is equally true that the fruits of Akhbārī traditionalism in the form of collections of *ḥadīth* was fully appropriated by orthodox Shiᶜism. As we shall see, when Akhbārism was "overcome" by the *Uṣūlī* movement in the closing decades of the eighteenth century, the collections of traditions such as Fayḍ's *Wāfī*, al-Ḥurr al-ᶜĀmilī's *Wasāᵓil*, and Majlisī's own *Biḥār* served as invaluable and indispensable sources upon which the value-rational ingenuity of the *Uṣūlī* jurists in creation of new legal norms could be exercised. In fact, it does not seem to be an exaggeration to say that the accumulation of traditions in this period was a precondition for the revival of jurisprudence, which aimed both at the harmonization of the traditions as normative stereotypes and the deduction of further positive (*waḍᶜī*) norms.

Returning to the immediate historical context and strategy of Majlisī and Qumī, it is hardly surprising that the dogmatic reactionaries in their camp invariably accused their opponents of heresy and of Sufism. It was in these terms that Shaykh ᶜAlī b. Muḥammad al-ᶜĀmilī, (d. 1691–92/1103), an immigrant to Isfahan, attacked Fayḍ and Sabzavārī. Al-Ḥurr al-ᶜAīmilī, the *Shaykh al-Islām* of Mashhad, another immigrant doctor, used his specialty to adduce 1,000 traditions against the Sufis. Mullā Aḥmad Tunī, an *ᶜālim* from Khurasan, joined the struggle on the side of the dogmatists, and Niᶜmatullāh Jazāᵓirī of Shūshtar (d. 1700/1112) wrote a posthumous attack on Shaykh-e Bahāᵓī for his association with the "heretics, Sufis and lovers—[*ᶜushshāq*], i.e., those believed in the Sufi doctrine of divine love."[160] Above all, Majlisī the Younger, having made some qualified statements justifying the Sufis,[161] finally took pains to explain his father's proneness to Sufism as insincere and tactical, and embarked on a wholesale attack on the mystical tradition.[162] It should be noted that the party of dogmatic reaction could also enlist the support of the Shiᶜite *ᶜulamāᵓ* abroad. Thus

Shaykh ʿAlī b. Muḥammad (fl. 1660s and 1670s/1070s and 1080s) wrote polemics against both Mullā Muḥsin Fayḍ and Mullā Muḥammad Bāqir Sabzavārī.[163]

It is highly significant that, hand in hand with the accusations of heresy and Sufism, went the accusation of faulty formal comportment in different rituals and prayers and criticisms for incorrect Arabic pronunciation. In these finicky criticisms of the philosophical party for using the incorrect vowels, "like the masses," and insistence on ritualistically proper, guttural pronunciation in an alien language,[164] we can see the manifestations of ritualized style of the hierocracy, which, since the beginning of the nineteenth century, has been captured in the stereotype of the hypocritical and obscurantist *mullā*, notably by the poet Qāʾānī.[165]

Though written much later in the nineteenth century, Riḍā Qulī Khān Hidāyat's statement on the suppression of Sufism and of *ʿirfān* is worth quoting for its identification of the salient elements of late Safavid "high" Sufism. After reporting the destruction of the convent of Mullā Muḥsin Fayḍ and the massacre of its Sufis by the order of Shāh Sulṭān-Ḥusayn, Hidāyat remarks:

> As the foundation of the livelihood of the Men of the Path came to an end, they called the Lords of Asceticism dry-headed, and named the Men of Investigation, imitators, the Philosophers, innovators, and the Men of Gnosis [*ʿurafāʾ*] inventors. They prevented the Men of Reflection from the remembrance [of God—*dhikr*] and tore asunder the books of the Sufi *silsilas*.[166]

With the decline of gnostic philosophy taught in the *madrasas* of Isfahan and Shiraz and the devastation of the cities by the Afghan invaders after 1722, recluse Sufis remained on the scene as the only surviving bearers of the mystical tradition of "high" Sufism.[167]

Hand in hand with the victory of the dogmatic party over the proponents of gnostic Shiʿism went the institutional consolidation of the Shiʿite hierocracy. The ascendancy of dogmatic religious professionals was signaled by Majlisī's appointment in 1687/1098 as the *Shaykh al-Islām* of the capital, Isfahan.[168] A Shiʿite hierocracy, differentiated from the caesaropapist state though still in uneasy coexistence with the countervailing power of the clerical notables, had come into being. The institutional consolidation of this hierocracy over the decade following Majlisī's death is attested to by the creation of the office of *Mullā-bāshī* as its head:

> On the last Sunday of the month of Rabīʿ al-Thānī of the year 1124 [June 15, 1712], the Illustrious Vice-gerency and Exalted Majesty ordered that His Excellency the *Mujtahid* of the Age, Amīr Muḥammad Bāqir, may God protect him from harm, be the leader [*raʾīs*] of all the *ʿulamāʾ*, and the religious notables, and the dignitaries, and that in the assembly of His Majesty no one have priority over the *Mujtahid* of the Age in seating or standing. That he deliver the reports, and that everyone give precedence and priority to that

most learned of the *ᶜulamā*ʾ. In short, that none of the *ṣadr*s and the *ᶜulamā*ʾ and the *sayyids* have precedence over him in any matter.[169]

On his tombstone, Mīr Muḥammad Bāqir Khātūn-ābādī is identified as the first rector of the *madrasa* in *Chahār-bāgh*, the tutor of Shāh Sulṭān-Ḥusayn, and the *Mullā-bāshī*. After the death of Mīr Muḥammad Bāqir in 1715/1127, "the learned Mullā Muḥammad Ḥusayn, son of Mullā Shāh-Muḥammad of Tabriz, was appointed *Mullā-bāshī*." [170]

In view of the caesaropapist authority of the ruler, and given the patrimonial nature of Safavid government, the designations of *Mullā-bāshī* or chaplain of the royal household seems to have been the logical title for the position that Majlisī had in fact created for himself as the *Shaykh al-Islām* of Isfahan, which subsequently became a distinct office—namely, the head of an institutionally differentiated but heterocephalous hierocracy.

5.4 Sociological Properties of Gnostic and Orthodox Shiᶜism as Determinants of the Final Consolidation of the Shiᶜite Hierocracy

The dogmatic party had a tremendous advantage over the proponents of gnostic Shiᶜism in emphasizing and exploiting the charismatic quality and hierocratic aspect of religious authority. The attainment of gnosis is inevitably the prerogative of the spiritual elite, and its pursuit is largely an asocial matter. Routine professional guidance of the masses to attain salvation appears as religiously based worldly dominion, and is seen as motivated by worldly ambition, and love of power and fame.[171] "Know that the Traditions in derogation of the world, of the seeking of fame among men, and of sociability with men [*al-istīnās bi'l-nās*] are many and famous," wrote Mullā Ṣadrā in his *Breaking of the Idols of Ignorance*.[172] With its uncompromising intellectualism and indifference to the pedestrian religious needs and concerns of the masses, gnostic Shiᶜism of the seventeenth century militated against the formation of a popularly rooted hierocracy, and, faced with the rivalry of a clamoring dogmatic party from within the hierocracy, was doomed to failure once its supreme political patronage was withdrawn.

The comparison between gnostic Shiᶜism and Lutheranism is instructive in this regard: "Luther was completely indifferent towards the organization of the church as long as the Word could be spread in purity." [173] Mullā Ṣadrā would go further, and consider in political interest on the part of the *ᶜulamā*ʾ in the maintenance of hierocratic domination a deflection from and hindrance of the true interpretation of the Word and hence salvation through gnosis. He condemns hierocratic domination outright as *worldly* domination and as such indistinct from political domination. The legitimation of all hierocratic office is radically undermined.

By contrast, the dogmatic party under the leadership of Muḥammad Bāqir Majlisī could and did make a determined effort to consolidate the hierocratic domination over the masses. Majlisī's massive output of religious writings reached down to the masses and succeeded in capturing their imagination and enlisting their loyalty. For the philosophers' incomprehensible notion of innerworldly *maᶜād*, he produced fantastically detailed pictures of paradise and hell and lurid accounts of the questioning of the dead in their graves; for their abstract discussions of God as "necessary existence" he substituted simplistic and rigidly dogmatic statements of the tenets of the Shīᶜite creed.

Mullā Ṣadrā fulminated against the wandering dervishes, the *qalandar*s, and expressed concern that not only the masses (*ᶜawāmm*) but also "men of crafts and industry" were leaving their occupations to follow these Sufi mystagogues.[174] But given the pattern of social distribution of knowledge at his time, his gnostic philosophy, even in the form popularized by some of his disciples such as ᶜAbd al-Razzāq Lāhījī, could at best have an impact on some of the more literate "men of crafts and industry" and could not hope to compete with the *qalandar* mystagogues and thaumaturgists in enlisting the masses. The group that could do this was the dogmatic party of the Shiᶜite hierocracy. It could do so by institutionalizing thaumaturgy and miracle working in a slightly sublimated form, by "shiᶜitizing" popular rituals, by incorporating a large body of popular superstitions, and, finally, by stating the main tenets of the Shiᶜite creed in dogmatic terms easily graspable by the illiterate masses.

Along with the dogmatic party's dissemination of Shiᶜite dogma, sacred history, and devotional blueprints went the ritualistic stereotypification of religious functions—inordinate attention to the appropriateness of specific prayers for specific days of the year and for specific occasions, emphasis on the correctness of accent and Arabic pronunciation, on the correct number of ritualistic repetitions of specific verses of the Qurᵓan, and the like. Nor did the religious professional (*mullā*s) hesitate to dabble in the important popular parareligious practices such as charm writing (*duᶜā nivīsī*), in addition to the less obviously quasi-magical and very widespread practice of *istikhāra* (consultation of the Qurᵓan to determine whether or not to undertake a specific action), which they monopolized.[175] These practices amounted to deliberate obfuscation of the rational content of communication between the religious professional and the layman in favor of the ritualization of its form, which had tremendous appeal to the religious propensities of the illiterate masses. This ritualization, together with the quasi-magical functions, greatly enhanced the "hierocratic"—as distinct from the purely juristic—aspect of the *ᶜulamā*ᵓ's authority over the mass of Shiᶜite believers.

Gnostic Shiᶜism implied a sharp religious stratification into the spiritual élite (*khawāṣṣ*) and the masses (*ᶜawāmm*). The gnostic perception of the face of God in all beings was a privilege from which the masses were barred.[176] Given the widespread illiteracy and the skewed distribution of knowledge, any feasible social arrangement to regulate the relationship between the (true) men of religion and the masses would involve a structure of extracognitive or extraspiritual domination, which, as we have seen, Mullā Ṣudrā firmly rejected in his vehement criticism of the popular Sufi shaykhs and of the worldly *ᶜulamāʾ* of the surface or "huskers" (*ᶜulamāʾ al-qishr*).[177] By contrast, religious stratification was far from posing an insoluble problem for Majlisī and his party. On the contrary, it was used as the basis for the creation of a firm and lasting structure of hierocratic domination. Though heartily contemptuous of the masses,[178] Majlisī had no scruples about stooping to conquer.

Though for strategic reasons he was not unwont to try to distort and preempt positively valued terms such as *ᶜārif* (man of gnosis or knowledge) from the philosophers' vocabulary,[179] Majlisī attacked the philosophers in his words as well as his deeds: philosophy—this irreligious "innovation" of the Greek infidels—implied a presumptuous use of human reason when all the necessary and correct guidelines were laid down for mankind in the teachings of the Prophet and the Imams; it was therefore reprehensible. It goes without saying that mystical notions were heretical and Sufism a foul and hellish growth.[180]

Mullā Muḥammad Ṭāhir Qumī was even more vehement in his attacks and more insistent in coupling the twin anathemas (*kufr*) of Sufism and philosophy. He asserted that the doctrine of the philosophers was "contrary to the religion of Islam and the content of the Verses of the Qurʾan." The caliph al-Maʾmūn took the books of philosophy from the king of the Franks and circulated them among the Sunnis. Fārābī and Ibn Sīnā (Avicenna), who cultivated this form of irreligion, were, furthermore, afflicted with melancholia. Qumī continues his *ad hominem* attack against the philosophers by pointing out that Ibn Sīnā was known to be a wine drinker, and Fārābī played musical instruments well. The Shiᶜites, by contrast, are said to have opposed the irreligious philosophers, and are commended for having killed the great mystic Suhrawardī in Aleppo because of his attention to philosophy.[181]

On the constructive side, Majlisī's efforts included the codification of religious and parareligious practices of the Shiᶜite religious professionals. His manual *Mishkāt al-Anwār* begins with the correct manners of reading the Qurʾan (including the proper preliminary ablution, the manner of concluding), and moves on to prescribe numerous prayers (sing. *duᶜa*) to cure numerous illnesses, toothaches, headaches, and the like, and to prevent earthquakes and natural disasters. He ends with the discussion of the appropriate invocations (*adhkār*) at the end of the daily prayers. In *Zād al-Maᶜād*, he provides religious professionals with a compendium of supererogatory prayers prescribed for specific days of the year. Finally, he attempts to capture some territory for the religious professionals from the practicioners in the neighboring parareligious fields of astronomy and divination. In *Ikhtiyārāt*, basing his prescriptions on a mixture of considerations drawn from astrology, geography, and sacred history, he determines the appropriateness of the days of the year for specific activities, the significance of natural and astral phenomena, the proper times, places, and conditions of copulation, the hours of *istikhāra*, and the days and manner of seeking help from the "men of the invisible world" (*rijāl al-ghayb*). It is interesting that in conjunction with this last topic, Majlisī has to admit the absence of reference in the traditions gathered by the Shiᶜite scholars to the "men of the invisible world," but opines that they must be the souls of the fourteen Immaculates (the Prophet, Fāṭima, and the twelve Imams), and of the prophets Khiḍr and Elīās, who are identified by the Sufis as the "poles" (of the universe; sing. *Quṭb*).[182] Here we gain the first glimpse into Majlisī's strategy for undermining popular Sufism through the preemptive appropriation of its notions. We shall see in the following chapter how this strategy is followed to appropriate the Sufi shaykhs' function of divine intercession exclusively and in a sublimated fashion for the vividly depicted, even though otherworldly, Imams.

In view of its intrinsic sociological properties, the eventual triumph of Shiᶜite orthodoxy is not surprising. With the accession of Shāh Sulṭān-Ḥusayn, in whose coronation Majlisī took the leading part, the triumph of the Shiᶜite hierocracy became definitive. Secure in his office in the Safavid state and with great influence over the new pious king, Sulṭān-Ḥusayn, Majlisī immediately embarked on a vigorous religious policy which was inaugurated with a strict prohibition of wine drinking and banishment of the Sufis of Isfahan, and proceeded with the large-scale conversion of the minorities, earning him the title of *Dīn-parvar*—the nurturer of religion.[183] He also vehemently opposed gnostic Shiᶜism and firmly demanded doctrinal compliance with his orthodox statements of Shiᶜism. Thus Shiᶜite orthodoxy, as initially embodied in his writings, was born.

Majlisī's writings have enjoyed tremendous popularity through the nineteenth century down to the present time, and there is hardly a feature of contemporary Shiᶜism that is not either fully depicted or at least presaged in his writings. It must be admitted that it is with this hindsight that I have talked of the "triumph" of the Shiᶜite hierocracy under the leadership of Majlisī. But to avoid any misrepresentation of the course of events, it should be pointed out that at the close of the Safavid era, the triumph of the hierocracy does not appear as definitive. It is true that Majlisī did institute the persecution of the gnostic philosophers alongside the Sufis—not distinguishing between the two—and that their persecution continued after Majlisī's death, as is epitomized in the tragic banishment of the philosopher Muḥammad Ṣādiq Ardistānī (d. 1721–22/1134), leading to the death of his children, and in the trepidations of many another gnostic philosopher in the early decades of the eighteenth century.[184] Nevertheless, Ḥazīn's valuable autobiography leaves us in no doubt about the extensiveness of the incidence of the gnostic-philosophical outlook among the literati of the first decades of the eighteenth century.[185]

Be that as it may, the gnostic Shiᶜism of the philosophers of the school of Isfahan, severely debilitated by Majlisī, was forced after his death to subsist *outside* the Shiᶜite hierocracy, and was thus perhaps doomed to virtual extinction. After decades of devastation and civil war in the eighteenth century, from dominating the main stream of Shiᶜism in the seventeenth century, gnostic philosophy of the school of Isfahan was carried to the nineteenth century as a rivulet, owing its continued flow in some measure to the unusual longevity and energy of its sole important exponent in Isfahan, Mullā ᶜAlī Nūrī (d. 1830–31/1246); and, despite the brilliance of Mullā Hādī Sabzavārī (d. 1869–70/1289) in the nineteenth century, it ceased to be a significant element in the culture of the Shiᶜite Iran in the second half of the nineteenth century.

Though not necessarily with the foresight of helping our exposition by the provision of a felicitous contrast, Mīrzā Muḥammad Riḍā Ṣahbā Qumsheh-ī, a contemporary of Mullā Hādī and the foremost bearer of the philosophical tradition after his death, and Mullā ᶜAlī Kanī, the most prominent member of the Shiᶜite hierocracy in Tehran, died on the same day in 1888–98/1306. A day of national mourning was declared for the passing away of the *mujtahid* and thousands took part in his funeral procession. But very few were seen taking part in the funeral procession of the philosopher, aside from his forlorn student and successor Mīrzā Abu'l-Ḥasan Jilveh (d. 1897/1314).[186]

Let us conclude by contrasting the (partial) failure of al-Karakī's attempt to take over the administrative-religious-legal complex of institutions on the basis of a Shiᶜite political ethic in the first decades of the sixteenth century, with Majlisī's success in the consolidation of a Shiᶜite hierocracy of religious professionals in the last decades of the seventeenth. Al-Karakī's weapon was the support of the monarch at the apex of the body politic. Majlisī, on the other hand, used Shiᶜism *qua* religion and irrespective of the specific content of its political ethic as a weapon for the enhancement of differentiated hierocratic domination directly upon the masses, without the intermediary of the state as the apparatus of political domination. It was on the basis of the groundwork laid by Majlisī that a Shiᶜite hierocracy, with firm roots among the people and therefore with a power base independent of the state, could emerge with the restoration of peace and stability under the Qājārs (1785–1925). This created the basic preconditions for the repeated occurrence of instances of hierocracy-state conflict, which are rare in the "caesaropapist" political tradition of Islam.

CHAPTER SIX

From Sectarian Shiᶜism to Shiᶜism as a National Religion

6.1 The Ascendancy of the Shiᶜite Doctors and the Containment of Mahdistic Chiliasm

The suppression of millenarian extremism among the Qizilbāsh by the Safavid rulers at the political level has its religious counterpart in the efforts of the Shiᶜite doctors to contain mahdistic chiliasm at the doctrinal level by means of religious instruction. To assert their authority in the regulation of the religious life of their lay congregations, the Shiᶜite *ᶜulamā*ʾ had to deal with the mahdistic tenet included in their doctrinal heritage.

As we have seen, in the tenth/fourth century two separate concepts of imamate and mahdihood were welded together, and the Hidden Imam emerged as a bipartite figure: as the Imam of the Age (*Imām-e Zamān*) he was said to fulfill the function of imamate, while as the Mahdi and the *Qāʾim* (redresser) he assumed the role of the paraclete. In the late tenth or early eleventh century, al-Mufīd put the return of the dead (*rajᶜa*) and the rising (*qiyām*) of the Mahdi together as the prelude to Resurrection (*Qiyāma*).[1] The notion of the Mahdi was accepted on the basis of the tradition attributed to the Prophet, which predicts the appearance of one of his descendants who "will fill the earth with equity and justice as it is filled with oppression and tyranny."[2] Al-Ṭūsī's account of the return of the Mahdi is nevertheless completely apocalyptic, and sets the apocalyptic tone for the subsequent Shiᶜite works on the topic, including those of the Safavid period. They tell us of the reign of total chaos and tyranny, the appearance of the *Dajjāl* (Antichrist) and of Sufyānī, the return of Imām Ḥusayn and of Jesus, and the armed rising of the entire believing community under the Mahdi's banner.[3]

Furthermore, from the European sources of the late Safavid period, we hear of an astonishing practice which must be presumed to have perpetuated some kind of apocalyptic mood. Though not as zealously expectant as the Sarbidārs, who sent the caparisoned horse to the gate of their city to accommodate the expected Mahdi every day, the Safavid monarchs kept a bevy of well-groomed horses in the richly endowed "stable of the Lord of the Age" (*ṭavīleh-ye ṣāḥib al-zamān*[4]) which were strictly reserved for his use upon *parousia*, but which were marched through the streets of the cities on ceremonial occasions. Two of the horses are reported to have been harnessed all the time, one for the Lord of the Age himself, the second for Jesus, who would also appear in his company. Chardin mentions the existence of the stable of the Lord of the Age not only in Isfahan, but also in Bandar ᶜAbbās, which allows us to infer that horses must have been maintained for his possible use in the major cities.[5]

Despite the retention of apocalyptic tenets and the institution of such practices, how can Safavid Shiᶜism be said to have contained the impulse to chiliasm? The statement of the Shiᶜite doctrine tended to do so, to some extent, through the obviation of the plausibility of the occurrence of the millennium in the present or foreseeable future. Already in the eleventh century, al-Ṭūsī had prohibited the fixing of a date for the reappearance of the Mahdi.[6] In the twelfth century, the author of *Kitāb al-Naqḍ* again ruled out the possibility of cabalistic determination of the time of *parousia*.[7] Furthermore, the juxtaposition of the *parousia* to otherworldly physical resurrection relegated it into as distant a future as possible. Thus Majlisī gave significance to the reign of the Mahdi at the end of time primarily as the earthly prelude to Resurrection and the Day of Judgment.[8] Du Mans's account of popular religious beliefs confirms that this association was as close in the mind of the Shiᶜites as in their religious writings.[9]

Nevertheless, the tenet of the return of the Mahdi itself remains potentially chiliastic. What was decisive for the containment of the chiliastic impulse was not so much the dogma as the attitude of its interpreters: the ascendancy of the Shiᶜite hierocracy assured the continued suppression of the chiliastic impulse, which, under their hierocratic control over the interpretation of dogma, ritual conduct, and prayer, was sublimated into pietistic passive expectancy. Al-Ṭūsī cites a tradition from the sixth Imam to establish that the reward for believing in the reappearance of the rule of the house of Muhammad is tantamount to martyrdom in the company of the Mahdi.[10] Consonantly with this attitude, subsequent Twelver Shiᶜite ethical manuals came to enjoin the virtue of *intiẓār* (patient expectation) of the Mahdi, which is interpreted as a sign of faith (*īmān*), and becomes a stabilized element in the devotional piety of believing Shiᶜites.[11]

The mahdihood of the Hidden Imam was only one aspect of the doctrine of occultation. In the heyday of chiliasm and before the consolidation of the Shiᶜite hierocracy—i.e., the early Safavid period—this aspect predominated, rendering the doctrine highly chiliastic. Qāḍī Nūrullāh Shūshtarī, in his section on holy places, mentions an island—the Jazīra-ye Akhḍar—fifteen days away from Andalusia, on which the Hidden Imam and "his sons and disciples" live, and tells us that the deputy of that holy region has ships brought to the island twice a year, and distributes their loads among the inhabitants. He appears to have based this retrospectively bizarre view on a treatise written by the order of Shāh Ismāʿīl I, on the "philosophy and expediency" of occultation. In it, the Imam and his sons and disciples are said to be engaged in the teaching and learning of the religious lore on the island, while armies stand in preparation outside the island, awaiting the Imam's word for the rising.[12]

With the ascendancy of the Shiʿite hierocracy in the late Safavid period, other elements of the doctrine of occultation, aiming at containing the potential to chiliastic action under a claimant to mahdihood, tended to come to the foreground. Following al-Ṭūsī closely, Majlisī insists that the Hidden Imam was alive and lives on earth, and tries to establish that his longevity had precedence among biblical figures, and that it is biologically possible. He alleges that the Imam has been seen from time to time and dreamt of frequently, has performed many miracles, and that he watches over the affairs of his people and takes part, unrecognized, in the Ḥajj ceremony at Mecca.[13] Above all, the Shiʿite community is said to benefit from his presence in spite of concealment: in the first section of his treatise on imamate, Majlisī enumerates these benefits.[14] Nor does Majlisī omit to reiterate the message purportedly handed down by the Hidden Imam to disqualify the potential claimants to authority delegated from the Lord of the Age: "If they claim that they have seen and recognized [him] at that time, they are lying, and if, through claims to seeing [him] they claim vicegerency [*niyābat*], they are lying."[15]

Thus, though the Shiʿite tenet on the return of the Mahdi remains incurably millenarian, the doctrine of occultation, as interpreted by the ascendant hierocracy, removes all plausible justifications for the expectations of imminent *parousia*.

With the establishment of Twelver Shiʿism under the Safavids, the Shiʿite hierocracy, while allowing for the intermittent appearance of the Imam and especially for visits and favors he vouchsafes upon the prominent *ʿulamāʾ*, and attempting to reserve attenuated forms of contact with the Hidden Imam through dreams and visions as ther own prerogative,[16] staunchly opposed any attempt to translate the eschatology into this-worldly millenarianism on the basis of mahdistic and epiphanic claims. Any such attempt would involve a radical break with the Shiʿite orthodoxy of the *ʿulamāʾ*, and was bound to be considered by them a reversion to extremism and, as such, cardinal heresy.

As regards gnostic Shiʿism, consonantly with the emphasis on the initiatory functions of the Imam (*vilāyat*), the occultation of the Imam of the Age facilitated an innerworldly transposition of the orthodox otherworldly eschatology into an eschatology of the soul through spiritual ascent and perfection. According to Corbin,

> the idea of the occultation of the Imam forbids all socialization of the spiritual, all materialization of the spiritual hierarchies and forms which would identify these with the constituted bodies of the external, visible history; this idea is only compatible with the structure of a spiritual sodality, a pure *ecclesia spiritualis*.[17]

As was pointed out, gnostic Shiᶜism survived the collapse of the Safavid state and remained a significant mode of religiosity in the eighteenth century. It is from the second half of the eighteenth century that we have a highly significant statement by Āqā Muḥammad Bīdābādī (d. 1783–84/1197 or 1198) on the purely spiritual interpretation of the vicegerency of the Hidden Imam. Acording to Bīdābādī, it is the perfect mystical guide who can claim this vicegerency. When such a person attains the highest stage of spiritual perfection, that is, when he finally

> reaches clarity of consciousness after obliteration [of the ego] and obtains general persistence [in God] at the same time as annihilation [of the ego], and the secret meaning of "Servanthood [ᶜ*ubūdiyyat*] is an essence whose foundation is Divinity [*rubūbiyya*]" is discovered and made apparent to him, in this station [*maqām*] he has reached the rank of Deputyship [*khilāfat*], as is intended by the Exalted God in, "We have appointed a Deputy [*khalīfa*] on earth." In this rank it is appropriate for him to call people to God, and he will be the General and even the Special [*khāṣṣ*] Vicegerent of the Proof of God upon the Earth [i.e., the Hidden Imam] according to the invisible/transcendental [*ghaibī*] indication of that personage.

Bībābādī proceeds to state that the attainment of this spiritual rank is conditional upon the completion of all the detailed requirements pertaining to each and every station of spiritual advancement. Otherwise, the seeker would "remain on the first step [and] egotism [*anāniyyat*] and pharaonism [*fir*ᶜ*awniyyat*] will bud in his soul."[18]

Thus, so long as the gnostic masters could maintain the spiritual discipline of the Sufi mystical tradition, pharaonism would be curbed and chiliasm contained.

6.2 The Transformation of the Sectarian Orientation of Shiᶜism: Orthodox Shiᶜism as an Established Religion

Max Weber has drawn our attention to the differential function of salvation religions for higher and lower strata: legitimation for the privileged strata and compensation for disprivileged groups.[19] In becoming the national religion of Iran under the Safavids, Shiᶜism had to perform both these functions. It drew on the appropriate elements in its tradition to provide legitimation primarily for the rulers but also for the politically privileged strata in its glorification of the charisma of prophetic lineage. This legitimation constituted a theodicy of good fortune for the Safavid rulers and the clerical notables (*sayyids*). Shiᶜism also drew on its tradition to provide compensation for the disprivileged groups, the bulk of the nation under its spiritual custody, in the forms of a theodicy of suffering centered on the tragedy of Ḥusayn's martyrdom in Karbalā and, more importantly, of an otherworldly soteriology.

To establish their hierocratic domination over the masses in Iran, the Shiᶜite doctors had to take two sets of factors into account: the predispositions and religious demand of the lay masses, and the services required by the rulers in exchange for which the indispensable royal political support could be secured. Under the impact of these two sets of factors, the "established" or orthodox Shiᶜism that the doctors of Safavid period sanctioned and propagated came to differ in some important respects from the Shiᶜism of the sectarian phase, a religion of urban minorities that had borne the imprint of the outlook of their literate dominant strata.

The basic religious predispositions and demands of the masses are marked by the congeniality of savior soteriology and the desire for solicitation of supernatural powers for earthly benefits such as good health and fulfillment of wishes. In the fourteenth and fifteenth centuries, the lay masses' demand for salvation was met by living saviors: the Sufi shaykhs and the claimant to mahdihood. For these the Shiᶜite religious professionals had to substitute acceptable otherworldly saviors. These same otherworldly saviors could then be solicited and induced to use their supernatural powers for the worldly benefit of the believers.

As is usually the case, the pressure emanating from mass religiosity could be responded to in a manner consistent with the mutual accommodation of the hierocracy and the ruler. In Weber's formulation,

> as a rule, a compromise is concluded between the other-worldly and the this worldly powers; this is indeed in their mutual interest. The political power can offer exceedingly valuable support to the hierocracy as the *branchium saeculare* for the annihilation of the heretics and the exaction of taxes. In turn, two qualities of the hierocracy recommend an alliance to the political authorities. First of all, as a legitimating power . . . hierocracy is the incomparable means of domesticating the subjects in things great and little.[20]

In the following pages, we shall consider all the elements of this rather complex transaction. The state's suppression of Sunnism for the benefit of the hierocracy is discussed in chapter 8, and the hierocracy's legitimation of rulership in chapter 7. Here, we shall confine ourselves to the modification undergone by Shiᶜism in the transition from the sectarian to the established phase—very roughly corresponding to the "Church" phase of Christianity in Troeltsch—under the concurrent influence of mass religiosity and political interests of the rulers.

Sectarian Shiᶜism already possessed a popular theodicy of suffering. We have encountered the popular recitals commemorating the martyrdom of Ḥusayn and his family in the Buyid and Saljuq periods. During the Mongol period, these were elaborated into a powerfully emotive theodicy of suffering in Ibn Ṭāwūs's (d. 1259–60/665) *al-Luhuf ʿala Qatlī al-Tuhuf*. In the subsequent era of religious eclecticism, the second half of the fifteenth century, it was taken up and developed by the Naqshbandī philosopher and moralist Mullā Ḥusayn Vāʿiẓ-e Kāshifī (d. 1504–5/910). Under the Safavids, this Shiʿite theodicy of suffering became an important element in popular religion. It had its most eloquent expression in the poetry of Muḥtasham-e Kāshānī in the sixteenth century. The afflictions and martyrdom of the house of the Prophet—the quintessential prototype of senselessly unjust suffering in this world—is endowed with cosmic significance and finds an otherworldly resolution:

> When they summoned mankind to the table of sorrow, they first issued the summons to the hierocracy of the Prophets.
>
> When it came to the turn of the 'Friends of God,' Heaven trembled at the blow which they smote on the head of the Lion of God [i.e., ʿAlī].
>
> . . . .
>
> Then they tore up from Madina and pitched at Karbalā those pavilions to which even the angels were denied entrance.
>
> Many tall palm-trees from the grove of the 'Family of the Cloak' did the people of Kufa fell in that plain with the axe of malice.
>
> . . . .
>
> And the Trusted Spirit [Gabriel] laid his head in shame on his knees, and the eye of the sun was darkened at the sight.
>
> . . . .
>
> That company, whose ranks were broken by the strike of Karbalā, at the Resurrection in serried ranks will break the ranks of the uprisen.
>
> . . . .
>
> Then [finally] they raise on a spear-point that Head [i.e., the head of Imām Ḥusayn] from whose locks Gabriel washes the dust with the water of Salsabīl [a river in paradise].[21]

Three important features of the popular Shiʿite religiosity of the last quarter of the sixteenth century stand out in the critical account given by Mīr Makhdūm Sharīfī. The first is the continuation of *laʿn* or *sább*—cursing of the three rightly guided caliphs—which reflects the new and violent anti-Sunnism characteristic of Safavid Shiʿism. We know that in 1511–12/917 al-Karakī wrote a tract on the "incumbency" of *laʿn*.[22] According to Mīr Makhdūm, the cursing of the second caliph ʿUmar was even believed to cure diseases and ward off misfortune. The second is the importance of pilgrimage [*ziyārat*] to the shrines of the Imams and *imām-zādeh*s—descendants of Imams—which, according to Mīr Makhdūm's intelligent judgment, reduces man's desire for *ḥajj*—the pilgrimage to Mecca. Finally, over and above the belief in the potency of the Imams and *imām-zādehs* to intercede on behalf of the pilgrim with God and to grant his wishes, we find a strong popular belief in the virtual omnipotence of the First Imam, ʿAlī, in fulfilling the worldly wishes of the believers and in interceding for them with God upon the believer's solicitation. This belief is epitomized in the simple verses of the poet Ḥayratī, quoted by Mīr Makhdūm:

> O Ḥayratī! Whatever you seek from God
> ʿAlī the excellent Friend of God will give
> Should God not grant your object of desire
> It His Highness [Majesty] ʿAlī the Fulfiller will grant.[23]

A reference in *Majālis al-Muʾminīn* to ʿAlī as "His Highness the Commander [of the Faithful] the owner of the *Kawthar* pond"—a pond whose water the Imam will sprinkle on the believing Shiʿites in the hereafter before their admission to paradise—brings out ʿAlī's role of intercessor in the other world.[24]

In a mid-seventeenth-century work, we are given evidence of a vigorous effort by the Shiʿite hierocracy to extend the cursing of the three rightly guided caliphs to Abū Ḥanīfa, the founder of the rite subscribed to by the Ottomans. The shah is enjoined to support the Shiʿite hierocracy because following Abū Ḥanīfa is said to be tantamount to loyalty to the Ottoman sultan. The work also shows the importance of a correlative of *laʿn*, namely *tavallāʾ* (befriending [of the Imams]) and *tabarrāʾ* (avoidance [of the enemies]): the author identifies the befriending of the friend of God, the Imam, as "loving in God" (*ḥubb fi Allāh*), and the avoidance and enmity of their enemies as "hating in God." It is stated as the belief of the Shiʿite doctors in the necessity of "imploring and clinging and cleaving to the Immaculate House of the Prophet and the righteous Imams, may peace be upon them, who are the Ark of salvation. Happiness and salvation in the abode of permanence is not possible without this and without avoidance of their enemies."[25]

The anti-Sunni sentiment reflected in the vilification of the three rightly guided caliphs was subdued in al-Murtaḍā's treatise on the imamate, the *Shāfī*, but became pronounced in the ʿAllāma's treatise on imamate, the *Minhāj al-Karāma*.[26] This is intelligible in light of al-Ḥillī's effort to use the Mongol rulers for the propagation of Shiʿism in the way al-Karakī used the Safavid rulers. When Shiʿism finally was established as the state religion in the Safavid period, the anti-Sunni polemic and the vilification of the three rightly guided caliphs became particularly vehement. In his Persian writings, Majlisī devoted much energy to the denunciation of the first three caliphs as the usurpers of ʿAlī's right to rule.[27] It is interesting to note that the "Book of Sedition," devoted to the vilification of the caliphs, was one of the first books of Majlisī's *Biḥār al-Anwār* to be translated from Arabic into Persian by one of his nephews.[28]

One certain way to befriend the Imams, to implore them, and to cleave and cling to them, was by visiting the shrines of their putative descendants, the *imām-zādehs*, most of which were doubtless formerly the shrines of the Sufi saints. The importance of shrines of the real or putative *imām-zādehs* in popular religiosity—a feature of popular Sufism taken over by Safavid Shiᶜism—is clearly shown in the seventeenth-century European sources.[29] These sources also highlight another important characteristic of orthodox Shiᶜism. With his usual perceptiveness, Chardin remarks that the Persians have a lively persuasion of another life, and speak of death calmly.[30] Du Mans mentions, as one of the religious feasts, the Night of Transference (*shab-e barāt*), when angels bring sheets of the great books where the names of the living are recorded. On that night, people go to cemeteries and take *mullās* with them to read the Qurʾan.[31]

Among the Shiᶜite doctors who responded to the predispositions of the masses and thus won their exclusive religious allegiance in the seventeenth century, Mullā Muḥammad Tāhir Qumī and Majlisī the Younger played an important role in giving Shiᶜism a markedly otherworldly outlook, which they sought to propagate widely in their writings *in Persian* (Arabic being the language used for communication aimed at the more restricted audience of religious scholars).

Mullā Muḥammad Ṭahir Qumī wrote a tract entitled *The Curing of the Soul* (*Muᶜālijat al-Nafs*), in which the life in this world is presented as but a transient stage to life in the hereafter (*Ākhirat*), a stage full of distractions perilous to the salvation of the soul. The sections of the tract systematically characterize "the world" (*Dunyā*) with the aid of a series of pejorative images: an ugly crone, a snake, a putrifying dead bride, the hiding place of the ghouls and monsters engaged in highway robbery, a hospital, a sharp and life-taking sword, a beautiful but treacherous woman, and a luring island that traps the foolish passengers from their salvational voyage on the ark of sacred law, thus preventing them from arriving at their destination in the other world. In another tract, *The Awakening of the Sleepers* (*tanbīh al-rāqidīn*), Qumī reminds the believers of the numerous benefits of the remembrance of death. He cites numerous traditions "on the incitement to the remembrance of death and the preparation therefor." He also provides the reader with various formulas for "conversation with the Lords of the Graves." In a third tract, he writes of the "utility of two palm leaves" buried with the dead in reducing the "pressure of the grave," and explains why the Shiᶜites diverge from the Sunnis in pursuing this practice.[32] Finally, he defines Resurrection (*maᶜād*) as follows:

> the belief in reviving in the grave and the events of the grave [the questioning of the dead by Nakīr and Munkir] and the belief in the resurrection on the Day of Judgment for rendering account, and the speaking of the limbs, and the [bridge of] Ṣirāṭ [leading to paradise], and the intercession [of the Imams] and heaven and hell.[33]

The more decisive and widespread propagation of the tenets of Twelver Shiᶜism among the population of Iran took place under the direction of Majlisī, and went hand in hand with the incorporation of many aspects of popular religion. This is reflected in Majlisī's writings, which were much more voluminous and systematic than Qumī's occasional tracts and came to constitute the lucid and authoritative exposition of Shiᶜite orthodoxy. At his hands, the sectarian religiosity of the early Imāmiyya underwent the definitive change in the direction of otherworldliness. I shall try to elucidate this change by contrasting *Ḥaqq al-Yaqīn*, his authoritative and comprehensive statement in Persian of the Shiᶜite creed, with Kulaynī's *Uṣūl* and the ᶜAllāma al-Ḥillī's concise *Bāb al-Ḥādī ᶜAshar*, which are representative of the Shiᶜism of the sectarian period.

In contrast to Kulaynī's *Uṣūl*, the "virtue of knowledge" and the contrast between reason (*ᶜaql*) and ignorance (*jahl*) receive no attention. Faith (*īmān*) and infidelity (*kufr*) are summarily treated at the end. The section on God and his attributes is very brief. (This contrasts even more sharply with the attention the topic received in al-Ḥillī's statement.) In al-Ḥillī's treatise, the philosophical section on *ᶜAdl* (the justice of God) is pivotal. It seeks to demonstrate how the will of God operates in the universe compatibly with the free will of man, how *Lutf* (grace) is incumbent upon God, and how his benevolence would not tolerate the prevalence of evil and the adversity of men. It is largely on this principle that the explanation of prophecy, imamate, and Resurrection rests. *Ḥaqq al-Yaqīn* contains no chapter, section, or subsection on justice.[34] Instead, the bulk of Majlisī's book is taken up by two topics that had received much less attention in the earlier works: the denigration of the three rightly guided caliphs and Resurrection.[35]

In Majlisī's writings, eschatology is made the cornerstone of orthodox religiosity: the end of time, described in lurid detail, is said to precede Resurrection.[36] Physical resurrection is proven, and we are told of the punishment by physical fire, entry into the physical paradise, the details of the end of time, the rising of Gog and Magog, the disfigurations of things, the proceedings in the other world on the Day of Judgment, the crossing of the bridge Ṣirāṭ (a bridge which is finer than a hair, sharper than a sword, and hotter than fire, and has to be crossed to reach paradise) and the selection of the saved and the condemned by the Prophet and the Imams, and other engaging topics.

As we have seen, our sixteenth-century polemicist Mīr Makhdūm had noted the substitution of *ziyārat* for *ḥajj*, and correctly emphasized that the two kinds of pilgrimage are in an important respect antithetical. While the pilgrimage to Mecca (*ḥajj*) impressed upon the pilgrim the absolute transcendence of God and the universality of the Muslim community, pilgrimage to shrines of the Imams only fostered the cult of otherworldly saviors and intercessors. Pilgrimage to shrines, which had been recommended by the early Imāmī theologians but which had been given relatively little importance, became a major feature of Persian

Shiʿism. *Ziyārat-nāmeh*s, or special prayers to be read at different shrines, proliferated. Majlisī devoted an entire book in Persian to the topic, the *Tuḥfat al-Zāʾir*.

On the subject of "the Excellence of Prayer [*duʿā*] and Its Utilities," Majlisī writes: "Know that the most excellent of devotional practices [*ʿibādāt*] and the shortest way of nearness of the creature to the [divine] Fulfiller of Needs is the way of prayer, beseeching lamentation [*taḍrruʿ*], and supplication [*munājāt*]."[37] Supererogatory prayers, suitable for a variety of specific purposes, are rewarded by God both in this world—through granting of wishes—and in the other world.[38] Majlisī's *Zād al-Maʿād* contains numerous examples of the calculus of otherworldly rewards for supererogatory acts of piety such as special prayers and fasting appropriate for specific days and months of the year, as well as numerous this-worldly benefits of *duʿās* for curing stuttering, various diseases and aches, and for avoiding abortion and the like.

The shift of emphasis in the relative importance of *ḥajj* and *ziyārāt* (pilgrimages to shrines) is best brought out by a comparison of the number of pages devoted to these topics in the "Four Books" (written in the tenth/fourth and eleventh/fifth centuries) and in Majlisī's encyclopedic compendium, *Biḥār al-Anwar* (see table 6.1). In addition, al-Ṭūsī's more concise *al-Nihāya* is entered in parentheses.

TABLE 6.1

	Pages	
	Ḥajj	*Ziyārāt*
I. Kulaynī, *al-Kāfī* (*Furūʿ*) (early tenth/fourth century)	197	42
II. Ibn Bābūya, *Man la yaḥḍuruhu 'l-faqīh* (late tenth/fourth century)	149	39
III. al-Ṭūsī, *al-Istibṣār* (eleventh century)	198	—
IV. al-Ṭūsī, *Tahdhīb al-Aḥkām* (eleventh century)	493	118
(al-Ṭūsī, *al-Nihāya*)	(67)	(—)
Majlisī, *Biḥār al-Anwār* (late seventeenth century)	387	1055

It is extremely interesting to observe that the Shiʿite theologians of Jabal al-ʿĀmil do not seem to have modified the relative salience given to *ḥajj* and *ziyārāt* in the "Four Books." One such theologian, the famous al-Ḥurr al-ʿĀmilī, the contemporary of Majlisī, did not come to Iran until he was forty. The ratio of the number of pages devoted to *ḥajj* and *ziyārāt* respectively in his massive *Wasāʾil al-Shīʿa* is similar to the ratio found in the "Four Books" (see table 6.2).[39]

TABLE 6.2

	Ḥajj	*Ziyārāt*
al-Ḥurr al-ʿĀmilī, *Wasāʾil al-Shīʿa* (late seventeenth century)	1402	235

Once eschatology is made the cornerstone of orthodox religiosity, the intercession of the Imams is substituted for that of the Sufi saints[40] and the Imams are cast primarily into the role of otherworldly saviors and intercessors with God: as the author of *Himam al-Thawāqib* untiringly repeats, the Imams are the "ark of salvation" (*safīna-ye najāt*) or, as Majlisī states, "Guidance and salvation cannot be found except through the Imams, and they are the mediators between God and mankind; without knowing them it is impossible for me to avoid the punishment of God."[41] These superhuman saviors, these "Imams of the *jinn* and of mankind,"[42] determine who should enter paradise and who should be condemned to hell. Their power of intercession can be solicited by visitation to their shrines and by special prayers. In the popular mind, the Imams thus became the figures of an apolitical and otherworldly soteriology whose miraculous intervention in daily life can be solicited by supplication and prayer at their shrines or those of their putative descendants.

To conclude, in becoming the national religion of Iran, the preponderantly inner-worldly sectarian Shiʿism was appreciably modified. It became more anti-Sunni, and above all markedly more otherworldly, with the Imams dominating its soteriology as saviors in the hereafter.

CHAPTER SEVEN

Two Variants of Shiᶜism and Their Respective Political Implications; The Political Ethics of Safavid Shiᶜism

7.1 The Two Types of Shiᶜite Religiosity and Their Influence on Political Attitudes

It should be clear from chapter 5 that until the very end of the Safavid era when a Shiᶜite hierocracy was consolidated and prevailed upon the ruler to take severe measures to establish religious uniformity and orthodoxy throughout Iran, the religious topography of the country was varied. Two distinct variants of Shiᶜism have been adumbrated as the most significant modes of religiosity in the Safavid period. As these variants have very different political implications, we need to consider them separately.

7.1.1 Orthodox Shīᶜism: Otherworldly Soteriology and Fatalistic Political Submissiveness

The otherworldly soteriology of orthodox Shiᶜism implied a considerable shift of religious attachment from the law of God and from the constitutive tradition of the Prophet to the personal figures of the Imams as saviors. As eschatology and soteriology became the cornerstones of popular Shiᶜism, and with the Imams as the otherworldly saviors of the Shiᶜite soteriology, imamate lost all connotation of political leadership.[1] This is true also as regards the Hidden Imam. The chiliasm of the mahdistic tenet was sublimated in ritualistic prayer, transposing the Mahdi into a preponderantly otherworldly savior. In the *duᶜā-ye nudba* (prayer of lamentation), a supplication addressed to the Hidden Imam, which according to Majlisī would assure the believer a place among the companions of the Mahdi if read on forty mornings, the supplicant, having ritualistically requested God to expedite the return of the Hidden Imam, makes various references to the *Kawthar* pond, whose water assures salvation in the hereafter. Significantly, he ends by beseeching God for the water of the "pond of his [the Hidden Imam's] forefather [ʿAlī]," that is, the *kawthar* pond, in the Hidden Imam's bowl and by his hand.[2]

The otherworldly soteriology of orthodox Shiʿism did not foster chiliasm, and did not impinge upon politics by posing a this-worldly ideal. On the contrary, it implied a serious devaluation of the political sphere, a devaluation, however, which in practice made for distraction rather than disobedience. The most important practical consequence of this devaluation of the political sphere was thus the enfeebling of the propensity to religiously regulated political action. It involved a devaluation of earthly powers and of temporal rule that was devoid of practical consequences. Even the kings paid lip service to the inferiority of the political to the religious sphere: Shāh ʿAbbās the Great officially called himself the Dog of the Threshold of ʿAlī (*kalb-e āstān-e ʿAlī*) and the Dog of the Threshold of *vilāyat* (= imamate [of ʿAlī]).[3] To emphasize the superiority of religion over earthly kingship, ʿAbbās I reportedly walked behind the eminent *ʿālim*, Mullā ʿAbdullāh Tunī, while the latter rode ahead of him in Shah Square in Isfahan.[4] Similarly, Sulṭān-Ḥusayn typically signed a *farmān* issued the year before the Afghan invasion as the "Most Humble Dog of the Commander of the Faithful [i.e., ʿAlī], Sulṭān-Ḥusayn."[5] It is crucial to note, however, that an independent organization as the institutional embodiment of religion had not emerged; the admission of the superiority of religion over kingship was therefore not politically costly, as the vastly superior otherworldly powers did not make a habit of bridging the hiatus that separated them from this world, and their as-yet-dependent representatives could not effectively impinge upon the political sphere by detracting from the earthly majesty of the ruler.

In this context, let us refer to a letter supposedly written by Mullā Aḥmad Ardabīlī to ʿAbbās I. The reference it makes to the "borrowed kingdom" (*mulk-e ʿāriya*) has been cited as evidence that government was considered usurpatory even in the heyday of the Safavid empire.[6] I have argued elsewhere that the authenticity of the letter is dubious.[7] In all likelihood, Mullā Aḥmad did write a letter addressing the ruler as "dearest brother," but the letter was addressed to Ṭahmāsp and not to ʿAbbās I.[8]

This notwithstanding, the tone of the note and the reference to God's forgiveness (in the other world) makes it fairly clear that what is invoked is a contract between the ruler's this-worldly kingdom and the realm of the omnipotent God. There certainly is no intimation of the shah's having usurped the Imam's kingdom, and a fortiori it is incorrect to suppose any allusion to the shah's usurpation of the kingdom of the *ʿulamāʾ*. Ṭahmāsp is said to have willed that the letter from the Mullā, in which he was addressed as "dearest brother," be put in his shroud so as to aid him during the inquisition of Nakīr and Munkir in his grave.[9]

As regards the motivation to uphold the prevalent normative order legitimating political domination, certain correlates of otherworldliness are of decisive importance. "Know," Majlisī enjoins the reader, "that reliance on God [*tawakkul*], surrender of the will [to God, *tafwiḍ*], contentment [*riḍā*], and resignation [*taslīm*] are the great pillars of faith [*īmān*]."[10] Men inculcated with this cluster of attitudes, which the Victorian orientalists came to refer to as fatalism, were likely to submit to political domination and accept the existing order and the norms it imposed, especially as the Safavids claimed to be the descendants of the otherworldly saviors—the Imams. This is borne out by Chardin, who duly recorded the resignation of the Persians, and reported with bemusement their sincere devotion to their kings even though they were considered tyrannical and arbitrary.[11] Thus, otherworldly soteriology of orthodox Shiᶜism did indeed serve as the "opium of the masses."

7.1.2 Gnostic Shiᶜism: Innerworldly Soteriology and Political Indifferentism

For gnostic Shiᶜism,[12] imamate ceases to be the central concept of a theological system which is a substitute for *political* theory, and acquires a different and fundamentally spiritualized significance. The spiritualization of the notion of imamate enhances the differentiation of the religious (spiritual) and the political spheres.

Qāḍī Saᶜīd Qumī (d. 1691), a representative of gnostic Shiᶜism, insists upon the essentially religious significance of the imamate as "spiritual sovereignty." In this light,

> there could even be more advantage to the Occultation of the Imam because the authority of a spiritual presence is essentially oriented to the transcendent world whereas material power only concerns this world. This temporal power would only be a supplementary divine grace *whose non-necessity is evident*.[13]

The physical absence of the Imam from this world and his spiritual presence in the inner world attests to the insignificance of the things of this world and of temporal rule, which is therefore seen as profane and devoid of relevance to religious (spiritual) concerns. According to Qāḍī Saᶜīd, imamate consists in religious caliphate (*khilāfa dīniyya*), and spiritual sovereignty (*salṭanat maᶜnawiyya*).[14] The unambiguously innerworldly connotation of the word *maᶜnawiyya* leaves us in no doubt that Qāḍī Saᶜīd's position entails not the rejection of temporal sovereignty in favor of this-worldly theocracy, but the radical devaluation of earthly sovereignty and the spiritual irrelevance of worldly power.

This radical devaluation of earthly sovereignty is brought out much more clearly in a brief but important tract by Mullā Muḥsin Fayḍ, the *Āʾīneh-ye Shāhī* ("The Mirror for the King"), written for ᶜAbbās II.

Fayḍ's "Mirror" is worlds apart from the traditional "mirrors for princes." It sets worldly sovereignty, presented most briefly, in the context of a gnostic/

philosophical *imago mundi*. Men are said to be governed by five "Governing Faculties" (*ḥukkām*, literally "governors"). These are divided into two pairs of corresponding "inner" and "external" faculties, followed by a last one. The first pair are the most relevant to spiritual salvation through gnosis; the last faculty is the least. The faculties are reason (*ᶜaql*) and sacred law (*sharᶜ*), nature (*ṭabᶜ*) and habit (*ᶜādat*)—which may derived either from sacred law or reason—and, finally, custom (*ᶜurf*), defined as man-made law. Sovereignty (*salṭanat*) is valid and legitimate only as regards this last governing faculty, custom, and, correspondingly, the lowest level of esoteric reality: "Sovereignty is to sacred law as the body is to the soul." However, as Fayḍ makes clear later, the sacred law that he has in mind is equivalent to the commandments of the Prophet and the Imams as the "Lieutenants of Perfect Reason." It is to be grasped directly with the aid of God, the most sovereign of the faculties (*aḥkam al-ḥākimīn*), and without the mediation of the jurists, whose practice in fact amounts to the adulteration of sacred law by custom. If the king follows the (spirit of) sacred law, he infuses soul into the body politic; otherwise it remains under the dominion of the lowest of men's governing faculties, which ought not to be obeyed whenever its dictates conflict with those of the superior faculties. But all these considerations receive attention only in proportion to their importance in the perspective of a spiritual teleology whose goal is gnosis. Having apprehended the significance of the five governing faculties, man should proceed with the knowledge of the self through the hermeneutic comprehension of sacred law through the employment of reason, and through seeking the aid of God—the sovereign faculty—by means of prayer and supplication. In this manner, man may transcend exoteric reality and grasp the structure of existence through the certain science (*ᶜilm al-yaqīn*). Through the knowledge of the self (soul)—*nafs*—man can assure the dominion of reason (the highest of the governing faculties) within himself and become consubstantial with angels, "as reason and the angels belong to the same order of reality."[15]

Here we have a radical devaluation not only of political domination but also of the political sphere in general and of political action. What is implied is an attitude not of oppositional political activism, but of radical political indifferentism. We may therefore speak of gnostic Shiᶜism as fundamentally apolitical. "In Catholicism," writes Troeltsch, "State belongs to natural existence, above which there rises the supernatural stage of Grace, which is completely indifferent to the State."[16] We may say the same is true for gnostic Shiᶜism but must add that for the latter the stage of spiritual grace is in principle ever attainable by effort, and therefore natural exoteric reality is ever radically devalued.

Thus *ᶜirfān* has no direct consequences for political action and no direct impact on the political order. Indirectly, however, like Lutheran mysticism,[17] it undermines hierocratic authority—lessening the importance of hierocratic action and thereby strengthening the hand of the state—and consequently the preponderance of state-initiated acts in the overall pattern of societal action.

As regards to the public observance of religious ethics, the antilegalistic bent of gnostic Shiᶜism made it antipathetic toward ethical rigorism and the zealous enforcement of morals. In a letter dated 1661–62/1072, Mullā Muḥsin Fayḍ disapproves of his correspondent's moralistic zeal in demanding the forcible "forbidding of the reprehensible," pointing out that now is the time of cessation (*hudna*), and adding that if the time were ripe for such action, the Lord of Time would have been present.[18] ᶜAbd al-Razzāq Lāhījī would go even further and would not hesitate to write poetry on the benefits of wine.[19]

7.2 The Normative Regulation of the Safavid Political Order

7.2.1 The Official Political Ethic

ᶜAbbās I ordered Bahāʾ al-Dīn ᶜĀmilī to compile a legal compendium for practical use in his kingdom. The work began under the supervision of ᶜĀmilī and was completed after his death by one of his students.[20] The compilation was published as the *Jāmiᶜ ᶜAbbāsī*, and remained the official legal manual throughout the seventeenth century.[21] As it was the officially recognized guide for the religious courts of the realm as well as for the cautelary advice given by the religious jurists to individual believers, its ethico-legal provisions with their political implications may be referred to as the "official" political ethic of the seventeenth and early eighteenth centuries.

The discussion of "enjoining the good" and "forbidding the evil" in *Jāmiᶜ ᶜAbbāsī* is brief, and does not show any major change from the sectarian phase of Shiᶜism. Though these ethical obligations are considered "individually incumbent" (*ᶜaynī*), the conditions for their incumbency in reality restricts them to nonviolent persuasion in cases where no damage to Muslims is likely to ensue. Disagreement among authorities on many of the related issues is reported, most notably the disagreement as to whether the *mujtahid* is permitted to enforce the punishments explicitly decreed by the Qurʾan (*ḥudūd*) during the occultation of the Imam. The brief chapter ends by an affirmation that the argument in favor of permissibility is the stronger, and that the *mujtahid* may enforce these punishments provided that they do not involve death or injury.[22]

The discussion of *jihād* (holy war), on the other hand, departs from the unenthusiastic interpretations of the sectarian phase, a development reflecting the consequences of the establishment of Shiᶜism as the religion of a state engaged in warfare against non-Muslims. It discusses the definition of the wars that can be considered *jihād*, and the detailed regulation of the division of booty and appropriation of the captives. The criterion for when the "peoples of the book" can be considered "infidels" (*kuffār-e ḥarbī*) is set out with the intention of bringing the frequent Safavid wars against the Georgians within the ambit of regulation of the sacred law.[23]

During the reign of Shāh Suleymān, several translations into Persian were made of ᶜAlī's instructions to his appointee, Mālik, the governor of Egypt, including one by Muḥammad Bāqir Majlisī himself.[24] These translations of the "Covenant [*ᶜahd-nāmeh*] of Mālik Ashtar," considered a blueprint for exemplary political rule and humane government according to justice and equity, represent attempts to incorporate the ethos of Sasanian patrimonialism into Shiᶜite ethics. The "Covenant" which, as we have seen, was first attributed to ᶜAlī by Sharīf al-Raḍī in the eleventh/fifth century, enjoins the strict observance of the norms of justice upon the delegate. It does contain references to certain specific practices, such as a strong condemnation of hoarding, but is substantively very akin to the ethos of patrimonialism both in specific matters such as accessibility of the ruler to the subjects and in the overwhelming general emphasis on justice.

Majlisī also turns to the ethics of kingly patrimonialism in his other works. In a section of the *ᶜAyn al-Ḥayāt*, "On the Rights of Kings, Obedience to Them, Praying for Their Moral Probity [*ṣalāḥ*], and Not Disputing Their Majesty," Majlisī writes:

> Know that the Kings of the Right Religion [*dīn-e ḥaqq*] have many rights upon their subjects, as they protect them and repel the enemies of Religion from them, and [as] their religion, life, property, and honor is secure through the protection of the kings. Therefore, [the subjects] must pray for the kings and recognize their rights.

Furthermore, Majlisī affirms that even if the kings are tyrannical and unjust one must obey them and pray for their improvement, because by disobeying them one brings afflictions upon oneself, which is forbidden by the ethically incumbent *taqiyya* (dissimulation of faith to assure survival) and by a categorical dictate of the Prophet. The Seventh Imam is also cited through "authentic attribution" as commanding a group of Shiᶜites to pray to God for the preservation of the king if he is just, and for the improvement of his character if he is oppressive and tyrannical, as their interest is verily in the interest of their king. In addition, Majlisī relates the exemplary story of Abraham and the king of the Copts (*qibṭ*) [*sic*]. The king coveted Abraham's wife, Sarah. Abraham did not oppose him violently, and did not rebel, but prayed to God. Thrice the king extended his hand toward Sarah, and thrice God petrified it in response to Abraham's prayers. The king repented, revered and respected Abraham, and made him a gift of a beautiful Coptic slave to serve Sarah: no other than Hagar, the mother of Ishmael.[25]

Correspondingly, the kings and those commanding authority should observe the rights of the subjects and rule them with justice "like a benign father" in order to avoid the decline of the kingdom and to escape punishment in the hereafter.[26] Finally, Majlisī, very much along the path paved by al-Murtaḍā, also recommends morally responsible association with kings and governors, not only to avoid endangering lives and property (as required by the duty of *taqiyya*) but also with more positive aims: to alleviate oppression and further the cause of justice and the well-being of the faithful, and to admonish those who yield political power to improve their morality.[27]

Let us be careful in characterizing the precise nature of Majlisī's addition to the "official" political ethic of Shiᶜism. It was the hierocracy's legitimation of kingship as *temporal* rule, and amounted to granting religious sanction to the legitimation of *political* domination according to the principles of the patrimonial theories of kingship. As we shall see in the following chapter, this did not endow the office of the king with any *religious* authority, and therefore did *not* mean a justification of Safavid domination as "caesaropapist." Majlisī's adoption of the ethos of patrimonialism and his justification of kingship as temporal rule were consistent with the Shiᶜite separation of political and religious authority. At the same time, it can be presumed to have gained the support of the ruler for the nascent hierocracy by impressing upon him the latter's prospective rule as the legitimators of political domination. However, even though he found it expedient to turn a blind eye on them, Majlisī stopped short of endorsing the Safavid rulers' "extremist" claims to supreme political *and* religious authority. That Majlisī reserved religious authority for the Shiᶜite doctor is clearly shown by another passage in *ᶜAyn al-Ḥayāt* in which the Prophet is reported to have said:

> "There are two classes [*ṣinf*] in my community such that if they are righteous and worthy my community will also be righteous, and if they are corrupt, my community will also be corrupt." The Companions asked him who these two classes were. He replied that they were the *fuqahā*ᵓ [jurists] and the *umarā*ᵓ [princes].[28]

7.2.2 The Shiᶜite Hierocracy as the Legitimator of Rulership

Legitimation may result from writings on political ethics but also needs to be effected by ritual. Coronation is the most important ritual of legitimation. In Safavid times, it was performed by the foremost religious dignitary of the realm: the Mujtahid of the Age, a descendant of al-Karakī, in the sixteenth century, and the *Shaykh al-Islām* of Isfahan in the seventeenth. This function derives not from the provisions of the sacred law, but from the nature of the institution of hierocracy as the social embodiment of religious charisma. As religion was to guide life in general, religious charisma could bestow legitimacy on a variety of nonreligious activities. In this capacity, the hierocracy could *legitimize* secular activities, including rulership, without sacralizing them.

When Shiᶜism ceased to be a sectarian religion and became the established religion of the state, the Shiᶜite hierocracy found a new role and function in the legitimation of rulership. The occasion *par excellence* when the hierocracy could perform the role of legitimator of kingship was the ceremony of coronation.

Al-Karakī's son, Shaykh ᶜAbd al-ᶜĀlī, and Mīr Sayyid ᶜAlī Jabal-ᶜĀmilī, spread the "rug of sovereignty" for the ascension of Ismāᶜīl II (1577/985) and Muḥammad Khudā-Bandeh (1580/988) respectively.[29] In the seventeenth century, when Isfahan became the permanent capital of the Safavid rulers, the function of inaugurating a new monarch was entrusted to the Shaykh al-Islām of the capital. Mīr Dāmād conducted the coronation of Ṣafī, and Majliṣī that of Sulṭān-Ḥusayn.[30] For superstitious reasons, Suleymān had two coronations, of which Chardin supplies us with an extensive account that clearly brings out the legitimatory role of the *Shaykh al-Islām* and other religious functionaries. During the coronation in 1667/1077, of which Chardin was an eyewitness, the *Shaykh al-Islām* crowned Suleymān and girded him with the sword and dagger. The *khuṭba* (sermon) was then delivered by another religious dignitary, Mīrzā Rafīᶜā. In it, the benefaction and prayer of the hierocracy was bestowed upon the king as the shadow of God and "illustrious Branch of the Imamic Race," who is "according to the true Law become the Lieutenant of the Monarch of all the Earth, and Lawful Lord of the World [i.e., the Hidden Imam]." By divine revelation, the subjects are said to be

> bound to obey Kings, as being the Valie or Sovereign Lieutenants of God, *Gaanit-chin* [*jānishīn*], sitting in his place on Earth, and that we ought to submit to their Commands, without examining whether they be just or not. In . . . submitting to their Commands we submit at the same time to the Holy Books in all things. . . .[31]

Finally, the *Shaykh al-Islām* bowed three times in front of the king and read a prayer (*duᶜā*) for the longevity of the king and the prosperity of the subjects.[32]

Here we have the *Shaykh al-Islām* of the capital ritually carrying out the prayer for the preservation of the king, as was to be prescribed in Majlisī's political ethic. In a *farmān* issued in 1703/1115, granting a stipend to the *sayyid*s descending from Mīr ᶜAbd al-Razzāq, Shāh Sulṭān-Ḥusayn typically reminds them of their duty in exchange: *duᶜā-gūʾī*—praying (for the everlasting fortune of the dynasty).[33] Furthermore, we even know that the phrase "May the king, from whom all our fortunes flow live forever," was included in the daily prayers, presumably as a supererogatory *duᶜā*.[34] This blessing or legitimating of the king as the head of the body politic through prayer, so much in congruence with the soteriological character of orthodox Shiᶜism, proved to be a lasting function of the hierocracy in Qājār polity.

7.2.3 The Principles of Safavid Legitimacy and Their Partial Lack of Congruence with Twelver Shiᶜism

As might be expected, some Shiᶜite jurists and theologians hailed the creation of the first Shiᶜite empire in history as the forerunner of the kingdom of the Hidden Imam. Many considered obedience to the new Shiᶜite state as incumbent, and some did not hesitate to use the term *dawlat al-ḥaqq*,[35] which term al-Mufīd had reserved for the kingdom to be installed by the Mahdi himself.[36] In addition to this jubilant but specifically Shiᶜite glorification, much of the political culture prevailing at the time of the Safavid conquests was retained and used to strengthen the legitimacy of Safavid rule.

As has been pointed out, though ᶜAlid sentiments and ideas had permeated many parts of Iran by the late fifteenth century, Iran was still predominantly Sunni. Although Ismāᶜīl's claims to legitimate rulership were more extreme than those of his contemporaries, it was not unusual for Sunni rulers to claim legitimacy by styling themselves caliphs and Imams. This was so because in Sunnism, unlike Shiᶜism, the de facto depoliticization of the conception of imamate never occurred. Thus, in the later fifteenth century, Davvānī would call Ūzūn Ḥasan Imam and caliph; the last important Aqqūyūnlū monarch, Sulṭān Yaᶜqūb, was also referred to as Imam.[37] In the first decade of the sixteenth century, very probably with the intention of implying that his Uzbek patron was the legitimate leader of both Sunnis and Shiᶜites, Khunjī addresses him as *imām al-zamān* (Lord of the Age) and *khalīfat al-raḥmān*.[38] Neither Ismāᶜīl's "exaggerated" claims nor the Sunni claims to caliphate and imamate were compatible with the systematized Imāmī doctrine, for which imamate had become a theological concept and temporal rule been divested of a religious or quasi-religious character.

Ismāᶜīl's theophanic claims and the unusual and unstable convergence of the principal charismas of the warlord and of the holy imam, culminating in his claim to incarnate God, have been noted. Such intense personal charisma was in need of constant corroboration by external events as signs of divine favor. His defeat by the Ottomans in the battles of Qajdivān in 1512 and of Chaldirān in 1514 must therefore have been interpreted as an indication of the withdrawal of such divine favor. In fact, after Chaldirān, Ismāᶜīl avoided direct contact with his subjects, and even relegated the appointment of governors to his minister (*nāẓir-e dīvān-e aᶜlā*).[39] However, while the Turkman tribal element, highly prone to extremism, remained prominent in the polity, the veneration of the shah was resumed. The veneration of Shāh Ṭahmāsp as the Mahdi by his fanatical tribal *murīd*s (followers), who had to be suppressed as heretics, has been mentioned. We also have the Venetian envoy d'Alessandri's confirmation (1571) that his subjects "worship him not as a king, but as a god, on account of his descent from the line of ᶜAlī."[40]

Shāh Ṭahmāsp's piety is evident in his autobiography.[41] As we have seen, orthodox beliefs led him to confer the title of *nāʾib al-imām* (vicegerent of the Imam) upon the Shaykh al-Karakī. By reacting sharply to his own "exaggerated"—and therefore blasphemous—elevation to supreme politico-religious leadership, and by deferring to the learned doctors in matters of religion and sacred law, he renounced all pretensions to *religious* authority, whose ultimate source was thus admitted to rest not in the person of the charismatic leader but in holy scripture, and whose legitimate exercise was invested in the learned doctors of the Shiᶜite dogma and the sacred law. The pious Ṭahmāsp was thus instrumental in carrying out an essential step in the process of "rationalization" of the structure of domination away from the heritage of extremism—the fusion of religious and political authority—in the direction of greater congruence with the Twelver Shiᶜite world-view, which implied a high degree of de facto differentiation between the religious and the political spheres. But the process was arrested long before reaching its logical conclusion. Ṭahmāsp continued to claim religio-political legitimacy as a descendant of the Imams, and retained the requirement of *sajda* (prostration) on the part of his subjects—an act of veneration reserved for God in Shiᶜism as in Islam in general. This practice continued into the reign of ᶜAbbās I.[42]

With the military reforms of ᶜAbbās the Great, the Qizilbāsh tribal forces ceased to be the mainstay of the Safavid state. The Sufi principle legitimating the rule of the monarch as the *Murshid-e Kāmil* (the perfect spiritual guide) became dispensable. The rituals associated with this function were discontinued with the decline of the power of the Qizilbāsh tribes.[43] With the early Safavids the prayer rug of the Sufi shaykhs' *sajjādeh-ye irshād* had become one of the regalia used in coronations. In the coronation of Ismāᶜīl II, this rug is referred to as the *qālīcheh-ye salṭanat* (rug of sovereignty),[44] but it appears to have been totally eliminated from the coronation of Suleymān.[45] But even at the coronation of his predecessor, Shāh Ṣafī, when the immediate circumstances required the cooperation of the Qizilbāsh palace guards and assured the inclusion of the rug among the regalia for the last time, it is referred to as *qālīcheh-ye irshād* in one source (rug of Sufi guidance)[46] and *qālīcheh-ye ᶜadālat* (rug of justice)[47] in another. This ceremonial juxtaposition of the norms of *irshād* and justice, deriving respectively from the Sufi and the patrimonial ethos, illustrates the transition from the former to the latter norm, which aimed at legitimating Safavid rule in the eyes of the sedentary majority, and which was in fact completed by that time.

The legitimation of Safavid rule in the eyes of the peasantry and the urban population of course dates back to the very beginning of Safavid rule. This legitimation drew upon two normative sources. The first was nonproblematic, and has already been referred to in chapter 3. It consisted of the patrimonial ethos as embodied in the theories of kingship. The traditional conception and attributes of kingship were retained after the establishment of Shiᶜism under the Safavids. At the close of the fifteenth century (1495/900), Vāᶜiẓ-e Kāshifī had "applied the belief in *barakat* [charisma] to the person of the king implicitly [attaching] to him a spark of divine personality such as was attached, in popular religion preeminently to the person of Muhammad."[48] According to Chardin (in the late seventeenth century), the Persians "say that the Persons of their Kings are Sacred and Sanctified, in a peculiar manner above the rest of Mankind, and bring along with them wheresoever they come, Happiness and Benediction."[49] Thus, as Lambton points out, "the theory that the temporal ruler was the Shadow of God upon Earth remained the central theme" in the Safavid period.

According to the restatements of this theory, first and foremost, the king is the shadow of God on earth,[50] and disobeying kings is tantamount to disobeying God:[51] "disagreeing with kings is disgrace in this and fire in the other world."[52] Royalty and religion are intermixed. With some eclecticism, Qurʾanic verses, including the "authority verse," are also on occasion adduced to enjoin obedience to kings. Conversely, the primary ethical obligation of the king is to rule with justice and to eliminate oppression: "sovereignty may last with infidelity, but it will not last with tyranny," and "Verily, God commands justice and charity."[53]

Consonantly with these norms, the author of *Tārīkh-e ʿĀlam-ārā-ye ʿAbbāsī* presents Shāh ʿAbbās the Great as the paragon of all patrimonial virtues: the firmness of his religious beliefs, securing him God's favors, his justice, his severity and efficiency in statecraft, the security of roads and cities, his accessibility and avoidance of pomp, his patrimonial munificence, reflected in occasional tax exemptions, and his projects for urban and agricultural development are all greatly applauded. What is much more interesting from our point of view is that his official historian does not omit to emphasize ʿAbbās's direct and unmediated blessedness by the "grace of God." This grace is manifested in ʿAbbās's spectacular military victories, in his surviving lethal dangers, and also in astrological indications and astral events. Above all, it is manifested in ʿAbbās's miraculous deeds and elicitation of divine guidance through *istikhāra*.[54]

The second normative source was religion, drawn upon in a variety of ways, some of which proved problematical in the long run. As one would expect, traditions foretelling the advent of the Safavid reign to establish the true religion—Twelver Shiʿism—were produced, and the meritorious deed of the Safavids who spread Twelver Shiʿism after an eclipse of 900 years were greatly emphasized.[55] Not unlike the post-Reformation kings of Spain and France, who sported the title of "Most Catholic Majesty," the Safavid kings enjoyed the titles of *dīn-panāh* (protector/refuge of religion) and "Promoter of the Doctrine of the Church of the Twelve."[56]

Much less innocuously, another normative religious source was drawn upon: the heritage of extremism, or more specifically, the mahdistic tenet. The exploitation of the mahdistic tenet to provide legitimation for the caesaropapist politico-religious authority of the Safavid monarch was no doubt very effective in the short run, but in the long run proved problematic. Among the sources, the *Takmilat al-Akhbār* is of great value in showing the precise nature of this legitimation:

> The office of the Sovereignty of the world after the Prophet is reserved for the Commander of the Faithful [ʿAlī], and after Him, this exalted office belongs to the Twelve Imams; and anyone else who interferes in this matter is

> a tyrant. As the Ruler of the Age [*sulṭān-e zamān*] [and] the Lord of Command [*ṣāḥib-e amr*] . . . is absent, it is right and necessary that a person from the exalted dynasty of ᶜAlī and Fāṭima, who is competent for this task, should give currency to the Commandment[s] of the Imam of the Age among God's worshippers.[57]

The divergence from the writings of the Imāmī doctors on imamate is striking. From being a utopian theological substitute for political theory, the doctrine of imamate suddenly forms the basis for the sacralization of political authority through the charisma of lineage. In sharp contrast to the separation of the religious and the political spheres and the profanation of the latter, here we are witnessing an attempt to sacralize rulership through the fusion of religious and political domination. This attempt involves maximal *politicization* of the implications of the concept of imamate, with the emphasis shifting decisively from the quality of the Imam as the authoritative teacher in religion to his function of political leadership of the community. The millenarian consequences of this shift of emphasis is clear: it focuses attention squarely on the Imam in occultation, the Lord of the Age. Thus, beginning with the earliest Safavid chronicle, great emphasis is put on the precursorship of the Safavid monarchs.[58] I have already mentioned the references to Ismāᶜīl as the precursor of the Imam. Similarly, the author of *Takmilat al-Akhbār* calls Ṭahmāsp the aider of the Lord of the Age and, emphasizing his mission of preparing the world for the Imam's *parousia*, stresses that the end of time has the same numerological value as the year of Ṭahmāsp's ascension, and that the kingship of the end of time is reserved for him.[59] The same claim is made by other chronicles.[60]

Although legitimatory writings in this genre continued to be written in the seventeenth century, the Shiᶜite hierocracy began to have reservations about this approach as it ran counter to hierocratic efforts to contain mahdistic chiliasm. In order to ingratiate himself with the new ruler, Suleymān, Majlisī the Younger in *Rajᶜat*, one of his early works written in 1667–68/1078, had cited a tradition from the Sixth Imam foretelling the rise of the Safavids from Gilan as a prelude to the kingdom of the Mahdi. Safavid rule was to last for sixty-five more years until the date Majlisī had set for the return of the Mahdi on the basis of numerology. This kind of legitimation of Safavid reign was challenged by Mīr Lawḥī, who wrote a polemical tract attacking Majlisī after a dream on the birthday of the Hidden Imam some two or three years later. Mīr Lawḥī disputed the interpretation of the tradition in question, and considered the fixing of a date for the return of the Mahdi superstitious. He claimed that the legitimacy of the Safavid rulers, whose excellence and descent from the Imams puts them above all the rulers of the earth, need not be based on such shaky grounds.[61]

As we have seen, the suppression of chiliasm was both in the vital interest of the Shiᶜite hierocracy and politically expedient for the centralizing monarchs, and was therefore pursued in the sixteenth and early seventeenth centuries. After the subsidence of chiliasm, the formula that there be no gap between the reign of a monarch and the appearance of the Imam was expressed as a stylized, ritualized wish throughout the Safavid period,[62] and beyond it into the Qājār era. But the other element in the early legitimation of Safavid domination—their rule on behalf of the Hidden Imam and as the descendants of the holy Imams—continued to be greatly emphasized. This emphasis brought forth their charisma of lineage as the descendants of the seventh Imam, Mūsā al-Kāẓim, which, as Kasravī has shown, was in fact forged, but was nevertheless universally accepted.[63] In the seventeenth century, both the devotional attachment to the Imams fostered by Akhbārī traditionalism and the cult of the Imams as otherworldly saviors encouraged by orthodoxy worked in the direction of enhancing the Safavid charisma of holy lineage.

Devotional attachment to the Imams enhanced the charisma of lineage of the Safavid dynasty and enhanced the propensity on the part of their Shiʿite subjects to accept the legitimation of their rule, as set forth in statements such as the following by the historian of the reign of Shāh Ṣafī: "The relatedness of the Safavid Dynasty to the House of Prophecy and divinely ordained Sovereignty [*vilāyat*], and to the Dynasty of Prophethood and Imamate is clearer to mankind than the shining sun."[64]

No doubt relying on the same popular sentiment, Suleymān begins a *farmān* issued in 1684–85/1096 with the phrase "My Noble Forefather, My Glorious Great Ancestor."[65]

The charisma of holy lineage very effectively buttressed the legitimation of the ruler as the shadow of God on earth in accordance with the ethos of patrimonialism. At the same time, it legitimated the rulers' caesaropapist pretensions. This additional boon, however, introduced a contradictory element into the Safavid normative order. To analyze this contradiction, let us return to our sixteenth-century sources. Emphasizing the Safavids' charisma of lineage, the chroniclers sought to reconcile charismatic religio-political domination of the Shiʿite-Sufi extremists with the Imāmī doctrine. This attempt bypassed the Imam's function as the supreme authority in religious jurisprudence and dogma, which the Safavid monarch was not competent to exercise vicariously, and which Ṭahmāsp came to concede to al-Karakī, the Mujtahid of the Age. However, the contradiction between the extremist grounds of legitimacy of political rule and the logic of the Imāmī doctrine, which these theorists sought unsuccessfully to overcome, did not pass unnoticed. It was clearly perceived and emphasized by the Sunni Mīr Makhdūm, who remarked that the Shiʿites are forced to admit that Ṭahmāsp is not one of the twelve Imams, and are also forced to say that he is not a *mujtahid*; "yet they revere him with utmost veneration, believing him to be the Perfect Guide, the Pole and the Principle [of the universe]."[66] But the ordinary run of men were of course not unduly troubled by such inconsistencies.

Subsequently, in light of these contradictions, the excessive Mahdistic claims of Ismāʿīl I were modified into the claim that the Safavid shahs were the descendants of the Prophet and of ʿAlī and the vicars of the Hidden Imam, and ruling on his behalf. The shahs nevertheless arrogated to themselves the Imam's attribute of *ʿiṣmat* (sinlessness, infallibility).[67] It should be emphasized again that it was this principle of Safavid legitimacy that was flatly incompatible both with the explicit tenets of Twelver Shiʿism and with its implicit profanation of political power. The inconsistency between the secularization of political rulership, as logically entailed by the doctrine of occultation, and the Safavids' *religious* legitimation of their rule, amounted to the exploitation of the mahdistic tenet of the period of extremism as a most valuable normative asset. The might of the Safavids and their dynastic interest prevented the resolution of this inconsistency, but did not prevent it from constituting a latent source of tension which manifested itself from time to time in concrete events. For centuries to come, the constellation of political and hierocratic power in the polity did not allow the resolution of this contradiction.

The hierocracy of *mullā*s, who certainly needed the support of the rulers to consolidate their position vis-à-vis the clerical estate and lacked political power and an independent ecclesiastical organization, condoned the Safavid shah's caesaropapist legitimation consisting in their claims to vicegerency of the Hidden Imam (without, however, justifying it in their writings on political ethics or jurisprudence). As no organizational apparatus independent of the caesaropapist state existed, and faced with a powerful state, the nascent hierocracy could not exploit its domination over the masses at the psychological level as a secure basis for assertiveness. It compromised with ruling power in condoning its religious pretensions and caesaropapist legitimation. In fact, as we have seen, Majlisī was even happy to oblige and to grant Safavid rule full legitimacy, drawing largely on the political ethic of patrimonialism. However, it cannot be overemphasized that, even though sayings of the Prophet and the Imams are adduced to enjoin obedience to the temporal ruler, Majlisī *endorsed the legitimacy of kingship as temporal and not as religious and political rule*. Accepting the principles legitimating the *religious* authority of the Safavid monarchs would have meant the endorsement of the heritage of extremism, which was in contradiction with the Shiʿite doctrine and could therefore not be granted by its custodians. What Majlisī as the head of the hierocracy could and did do was to sanction the principles of legitimacy of patrimonial *temporal* rule, which, as such, were compatible with the secularity of political rulership as implied by the logic of the Shiʿite doctrine.

Furthermore, there were occasions on which the Safavid claims to supreme religio-political authority were not even condoned but were rejected outright. We know from Chardin's copious account that under ʿAbbās II, who decidedly favored the gnostic philosophers and the mystic virtuosi and from whom the dogmatic party could not hope for much, these claims came under the latter's fire of attack:

> How can it be possible, says the men of the church, that these impious kings, who are not constrained by the Sacred Law [*nā-muqayyad*] . . .•[who are] wine drinkers, and transported by passion, be the vicars of God; and that they have communication with heaven to receive the necessary light for the conduct of the believers?

Furthermore, claimed the dogmatic party, these kings hardly know how to read. How can they dispel the doubts of the believers?[68] As is bound to happen in ideological confrontations of this kind, the parties could not hesitate to exploit their opponents' principles if it suited them, and the assertion of the religio-political nature of supreme political authority was highly suitable for (unprincipled) exploitation by the dogmatic party. Commitment to logical rigor and consistency on the part of the worldly ambitious among the *mujtahid*s would not get in the way of their giving tacit encouragement to the view that they were sinless (or infallible), and that their existence was due to the grace that is incumbent upon God.[69] (In doing so, they were taking a leaf out of the book of the royal beneficiaries of the extremist heritage and arrogating to themselves qualities attributed to the Imams.) In a similar vein, they would press forward to assert that "the supreme throne of the universe belongs only to a *mujtahid*, . . . a man of sanctity and science. However, as the *mujtahid* is peaceable, he should have a king at his service to exercise his sword in the cause of justice as his minister."[70]

It should be emphasized that in putting forward their political counter-claims, the party of religious professionals was acting in its strategic interest in exploiting the flaws of the Safavid principles of legitimacy, which were the vestiges of extremism. It was according to these principles, and *not* on the basis of any Shiᶜite doctrine, that they asserted a *mujtahid* would be better qualified to rule than the king. The stance was no doubt profitable to the dogmatic party in their political struggle against the secularist ᶜAbbās II, but it could not be said to have been taken in accordance with Shiᶜite doctrine. In fact, given the absence of any jurisprudential theory of vicegerency, what seemed more consistent with the Shiᶜite theological tenet of *luṭf*—that the grace of God made the existence of the Imam necessary for every age—was the assertion made in the same period by the royalist Mullā Muḥammad Bāqir Sabzavārī, the *Shaykh al-Islām* of Isfahan and a man of far greater intellectual stature than Mullā Qāsim, who agitated against ᶜAbbās II. In the *Rawḍat al Anwār ᶜAbbāsī*, Sabzavārī states:

> No time is devoid of the existence of the Imam, but in certain periods the Imam is absent from the eyes of the human beings for some reasons and expediencies, but even then the world is prospering thanks to the emanation of His existence. . . . Now in this period where the Master of the Age . . . is absent, if there be no just and judicious king to administer and rule this world, the affairs will end in chaos and disintegration, and life will become impossible for everybody. But it is inevitable, and imperative, for people [to

be ruled by] a king who will rule with justice and follow the practice and tradition of the Imam.[71]

In any event, we know that the opinion of the *mullās* of the dogmatic party changed drastically once, under the leadership of Majlisī, they had gained the support of the monarch in their fight against the gnostic philosophers within the hierocracy. What the party of the dogmatic *fuqahā* were appealing to when in opposition was the extremist-type religiosity and gullibility of the masses, whose persistence was detected by Du Mans. According to Du Mans, this doctrinally undisciplined propensity could be activated by a *mujtahid* (we know that in fact it could be activated by any *mullā* or any *sayyid*) who, by claiming to be the *jānishīn-e imām* (vicegerent of the Imam) could entice the populace and "gather the people behind him like another Orpheus," a possibility of which political authorities were very mindful.[72] Another source leaves us in no doubt that Majlisī the Elder was the object of extremist adulation by the gullible masses. Mīr Lawḥī disappropvingly reports the rumor circulating among the "common people, more benighted than cattle," that when Majlisī returned from Mecca, Imām Ḥusayn and the Hidden Imam were seen holding his stirrups! After Majlisī's death, his coffin was broken to pieces by the populace, and the pieces were worn as amulets.[73]

The anomaly of the Safavid period was not the absence of political pretensions on the part of the hierocracy (as is implied by the current views of the political implications of Shiᶜism), but the religious pretensions of the Safavid rulers, which were a vestige of Shiᶜite extremism. However, even though the structure of domination that prevailed in the Safavid period contained a fundamental contradiction, it was highly stable. The contradiction remained unresolved because of the supremacy of the state, a supremacy that rested not only on overwhelming de facto power but also on the solid normative foundation of the patrimonial political ethos, in turn buttressed by the rulers' charisma of lineage as alleged descendants of the Seventh Imam.

It is therefore not surprising that the Safavid dynasty lasted over two centuries, and that its unrivaled legitimacy tenaciously persisted even after its overthrow by the Afghan invaders. In addition to the numerous contenders who claimed Safavid descent during the prolonged aftermath of the Afghan invasion, it should be remembered that half a century after the fall of Isfahan, Karīm Khān Zand (1750–79), who never assumed the title of shah, ruled as *vakīl al-raᶜāyā*, and would rebuke whomever called him king, reminding them that the king, Ismāᶜīl III the Safavid, was in Ābādeh (where he lived as a confined figurehead on a pension making knives); he would add that he himself was Ismāᶜīl III's steward (*kadkhudā*).[74] We may even go further and speculate that many of the false pretenders to Safavid descent through the interregnum were the types of local leader who would have claimed mahdihood in a different period.

The continuity with extremism in the Safavid principles of legitimacy made for the intrusion of religion into the structure of political domination. The virtually complete separation of the political and religious spheres implied by the pattern of the Shiʿite doctrinal belief system found a very imperfect translation in the societal structure of domination. The societal structure of domination resisted change in the direction of greater congruence with the normative logic of Twelver Shiʿism because of the contrary prevalence of *domination on the basis of charisma of lineage*, both at the apex of the body politic with the ruling dynasty and at the intermediate level with the clerical notables who persisted side by side with the professionalized hierocracy and whose members put forward an antijuristic religious doctrine of their own in the form of Akhbārī traditionalism.

CHAPTER EIGHT

Shiᶜism, the Patrimonial Political Ethos, and Sociopolitical Action

In the preceding chapters we have reviewed the two independent components of the normative order governing action in the political sphere: The ethos of patrimonialism and the political ethic of Shiᶜism. It is now time to consider the respective bearing of these components on practice, that is, their respective influence on action in the political sphere. We shall begin with an examination of the directive influence upon societal action of the Shiᶜite ethos, and of the ethos of patrimonialism. ("Religiously relevant" societal action in the form of the religious policy of the Safavid state and instances of "communal action" in the case of "politically conditioned" religious movements such as the Nūrbakhshiyya and the Niᶜmatullāhiyya were dealt with in chapter 4.)

8.1 Shiᶜism, the Patrimonial Ethos, and Societal Action

8.1.1 Royal Enactments and Reglementations

The determinative imprint of the norms of the patrimonial ethos on these enactments and administrative instructions is unmistakable, though incidental exhortative references are also made to the Qurʾan, such as the verse, "Verily God commands justice and charity and forbids tyranny"; a verse that in fact encapsulates the general principles of the patrimonial ethos.[1] The ethical content of these principles consists in exhortations to the governor to take care of the weak and the poor in particular, and to protect the subjects in general. Except for the specifically religiously oriented enactments to be considered presently, no material religious influence is detectable. This is the case even with the enactments of Ṭahmāsp, the most pious of the Safavid monarchs. In three *farmān*s inscribed in the main mosque of Kashan (1526, 1572, and 1573), which deal with a range of general topics, only at one point is the sacred law mentioned, and then in conjunction with justice as the means of extirpating oppression (*ẓulm*). For the rest, the *farmāns* are overwhelmingly couched in terms drawn from the theories of kingship centering around justice and patrimonial charity.[2] These same principles of the patrimonial ethos inform the reglementations of Ṭahmāsp's code for governors, the *Aʾīn-e Shāh Ṭahmāsp*. Of the sixty-nine articles, only two derive from the sacred law (the prohibitions of drinking and music making), while two (relating to inheritance of the heirless and the charitable care of the orphans) bypass the provisions of the sacred law.[3]

We now come to a group of enactments that are specifically oriented to the enforcement of the provisions of the sacred law (religiously conditioned societal acts in our terminology). Their incidence depended largely on the piety of the person of the king, and they therefore abound during the reign of Ṭahmāsp. After his famous repentance in 1534/941,[4] Ṭahmāsp issued *farmāns* closing taverns, opium houses, gambling houses, and brothels, consciously foregoing the considerable taxes (2,000 *tūmāns*) accruing to the royal treasury from these sources.[5] In another *farmān* inscribed in Kashan in that year, this time couched in terms of enjoining the good and forbidding the evil, shaving is also forbidden.[6] The governors were from time to time reminded to observe these prohibitions which "have by now [1570s] been observed for nearly forty years."[7] Another pious king, Sulṭān Muḥammad Khudā-Bandeh, also repented in 1583/991, manumitting thirty or forty slaves,[8] and issued a *farmān* forbidding wine drinking and pastimes prohibited by the sacred law.[9] It should be noted that even in these cases of specific, religiously oriented societal action, the enactments also include references to the patrimonial ethos and enjoin the care of the subjects.[10]

Two unusual acts by the pious Ṭahmāsp that are important for the consolidation of Shiʿism in a critical period should be mentioned. In 1555–56/963 he made his generals and notables repent collectively,[11] and in 1568–69/976 he ordered the *ʿulamāʾ* and the men of learning to engage in preaching.[12] Finally, one can mention ʿAbbās II's decision to induce voluntary conversion of the Jews by means of monetary incentive. In this meritorious religiously oriented societal act, 2,000 Jewish households were paid two *tūmāns* each for converting to Islam (the treasury also incurred the additional cost of foregoing the income for *jizya* previously levied on the new converts as the "protected people of the book").[13]

8.1.2 Personal Acts of Piety by the King and the Members of the Royal Household

As patrimonialism is sociologically characterized by the treatment of the kingdom as an extension of the household of the king,[14] we may consider the acts of the kings and their immediate siblings as "societal." Of these acts, a distinct group can be considered religiously oriented. This group includes pilgrimage to and repair of important shrines and to a lesser extent mosques, creation of religious endowments, and sponsorship of religious charities. When undertaken by the monarchs themselves, these had the important incidental effect of enhancing their legitimacy (which they quite possibly took into account). In the case of the female members of the royal household, however, the exclusively religious motivation of these pious acts is easier to discern.

We are told that Ṭahmāsp paid 80,000 *tūmān*s per annum to the holy shrines, including five *tūmān*s a day to the shrine of Mashhad, to be spent on food and beverage for charitable distribution.[15] ʿAbbās I twice undertook pilgrimages to Mashhad on foot, and in 1015 munificently endowed the shrine of the Eighth Imam in Mashhad with his vast estates, urban property, and much of his jewelry and other belongings.[16] In 1622–23/1032 he went on pilgrimage to the shrines of the Imams in Arabian Iraq.[17] Shāh Ṣafī, after the conquest of Ḥilla in 1631/1040, visited the shrine of Imām Ḥusayn in Karbalā and renovated the dome of the shrine of ʿAlī in Najaf.[18]

Ṭahmāsp's favorite sister, Sulṭāmun, who died in 1561–62/969, made her entire estate, including her jewelry, into a religious endowment.[19] The extant correspondence between Ṭahmāsp's wife and one of his sisters also indicates preoccupation with religious and charitable acts and with the repair of mosques.[20] Last but not least, the pious mother of Shāh Sulṭān-Ḥusayn built the magnificent Madrasa-ye Mādar-e Shāh in Isfahan and endowed it generously.[21]

8.1.3 Religiously Conditioned and Hierocratic Action through the State

This category of societal action aimed at the enforcement either of morals or orthodoxy. Under the pious Ṭahmāsp and his pious but ineffectual son Sulṭān Muḥammad Khudā-Bandeh, religiously oriented societal action aiming at the enforcement of the provisions of the sacred law emanated directly from the monarch. However, such action could also be initiated by clerical officials of the state. For instance, al-Karakī's student, Amīr Muʿizz al-Dīn Iṣfahānī (d. 1545–46/952), noted for his knowledge of the sacred law and his ethical rigorism, destroyed many "houses of sin" and sites of gambling, opium smoking, and wine drinking, and extirpated many a corrupt heretic.[22] Under the seventeenth-century monarchs, this kind of action was initiated either by clerical officials or by the hierocracy. Thus, when ʿAbbās II in his early teens appointed Sulṭān al-ʿUlamāʾ grand vizier in 1645/1055 "to strengthen the pillars of the sacred law," wine drinking and prostitution were forbidden by a royal decree. A number of Armenians were also forbidden to make sheepskin coats for sale to Muslims, even though this measure cost royal treasury much in foregone revenue.[23] The first act of the triumphant hierocracy under Majlisī was the decree prohibiting wine drinking, issued by Shāh Sulṭān-Ḥusayn at his request. Six thousand bottles of prime wine from the royal cellars were broken, and the prohibition was severely enforced.[24]

Under Shāh Ṣafī, the Shiᶜite *ᶜulamā*ʾ fulminated against the ruler's commissioning of a translation of the *Revival of the Religious Sciences* by the Sunni thinker al-Ghazālī, and demanded repressive measures against the Sunnis. However, Ṣafī paid no heed to their demands and they had to content themselves with writing polemical tracts against Sunnism.[25] Some six decades later, under Sulṭān-Ḥusayn, they were to have their way. The final wave of persecution of Sunnism thus came with the final triumph of the Shiᶜite hierocracy. As the *Skaykh al-Islām* of Isfahan, Majlisī pursued a vigorous policy of suppression of Sunnism and the conversion of Sunnis and other religious minorities. Persecutions are reported in the Sunni region of Lāristān[26] and elsewhere.[27] The sources make clear that not all the 70,000 non-Shiᶜites, whom the author of *Qiṣaṣ al-ᶜUlamā*ʾ accredits Majlisī with having converted, accepted Shiᶜism nonviolently, and merely by reading the massively voluminous popularized religious writings bearing his name.[28] In 1671–72/1082, we hear of a request for Shiᶜite missionaries for the region of Badakhshān in Afghanistan being granted by Shāh Suleymān.[29] Shiᶜite missionary activities coupled with persecution of Sunnism can be presumed to have been intensified after Majlisī's appointment as the *Shaykh al-Islām* of Isfahan. In fact, the repression he instituted can be counted as an important cause of the discontent of the Sunni population of Afghanistan, which led to the Afghan invasion and the overthrow of the Safavid dynasty.[30]

As was the case with the final suppression of Sunnism, the last wave of persecution of Sufism was initiated and carried out at the instigation of the Shiᶜite hierocracy. The Safavid state had no political motive for suppressing the individualistic ascetic, antinomian, or intellectualist Sufism of the second half of the seventeenth century, and, under ᶜAbbās II, greatly encouraged it. However, as we have seen, these varieties of Sufism came under the heavy attack of the emergent Shiᶜite hierocracy. There were sharp clashes between the dogmatic *ᶜulamā*ʾ and the Sufis during the reign of Suleymān.[31] Chardin relates the incident of a *faqih* being dragged down from the pulpit and beaten by four or five Sufis in his audience when he declared the shedding of the blood of Sufis lawful.[32] With the ascendancy of hierocracy under Sulṭān-Ḥusayn, persecution of the Sufis was instituted by Majlisī, who obtained a decree from the shah for their expulsion from the capital.[33] The persecution was continued by the first two *Mulla-bashi*s,[34] men of similarly rigid and dogmatic frame of mind, the latter of whom was apparently not even loath to commit acts of violence personally.[35]

8.1.4 Military Action

Military orgiasticism of the fanatically devoted tribal military force with which Ismāᶜīl built his vast empire is illustrated in some detail by the contemporary sources. The following is an account of the chiliastic enthusiasm of the Qizilbāsh:

> . . . many of [the Qizilbāsh warriors] enter into battle without armour, expecting their master Ismael to watch over them in the fight. There are also

> those others who go to battle without armour . . . rushing with naked breasts, crying, "Schiac, Shiac." The name of God is forgotten throughout Persia and only that of Ismael remembered; if any one falls when riding or dismounted he appeals to no other god but Shiac [shaykh or shah]. . . .[36]

In accounts of the battles given in the *Ross Anonymous*, prostrations and excited cries of "may my life be sacrificed for my *Murshid*" upon Ismāʿīl's appearance would precede the march to the battlefield.[37]

Nor could the military orgiasticism of the Qizilbāsh, drawing on central Asiastic shamanism, be considered in any way religiously disciplined. According to an eyewitness at the Battle of Marv (1510/916), after striking down his Uzbek archenemy, Shaybak Khān, Ismāʿīl turned to the Sufis and cried: "Whoever loves my head should eat of the flesh of this enemy," whereupon a crowd of Qizilbāsh Sufis descended like vultures upon the bloody and soil-covered corpse, fighting among each other with drawn swords for a morsel of the corpse's flesh.[38]

Under Ṭahmāsp certain aspects of military action came under ethical regulation, though it is difficult to determine when and how. In the last two decades of Ṭahmāsp's reign, the jurists apointed *qāḍī muʿaskar* (army judge) begin to figure prominently among the elite. During the Qizilbāsh interregnum, the importance of the office of *qāḍī muʿaskar* reached its height. It declined thereafter under ʿAbbās I. Strong emphasis is placed on the *lawfulness* of the appropriation of booty and captured women and children in the chronicles.[39] The jurists ruled that the Imam had made his share of captured women and children lawful as slaves to the Shiʿites during the occultation.[40] The detailed treatment of *jihād* in the *Jāmiʿ ʿAbbāsī*, by affirmation as well as by judicious omission, sanctions the appropriation of sons and wives of Christians, since Christians are "people of the book" who have become *ḥarbī*.[41]

However, the effectiveness of this ethical regulation depended on the maintenance of military discipline in general and had to be enforced from above. This is clearly borne out by an instance of the breakdown of military discipline that led to the massacre of the inhabitants of the old Shiʿite city of Sabzavār during the Qizilbāsh interregnum (1583/991). In this case, despite the exhortation of the *ʿulamāʾ* attached to the army, large-scale massacre, rape, and enslavement of boys and girls took place.[42] As one contemporary historian remarked about this flagrant violation of the dictates of the sacred law: "In short, what the Muslims do to the Georgian nation and the *kuffār-e ḥarbī*, the Qizilbāsh group did unto the innate Shiʿites of that city."[43]

ʿAbbās I's military reforms, especially the creation of a largely Georgian slave army and the recruitment of sedentary Persians,[44] entailed considerable rationalization of military organization. Furthermore, military forces came to include many recently islamized men, and men from urban backgrounds to whom the Qizilbāsh tradition of military chiliasm was most probably alien. Military action was largely secularized. Nevertheless, the army judge and his delegates continued to function in the army in the seventeenth century.[45] Though the office of *qāḍī muʿaskar* was never abolished, the description of his minor administrative function (of underwriting the soldiers' pay drafts) at the end of the Safavid era makes it clear that the religious aspects of this office had become less significant.[46]

8.1.5 Fiscal Action

One of al-Karakī's first acts in his attempt to weave Imāmī Shiʿism into the fabric of the Safavid body politic was to write a treatise on the lawfulness of *kharāj* (the land tax), by far the most important source of state revenue in a predominantly agrarian empire. Like his Ottoman counterpart Abu'l-Suʿūd some half a century later,[47] al-Karakī set out to prove that the *kharāj* was lawful; that is, in accordance with the sacred law.

In a preliminary manner, *kharāj* is differentiated from the religious taxes (*khums* and *zakāt*), and is said to be payable to the state. Different categories of land are described, and the land of the Safavid domains is said to belong to the category of *maftūḥ ʿunwatan*, on which the *kharāj* is leviable:[48] "The land tax and dues are like rent and *therefore determinable by custom*." [49] Whether or not it is wrongly appropriated by a tyrannical ruler (*sulṭān jāʾir*), who would be responsible before God for the wrong appropriation, its payment remains an ethically incumbent obligation (*ḥaqq sharʿī*) upon the cultivator, as it corresponds to the right of God, and "it is not permissible for he upon whom the *kharāj* . . . is incumbent to steal it or to repudiate it." [50] Thus the payment of the *kharāj* to the ruler, at the rate determined by custom, is incumbent upon the cultivator during the occultation of the Imam. This is so because the *kharāj* belongs to the Shiʿite community as a whole and not to the ruler, who is merely its caretaker.

As we have seen, al-Karakī's chief rival within the hierocracy, Al-Qaṭīfī, put forward a detailed refutation of al-Karakī, but it is very doubtful if the latter's views were allowed to find any currency among the people, whereas we know from the tract written by Aḥmad Ardabīlī some few decades later, upholding al-Qaṭīfī's basic position, that the collection of the *kharāj* was legitimized on the basis of al-Karakī's treatise. Ardabīlī's ruling that the payment of the *kharāj* is not incumbent upon the cultivator[51] was in turn refuted by a certain Shaykh Mājid al-Shaybānī, who reaffirmed al-Karakī's basic contentions that the *kharāj* is like legally contracted rent, and its payment is incumbent even if it is collected by a tyrannical ruler. In his argument, Shaykh Mājid also invoked the authority of the second martyr,[52] who, as we know, had gone even further than al-Karakī in legitimizing the *kharāj*.[53]

Unlike some ambiguous modernist attempts to bring fiscal action within the scope of the sacred law by admitting only the legitimacy of *zakāt* as the Islamic (i.e., religious) form of taxation, al-Karakī expressly states that land taxation belongs to the realm of the customary (*ʿurf*), its rate being accordingly determinable by custom (fifteen percent of the product appears to have been the basic rate at the time[54] and is as such sanctioned by al-Karakī). Al-Karakī is not extending religious law into the sphere of political economy; rather, recalling the distinction between the legitimatory power of the hierocracy over the secular spheres of life and their sacralization, we can see that this endeavor consists in supplying a hierocratic *legitimization* of secular land tenure and taxation.

Of course, once this legitimization was put forward in writing by the most eminent of the Shiᶜite jurists, the ideologues of the state would not hesitate to assert that land taxation was in accordance with "the *Sharīᶜa* of the Prophet."[55] Furthermore, al-Karakī's treatise established *kharāj* as a more legitimate form of taxation than other imposts. Thus, after one of his many dreams of the Hidden Imam in 1565/972, Ṭahmāsp would abolish the remainder of the *tamghāvāt*—levies on crafts and commerce—that were not explicitly justified by al-Karakī, and his official historian would write that he had abolished all the levies that were not established in Jaᶜfarī (i.e., Imāmī) Shiᶜism. Here an appeal to the patrimonial ethos is made side by side with stress on the conformity of taxation with the provisions of the sacred law. In the determination of taxes and state imposts, Ṭahmāsp is said to have applied the code (*qānūn-nāmcheh*) of Ūzūn Ḥasan Aqqūyūnlū, "who was the most just of the kings on the earth."[56] In actual practice, the provisions of the sacred law did not affect either the basic rates of taxation or the arbitrary additional levies of various governors, both of which came to be variously "determined by custom," and in fact increased in the seventeenth century.[57] Insofar as normative considerations played a part in taxation, as distinct from maximum taxability and degree of control of central government and the like, these were the norms of fairness and substantive justice belonging to the patrimonial ethos.

8.1.6 Sacred Law and Patrimonial "Custom" in the Administration of Justice

In chapter 5, I emphasized the trend toward the continuous decline in the importance of the office of the qadis throughout the sixteenth and seventeenth centuries. This decline, together with important inherent characteristics of the Shiᶜite legal system discussed in chapter 1, the role of the sacred law and of the religious courts in the overall Safavid system of administration of justice, was relatively unimpressive. By the second half of the seventeenth century, as Chardin would note, unlike the old times, the qadis had very little power,[58] and played a secondary role in the administration of justice. Their functions, as specified by the contemporary sources, were confined to the following: marriage and divorce, division of inheritance, preparation and endorsement of deeds of sale,[59] issuance of burial permits, certification of legal maturity (i.e., puberty [*bulūgh*]), and manumission.[60] In addition, diverse cases of litigation were brought before the qadis or the *Shaykh al-Islām*s and the *ṣadr*, who also had religious courts of an informally higher status. According to Chardin, cases of divorce were the most usual.[61]

The impact of the sacred law on social practice was also restricted by the insignificance of the muftis, whose influence on the development of law we have noted. According to Du Mans, the mufti, whose function is the declaration of what is "lawful" and "unlawful" and the issuance of legal opinions, is an important officer in Turkey: "Here, he is a miserable snake whom even his neighbors hardly know."[62] Du Mans also cites instances of employment of *ḥiyal* to give legal form to usurious transactions.

By contrast, secular, patrimonial administration of justice overwhelmingly predominated over the hierocratic administration of the sacred law. Chardin remarks that despite easy access, recourse to the religious tribunals were infrequent. By contrast, the massive bulk of the cases referred to the secular tribunals is striking. There were usually 7,000 or 8,000 and at times over 10,000 plaintiffs at the king's court. Not surprisingly, therefore, the secular administration of justice prevailed over the hierocratic "without the slightest resistance" despite the hypothetical supremacy of the sacred law. There were no conflicts between the religious (*sharʿī*) and the customary (*ʿurfī*) tribunals, and the former dared not protest against the encroachments of the latter especially as the qadis depended on temporal power for the execution of their verdict.[63]

What then were the characteristics of the patrimonial administration of justice that overwhelmingly dominated the Safavid judiciary organization, and what were the normative principles governing it? Here, Weber's admirable characterization of the patrimonial administration of justice of the "patriarchal" variety (as distinct from the "estate" type) is borne out at every point. As Weber noted, under patrimonialism, the distinction between administrative and judiciary is completely blurred and the administration of justice is subsumed under the ruler's "regulations" containing general directives to the officials of his realm.[64] This is well illustrated by Ṭahmāsp's code—the *Āʾīn-e Shāh Ṭahmāsp*—which consists of sixty-nine reglementations to the officials of his realm in which fairness in the administration of justice is incorporated in the general directives on just and benign administration, regulation of prices and care, and protection of the poor. The same is true of Ṭahmāsp's directives to individual governors.[65] The code also illustrates the substantive character of the patriarchal administration of justice centering on social justice and welfare. According to Weber, "in purely patriarchal administration of the law, the law is . . . thoroughly informal, as far as one may speak of law at all under such a system of pure 'regulations.'" Thus, monarchical patriarchalism, in striving for substantive justice, deprives law of its specialized character in order to formulate reglementations in such a way as to instruct the officials *and* enlighten the subjects.[66] Ṭahmāsp's code was in fact inscribed in stone in the major cities.[67]

The Safavid secular tribunals were the organizational embodiments of the patrimonial ethos. The supreme tribunal was that of the king, usually held by his delegate, the *Dīvān-begī*, or the secretary of the *dīvān-e aʿlā* at the gates of the royal palace. A distinctive feature of Safavid patrimonialism was the monarch's exclusive prerogative of passing the death sentence on a subject. In theory, it was possible to appeal to the king as the father of his subjects against all authorities, administrative or judiciary, and the plaintiffs could and did appear individually or *en masse* at the gates of his palace to make their complaints heard. In the cities other than the capital, provincial governors represented the king at the secular tribunals.[68]

Some of the cases brought before the secular tribunals concerned administrative matters, complaints against the officials, and taxation.[69] Another important group of cases had to do with criminal justice. As we have seen, the self-imposed idealistic limitation on the part of the jurists—as, for instance, reflected in the reiterated rules of evidence in *Jāmiᶜ ᶜAbbāsī*[70]—relegated this branch of administration of justice to the secular tribunals, which were in this capacity also referred to as the courts of the "four crimes" (*aḥdāth-e arbaᶜa*).[71] According to Chardin, criminal justice was exercised entirely independently of the sacred law by the *ᶜurf* magistrates, composed of the president of the *Dīvān*, the governor of the town, and the supervisor (*nāẓir*) of the king, who ruled by maxims founded on customs.[72]

Consonantly with the patrimonial ethos, great emphasis was put on the responsibility of governors for the safety of the roads and security within the cities. This accounts for the great security of roads at the end of Ṭahmāsp's reign and throughout the seventeenth century. An ordinance of Suleymān restated that the governors were responsible for compensating losses due to robbery.[73] Crimes against public order, including drunkenness, were severely punished, and the worst forms of capital punishment were reserved for highway robbers. Again, as a result of the tight ethical regulation of "fair" prices, weights, and measures, those selling short measures or above the tariff were also severely punished.[74]

Having delineated the secular judiciary organization, we may end by pointing out the role played by the *ṣadr* and his provincial deputies in the *legitimization* of *secular* administration of justice—a role akin to the hierocracy's legitimatory function in the political and fiscal spheres. The *ṣadr-e khāṣṣa* sat at the *dīvān-begī*'s supreme tribunals and put his seal to his verdicts. His deputies in the provincial cities (sing. *nāʾib al-ṣadāra*) similarly sat at the criminal (*aḥdāth*) courts of the governors and sanctioned the latter's sentences.[75] Over and above their legitimatory function, individual members of the hierocracy also on occasion took part in certain patrimonial judiciary processes. For example, a *farmān* issued by Shāh Sulṭān-Ḥusayn in 1695/1107 includes the *Shaykh al-Islām* of Gilan in a commission of inquiry appointed to investigate a complaint by a number of subjects from that province.[76] But such incorporations of the members of the hierocracy into the patrimonial judiciary process were in no way as common as in the Ottoman Empire.

8.2 Religion and Communal Action

8.2.1 Extremism and Political Rebellions

Although, as we have seen, the suppression of extremism had gone a long way under Ṭahmāsp, communal action motivated by popular Sufi and extremist religiosity reappear in the political arena during the Qizilbāsh interregnum and in sporadic instances thereafter during the reigns of ᶜAbbās I and Ṣafī. Though the mahdistic tenet was not explicitly activated in all instances, Shiᶜite-Sufi extremism is unmistakably the hallmark of all these political rebellions.

A set of rebellions occurred after the death of Ismāᶜīl II in 1577 in which it was not the Hidden Imam's but Ismāᶜīl II's alleged *parousia* that triggered off communal political action! After Ismāᶜīl's death, rumors spread that he had not died but had gone into "concealment" (*ghāʾib shodeh*) and would soon reappear (*ẓuhūr khāhad kard*) in Anatolia or India. For the first time in Sabzavār, a Qalandar dervish claimed to be Ismāᶜīl, and then another in Hamadan.[77] Then came the most important of the pseudo-Ismāᶜīls, another Qalandar in Kūh Gīlūyeh who resembled Ismāᶜīl II in appearance and rose (*khurūj kardeh*) with 10,000 men who accepted his claim to be Ismāᶜīl. He became known as Shāh-e Qalandar and also as Shāh Ismāᶜīl-e Qatīl, captured territory bordering on Dizfūl and Shūshtar, struck coins in his name, and ruled "with utmost ease and felicity"[78] for some years until he was captured and decapitated in 1582/990. His head was sent to the capital upon a spear and his territory recaptured.[79]

There may also have been other instances of appearances of peudo-Ismāᶜīls because we are told that during the first four or five years of Sulṭān Muḥammad's reign there was much talk about Ismāᶜīl among the people.[80]

In the rebellions under ᶜAbbās I and Ṣafī, the activation of the mahdistic tenet was much more explicit. In 1620/1029, a certain Sayyid Muḥammad, claiming descent from Shaykh Ṣafī, rose as an antimonarch in Gilan. He called himself the "Messenger of the Lord of the Age" (*rasūl-e ḥaḍrat-e ṣāḥib al-amr*), appointed *khalīfas*, and issued *farmāns* in a kingly fashion. Sayyid Muhammad and his followers were eliminated by Shāh ᶜAbbās.[81] This case illustrates that an extremist claim to legitimacy of political authority could henceforth be put forward only in revolutionary defiance of the Safavid normative order, and would be suppressed by the military force upholding it. Thus, when in 1631/1041 yet another attempt was made to harness extremist religiosity for chiliastic political action in revolutionary defiance of Shāh Ṣafī, the same ruthless fate awaited the new claimant to mahdihood. A certain Darvīsh Riḍā attributed to himself the power of "revelation and charismata" (*hashf va karāmāt*). Not unlike Mushaᶜshaᶜ and Ismāᶜīl I, he put forward a nuanced claim: "at times he called himself the Deputy of the Lord of the Age, and at times he claimed Mahdihood." Darvīsh Riḍā had a following among the Zanganeh tribe, but his uprising was speedily put down and he was killed.[82] Thenceforth, the claimants to mahdihood had to find a more congenial milieu. Thus we hear of a Shāh ʿĀrif Darvīsh, reputedly descending from Shāh Ṭasmāsp, who claimed to be the "Mahdi of the End of Time" in Kashmir, and was as such revered with the sublime act of worship—prostration.[83]

8.2.2 The Nuqṭavī Heresy

The military chiliasm of Qizilbāsh was not the only religious movement born out of the extremism of the fifteenth century. Another kindred phenomenon with a literate, urban following was the Nuqṭavī movement. The Nuqṭavī doctrine, formulated by Maḥmud Pasīkhānī, was a later offshoot of Ḥurūfism. Maḥmūd's follower, the Nuqṭaviyya, preserved the Ḥurūfīs' numerological cabalistic emphasis as well as the central belief in gnostic union with God through spiritual perfection, while adding a pronounced belief in metempsychosis or transmigration of souls.[84] In the sixteenth century the doctrine spread in Persian Iraq.[85] Ṭahmāsp took active measures to suppress the Nuqṭavī movement during the last decade of his reign. The Nuqṭavī poet Abu'l-Qāsim Amrī was blinded, in 1555–56/973, a Nuqṭavī community near Kashan was massacred in 1575–76/983, and a number of the Nuqṭavīs of Qazvin were imprisoned. Nevertheless, Nuqṭavism appears to have flourished after Ṭahmāsp's death. We hear of the Nuqṭavī presence in Kashan during the Qizilbāsh interregnum and of a Nuqṭavī rebellion under the leadership of the blind poet, Amrī, in Shiraz a few years after ʿAbbās I's ascension (1590–91/999).[86] By the sixth year of ʿAbbās's reign, the Nuqṭavīs under the leadership of Darvīsh Khusraw, were well established in the capital, Qazvin. According to one account, some 200 persons were constantly present in their *tekke*, which was frequented by ʿAbbās himself, and consequently by a number of generals and high government functionaries.[87] Despite the subsequent rationalizations of the chroniclers, it is clear that ʿAbbās was for a time keenly interested in the Nuqṭavī doctrine.[88] In fact, they considered him the "perfect trustee" (*amīn-e kāmil*) whose initiation was complete under the instruction of two dervishes who had attained unity with God.[89] At the turn of the year 1002 (1593), the Nuqṭavīs, on the basis of their numerology, predicted the coming of the Lord of the Age, whose most likely incarnation was ʿAbbās himself. However, ʿAbbās's official astrologer had a more ominous prediction based on the appearance of a certain star. The astrologer's opinion finally prevailed upon ʿAbbās. He put one of the leading Nuqṭavīs on the throne as king and had him assassinated after three days, thereby fulfilling the astrologer's prediction.[90] Thereupon ʿAbbās embarked on a policy of ferocious suppression of the Nuqṭavīs. Darvīsh Khusraw was tried for heresy by an inquisitorial gathering of the *ʿulamā*ʾ, and hanged. A prominent Nuqṭavī physician, Mawlānā Salmān, was also condemned to imprisonment by the *ʿulamā*ʾ but put to death by ʿAbbās's order. ʿAbbās also sent orders to Kashan and Isfahan for the extirpation of Khusraw's followers, and killed the leader of the Kashan community with his own hands. Some years later he killed the two dervishes who had allegedly initiated him to the secret Nuqṭavī teachings.[91]

The suppression of the Nuqṭaviyya indicated ʿAbbās's definitive rejection of extremism and the adoption of an unmistakably antimillenarian religious policy in favor of the Shiʿite hierocracy. In 1594/1003, a large number of the *ʿulamāʾ* and theological students were lavishly entertained in Qazvin. Special royal favor was bestowed upon the eminent *ʿālim* Shaykh Bahāʾ al-Dīn ʿĀmilī.[92]

As was pointed out, the Nuqṭavī heresy, like its Ḥurūfī parent, was an urban religious movement adhered to by literate craftsmen, artists, and poets. With the persecutions initiated by Ṭahmāsp and vigorously resumed by ʿAbbās, many Nuqṭavīs, including a truly impressive number of poets, fled to India, Emperor Akbar's land of religious freedom. Even though years later, in 1660, we still hear of a certain despised dervish-type group in Isfahan referred to as the Maḥmūdīs, with ideas akin to those of the Nuqṭaviyya,[93] it is clear that the increasing prominence of the Shiʿite hierocracy in the polity had left relatively little room for aberrant sectarian groups.

8.2.3 Communal Action Led by Shiʿite Clerics

Commenting on the (inevitable) tension between political and hierocratic domination, Weber remarks:

> In general, the subjugation of religious to royal authority was most successful when religious qualification still functioned as a magical charisma of its bearers and had not yet been rationalized into a bureaucratic apparatus with its own doctrinal system—two usually related phenomena; subjugation was feasible especially when ethics or salvation were not yet dominant in religious thought or had been abandoned again. But wherever they prevail, hierocracy is often invincible, and secular authority must compromise with it. . . . But wherever religious charisma developed a doctrinal system and an organizational apparatus, the caesaropapist state, too, contained a strong hierocratic admixture.[94]

Although in the Safavid period religious charisma did not develop an organizational apparatus independent of the state, it did possess a doctrinal system. Despite the accretion of quasi-magical and otherworldly cultic trappings in the course of its popularization, this doctrinal system still gave a prominent place to the ethics of salvation. As the custodians of the Shiʿite doctrine, the individual members of the hierocracy felt constrained, to varying degrees according to the circumstances, to take up their obligation of enjoining the good and forbidding the evil by insisting on the observance of the ethics of the sacred law.

The ethics of salvation contained in the sacred law could, and at times did, give rise to oppositional communal action in the form of religiously motivated protest. It could thus constitute a source of tension between the dogmatic party of the emergent hierocracy and the state. Though the shah had the right to rule and could claim God's blessing, he was in no way above the sacred law and could not infringe its rules with impunity. Though the Shiʿite *ʿulamāʾ* did not partake of the authority and the charisma of the Imam as the supreme political leader and were in no way entitled to political rule, they were privileged by their knowledge of the sacred law and could, in their capacity as its guardians and learned advisors to believers—in exactly the same way as their Sunni counterparts or Byzantine monks[95]—denounce any infringement of the sacred law by the ruler, and blast against the immoralities of the court.

It was not as rivals for political rule but as exponents of the Islamic ethic of salvation that the state had to contend with the "turbaned class." This presented no problem to Ṭahmāsp and ᶜAbbās I because of their great piety and their great power. With the less pious Safavid shahs, however, the problem arose occasionally.

The Safavid monarchs of the seventeenth century, in addition to their numerous wives and concubines, enjoyed the company of dancers and harlots. Above all they were very bibulous, not only privately but also in public. In fact, the *ṣadr* and the *Shaykh al-Islām* of Isfahan had to be absent in many of the king's official banquets so as not to be seen as giving their tacit approval to wine drinking—a blatant infringement of the sacred law.[96]

As ᶜAbbās II's official historian sychophantically put it, "even though He drinks ceaselessly from morning till evening, drunkenness is not shown on His face!"[97] Furthermore, the epicurian secularism of ᶜAbbās II, which found such physical embodiment as the sumptuous Garden of Peacocks (*ṭāvūs-khāneh*) in Isfahan,[98] was reflected in his preference for mysticism and in his unfavorable disposition toward the dogmatic party within the hierocracy. ᶜAbbās II left the post of the *ṣadr* vacant for the last eighteen months of his reign, and the stringent economies introduced in his reform of the administration of the religious endowments can safely be presumed to have hurt dogmatic clerics more than the favored gnostic philosophers.[99] All this sharpened the propensity of the party of dogmatic reaction to take up the ethically incumbent duties of enjoining the good and forbidding the evil. During the last year of ᶜAbbās II's reign, with the connivance of the *Shaykh al-Islām* of Isfahan and the *Dīvān-begī*, a certain Mullā Qāsim, who had formerly been but a schoolmaster, started his public denunciation of ᶜAbbās II in a suburb of Isfahan. He attracted many people to his sermons and preached that the king and his court were abominations: they were "violaters of the sacred law." God would exterminate the accursed branch, establishing "another branch of pure Imams." The branch he had in mind was to begin with the son of the *Shaykh al-Islām*, who was a grandson of ᶜAbbās the Great (and therefore possessed the [sacred] charisma of Safavid lineage), and who, as the pious son of the foremost jurist, would not infringe the sacred law. The episode ended quite unspectacularly. ᶜAbbās II did no more than to banish Mullā Qāsim from Isfahan to Shiraz and after six months of unrestrained preaching. The *Shaykh al-Islām* and his son threw themselves on the shah's feet, were forgiven, and even received favors. Nothing was done to Mullā Qāsim's other benefactor, the *Dīvān-begī*.[100]

Let us digress briefly to comment on the prevalent view on Shiᶜism and politics, whose proponents indiscriminately cite the episode of Mullā Qāsim, and Du Mans's speculation regarding the possibility of a *mujtahid* leading communal political action as proof of the alleged illegitimacy of all government according to Twelver Shiᶜism. On the basis of our analytical distinctions, we are able, first of all, to point out we are dealing with two types of action. The latter is akin to extremist communal action, which draws on ethically undisciplined religiosity, while the *ethical* motivation in the agitation of Mullā Qāsim is quite clear. Second, neither of the two cases is relevant to the issue of legitimacy of government in Twelver Shiᶜism. Du Mans's hypothetical communal action does not stem from a challenge to the legitimacy of Safavid rule, *but in accordance with extremism and not Twelver Shiᶜite doctrine*. As for Mullā Qāsim, he did not challenge the legitimacy either of the Safavid dynasty or of government in general, but attacked the king and his entourage for their *infringements of the sharīᶜa*. His agitation represents a type of phenomenon found in all world religions, when the ethics of salvation provides a religious source for oppositional communal action, typically led by low-ranking members of the hierocracy.[101]

There are also other instances of "religiously conditioned" and "politically relevant" communal action led by the *ᶜulamā*ʾ. These are analytically less interesting. Some are haphazard: for example, during the political instability of the Qizilbāsh interregnum, we hear of communal political action in the form of riots led by a certain preacher (*vāᶜiẓ*), Mullā Ḥasan Khwānsārī, and a group of low-ranking religious men during the siege of Kashan.[102] Others involved cases of bigotry and communal action with political repercussions. These consisted in the incitement of the populace against the religious minorities, as an example of which we may cite the attempt at coercive conversion of Donna Theresa, the wife of Sir Robert Shirley, after his death. The agitation involved the *Shaykh al-Islām* of Isfahan and a number of *mullā*s, and would have cost Donna Theresa her life had political authorities not shown firmness.[103] This latter type is more noteworthy as it presages the roles of the *ᶜulamā*ʾ as inciters of rabid bigotry against the Sufis and real and alleged Bābīs in the nineteenth century.

CHAPTER NINE

World-rejecting Tendencies in the Shiᶜite Religion

In contrast to primitive religions or cosmologies, the world religions of salvation have a clearly delimited religious sphere immediately relevant to the pursuit of salvation in relation to which the residual social institutions can be conceived of as the "world." Not surprisingly, the "world" appears not only as the realm of the profane but also is negatively evaluated because activity within it is considered a baneful distraction from the pursuit of salvation. In early Christianity, "with the idea of the sacerdoctal and sacramental Church as the *civitas Dei*, . . . the opposite idea of the 'world' as the kingdom of Satan in which there is nothing but perdition and impotence was intensified."[1]

Although the conception of the church as the *civitas Dei* has no equivalent in Islam, the notion of "*dunya*" contrasted doubly to "*dīn*" (religion) and "*ākhirat*" (the hereafter), corresponds reasonably closely to its literal equivalent the "world," and has been the object of instances of both rejection and subjugation to religious governance in the history of Islam. Furthermore, in Islam as in Christianity, the state is clearly included among the institutions of the "world."

9.1 Religious Rejection of Earthly Powers

9.1.1 In Theory

Tendencies in the world religions to reject the world have not spared kingship, the institution presiding over it. Given the age-old tendency toward political apotheosis in the form of sacral kingship, these world religions have at times been violent in this rejection.

Despite his generally erroneous view of kingship in ancient Israel, Frankfort correctly perceives this fundamental antipathy between sacral kingship and monotheistic religions. Such antipathy was entailed by the insistence of the Hebrew prophets on the uniqueness and transcendence of God: "The predominant accusation of the prophets against the kings was faithlessness to Yahweh, a 'seduction' of his chosen people (e.g. II Kings 21:9–11) so that they followed the ways of the gentiles." [2] In Christianity, the most vehement rejection of earthly power is contained in the Book of Revelation, where it is presented as quintessentially evil and opposed to the kingdom of God, being destined, therefore, for destruction by God at the climax of history when he lays bare his arm.[3] Saint Augustine declares "the *regnum*, the state in the narrow sense of rule, [to be] essentially a great band of robbers, *since* it is devoid of justice or at any rate *when* it is devoid of justice." [4] To take an example of antipathy to political power in Eastern Christianity, we may mention Athanasius (d. 373), who, in his *History of the Arians* "compared the Emperor with Ahab, with Belshazzar, and with the Pharaohs," and considered him the forerunner of the Antichrist.[5]

Religious antipathy to political power entails a negative evaluation of the political sphere. However, like so many other religious phenomena, antipathy to political powers has a Janus face. Monasticism and asceticism, the two most important institutionalized forms of rejection of the world in Christianity, could, and under suitable circumstances did, change their posture from withdrawal from the world to the attempt to gain mastery over it.[6] Likewise, the world-rejecting antipathy to political power may move from a position of rejection with a view to withdrawal from the political sphere to one of rejection with a view to subjugation and subordination of political power. The more uncompromising position of withdrawal from the political sphere and avoidance of contact with political powers appears to be tampered in the direction of subjugation only with the growing power of the hierocracy. There seems to be substantial agreement that the crucial transition in Western Christianity took place under Gregory VII (d. 1085). According to Tellenbach,

> Gregory stands at the greatest—from the spiritual point of view perhaps the only—turning point in the history of Catholic Christendom; in his time the policy of converting the world gained once and for all the upper hand over the policy of withdrawing from it: the world was drawn into the Church, and the leading spirits of the new age made it their aim to establish the right order in this united Christian world. In their eyes, however, the most immediate task seemed to be that of successfully asserting the supremacy of the "Servant of the servants of God" over the kings of the earth.[7]

In Shiʿism, by contrast, although movement in the direction of this transition is discernible with the emergence of an autonomous hierocracy in the early decades of the nineteenth century, antipathy to political power overwhelmingly took the form of rejection accompanied by pious withdrawal from politics. The attempt to subjugate and appropriate political power does not make its appearance until the present century (see the epilogue). By contrast, instances of antipathy to earthly power in the form of withdrawal from the political sphere abound throughout the period under consideration.

Early Islam was vehemently opposed to worldly kingship: "It could not but consider the application of the name king of kings (*shāhanshāh*) to any human being as obnoxious and blasphemous." In a well-authenticated tradition, the Prophet is reported as saying: "The vilest [*akhnaʿ*] name in the eyes of God on the day of resurrection is [that of] a man who calls himself king of kings [*malik al-amlāk*]" (an early transmitter explains that the expression refers to *shāhanshāh*).[8]

Islam did not succeed in eradicating or modifying kingship, but the attitude of the Prophet persisted among his "depositories," the *ʿulamāʾ*. Kulaynī strongly denounces those who seek worldly power. "The quest for (political) leadership" (*ṭalab al-riʾāsa*) is dealt with under *kufr* (infidelity, irreligion), and Imam Jaʿfar al-Ṣādiq is thus quoted: "He who seeks leadership perishes."[9] It would be wrong to assume that the pious rejection of political power and its pursuit is specific to Shiʿism. Among the Sunnis too, one frequently comes across the view that the *ʿulamāʾ* "are the depositories of the prophets; yet when they draw near to the rulers and take part in the dealings of this world they betray the prophets. One should beware of such scholars and avoid them."[10]

The problem of the (lack of) propriety of the "association with the sultan" was often discussed in medieval legal and moral texts. Ghazālī devotes a chapter of the *Revival of the Religious Sciences* to the permissible and the forbidden in association with tyrannical rulers. In it, he quotes the tradition attributed to the prophet by Abū Dharr: "whenever a man accedes to authority, he drifts away from God." Ghazālī goes on to argue that

> when a religious scholar meets a corrupt ruler in public, he should honor him, so as not to incite to rebellion, which Islam strictly forbids. On the other hand, when meeting the ruler in private, the scholar must not even rise before him—in order to show him the superiority of religion.[11]

In a subsequent chapter on enjoining the good and forbidding the evil upon the *amīr*s and the sultans, Ghazālī cites another tradition: "the most excellent of the *jihād*s is the utterance of truth in front of the tyrannical sultan."[12]

The separation of the religious sphere from the political reinforced the pious attitude of withdrawal from politics in Shiʿism. What perpetuated this separation and assured that it would be accompanied by a negative evaluation of the political sphere was the existence of the theory of imamate as a utopian substitute for political theory.

It is instructive to look up the Shiʿite interpretations of the "authority verse" (4:59) in the two major Qurʾān commentaries of the sectarian period: al-Ṭūsī's

(d. 1067) *Tibyan* and al-Tabrisī's (d. 1153 or 1158) *Majmaʾ al-Bayan*. Both al-Ṭūsī and al-Tabrisī assert that "those in authority" (*ulu'l-amr*) are neither the secular rulers (*amīrs*) nor the *ʿulamāʾ*—neither of whom are immune from error and sin—but rather the infallible Imams.[13]

As is the case with the arguments in favor of divinely appointed imamate in general, these two most authoritative commentaries on the Qurʾan put forward an invidious contrast with the actual ruler which entails a negative evaluation of political power. By insisting that the true *ulu'l-amr*, those entitled to rule, are the long-dead or hidden Imams, but without clarifying their relationship to the actual holders of power and without elaborating on the latter's functions and obligations either in connection with the notion of "trust" (*amāna*) from the previous verse (4:58) or otherwise, al-Ṭūsī and al-Tabrisī reinforced the gap between the actuality of political rule and the religious sources of normative orientation, a gap that was to remain unbridged. This detachment of the religious and political spheres entailed the rejection of earthly power and pious withdrawal from the political sphere.

Turning now to the Safavid period, in the Muqaddas's commentary on the "authority verses" of the Qurʾan in *Zubdat al-Bayān fī Aḥkām al-Qurʾān*, "imamate" and "caliphate" are said to be among the "trusts" (*amānāt*) to be returned to those entitled to them, but no other "trust" is mentioned.[14] The Muqaddas vehemently attacks the Sunni interpretation of the authority verse as enjoining unconditional obedience to the ruler even when he is tyrannical. However, to establish the illegitimacy of the commands of tyrannical ruler, he does quote, with at least partial implicit approval, the commentary of the Muʿtazilite Zamakhsharī in *al-Kashshāf*, which takes the phrase "those in authority" (*ulu'l-amr*) to refer to righteous princes (*umarāʾ al-ḥaqq*).[15] This notwithstanding, he then turns to al-Tabrisī's above-mentioned interpretation, and concludes by affirming that the rulers cannot be considered on a par with God and his Prophet and therefore entitled to the same kind of obedience. Therefore, the phrase "those in authority" must refer to the house of the Prophet—i.e., Fāṭima and the infallible Imams.[16]

Not only does the Muqaddas set Zamakhsharī's restriction of "those in authority" to the righteous prince in favorable contrast to the view of the Sunni apologists of absolute and unconditional obedience to any ruler, but in the ensuing sections he stresses the necessity of ruling with justice among men. Yet he does not move in the direction of elaborating a positive political ethic, and is content with the doctrine of imamate as a utopian substitute for political theory. This reliance on the doctrine of imamate in general and ʿAlid legitimacy in particular as a pseudo-political theory of authority emerges even more clearly in another work, where the Muqaddas, in a typically Shiʿite polemic, attacks the Sunnis for restricting the conception of imamate to "apparent sovereignty" (*salṭanat-e ẓāhirī*).[17]

In short, Ardabīlī's commentary does not basically differ from those of Tabrisī and Ṭūsī. In all cases, we are given a utopian substitute for a theory of authority that presents temporal power in invidious contrast to historical imamate, thereby not only secularizing it but also evaluating it negatively.

9.1.2 In Practice

As we have seen, al-Karakī's positive political attitude was staunchly criticized by Ibrāhīm al-Qaṭīfī and by Aḥmad Ardabīlī, the Muqaddas, both of whom upheld the ideal of pious antipathy to political power, albeit from different motives. The Muqaddas shunned all involvement with the rulers. Even though many other eminent *ᶜulamāʾ* did accept office under the Safavids, the justifications of cooperation with the temporal ruler were often conditional, cautious, and circumspect.

Many *mujtahid*s were reluctant to accept governmental positions and open favors. The Shaykh al-Bahāʾī reluctantly accepted the office of *Shaykh al-Islām* at the insistence of Shāh ᶜAbbās, but resigned after a brief period and could not be prevailed upon to accept an office again. Many other pious *ᶜulamāʾ* regarded involvement in politics and association with the ruler with deep suspicion and moral disapproval. Shaykh Zayn al-Dīn, the second martyr (d. 1557–58/965), attributed the decline in the authority of the men of religion (*ahl-e dīn*) to their involvement with men of the world (*ahl-e dunyā*) and in worldly affairs. Two other famous Syrian *mujtahid*s, Sayyid ᶜAlī Nūr al-Dīn (d. 1657–58/1068) and his brother Sayyid Muḥammad Shams al-Dīn, fearing to be summoned by ᶜAbbās I and forced to associate with him, dared not undertake the pilgrimage to the shrine of the Eight Imam in Mashhad.[18]

It goes without saying that norms are often broken in practice. Yet their validity as norms is all the more attested to if the norm-breakers acknowledge it. Even such an eminently political theologian as Majlisī felt constrained to pay lip service to the ideal of pious antipathy to political involvement, and wrote "on the iniquities of nearness to kings."[19] When the office of the *shaykh al-Islām* of Isfahan fell vacant after the death of Majlisī's successor Shaykh Jaᶜfar Kamareh-ī in 1703–4/1115, the first two candidates for the office firmly refused to accept it.[20] A third candidate, whose nepotism and venality subsequently became evident, accepted the office. However, the astrologer, the court historian, and another courtier had a secret bet with the king, believing that the "dignified and learned *sayyid*" could not be prevailed upon to accept the post.[21]

The author of *Vaqāyiᶜ al-Sanīn*, himself from a prominent family of clerical notables, in his moral evaluation of the prominent *ᶜulamāʾ* who occupied religio-administrative offices repeatedly states that the man in question "except for accepting office, had no blemish."[22] Conversely, the Safavid historians mention the cases of refusal to accept office, prebends, and gifts from the ruler by men of religion with the greatest admiration and as the sign of moral excellence and piety.

The author of *Ḥabīb al-Siyar*, for instance, admires Qāḍī Naṣrullāh Baghdādī "who reached the limit of *ijtihād*, . . . [and] never accepted a land grant [*surūrghāl*]." [23] Another historian tells us of the eminent Mawlānā Muḥammad Muqīm Yazdī, the "Honor of the Searchers [of truth] and the Proof to the Scholars of the Traditions," who never accepted gifts, land grants, stipends, or supplementary assistance from any king or from any *ṣadr*. Similarly, the less renowned Mawlānā ʿAbdullāh ʿĀdil "never accepted stipends or supplementary assistance from kings or *ṣadr*s." [24]

However, in reality only the elite (*khavāṣṣ*) of the religious community could aspire to uphold the ideal of pious excellence. As for the laymen who could not boast of attaining such excellence, involvement with political power as such was not a necessary evil but a matter of religio-ethical indifference, regulated by the norms of the patrimonial political theory.

9.2 The Ethical Character of Shiʿite Jurisprudence in the Safavid Period and Its Inhibitory Consequences for the Rationalization of Legal Administration

There are instances in which the pious antipathy of the scholars to involvement in worldly affairs went so far as the refusal to engage in jurisprudence. The pious Ibn Ṭāwūs in the thirteenth/seventh century had a complete aversion to *fiqh*, which accounts for the absence of legal works in his very copious writings.[25] The same attitude was no doubt shared by some of the Akhbārī traditionalists of the seventeenth century. Nevertheless, in the Safavid period the formal recognition of *ijtihād* did facilitate the updating of law through the inclusion and extension or omission of topics. This was in fact done under the direction of Shaykh-e Bahāʾī, whose *Jāmiʿ ʿAbbāsī*, as we have seen, became the official legal compendium in the seventeenth century. *Jāmiʿ ʿAbbāsī* represents a serious effort to embrace the world and bring it under the normative governance of the sacred law. In each section, many relevant practical guidelines are appended to the formal ethical categories of the "incumbent," the "commendable," the "reprehensible," and the "forbidden" under the rubric of "traditional practices" (*sunnat*), thereby granting recognition, and by clear implication assent, to many matters of practical relevance not covered by the details of the sacred law. The positive attitude toward the administration of the sacred law is emphatic. Carrying out the duty of qadiship is declared "collectively incumbent" (*vājib kifāʾī*), and under certain circumstances even "individually incumbent" (*vājib ʿaynī*), and the acceptance of the office from a tyrannical ruler is declared permissible along the lines determined by al-Murtaḍā.[26]

Yet, despite Shaykh-e Bahāʾī's intention and serious effort, he did not succeed in bringing the administration of the law within the jurisdiction of the qadis or in subjecting it to formal rationalization. The reason for this failure is to be sought in the self-limiting nature and aims of Shiᶜite value-rational jurisprudence and the primacy of ethical considerations in the administration of justice.

First and foremost, the overriding ethical concern, the concern for implementation of (substantive) justice in each concrete case, minimized the urge toward the rationalization of procedure. In *Jāmiᶜ ᶜAbbāsī*, the function of the judge is at times not distinguished from that of the arbitrator, and the judge is urged not to refrain from "inculcating" and "guiding" the parties if he can do so with impartiality. The qadi is urged to annul his verdict if he subsequently comes across a contrary passage in the "sources" (the Qurʾān, the traditions, or consensus) whether or not his verdict has in the meantime been confirmed by another judge. The same possibility of annulment seems to have existed in the cases where the probity of the witnesses subsequently became questionable.

The same moral concern gives a strongly *personal* character to the administration of the sacred law. The *person* of the plaintiff, the *person* of the defendant (hence the importance of their presence) and the *person* of the witness(es) (hence the importance of their moral probity) completely eclipse the concern for objective evidence and for written documentation. Even in cases of one-sided and two-sided transactions (*īqāᶜāt* and *ᶜuqūd*), the production of the relevant documents is said to be inadequate and the presence and verbal testimony of the parties indispensable. Inordinate emphasis is put on the importance of swearing upon oath at the expense of objective evidence. Similarly the testimonies of the witnesses weighed according to their degree of moral probity (*ᶜadālat*), again without any concern for the assessment of objective evidence.

Another very interesting type of self-limitation consists of the judges' attempt to keep in abeyance some of the specific commandments in the "sources" to which all Islamic jurisprudence is irrevocably and rigidly moored. The specific Qurʾān punishments for adultery, theft, and drunkenness in the *ḥudūd* had throughout the ages posed a problem for the qadi because of their excessive harshness. The *Jāmiᶜ* attempted to circumvent the problem by citing among the "traditional practices" (*sunnat*), with obvious approval, the norm "that if someone confesses to a *ḥadd*, the qadi should so act as to make it likely for him to deny it and be rescued from the *ḥadd* [punishment]." [27]

Finally, we should mention a certain indifference to positivism induced by stereotypified formalism. Despite the expression of the necessity of the administration of justice irrespective of the moral qualities of actual rulers, the *Jāmiᶜ* gives us a disquisition on the "three ways of confirming the appointment of the qadi by the Imam," [28] imperturbed by its irrelevance during the occultation and in complete disregard of the actual procedures for the appointment of the qadis.

Turning now from theory to practice, there are indications that the jurists did conceive of the application of the sacred law in an imperfect world as inherently unpractical. Responding to the accusation that the paucity of judges in

Shiʿite Iran left the execution of the provisions of the sacred law—especially the *ḥudūd*—in abeyance, our Shiʿite polemicist took it for granted that even if 1,000 qadis and *mujtahid*s existed, they would not be able (*mutamakkin*) to implement the sacred law and his Sunni opponent would still be able to say that the commandments of the sacred law were not executed.[29]

The indifference of jurisprudential value-rationalism to administrative procedures left the judiciary processes extremely informal. Chardin was impressed by the extreme informality of legal procedures. He stated that the ease of pleading in Persia was the greatest in the world. The defendant is summoned by the qadi's valet in the simplest manner.

There were advocates, but their role was very minor and their status low. In an amusing entry in his bibliographical compendium, Naṣrābādī mentions a certain Shaykh Allāh Qulī who frequented the houses of the qadis and would act as advocate for people. He then makes the remark that "as this sort of thing comes to no good end, he became blind in both eyes and lived in utmost adversity."[30] During the hearing the qadi occasionally became angry and swore at the defendant.[31] Du Mans also noted the complete lack of procedural formality. There was no palace of justice. The qadi set in a room in his house, did not refrain from swearing, and pronounced his sentence summarily. Du Mans was also struck by the lack of rationality in the judiciary organization. There was no coordination between the various judges, and a European-type hierarchical judiciary organization with rationalized possibility of appeals was totally absent.[32] All this substantiates Weber's proposition that the primacy of ethical considerations in theocratic administration of justice entails indifference or aversion to formalism.[33]

The restricted application of the sacred law through the hierocratic administration of justice of course did not affect the sacred law's supreme and unquestionable legitimacy as divine ethico-religious law, nor its claim to the all-embracing *ethical* regulation of social life, both of which manifested themselves in a number of ways. An interesting illustration of the latter point is to be found in Du Mans's account of the revenues of the high functionaries of the Safavid state, whose earnings are divided into "lawful" (*ḥalāl*) and "unlawful" (*ḥarām*), with the respective figures being given separately in each case.[34] As regards legitimacy, many jurists would restrict it to the hierocratic administration of justice, and were reluctant to grant explicit legitimacy to "customary law" (*ʿurf*) as administered by the temporal tribunals. In fact, according to Chardin, the pious Persians and the *ʿulamāʾ* contrasted the verdicts of the *ʿurf* tribunals to those of the religious courts, and considered them tyrannical.[35]

Thus in the administration of justice, as with government, an invidious dichotomy between the religious and the temporal was created which entailed a negative evaluation of the temporal, but no attempt was made to subjugate the latter to the former.

Conclusion to Part Two

The Safavids succeeded in establishing Shiʿism as the religion of their empire. Two factors stand out as the causal determinants of this process of religious evolution: "reason of state" or the political interests of the Safavid rulers, and the dogmatic and institutional interests of the nascent Shiʿite hierocracy. The first factor was operative from the outset; the second became so mainly in the latter part of the Safavid period.

The suppression of extremism was determined almost entirely by reasons of state, which were twofold. The first motive for the suppression was the need to rationalize the form of political domination into an enduring and stable structure suitable for the administration of a centralized empire, a need that was incompatible with the intense and therefore volatile millenarian expectations associated with extremism. The second related political motive underlying the suppression of extremism was the need for the institutionalized domestication of the sedentary as well as the nomadic tribal masses, which in turn required a more dogmatic and otherworldly type of religion than the this-worldly extremist millenarianism.

The suppression of Sunnism at the beginning of the sixteenth century, dictated by reasons of state, was achieved with much violence but very rapidly by Ismāʿīl I. However, before the consolidation of a Shiʿite hierocracy in Iran—that is, for over one and a half centuries following the establishment of the Safavid dynasty—while the gradual dissemination of the Shiʿite doctrine continued, the persecution of Sunnism occurred only sporadically and on a limited local scale with no signs of general alarm and apprehension on the part of the state. The vigorous attempt at the systematic eradication of Sunnism, whose motivation was dogmatic and which proved politically disastrous, came much later. The massive repression of Sunnism, aiming at the imposition of doctrinal uniformity over the Safavid dominions, was initiated by the Shiᶜite hierocracy in the closing decade of the seventeenth century, and was vigorously continued until the fall of Isfahan in 1722.

The suppression of Sufism took place in two distinct stages. The first, completed under ᶜAbbās the Great, consisted in the suppression of popular Sufism. It took the form of the eradication of the organized Sufi orders that presented a political threat to Safavid supremacy. The Safavid state, however, could afford to, and did, tolerate—and under ᶜAbbās II actively encouraged—the apolitical "high" Sufism of the ascetic virtuosi and the mystically oriented literati.

The second stage of the suppression of Sufism, beginning under Suleymān and gathering momentum under Shāh Sulṭān-Ḥusayn, took the form of the repression of "high" Sufism or *ᶜirfān*. In marked contrast to the political motivation of the first stage, its motivating force was the dogmatic and institutional interest of the emergent Shiᶜite hierocracy.

From its foundation to its very last days, the Safavid polity was unmistakably caesaropapist. The religious institutions were incorporated into the state. The rulers possessed great charisma of lineage as descendants of the Imams, and even claimed an attribute of the Imams: infallibility or sinlessness.

The normative governance of political action in the Safavid state had two distinct bases: the ethos of patrimonialism and the Shiᶜite religion. The former emerges as preponderant influence in the normative regulation of societal action, while communal oppositional action and can be seen to have drawn on religious motives.

In the course of the sixteenth century, the fusion of the religious and political spheres, and of political and hierocratic domination, belonging to the period of mahdistic extremism receded with the imposition of Twelver Shiᶜism, which resulted in the progressive *differentiation* of the religious and the political spheres and of religious and political domination. For the first six or seven decades of the seventeenth century, the fundamental separation of religious and political authority in the Shiᶜite world view manifested itself mainly in the form of the differentiation of an innerworldly spiritual sphere from the mundane sphere of politics and earthly domination. The laity, however, was precluded from access to this spiritual sphere through gnosis, and submitted to the caesaropapist domination of the Safavid ruler and to the religio-political authority of the notables, the *sayyid*s, of the clerical estate.

However, throughout this period, the lay masses also submitted to a growing group of Shiᶜite *ᶜulamāʾ* whose domination was exclusively religious. In the last four decades of the seventeenth century, this group of religious professionals consolidated their position and emerged as a Shiᶜite hierocracy, albeit a heteronomous and a heterocephalous hierocracy within the Safavid caesaropapist state.

The fundamental separation of religious and political authority in the Shiᶜite normative image of the world came closer to finding a corresponding institutional translation.

In fact, it is even possible to speak of the hierocracy state relationships in the late Safavid period in terms of concordant and discordant acts. In the former category one can mention the religiously relevant political action of the suppression of Sunnism, Sufism, and gnostic philosophy by the Safavid state in the late seventeenth and early eighteenth centuries in exchange for (1) the politically relevant religious action of domestication of the masses through the propagation of otherworldly orthodoxy and for (2) the politically conditioned religious action of legitimation of rulership by the hierocracy. In the discordant category should be mentioned ᶜAbbās II's encouragement of Sufism and gnostic philosophy retaliated by Mullā Qāsim's championship of Shiᶜite ethics and denunciation of the ruler for infringing the sacred law.

In contrast to Ottoman caliphate,[1] the normative foundations on which the caesaropapism of the Safavid Empire rested contained a fundamental contradiction which remained unresolved because of the overwhelming power of the state. Especially in view of their vulnerability and the rivalry of the intellectual representatives of the clerical estate, the Shiᶜite hierocracy under Majlisī had to condone the religious pretensions of the Safavid kings, which were vestiges of aberrant Shiᶜite extremism and were in contradiction both with the explicit tenets of Twelver Shiᶜism and with its implicit profanation of temporal rule. The continuity with aberrant extremism in the Safavid principles of legitimacy made for the intrusion of religion into the structure of political domination. The virtually complete separation of the political and the religious spheres implied by the pattern of the Shiᶜite doctrine found a very imperfect translation in the societal structure of domination. Meanwhile, all tendency toward reduction of the incongruence between the societal structure of domination and the logic of the world image projected by Shiᶜite doctrine was curbed by the Safavid dynastic interest in the preservation of the heritage of mahdistic extremism.

PART THREE

The Shiʿite Hierocracy and the State, 1785–1890

Introduction to Part Three

The overthrow of the Safavids by the Sunni Afghans from the periphery of their empire in 1722 resulted in the devastation of the cities, the ruin of the economy, and a pronounced reassertion of the nomadic tribal element in the polity. During the interlude preceding the formal institution of a lasting dynasty by Āqā Muḥammad Khān Qājār in 1796, the newly consolidated Shiʿite hierocracy as well as the clerical estate suffered severe blows, and temporal rule was deliberately shorn of all hierocratic trappings.

There can be little doubt that Nādir Shāh Afshār's (1736–47) religious policy was determined not by his religious convictions but by his goal of consolidating his rule over an Eastern pan-Islamic empire. Considerable evidence has recently been brought to light to suggest Nādir's Shiʿite background.[1] However, it is equally clear that he had no personal religious convictions, and is said by his physician to have compared himself as a great military man to Muhammad and ʿAlī.[2] He also commissioned the translation of the Qurʾān, the Old Testament, and the Gospels into Persian; and, when receiving the Muslim, Christian, and Jewish scholars upon the completion of their work in 1741, he reportedly derided all three doctrines and said that he himself was capable of inventing a better religion.[3]

It was Nādir's imperialism and his extensive military campaigns that dictated his firm and high-handed religious policy. To maintain his massive army, Nādir exploited every possible source of revenue and taxation and did not hesitate to authorize the systematic confiscation of all religious endowments. This policy was progressively implemented until the time of his death, and very seriously undermined the economic basis of religious activities, as many of the religious endowments were confiscated by the state and many more usurpsed as private property by their administrators and others who did not produce the endowment deeds.[4] In connection with this policy, Nādir summoned the *ṣadr* in Isfahan and asked him why he thought the *ʿulamāʾ* and the religious students were entitled to enjoy the enormous revenue of the religious endowments. The *ṣadr* replied that it was because of their function of praying for the perpetuity of the reign of the king. Nādir replied that their prayers were evidently unheeded as they could not forestall the Afghan disaster, and ordered the confiscation of the religious endowments and the discontinuation of most of the stipends.[5] Nādir also had the last Safavid-appointed *Mullā-bāshī* strangled with a bowstring upon succession.[6] Nādir thus dealt the Shiʿite hierocracy a severe blow.

Not only did Nādir not consider the hierocracy's legitimation of temporal rule through praying (*duʿā-gūʾī*) dispensable, but from the very outset he conceived of his prospective empire as the diametrical opposite of the Safavid Ismāʿīl's. Upon his election as king by the assembly he had convoked at the plain of Mughān in 1736/1148, Nādir made it a condition for his accepting the crown that the people of Iran foreswear the aberrant religion of Ismāʿīl, which had been the cause of centuries of dissent and bloodshed among the Muslims, and rejoin the mainstream of Sunni Islam. They would be allowed, however, to continue to subscribe to Twelver Shiʿite law as the legal school of Jaʿfar al-Ṣādiq, being considered the followers of a fifth official *madhhab*.[7]

Even before he began to rule in his own name, Nādir had forbidden the cursing of the first three rightly guided caliphs, ordered that their praise be restored to the *khutba*, and discouraged the Shiʿite religious ceremonies of Muḥarram and the *Ghadīr-e Khum*.[8] Later as king of Iran he sought the Ottoman sultan's recognition of Twelver Shiʿism as the Jaʿfarī *madhhab* in his peace negotiations.[9] In 1743, taking a large group of *ʿulamāʾ* from his domains in Transoxiana, Afghanistan, and Iran under the leadership of his *Mullā-bāshī*, ʿAlī Akbar, he marched on to the Arab Iraq. Having visited both the Shiʿite holy shrines and the tomb of Abū Ḥanīfa in Baghdad, with the collaboration of Aḥmad Pasha, the Ottoman governor of Baghdad, he summoned the Sunni *ʿulamāʾ* of Arab Iraq and secured their signatures, alongside those accompanying him, upon a document drawn up by his secretary. The Shiʿite *ʿulamāʾ* acknowledged the aberrance of the beliefs introduced by Ismāʿīl and the legitimacy of the first three rightly guided caliphs. The Sunnis in turn recognized Twelver Shiʿism as the fifth *madhhab*.[10] This first pan-Islamic document of modern times, bearing the signatures of fity-six religious dignitaries, was then signed and sealed by the Muftī of Baghdad, who thus bestowed upon it the Ottoman sultan's implicit recognition.[11] On behalf of the Shiʿite hierocracy, ʿAlī Akbar, the *Mullā-bāshī*, was forced to admit the legitimacy of the rightly guided caliphs and praised them from the pulpit of the Friday Mosque in Kufa.[12]

Nādir's policy of suppression of Shiʿism and promotion of pan-Islamism collapsed together with his empire with his assassination in 1747. His nephew and immediate successor, ʿĀdil Shāh, cited Nādir's abandonment and suppression of

Shiᶜism as a cause of his assassination, and chose the Shiᶜite formula "Slave of the King of *vilāyat*, ᶜAlī" for his seal.[13] Nevertheless, Nādir's religious policy was of crucial significance in instituting a definitive break with the Safavid era through the systematic exclusion of religion from political organization. This was achieved by the virtual liquidation of the hierocracy as a branch of the Safavid caesaropapist state *and* by emphatically divesting temporal rule of hierocratic trappings. It was with this latter aim in mind that Nādir forbade the utterance of the phrase "May the King, from whom all our fortune flows, live forever" in the public prayers of governors.[14]

The next important ruler of the interregnum, Karīm Khān Zand (1750–79), was said by one of the more pious chroniclers of his reign never to have performed his prayers during the whole of his life, and to have regarded the *ᶜulamāᵓ* and the religious students as parasites.[15] Karīm Khān's successors, like those of Nādir Shāh ruling contemporaneously with them in northwestern Iran, were no more favorably disposed toward the *ᶜulamāᵓ*.[16]

In his coronation in 1796, Āqā Muḥammad Khān Qājār, the de facto ruler of most of Iran since 1785, emphatically affirmed his adherence to Shiᶜism. He wore a sword that had been left in the tomb of Ismāᶜīl, who had established Twelver Shiᶜism in Iran.[17] His pious nephew succeeded him as Fatḥ ᶜAlī Shāh in 1797 and during his long reign pursued a Shiᶜite religious policy of momentous consequences.

The religious policy of the Afshārs and the Zands during the interregnum resulted in a sharp decline of the *madrasa*s and torpor befell all centers of religious learning. The rigors of Nādir's persecution and of the ensuing anarchy forced the Shiᶜite *ᶜulamāᵓ* to subsist on their own resources, totally independent of the state. After the removal of state support in the form of the provision of offices and subventions from the religious endowments, the most notable resource that enabled the Shiᶜite men of religion to survive and reconstitute a hierocracy by the end of the eighteenth century was the close primordial ties between its leading members. Kinship performed the crucial function of substituting for the state-dependent institutional ties, and enabled two frequently intermarrying lateral branches of Majlisī's family, the Bihbihānī and the Ṭabātabāᵓī families,[18] to persist as the prominent members of the clerical sodality (*Rechtsgenossenschaft*). Toward the end of the interregnum, these prominent families rallied others under the leadership of Āqā Muḥammad Bāqir Bihbihānī (1705–1803) launched and sustained a vigorous religious movement known as the Uṣūlī movement. Bihbihānī, a relative of Majlisī, whom he appears to have been named after, vehemently attacked the Akhbārī position and revived jurisprudential rationalism. The Uṣūlī movement soon became the dominant intellectual trend in nineteenth-century Shiᶜism. Bihbihānī thus trained a number of outstanding *mujtahid*s in Arab Iraq, who constituted a pool of first-rate religious scholars to be drawn upon by Fatḥ ᶜAlī Shāh in his attempt to re-create a Shiᶜite polity in Iran.

In his piety, Fatḥ ʿAlī Shāh is the Qājār counterpart of the Safavid Ṭahmāsp. He took great interest in doctrinal matters and is said to have been an accomplished religious scholar. He built mosques, embellished shrines, and commissioned many works of theology. He exempted the inhabitants of the religious city of Qum from taxation, and built the important Fayḍiyya *madrasa* near the shrine. With his encouragement, Tehran became a center of religious learning.[19] One of his courtiers, Muḥammad Ḥusayn Khạn Marvī, founded a well-endowed school in the capital.[20] Another nobleman, Ḥajj Muḥammad Ḥusayn Khān Ṣadr, built the famous Ṣadr School in Isfahan.[21] Fatḥ ʿAlī Shāh cultivated excellent personal relationships with the eminent *mujtahid*s of his time, most of whom had been the students of Bihbihānī and who had returned to settle in Iran at his invitation. He greatly favored Mīrzā Abuʾl-Qāsim Qumī, who settled in Qum; Mullā Aḥmad Narāqī, who returned from Arab Iraq to his native Kashan; and Ḥạjjī Ibrāhīm Karbāsī and Ḥajjī Muḥammad Bāqir Shaftī, who lived in Isfahan and revitalized its *madrasa*s after the long period of decay. Fatḥ ʿAlī Shāh encouraged the settlement of the *ʿulamāʾ* in various parts of the country through the distributions of largesse and by appointing them *shaykh al-Islām*s and leaders of the Friday prayer (sing. *imām jumʿa*), and showed them great respect, often soliciting their advice and accepting their intercession.[22]

With Fatḥ ʿAlī Shāh's religious policy, the revival of religious learning that had been started in Arab Iraq by Bihbihānī was given a tremendous boost. Furthermore, the major cities of Iran, especially Isfahan, reemerged as the centers of religious activity. Thus the vigor of the Uṣūlī movement and the religious policy of the Qājār monarch combined to make the first half of the nineteenth century a period of intense religious scholarly activity as lively as any since Buyid times. The consolidation of the Shiʿite hierocracy in Iran was virtually complete under Fatḥ ʿAlī Shāh and could not be affected by the reversal of state policy under his successor, Muḥammad Shah (1834–48). The center of gravity of religious activity for a time shifted from Arab Iraq to Iran itself, where the majority of the eminent *mujtahid*s came to reside and engage in teaching.[23]

With the sharp decline of hierocratic power during the post-Safavid interregnum, Sufism had experienced a revival. The Shiʿite hierocracy immediately perceived the threat posed by the Sufi shaykhs to their religious authority. At their behest, Fatḥ ʿAlī Shāh pursued a vigorous policy of suppression of popular Sufism. This repressive policy succeeded in stemming the tide of popular Sufism. Though Fatḥ ʿAlī's grandson and successor Muḥammad Shah (1834–48) was a practicing Sufi and, before long, appointed his Sufi *directeur de conscience* prime minister, popular religiosity was by then so securely dominated by the Shiʿite doctors that Sufism did not penetrate beyond the courtly circles into the lower layers of society. Consequently, in striking contrast to the rest of the Islamic world, Sufism in Iran became a predominantly aristocratic religious movement and has remained so to this date.

No evidence can attest more eloquently to the effectiveness with which Majlisī created a psychological basis for hierocratic domination among the masses than the tremendous power gained by the returning members of the Shiᶜite hierocracy in the first decades of the nineteenth century. Through his popularization of Shiᶜism, Majlīsī had secured the religious loyalty of the masses, precluding the influence of the Sufi shaykhs upon them. The loyalty to Twelver Shiᶜism he had thus ingrained in the masses through the preemptive incorporation of popular peripheral beliefs and practices, made the authority of its custodians acceptable as the unrivaled religious authority.

Otherworldly Shiᶜism as first popularized by Majlisī continued to hold a firm grip on the masses. Shiᶜite otherworldly eschatology was given a simplified and clear exposition in the popular works of the period such as the *ᶜAqāʾid al-Shīᶜa* by ᶜAlī Asghar Burūjirdī—which gives even greater attention than did Majlisī to topics of the inquisition in the grave by Nakīr and Munkir, the Greater and the Lesser Resurrections (the latter being the return of the Hidden Imam as the Mahdi at the end of time), the seven hells, purgatory, and paradise.[24] The pious *ᶜulamāʾ* were greatly revered for their power of *shafāᶜa* (intercession) in the hereafter by those whose psychological propensities were shaped by post-Safavid otherworldly Shiᶜism. Prince Muḥammad ᶜAlī Mīrzā, one of the numerous sons of Fatḥ ᶜAlī Shāh and the governor of Kirmanshah, insistently purchased one of the gates of paradise from Shaykh Aḥmad Aḥsāᶜi and another from Sayyid Riḍā, son of the eminent theologian Sayyid Mahdī Baḥr al-ᶜUlūm, and ordered that both deeds of sale be wrapped up with him in his shroud.

By lessening the propensity to religiously motivated political action in opposition to the status quo, the otherworldly religiosity of the Shiᶜite masses made for their domestication and political submissiveness. However, with royal political power totally divested of hierocratic pretensions, the Shiᶜite hierocracy was also able to harness this otherworldly psychological disposition of the believing masses to the institutional consolidation of religious domination. This consolidation was virtually complete under Fatḥ ᶜAlī Shāh and could not be affected by the policy of his successor, Muḥammad Shāh. In marked contrast to the Ottoman Empire, where the hierocracy was firmly incorporated into the caesaropapist state while religious domination over the masses rested largely with the Sufi shaykhs and dervishes,[25] the Shiᶜite hierocracy of Iran had somewhat tenuous and informal ties with a weak central government while it firmly dominated the masses by its exclusive religious authority.

What is just as important as the absence of a viable challenge to the religious authority of the hierocracy from the Sufi mystagogues was the liquidation of the estate of clerical notables. The loss of favor of the central government can be assumed to have very adversely affected the economic and political bases of domination of the families of clerical notables, the *sayyid*s. Furthermore, the office of the qadi, a prerogative of this estate, declined even more sharply during the post-Safavid interregnum than during the previous centuries. Under the early Qājārs, the *shaykh al-Islām*s and the *mujtahid*s carried out the administration of the sacred law in their courts, largely obviating the need for the office of the qadis, who appear as the subordinates of the *shaykh al-Islām* in early nineteenth century.[26] It is true that certain *sayyid*s without religious learning, maintaining themselves on charity of others, could be found in the Qājār period, but they completely lacked the power and prestige of the Safavid notables[27] and could aspire to such power and prestige only through the acquisition of learning and entry into the ranks of the hierocracy. In contrast to the Safavid period, prophetic descent was now often used by the scions of the locally prominent *sayyid* families for entry into the ranks of the hierocracy rather than the service of the state.

Thus, in the early decades of the nineteenth century, the three major obstacles to the consolidation of autonomous hierocratic power were definitively removed: royalty renounced all hierocratic pretensions, the estate of clerical notables was liquidated as such (many of its members being absorbed into the hierocracy), and popular Sufism was virtually extirpated.

CHAPTER TEN

The Impact of Shiᶜism on the Qājār Polity and Its Limits

10.1 Normative and De Facto Separation of Political and Hierocratic Domination in the Qājār Polity

As we have seen, Nādir sought to effect a definitive break with Safavid rule and its principles of legitimacy of kingship. He sought to obliterate the hierocratic trappings of temporal rule (a vestige of extremism perpetuated by the Safavids), as these would restrict legitimate rule to a member of the Safavid house. To emphasize this break, as we have seen, he went so far as to disown Shiᶜism. Furthermore, in a deliberate attempt to reverse the abandonment of the glorification of Genghis-Khanid descent as a "branch of the tree of unbelief" by Ismāᶜīl, Nādir tried to revive the pre-Safavid Turkman tribal principles of legitimacy, which had not been given currency since the fifteenth century.[1] In a letter to the Ottoman grand vizier, Nādir states that the dignitaries of Iran gathered in the plain of Mughān "elected our august Majesty to kingship and sovereignty which are the hereditary prerogatives of the noble Turkman tribe."[2] Mullā ᶜAlī Akbar, his *Mullā-bāshī*, opens his pan-Islamic sermon in Kufa with the eulogy of Nādir not only as the shadow of God on earth, but also as the scion of the Turkman tree and heir to Genghis Khan.[3]

However, after Nādir's death, Safavid descent, often with a marked emphasis on its religious character, remained the most viable ground of legitimacy for rulership. Karīm Khān Zand sought a compromise solution to the problem of legitimacy by maintaining an incarcerated Safavid figurehead as Shāh Ismāᶜīl III while calling himself *vakīl al-raᶜāyā* (deputy of the subjects).[4] Meanwhile, a serious attempt was made to revive Safavid caesaropapism, with a strong emphasis being put on the religious character of the rule of the Safavid descendants of the Imams. Mīr Muḥammad, a grandson of Shāh Suleymān, specialized in the study of the religious sciences and became known as Mīr Muḥammad Mujtahid. In the years of anarchy that followed Nạdir's assassination, he was drawn into politics by the Safavid loyalists and ruled in Mashhad for forty days in 1163 (January–February 1750) as Suleymān II. But this last attempt at the revival of the Safavid hierocratic caesaropapism collapsed, and Mīr Muḥammad, who had already been blinded, also had to suffer the mutilation of his tongue.[5]

Āqā Muḥammad Khān, the founder of the Qājār dynasty, affirmed the continued adherence of his state to the Twelver Shiᶜism established in Iran by the Safavids. Especially in view of his lay descent, this fact made it all the more imperative for him to establish his rule and that of his dynasty as *temporal*. This could only be done by the exclusion of hierocratic pretensions resting on charisma of holy lineage, which, if retained, would have made a Safavid pretender appear more qualified to rule.

Āqā Muḥammad Khān did not live long enough after his coronation to deal with this problem, but his successor Fatḥ ᶜAlī Shāh did. As a new dynasty, the need to legitimate their rule must have been felt acutely by the first Qājār monarchs. As Weber remarks, "if the legitimacy of the ruler is not clearly identifiable through hereditary charisma, another charismatic power is needed; normally this can only be hierocracy."[6] In the need to secure such legitimation, Fatḥ ᶜAlī Shāh turned to the Shiᶜite hierocracy, many of whose prominent members responded favorably most notably, Mīrzā Abu'l-Qāsim Qumī, the Muḥaqqiq, and Sayyid Jaᶜfar Kashfī. Against this background, the interest of Fatḥ ᶜAlī in securing a firm de jure basis for the legitimacy of Qājār rule, and the doctrinal interest of the supportive *ᶜulamā᾽* in the removal of inconsistencies between Shiᶜite doctrine and the principles of legitimacy of the Safavid era, resulted in the completion of the process of rationalization of the normative order governing political and hierocratic domination in the direction of greater congruence with the logic of Twelver Shiᶜism.

With the destruction of the edifice of the Safavid caesaropapist state and the renunciation of its normative basis, and with the reestablishment of the Shiᶜite hierocracy in the early decades of the nineteenth century, a separation of political and hierocratic domination congruent with the normative logic of Twelver Shiᶜism within the polity had in fact come into existence. Against this background, the compatibility of the patrimonial theories of kingship and justice with Twelver Shiᶜism was explicitly stated and elaborately amplified. What is even more momentous is that in the first decades of the nineteenth century we find the culmination of the efforts of al-Murtaḍā and al-Karakī aiming at the overcoming of pious political indifferentism through the creation of a positive political ethic. Consonantly with the logic of Shiᶜism, the blessing of the Hidden Imam came to be bestowed upon the king as *temporal* ruler. Thus, in the reign of the pious Fatḥ ᶜAlī Shāh, we witness the consolidation of a Twelver Shiᶜite polity in Iran in which the Shiᶜite normative pattern bearing on political and hierocratic domination found as close an institutional translation as it was ever likely to have.

10.1.1 The Legitimation of Political and Hierocratic Domination

There are a number of works written by the literati during Fatḥ ᶜAlī's reign that belong to the traditional genre of patrimonial political theory. When, in the early years of Fatḥ ᶜAlī's reign, the eminent *mujtahid* Mīrzā Abu'l-Qāsim Qumī (d. 1817–18/1233) set forth the principles of legitimacy of temporal rule, he too, by and large, reiterated the patrimonial theories of kingship. However, there were some important qualifications.

For Mīrzā Abu'l-Qāsim as for all previous political theorists, the fundamental basis of legitimate rulership was justice, and he considered the king the shadow of God on earth. But he stressed the necessity of the correct *interpretation* of the term "shadow of God on earth," and in explicating its "three meanings" he took great care not to repeat any of the Safavids' claims. In fact, his interpretation emphatically divests the ruler of divine power and divine attributes, and, most importantly, links the term with justice and equity as the "shadow of divine justice." Mīrzā Abu'l-Qāsim states that God has made the king His lieutenant (*jānishīn*) on earth (not the *jānishīn* of the Hidden Imam, as the Safavids claimed to be), but immediately proceeds to emphasize the responsibilities implied by such an appointment. In sharp and, one is tempted to say, deliberate contrast to the Safavids' claim to infallibility, he writes that the actions of the king are not necessitated by divine decree. The king's rule is a trial; he is not absolved from performing his ethical duties by virtue of kingship, and will be punished by God for all evil doing. Finally, Mīrzā Abu'l-Qāsim stresses the interdependence of kingship and religion, noting the differentiation of political and hierocratic functions: kings were needed for the preservation of order, the *ᶜulamaᵓ* for the protection of religion.[7]

Even though these modifications of the patrimonial theory are important in themselves, Mīrzā Abu'l-Qāsim did not take the step of legitimating the temporal rule in terms of Shiᶜite doctrine. This momentous step was taken by a prominent member of the Shiᶜite hierocracy belonging to the subsequent generation, and became possible when nearly a quarter of a century of stable Qājār rule, accompanied by economic prosperity, had transformed the conception of the Safavid era from the Golden Age of the anarchical interregnum to a vague and fast-receding historical memory. In the meantime, the demise of Akhbārī traditionalism and the decline of the charisma of Prophetic lineage fostered by it, had relegated the heritage of extremism to oblivion. Against this background, the legitimation of temporal rule could once again be related to the theories of imamate and occultation, but this time in terms not of extremism but of Twelver Shiᶜism.

An interesting testimony from the period of transition to the full autonomy of the hierocracy is supplied by the grandson of Bihbihānī, Aḥmad ᶜAlī, in

1809/1224. In his autobiography, having profusely praised Āqā Muḥammad Khān and Fatḥ ʿAlī Shāh as shadow of God, he comments on Fatḥ ʿAlī's confirmation of his brother in positions held by his deceased father, Āqā Muḥammad ʿAlī Bihbihānī (d. 1801–2/1216):

> From the threshold of the august king, protector of the world, Shadow of God, letters containing condolences and orders for holding of mourning services arrived; and the affairs in charge of the deceased [in the region of Kirmānshāh] . . . , *in addition to [being a] divine commission*, were entrusted to him [the author's brother] by the king, the Protector of religion.[8]

Bihbihānī thus claims direct divine commission in addition to delegation of authority by the shadow of God.

The final resolution of the normative problem of the legitimacy of political and hierocratic domination was facilitated by an instance of cooperation between the state and the hierocracy as the two organs of the reconstituted Shiʿite polity. The occasion came during the first Perso-Russian War (1810–13) with the initiative taken by ʿĪsa Qāʾim Maqām, the minister of the reforming regent and crown prince, ʿAbbās Mīrzā, who tried to enlist the support of the Shiʿite hierocracy in the declaration of *jihād* against the infidel Russians. He dispatched envoys to Arab Iraq and Isfahan to solicit the Shiʿite hierocracy for injunctions and tracts on holy war. Many such *fatwā*s and treatises were obtained and assembled in a volume entitled *Risāla-ye Jihādiyya*. A crucially important byproduct of this venture was the clarification of the foundations of hierocratic authority de jure.

The most eminent *mujtahid* of the time and the doyen of the hierocracy, Shaykh Jaʿfar, the *Kāshif al-Ghiṭāʾ* (d. 1812–13/1127–28) responded by a long declaration (in Arabic) making the waging of war against the Russians incumbent; and authorizing Fatḥ ʿAlī Shāh to conduct the *jihād* against the Russians on behalf of the Imam of the Age. He explained that his power to authorize the king rested on the *mujtahid*s' collective office of *niyābat-e ʿāmma* (general vicegerency). Shaykh Jaʿfar did explain that the defense of Islam through *jihād*, a duty of the Imam according to the sacred law, falls upon the *mujtahid*s by virtue of their general vicegerency during the occultation. He also explained that it was this duty, and his recognition as a *nāʾib ʿāmm*, that empowered him to authorize the sultan. Nevertheless, Shaykh Jaʿfar's use of the phrase "I give permission" (*faqad adhintu*), though logically unobjectionable, could be viewed as arrogant. Lambton is therefore correct in supposing that Shaykh Jaʿfar's declaration, like those of some of the other *mujtahid*s "carried with it the important corollary that they could give by this authorization validity, or at least temporary validity, to the rule of a shah whom they appointed to engage in *jihād*."[9] However, it should also be noted that the ministers of the Qājār state who initiated and pursued the *jihād* policy, Qāʾim Maqām the Elder and his son Mīrzā Abu'l-Qāsim, Qāʾim Maqām the Younger, were quite mindful of this hierocratic pretension and took prompt steps to rectify it. Qāʾim Maqām the Elder's name appears as the author of a slim volume in Persian summarizing the views of the Shiᶜite hierocracy on *jihād*. After being carefully read and approved by Fatḥ ᶜAlī Shāh,[10] it was printed in Tabriz in 1818 as *Kitāb al-Jihādiyya* and can safely be assumed to have been fairly widely read as one of the earliest printed books. Qāʾim Maqām of course states that the late Shaykh Jaᶜfar authorized Fatḥ ᶜAlī Shāh on behalf of the Imam to engage in *jihād*.[11] However, in a later passage he takes care, in referring to a treatise by the shaykh, to quote him as saying "if I be a man of *ijtihād* and worthy of the vicegerency of the Imam, peace be upon Him, I give permission to the ruler etc."[12] Similarly, Qāʾim Maqām the Younger, in his well-known preface to the longer *Jihādiyya*, is as clear as he can be without compromising his consummately ornate literary style, about the basis of the hierocratic authority of the *mujtahid*s, and about the appropriateness of its exercise in authorizing the king to engage in *jihād*: When the sun of imamate passed beneath the veil of occultation, the star of vicegerency was still left visible for the guidance of the world. Ethical duties remained just as binding, the commandments of the sacred law being those given in the "Book" (of God) and by the "Household" (of the Prophet). The function of the *mujtahid*s embodying the "star of vicegerency" is the protection of the sacred law and the observance of its provisions. In fulfillment of this function of guidance of the believers, they have explained the commandments of the sacred law regarding holy war, and authorized the "*shāhanshāh* of the world and of religion"[13] to unsheath his sword at the service of religion to become the reviver of the tradition of *jihād*.

Thus the important consequence of the *jihād* episode was that it gave the Shiᶜite hierocracy the opportunity to publicize the concept of general vicegerency (of the Hidden Imam) as the basis of *hierocratic* authority, de jure, *and* to secure its respectful acknowledgment by the spokesmen for the Qājār state. What remained to be done was the legitimation of *political* authority in a manner consistent with Shiᶜite doctrine. This was done by a prominent member of the Shiᶜite hierocracy, Āqā Sayyid Jaᶜfar ibn Abī Isḥāq Kashfī (d. 1850–51/1267).[14] In *Tuḥfat al-Mulūk*, written in 1817–18/1233, Kashfī at last put forward a systematic treatment of political and hierocratic domination within a unified *Shiᶜite* normative perspective.[15] Kashfī could go beyond Qumī's reiteration of the patrimonial ethos and produce a consistently *Shiᶜite* political theory incorporating the authority of the Imam of the Age with reference to the doctrines of imamate and occultation.

With the conclusion of historical imamate in the form of occultation of the Imam of the Age, the twin functions of imamate—supreme political and religious leadership of the community—devolved upon two groups entitled to his deputyship or vicegerency (*niyāba*), the rulers and the *ᶜulamāʾ*:

> Thus it becomes clear that the *mujtahid*s and the rulers both hold the same office, which office is the office of imamate, transferred to them from the Imam through vicegerency, and consisting of two pillars [*rukn*]: knowledge of the prophetic matters, which is called religion; and the implementation of the same in the course of imposing order upon the world, which is termed kingship or sovereignty. These two pillars are also referred to as "the sword" and "the pen" or "the sword" and "knowledge." Both these pillars were found in combination in the imam . . . and they should similarly coexist in the person who is his deputy. But the *ᶜulamā*ᵓ and the *mujtahid*s, because of the contention of the rulers with them leading to sedition and anarchy, have abandoned sovereignty and the organ of the sword. Similarly the rulers, because of their inclination from the beginning of sovereignty toward the baser world—that is, mere worldly sovereignty consisting solely in the imposition of order in the world—have foregone the acquisition of the knowledge of religion and understanding of the prophetic matters, and have made do with the science of politics only. *Thus, the function of vicegerency inevitably became divided between the ᶜulamā*ᵓ *and the rulers.*[16]

Doubtless to stress the importance of maintaining the concord established between the hierocracy and the state in the contemporary reconstituted Shiᶜite polity, Kashfī continues his disquisition:

> In some ages, [the rulers and the *ᶜulamā*ᵓ] cooperated with mutual consensus and ruled and directed the subjects through partnership and cooperation. . . . At other times, they became mutually antagonistic and parted from each other. Consequently religion and sovereignty, which must be conjoint, became separated from each other. The knowledge of the *ᶜulamā*ᵓ and the endeavor of *mujtahid*s became stagnant because of disorder. Similarly, the sovereignty of the rulers, because of its divorce from the upholding of religion and the traditions of the sacred law, became sheer sovereignty. The matter of politics and vicegerency . . . became disturbed, and both groups fell short of [discharging] the office of vicegerency.[17]

After thus deriving his theory of the two powers from the doctrine of imamate (*pace* the Shiᶜite commentators on the Qurᵓan), Sayyid Jaᶜfar is able to adduce the "authority verse" of the Qurᵓan as enjoining obedience to the just ruler.[18]

Kashfī, a rationalist (*uṣūlī*) jurist,[19] had stated at the outset of the chapter that, as men left to themselves are *lupus lupendi*, they need a ruler. Obedience to this ruler is necessary to prevent anarchy, and therefore incumbent upon men according to the dictates of reason.[20] He returns to the employment of "reason" (formally admitted by the *Uṣūlī* school as a fourth basis for the validity of legal norms) in an original instance of *ijtihād* (deduction of legal norms) with the aim of deriving the legitimacy of political and hierocratic domination as differentiated instances of vicegerency of the Imam from the "sources" of sacred law.

Āqā Sayyid Jaᶜfar cites the tradition related by Ibn Ḥanẓala: "Look to him who is among you and has explored our 'lawful' and 'unlawful' and knows our commandments," as the basis of the *niyābat-e ᶜāmma* of the *mujtahids*,[21] and proceeds with a consideration of ᶜAlī's instructions to Mālik al-Ashtar—the famous covenant (*ᶜahdnāmeh*) we have already mentioned—to derive a second category of *niyāba*. Mālik is said to be the *nāᵓib khāṣṣ* (specified deputy)[22] and ᶜAlī's delegation of authority to him sets the precedent for the *niyābat-e khāṣṣa*. It follows that

> in these times when "knowledge" and the "sword" have become separated from each other, and knowledge is lodged with the *ᶜulamāᵓ* and the *mujtahids* and the sword with the [political] leaders and the rulers, the instructions of the covenant which relate to the organ of knowledge and the conditions of the *ᶜulamāᵓ* regard the *mujtahids* and men of knowledge; and those which relate to the organ of the sword and the affair of sovereignty and politics and order regard the kings and rulers. As we have mentioned, the rulers who act according to those clauses [of the covenant] which relate to and regard them is of course the "specified deputy" [*nāᵓ ib-e khāṣṣ*] of the Imam. Similarly, the *mujtahids* who act according to those clauses which relate to and regard them, of course they too are the "specified deputy" of the Imam. And this covenant is the proof of the "specified vicegerency" [*niyābat-e khāṣṣa*] of these two groups of men.[23]

Kashfī then reproduces the covenant (which, as words of the first Imam constitutes a "source" of law in Twelver Shiᶜism) together with its Persian translation.[24]

Another important feature of Kashfī's political tract is the consistent and successful integration of the patrimonial theories of kingship, with a cursory mention of the phrase "shadow of God on earth" and copious emphasis on justice, "paternalism" (*abaviyya*), and finally on charity. In fact, both explicitly and by clear implication, justice is made the condition of legitimacy of temporal rule and the qualification of the ruler for the "specified vicegerency" of the Imam.[25]

Kashfī's theory does not invest the ruler with any hierocratic authority. He does put forward a novel and broad interpretation of the notion of "specified vicegerency," but only to provide religious legitimation for kingly rule as (differentiated) secular political domination. Differentiated hierocratic authority is said to devolve on the *mujtahids* through their collective office of "general vicegerency." Kashfī legitimizes just rulership as tantamount to the vicegerency of the Imam only in temporal matters. Thus, while Fatḥ ᶜAlī Shāh's contemporary Naṣīr al-Dīn Ḥaydar, the Shiᶜite king of Oudh, struck coins in 1830 bearing the inscription, "The Nāᵓib of Mahdī, Naṣīr al-Dīn Ḥaydar, the King . . ."[26] the clear separation of the political and the religious spheres and the renunciation of the Safavid heritage in Qājār Iran precluded any such designation of the ruler. It should be pointed out, however, that, in practice the king did retain some of the Safavids' "caesaropapist" prerogatives regarding a number of important clerical appointments.

The importance of Kashfī's political theory cannot be exaggerated. It is a consistent synthesis of the traditional Persian theories of kingship and the Shiᶜite doctrines of imamate and occultation. As such, it represents not only the removal of the anomalies of Safavid legitimacy but also the definitive reconciliation of the secular and the religious cultures of premodern Iran.

Temporal power, in turn, acknowledged the uncontested religious authority as the general vicegerents of the Imam *and* their prerogative to legitimate temporal authority in that capacity. At the very outset of his reign, Fatḥ ᶜAlī Shāh sent money to the *ᶜulamāʾ* so that they would absolve the oppressive wrongdoings of the wielders of temporal authority (*radd-e maẓālim*), and asserted that he was ruling on behalf of the *mujtahid*s of the age.[27]

We find Kashfī's dualistic theory of legitimate authority restated in the second half of the nineteenth century. For instance, the theory is set forth in an important letter to Nāṣir al-Dīn Shāh (1848–96) written in 1873, by the influential *mujtahid* of Tehran, Mullā ᶜAlī Kanī, who, upon his death in 1888/1306, was ceremoniously mourned by the population of the capital as the deceased "vicegerent [*nāʾib*] of the Prophet."[28] Denying all intention of stepping beyond the limits set to hierocratic authority by the prevalent consensus on the division of labor in the polity, Kanī expressly upheld the theory of the two powers. Having asserted the unity of the offices or functions of "sovereignty" (*salṭanat*) and "knowledge" (*ᶜilm*), i.e., of political and religious authority under the Prophet and the Imams, Kanī turned to their separation during the "times of occultation." During the occultation, God has appointed a "vicegerent" (*nāʾib*) for each of the Imam's functions or offices: the *ᶜulamāʾ*, as the embodiments of knowledge, as the vicegerents for the religious office, and the "rulers [*salaṭīn*] of Islam," as the vicegerents for the office of sovereignty, for the maintenance of law and order and for the protection of the subjects.[29]

The theory of dual power during the occultation of the Imam is upheld by the foremost religious authority of the closing decade of the nineteenth century, Mīrzā Muḥammad Ḥasan Shīrāzī. In response to the request to intervene in politics concerning the question of imported sugar, the Mīrzā restated this theory with an interesting nuance, using the terms *dawlat* (government) and *millat* (community) as the respective repositories of executive and religious authority:

> In the ages when government [*dawlat*] and community [*millat*] were established in one place, as at the time of the Seal of the Prophets, political duties regarding this kind of general affairs [*umūr ᶜāmma*] were entrusted to that same person. Now that according to the requirements of divine wisdom each is found in a separate place, it is upon both these [powers] to aid each other in protecting the religion and worldly interests [*dīn va dunyā*] of the servants of God and the safeguarding of the citadel of Islam [*bayḍa-ye Islām*] during the occultation of the Lord of Time.[30]

However, the theory of the two powers was not legally binding for the members of the hierocracy. The Shiᶜite sacred law was a "jurists' law" to be interpreted in each and every case by the independent *mujtahid*. Especially in view of the tremendous enhancement of hierocratic domination, there was nothing other than pious indifference to political power to prevent the individual doctors from putting forward a variety of more or less pretentious or more or less realistic claims. In interpreting the extent of the authority of their collective office of vicegerency, the doctors arrogated to themselves the power of making clean the goods and property wrongfully acquired by the ruler and his officials as well as private individuals in exchange for receiving the booty tax (*khums*), rent (on inadvertently usurped property), and alms.[31] Nevertheless, because it successfully reconciles the ethos of patrimonial kingship and the political ethic of Twelver Shiᶜism and because it adequately reflects the institutional division of authority between the state and the hierocracy, Kashfī's political theory can be taken to represent the unified normative order that governed the relations of authority in the Qājār body politic.

To conclude our survey of Shīite political theory, the king remained, as he had always been, the shadow of God on earth or his shadow on the temporal world, while the designation "vicegerent of the Imam" and the uncontested religious authority of the most eminent of the *mujtahid*s was fully acknowledged by the official spokesman for the royal court in the latter part of the century.[32] There was little change in the notion of the king as the shadow of God on earth, but with Kashfī we do find a more thoroughly consistent legitimation of kingship as secular rule on the part of the hierocracy. The posture of the hierocracy toward the legitimated temporal ruler continued to be what had been affirmed by Majlisī two centuries earlier.[33] Throughout the nineteenth century, *duᶜā-gūʾī* or praying for the preservation of the king, who, against the background of European imperialist encroachments, came more emphatically to be referred to as the *pādishāh-e Islām* (king of Islam) or the "*pādishāh* [king] of the Shiᶜite nation," remained the self-defined function of politically active members of the hierocracy, including those who led the nationalist opposition movement in the closing decade of the nineteenth century.[34] Both sides thus recognized and reaffirmed the prevailing division of political and hierocratic authority in Iran's definitively reconstituted Shiᶜite polity.

10.1.2 The Institutional Autonomy of the Hierocracy from the State

In 1791/1205, Āqā Muḥammad Khān Qājār sent his *Mullā-bāshī*, Mullā Muḥammad Ḥusayn of Māzandarān, to Kirmānshāh to invite Āqā Muḥammad ᶜAlī Mujtahid, the son of Āqā Muḥammad Bāqir Bihbihānī, to the capital. This mission marked the beginning of the *rapprochement* between the Qājār state and the Shi^cite hierocracy, and decisively sealed the fate of the office of the *Mullā-bāshī*. The *Mullā-bāshī* still remained the chaplain of the royal household, but, given the autocephaly of the Shiʿite hierocracy and its independence from the patrimonial government, his jurisdiction no longer extended beyond the Qājār household. With a handful of eminent *mujtahid*s acquiring enormous power and prestige as the heads of an autonomous Shiʿite hierocracy during the reign of Fatḥ ʿAlī Shāh, the office of the royal chaplain, the *Mullā-bāshī*, withered away.[35]

The separation of political and hierocratic domination in nineteenth-century Iran was made possible by the financial autonomy of the hierocracy, and by its appropriation of extensive judiciary functions that were independent of state control.

Taxation did not really have much relevance to the issue of *jihād*, yet it was treated at some length by the jurists who wrote on the topic in connection with the first Perso-Russian War. Ostensibly, their purpose was to legitimize the land tax (*kharāj*) by reiterating and affirming the Shaykh al-Karakī's argument in the sixteenth century. The land of Iran was said to be subject to *kharāj*. As for the collection of *kharāj*, "during the occultation of the Imam, peace be upon him, should his *nāʾib ʿāmm* be unable to perform this task, he should authorize the rulers [*umarāʾ*] of Islam [to do so], and even if he does not give such authorization, the matter still pertains to the rulers of Islam."[36]

However, in view of the trend in land tenure that had already set in and that was to remove the semblance of the dues levied by the landowners on peasants from "taxation,"[37] it is extremely doubtful that the state either needed or had asked for the hierocracy's legitimization of the land tax along the above lines. It is when the *mujtahid*s move on to consider other forms of taxation, i.e., the religious taxes, that their motive for the inclusion of the topic of taxation in their writings on *jihād* becomes apparent. In Shiʿism, by far the more important of the two categories of religious taxes is the *khums*, which is considered leviable upon all gainful activity. After explaining that one-half of the *khums* belongs to orphans and the poor, and the other half is the "share of the Imam" (*sahm-i imām*), the *mujtahids* (by virtue of their "general vicegerency") authorize the king to avail himself of the "share of the Imam" for arming the warriors of faith.[38]

The collection of the religious taxes by the *mujtahid*s had sustained the *Uṣūlī* movement and constituted the economic basis of their independent religious and scholarly activity. By seizing the opportunity offered to them for publicizing their views through the state, and therefore with the latter's tacit endorsement, the Shiʿite *ʿulamāʾ* made the gesture of putting the "share of the Imam" at the disposal of the king for the duration of the war, thereby establishing their exclusive claim to the appropriation of this religious tax once the Perso-Russian War ended. Thus this crucial financial basis of the independence of the Shiʿite hierocracy was written into what amounted to an implicit concordat between the hierocracy and the state. With this agreement, the separation of hierocracy and the state found a secure financial basis.

The importance of this novel development in securing the relative financial autonomy of the Shiᶜite hierocracy cannot be overemphasized. The jurists of the sectarian period had not laid down any provisions for the collection of the "share of the Imam," and had envisioned its burial, pending the reappearance of the Hidden Imam, or its payment to whomever was entitled to the rest of the *khums*. The *Jāmiᶜ ᶜAbbāsī* puts forward the significant rule that it be paid to the *mujtahids*. However, there is no evidence that this rule was ever enforced or widely practiced. On the contrary, Du Mans states that *khums* was paid to the clerical notables (who, as *sayyids*, were entitled to the other part of it). In any event, the rise of Akhbārī traditionalism discredited the claim of the *mujtahids* to entitlement to *khums*. Al-Ḥurr al-ᶜĀmilī, having stated that the *khums* should be discharged after deductions are made for the maintenance of the self and family and the *kharāj* of the ruler, adds that one-half of it belongs to the Imam specifically (*khāṣṣatan*), thus implying its nontransferability. In any event, there is no provision whatsoever for the collection of the *khums* by the jurists and the *mujtahids* in his *wasāʾil*. Against this background, the significance of the impact of the *Uṣūlī* revival of the authority of the jurists can be seen by the fact that Shaykh Jaᶜfar Najafī not only made regular trips to Iran to collect *khums* and absolution payment for oppressive wrongdoings (*radd-e maẓālim*) but reportedly went so far as to consider anyone who withheld the payment of *khums* as a rebel against the Imam and his vicegerent.[39]

The *Uṣūlī* movement reestablished and greatly enhanced the juristic authority of the Shiᶜite hierocracy. The lengthiest discussions of *ijtihād* and its corrective *taqlīd* (following) occur in the early works of the period of anti-Akhbārī assertiveness such as Mīrzā Abu'l-Qāsim Qumī's *Qawānīn al-Uṣūl*, and Sayyid Muḥammad ibn ᶜAlī Ṭabāṭabāʾī's (d. 1826–72/1242) *Mafātīḥ al-Uṣūl*. There, the brunt of the arguments are for the "permissibility" (*jawāz*) of *taqlīd*, and correspondingly for the "nonincumbency of *ijtihād* upon each and every individual"[40]: following (a *mujtahid*) in the *furūᶜ* (derivative matters of sacred law) is permissible. It is not incumbent upon each and every individual to acquire the necessary knowledge to embark upon *ijtihād* himself, as such an attempt would prevent him from gaining his livelihood. He may therefore follow the rulings of a specialist who is competent to exercise *ijtihād*. There follow enumerations of qualifications of the *mujtahids* and rules for choosing among them for the layman. Finally, *taqlīd* of a deceased *mujtahid* is definitively ruled out, as no age is devoid of the proof of God—i.e., the Hidden Imam.[41] However, there is no explicit assertion of the incumbency of obedience to the *mujtahids*. What emerges clearly is that the aim of these writings is to legitimate professional specialization in jurisprudence by overcoming the objections of the Akhbārī traditionalists.

Once this task was accomplished, the discussion of the topic ceased to be controversial and received little attention. As Gorjī has remarked the topic does not really belong to the jurisprudential methodology, and was in fact omitted from Anṣārī's *Farāʾid al-Uṣūl*.[42]

Once the objections to *ijtihād* had been overruled and the practice of *ijtihād* taken for granted, the *mujtahid*s could then proceed, as they in fact did, to claim the *niyābat-e ʿāmma* (general vicegerency) of the Imam on its basis. Furthermore, the obligation of the believer to observe the sacred law was of course given. As Scarcia has remarked, in the Shiʿite legal system the layman cannot understand the code, and needs the help of a jurist to determine the binding legal norm.[43] The incumbency of the observance of the sacred law in fact necessitated recourse to its authoritative interpreters. Thus, in his *Awāʾid al-Ayyām*, Mullā Aḥmad Narāqī (d. 1828–29) would rule on the "incumbency of following upon the common man [*ʿāmmī*]". In the same work he adduces a number of traditions to establish the general vicegerency of the jurists, using the term *vilāya* to denote the latter's delegated authority on behalf of the Hidden Imam during the occultation.[44] But perhaps the most influential and concise discussion of the concept is found in the *Jawāhir al-Kalām* of Shaykh Muḥammad Ḥasan Najafī (d. 1850/1266). Shaykh Muḥammad Ḥasan adduces the traditions of Ibn Ḥanẓala and of Abū Khadīja and the ordinance handed down by the Hidden Imam to affirm and establish the general or collective authority (*vilāya ʿāmma*) of the Shiʿite jurists on behalf of the Hidden Imam by virtue of their knowledge of the commandments of the sacred law and the methods of deriving them. The authority of the hierocracy is said to extend to every field except where the Imams knew of its inability to exercise authority, such as in a *jihād* for the propagation of faith, which would require a commander and armies, and like matters that would necessitate the appearance of the rightful reign (of the Imam; *dawlat al-ḥaqq*).[45]

The world-embracing aspect of the rationalism of the early phase of the *Uṣūlī* movement in the first decades of the nineteenth century was reflected in the formal elevation of reason into a "proof" of validity of legal norms, and the formal qualification of such proofs as the "four proofs" (*adilla*). Reason was exercised more freely in the creation of norms in the early than in the later phase. The category *ḥukm ʿaqlī mustaqill*[46] (independent rational norm) recognized as valid by the *Uṣūlī* jurists was referred to by Kashfī in his aforementioned political treatise. Another case of exercise of *ijtihād* which was intended to increase the impingement of the Shiʿite religion upon "the world" and had momentous consequences was Sayyid Muḥammad Bāqir Shaftī's (d. 1844/1260) treatise on "the incumbency of the implementation of the *ḥudūd* upon the *mujtahid*s during the occultation of the Imam." Shaftī thus diverged from the *Jāmiʿ ʿAbbāsī*'s cautious justification of the implementation of the *ḥudūd* in general, and, even more sharply, from its prohibition of their implementation in cases requiring capital punishment. Furthermore, to set an example, he himself proceeded to implement the *ḥudūd* vigorously, and is said to have executed some seventy persons.[47] Thus the abeyance of *ḥudūd* according to the sacred law, bemoaned by our sixteenth-century polemicists, ceased to be the case, in Isfahan at any rate. Though the other *mujtahid*s did not follow Shaftī in this particular respect, his legal writings, as well as those of Shaykh Muḥammad Ḥasan Najafī a generation later, were indicative of a much more positive attitude of the *mujtahid*s toward the administration of law.

In fact, in this phase, the *Uṣūlī* movement made not only theoretical jurisprudence but its application a very important component of the activity of religious professionals. The courts of the *mujtahid*s and other prominent members of the hierocracy such as the *shaykh al-Islām* and the *imām-jumᶜa* enjoyed an unprecedented level of activity,[48] eclipsing totally the courts of the qadis, whose offices, in the course of the century, turned into sinecures or went out of existence. The virtual disappearance of state-appointed qadis represented yet another change away from the Safavid "caesaropapist" constitution in the direction of a sharper bifurcation between the state and the hierocracy. This trend was encouraged by Fatḥ ᶜAlī Shāh, who personally referred cases to the courts of the eminent *mujtahid*s. Though the *ᶜurf* jurisdiction, with its typical patrimonial features (such as the lack of clear differentiation between administration and adjudication and the king's prerogative of passing death sentences), remained very widespread, the religious courts reached the peak of their importance in Iran's judiciary organization.[49]

Thus, in the reconstituted Shiᶜite polity of Fatḥ ᶜAlī Shāh, the hierocracy found an enlarged role in the administration of justice much more congruent with the legal authority they were entitled to according to Twelver Shiᶜism than had been the case under the Safavids. In this respect, too, the institutional translation of the Shiᶜite religious system reached its furthest point.

10.1.3 A Polemical Digression on Legitimacy

As we have seen on various occasions, for the Shiᶜites the Hidden Imam is the Imam of the Age (*imām-e zamān*) and the proof (*ḥujjat*) of God. He is alive but performs the essential function of the imamate of the age in "concealment." The proof of his existence is that, owing to the grace (*luṭf*) of God—a tenet of Twelver theology that has already been mentioned—it is incumbent upon Him to appoint an Imam for each age to guide the believers. Since al-Ṭūsī, the Shiᶜite theologians have insisted that the Hidden Imam is alive and carries out the essential functions of the Imamate of the Age. Now, *when and if* the ruler claimed imamate, the Shiᶜites would consider him a usurper of the right of the Hidden Imam and therefore illegitimate. As Madelung has pointed out, this was the case with the ᶜAbbasid caliphs who *claimed imamate* and thus the religious authority that was the Imams' alone. But as the Shiᶜite jurists recognized immediately after the overthrow of the ᶜAbbasid caliphate, a temporal ruler without pretensions to the religious authority of the Imam would no longer be a usurper, and the legitimacy of his temporal rule would be conditional upon his justice.[50]

Once the distinction between the time of absence and the time of *parousia* of the Imam is made, the notion of usurpation and illegitimacy of temporal rule[51] can be seen as truly absurd. When the Hidden Imam does appear, it is incumbent upon the ruler to join the ranks of his followers, and he would be a usurper if he failed to do so. But it is preposterous to suggest that all government is "inescapably usurpatory" *in the time of occultation*. One may well say that the Hidden Imam is the true sovereign of the Shiᶜite polity in the sense that the enthroned Christ is depicted as the true ruler of the Christian empire in the mosaic above the imperial gate of Hagia Sophia. But as the true sovereignty of Christ in no way implied the illegitimacy of Emperor Leo VI, depicted as crowned but prostrate before Christ, the true sovereignty of the Hidden Imam is in no way incompatible with the legitimate rulership of a just king. As we have seen, the Safavid rulers kept harnessed horses ready for the Imam, should he decide to appear and avail himself of them. In the event, the Qājār rulers were also undoubtedly ready to serve the reappearing Lord of Time and considered such service the utmost honor. The Qājār historian and man of letters, Rustam al-Ḥukamāᵓ, considered the return of the Imam of the Age imminent. It is interesting to note that in his prediction, "one of the sons of Fatḥ ᶜAlī Shāh would ascend the throne as the *nāᵓib* of the Imam in 1835–36/1251. He would follow the path of justice and equity, but in 1849–50/1266, after unbelief [*kufr*] had been victorious over Islam, the Imam himself would appear from Medina, overthrow unbelief and polytheism, destroy tyranny and error, and conquer the world."[52] Here, to emphasize a very obvious point, legitimate kingship and the absence of the Hidden Imam are conceived as fully congruent.

To conclude, therefore, no Shīite doctrine of illegitimacy of government during the occultation can be found in the legal literature for the entire period under study.

10.2 The "Value-Rationalism" of the Shiᶜite Jurisprudence and Pious Withdrawal from Politics

So far we have been considering the factors that facilitated the impact of Shiᶜism as a world religion on the societal structure of domination in nineteenth-century Iran. We must now focus on some of the inherent limitations that restricted this impact and at times necessitated reversals in the process of rationalization of the constitution of the polity.

The history of the *Uṣūlī* movement provides us with a very interesting concrete case of striving for what Weber termed "value-rationality." As we have recently been reminded, the concept makes its appearance very late in Weber's writings, interestingly, in the period in which he formulated his precepts on the "religious rejections of the world."[53] This conjunction is far from accidental. Weber paid special attention to the formulation of the concept of value-rationality at the time when he was impressed by the tension created by the inevitable incompatibilities between the rationalization of life in view of the attainment of salvation as the ultimate religious value and the instrumental and formal rationalization of social action in the light of economic, political, aesthetic, and other interests.

As we have seen, Weber emphasized the fusion of legal rules and ethical demands in sacred laws that results in indifference or aversion to positivistic formalism. For this reason, he had been content to underscore the "irrational" character of sacred law in general of Shi'ite sacred law in particular.[54] What Weber had precluded from his analysis of Shi'ite and other systems of sacred law were the procedures for the determination of the "substantive" rationality—i.e., value-rationality—of legal norms within these systems. Our examination of these procedures in the case of *Uṣūlī* jurisprudence indicates a more complex picture than the one envisaged by Weber, while in part also demonstrating the general inhibitory consequences of value-rationalism for positivistic formalization and codification. The concern with the value-rationality of legal norms did in fact, contrary to Weber's argument, result in the generation of a set of legal principles that could also be applied to the rationalization of public law—and consequently of the political sphere. As we have seen, this was in fact partly the case with the application of rational jurisprudential method by Kashfī and Shaftī. At the same time, however, the application of the principles of jurisprudence to the field of public law was arrested by the ethical involution stemming from the introversion of hierocratic jurisprudence. The tendency toward ethical involution can in turn be seen to stand in a mutually supportive relationship to the world-rejecting tendencies of the religious rationalization of life, which, from the political viewpoint, entailed withdrawal from the sphere of politics and indifference to public law.

The tension between religious rationalism and politics and the various modes of its resolution is strikingly illustrated by the paradoxical consequences of the *Uṣūlī* movement for the rationalization of the societal structure of domination (or of public law). Gorjī has distinguished two phases of this movement: the defeat of Akhbārī traditionalism and the revival of the *uṣūl al-fiqh* (principles of jurisprudence) in the late decades of the eighteenth and the early nineteenth century; and the period of technical maturity inaugurated by Shaykh Murtaḍā Anṣārī's (d. 1864/1281) *Farā'id al-Uṣūl* (the second half of the nineteenth century).[55] In the first phase, when the degree of technical rationality of the jurisprudential methodology was lower, we witness a considerable impact on the constitution of the polity, while, paradoxically, the perfection of value-rational techniques for the derivation of the ethically and legally binding "norms" (*aḥkām*) in the second phase can be seen to deflect the Shi'ite jurists' attention from positive public law. With the progressive rationalization of methodology in the second phase, ethical involution set in: the concern with value-rationalism decisively predominated and the impact on positive law became quite negligible. Instead, the ethical introversionism of *Uṣūlī* jurisprudence reinforced the attitude of pious antipathy to temporal power and of political indifferentism.

As Coulson has remarked, the great moral concern of the jurists in general set self-imposed limits on the rationalization of the legal system.[56] In the preceding pages I have been arguing that the favorable conditions created by the first Qājārs, certain *mujtahid*s like Kashfī and Shaftī did overcome these pious limitations and took an active part in the administration of justice. However, even a *mujtahid* like Shaykh Muḥammad Ḥasan Najafī, who similarly ruled in favor of the incumbency of administration of *ḥudūd* during the occultation and emphasized the general vicegerency of the jurists, exhibited the pious mistrust of worldly involvement to the extent that he accused some of the doctors ruling in favor of the incumbency of Friday prayer during the occultation of the "love of leadership [*riyāsa*] and earthly dominion [*salṭana*]".[57] Furthermore, there were many *mujtahid*s who did not follow his example and continued to adhere to the ideal of pious antipathy toward all worldly activity including the administration of justice. Among these, we may name the greatest jurist of the century, Shaykh Murtaḍā Anṣārī.

The overriding concern with ethics and morality made *Uṣūlī* jurisprudence often militate against the rationalization of practice even in the first period. For instance, the author of *Mafātīḥ al-Uṣūl* refused to accept that a transaction involving "positive rules" (*aḥkām waḍʿiyya*) could be valid if concluded in a formally correct manner. He maintained that in order for such transactions to be valid, it was necessary for the parties to the transaction to *believe*, either through independent exercise of judgment or through following an authority, in the lawfulness of their action.[58] Nevertheless, as we have seen, in this period reason was fairly freely applied by Kashfī to matters not covered by the letter of the sacred law. The subsequent rationalization of the jurisprudential methodology consisted precisely in the systematically more rigorous ethically oriented rules for the employment of reason, thus progressively constraining its free exercise.

Anṣārī certainly did uphold the attitude of pious antipathy to judiciary practice. According to his biographer, the shaykh was so pious and God-fearing that he would refrain from issuing binding injunctions as far as possible. When a disciple of his protested against this fact, the shaykh replied that he was courageous and even foolhardy in this respect compared to his teacher Shaykh ʿAlī. The latter found his followers' seeking of rulings from him "in matters not necessary to religion" more unpalatable to him than a wound from a dagger.[59]

This attitude was reflected in the direction in which Anṣārī steered the *Uṣūlī* movement. It also constituted a severe self-limitation on the scope of hierocratic jurisdiction in the overall legal system, which in part explains the continued importance of "customary" (*ʿurf*) tribunals under the jurisdiction of secular authorities.

Anṣārī's treatise, the *Farāʾid al-Uṣūl*, contains three parts: the first is on the determination of legal norms with certainty (*qaṭᶜ*), the second on their determination through "valid conjecture" (*ẓann muᶜtabar*), and the third on their determination through the employment of "practical principles" (*uṣūl ᶜamaliyya*). The first part regards cases where unambiguous norms can be found *in the sources*, and there is no need for the employment of reason. The second regards cases where reason in the form of rational methodology is painstakingly employed to create (insulated and individual) binding legal norms. The third and last part occupies most of the book.[60] It represents Anṣārī's major contribution, and consists of a consideration of the four practical principles, which have been described as "emanations of reason."[61] It is fascinating to note that these practical emanations of reason consist not in the systematization of rationalization and modification of norms already derived by the first two groups of methodological procedures, but in the creation of analogous "apparent norms" (sing. *ḥukm ẓāhirī*, in contrast to "real" or "certain" [*wāqiᶜī*] norms) regarding "apparent duties" (sing. *taklīf ẓāhirī*) in areas not covered by "certain norms" or "valid conjectures," and only in these areas.[62] The antithetical relationship between this rationalization of the *method* for ascertaining the moral-legal status of single acts through textual and grammatical analysis and the formal rationalization and codification of law should be obvious. With Anṣārī the moral, ethical orientation of value-rational jurisprudential methodology, already pronounced in the preceding phase, overwhelmingly swamped all consideration for positive law. Not legal practicality and systematization of positive law but ethical introversion became the hallmark of *Uṣūlī* rationalism.

Anṣārī's fastidious concern for the value-rationality of specific legal norms meant that their conformity to the ultimate values as determined by the divine purpose as revealed in the book of God and the sayings and deeds of the Prophet and the infallible Imams, either with certainty or through valid conjecture, was to be established in as compelling and stringent a rational fashion as possible in order to dispel all justifiable doubt about any possible transgression of the divine law. This explains Anṣārī's indifference to the central issues of public law, which required a latitude in the interpretation of the exiguous "sources" incompatible with the stringency with which the rational method of inference was to be applied. In fact, parting company with Kashfī and Shaftī as well as Narāqī and Najafī, he would not even countenance an *ex cathedra* legitimation of the "general vicegerency" of the *ᶜulamāʾ* as jurists, which according to him could not be firmly deduced from the "sources" of the sacred law.[63]

Thus the mature phase of value-rationalism in Shiᶜite jurisprudence, beginning in the middle decades of the nineteenth century, was destined to have no impact on the judiciary framework or on the constitution of the polity.

CHAPTER ELEVEN

Religion and Sociopolitical Action in the Qājār Polity

11.1 Societal Action: Collaboration and Discord between the Hierocracy and the State

The creation of a unified normative order regulating political and hierocratic domination of course did not eliminate conflicts between the hierocracy and the state but rather established the framework within which these conflicts would be played out, along with much cooperation.

As we have seen, in Max Weber's discussion of institutionalization of charisma, one finds two basic types of charisma whose antagonism he considers primeval: the political and the religious, as prototypically embodied in the warlord and the divinely inspired. Weber's juxtaposed and analogous definitions of ruling organization/hierocratic organization and state/church replicate this dichotomy at the organizational level.[1] After the fall of the Safavid dynasty, whose rulers enjoyed a caesaropapist admixture of political and religious authority, religious charisma came to reside exclusively with the men of religion. With the separation of political and hierocratic domination under the Qājārs, political and religious charisma in institutionalized form could, and in the instance to be described did, face each other in stark mutual antithesis.

Sayyid Muḥammad Bāqir Shaftī (d. 1844/1260), whose insistence on the administration of the Sacred Law during the occultation of the Imam has already been noted, was undoubtedly the most powerful—and the wealthiest—of the Shiᶜite *ᶜulamāᵓ* residing in Iran after the death of Mīrzā Abu'l-Qāsim Qumī. He is probably the first religious dignitary to be given the title of *ḥujjat al-Islām* (proof of Islam).[2] He never visited any of the governors of Isfahan, and would receive them with utmost disdain. He would pay visits to the king whenever he was in Isfahan, but even then with much arrogance. When he was taken to visit Fatḥ ᶜAlī

Shah for the first time, the king granted him the usual favor of making a request. The "proof of Islam" saw this as an opportunity to remind the earthly ruler of the antithesis of divine and worldly charisma which they respectively represented. He asked that the royal *naqāreh-khāneh* (music house), indispensable for ceremonial regal pomp, be banned. The king remained silent, and the point was not lost on him. When the Sayyid left, he marvelled at how he could have dared to ask for the banning of the "royal *naqāreh-khāneh* which is the insignia of kingship."

The stark opposition between the two forms of charisma was brought out much more clearly in Shaftī's encounters with Muḥammad Shāh. When riding on a mule on his way to visit the king, Shaftī, the "proof of Islam," had a cantor walk in front of him reciting the Qurʾan. As they approached the royal residence, surrounded by a crowd kissing Shaftī's hands, his mule, and the mule's hooves, he ordered the cantor to recite the verse, "We sent a Prophet to the Pharoah [the symbol of worldly despotism] and the Pharoah rebelled against the Prophet." When returning his call, Muḥammad Shāh made the *naqāreh* precede him with ceremonious pomp. Shaftī was coming to the gates of his house to welcome the king, but, "upon hearing the sound of the *naqāreh*, he raised his hands toward the sky and implored: 'Oh God, do not wish the humiliation of the descendants of Fatima the Radiant [the daughter of the Prophet] any more!' and returned to his house."[3]

Needless to say, there was no need for constant expression of this potential antagonism between political and religious charisma, which in fact remained completely latent, allowing much cooperation between the hierocracy and the state. It is important to note that this cooperation was even extended to the political sphere proper: one can cite numerous instances of the *ʿulamāʾ*'s intercession in internal political disputes and in its diplomatic relations with the Ottoman Empire. The Shiʿite religious dignitaries residing in the holy cities of Iraq often mediated between the Qājārs and the Ottoman governors of Arab Iraq in order to settle important disputes.[4]

The tension between the hierocracy and the state reached its highest point under Muḥammad Shāh. The tension was provoked by Muḥammad Shāh's Sufism and his anticlerical attitude. Owing to the fact that the hierocracy, though formally acephalous, was dominated by Shaftī and a handful of other *mujtahid*s, hierocratic opposition to the state became polarized. However, the tension between the hierocracy and the state abated during the long reign of the subsequent monarch, Nāṣir al-Dīn (1848–96), until it suddenly flared up in the last decade of the nineteenth century.

11.1.1 Religiously Relevant Policies of the Qājār Rulers and Acts of the Ruling Stratum

There seems no need to compile a list of the genuine or calculated acts of piety such as pilgrimages and endowments of holy shrines by the Qājār rulers since many of these are mentioned in detail by Algar.[5] Of far greater importance is Fatḥ ʿAlī Shāh's religious policy, sketched in the introduction to part 3, which comprises the most crucial religiously relevant set of "societal actions" initiated by the state.

In this section, we shall devote our attention to another aspect of the religious policy of Fatḥ ʿAlī Shāh, and especially of his successor Muḥammad Shāh, a policy that was politically conditioned at least insofar as it aimed at the domestication of the masses independently of the hierocracy and at increasing the control of the state and the ruling elite over popular religion—i.e., the development of passion plays, the *taʿzieh*.

Under the Safavids, the mourning ceremonies commemorating the martyrdom of Ḥusayn were an important component of popular religion, but there were other equally important ceremonies connected with the figure of ʿAlī.[6] Furthermore, it is extremely unlikely that there were any theatrical representations of the events of Karbalā.[7] Fatḥ ʿAlī Shāh gave considerable impetus to the development of passion plays on the martyrdom of Ḥusayn and the tragedy of Karbalā. These were at first performed in the houses of notables as a part of the ceremonies of the month of Muharram alongside long recitations of the afflictions of the house of the Prophet, known as *rawḍa-khwānī*. During Fatḥ ʿAlī Shāh's reign a small number of fixed *takiyeh*s (theaters) were built specifically for *taʿzieh*, most notably that of his foreign minister Ḥajjī Mīrzā Abuʾl-Ḥasan Khān. Under Muḥammad Shāh, the prime minister Ḥajjī Mīrzā Āqāsī built a sumptuous *takiyeh*, which was attended regularly by the crown prince, the high officials of the state, and the high ranking diplomats. Mindful of the hostility of the hierocracy, the Sufi prime minister was eager to establish a measure of control over popular religion and to that end greatly encouraged the development of the passion plays. *Takiyeh*s built by the notables mushroomed in Tehran and the major cities. A French diplomat wrote that during his stay in Tehran in 1842–43, fifty-eight *takiyeh*s were built. The process culminated in the erection of the famous Takiyeh Dowlat (*takiyeh* of the state) under Nāsir al-Dīn Shāh (1848–96). On the literary plane, Qāʾanī and Yaghmā Jandaqī produced variations in verse on the themes of the tragedy, and, with the advent of printing, the scripts of some eighty of the passion plays were produced and sold to an avid public.[8]

It is important to note that the vigorous development of the *taʿzieh* took place despite the opposition of the jurists in the upper echelons of the hierocracy. The hierocracy could not curb the development of *taʿzieh* because of its total organizational amorphousness. The disapproving *mujtahid*s had no disciplinary machinery for controlling the clerics who took part in them. The *taʿzieh* and the *rawḍa-khwānī* conjoined with it became the source of livelihood for a new type of religious professional, typically drawn from among the dispossessed real or putative *sayyids*: the *rawḍa-khwān*, who was modestly paid and of low prestige.

The *taʿzieh* became tremendously popular among the people. Not only were they affected as audience, but they actively participated in the flagellant processions accompanying the ceremonies. We also know that the guilds of the bazaar zealously competed in the preparation of the feast of Ḥusayn and the decoration of the *takiyeh* of Ḥajjī Mīrzā Āqāsī. As Calmard rightly emphasizes, the spread of *taᶜzieh* enhanced the political domination of the monarchy and the patrons among the nobility who controlled this branch of religious activity. This is especially so in that poems in praise of the shah preceded the beginning of *sineh-zani* (beating of the chest) during the ceremonies. Furthermore, because of its tremendous cathartic effect on the spectators, the ceremonies acted as channels of discharge of potentially rebellious energy and thus aided the domestication of the masses.[9] Yet, as we shall see, these ritual reenactments of the tragedy of Karbalā made the Shiᶜite theodicy of misfortune a source of powerfully emotive notions and imagery, which could also be drawn upon to motivate communal oppositional action, both by the hierocracy and by chiliastic revolutionaries.

11.1.2 Military Action

The issue of the bearing of religion on military action arose in the decisive instance of cooperation of the hierocracy and the state during the first Perso-Russian War.

The attempt to mobilize the masses for war through the religious motivation of military action in defense of Islam against the Russian infidels appears to have been highly successful at first—perhaps even too successful in that it was one of the factors that forced the reluctant Fatḥ ᶜAlī Shāh into a disastrous second war with Russia. But this sacralization of military action as *jihād* could not be effectively repeated. Thereafter, similar attempts quickly became subject to the law of diminishing returns. The preaching of holy war against the Sunni Afghans fell flat under Muḥammad Shāh, and the more sustained attempt to mobilize the masses for a holy war against the British in 1856–57 was given up as a fiasco.[10]

What interests us is not the detailed history of these attempts but the logic of making military action religiously significant. It is interesting to note that both religious *credenda* or beliefs and religious *miranda* or emotive symbols and imagery[11] appear as the instruments of sacralization of military action. The *miranda* are taken from the Shiᶜite theodicy of suffering, and relate to the martyrdom of the Third Imam. This "Lord of the Martyrs" was said to be beckoning the believers to his aid and the warriors of faith were advised to carry small plaques made with the dust of his tomb to the battlefield. But the use of *miranda*, which has the effect of inducing an enthusiasm akin to those of the chiliastic warriors of the fifteenth and early sixteenth centuries, is clearly secondary. Even more ancillary is the promise of the *ᶜulamāʾ*, who, acting as the spokesmen for the otherworldly orthodox soteriology, pledged to "intercede" for the warriors of faith in the hereafter.[12] It is rather the Shiᶜite *credenda* or beliefs that are primarily drawn upon. For the nineteenth-century warriors, in contrast to the chiliastic holy warriors of the early Safavid times, the religious motivation to military action had firm ethical roots. It was first and foremost the provisions of the Shiᶜite ethics of salvation regarding holy war that were drawn upon by the *mujtahids* as its authoritative interpreters in order to endow military action against the Russians with soteriological significance. The *mujtahids* wrote expositions of a somewhat neglected section of the sacred law,[13] in light of which they exercised their *ijtihād* and ruled that it was the "individually incumbent" (*wajib ᶜaynī*) duty of the Shiᶜites under the circumstances to wage war against Russia.[14] In doing so, they sought to motivate the believers to military action in fulfillment of their ethical duties.

11.1.3 The Dependence of the Hierocracy on the State in the First Half of the Nineteenth Century

The Shiᶜite hierocracy that emerged with firm roots in Iran in the first half of the nineteenth century was an autonomous institution. Organizationally, however, it was amorphous. The collapse of the Safavid state entailed the removal of the underlying centralized financial control of the *ṣadr*, while the theoretical equality of the *mujtahid* tended to result in the acephaly of the hierocracy. Thus there existed no hierarchical religious organization. Instead, the hierocracy was very steeply stratified in terms of status honor into the venerable *mujtahids* and the great bulk of the *mullās*.

Malcolm noted the sharp division between the higher and lower ranks of the hierocracy at the beginning of the nineteenth century.[15] Some quarter of a century later, Sepsis similarly noted that the *mujtahids* were the objects of veneration, surrounded by *sayyids* who were far from enjoying a similar rank. On the contrary, a hiatus separated the lower ranks, who did not receive such reverence and were of great ignorance and cupidity.[16] The hierarchy of deference within the religious community came to assume the curious shape of what amounted to a sharply stratified dichotomy. It is quite possible that there was some status stratification at the lower level of the dichotomy among the congeries of rustic *mullās*, simple *sayyids*, and *rawḍa-khwāns*, but this seems irrelevant from the viewpoint of the initiation of hierocratic action. What is important is the pressure for obliteration of formal ranking in the upper sector of the hierocracy.

The doctrine of *ijtihād* had much to do with this obliteration. Two related aspects of the development of the doctrine of *ijtihād* in this period tended to depress the status honor of non-*mujtahids*, resulting in their ousting from the upper sector of the deference hierarchy. One was a trend toward denying the validity of the endeavor of the "specialized *mujtahid*" (*mujtahid mutajazzī*), and restricting the validity of *ijtihād* to the "absolute *mujtahid*" (*mujtahid muṭlaq*).[17] This had the effect of lowering the status of those who had mastered only one or two branches of the religious sciences. A second factor was the restriction of *ᶜamal bi' l-iḥtiyāt* (acting with caution) for those about to reach the level of *ijtihād*. Thus the author of *Mafātiḥ*, stressing the ethical desirability of avoiding mistakes in the fulfillment of religious duties, devoted a section to arguing for the "necessity of following a *mujtahid* for him who has not [yet] reached the rank of *ijtihād*." This again had the effect of dividing the learned section of the hierocracy into the *mujtahid*s and the non-*mujtahid*s, who were increasingly pressed to assume the rank of *muqallid* (followers). On the other hand, the "impermissibility of *taqlīd* for one *mujtahid* from another" set real limits to formal stratification in terms of ranks at the highest level.[18]

The hierocracy had no administrative staff for the execution of the verdicts of the religious courts, which therefore had to be referred to secular authorities. Furthermore, the absence of hierarchical ranking among the religious courts meant that the litigants could obtain different verdicts from different religious courts for the same case. The secular authorities could then choose which verdict to enforce, usually in light of the bribes the parties to the case were able to offer them.[19] The amorphous organization of the hierocracy was reflected in the procedurally uninstitutionalized manner in which the weapon of excommunication (*takfīr*) was used and abused by the individual *ʿulamāʾ*. In the absence of organizational control, excommunication or the threat thereof could easily be used for personal gain. What was more serious was its frequent use by the *ʿulamāʾ* against one another.[20] Despite the inevitable debasement resulting from its abuse, however, excommunication remained a powerful weapon, especially in doctrinal matters, as it was always possible for one *mujtahid*'s *takfīr* to be subsequently endorsed by others.[21]

Because of the absence of a hierarchical organization, the members of the hierocracy had to initiate action as individuals or as small groups. In very rare instances, individual *mujtahid*s did set up small hierocratic patrimonies as "states within states." This was the case with Shaftī, who set up such a hierocratic patrimony in Isfahan during the reign of Muḥammad Shāh, making use of the *lūṭī*s (a "Mafioso" group of strongmen of city quarters engaged in the extraction of protection money and occasional brigandage) as its "executive arm."[22]

But in general hierocratic action could be launched either through the state or by mobilizing the populace. The initiation of action through the state was problematic and always had to be "negotiated" through the *shaykh al-Islām*s as intermediaries. As has been pointed out, the *ʿulamāʾ* were unable to initiate any such action in a matter so intimately related to religion as the spread of the passion plays. This was so because the religious policy of the state in this regard was diametrically opposed to their doctrinal interests. However, in two other matters of great religious concern they did succeed in initiating societal action through the state, with varying effectiveness.

As the custodians of Shiʿite orthodoxy, the hierocracy was alarmed at the reemergence and spread of Sufism at the end of the eighteenth century. The *ʿulamāʾ*

did initiate firm and violent communal and societal action, which was in fact effective in curbing the spread of Sufism among the masses. By vigorously opposing the Sufis, the Shiᶜite hierocracy succeeding in maintaining their domination over the masses, so deeply imbued with the otherworldly post-Majlisī orthodox Shiᶜism. Consequently, despite the persistence of such a plebeian order as the Khaksar and the acceptance of lower-class adepts by other orders, Sufism in Iran became a predominantly aristocratic religious movement, in striking contrast to the rest of the Islamic world.

If Malcolm can be relied upon, with the return of Maᶜṣūm ᶜAlī Shāh, the *Pīr* (spiritual guide) of the Niᶜmatullāhī order, and his disciples from the Deccan during the last years of Karīm Khān's reign, Sufism spread very rapidly. Malcolm's informants give an incredibly high estimate of the adherents to Sufism, which is put at 300,000. With the ending of the anarchic interregnum and the reestablishment of peace by the Qājārs, the champions of Shiᶜite orthodoxy had no difficulty in persuading the pious Fatḥ ᶜAlī Shāh to take firm action to suppress Sufism. The *mujtahid* who tirelessly led the anti-Sufi campaign was Āqā Muḥammad ᶜAlī Bihbihānī, son of the founder of the *Uṣulī* movement, whose rabid violence against the Sufis earned him the title of *ṣūfī-kosh* (killer of the Sufis). Malcolm reports firm repressive measures taken by Fatḥ ᶜAlī Shāh.[23] This is confirmed by the *ṣūfī-kosh*'s grossly vituperative tracts against the Sufis, where he praises the king for such action. Āqā Muḥammad ᶜAlī persuaded Fatḥ ᶜAlī Shāh to expel all the Sufis from Tehran. It appears that the shah also ordered a number of important Sufis to be arrested and sent to Āqā Muḥammad ᶜAlī in Kirmanshah for condemnation to death for heresy.[24] It is interesting to note that Bihbihānī's son viewed this collaboration between his father and Fatḥ ᶜAlī Shāh as parallel to the ideal model of late Safavid cooperation between the state and the hierocracy, which had resulted in the propagation of the Shiᶜite religion through the pen of his ancestor Majlisī and the sword of the Safavid rulers.[25]

In 1819–20/1235, the *ᶜulamāʾ* of Gilan, alarmed at the vitality of Niᶜmatullāhī Sufism in Rasht under the guidance of Ḥājj Muḥammad Jaᶜfar (Majdhūb ᶜAlī Shāh), petitioned Fatḥ ᶜAlī to suppress the activities of the Niᶜmatullāhī order, alleging that the Sufis were contemplating political rulership. Fatḥ ᶜAlī Shāh dismissed the state official in question and imposed the crashing fine of 1,000 or 2,000 tomans on the order, dispatching a military cohort to extract it.[26]

Muḥammad Shāh was himself a Sufi, and appointed his Sufi guide Ḥājj Mīrzā Āqāsī prime minister as soon as he could. The Shiᶜite hierocracy could therefore no longer initiate repressive action through the state. However, the *ᶜulamāʾ* did use the hierocratic offices they occupied to check the spread of Sufism to the lower strata of society. For instance, in 1836, at the end of the month of Ramadan, the *Imām Jumᶜa* of Tehran "in Hajee Meerza Aghassee's presence, denounced the Soofies from his pulpit, called them 'sons of burnt fathers' and 'defiled mothers,' recommended their immediate extermination, and devoted them to future damnation."[27]

The complete dependency of the hierocracy on the state for initiation of societal action in defense of religious orthodoxy is illustrated by the part they played in the arrest and eventual execution of the Bāb. Sayyid ʿAli Muḥammad Shīrāzī, the Bāb, reactivated the mahdistic tenet by claiming to be an agent of fresh revelation. The proclamation of his mission came in 1844 with the words, "I bear witness that ʿAlī Muḥammad is the remnant [*baqiyya*] of God," diffused from the minaret of the mosque of Āqā Qāsim in Shiraz by an early convert. Bābism as a new religion claiming to supersede Shiʿism was of course sheer heresy, and the guardians of orthodoxy could be expected to react. The *ʿulamāʾ* of Shiraz persuaded the governor to punish the Bābīs, and bring the Bāb to Shiraz to face an inquisitional confrontation with them. Subsequent action of the governor depended on the orders he received from Tehran, and despite the pressure put by Shaykh ʿAbd al-Ḥusayn Mujtahid on the prime minister, the latter only ordered that the Bāb be confined to his house, causing the dissatisfaction of the *ʿulamāʾ* by his laxity. Subsequently the Bāb was transferred to Isfahan, where he even enjoyed the protection of its powerful governor, Mīrzā Manūchihr Khān Muʿtamid al-Dawla. Upon the latter's death, he was arrested and sent to Mākū, and then to the fortress of Chihrīq. The *ʿulamāʾ* of the nearby city of Tabriz were granted an inquisitorial session with the Bāb, and the *Shaykh al-Islām* even had the satisfaction of beating the arch-heretic in person, but the Bāb was taken back to his prison alive. Despite several *fatwā*s condemning him to death for heresy (and despite the beginning of the Bābī insurrections), Ḥājjī Mīrzā Āqāsī did not put him to death. It was only after the more serious insurrection of Zanjān in 1850, and primarily for political reasons, that Amīr Kabīr, Āqāsī's successor under the new shah, eventually responded to six years of relentless clerical pressure and ordered the execution of the Bāb. Therefore, the final putting to death of the arch-heretic can hardly be considered the simple execution of the injunctions of the hierocracy.[28]

11.1.4 The Organizational Characteristics of the Shiʿite Hierocracy in the Second Half of the Nineteenth Century and Their Consequences

Kashī had stressed that the king needed the *ʿulamāʾ* and the *ʿulamāʾ* needed the king. In the second half of the nineteenth century, the dependence of the *ʿulamāʾ* on the king became considerably greater.

A crucially important fact that has not been noted in the literature is the massive increase in the number of *mujtahid*s in the second half of the nineteenth century. In the second half of the seventeenth century, Chardin had remarked that the *mujtahid*s were very few.[29] Writing during the second decade of the nineteenth century, Malcolm stated: "There are seldom more than three or four mooshtaheds."[30] The total number of *mujtahid*s in the first four decades of the nineteenth century was certainly less than a dozen. Let us compare this period with the first forty years of Nāṣir al-Dīn Shāh's reign (1848–88). Nearly one-half of the 359 noteworthy *ʿulamāʾ* of the period mentioned by Iʿtimād al-Salṭana in *al-Maʾāthir wa'l-Āthār*, or some 175 persons, are, either explicitly or by inference, classifiable as *mujtahid*.[31] At the end of the nineteenth century, the inflation of the rank of *mujtahid*s got worse. A single scholar, the famous Ākhūnd Khurāsānī is said by a careful author to have trained at least 120 "definitive" (*musallam*) *mujtahids*.[32] The title of *ḥujjat al-Islām*, "proof of Islam," too, having been conferred upon an eminent *mujtahid* of Kashan after Shaftī,[33] depreciated very sharply thereafter.

Its rapid growth during the second half of the century gave the hierarchy of deference a very large undifferentiated sector. To this upper sector of the hierocracy was appended a group of non-*mujtahid*s, who owned their prestige to their offices. This latter group consisted of *shaykh al-Islām*s and *imām jumʿa*s, appointed by the government, directors and professors of the seminaries, and finally prayer leaders of the mosques. There were no organizational links between the holders of these offices and the *mujtahid*s, their overlapping relationship being determined by their respective position in the hierarchy of deference.

The absence of any hierarchical organization had a number of important consequences. The clearly defined and sharply stratified hierarchy of deference was incapable of generating action, or of controlling the individual members and disciplining them as a unified organization and in consistent pursuit of doctrinal and institutional interests. The incipient modernization of the state in the second half of the nineteenth century entailed actual and planned encroachments upon the judiciary prerogatives of the *ʿulamāʾ*[34] and upon their control over the *awqāf*,[35] and thus threatened their institutional vested interests. Yet the Shiʿite hierocracy did not react as an institution, and many of its members continued to display accommodating docility toward the government. As an organization, the hierocracy was poorly isolated from its sociopolitical environment and was therefore permeable by environmental forces. The forces of its political environment, extraneous factors emanating from the interests of the state or of social groups, could easily impinge upon the action of the hierocracy or prevent such action from being initiated. Let us illustrate the point with an important example. Until the 1880s, Nāṣir al-Dīn Shāh's public behavior was decorous from the religious point of view. The new year (*Nō-rūz*) royal audience in 1881, for instance, was marked by the presence of the most respected *mujtahid*s of the capital. From 1885 onwards, the aging monarch's rampant pederastic proclivities filled the new year royal audiences with young children donning the mantles of the highest officials of the state. Nāṣir al-Dīn's love for his favorite, Malījak II, became increasingly engrossing and scandalous. We hear of the people grumbling profusely, but not the hierocracy. On the contrary, some of the most eminent *mujtahid*s of Tehran unmistakably condoned the immorality of the shah and his debauched prime minister, Amīn al-Sulṭān, who was the object of their constant flattery. It was only with the advent of a countervailing extraneous factor in the form of the agitation of the reformers and the merchants opposed to autocracy in general and to injurious concessions to foreign entrepreneurs, and at the direct instigation of the famous advocate of reform, Afghānī, that the hierocracy received the decisive impetus to speak out against the ruler as the custodian of religion and morality. It was only then that the king's pederasty and the journey of the harem favorite, a Muslim woman, to Europe for an eye operation would be publicly denounced, and the cries of "Woe to religion, woes to the sacred law" be raised from the pulpits of the important mosques.[36]

In contrast to the inability of the Shiᶜite hierocracy to initiate institutionalized action in pursuit of its institutional and doctrinal interests, the absence of an authoritative hierarchy and of disciplinary procedures meant that the *ᶜulamāʾ* could engage in politics in pursuit of personal gain with complete immunity. Paradoxically, their engagement in politics, institutionalized as their crucial role of mediation and intercession in political conflict, was premised on their material disinterestedness. However, against the background of a "push" factor consisting of the immense growth in the number of *ᶜulamāʾ* and intensified competition for the control of *awqāf*, professorships and directorships of schools, as well as the offices of *imām jumᶜa* and *shaykh al-Islām*, and the "pull" factor of the spoils to be gained in the highly factionalized late Qājār period, the involvement of the *ᶜulamāʾ* in pursuit of personal interests and material gain became extremely common. For instance, they frequently acted as political brokers to secure appointments of local governors and state officials and often engaged in the hoarding of grain in collusion with the latter.

Consequently, the age-old rift between the worldly *ᶜulamāʾ* and those who upheld the ideal of pious aloofness to all political involvement was sharpened. The former group as a rule showed little hesitation in using their hierocratic domination over the masses as an asset to enter the political arena in pursuit of material gain with the help of the state, in exchange for which they were on occasion ready to act as the legitimators of Qājār rule by praying for its glory (*duᶜā-gūʾī*) and cooperating with the ruler.[37] Those who did not tended to uphold the attitude of pious distrust of politics, and withdrew from all entanglements with the earthly powers into religious scholarship in the holy centers of Arab Iraq.

Alongside the organizational amorphousness of the hierocracy and the massive growth of its upper section, a contrary trend toward stratification at the apex of the hierocracy—and only at the apex—had set in. Already in the first half of the century, Fatḥ ᶜAlī Shāh had been greatly displeased to see a loaded elephant carrying the "share of the Imām" from his Shiᶜite followers in India to Shaftī, the "proof of Islam."[38] Shaykh Murtaḍā Anṣārī, emerging as the vicegerent of the Imam in the subsequent period, is said to have received some 200,000 *tūmān*s annually on behalf of the Imam.[39] In this manner, especially with the improved channels of communication in the second half of the nineteenth century, what amounted to the designation of the vicegerents of the Imam by the Shiʿite community through payment of their religious taxes, worked indirectly to stratify the Shiʿite hierarchy at the very highest level. The acephaly of the Shiʿite hierocracy, which was a feature of the first half of the nineteenth century, came to an end. Mīrzā Muḥammad Ḥasan Shīrāzī (d. 1895/1312) in due course succeeded Anṣārī as the vicegerent of the Imam. This development enhanced the capacity of the head of the hierocracy to mobilize mass action in situations of national crisis, even though the plethora of independent *mujtahid*s precluded unified routine action by the religious institution.

11.1.5 The Rift Between the Hierocracy and the State

The confrontation between Muḥammad Shāh and Shaftī belongs to the period in which the tension between the hierocracy and the state reached its highest point. Owing to the fact that the hierocracy, though formally acephalous, was dominated by Shaftī and a handful of other *mujtahid*s in this period, hierocratic opposition to the state became polarized and led to serious disturbances in Isfahan and Shiraz in 1839–40. However, the state was victorious. Muḥammad Shāh himself put down these disturbances in 1840, and humbled Shaftī and the *mujtahid* of Shiraz.[40]

The tension between the hierocracy and the state remained high during the first years of the reign of Nāṣir al-Dīn Shāh (1848–96), whose first prime minister, Amīr Kabīr, immediately embarked on a policy of strengthening the central government. But the tension abated in the 1850s as a result of judicious gestures by the young monarch.[41] The hierocracy-state relationship remained reasonable for some four decades until a critical conflict between the two suddenly flared up in the last decade of the nineteenth century. Throughout this period the state was very much the dominant partner in the dual polity. The hierocracy remained cooperative, and many of its members established close ties with the Qājār political elite.

Nevertheless, at least in one respect the rift under Muḥammad Shāh was never repaired: the Shiʿite hierocracy lost its role as the legitimator of the monarchy. By some curious coincidence, the reign of Muḥammad Shāh, which marked the sharp rift between the Qājār state and the Shiʿite hierocracy, also marked the beginning of a keener interest in the pre-Islamic imperial past, an interest that was to reach its culmination under the Pahlavīs. It was to Muḥammad Shāh that Sir Henry Rawlinson presented the first Persian translation of the inscriptions on Bisutūn, and it was one of Muḥammad Shāh's sons who wrote a history of ancient Iran after centuries of relative neglect. Whether for this or for other reasons, the state no longer sought any formal legitimatory action from the hierocracy. Beyond the cessation of this legitimatory function, the rift between the hierocracy and the state would not become critical so long as the attempts at centralization and modernization of the state remained feeble and largely ineffective, as they did in the nineteenth century. (The rift was to become critical and irreparable only in the twentieth century with the effective measures toward centralization and modernization of the state under the Pahlavīs.)

Toward the end of his reign, alarmed by the spread of Western political ideas, especially by what he referred to as "nihilism," Nāsir al-Dīn Shāh did seek religious legitimation for monarchical rule, and a number of treatises were produced. One such treatise by Ḥājj Muḥammad Nāʾīnī emphasized the "incumbency of monarchy" and the incumbency of working for government along the lines of al-Murtaḍā's political ethic.[42] One clerical author went too far, claiming that the "authority verse" of the Qurʾan referred to the king, and consequently incurred excommunication from other members of the hierocracy.[43]

Another legacy of Muḥammad Shāh's period is worth mentioning in this connection: the persistence of Sufism in the courtly circles, among the literate strata in the capital,[44] and in one or two other cities, notably Shiraz. Considering the capital a safer refuge "for a group like us," especially under Nāṣir al-Dīn Shāh, Ṣafī-ʿAlī Shāh of Isfahan (d. 1899/1316), the guide of the Niʿmatullahī order, moved to Tehran and spent over two decades in the gradual cultivation of "high" Sufism and gnosis among a select circle of literati.[45] It is therefore not surprising to find a Sufi amongst the latter-day legitimators of monarchy. Mīrzā Muḥammad Dhu'l-Riyāsatayn (d. ca. 1894–95/1312), in a treatise on the "incumbency of praying for the king," written to allay criticisms of Nāṣir al-Dīn's wasteful trips to Europe and the extravagant favors he bestowed upon the male harem favorite, ʿAzīz al-Sulṭān, takes on the *ʿulamāʾ*'s traditional function of *duʿā-gūʾī* (praying for the king). He is cautious in saying that "according to one interpretation" the "authority verse" refers to the king, but categorical in stating that the king is appointed by the Imam, peace be upon him, the Lord of Time. Praying for the king is an incumbent duty, especially upon the *ʿulamāʾ*, who can propagate religion and learning in the peace and security provided by him, and especially in the light of the king's respect for the sacred law and its interpreters, those in the clerical garb.[46]

To conclude, despite the cooperation of individual clerics, Nāṣir al-Dīn's solicitation of legitimation met with a somewhat lukewarm response from the Shiʿite hierocracy, which was no longer accustomed to performing the legitimatory function, and was increasingly alienated from the state and increasingly reliant on the people, by now massively opposed to it (see section 11.2.1 immediately below).

11.2 Communal Action

11.2.1 Communal Action Led by the Members of the Hierocracy

The amorphousness of the Shiᶜite hierocracy meant that most actions initiated by its members were communal action through the mobilization of the masses outside the framework of the religious institutions. Of these, the most important and recurrent were acts of violence against the Sufis (and later real or alleged heretics—i.e., Bābīs) and the rousing of the populace against non-Muslims and religious minorities. In addition, under Muḥammad Shāh, we have an interesting case of oppositional agitation against Qājār government.

The *ᶜulamā*ᵓ began to instigate and organize acts of violence and terror against the Sufis long before the reign of Fatḥ ᶜAlī Shāh, when they were able to rely on the coercive power of the state. As has been briefly pointed out, Maᶜṣūm ᶜAlī Shāh Dakkanī arrived in Shiraz during the last three years of Karī Khān's reign. In 1790/1205, Mushtāq ᶜAlī Shāh, a handsome disciple of his in Kirman, was violently killed by a mob incited by Mullā ᶜAbdullāh Mujtahid.[47] Maᶜṣūm ᶜAlī Shāh himself resided in Shiraz until 1792/1206. In that year, at the instigation of the *ᶜulamā*ᵓ, he was hounded from Shiraz to Isfahan. He was subsequently hounded from Isfahan and killed by the order of Āqā Muḥammad ᶜAlī, the *Ṣūfī-kosh*, around the year 1800.[48] With the repressive policy of Fatḥ ᶜAlī Shāh, Sufism became confined to literate circles without reaching down to the populace, and the need for this type of action was more or less obviated.

The masses were particularly prone to incitement against the non-Muslims and religious minorities by any troublesome *mullā*. In 1814–15/1229, a Ḥājj Mullā Muḥammad Zanjānī incited a group of his followers to break the wine bottles and to loot the houses of the Armenian community in Tehran; for this action he was banished from the capital.[49] In 1815/1230, a certain Mullā Ḥusayn incited the populace of Yazd, who killed Shāh Khalīlullāh, the leader of the Nizārī Ismāᶜīlīs in Yazd. We also know of an Akhūnd Mullā ᶜAlī Akbar, who from 1838/1254 onwards, under the pretext of "enjoining the good," caused considerable repression of the Zoroastrians of Yazd. Also in the later 1830s, Āqā Sayyid Muḥammad, the *Imām Jumᶜa* of Isfahan, ordered the water supply of the Jews of that city to be cut off.[50]

We have a fascinating report from the Frenchmen Sepsis in 1843 about disgruntlement and oppositional agitation of the *mullā*s against the government of Muḥammad Shāh and his Sufi prime minister. We hear of an accusation concocted by the *mullā*s to rouse the masses, with a keen insight into their disposition as molded by the passion plays and the tragedy of Karbalā. Rumors circulated that the Qājār tribe assisted Yazid, the Umayyad tyrant, in his war against Imām Ḥusayn and his household.[51] It is very interesting to learn from other sources that in this episode the *mullā*s were acting in alliance with and at the instigation of Safavid *sayyids*. The Shiᶜite hierocracy appears to have kept its links with the Safavid descendants long after the brief reign of Suleymān II in 1750. As in connection with the agitation reported by Sepsis, we still hear of a Safavid pretender with clerical support during the reign of Muḥammad Shāh and in the period immediately following his death. The Safavid legitimists circulated the rumor that the Qājārs had been ordered by Nādir Shāh's son to kill ᶜAbbās III the Safavid with the dagger of Shimr (the killer of Imām Ḥusayn), which was still in their possession.[52] The same rumors were to circulate during the popular agitations at the end of the nineteenth and beginning of the twentieth century.

Of far greater significance than the above incidents was the communal action of the populace of Tehran under the leadership of Mīrzā Mashīḥ Mujtahid, which led to the killing of the Russian envoy Griboyedov in the aftermath of the second Perso-Russian War in 1829. The *ᶜulamāᵓ* were drawn into the incident by the group attempting to secure the release of two Georgian women, members of a nobleman's household, who were converts to Islam and were allegedly interned by force by the Russian envoy. An important *mujtahid*, Ḥājjī Mīrzā Masīḥ, having issued an injunction declaring the rescuing of Muslim women from the hands of the infidels in accordance with the sacred law, led the populace of Tehran in the siege of the envoy's residence. The populace was outraged at the state's silence in the matter and the failure of the "King of Islam" (*pādishāh-e Islām*) to protect the rights of the two Muslim women and their relatives against the arrogant Russian envoy. "They said bluntly," writes the Qājār court historian, "if the government should order us [to act] against our will, we shall collectively abjure allegiance to the king." The king, having failed to protect the "people of Islam," did not dare protect the diplomat against their rage. Griboyedov and thirty-seven of his companions were massacred.[53]

The episode is of great significance as the first instance in which a prominent member of the Shiᶜite hierocracy assumes leadership of the people, conceived of as the Islamic nation or community, when the "King of Islam" is found delinquent in discharging his responsibility of protecting the Islamic nation against the foreign powers. As such, it foreshadows the hierocratic leadership of the protest movements of 1890–91 and of the 1970s.

If the absence of a hierarchical organization and the easily exploitable rivalry among the *ᶜulamāᵓ* made the hierocracy responsive to the demands of the state, the normative order legitimating hierocratic domination contained features that also assured the responsiveness of the hierocracy to the demands of the people. So far, our purpose has been to sketch the *differentiation* of political and hierocratic domination in Qājār Iran in contrast to the preceding Safavid societal structure of domination. Now one important qualification must be introduced. There remained an important area of overlap: his "caesaropapist" prerogatives over a number of clerical appointments apart, the shah, even though his authority over his subjects did not extend beyond matters temporal, was the "King of Islam and of the Shiᶜite nation." On the surface this meant that his authority was more extensive than that of a secular ruler, strictly speaking. But so was his responsibility: the protection of Islam and of the Shiᶜite nation against the encroachments of the infidels—a responsibility whose discharge an autonomous hierocracy, in response to popular demand, could insist upon. What underlay the issue—and here the comparative sociologist must place Shiᶜism squarely in the same category as Sunni Islam as against Western Christianity in modern times[54]—was the absence of any differentiation between the Shiᶜite Islam as a religious belief system from the conception of the Shiᶜite community as an autonomous social order. In other words, there existed no conception of a secular society. If the ruler failed to carry out his foremost duty of the protection of Islam and of the Shiᶜite nation or community, the hierocracy would consider it incumbent upon them to carry out this obligation by assuming the leadership of the nation conceived of as no other than the Shiᶜite community.[55] This was in fact precisely the inference Mīrzā Muḥammad Ḥasan Shīrāzī made when affirming the theory of the two powers: if the government (*dawlat*) that is in charge of executive matters during the occultation fails to carry out its duty of the protection of religion and interests of the subjects, the Shiᶜite community (*millat*) will, under hierocratic leadership, do whatever is necessary, because it is responsible to the Lord of Time.[56]

It is thus not surprising that confrontations with foreign powers in which the ruler proved unwilling or unable to act in accordance with the wish of the people constituted the typical situation in which prominent members of the Shiᶜite community would be called upon to assume the leadership of the people. This was certainly the case with Mīrzā Masīḥ in 1829. There were other similar instances. In 1843, the sack of the holy Shiᶜite city of Karbalā by the Ottoman governor of Arab Iraq and the inaction of the Qājār government provoked Shaftī to announce that he would dispatch an army against Baghdad "whatever the intentions of the shah."[57] (In fact, however, he never did.) In 1873, Mullā ᶜAlī Kanī, speaking in part on behalf of the Iranian merchants, reprimanded Nāṣir al-Dīn Shāh for neglecting the interests of the nation by granting concessions to foreign entrepreneurs backed by imperialist powers.[58]

11.2.2 Shaykhism: A Religious Movement and Its Political Conditioning

It is worth emphasizing that the consolidation of the Shiᶜite hierocracy went hand in hand with the growth and dominance of the *Uṣūlī* movement. Not surprisingly, therefore, we witness the continuation of Majlisī's policy of discouragement and elimination of gnostic Shiᶜism (*ᶜirfān*), now coupled with a vigorous campaign against Akhbārī traditionalism and the exclusion of the Akhbārīs from the Shiᶜite hierocracy. As a consequence of this development, Shaykh Aḥmad Aḥsāʾī (d. 1826/1241), the champion of Akhbārī traditionalism and of *ᶜirfān*, and his followers were forced to become a sect through expulsion from Twelver Shiᶜism by the triumphant *Uṣūlī*s, who emerged as the guardians of Shiᶜite orthodoxy.

Shaykh Aḥmad Aḥsāʾī was the philosophical heir to Mullā Ṣadrā, albeit a critical and discerningly selective heir, and as such the champion of gnostic Shiᶜism. He was excommunicated by the Shiᶜite hierocracy on account of his spiritualized interpretation of Resurrection and the journey of the Prophet to the heavens (*miᶜrāj*).[59] His excommunication (*takfīr*) and the Shiᶜite hierocracy's relentless opposition to him and his successors, Sayyid Kāẓim Rashtī (d. 1843/1259) and Ḥājj Mīrzā Muḥammad Karīm Khān Kirmānī (d. 1870/1288) who was a close relative of the king, created a schism between the Shaykhīs (thus designated for following Shaykh Aḥmad) and the Bālāsarīs (the remaining Shiᶜites).[60] Thus, with a schismatic convulsion, gnostic Shiᶜism in the new form of Shaykhism was forever banished to the heretical periphery.

Despite the great prominence of Shaykh Aḥmad, the sociological properties of gnostic Shiᶜism referred to in chapter 5 also doomed Shaykhism to failure in its struggle with the Shiᶜite hierocracy. It was relegated to the sectarian periphery of society and withered once Fatḥ ᶜAlī Shāh's support ended with his death. Shaykhism continued to survive in Tabriz and flourished in Kirman, where, significantly, political power was in the Shaykhīs' hands owing to the fact that Muḥammad Karīm Khān belonged to the Qājār family.

With the existence of an autonomous Shiᶜite hierocracy that was capable of initiating persecution of the Shaykhīs either by issuing "injunctions" to the people or demanding action from political authorities, the "political conditioning" of the movement meant that it had to orient itself not only toward the state but also toward the hierocracy. This political conditioning through orientation toward the state took the form of Ḥājj Muḥammad Karīm Khān's repeated disclaimers that being the "perfect Shiᶜite" in the eye of his followers did not entitle him to political authority,[61] and eventually reinforced a purely spiritual interpretation of the Shaykhī tenet of the Fourth Pillar (*rukn-e rābiᶜ*) purely as an *ecclesia spiritualis* of which men become members through ascending the ladder of spiritual perfection.[62]

The political conditioning resulting from the movement's orientation toward the Shiᶜite hierocracy took the form of insistence on *taqiyya* (dissimulation of faith to assure survival): "The greatest of the ethical duties, is the observance of the rights of the brethren in faith, and the *taqiyya*." Furthermore, "the harm resulting from him who does not observe the *taqiyya* is graver than that deriving from the Sunni and the Infidel, may God curse them."[63]

11.2.3 The Mahdism of the Bāb and the Bābī Chiliastic Uprisings

In 1844/1260, 1,000 lunar years after the occultation of the Twelfth Imam, extremist Shiᶜite millenarianism flared up after centuries of dormancy with the mahdistic claim of Sayyid ᶜAlī Muḥammad of Shiraz, the Bāb, and resulted in a series of chiliastic Bābī uprisings in the mid-nineteenth century.[64]

Bābism as an Instance of Shiᶜite Millenarianism in Comparison with Ḥurūf-

ism. First and foremost, it should be emphasized that Bābism unmistakably belongs to the tradition of extremist Shiᶜite millenarianism, and bears a striking resemblance to the Ḥurūfī movement. Mīrzā ᶜAlī Muḥammad at first claimed to be the Bāb (gate) to the Hidden Imam, but soon relegated the position of the Bāb to a disciple and claimed mahdihood as the "Qaᶜim [redresser] of the house of Muhammad."[65] After claiming mahdihood in prison, he proceeded to write his new dispensation in *Bayān*, a dispensation with a strong pantheistic and gnostic character, which allowed him to claim divinity while enabling his disciples to claim divine inspiration as new incarnations of the archetypes that had assumed the human forms of Muhammad, Fāṭima, and the Imams during the previous cycle of manifestation (*ẓuhūr*).[66] Like the Ḥurūfī religion, Bābism put great importance on the cabalistic significance of numbers and letters, and on the "incarnation" of the significant letters by the disciples of the initiator of the new cycle of divine manifestation in the form of the "living letters" (*ḥurūf-e ḥayy*).[67] The similarity extended not only to the prominence of a woman among the leaders of the movement but also the identity of the title of *Qurrat al-ᶜAyn* assumed both by the daughter of Faḍl Allāh Ḥurūfī and the martyred Bābī heroine and poet, the Ṭāhira.

In one important respect, however, the Bāb's new dispensation differed from the Ḥurūfī mystery religion. The *Bayān* contains detailed ethical regulations covering most areas of social and personal life, so much so that a later convert to Bahāʾism explained his motive for conversion as release from constrictive and rigorous ethical rules which he found stifling.[68] This, however, points to a tension in Bābism that was present from the very beginning, the tension between chiliasm and ethical rigorism, whose social and ideological roots are treated below. Though undoubtedly reflecting the intention of the Bāb, it is difficult to assess the immediate reception of his ethical regulations by his followers. While one group of converts, predominantly the craftsmen and merchants, can be presumed to have found them palatable, another group, chiefly the young seminarians (*ṭullāb*) hankering after chiliastic action, could not have cared much for them.

Finally, as was the case with the Ḥurūfīs, the initial difficulties encountered by the Bābīs, and especially the failure of their armed uprisings, generated intense messianism. This messianism was reflected in, and in turn encouraged by, the Bāb's foretelling of a new cycle of resurrection (*qiyāmat*),[69] which eventually culminated in the Bahāʾ Allāh's (d. 1892) claim to inaugurate a new cycle of manifestation as "he whom God shall make manifest" (*man yuẓhiruhu 'llāh*).

The Social and Religious Background of the Bābī Converts. As Amanat emphasizes, at the beginning Bābism was a clerical movement among the young seminarians, overwhelmingly from humble social origins, whose messianic yearnings had been kindled by the Shaykhī movement under the leadership of Sayyid Kāẓim Rashtī.[70] Throughout its brief history, the large proportion of clerics, including a small number of *mujtahid*s, in the Bābī movement is striking.[71] This important fact establishes Bābism as an authentic instance of the unfolding of the mahdistic tenet in chiliastic religio-political action in Shiᶜism. It also illustrates the difficulty of the Shiᶜite hierocracy in enforcing religious discipline among its members, especially among the lower ranks.

However, the Bābī movement did not, by any means, remain confined to young clerical circles. Proselytizing began very soon and was immediately successful, especially in the cities. Not unlike the Ḥurūfīs, many of the Bābī converts were urban craftsmen and merchants, a fact reflected in the attention paid by the Bāb to commerce in his writings.[72] In fact, the merchants and guildsmen very soon came to constitute the second largest group of Bābī converts,[73] and, in the long run, a more solid social basis for the continued development of the Bābī religion.

Of equal importance to the social background of the Bābīs was their religious background. Amanat shows convincingly that conversion to Bābism was most successful among Shaykhī groups and in Shaykhī districts, both with regard to the seminarians and the mercantile group.[74] From our point of view, it thus seems plausible to regard Bābism as representing the politicization of the Shaykhī religious movement. Many politicized Shaykhīs who were dissatisfied with the quietistic response of the movement's leaders to its political conditioning joined the Bābīs and helped to convert other Shaykhīs to Bābism.

I have already had occasion to point out that the diverse social composition of the Bābīs caused considerable tension which was reflected in the somewhat uneasy coexistence of millenarian activism and ethical rigorism in the turbulent first decade of Bābī history. In this history, Amanat detects a moderate tendency—and, one may add, a rigorous ethical orientation—represented by the Bāb himself and the merchants and craftsmen, and a militant tendency (along with an activist, chiliastic orientation) represented by the politicized ex-Shaykhi seminarians. It was the militant tendency that gained the upper hand in 1848.[75] The moderate tendency was to prevail only decades later with the transformation of the Bābī religion into Bahāʾism.

Chiliasm in the Bābi Uprisings of 1848–50. In expounding his views on the cycles of divine manifestation, the Bāb put forward a novel interpretation of *qiyāmat* (resurrection, according to the orthodox conception, of the dead) as the this-worldly culmination of the previous revelation. The earliest history of the Bābī movement, while elaborating on this conception of this-worldly resurrection, emphasizes the necessity and inevitability of dissension and disorder (*fitna*) accompanying it.[76] In 1848, the prolonged imprisonment of the Bāb and the death of Muḥammad Shāh persuaded the Bābīs that the hour for the rising had come. In a tumultuous gathering in Badasht, Qurrat al-ᶜAyn, the champion of chiliastic action, despite the opposition of the advocates of ethical rigorism, publicly removed her veil and declared the coming of resurrection and the abeyance of the sacred law:

> It is declared in many Traditions touching the religion of the Redresser [*Qāʾim*] that it shall abrogate all [previous] religions, for "the perfection of

> the doctrine of Divine Unity is the negation of [all] predicates from Him," and "mankind shall become a single church," and He will make all religions one. . . . The essence of His religion is the Doctrine of Unity, and Wisdom and Love: all around us is the *Qibla* [the point in the direction of Mecca to which one turns in prayer], and this is the meaning of "Whithersoever you turn, there is the Face of God" [Qurʾan, 3:25], and the realization of "He it is who is manifest in every manifestation"; although His manifestation will be the last, as, for instance, . . . is nineteen Gates [*Bāb*], which is the number of the Unity [*Vāḥid*]. *And should men not be able to receive the doctrine of the Unity at the beginning of the Manifestation, ordinances and restrictions will again be prescribed for them*, till they acquire such powers, when these in turn will be abolished. But during the continuance of the Return [*Rajᶜat*] the veils will gradually be lifted, till the verities [of religion] be established, and men learn to explore the Prophetic Mystery, which is the Paradise of Primal Unity [*Jannat-e Aḥadiyyat*].[77]

Many of the Bābīs present proceeded to Mazandaran to start the uprising, while another group independently arrived from Khurasan. The Bāb's approval reportedly came in the form of a letter containing the following passage: "They [the Bābīs] shall descend from the Green Isle [*Jazīrat al Khaḍrā'*; Māzandarān] unto the mountain of Zawrā' [Tehran], and shall slay about twelve thousand of the Turks."[78] The planned uprising began with the occupation of the shrine of Shaykh-e Ṭabarsī near Bārfurūsh (present-day Bābol) in 1848 and continued into the early months of 1849. It was a truly chiliastic uprising in which the leaders, most notably Ḥājj Muḥammad ᶜAlī Bārfurūshī, the Quddūs, and Mullā Ḥusayn Bushrūyeh, assumed to be reincarnations of important personnages in Judeo-Christian and Islamic history. In 1850, chiliastic uprisings followed in Zanjān in central Iran and in Nayrīz in Fars. These uprisings, like that of Shaykh-e Ṭabarsī, were bloodily suppressed, and the Bāb was executed (1850). Minor uprisings and an attempt to assassinate Nāṣir al-Dīn Shāh caused another wave of persecution and massacre of the Bābīs in 1852.

To understand the mood of pantheistic chiliasm that made the Bābīs so ready to court martyrdom, one could not do better than cite a poem attributed to Qurrat al-ᶜAyn:

> The effulgence of thy face flashed forth and the rays of thy visage arose on high;
> Then speak the word, "Am I not your Lord?" and "Thou art, Thou art!" we will all reply [Qurʾan, 7:171].
> Thy trumpet-call "Am I not?" to greet how loud the drums of affliction beat!
> At the gates of my heart there tramp the feet and camp the host of calamity.
> That fair moon's love is enough, I trow, for me, for he laughed at the hail of woe,
> And triumphant cried, as he sunk below, "The Martyr of Karbalā am I!"[79]

Of the Bābī uprisings, the first, the one in the shrine of Shaykh-e Ṭabarsī was the ideologically most important, being the purest manifestation of Bābī chiliasm. It is therefore not surprising that its bearers were the group we have characterized as the party of chiliastic activism. Of the 222 participants in it with known occupations (360 persons were identified), some sixty percent were clerics, twenty-six percent guildsmen, and less than two percent merchants.[80]

Bābism was the last serious revolutionary threat from within the Shiᶜite religious tradition to the Qājār polity, abrogating its dual normative order and being vehemently opposed to both its organs: the monarchical state and the Shiᶜite hierocracy. Although the "reasons of state" were ultimately the more decisive, the hierocracy fully sanctioned the suppression of the Bābī heresy, and throughout took an active part in it. Thus the state and the hierocracy acted in concord in putting an end to this extremist threat to the existing order.

Conclusion to Part Three

> If the hierocracy is willing to legitimize political rule through domestication of the people by using religious, sacred, and supernatural means, the political rulers will in turn extend religious uniformity over the entire country by removing dissenters and heretics and forcing other religious groups to accept the officially approved religion.[1]

Murvar's general formulation of the basic transaction between the hierocracy and the state aptly describes the Shiᶜite hierocracy's politically-relevant religious action of domestication of the masses and of the legitimation of temporal power in exchange for the Safavid and Qājār states' religiously relevant political acts of suppression of Sunnism, extremist millenarianism, philosophical dissent, and Sufism during the periods 1687–1722 and 1785–1850.

The benefits of this transaction were, in the long run, far greater to the hierocracy than to the state. Beginning from a position of uneasy coexistence with a hostile estate of clerical notables who enjoyed considerable political power in 1687, the Shiᶜite hierocracy successfully used the power of the state to establish its monopolistic hierocratic domination over the vast majority of the population of Iran. What it offered the state in return was also highly beneficial to itself. Although the domestication of the masses did have advantages for the political powers, it also greatly enhanced hierocratic domination over the masses. Finally, by assuming the function of legitimation of political rulership, the hierocracy contributed to the eventual removal of extremist adultation of the ruler. Safavid caesaropapism born of Shiᶜite extremism was replaced by the consistent Twelver Shiᶜite dualism of political and hierocratic domination in the Qājār polity.

Many extrareligious factors contributed to the success of Safavid mahdistic millenarianism, to the consequent establishment of Shiᶜism as the state religion of Iran, and to the final consolidation of the Shiᶜite hierocracy in the nineteenth century. The political sphere impinged upon the religious as frequently as the religious sphere impinged upon the political. Men's extrareligious orientations and political and institutional aims colored their religious stands in specific instances and determined the course of their concrete actions. Yet the separation of religious and political spheres and the corresponding differentiation of religious and political authority in the Shiᶜite world image, did, overriding hosts of interpenetrating concordant and contrary mediating forces, determine the track along which societal change unfolded. After for centuries taking the form of rejection of the world and creation of an inner spiritual sphere, the dualistic world image of Shiᶜism, in stages and with retardations and syncopations, intruded into the realm of social organization and was translated into a correspondingly autonomous religious institution. A Shiᶜite hierocracy independent of the state came into being as the institutional embodiment of differentiated religious authority. At the same time, rulership was shorn of its caesaropapist religious trappings and came to rest on the basis of the patrimonial principles of legitimacy. The Shiᶜite hierocracy accepted these principles as the appropriate norms for the regulation of the political sphere. So long as the ruler acted in accordance with these norms—most notably so long as he ruled with justice—he held legitimate authority on behalf of the Hidden Imam *in the political sphere*. The hierocracy, needless to say, was the depository of the authority of the Hidden Imam *in the religious sphere*. The state and the hierocracy thus constituted the two—and the only two—organs of the legitimate structure of domination in the Qājār polity.

With the consolidation of an autonomous Shiᶜite hierocracy monopolizing the guardianship and authoritative interpretation of Shiᶜite doctrine, the variegated religious topography of the Safavid period, made possible by the heterocephaly and the heteronomy of the hierocracy, gave way to a stifling uniformity of religious outlook. The autonomous hierocracy by and large succeeded in establishing its monopolistic control over the religious life of the population of Iran, and acted with effectiveness to enforce a rigid and otherworldly dogmatism. Philosophy declined sharply, Sufism was effectively contained, largely within the aristocratic circles none too susceptible to hierocratic influence, innerworldly gnostic Shiᶜism was expelled to the heretical sectarian periphery of religious society (Shaykhism) or to the private sphere created by the pious individual through withdrawal from the world, and mahdistic millenarianism was predictably suppressed as arch-heresy (Bābism). The autonomy of the hierocracy thus underlay the final maximal impact of Shiᶜism on Iran's premodern polity and society.

However, despite its autonomy, the organizational amorphousness of the Shiᶜite hierocracy was a serious hindrance to effective organized hierocratic action—that is, action carried out independently of the state *or* the masses. Furthermore, the absence of a hierarchical organization enabled the Qājār rulers to retain the caesaropapist prerogatives of their Safavid predecessors in making a number of important ecclesiastical appointments.

CHAPTER TWELVE

General Conclusion

12.1 The Shiᶜite Religion and Societal Change in Premodern Iran

What can we conclude from our analysis of Shiᶜism as a world religion about its role in societal change? We began our study with the definitive separation of religious and political authority during the formative period of the history of Twelver Shiᶜism, that is, the eighth / second century. It was argued that the development of Imāmī Shiᶜism into a sectarian religion within the Islamic body politic entailed a de facto depoliticization of the conception of religious leadership, the imamate. The gradual delimitation of the religious sphere by the corpus of religious literature on theology and jurisprudence, by omission, relegated temporal rule to the sphere of the profane. The sublimation of the mahdistic tenet in the doctrine of occultation assured the continued secularity of the political sphere to the end of time.

We then witnessed the variety of forms in which the definitive separation of religious and political authority made its impact manifest during subsequent ages: the political pragmatism of the Shiᶜite sectarians, the political indifferentism of innerworldly gnostic Shiᶜism, and, finally, the disengagement of the hierocracy from the caesaropapist state and its emergence as the autonomous guardian of orthodox Shiᶜism. In each of these successive periods, the fundamental separation of religious and political authority entailed by the *ratio* of the Twelver Shiᶜite doctrine did not determine the course of evolution in detail but *constrained the range of possible eventual outcomes through the requirement of consistency*.

With the eventual consolidation of an autonomous hierocracy in the nineteenth century, Twelver Shiᶜism completed its revolutionary impact on the constitution of Iran's premodern polity. In Iran alone, the political monism typical in Islam, whose caesaropapist features had in fact been sharpened by the Safavid extremist heritage, was transformed into the dualistic Qājār polity. Differentiated religious authority found autonomous institutional embodiment in a Shiʿite hierocracy independent of the state. The separation of the religious and the political spheres no longer required an overwhelmingly innerworldly and pietistic delimitation of the former but could find an adequate institutional translation in the division of labor within the polity—i.e., in a new balance between political and hierocratic powers in the societal structure of domination. The normative and de facto separation of political and hierocratic domination that prevailed undisturbed during the nineteenth century reflected the indelible impact of Shiʿism on the social structure of premodern Iran.

12.2 Shiʿism, Political Action, and Political Attitudes

We have examined several instances of revolutionary political action in the form of millenarianism generated by the activation of the mahdistic tenet. In these instances, the prevalent normative order was rejected and replaced by a new one. The mahdistic tenet motivated men to challenge the validity of the normative order and to abrogate it. The ensuing chiliastic action thus brought about revolutionary change. In view of the inadequate treatment of mysticism in the sociology of religion, it should be pointed out that the research here confirms the following. Mysticism, like asceticism, has a Janus face.[1] In fact, all our cases of fourteenth- and fifteenth-century mahdistic millenarianism, arising from the background of the Sufi mystical tradition, offer concrete examples of transformation of Sufi mysticism into millenarian movements.

In sharp contrast to millenarian religiosity, there is a spectrum of religiously influenced political attitudes that make for stability and the upholding of the status quo. In early Catholicism, Troeltsch tells us, "the idea of the Kingdom of God was replaced by 'eschatology,' Heaven, Hell, and Purgatory, immortality and the future life."[2] This prototypical process was repeated by the Shiʿite hierocracy in the Safavid period in its attempt to contain chiliasm and discipline popular religiosity. In the second half of the seventeenth century, Shiʿism became markedly more otherworldly. The otherworldliness of late Safavid and Qājār Shiʿism entailed a drastic weakening of the propensity to religiously motivated this-worldly political action aiming at the overthrow of the existing order. On the contrary, the religiously conditioned political attitude fostered by orthodox Shiʿism had a pronounced fatalistic character, making for submissiveness to political authority.

Throughout the Safavid period, and less so in the Qājār era, along with the otherworldly orthodox Shiʿism and its concomitant political attitude we found another religiously conditioned political attitude with a high incidence among the intellectual elite: the attitude of political indifferentism, induced by the innerworldly soteriology of gnostic Shiᶜism.

Finally, we must recall the attitude of pious antipathy toward political power induced by the world-rejecting mode in Shiᶜite religiosity. While the ordinary Shiᶜites submitted to and worked with temporal authority, those who excelled in piety shunned entanglement with earthly powers.

12.3 Shiᶜism and the Principles of Legitimacy of Temporal Rule

The structure of domination that came to prevail in the Safavid period contained a fundamental contradiction that remained unresolved because of the overwhelming power of the state. This contradiction consisted in the monarch's pretension to hierocratic authority as the representative of the Imam of the Age, which was rooted in the extremist Shiᶜism of the Turkman tribesmen and was perpetuated by effective political power. The fall of the Safavid dynasty brought about a fundamental break with the historical heritage of the extremist period, whose beneficiaries were now overthrown. The hierocratic pretensions of the Safavids could not be reasserted by the new rulers on the basis of the Twelver Shiᶜite doctrine, whose independent custodians could, furthermore, dispense with the support of the rulers in the new configuration of political power. Consonantly with the differentiations of the political and the religious spheres implicit in the authoritative interpretations of the Shiᶜite belief system, political rule and hierocratic authority became definitively separated.

Shiᶜism thus made its impact by divesting kingship of religious pretensions, by secularizing rulership. However, the very fact of the separation of political and hierocratic domination, of the political and the religious spheres, meant that there would be no clash between Shiᶜism and the Persian patrimonial ethos, and that Shiᶜism would have virtually no substantive impact on the latter, which would therefore persist autonomously. The king remained the shadow of God on earth, unperturbed.

12.4 The State and the Shiᶜite Hierocracy

Majlisī and the dogmatic party of the late Safavid period used Shiᶜism *qua* religion as a weapon for the enhancement of differentiated hierocratic domination upon the masses and hence laid the foundation for an autonomous religious institution that was consolidated in the nineteenth century. Majlisī's appointment as the *Shaykh al-Islām* of Isfahan in 1687 and the creation of the office of *Mullā-bāshī* over a decade after his death (1712) marked the emergence of a differentiated albeit heteronomous and heterocephalous hierocracy. Having suffered the severance of its ties to the state during the Afshār-Zand interregnum, a Shiᶜite hierocracy headed by the *mujtahid*s consolidated itself as an institution independent of the state in the early decades of the nineteenth century.

As an autonomous structure of power, the Shiᶜite hierocracy was inevitably drawn into politics. "The extent," writes Eisenstadt regarding premodern politics, "to which the religious institutions were organizationally autonomous greatly influenced the degree to which they could participate in the central political struggle of a given society."[3] The hierocracy is typically drawn into politics as the protector of the poor and the weak, on the one hand, and the legitimator of ruling powers on the other. The intervention of the Shiᶜite hierocracy in the former capacity produced instances of mediation and communal action that have received considerable attention in the literature on the nineteenth century. Their involvement in politics in the latter capacity, however, requires a final comment. With the increasing degree of autonomy of the hierocracy, there is a tendency for it to dispute the immediate legitimacy of the king by the grace of God, and to insist on the mediation of religious authority. At the very beginning of this reign, Fāth ᶜAlī Shāh acknowledged that the legitimacy of his rule was mediated by hierocratic approval, and is reported to have said that he considered his kingship to be "on behalf of the *mujtahid*s of the age" and at the service of the "rightly guiding Imams."[4] In Western Christianity, the hierocratic power to bestow legitimacy upon temporal rulers came to constitute the basis of the canonists' claim to the theocratic monarchy of the pope. Against the imperial theorists who derived the authority of the emperor from God without intermediary, Alanus (writing between 1201 and 1210), whose position was adopted by the canonists in the thirteenth century and eventually promulgated in the famous bull *Unam Sanctum* (1302), argued that the emperor obtained the temporal sword from the pope, who was therefore the only one head of the Christian monarchy.[5] By comparison, the increasing dependence of the hierocracy on the state in Iran in the second half of the nineteenth century curbed all potential tendencies toward hierocratic monism. What produced some normative imbalance in the period was that the sluggishly centralizing and modernizing state increasingly dispensed with the legitimatory service of the hierocracy. Shiᶜite theocratic monism remained a surprise held in store for the last quarter of the twentieth century.

Epilogue
From the Rejection to the Subjugation of Earthly Powers

Comparative history teaches us that once the separation of political and hierocratic domination has been established, given the indisputable superiority of God over earthly powers, theocratic monism is but a further logical step which can, in theory, be taken at any time. Political-hierocratic dualism does often contain germs of hierocratic monism which may or may not develop depending on historical contingencies. In Western Christianity, the separation of hierocratic and political domination on the basis of the "freedom of the Church" was established under Gregory VII (d. 1085).[1] It was this separation and the consequent autonomy of the Church that paved the way for the theocratic monism of the later Middle Ages.

Once religious authority is embodied in an autonomous hierocratic organization, and is as such inevitably drawn into political processes, conversion of the world presents itself as a tempting—and with a suitable power constellation, perhaps a compelling—alternative to withdrawal from it.

Nevertheless, over a century had to go by before the crusade would show "to the alert and sensitive canonistic mind the immense possibilities that existed for the expansion of papal power" in the form of the papalist claims to world monarchy.[2] The connection seems far from fortuitous. The crusades brought to the foreground the Christian *identity*, thereby enhancing the pope's claim to the supreme leadership of the Christian community. Similarly, the impetus to the eventual development of claims to hierocratic monism out of Qājār political-hierocratic dualism came from the politicization of Islamic identity in confrontation with Western imperialism and political and cultural dominance.

In chapter 9, we noted that the negative evaluation of the political sphere, implying its rejection, can, under suitable circumstances, turn into a negative evaluation of the political sphere with the aim of its subjugation to religious authority—that is, into the advocacy of hierocratic monism.

In some of the early *Uṣūlī* justifications of hierocratic authority, as in Mullā Aḥmad Narāqī's (d. 1828–29) attempt to establish the authority of the religious jurist on behalf of the Imams, some movement in this direction is discernible, but the invidious contrast between religious and political authority remain unstated and implicit.[3] Thus, in the nineteenth century, the advocacy of theocratic monism was to remain a latent possibility, which was in fact not to be actualized until the recent decades of the present century.

The claims to hierocratic supremacy did not find public expression in confrontations with the state, and did not threaten the stability of the hierocracy-state relationship in the second half of the nineteenth century. The large increase in the number of *mujtahid*s and their considerable dependence on the state curbed any possible movement in the direction of hierocratic monism. In any event, possible claims to hierocratic supremacy could be countered by the reassertion of the patrimonial ethos of kingship by the partisans of the monarchical state on behalf of the shadow of God on earth.

Nothing from within Shiᶜism threatened the stability of the dual structure of domination in the reconstituted Shiᶜite polity of premodern Iran. The threat came from without: in the form of imperialist penetration, and of the impact of the West on the modernization of the state.

Parsons is correct in considering the absence of a structurally independent hierocracy as the most important single point of difference between Western Christianity and Islam.[4] The developments studied in this volume indicate that, in the first half of the nineteenth century, Shiᶜism markedly diverged from the general Islamic pattern, becoming more similar to Western Christianity. As was the case with the papacy in medieval Western Christianity, in sharp contrast to Byzantine caesaropapism and its Russian heir, it was the successful institutional translation of the separation of the religious and the political spheres that subsequently gave the Shiᶜite hierocracy tremendous *political* power as the independent custodians of religion and of the sacred law. At the same time, the persistence of the attitude of pious withdrawal from daily politics at the highest level of the hierocracy tremendously enhanced the effectiveness of their rare interventions in political crises when they could be prevailed upon to do so.

The separation of hierocratic domination from political domination in the nineteenth century had consequences that extend to the present day. In the context of the theory of the two powers, the absence of a secular conception of society meant that the hierocracy was called upon to assume the leadership of the nation when, in critical confrontations between the "Shiᶜite nation" and foreign powers, the ruler was seen to be failing to discharge his responsibility of protecting the nation's interests. Though, as we have seen, there were earlier precedents, by far the most important instance in which the hierocracy had to respond to the merchants' and nationalists' call to assume the leadership of the Shiᶜite nation in the name of their Hidden Imam was the granting of the notorious tobacco concession by Nāṣir al-Dīn Shāh to a British company, Regie. This action was perceived and denounced as delivering the Shiᶜite nation to the infidel imperialists,[5] and thus promoted the vigorous nationwide protest of 1891–92 which resulted in its repeal. What was decisive in this instance, as was largely the case during the Constitutional Revolution of 1905–11, was not so much the involvement of the worldly *ᶜulamāʾ* with routine political entanglements but the intervention of the highest-ranking member or members of the hierocracy residing in the holy cities of Iraq, who had firmly upheld the attitude of pious withdrawal from politics up until the time of the national emergency.

In the next important round of nationalist agitation and anti-imperialist confrontation, the period of the nationalization of oil (1950–53), the Shiᶜite nation was able to find a secular leader in the person of Musaddiq, thus obviating the need for the hierocracy to intervene in politics on behalf of its Hidden Imam. Not so in the sudden explosion of rage against the shah as the presumed lackey of American imperialism and propagator of an alien culture. The hierocracy once again assumed the position of national leadership in the political crisis of 1978, but this time the contending monarchical state collapsed totally. The hierocracy inherited the state from its last secular ruler on 11 February 1979.

The autonomy of the Shiᶜite hierocracy assured its survival and continued spiritual authority despite the relentless pressure from the state during the twentieth century. Though the modernization of the state entailed a drastic diminution of the social power of the hierocracy, it did not impair the legitimacy of the exclusive hierocratic authority of the *ᶜulamāʾ*, which had become definitively established in early nineteenth century, and which assured the continued financial autonomy of the hierocracy, and consequently its survival and virtually exclusive control over religious learning and the authoritative interpretation of the Shiᶜite religion.

"Since the outcome of the struggles between political and hierocratic power depends so largely upon historical 'accidents,' it is not easy to generalize about their determinants. In particular, these struggles are not determined by the general degree of religiosity among the people."[6] The decisive "accident" came in the form of the internal crumbling and collapse of the Pahlavī state. As a result of its continued autonomy, the Shiᶜite hierocracy did not disintegrate with the collapse of the monarchial state as did its heteronomous Ottoman and Russian counterparts. On the contrary, the Shiᶜite hierocracy, debilitated though it was, emerged as the decisive institution in the power vacuum created in Iran's atomized society by the sudden collapse of the monarchy and the paralysis of the state in 1979.

Finally, the autonomy of the hierocracy facilitated its isolation from the state and made it completely immune from secular influences. Although—or probably because—the modern state wrested the national judiciary and educational system from the control of the hierocracy, it did not have the slightest secularizing effect on the organizational structure or the cultural outlook of the hierocracy. Unlike the Ottoman qadis, the Shiᶜite *mujtahids* were not the officials of the state and did not have to deal with the problem of modernization of the legal system. Jevdet Pasha, the Ottoman qadi who became a minister of the sultan's state in order to implement legal reform of the empire, has no counterpart in the nineteenth- or twentieth-century Iran. Similarly, the exclusion of the *ᶜulamāᵓ* from diplomacy and the elimination of their function of mediation in political disputes completely isolated the hierocracy from political currents.

In the latter part of the nineteenth and the opening decade of the twentieth century, we encounter two rival normative orders bearing on political domination: the democratic principles of (legitimate) government and the traditional theories of kingship. The impact of Western political philosophy began to be felt in Iran in the last quarter of the nineteenth century. The first decade of the twentieth century witnessed Iran's entry into the age of modern politics with the Constitutional Revolution of 1905–6.

During the Constitutional Revolution, a number of prominent Shiᶜite jurists supported the Constitutionalist movement and wrote political tracts justifying parliamentary democracy. From our point of view, these tracts can be seen as attempts to address the twin questions of the legitimation of parliamentary legislation and the legitimation of democratic government.

However, clerical writings were flawed by a number of important misconceptions regarding the nature and underlying principles of parliamentary democracy. The serious secularizing implications of legislation were played down, and a number of flat contradictions between Islamic and liberal political concepts were ignored. Therefore these tracts were not to serve as the basis for a modernized Shiᶜite political ethic once these implications became clear. The pro-Constitution jurists soon found themselves on the defensive. The reactionary camp within the Shiᶜite hierocracy continued to gain in strength and was unmistakably predominant by the beginning of the second decade of the century.

From 1911 onwards, the Shiᶜite hierocracy withdrew from the political arena after its complete disillusionment with Constitutionalism.[7] The advent of parliamentary democracy, and then the establishment of the Pahlavī regime a decade later, not only perpetuated the withdrawal of the hierocracy from the process of legitimation (which had continued to be the case since the reign of Muḥammad Shāh Qājār, except for Nāṣir al-Dīn Shāh's feeble attempt to revive it and for the more significant attempt to legitimate monarchical autocracy under Muḥammad ᶜAlī Shāh [1907–09] by Shaykh Faḍl Allāh Nūrī[8]) but assured the *ᶜulamāᵓ*'s increasingly total exclusion from the polity. The Shiᶜite hierocracy became deeply alienated from the modernized Pahlavī state and the increasingly secularized political elite that dominated it. The hierocracy's opposition to the etatist regime assumed the form of a staunchly uncompromising traditionalism, coupled with a strong tendency to reject the political order from which it had been systematically excluded for over half a century.

To find ideological ammunition in their bid to overthrow the Pahlavī regime from the late 1960s onwards, Khumaynī and some other *mullāh*s naturally turned to the Shiᶜite tradition. In doing so, they reactivated the process that had unfolded in the early nineteenth century equilibrium between political and hierocratic domination.

The hierocracy no longer felt itself bound by the implicit Qājār concordat (in part retained in the Constitution of 1906–7), which had been so arrogantly trampled upon by the state. Total exclusion from the political order obviated the need for any realistic acknowledgment of the balance of political and hierocratic power, while the hierocracy's isolation from the Western-oriented political and bureaucratic elite precluded the making of any concessions to the latter's viewpoint to achieve a consensus. Over the past two decades, the state's intensified encroachment upon the sphere that had been under the control of the religious institution forced a number of leading *mujtahid*s to abandon the involuted value-rationalism of religious jurisprudence, and to couple their championship of the menaced Islamic traditions with counterclaims of hierocratic monism. Āyatullāh Rūḥullāh Khumaynī and others extended the highly technical and specific discussion of the rights of the gerent into a political theory that proposed theocratic monism in the form of the "sovereignty of the jurist."[9] They did so without any communication or discussion with the secular elite, and the theory of the sovereignty of the religious jurist was put forward as the Islamic alternative by the largely lower-middle-class traditionalist party in its fight against the Pahlavī regime. Though it is by no means difficult to observe the persistence of the attitude of pious withdrawal from politics at the highest ehelons of the triumphant hierocracy, its politically active members under the leadership of Khumaynī, facing a paralyzed and completely servile state, incorporated their theory of hierocratic monism into a new constitution that was ratified by the referendum of 2–3 December 1979.[10] The result was the establishment of Shiᶜite theocratic monism in Iran, the like of which the late medieval popes advocated but never had the possibility to implement except in the territories under their direct administration. This bold and successful attempt to embrace the world by capturing the pinnacle of political power means that the period of theocratic monism is bound to be the period of maximum compromise of Shiᶜism with the world and its profound transformation, since, for the first time, Shiᶜism finds itself deeply entangled in innumerable hosts of mundane affairs.

We have said so far that the advent of democratic theories of government in modern times gnawed at the traditional principles of legitimacy of kingship. The Shiᶜite principles of legitimate juristic authority, having spent their force in creating Qājār dualism, remained in dormancy for over a century to be discovered by the beleaguered *mullāhs* in the late 1960s and early 1970s, and to be modified into a theory of theocratic monism, and as such to assume the character of a miraculously revealed panacea to reverse imitative Westernization and to cure the strains of the rapidly emerging industrial society. But this is not the end of the story. To mobilize the masses effectively for his Islamic revolution, Khumaynī not only drew on upon the Shiᶜite principle of juristic authority in order to extend it to matters political as well as religious, but also revived the mahdistic principle of authority in a modified form. Versed in Bīdābādī's tradition of gnostic Shiᶜism but ignoring the latter's warning concerning the possibility of arrested spiritual development at the level of "egotism" and "pharaonism,"[11] Khumaynī decided to call the people to God by means of revolutionary political action. He took the unprecedented step of assuming the title of Imam, conferred upon him by his militant followers, and put forward a radically novel interpretation of imamate as continuous (*mustamarr*) leadership, which was duly incorporated into the Constitution of the Islamic Republic of Iran. It would indeed not be too much of an exaggeration to suggest that, owing to the intense political conditioning of the Shiᶜite traditionalist movement that was launched in defense of Shiᶜite Islam and its custodians against Pahlavī modernization and centralization, 130 years after the execution of the Bāb, *ghuluww* (extremism) succeeded in conquering the Shiᶜite hierocracy itself.

The reader will recall that the mahdistic principle enabled the founder of the Safavid empire to conquer Iran and establish Shiᶜism, but that in the long run it clashed with the juristic principle of authority. The very same inconsistency has already produced something of a crisis of legitimacy, which is certain to become acute after the death of the charismatic leader of the Islamic revolution. Elements of neo-*ghuluww* were present from the very beginning of the revolutionary process, as for instance in the discussions among the anti-shah demonstrators as to whether Khumaynī was the Hidden Imam or merely the introduction to him. By 1982, Fakhr al-Dīn Ḥijāzī, perhaps the most important demagogue of the Islamic Republican Party, would openly implore Khumaynī to drop the veil if he indeed was the Mahdi himself. As is proper for such occasions, the Imam would of course observe nobly ambiguous silence.[12] In fact, the unprecedented "dismissal" of Sharī ᶜat-madārī from the rank of grand āyatullāh by some seventeen out of over forty professors of the Qum theological seminaries who could be prevailed upon to do so in April 1982, and the intimidation and silencing of other grand āyatullāhs opposed to Khumaynī's theory of hierocratic monism, signaled a serious setback for the juristic principle of authority and indicated that the mahdistic principle had gained the upper hand. Other indications also confirm the ascendancy of mahdism and the onset of a reaction to it from within the Shiᶜite community.

In a speech to the Islamic Parliament in October 1982, Ḥujjat al-Islām Riḍvānī, the deputy from the town of Fīrūzābad, predicted the success of the war against

Iraq as a prelude to marching on Jerusalem. Adducing a number of traditions relating to the Mahdi, he added that the purpose of the march on Jerusalem was to acclaim the reappearance of the Hidden Imam as the Mahdi, and to witness the reappearance of Jesus Christ and his final conversion to Islam by the Mahdi. It is interesting to note that the Ḥujjatī group—so named after the Hidden Imam as the *ḥujjat* (proof) of God, and a powerful oppositional group within the Islamic Republic—rejects the legitimacy of Khumaynī's theocratic monism because it entails the usurpation of the right of the Mahdi. Khumaynī's followers have reacted by coining the phrase, highly reminiscent of early Safavid legitimatory motifs,[13] "O God, keep Khumaynī until the revolution of the Mahdi." The Mahdi has reportedly been seen on the front and, on one occasion, told an injured volunteer, "Your prayer, 'O God, O God, keep Khumaynī until the revolution of the Mahdi,' has expedited my advent by a few hundred years."[14]

To complicate matters further, Khumaynī has created an Islamic Parliament that has engaged in legislation since its institution. Although he initially considered this a necessary concession to nationalists and democrats and a transitional step, Khumaynī has come to appreciate the loyalty of the Majlis, and has reportedly grown to like it. Furthermore, institutions, once created, in turn give rise to new constellations of interests. The Majlis is no exception, and has given rise to a significant social group with a vested interest in upholding the legitimacy of parliamentary legislation. The reconciliation of the legitimacy of parliamentary legislation with the Shiᶜite principle of juristic authority—especially in its present extended, theocratic form—poses problems as serious as any arising from the inconsistency of the Shiᶜite mahdistic and juristic principles of domination.

The coincidence of these three distinct principles of legitimate domination has already created a crisis of legitimacy and set in motion attempts at its resolution and thus the process of rationalization. To the two contradictory but recognizably Shiᶜite principles of authority—the juristic and the mahdistic—is now added a third pertaining to parliamentary legislation. It is quite likely that a completely satisfactory resolution will never be reached. It is also likely that the process of rationalization will be more condensed in time than was the corresponding one in premodern Iran. However, once the process is set in motion, as it has been, the logic of the Shiᶜite doctrine will not determine its course of evolution in detail, but is bound to constrain the range of eventual viable outcomes through the requirement of consistency.

List of Abbreviations

Journals and Contemporary Publications

AION	*Annali dell'Istituto Universitario Orientale di Napoli*
BSOAS	*Bulletin of the School of Oriental and African Studies* (London)
Ec. & S.	M. Weber, *Economy and Society*, G. Roth and C. Wittich, eds. (Berkeley and Los Angeles: University of California Press, 1978)
EI and EI^{2}	*Encyclopaedia of Islam* (first and second editions), H. H.
Essays	Gerth and C. Wright Mills, trans. and ed., in *Max Weber: Essays in Sociology* (New York: Oxford University Press, 1946)
IJMES	*International Journal of Middle East Studies*
IS	*Iranian Studies*
JESHO	*Journal of the Economic and Social History of the Orient*
JRAS	*Journal of the Royal Asiatic Society*
REI	*Revue des études islamiques*
Shiʿisme	*Le Shiʿisme imâmite* (Colloque de Strasbourg) (Paris: Presses Universitaires de France, 1970)
SI	*Studia Islamica*
ZDMG	*Zeitschrift der deutschen morgenlandischen Gesellschaft*

Primary Sources

Ab. N.	Mīrzā Muḥammad Tāhir Vahīd Qazvīnī, *ʿAbbās-nāmeh*, I. Dihgān, ed. (Tehran, 1951/1329)

Ah. T.	Ḥasan Rūmlū, *Aḥsan al-Tawārīkh*, C. N. Seddon, ed. (Baroda: Oriental Institute, 1931)
Arb.	Mīr Muḥammad Ḥusaynī (Mīr Lawḥī), *Arbaʿīn*, Central Library of Tehran University, MS 1154 (Mishkāt Collection, no. 619)
A. Sh.	Mullā Muḥsin Fayḍ, *Āʾīneh-ye Shāhī*, published in his *Risālāt* (Shiraz: Musavi, 1941/1320)
A. Sh. Tp.	*Āʾīn-e Shāh Ṭahmāsp-e Ṣafavī dar Qānūn-e Salṭanat*, printed by M. T. Dānish-pajūh in *Barrasīhā-ye Tārīkhī* 7, no. 1 (1972/1351)
Asnad Ab.	A.-H. Navāʾī, ed., *Asnād va Mukātibāt-e Tārīkhī*; *Shāh ʿAbbās Avval* (Tehran, 1973/1352)
Asnad Q.	J. Qāʾim-maqāmī, ed., *Yikṣad va Panjāh Sanad-e Tārīkhī* (Tehran 1969/1348)
Asnad Tp.	A. H. Navāʾī, *Shāh Ṭahmāsp-e Ṣafavī, Majmūʿa-ye Asnād va Mukātibāt-e Tārīkhī* (Tehran, 1970/1350)
Ay. H.	Muḥammad Bāqir Majlisī, *ʿAyn al-Ḥayāt* (Tehran: ʿIlmī, 1954/1333)
B. Si.	Zayn al-ʿĀbidīn Shīrvānī, *Bustān al-Siyāḥa* (Shiraz, 1923–24/1342 Q)
Carmelites	*A Chronicle of the Carmelites in Persia and the Papal Mission of the XVIIth and XVIIIth Centuries*, 2 vols. (London, 1939)
Chardin	J. Chardin, *Les Voyages du Chevalier Chardin en Perse*, 10 vols., L. Langlès, ed. (Paris, 1811)
Dh. U. Sh.	Sayyid al-Murtaḍā, *al-Dharīʿa ilā Uṣūl al-Sharīʿa*, A.-Q. Gorjī, ed. (Tehran: Tehran University Press, 1969–70/1348)
Du Mans	Rafael Du Mans, *Estat de la Perse en 1660*, C. Schefer, ed. (Paris, 1890)
F. D.	Muḥammad Tāhir ibn Muḥammad Ḥusayn (Qumī), *al-Fawāʾid al-Dīniyya*, Central Library of Tehran University, MS 2479
Gemelli	"A Voyage Round the World," J. F. Gemelli/Careri (visited Iran in 1694) in J. Churchill, ed., *A Collection of Voyages*, vol. 4 (London, 1704)
H. S.	Khwānd Amīr (Ghiyāth al-Dīn ibn Humām al-Dīn al-Ḥusaynī), *Ḥabīb al Siyar*, 4 vols., J. Homāʾī, ed. (Tehran: Khayyam, 1954)
H. Sh.	Mullā Aḥmad Ardabīlī, *Ḥadīqat al-Shīʿa* (Tehran: ʿIlmiyya Islāmiyya, n.d.)

Hm. Th.	ᶜAlī-Naqī Ṭughāʾī, *Himam al-Thawāqib*, Library of Sipahsālār Madrasa, MS 1845.
Ht. Q.	Muḥammad Bāqir Majlisī, *Ḥayāt al-Qulūb, III: dar Imāmat* (Tehran, 1955/1374 Q.)
H. Yq.	Muḥammad Bāqir Majlisī, *Ḥaqq al-Yaqīn* (Tehran, 1968/1347)
J. Ab.	Bahāʾ al-Dīn ᶜĀmilī, *Jāmiᶜ ᶜAbbāsī* (Bombay, 1901–2/1319 Q.; reissued by Intishārāt-e Farahānī in Tehran, n.d.)
J. M.	Muḥammad Mufīd, *Jāmiᶜ Mufīdī*, 3 vols., I. Afshār, ed. (Tehran, 1961/1340)
Kaempfer	Engelbert Kaempfer, *Dar Darbar-e Shāhanshāhān-e Īrān*, trans. K. Jahāndārī (Tehran, 1971/1350), being the Persian translation of *Amoenitatam exoticarum politico-physico-medicarum Fasciculi V* (Lemgo, 1712)
K. A. J.	Ṣadr al-Dīn Muḥammad Shīrāzī, *Kasr Aṣnām al-Jāhiliyya*, M. T. Dānish-pajūh, ed. (Tehran, 1962/1340)
K. Gh.	Ḥasan al-Ṭūsī, *Kitāb al-Ghayba*, Āqā Buzurg Tihrānī, ed. (Najaf, 1965–66/1385 Q.)
Khj.	ᶜAlī al-Karakī al-ᶜĀmilī et al., *al-Riḍāiyyāt waʾl-Kharājiyyāt* (Tehran, 1895–6/1313 Q.)
Kh. T.	Qāḍī Aḥmad Qumī, *Khulāṣat al-Tawārīkh*, Preussiche (now Deutsche) Staatsbibliothek, Berlin, MS Orient. fol. 2202.
K. Mk.	Mullā Muḥsin Fayḍ, *Kalamāt-e Maknūneh* (Tehran, 1898–99/1316 Q.)
K. Nq.	ᶜAbd al-Jalīl al-Qazvīnī al-Rāzī, *Kitāb al-Naqḍ*, S. J. Ḥusaynī Urmavī, ed. (Tehran, 1952/1331)
Malcolm	Sir John Malcolm, *History of Persia*, 2 vols. (London, 1829)
M. Din	Shaykh Ḥasan ibn Zayn al-Dīn, *Maᶜālim al-Dīn wa Malādh al-Mujtahidin* (Tehran: ᶜIlmiyya Islāmiyya, 1958/1378 Q.)
Mj. B.	Faḍl ibn Ḥasan al-Ṭabrisī, *Tafsīr Majmaᶜ al-Bayān*, Aḥmad Bihishtī, trans. (Qum, 1970–71/1349)
Mj. T.	Mīrzā Muḥammad Khalīl Marᶜashī Ṣafavī, *Majmaᶜ al-Tawārīkh*, A. Iqbāl, ed. (Tehran, 1949/1328)
M. M.	Qāḍi Nūrullāh Shūshtarī, *Majālis al-Muʾminīn*, 2 vols. (Tehran: Islāmiyya, 1975–76/1354)
M. Nw.	Qāḍī Nūrullāh Shūshtarī, *Maṣāʾib al-Nawāṣib*, Library of Majlis (Tehran), MS 2036
Mrt. A.	Aḥmad Bahbahani, *Miratu-l-Aḥwal Jahan Numa*, British Library Or MS Add. 24052

M. U.	Sayyid Muḥammad Ṭabāṭabāʾī, *Mafātiḥ al-Uṣūl* (Tehran, n.d.; pages unnumbered)
Mukhtasar	Abuʾl-Qāsim Najm al-Dīn Jaʿfar b. al-Ḥasan al-Ḥillī, *al-Mukhtaṣar al-Nāfiʿ fi Fiqh al-Imāmiyya* (Najaf, 1964/1383)
M. W.	Ibn al-Muṭahhar al-Ḥillī, *Mabādī al-Wusūl ilā ʿilm al-Uṣūl* (Najaf, 1970)
Narrative	*A Narrative of Italian Travels in Persia in the Fifteenth and Sixteenth Centuries*, Hakluyt Society, vol. 49, pt. 2 (London, 1873)
N.B.R.	Mīr Makhdūm Shīrāzi, *al-Nawāqiḍ li-Bunyān al-Rawāfiḍ*, British Library MS Or 7991
Nihaya	Muḥammad b. al-Ḥasan al-Ṭūsī, *al-Nihāya fi Mujarrad al-Fiqh waʾl-Fatāwā* (Tehran, 1963/1342)
Nq. A.	Maḥmūd Afūshteh-yi Naṭanzī, *Nuqāwat al-Āthār fi Dhikr al-Akhyār*, E. Ishrāqī, ed. (Tehran, 1971/1350)
N. Tkh.	Mīrzā Muḥammad Taqī Sipihr, *Nāsikh al-Tawārīkh*, 4 vols., M. B. Bihbūdī, ed. (Tehran: Islamiyya, 1965–66/1344)
Nurbakhsh	The Writings of Sayyid Muḥammad Nūrbakhsh, published in J. Sadaqiyānlū, *Taḥqīq dar Aḥvāl va Āthār-e Sayyid Muḥammad Nūrbakhsh Uvaysī Quhistānī* (Tehran, 1972/1351)
Olearius	Adam Olearius, *Relation du voyage en Moscovie et en Perse* (Paris, 1656)
Q. Kh.	Valī Qulī Shāmlū, *Qiṣaṣ al-Khāqānī*, British Library Add. MS 7656
Q. U.	Muḥammad Tunikābunī, *Qiṣaṣ al-ʿUlamāʾ* (Tehran: ʿIlmiyya Islāmiyya, n.d. [1878])
Q. Usul.	Abu'l-Qāsim Qumī, *Qawānīn al-Uṣūl* (Tehran, n.d.)
R. Ad.	M. A. Mudarris, *Rayḥānat al-Adab*, 8 vols. (Tabriz, 1967)
R. J.	Muḥammad Bāqir Khwānsārī, *Rawḍāt al-Jannāt fi Aḥwāl al-ʿUlamāʾ wa'l-Sādāt* M. A. Rawḍātī, ed. (Tehran, 1947/1367 Q.)
R. J. J. J.	Ḥāfiz Ḥusayn Karbalāʾī Tabrīzī, *Rawḍat al-Jinān va Jannāt al-Janān*, 2 vols., J. Sulṭān al-Qurrāʾī, ed. (Tehran, 1965/1344)
Ross. Anon.	Anonymous history of Shāh Ismāʿīl, British Library MS Or 3248 (*Ross Anonymous*)
R. S. J.	Muḥammad Bāqir Majlisī, *Risāla-ye Suʾāl va Javāb*, printed together with *Tadhkirat al-Awliyāʾ* etc. (Tabriz, 1953/1332)

R. S. N.	Riḍā Qulī Khān Hidāyat, *Rawḍat al-Ṣafā-ye Nāṣirī*, 10 vols. (Tehran, 1960–61 / 1339)
R. T. S.	Muḥammad Taqī Majlisī, *Risāla-ye Tashvīq-e Sālikīn*, printed together with R. S. J. (above), etc. (Tabriz, 1953 / 1332)
Sanson	Sanson (missionary), *The Present State of Persia*, (London, 1695)
Seh Asl	Ṣadr al-Dīn Muḥammad ibn Ibrāhīm Shīrāzī, *Risāla-ye Seh Aṣl*, S. H. Nasr, ed. (Tehran: Tehran University Press, 1961 / 1340)
Shar. Is.	Abuʾl-Qāsim Najm al-Dīn Jaʿfar al-Ḥillī, *Sharayiʿ al-Islām*, Persian trans., M. T. Dānish-pajūh, ed., 4 vols. (Tehran: Tehran University Press, 1967–74 / 1346–53)
T. A. Ab.	Iskandar Beg Turkamān, Munshī, *Tārīkh-e ʿĀlam-ārā-ye ʿAbbāsī*, 2 vols. (Tehran, 1971 / 1350)
T. Akh.	Zayn al-Dīn ʿAlī ibn ʿAbdulmuʾmin, *Takmilat al-Akhbār* (1571 / 979), University of Tehran Microfilm #1981 (folios unnumbered)
Tibyan	Ḥasan al-Ṭūsī, *Tafsīr al-Tibyān* (Najaf, 1957)
Th. M.	Sayyid Jaʿfar Kashfī, *Tuḥfat al-Mulūk* (Tehran, 1857 / 1273 Q.)
T. Hq.	Maʿṣūm ʿAlī Shāh, *Ṭarāʾiq al-Ḥaqāʾiq*, 3 vols., M. J. Maḥjūb, ed. (Tehran, 1960 / 1339)
T. J. A.	Qāḍī Aḥmad Ghaffārī, *Tārīkh-e Jahān-ārā* (Tehran: Hafiz, n.d.)
Tk. H. L.	*Tadhkira-ye Ḥazīn-e Lāhījī*, published as *The Life of Sheikh Mohammed Ali Hazin*, F. C. Belfour, ed. (London, 1831)
Tk. M.	*Tadhkirat al-Mūlūk*, V. Minorsky, ed. (London: E. J. W. Gibb Memorial Series, n.s., 16, 1943)
Tk. N.	Mīrzā Muḥammad Ṭāhir Naṣrābādī, *Tadhkira-ye Naṣrābādī*, V. Dastgirdī, ed. (Tehran: Furūghī, 1973 / 1352)
T. Ol.	ʿAbdullāh ibn Muḥammad al-Qāshānī, *Tārīkh-e Ōljeitū*, M. Hambly, ed. (Tehran, 1969–70 / 1348)
T. Sh. Tp.	*Memoirs of Shah Tahmasp* [*Tadhkira-ye Shāh Ṭahmāsp*] Calcutta, 1912
Tuh. A.	Mullā Muḥammad Ṭāhir Qumī, *Tuḥfat al-Akhyār* (Qum, 1973 / 1393 Q.)
T. W.	[Ibn al-Muṭahhar] ʿAllāma al-Ḥillī, *Tahdhīb al-Wusūl ilā ʿIlm al-Uṣūl* (Tehran, 1890–91 / 1308 Q.)
U. Kafi	Muḥammad b. Yaʿqūb al-Kulaynī al-Rāzī, *Uṣūl al-Kāfī*, with Persian trans. and comm. by J. Muṣṭafavī (Tehran, n.d.)

V. S. A.	Sayyid ᶜAbd al-Ḥusayn Khātūnābādī, *Vaqāyiᶜ al-Sanīn va'l-Aᶜvam* (Tehran: Islamiyya, 1973/1352)
Z. B.	Mullā Aḥmad Muqqaddas Ardabīlī, *Zubdat al-Bayān fi Aḥkām al-Qur'ān* (Tehran 1966–67/1386 Q.)
Zd. M.	Muḥammad Bāqir Majlisī, *Zad al-Maᶜād* (Tehran, 1902–3/1320 Q.)
Z. T. A. Ab.	Iskandar Beg Turkamān and Muḥammad ibn Yusūf, *Dhayl-e Tārīkh-e ᶜĀlam-ārā-ye ᶜAbbāsī*, Suheylī Khwansārī, ed. (Tehran: Islāmiyya, 1938–39/1317)
Z. U.	Bahā' al-Dīn ᶜĀmilī, *Zubdat al-Uṣūl* (?, 1851/1267 Q.)

Notes

General Introduction

1. Ec. & S.:25
2. Ec. & S.:245, 1116–17
3. Cf. Ec. & S.:30–31
4. The exception being Weber's treatment of the normative order in imperial China, alluded to in chapter 3 below.
5. E. Troeltsch, *The Social Teachings of the Christian Churches*, 2 vols., O. Wyon, trans. (London, 1931).
6. *Essays*:280.
7. Ec. & S.:1135–43.
8. Ec. & S., chap. 14, esp. section 10.
9. Ec. & S.:54.
10. Ec. & S.:1159–60.
11. Ec. & S.:1162.
12. E. Benveniste, *Le Vocabulaire des institutions indo-européennes*, vol. 2. *Pouvoir, droit, religion* (Paris, 1969):20.
13. A. M. Hocart, *Kings and Councillors: An Essay in the Comparative Anatomy of Human Society* (Chicago, 1970 [1936]), pp. 161, 167.
14. See further, chap. 2, section 2.1.
15. Ec. & S.:953, emphasis added.
16. Ec. & S.:1078–81.
17. Ec. & S.:954.
18. Ec. & S.:248–49.
19. Incidentally, both these pictures resemble Weber's characterization of sultanism as the extreme case of unprincipled and arbitrary personal rule (Ec. & S.:231–32).
20. Ec. & S.:32.
21. Ec. & S.:32.

22. Ec. & S.:36.
23. Ec. & S.:25.
24. Ec. & S.:327.
25. Ec. & S.:326–27.
26. See below, pp. 188–89.
27. See especially chap. 1, section 3.
28. Ec. & S.:36ff.
29. In this regard I diverge from Weber who defines "Church" exclusively in organizational terms and considers it applicable to Islam (Ec. & S.:54, 1164).
30. Troeltsch:330.
31. Ec. & S.:695, 1012, 1028.
32. This is my assessment. A case against the application of the term "hierocracy" could be made if a somewhat more stringent criterion of hierarchical organization were adopted.
33. See below, pp. 133–34.
34. Ec. & S.:544–51.
35. Ec. & S.:576–97.
36. "Religious Rejections of the World and Their Direction," in *Essays*:323–59: Here, the basic underlying assumption is that "rationality, in the sense of logical or teleological 'consistency,' of an intellectual-theoretical or practical-ethical attitude has and always has had power over man, however limited and unstable this power is and always has been in the face of other forces of historical life.

"Religious interpretations of the world and ethics of religions created by intellectuals and meant to be rational have been strongly exposed to the imperative of consistency. The effect of the *ratio*, especially of a teleological deduction of practical postulates, is in some way, and often very strongly, noticeable among all religious ethics" (*Essays*:324).

37. *Essays*:323, emphasis added.
38. Ec. & S.:576.
39. Ec. & S.:593.
40. *Essays*:326: "The conflict of ascetic ethics, as well as of the mystically oriented temper of brotherly love, with the apparatus of domination which is basic to all political institutions has produced the most varied types of tension and compromise."
41. Ec. & S.:623–27.
42. Ec. & S.:623–27.
43. H. R. Niebuhr, *The Social Sources of Denominationalism* (New York, 1929). Niebuhr's focus is exclusively on the world-embracing tendency and its consequences.
44. M. Weber, *Religion of India* (New York, 1958), pp. 181–84.
45. See S. J. Tambiah, "Buddhism and This-Worldly Activity," *Modern Asian Studies* 7, no. 1 (1973):1–20.
46. My schema is modeled on Weber's analytical distinction between "economic action" and "economically oriented action" but with two dimensions—the religious and the political—instead of one. Weber does define the term "politically oriented action" (Ec. & S.:54–55) but does not proceed to subdivide the category, as he does with "economically oriented action" (Ec. & S.:64).
47. My definitions of "societal" and "communal" action are not those of Weber (Ec. & S.:40–41).

48. Malcolm 2:315.

49. A. de Tocqueville, *Oeuvres complètes, IX: Correspondance d'Alexis de Tocqueville et d'Arthur de Gobineau*, J. P. Mayer, ed. (Paris: Gallimard, 2nd edition, 1959), pp. 285–87.

50. Ec. & S.: 1147.

51. Ec. & S.: 1175.

52. Ec. & S.: 831.

53. Ec. & S.: 822–23.

54. Weber's comparative remarks on the absence of caesaropapist legitimacy of the shahs combined with certain caesaropapist privileges in practice are correct.

55. See especially A. K. S. Lambton, "The Persian *ᶜulamā*ʾ and Constitutional Reform" (*Shiᶜisme*: 245–69); N. R. Keddie, "The Roots of the Ulama's Power in Modern Iran," in *Scholars, Saints and Sufis, Muslim Institutions since 1500* (Berkeley, 1972); and H. Algar, *Religion and the State in Iran: 1785–1906* (Berkeley, 1969) and "The Oppositional Role of the Ulama in 20th Century Iran," in *Scholars, Saints and Sufis*.

56. See W. Madelung, "A Treatise of the Sharīf al-Murtaḍā on the Legality of Working for the Government (*Masʾala fi'l-ᶜamal maᶜ al-sulṭān*)," BSOAS 43 (1980) and his "Authority in Twelver Shiᶜism in the Absence of the Imam," in G. Makdisi et al., *La Notion d'autorité au moyen age: Islam, Byzance, Occident: Colloques internationaux de la Napoule, 1978* (Paris: Presses universitaires de France, 1982); J. Eliash, "The *Ithnā ᶜasharī* Juristic Theory of Legal and Political Authority," SI 29 (1969) and his "Some Misconceptions Regarding the Juridical Status of the Iranian *ᶜulamā*ʾ" IJMES, 10 (1979): H. Enayat, *Modern Islamic Political Thought*, (London: Macmillan, 1982), p. 12 and n. 11, pp. 195–96; and my "Religion, Political Action and Legitimate Domination in Shiᶜite Iran: fourteenth to eighteenth centuries A.D.," *Archives européennes de sociologie* 20 (1979) and "The Shiᶜite Hierocracy and the State in Pre-modern Iran: 1785–1890," *Archives européennes de sociologie* 22 (1981).

57. See especially chaps. 7 and 10, below.

58. See N. Calder, "Accommodation and Revolution in Imāmī Shīᶜī Jurisprudence: Khumaynī and the Classical Tradition," *Middle Eastern Studies* 18 (1982). Calder's disregard of Madelung's very specific quotation from and reference to al-Ṭūsī's *Nihāya* ("A Treatise," p. 30) and of his equally precise reference (p. 31, n.37) to the endorsement of al-Ṭūsī's position in the *Sarāʾir* of Ibn Idrīs al-Ḥillī—who, interestingly, was among the foremost later critics of al-Ṭūsī—is puzzling. Equally puzzling is Lambton's citation of the Persian translation of another text from the *Nihāya* which, in any event, does not support her position (A. K. S. Lambton, *State and Government in Medieval Islam: An Introduction to the Study of the Islamic Political Theory of the Jurists* [Oxford, 1981], p. 244, n.7). The group of Western scholars writing on nineteenth-century Iran stated their argument in general terms without any reference to Shiᶜite juristic writings from the earlier periods—or, for that matter, from the nineteenth century. Calder's statements are all the more seriously misleading in that he has studied the earlier sources. It is to be regretted that his otherwise valuable work on Shiᶜite jurisprudence (N. Calder, "The Structure of Authority in Imāmī Shīᶜī Jurisprudence," unpublished Ph.D. thesis, University of London, 1980, henceforth Calder) is vitiated by non sequitur allegations of inevitable illegitimacy of de facto powers and by the anachronistic bias in the interpretation of the earlier periods.

Calder is aware of the profuse praise for the Īl-Khān ruler, Öljeitü, in al-Ḥillī's *Minhāj al-Karāma*, a treatise devoted to the exposition of the doctrine of imamate—which allegedly entails the denial of legitimacy of temporal rule—and of al-Karaki's "exordium of praise for Safavid rulers" in his major legal compendium, *Jāmiᶜ al-Maqāṣid* (Calder, pp. 82, 157). Nevertheless, he persists in drumming the illegitimacy of all government. In the above-cited article, Calder's use of phrases such as "the *jāʾir* Sulṭān Ṭahmāsp," (p. 6) which have the appearance of a close paraphrase of the sources, borders on willful deception. In fact, the very collection of legal treatises he refers to in connection with that phrase contains a clear statement by the Safavid jurist al-Qaṭīfī that the term *jāʾir* is specific to a person with a false claim to the imamate (Khj.: 164; Madelung, "Authority in Twelver Shiᶜism," p. 172, n.9). This means that Ṭahmāsp and other rulers are *not jāʾir*. On the other hand, the term *dawlat al-ḥaqq*, which can be exactly and accurately rendered "legitimate government" *is* employed by the Shiᶜite doctors of the period to refer to Safavid rule (see p. 179 below).

The occultation of the Twelfth Imam does inaugurate a period in which divinely inspired and *infallible* authority in religion and in political leadership cannot obtain. But while appreciative of the gradual establishment of "valid opinion" (*ẓann muᶜtabar*) as the relevant criterion for legitimacy of legal norms during the occultation, Calder fails to note the inevitable change in the criterion of legitimacy of political authority which is the exact logical parallel of the change in the criterion of legitimacy of religio-legal authority.

Calder has studied Shiᶜite jurisprudence, but his notion of "legitimacy" is doubtless not a category of Shiᶜite law. Like Western observers from Gobineau to Algar, he misapplies the concept in a manner reminiscent of the early anthropologists' if-I-were-a-horse-type characterization of the mentality of the primitives. Like theirs, Calder's implicit assumption is that if the Shiᶜite theory of historical imamate of ᶜAlī and his descendants were positive public law of the period of occultation—i.e., if it were tantamount to modern constitutional theory—temporal rulers would be illegitimate until the end of time. As has been pointed out, the assumption is false.

59. H. Corbin, *Histoire de la philosophie islamiques* (Paris, 1964), p. 59.

60. S. H. Nasr, "Le Shiᶜisme et le Soufisme: Leur relations principielles et historiques," *Shiᶜisme*: 215–33.

61. Even looking at the mid-seventeenth century, the period for which the Corbin-Nasr thesis has the highest plausibility, we find not only the endorsement of Āmulī's dictum on the identity of Sufism and Shiᶜism—which constitutes the core of Corbin's thesis (R.T.S.: 18)—but also the frequent accusatory coupling of Sufism with Sunnism (Tuh. A.: 113–43).

Introduction to Part 1

1. S. H. M. Jafri, *Origins and Early Development of Shiᶜa Islam* (London: Longman, 1979), pp. 222–33.

2. U. Kafi, 3: 38–45.

3. See W. Madelung, "Imamism and Muᶜtazilite Theology," *Shiᶜisme*: 13–29.

4. See R. Brunschvig, "Les UṢŪL AL-FIQH imâmites a leur stade ancien (X_e et XI_e siècles)," *Shiᶜisme*: 201–12.

5. M. J. McDermott, *The Theology of al-Shaykh al-Mufīd* (Beirut, 1970), p. 243.
6. K. Nq.:618.
7. See W. Madelung, "The Spread of Maturidism and the Turks," in *ACTAS do IV Congresso de Estudos Arabes e Islamicos* (Leiden: Brill, 1971), pp. 109–68.
8. Ibid., p. 138–41.
9. K. Nq.
10. The Īl-Khāns were the autonomous Mongol dynasty who ruled in Iran after the division of the Mongol Empire until its disintegration in 1335/735.
11. T. Ol.:90–95, 100–101; A. Bausani, "Religion under the Mongols," *Cambridge History of Iran* 5:544.
12. Strong Sunni resistance was encountered in Isfahan. (A. Iqbāl Āshtiyānī, *Tārīkh-e Mughul*, 4th impression [Tehran 1977–78/1356], pp. 316–18) When Sayyid Tāj al-Dīn fell into disgrace and was executed by Öljeitü's order in 1311–12/711, his body was savagely torn to pieces by the Ḥanbalīs and distributed in their community in Baghdad. The incident, which made Öljeitü deprive the Ḥanbalī community of Baghdad of their own qadi and put them under the jurisdiction of a Shāfiʿī judge, is indicative of the resentment caused by the pro-Shiʿite policies of Öljeitü. (T. Ol.:132–33; ʿAbd al-Ḥusayn Aḥmad Amīnī, *Shahīdān-e Rāh-e Faḍilat*, Persian Translation of *Shuhadāʾ al-Fāḍila* [Tehran, n.d.], pp. 130–33)
13. T. Ol.:107–8; M. Murtazavi, "Dīn va Madhhab dar ʿAhd-e Īl-Khānān," in *Taḥqīq dar bāreh-ye Dawreh-ye Īl-Khānān-e Irān* (Tehran, 1963/1341), pp. 1–88.
14. M. Murtazavi, "Taṣawwuf dar Dawreh-ye Īl-Khānān," *Taḥqīq*, pp. 89–130.
15. M. G. S. Hodgson, *The Venture of Islam* (Chicago, 1974), 2:279–84; Iqbāl, *Tārīkh-e Mughul*, pp. 466, 498–99.
16. T. Ol.:90–95, 132.
17. S. Nafīsī, "Saʿd al-Dīn Ḥamūya," *Yadigār* 1 no. 10 (1945):43.; M. Molé, "Les Kubrawiya entre Sunnisme et Shiisme aux huitième et neuvième siècles de l'Hégire," *REI* 29 (1961):61–142.
18. See below, chapter 2, section 2.1.2
19. Bausani, p. 547.
20. See also the introduction to part 2.
21. This group was known as the *tafḍīlī* Sunnis. See M. Dj. Mahdjoub, "The Evolution of the Popular Eulogy of the Imams among the Shiʿa," in S. A. Arjomand, ed., *Authority and Political Culture in Shiʿism* (Albany: SUNY Press, 1987).

Chapter 1

1. G. E. von Grunebaum opens his chapter on the body politic as follows: "Islam is the community of Allah. He is the living truth to which it owes its life. He is the center and the goal of its spiritual experience. *But he is also the mundane head of his community which he not only rules but governs*" (von Grunebaum, *Medieval Islam* [Chicago, 1954], p. 12). The underlined assertion is in my view untenable.
2. As an example, sūra 64, verse 1 can be cited: "All that is in the heavens and the earth magnifies God. His is the Kingdom, and His is the praise, And He is powerful over everything" (A. J. Arberry, trans.). One of the most recurrent phrases of the Qurʾan is "and for

God is the kingdom of the heavens and of the earth" (3:189; 5:19–20; 7:157; 24:42; 42:49; 45:26; 48:14).

3. See M. Weber, *Ancient Judaism* (New York, 1952), pp. 118–31.

4. See the Qur'an, sūra 25, al-Furqān ("Salvation"), esp. verse 56: "We have sent thee not, except good tidings to bear, and warning" (A. J. Arberry, trans.). Tor Andrae describes the typical rhetorical scheme of the sūras of the Qur'an as (1) a description of the blessings of God; (2) the duty of man in obedience to God; (3) judgment and retribution that shall come upon those who do not fulfill this duty (and rewards for those who do); see Tor Andrae, *Muhammad: The Man and His Faith* (New York, 1936), p. 126. It is true that the Qur'an does frequently speak of a judgment of God in history upon peoples incurring his wrath by their moral corruption. This, however, is not the case as regards the individuals whose soteriological calculus must necessarily have an otherworldly character.

5. M. A. Shaban, *Islamic History: A New Interpretation* (Cambridge, 1971) 1, esp. pp. 62, 73, 79–80.

6. Ira M. Lapidus, "The Separation of State and Religion in the Development of Early Islamic Society," *IJMES* 6 (1975):363–85.

7. Ibid., pp. 382–83.

8. M. G. S. Hodgson, "How Did the Early Shīʿa Become Sectarian?" *Journal of the American Oriental Society* 75 (1955):1–15. Hodgson's otherwise excellent account does not pay enough attention to the historical importance of Muḥammad al-Bāqir as the founder of Imāmī jurisprudence.

9. A. Iqbāl, *Khāndān-e Nawbakhtī* (Tehran 1932/1311), pp. 65–66, 75; Hodgson, p. 12. In this respect, their attitude is diametrically opposed to that of al-Bāqir's half-brother, Zayd ibn ʿAlī (d.740), the founder of the Zaydī branch of Shiʿism, who insisted on the taking up of arms as a condition of imamate. See Jafri, pp. 251–52, 265–66; H. Laoust, *Les Schismes dans l'Islam* (Paris, 1965), p. 35.

10. Jafri, p. 273.

11. See I. Goldziher, *Muslim Studies* (London, 1971 [1889–90]), 2:60–64; C. Cahen, "The Body Politic," in G. E. von Grunebaum, ed., *Unity and Diversity in Muslim Civilization* (Chicago, 1955), esp. pp. 137–39 and p. 149; Jafri, p. 281.

12. A. M. Schimmel, *Mystical Dimensions of Islam* (Chapel Hill, 1975), pp. 41, 83, 191; Laoust, p. 67.

13. Hodgson, pp. 1–8; M. J. Mashkūr, "Negāhī be Madhāhib-e Shīʿa va dīgar-e Firqa-hā-ye Islām tā Pāyān-e Qarn-e Sevvum-e Hijrī," introduction to his *Tarjuma-ye Firaq al-Shīʿa-ye Nawbakhtī* (Tehran, 1974/1353), pp. 193–96.

14. Calder, pp. 7–8.

15. Jafri, pp. 250, 253–55; Laoust, p. 33. The important role of al-Bāqir in laying the foundation of the Shiʿite legal system is recorded in the following statement by Kashshī in his *Rijāl*: "Before the Imamate of Muḥammad al-Bāqir the Shiʿites did not know what was lawful and what was unlawful, except what they learned from the [other] people; until Abū Jaʿfar [Al-Bāqir] became the Imam, and he taught them and explained to them the knowledge [of law], and they began to teach other people from whom they were previously learning" (trans. Jafri, p. 253).

16. Iqbāl, pp. 70–71; Jafri, pp. 289–310.

17. Jafri, p. 294.

18. W. Madelung, HISHĀM b. al-ḤAKAM, EI², 3:497.

19. See Modarresi Tabataba'i's forthcoming book, *Introduction to Shi'i Law* (sources: Kashshī's *Rijāl*, al-Ḥurr al'Āmilī, *Wasā'il*, Baḥr al-'Ulūm's *Rijāl*, etc.). The manuscript was kindly lent me by Dr. Modarresi.

20. Laoust, p. 100.

21. Hodgson, p. 10; emphasis added.

22. Ibid., p. 11; emphasis added.

23. Hodgson, p. 13.

24. Khj.:35–36.

25. Jafri, p. 298.

26. Ibn Bābūya, *Kitāb al-I'tiqād*, section (b) 39.

27. Shahrastānī, *al-Millal va'l-Nihal*; Persian translated and edited by M. R. Jalālī Nā'īnī (Tehran, 1971/1350), p. 122.

28. Qur'an, 3:7.

29. A. A. Sachedina, *Islamic Messianism: The Idea of the Mahdi in Twelver Shi'ism* (New York: SUNY Press, 1981); appendix, pp. 184–95.

30. Ibn Bābūya had considered the Imams immune from greater and lesser sins but liable to inadvertent error (*sahw*). By the time of al-Ṭūsī, the assertion of infallibility of the Imams became more categorical. His teacher al-Murtaḍā considered the Imams immune from both sin and inadvertent error. See W. Madelung, 'IṢMA, EI^2, 4:182; Lambton, *State and Government in Medieval Islam*, pp. 230–31.

31. K. Gh.:4–9.

32. The Mu'tazilite Qāḍī 'Abd al-Jabbār would typically attack the Imāmīs as follows: "and as for those who say there is a need for the Imam because he is *lutf* [grace] in the religion . . . how do they permit the Imam to be in occultation from the *umma* for such a long time, when his existence is *lutf* in the religion and when he is so badly needed" (cited in Sachedina, p. 133).

33. *al-Bābu'l-Ḥādī 'Ashar*, trans. W. M. Miller, (London, 1928), p. 62.

34. H. Laoust, "La Critique du Sunnisme daus la doctrine d'Al-Ḥillī," *REI* 24 (1966):51.

35. Madelung, "IMĀMA," EI^2, 3:1168.

36. G. Scarcia, "A proposito del problema della sovranita presso gli Imamiti," AION 7 (1957):118–19.

37. See W. Madelung, "New Documents Concerning al-Ma'mūn, al-Faḍl b. Sahl and 'Alī al-Riḍā," in Wadad al-Qadi, ed., *Studia Arabica et Islamica* (Beirut, 1981), pp. 345–46.

38. Sachedina, pp. 60–61.

39. Nawbakhtī, *Firaq al-Shī'a*, nos. 108, 118–24, 143–44 (Persian trans.: pp. 100, 118–22, 139–42).

40. Three sects, according to Nawbakhtī (*Firaq al-Shī'a*). Sa'd b. 'Abdullāh al-Ash'arī mentions a fourth sect (in the *Sawād al-Kūfa*) holding this belief, adding that their number was small. See *Kitāb al-Maqālāt va-l-Firaq*, M.J. Mashkūr, ed. (Tehran, 1963), p. 114 (no. 215). (Shahristānī [*al-Milal va'l-Nihal*] also mentions three such sects.) Among the twenty sects listed by Iqbāl on the basis also of slightly later sources (not counting the sect reported by al-Ash'arī, but counting separately a sect reported by Shahristānī only), we find six sects adhering to this belief. See Iqbāl, *Khāndān*, pp. 161–65.

41. Sachedina, pp. 49–50; emphasis added.

42. Sachedina, p. 93.

43. Shaban 2:46. This outlook was reinforced as a result of the persecution instituted by al-Mutawakkil in the second half of the nineteenth century. See Sachedina, p. 28.

44. Sachedina, pp. 90–91.

45. K. Gh.:223–26, 237–38.

46. Massignon 1:362–66, 465.

47. They appear to have modeled their belief after the Wāqifiyya, who considered Mūsā al-Kāẓim, the Seventh Imam, the Mahdi.

48. Sachedina, p. 43.

49. Massignon 1:360.

50. Iqbāl, Khāndān, pp. 100–101, 112–14; Massignon 1:362, 373, 376–77. The belief in the advent of the Qā'im and the Mahdi, and the inherence of God (*ḥulūl*) in the person of the imam, were among the most dangerous of tenets of the dissident extremists. As the principal theologian of the Imāmī religious institution, Abū Sahl had to contend with these tenets. In addition to rejecting mahdistic chiliasm, he affirmed the absurdity of *ḥulūl*: divine inherence in any human being, including the Imam (ibid, p. 360).

51. Ibid. 1:355–56.

52. Iqbāl, *Khāndān*, p. 237.

53. K. Gh.:241; Sachedina, p. 95.

54. K. Gh.:243.

55. E. Kohlberg, "From Imāmiyya to Ithnā-ᶜAshariyya", BSOAS 39 (1976).

56. Sachedina, p. 82.

57. This traditionalist doctrine of occultation was buttressed by arguments from the Qur'an and from the Bible and Jewish tradition. See Kohlberg, pp. 525–28.

58. Sachedina, pp. 57–71, 171.

59. Ibid., p. 58.

60. D. Sourdel, "Les Conceptions Imamites au début du XI siècle d'apres le Shaykh al-Mufīd," in D. S. Richards, ed., *Islamic Civilization 950–1150* (Oxford: Cassirer, 1973), p. 198.

61. The assertion that there are two forms of *ghayba* is made by al-Nuᶜ mānī in his *Kitāb al-Ghayba*, written ca. 953/342 (Kohlberg, p. 528).

62. K. Gh.:4. A third, logically redundant principle is also mentioned: that the truth is not outside the community.

63. Ibid., pp. 3–4.

64. Ibid., pp. 73, 203–9.

65. *Muᶜtaqad al-Imāmiyya*, pp. 122–23.

66. Scarcia, "A proposito del problema della sovranita presso gli imamiti," p. 99.

67. The most significant differences regard the rules of inheritance (N. J. Coulson, *A History of Islamic Law* [Edinburgh, 1964], pp. 110–14). For the enumeration of the other (very minor) differences, see J. Schacht, *Origins of Muhammadan Jurisprudence* (Oxford, 1950), part 4, chap. 9; and Y. Linant de Bellefonds, "Le droit imâmite," *Shiᶜisme*: 183–99. The differences regarding the *uṣūl al-fiqh* will be alluded to below.

68. Ec. & S.:810–11.

69. Ibid., pp. 789–90.

70. Goldziher 2:41–42.

71. Coulson, *History*, p. 37; Schacht, *Origins*, pp. 283–87.

72. J. Schacht, *An Introduction to Islamic Law* (Oxford, 1964), p. 27. Emphasis added.

73. Abū Ḥanīfa persistently refused to accept the office of qadi (Shorter EI: 9). Furthermore, "not being a kadi, Abū Ḥanīfa was less restricted than ibn Abī Laylā [his contemporary and a qadi of Kufa] by consideration of day-to-day practice. . . . A high degree of reasoning, often somewhat ruthless and unbalanced, with little regard for practice, is typical of Abū Ḥanīfa's legal thought as a whole" (Schacht, *Introduction*, p. 44).

74. Goldziher 2: 198–99.

75. Ibid. 2: 78–81. This is so even though the more conservative among the traditionalist party refused to accept even the limited ancillary role al-Shāfiʿī conceded to legal reasoning.

76. Schacht, *Origins*, pp. 284, 286.

77. Ibid., pp. 4–20, esp. 16.

78. Coulson, *History*, pp. 53–61.

79. Ec. & S.: 813–14.

80. Schacht, *Introduction*, p. 5.

81. S. Kalberg, "Max Weber's Types of Rationality: Cornerstones for the Analysis of Rationalization Processes in History," *American Journal of Sociology* 85, no. 5 (1980): 1155, 1161.

82. W. Schluchter, *The Rise of Western Rationalism: Max Weber's Developmental History* (California University Press, 1981), pp. 87–99.

83. Ec. & S.: 857. Weber uses the expression in the phrase "patrimonial substantive rationalism," which is rightly said not to provide much stimulation for formal legal thought.

84. J. Schacht, "Zur soziologischen Betrachtung des islamischen Rechts," *Der Islam* 22 (1935): 215.

85. Schacht, *Origins*, p. 97.

86. Goldziher, Z.: 215–17, 232.

87. Ibid., 2: 249–50.

88. Ibid., 2: 234.

89. Ibid., 2: 140–41.

90. Ec. & S.: 816.

91. Schacht, *Origins*, pp. 95, 102.

92. Ibid., p. 71.

93. Coulson, *History*, p. 82.

94. Schacht, *Introduction*, pp. 74–75.

95. W. Ullmann, *A Short History of the Papacy in the Middle Ages* (London, 1972), p. 162.

96. Schacht, *Introduction*, pp. 77, 84.

97. In Christianity, where, owing to the existence of the Church, canon law did not become a "jurists' law," the mixture of legislative and moral considerations resulted in a much smaller loss of distinctness between the ethical and the legal (Ec. & S.: 829).

98. Goldziher 2: 48; Coulson, *Conflicts*, pp. 58–60.

99. Ibid., pp. 63–64; *History*, p. 125. No written or circumstantial evidence was admitted, and there was no cross-examination of the witness.

100. Schacht, "Zur soziologischen Betrachtung," p. 222.

101. Coulson, *History*, pp. 123, 128–29, 132–33. The exception that proves the rule is the Mālikī school in Morocco and the West. It was unique among the schools in attaching importance to practice. The Mālikī qadis have played a role in public law (justified by their doctrine of *siyāsat al-sharʿiyya*) and have had coercive power. The power of the governors' temporal tribunals (*maẓālim*) have been correspondingly more restricted (Coulson, *History*, pp. 144–47; M. Khadduri and S. Liebesney, eds., *Law in the Middle East* [Washington, 1955], pp. 260–61).

102. S. H. Nasr and M. Mutahhari, "The Religious Sciences," *The Cambridge History of Iran* (Cambridge, 1975), 4:472.

103. Troeltsch, pp. 80–81 and n.35d. Centuries later this typical sectarian process repeated itself among the Moravian Brethren until 1500, when the sect developed a more positive attitude toward the world, the state, and courts of law (ibid., p. 368).

104. U. Kafi, chapter on *qaḍā*; Calder, p. 71.

105. *Nihāya*:304; cf. Lambton, *State and Government in Medieval Islam*, p. 252.

106. Calder, pp. 62–69.

107. L. Binder, "The Proofs of Islam: Religion and Politics in Iran," *Arabic and Islamic Studies in Honor of Hamilton A. R. Gibb* (Leiden, 1966), pp. 122–38.

108. Calder, pp. 78–80, 101–5.

109. Ec. & S.:784–88.

110. Calder, chap. 7.

111. Dh. U. Sh.:2–3.

112. Dh. U. Sh.:xxxii, 606; Brunschvig, p. 210: Certain specific practical problems were excepted. With regard to these, *ijtihād* was considered valid.

113. Dh. U. Sh.:xxxi, 519ff.

114. Dh. U. Sh.:810–11.

115. Dh. U. Sh.:824, 826.

116. Our discussion of al-Ṭūsī and the critical reaction to his legal system draws heavily on Dr. H. Modarresi Tabatabaʾi's forthcoming *Introduction to Shiʿi Law.*

117. Schacht, "Zur soziologischen Betrachtung," p. 208.

118. R. Ad. 8:73.

119. Modaressi, forthcoming *Introduction to Shīʿi Law.*

120. Dh. U. Sh.:xxxii, 606.

121. G. Scarcia, "Intorno alle controversie tra Uṣūlī e Akhbārī presso gli imamiti," *Revista degli Studi Orientali* 33 (1958):232–34. According to post-Buyid Shiʿism, the *ijmāʿ* constitutes proof of validity of a legal norm only if it is "discovering" (*kāshif*) of the opinion of the infallible Imam and not per se. On the other hand, the opinion of the Imam by itself constitutes *ijmāʿ*. This nugatory interpretation disposes of the principle of *ijmāʿ* in reality despite its formal retention.

122. Madelung, "Authority in Twelver Shiʿism," p. 168.

123. D. U. Sh.: Gorjī's *Introduction*, pp. v–vi.

124. K. Nq.:84. J. Calmard, "Le Chiisme imamite en Iran a l'époque seldjoukide d'après le *Kitāb al-Naqḍ*," in *Le monde iranien et l'Islam* 1 (1971):43–67. Random enumerations of the occupations of the Imāmīs in four passages of K. Nq. by the Sunni opponent of the author (in which adjective and pejorative terms at times appear instead of identification of the profession) yields the following list focusing on the lower ranks:

Profession	*Number of times referred to*
Military (at the service of the state or retinues in private armies)	5
Cobbler	3
Weaver	2
Hatter	2
Local land-owning notables	2
Tanner	1
Unidentifiable	1

(K. Nq.:296, 474, 583, 648; Calmard, p. 53. Calmard incorrectly interprets the term *kiyākān*, which I have rendered as "local land-owning notables," to mean "peasants").

In response, the author points to the more elevated professions occupied by the Shiᶜites (K. Nq.:475; Calmard, p. 54). Again, the military profession—strongmen of the city quarters, commanders, and generals—features prominently. To these are added the *ᶜulamāʾ*, the notables (*sayyids*), and the dignitaries of various cities, and high government functionaries and viziers.

125. A. Bausani, "Religion in the Saljuq Period," in J. A. Boyle, ed., *The Cambridge History of Iran* (Cambridge, 1968), 5:293–94.

126. Iqbāl, *Khāndān*; L. Massignon, *La Passion de Ḥusayn Ibn Manṣūr Ḥallāj*, new ed. (Paris, 1975), 1:351ff.

127. Laoust, *Schismes*, pp. 74, 166; Madelung "A Treatise," pp. 18–19.

128. Madelung, Lectures on History of Shiᶜism; Laoust, *Schismes*, p. 223.

129. Iqbāl, *Tārīkh-e Mughul*, pp. 185–89.

130. Calmard, pp. 58–59.

131. *Rāḥat al-Ṣudūr*, Muhammad Iqbal, ed. (London, 1921), pp. 31–33.

132. al-Ḥurr al-ᶜĀmilī, *Amal al-Āmil*, Sayyid Aḥmad al-Ḥusaynī, ed. (Baghdad, 1965–66/1385Q), 2:201.

133. Rashīd al-Dīn Faḍl Allāh, *Jāmiᶜ al-Tawārīkh*, B. Karīmī, ed. (Tehran: Iqbāl, n.d.), 2:715.

134. On Ibn Ṭāwūs, see R. Strothmann, *Zwölferschiᶜa* (Leipzig, 1926).

135. Iqbāl, *Tārīkh-e Mughul*, p. 504.

136. W. Madelung, HISHĀM b. al-ḤAKAM, EI² 3:497.

137. Al-Yaᶜqūbī, *Tārīkh*, M. Th. Houtsma, ed. (Leiden, 1883), 2:551.

138. See above, p. 57.

139. Al-Yaᶜqūbī 2:500.

140. The topics under which the traditions of the Imams are systematically compiled in *Uṣūl al-Kāfī* are instructive in showing the range of concerns of the religious scholarship of the period which is in turn illustrative of the type of religiosity it tended to cultivate. It is significant that before the topic of the "unity of God" (*Tawḥīd*) which is dealt with in the third book of the *Uṣūl*, Kulaynī includes two books containing traditions dealing with reason and knowledge. The first is entitled the "Book of Reason and of Ignorance," where the latter is presented as the primordial obstacle to salvation. The second, the "Book of the Virtue of Knowledge," stresses the relevance of knowledge to salvation.

The fourth book, the "Book of the Proof [or Evidence, of God]," deals with imamate along the lines indicated above; the Imam is the proof (evidence) of God to mankind. The fifth book, the "Book of Faith and Infidelity [Unbelief]" deals at great length with the issue of faith, and elaborates, through the arrangement of the appropriate traditions, an ethic of brotherly love amongst the community of the faithful. A shorter space is allotted to the treatment of unbelief (*kufr*) and its manifestation, the enumerated categories of sin. These two books form the bulk of *Uṣūl al-Kāfī* and its most important part. The sixth book, the "Book of Prayer," deals with devotional piety; "The Prayer is the Weapon of the Faithful [Believer]" (4:21: ان الدعا سلاح المؤمن). Finally, there are two brief books, on the excellence of the Qurʾan and on society/livelihood (*al-ʿIshra*).

141. Troeltsch, p. 82.

142. Madelung, "Imamism and Theology," in *Shiʿisme*.

143. R. Mottahedeh, *Loyalty and Leadership in an Early Islamic Society* (Princeton, 1980), pp. 149–50.

144. Weber, *Ancient Judaism*, pp. 392–94. Al-Kulaynī was greatly concerned with about the dangers of accepting remuneration for judging, and even al-Ṭūsī considered unpaid judging more meritorious. See Calder, pp. 74–76.

145. Troeltsch, pp. 159, 259–62. Melanchton's acceptance of natural law for Lutheranism proceeds along comparable lines (ibid., p. 536).

146. Modarresi, forthcoming *Introduction to Shiʿi Law*.

147. Cited in translation by McDermott, p. 282.

148. W. al-Qadi, "An Early Fatimid Political Document," *SI* 48 (1978):71–108, esp. 79–80.

149. E. Kohlberg, "The Development of the Imāmī Shiʿi Doctrine of *Jihād*," *ZDMG* 126 (1976):78.

150. Ibid., pp. 66–69.

151. *Nihāya*:293.

152. A. K. S. Lambton, "A Nineteenth-Century View of *Jihād*," *SI* 32 (1970):181–83; Shar. Is., 3:109–36.

153. *Muʿtaqad al-Imāmiyya*, M. T. Dānish-pajūh, ed. (Tehran, 1961/1339), p. 340.

154. *Nihāya* 1:302.

155. Ibid., p. 303.

156. Ibid., p. 302.

157. *Mukhtaṣar*:143.

158. Dh. U. Sh.: introduction, vi.

159. McDermott, p. 283.

160. Madelung, "A Treatise," pp. 22, 24–25.

161. Ibid., pp. 22–29. It should be noted in passing that Calvin's view on the ethical merits of active participation in official positions is quite similar to al-Murtaḍā's political ethic. See Troeltsch, p. 600.

162. *Nihāya*:305.

163. *Nihāya*:358. Note that the identical phrases used to describe the ethically proper discharge of authority by the ruler and by the holder of office on his behalf leave no room for doubt. Al-Ṭūsī is referring to an actual ruler and not the Imam as Lambton and Calder claim. Lambton and Calder do not differentiate, as they should, between al-Ṭūsī's use of the phrases *sulṭān al-ḥaqq*, which refers to the Hidden Imam, and *sulṭān al-ʿādil* or *sulṭān*

al-waqt, both of which refer to actual rulers. I have sought to do so by rendering the former as the "true sovereign" and the latters as the "just ruler" or the "ruler of the time."

164. "As regards the tyrannical ruler, when a person knows or thinks probable that, owing to the undertaking of office on his [i.e., the tyrannical ruler's] behalf, it is possible to attain the implementation of the *ḥudūd* and the commanding of the good and the forbidding of the reprehensible, the distribution of religious taxes and charities to those entitled to them, and that there is nothing in all this to disturb [the observance of] an incumbent [duty] . . . it is commendable that he proceed to undertake office on their [i.e., the brethren's] behalf"[179] (*Nihaya*: 358. Cf Lambton's translation, *State and Government in Medieval Islam*, p. 255).

165. Shar. Is. 2: 138–39.

166. *Mukhtaṣar*: 279; Shar. Is. 4: 68.

167. K. Nq.: 45.

168. Ibid., p. 504. Elsewhere, Qāḍī ᶜAbd al-Jalīl mentions the prophecy of a poet at the time of the Sixth Imam to the effect that the Turks will aid the victory of the Mahdi at the end of time (p. 511).

169. Ibid., e.g., p. 7.

Chapter 2

1. A. H. Zarrinkoob, "Persian Sufism in Historical Perspective," *IS* 3 (1970): 177.

2. Murtazavi, pp. 98–102.

3. The term *ghuluww* ("extremism") is used to denote dogmatically undisciplined extremist religiosity. I do not intend to imply any historical or ideological connection between the various religio-political movements of the post-Mongol period and the early Shiᶜite *ghulāt*.

4. C. Cahen, "Le problème du Shiᶜisme dans l'Asie Mineure turque preottomane," *Shiᶜisme*: 126.

5. See I. P. Petrushevsky, *Islām dar Irān*, Persian trans. by K. Keshāvarz (Tehran, 1971–72/1350), chap. 13.

6. Murtazavi, p. 87.

7. Mīr Ẓahīr al-Dīn Marᶜashī, *Tarīkh-e Ṭabaristān va Rūyān va Māzandarān*, M. H. Tasbiḥī, ed. (Tehran, 1966/1345); I. P. Petrushevsky, *Kishāvarzī va Munāsibāt-e Arḍī dar Īrān-e ᶜAhd-e Mughul*, Persian trans. of *Zemledelie i agrarnie otnosheniya v Irane XIII–XIV vekov* by K. Kishāvarz (Tehran 1976–7/1355), pp. 909–17 (henceforth, Petrushevsky).

8. Marᶜashī, pp. 166ff, 182–83, 185, 187, 192, 201–2.

9. Petrushevsky, pp. 828–32.

10. J. M. Smith, Jr., *The History of the Sarbidar Dynasty, 1336–1381* A.D., *and Its Sources* (The Hague/Paris, 1970), p. 133.

11. M. M. 2: 365.

12. Petrushevsky, pp. 877–80; Smith, p. 133.

13. Petrushevsky, pp. 891–92.

14. Petrushevsky, pp. 895ff.; Smith, pp. 146ff.

15. Smith, pp. 55–56. An apocalyptic tradition reported from the Eleventh Imam concerning the eventual *parousia* of his son relates: "Indeed God will hide His friend (*walī*)

from the people and conceal him from his slaves, and no one shall see him until Gabriel brings forward his horse for him . . ." (cited by Sachedina, p. 82). The practice of saddling a horse for the Hidden Imam in Kashan in the early 13th century is reported by Yāqūt; Ibn Baṭūṭa reports the same in Ḥilla in the mid-14th century.

16. It is interesting to note that innovating extensions of the scope of the sacred law is usually achieved by breaching the principle of the axiological supremacy of the traditions. The Shahīd is reported to have written the *Lumᶜa* secretly in seven days, constantly fearing to be caught in the act by the Sunni *ᶜulamā'* of his acquaintance (*Amal al-Āmil* 1:183; editorial note 1). The story illustrates the fact that in practice major advances in law finding occur without meticulous examination of the traditions and thus in disregard of a cardinal axiological principle of the traditionalist value-rationalism of Shiᶜite jurisprudence.

17. Cited in Calder, p. 82.

18. Cited in Calder, p. 162; emphasis added.

19. A. Bausani, ḤURŪFIYYA in *EI*² 3:600; H. Algar, ASTARABĀDĪ, Fazlollāh, *Encyclopedia Iranica*, forthcoming.

20. E. G. Browne, "Further Notes on the Literature of the Ḥurūfīs and Their Connection with the Bektāshī Order of Dervishes," *JRAS* (1907):541–42.

21. A. Bausani, *Persia religiosa* (Milan, 1959), p. 364.

22. Bausani, ḤURŪFIYYA, p. 601; E. G. Browne, "Some Notes on the Literature and Doctrines of the Ḥurūfī Sect," *JRAS* (1898); R. Tevfiq, "Etude sur la religion des Ḥourūfis," in C. Huart, ed., *Textes persans relatifs à la secte des Ḥourūfis* (London, 1909); and H. Ritter, "Die Anfange der Ḥurufisekte," *Oriens* 7 (1954):1–54.

23. E. G. Browne, *Literary History of Persia* (Cambridge, 1924), 3:365–75; Petrushevsky, pp. 322ff.

24. See Browne, "Some Notes," pp. 81–82.

25. Browne, "Further Notes," p. 541.

26. Ḥurūfī verse cited and translated by Browne, "Some Notes," p. 65.

27. Ritter, pp. 25–28.

28. M. J. Mashkūr, *Tārīkh-e Tabrīz tā Pāyān-e Qarn-e Nuhum-e Hijrī* (Tehran, 1973–74/1352), p. 692; Petrushevsky, pp. 323–24.

29. Algar, ASTARABĀDĪ, Fazlollāh.

30. R.J.J.J. 1:478–81.

31. Mashkūr, *Tārīkh-e Tabrīz*, p. 698. See Qurᵓan 32:17 for the connotation of *qurra aᶜyunin* as eschatological recompense.

32. R. M. Savory, "A 15th Century Safavid Propagandist at Harat," in D. Sinor, ed., *American Oriental Society, Middle West Branch: Semi-Centennial Volume* (Bloomington, 1969); Browne, *Literary History of Persia* 3:473–75; Mīrkhwānd, *Rawḍat al-Ṣafā* (Tehran, 1960/1339), 4:692–94.

33. For the Ismāᶜīlīs, see M. G. S. Hodgson, *The Order of Assassins: The Struggle of Early Nizari Ismāᶜīlīs Against the Islamic World* (The Hague, 1955).

34. R.J.J.J. 2:583.

35. This point is not adequately stressed by Molé.

36. M. M. 2:148, 583.

37. R.J.J.J. 2:250. Qāḍī Nūrullāh concurs on the fairly passive role of Nūrbakhsh: "He called Sayyid Muhammad Nūrbakhsh Mahdi and Imam" (M. M. 2:144).

38. Molé, pp. 132–33.

39. Nūrbakhsh: 151.
40. M. M. 2: 146.
41. Nūrbakhsh: 73–77.
42. Reproduced in R.J.J.J. 2: 583–584.
43. Molé, p. 136.
44. This is borne out by the *ḥadīth*: "The *Sharīʿa* is my words, the *Ṭarīqa* my action, and *Ḥaqīqa* my status."
45. Nūrbakhsh. The jurists are disdainfully referred to in such terms as the "people of the exterior" (*ahl-e ẓāhir*) or the "shallow scholars" (*ʿulamā-ye qishrī*).
46. M.M. 2: 147.
47. See A. Kasravī, *Tārīkh-e Pānṣad Sāla-ye Khūzistān*, 3rd ed. (Tehran, 1951/1330), pp. 1–52, 313–18; and V. Minorsky, "MUSHAʿSHAʿ," *EI Supplement* (1937).
48. Cited in Petrushevsky, *Islām dar Īrān*, p. 381.
49. Kasravī, p. 34, 313, 317–18.
50. H. S. 4: 496–97; *Ross Anon.*: 147a–b.
51. Minorsky, p. 162; Kasravī, pp. 74–75.
52. M. M. Mazzaoui, *The Origins of the Safavids: Shiʿism, Sufism and the Ghulāt* (Wiesbaden, 1972), pp. 66–67.
53. See P. Wittek, *The Rise of the Ottoman Empire* (London, 1938).
54. Mazzaoui, pp. 54, 56, 62–63.
55. *Silsilat al-Nasab*, Iranschahr, ed., pp. 50; cited by J. Aubin, "Shah Ismāʿīl et les notables de l'Iraq persan," *JESHO* 2 (1959): 46.
56. G. Sarwar, *History of Shah Ismāʿīl Sefavi* (Aligarh, 1939), pp. 23–24.
57. A. Kasravī, *Shaykh Ṣafī va Tabārash* (Tehran, 1977 [1944]), p. 40.
58. Mazzaoui, p. 72.
59. V. Minorsky, "Persia in A.D. 1478–1490," *An Abridged Translation of Faḍlullāh B. Ruzbihān Khunjī's Tārīkh-i ʿĀlam-ārā-yi Amīnī* (London, 1957), p. 63.
60. *Tārīkh-i ʿĀlam-ārā-y Amīnī*: بعوض قلم بر کتاب جلیل شمشیر بر کلاب اردبیل راندی
61. *Tārīkh-e ʿĀlam-ārā-ye Amīnī*, unpublished edition: خلفای پدر از هر سو بدو رو آوردند و دعوای الوهیت او را بشهادت سفاهت آشکار کردند. شیخ زاده را وفور طاعت مردم روم بر کسب اخلاق مذموم و اطوار مشئوم باعث آمد.

I am grateful to Professor John Woods for kindly putting this edition at my disposal.
62. Minorsky, *Persia in* A.D. *1478–1490*, pp. 65–67.
63. I. Melikoff, "Le problème Kizilbaš," *Turcica* 6 (1975), esp. pp. 58–61.
64. V. Minorsky, "The Poetry of Shāh Ismāʿīl I," *BSOAS* 10 (1942): 1049a.
65. T. Akh., III reproduced as f. 243(a) in facsimile in O. A. Efendiev, *Obrazovanie Azerbaidzhanskogo gosudarstva Sefevidov* (Baku, 1961):

بروانجات مشتمل بر استحضار منتظران ظهور آن اعلی حضرت که مقدمه
حضرت صاحب الزمان است بهر جانب رفت.

66. *Ross Anon.*: ff. 18(b), 43–45, 64(b), 71(a), 74(b) 87(a), 128(b), 140(b), 232(a). See also E. Glassen, "Schah Ismāʿīl, ein Mahdi der Anatolischen Turkmenen?" *ZDMG* 121 (1971): 61–69.
67. Melikoff, p. 65.
68. Minorsky, "Poetry," p. 1026a.

69. Ibid., pp. 1048a–1049a. The last phrase of verse 5 has been repeated to render the emphasis of the original; otherwise Minorsky's translation.

70. A comparison with Sunni *ghazā* bears this out. As both the Ottoman and the Safavid Empires were born out of *ghāzī* principalities, such a comparison is highly instructive. Wittek outlines the clear traces of a ceremony of investiture in which the frontier ruler is granted the title of *ghāzī*. In the course of such a ceremony, the shaykh of the Mevlevī dervish order designated the emir of the house of Aydin as the "Sultan of the *ghāzīs*," giving him a war club which the emir laid on his head and said: "With this club I first subdue all my passions and then kill all enemies of faith" (Wittek, p. 39). In this situation the *ghāzī* leader enjoyed the charisma of the warlord, and sought divine blessing from the shaykh, who possessed hieratic charisma and dispensed it in the name of Islam. This made the Islamic "political ethic" operative as a normative force regulating the conduct of the frontier warriors. According to Inalcik, "by God's command the *ghazā* had to be fought against the infidels' dominions. . . . According to the *Sharīʿa* the property of the infidels, captured in these raids, could be legally kept as booty, their country could be destroyed and the population taken into captivity or killed. The actions of the ghāzīs were regulated by the *Sharīʿa* to which they paid heed." The early Ottoman sultans attached the greatest importance to their reputation as *ghāzīs*. After the establishment of the Ottoman Empire, "they claimed to succeed the Prophet and the Patriarchal Caliphs as 'the best of *ghāzīs* and the fighters of the Holy War'" *(Cambridge History of Islam* 1:269, 290, 320). Thus an explicit item of the political ethic of Islam gave birth to a highly effective principle of legitimacy.

Let us consider a very different example of Sunni *ghazā*, taken from the history of islamization of eastern Afghanistan in 1580s: the *ghazā* of the Sunni Darvīsh Muḥammad of the Naqshbandī order, as documented by the chronicle of his campaigns, *Ṣifat-nāma-ye Darvīsh Muḥammad Khān-e Ghāzī* (ed. G. Scarcia [Rome, 1965]). Here, even though the warlord (*pahlavān* [hero]) is at the same time the divinely inspired dervish, the Islamic influence is fully operative. The *ghāzī* hero (the *pahlavān*) is in no way privileged by direct contact with God. He obtained his supernatural valor by soliciting God's succor, i.e., by entreaties and supplications (*taḍarruʿ va iltimās*) during daily and special prayers (*namāz, duʿā va munājāt*). We are told: "The *pahlavān* (hero) sought succour from God (may He be exalted and praised) and from the indwellers of the tombs, and set out to fight the unbelievers" (ibid., p. 55). His followers were enjoined to wage holy war; if they die they go to paradise, as "*ghāzīs* and martyrs (the fallen in the Holy War) are accepted by God" (ibid., pp. 36–37), and because "whoever dies in *ghazā* will attain eternal happiness and eternal life and all his past sins will be effaced and forgiven" (G. Scarcia, "Dal ms., 'Egerton 1104' del 'British museum,' etc.," *AION* 14, no. 2 (1964):242–43).

In the case of Darvīsh Muḥammad Khān-e Ghāzī, despite the fusions of the military and hieratic charisma, the transcendence of God is preserved and the autonomy of his revealed normative order unimpaired.

Chapter 3

1. Hocart, pp. 60–61, 72, 97, 142–49.
2. H. Frankfort, *Kingship and the Gods* (Chicago, 1948, 1978), pp. 3, 6, 51, 158, 231, 239–40.

3. Hocart, pp. 80, 82.

4. A. R. Johnson, *Sacral Kingship in Ancient Israel* (Cardiff, 1955); S. Mowinckel, "General Oriental and Specific Israelite Elements in the Israelite conception of the Sacral Kingdom," *La Regalita Sacra*, pp. 283–93; Parker, p. 6.

5. A. R. Johnson, "Hebrew Conceptions of Kingship," in S. H. Hooke, ed., *Myth, Ritual and Kingship* (Oxford, 1958), pp. 205–9.

6. Ibid., pp. 234–35. According to Johnson such eschatological orientation was already discernible at the time of Davidic kingdom.

7. H. A. R. Gibb, *Studies on the Civilization of Islam*, S. J. Shaw and W. R. Polk, eds. (Boston, 1962), p. 45.

8. Troeltsch, pp. 145–46.

9. N. H. Baynes, "Eusebius and the Christian Empire," *Byzantine Studies and Other Essays* (London, 1955), pp. 168–72.

10. E. Barker, *From Alexander to Constantine* (Oxford, 1956), pp. 369–95; emphasis added. Furthermore, kingship is an imitation of divinity just as ordinary men are imitators of kingship (ibid., p. 366).

11. Ibid., pp. 478–79.

12. W. Ensslin, "The Government and Administration of the Byzantine Empire," chapter 20 of *The Cambridge Medieval History. IV: The Byzantine Empire* (Cambridge, 1967), part 2, p. 8.

13. S. Runciman, *Byzantine Theocracy* (Cambridge, 1977), pp. 37, 159.

14. N. H. Baynes and H. St. L. B. Moss, *Byzantium: An Introduction to East Roman Civilization* (Oxford, 1961), p. 385.

15. G. Tellenbach, *Church, State and Christian Society at the Time of the Investiture Contest* (New York, 1959 [Leipzig, 1936]), p. 29.

16. Reproduced in B. Tierney, *The Crisis of Church and State: 1050–1300* (New Jersey, 1964), p. 13.

17. F. Kern, *Kingship and Law in the Middle Ages*, S. B. Chrimes, trans. (Oxford, 1968), p. 53.

18. J. M. Wallace-Hadrill, *Early Germanic Kingship in England and on the Continent* (Oxford, 1971), pp. 130–31.

19. Kern, pp. 54–56.

20. Ullmann, pp. 188, 211.

21. At least until the advent of Gallicanism, when the quasi-episcopal claims of the Most Christian Kings came to contain uncanonical elements somewhat akin to those contained in the Safavid principles of caesaropapist legitimacy. See Kern, pp. 58–59.

22. A. Basu, "Hindu Doctrine of Divine Kingship," *La Regalita Sacra*, pp. 167–71.

23. L. Dumont, "The Conception of Kingship in Ancient India," *Religion, Politics and History in India* (Paris, 1970), esp. pp. 68, 80, 86.

24. Frankfort, pp. 337–38; R. N. Frye, "The Charisma of Kingship in Ancient Iran," *Iranica Antiqua* 4 (1964): 37–42.

25. A. Christensen, *Les Kayanids* (Copenhagen, 1931), pp. 17–23, 33–35.

26. H. W. Bailey, *Zoroastrian Problems in the Ninth-Century Books* (Oxford, 1970), pp. 2–4, 23–24.

27. Christensen, pp. 21–25.

28. Bailey, pp. 19, 25–26, 29.

29. Benveniste 2:20–21.

30. Cited in G. Widengren, "The Sacral Kingship of Iran," *La Regalita Sacra*, pp. 245–246, 250.

31. Bailey, pp. 30, 48 (source: *Kārnāmak-e Ardashīr-e Pāpakān*).

32. M. Boyce, *The Letter of Tansar* (Rome: Is.M.E.O., 1968), introduction, esp. pp. 14–22.

33. Ibn Isfandīyār, *Nāmeh-ye Tansar*, M. Mīnuvī, ed. (Tehran, 1932–33/1311), p. 8:

عجب مدار از حرص و رغبت من بصلاح دنیا برای استقامت. احکام دین چه دین و ملک هر دو بیک شکم زادند دو سیده [دو بنده]
هرگز از یکدیگر جدا نشوند و صلاح و فساد و صحت و سقم هر دو یک مزاج دارد.

Cf. Boyce's translation, pp. 33–34.

34. R. C. Zaehner, *The Dawn and Twilight of Zoroastrianism* (New York, 1961), pp. 296–99.

35. R. C. Zaehner, *The Teachings of the Magi* (New York, 1976), pp. 85, 89–94. (source: *Dēnkart*.)

36. Zaehner, *Dawn and Twilight*, p. 299.

37. Bailey, pp. 59, 61–63.

38. Widengren, p. 246.

39. J. Duchesne-Guillemin, *Zoroastrianism: Symbols and Values* (New York, 1966), pp. 122–25.

40. M. Weber, *Religion of China* (Glencoe, 1951), p. 28.

41. M. Weber, *The Religion of India* (Glencoe: Free Press, 1958), p. 142.

42. This is the sense of Weber's assertion that the "welfare state" is the legend (read political ethos) of patrimonialism (Ec. & S.: 1107).

43. M. Grignaschi, "Quelques spécimens de la littérature sassanide conservés dans bibliothèques d'Istanbul," *Journal Asiatique* 254 (1966), Arabic text, p. 49, French trans., p. 70.

44. H. Busse, "The Revival of Persian Kingship Under the Buyids," *Islamic Civilization 950–1150*, D. S. Richards, ed. (London, 1973), p. 55.

45. S. Sperl, "Islamic Kingship and Arabic Panegyric Poetry in the Early 9th Century," *Journal of Arabic Literature*, 8 (1977), pp. 21, 24.

46. W. Madelung, "The Assumption of the Title of *Shāhanshāh* by the Buyids and the Reign of the Daylam (*Dawlat al-Daylam*)," *Journal of Near Eastern Studies* 28 (1969); H. Busse, "Persian Kingship," p. 65.

47. A. H. H. O. M. Dawood, "A Comparative Study of Arabic and Persian Mirrors for Princes from the Second to the Sixth Century A.H." unpublished Ph.D. thesis, University of London, 1965, pp. 57–59.

48. A. K. S. Lambton, "Justice in the Medieval Persian Theory of Kingship," *SI* 17 (1962): 101–2, 119; see also A. K. S. Lambton, "The Theory of Kingship in the *Naṣīḥat al-Mulūk* of Ghazālī," *Islamic Quarterly* 1 (1954); F. R. C. Bagley, ed. and trans., *Ghazālī's Book of Counsel for Kings* (London, 1964).

49. Niẓām Al-Mulk, *Siyar al-Mulūk*, H. Darke, ed. (Tehran, 1976), pp. 79–80.

50. *A Mirror for Princes, the Qābūs Nāma by Kai Kā'ūs ibn Iskandar, Prince of Gurgān* trans. and intro. by Ruben Levy (New York, 1951), p. 213.

51. Bagley, p. 15.

52. *Siyar al-Mulūk*, p. 43.
53. Gibb, p. 143.
54. Bagley, p. xl.
55. Naṣīr al-Dīn Ṭūsī, *Akhlāq-e Nāṣirī* (Lahore, 1952), pp. 117–18, 280–81, 302–3, 307–8.
56. E. I. J. Rosenthal, *Political Thought in Medieval Islam* (Cambridge, 1958), pp. 212–14, 216, 220.
57. Cited by J. E. Woods, *The Aqqūyūnlū: Clan, Confederation, Empire* (Minneapolis, 1976), pp. 117–18.
58. Cited in R. Bendix, *Kings or People: Power and the Mandate to Rule* (California, 1978), p. 51.
59. Kern, p. 21; Bendix, p. 25.
60. W. W. Tarn, *Hellenistic Civilization*, 3rd edition (New York, 1961), p. 340.
61. Bailey, p. 40.
62. Procopius, *The Secret History* (Hammondsworth, 1966), p. 90.
63. Mottahedeh, p. 185.
64. Cited by Mottahedeh, pp. 186–87.
65. J.-P. Roux, "L'Origine céleste de la souveraineté dans les inscriptions paléo-turques de Mongolie et de Sibérie," *La Regalita Sacra*, pp. 231–42.
66. Woods, pp. 4–5, 13, 67, 249.
67. E.g. Bagley, pp. 44ff.
68. Kautilya, *Artha-śāstra* in S. Radhakrishnan and C. A. Moore, eds., *A Source Book in Indian Philosophy* (Princeton, 1957), pp. 193–223.

Introduction to Part 2

1. See E. Glassen, *Die fruhen Safawiden nach Qasi Ahmad Qumi* (Freiburg, 1968), pp. 86–91.
2. *Ross Anon.*: ff. 74a–75b, Ah. T.: 61. It was not until the reign of Ṭahmāsp that this book was translated into Persian. See H. R. Roemer, "Problèmes de l'histoire safavide avant la stabilisation de la dynastie sous Shāh ᶜAbbās," *Actes Vᵉ Congres international d'Arabisants et d'Islamisants*, (? , 1970), p. 408.
3. M. M. 2:233–34.
4. B. Scarcia-Amoretti, "L'Islam in Persia fra Timur e Nadir," *Annali della Facolta di Lingue e Letterature Straniere Di Ca'Foscari* 13, no. 3 (1974), p. 69; Aubin, "Notables," p. 55, n. 2.
5. Ḥusayn Vāᶜiẓ Kāshifī, *Futuwwat-nāmeh-ye Sulṭānī*, M. J. Maḥjūb, ed. (Tehran, 1971/1350), pp. 286–87. ᶜAlī and the Sixth Imam, Jaᶜfar al-Ṣādiq, are mentioned in a fabric maker's code (*futuwwat-nāmeh*) probably dating from the fifteenth century. See the "Futuwwat-nāmeh-ye Chītsāzān" in *Rasāʾil-e Javān mardān*, ed. M. Ṣarrāfī, intro. H. Corbin, (Tehran, 1973/1352), p. 226.
6. H. Modarresi Tabatabaʾi, "Dhayl-e chand athar va katība-ye tārīkhī-ye dīgar," *Vahīd*, vi. 5 (1969/1348): 390–91.
7. See the accounts of the conquest of Herat—e.g., *Ross Anon.*: 194bff.; T. Akh., III under the year 916. As is pointed out below in the subsection 4.2 on Sufism (p. 112),

in 1503–4/909 there was a massacre of Sunni Sufis in Fars. In the course of this massacre, the *khaṭībs* (preachers) of Kāzirūn were also killed because of Sunnism (T. Akh., III).

8. See E. G. Browne, *Literary History of Persia* (Cambridge, 1924), 4:52–53.

9. *Ross. Anon.*: 183a. See also f. 270b, H.S. 4:508.

10. T. Akh., III, reproduced as f. 250b in O. A. Efendiev, *Obrazovanie Azerbaidzhanskogo gosudarstva Sefevidov* (Baku, 1961): که در تشیّع او ریب نبود

11. *Ross Anon.*: 113a, 198a; Kh. T.: ff. 102a–103.

12. See E. Glassen, "Schah Ismāʿīl I und die Theologen seiner Zeit," *Der Islam* (1971–72), pp. 254–68.

Chapter 4

1. *Ross. Anon.*: 74a.

2. G. Sarwar, *History of Shah Ismaʿil Safavi* (Aligarh, 1939).

3. R. M. Savory, "The Office of *Khalīfat al-Khulafāʾ* Under the Safavids," *Journal of American Oriental Society* 85 (1965): 497.

4. Narrative: 206.

5. Sarwar, p. 66.

6. Aubin, "Les Notables," pp. 37–81.

7. Tk. M., Minorsky's commentary: 126.

8. Narrative: 223.

9. Aubin, "La politique religieuse des Safavides," in *Shiʿisme*: 239; T. Akh., III (third *ṣaḥīfa*), pages unnumbered; T. Sh. Tp.: 16–17.

10. Kh. T.: 213.

11. Balbi, p. 282.

12. Savory, p. 500.

13. Kh. T.: 265a–266, Nq. A.: 34, Ah. T.: 486–87.

14. Asnad Ab. 1: 125, 2: 17; Falsafī 1: 184–85; H. R. Roemer, *Der Niedergang Irans nach dem Tode Ismaʿils des Grausamen 1577–1581* (Würzburg, 1939), p. 65.

15. This trend is unmistakable. From about the year 1000 A.H. (A.D. 1591–1592) we find the term *ikhlāṣ* (sincerity) and similar terms increasingly coupled with *shāh-sevanī* (e.g., Nq. A.: 288–89, T.A. Ab. 1: 431, 2: 617, 655, 734, 1000; Ab. N.: 109.)

16. T.A. Ab. 2: 882.

17. Falsafī 1: 184–86, 2: 123–27, 407.

18. Falsafī 2: 125–27. In his *Tārīkh-e ʿAbbāsī*, ʿAbbās's astrologer reports that in 1602/1010 an Uzbek guard was brought before ʿAbbās for interrogation in the vicinity of Balkh. "He looked down, did not reply and remained silent. [The executioners] . . . , upon the universally incumbent royal order, ate him alive" (cited by Falsafī 2: 126–27).

19. These include a confessional ceremony (*iʿtirāf*) (Falsafī 2: 407) and the distribution of bread, halva, and sweets among the congregation, in addition to the Sufi service of *dhikr-e jaliy* (the loud *dhikr*) conducted on Friday evenings in the "House of [the confession of] Unity" (*tawḥīd-khāneh*) adjoining the royal palace (Tk. M.: 55; Commentary: 126).

20. Du Mans: 16–17, 86–87. Curiously enough, the word *tāj* means "crown" in Persian.

21. Sanson: 27–29.

22. Aubin, "Politique religieuse," p. 240.
23. R.J.J.J. 1:490.
24. R.J.J.J. 2:159. In addition to the instances of reported eliminations of individual Sufis (e.g., R.J.J.J. 1:481–82, 2:88, T. Hq. 3:119), the effective suppression of Sufism under Ismāᶜīl can be inferred from the following fact. Roughly four times as many Sufis whose date of death is mentioned in R.J.J.J. (written 1582/990) died between 1496/900 and 1536/940, as compared for those who died after 940 or were still alive at the time of writing. (Bear in mind also the well-known longevity of the Sufi shaykhs.)
25. Aubin, "Les notables," p. 58 (source *Ross Anon.*).
26. Savory, "A 15th Century Safavid Propagandist at Harat," pp. 196–97.
27. R.J.J.J. 1:98–104, 214–16, 416–18, 602; Woods, *The Aqqūyūnlū*, p. 153.
28. H. Algar, "The Naqshbandī Order: A Preliminary Survey of Its History and Significance," *SI* 44 (1976): 139.
29. R.J.J.J. 1:214–16.
30. N.B.R.: f. 96b.
31. M. Nw.: section 4, subsection 14.
32. Savory, esp. p. 196.
33. R.J.J.J. 1:472, 476, 602 (notes); Woods, pp. 153, 166; T. Yazici, "GULSHANĪ," *EI*^{2}: 1136–37; B. G. Martin, "A Short History of the Khalwatī Order of Dervishes," in *Scholars, Saints and Sufis*, pp. 279–97.
34. W. Ivanow, "A Forgotten Branch of the Ismāᶜīlīs," *JRAS* 14 (1938): 57–79, esp. 61. Firishteh's biography of Shāh Ṭāhir is cited at length in T. Hq. 3: 134ff; see esp. 136–38. See also M.M. 2:234–37.
35. Asnad Tp.: 73–77.
36. Ibid., p. 101. In a letter to his former teacher, Shams Al-Dīn Khafrī, Ṭāhir expresses the hope to see him in person and continue the discussion orally.
37. T. Hq. 3:149.
38. Falsafī 3:44 (source: *Tārīkh-e Alfī*).
39. R.J.J.J. 2:159, 171, 186, 241–42.
40. T. Hq. 3:164–65.
41. Q. Kh.: 160a.
42. T. Hq. 3:216–19.
43. B. Si.: 194.
44. H. S. 4:611; J. M. 3, part 1: 104ff; T.A. Ab. 1:145; M. M. 2:149.
45. H. S. 4:612.
46. M. M. 2:152–53. We know that a disciple of Shams al-Dīn Muḥammad's in Khurasan was killed by the order of Ismāᶜīl's prime minister, Amīr Najm II (T. Hq. 3:119).
47. M. M. 1:521.
48. H. S. 4:612.
49. T. Akh. III.
50. Ah. T.: 279.
51. Ah. T.: 280. The family feud between Ṭahmāsp's minister, Qāḍī Jahān, and the Nūrbakhshes also appears as an important factor in the suppression of Qavām al-Dīn (Ah. T.: 374).
52. T.J.A.: 292–93; Ah. T.: 279–80; Kh. T.: 121a–122.
53. T.A. Ab. 1:150.

54. Mīrzā Muḥammad Taqī, son of Shāh Ḥisām al-Dīn Nūrbakhshī, held an important land assignment for two or three years, ca. 1656/1065, and his son Mīrzā Shāh Ḥisām al-Dīn is simply mentioned as living in the ancestral home in 1671/1082 (J. M. 3, pt. 1: 106–7).

55. T. Hq. 1:254.

56. T. Hq. 2:322.

57. S. Nafīsī, *Aḥvāl va Ashᶜār-e Shaykh-e Bahāʾī* (Tehran, 1937/1316), pp. 28–46. Despite the subsequent apologetics of the Shiᶜite hierocracy, there can be no doubt about Shaykh-e Bahāʾī's Sufi inclinations, which are fully confirmed by his poetry. See *Kuliyyāt-e Shaykh-e Bahāʾī*, G. Javāhirī, ed. (Tehran, n.d.), esp. pp. 4–7, 16–19, 29–33, 46–47). Nafīsī points out (pp. 51–52, 62–63) that even Bahāʾī's prayer books are permeated with the spirit of Sufi mysticism.

58. Ab. N.: 186, 221; R.S.N. 8:475, 483.

59. The section on the Nūrbakhshī order in Mullā Muḥammad Ṭāhir Qumī's book against the Sufis contains no information whatsoever on the organization or continued activity of the order in the seventeenth century (Tuh. A.: 202–7).

60. T. Hq. 3:163.

61. T. Hq. 3:49ff., 93–99; J. M. 3, pt. 1:47–49.

62. See H. Farzām, "Ikhtilāf-e Jāmī bā Shāh-e Valī," *Nashriyeh-ye Dānishkadeh-ye Adabiyyat-e Iṣfahān* 1 (1964/1343). See also his *Shāh-e Valī va Daᶜvī-ye Mahdavīyyat* (Isfahan, 1969/1348), pp. 23–24.

63. T. Akh. III, *Ross Anon.*, f. 208b; T. Hq. 3:100; J. M. 3, pt. 1:54–56.

64. In 1513/919 (T. Akh. III).

65. T. Hq. 3:100–101; J. M. 3, pt. 1:57, 62–63, 67. ᶜAbd al-Bāqī's son mediated between Ṭahmāsp and his rebellious brother Alqās in 1549/956 (T. Akh. III), and the burial of Ṭahmāsp's favorite sister in 1563–65/971-2 was entrusted to Shāh Nūr al-Dīn Niᶜmatullāh (T. Akh. III; T.J.A.: 299; Ah.T.: 422).

66. Kh. T.: 433a; J. M. 3, pt. 1:62–65; T.A. Ab. 1:145.

67. T. A. Ab. 1:425, 431, 437; J. M. 3, pt. 1:68ff.

68. Nq. A.: 366.

69. Nq. A.: 456–57.

70. J. M. 3, pt. 1:70–73.

71. J. M. 3, pt. 1:72, 76, 84.

72. T. Hq. 3:101.

73. R.J.J.J. 1:165.

74. In 1570, Alessandri mentions a particularly prolonged and ferocious faction fight between the "Nausitai"—presumably Niᶜmatīs—and the "Himicai"—presumably the Ḥaydarīs—who control five and four districts respectively, and whose mutual hatred has lasted over thirty years (Narrative: 224).

75. Falsafī 2:328 (source: *Tārīkh-e ᶜAbbāsī*).

76. Kaempfer: 137–38; Gemelli: 131; T. J. Krusinski, *The History of the Late Revolutions of Persia* (London, 1740), 1:92–93.

77. R.J.J.J. 1:467–68.

78. See p. 197 below.

79. T. A. Ab. 2:910.

80. Olearius: 382–83.

81. Du Mans: 216–17.
82. Sanson: 153–54.
83. A detailed study of R.J.J.J. and other sources is needed for the correct identification of many of the persons named, and especially of their affiliation. Pending the appearance of such a study, and on the basis of a very rough count and impressionistic assessment, table 4N.1 divides the readily identifiable Sufis among persons whose date of death is given into five categories, each category being chronologically subdivided by the year of Ismāʿīl I's death (1524/930).

TABLE 4N.1

	A	B
	d. 900–930[a] 1494–1524	d. 931–980s 1525–1570s
I. Sufis with specified affiliation:		
1. With *sayyids* and local orders.	10	6
2. With large (supralocal) orders only.	6 (or 7)	2
I. Total	16 (or 17)	8
II. Sufis of unspecified affiliation:		
3. Craftsmen and artisans	2 (or 3)	1 (or 3)
4. Literati (calligraphers, painters, scholars, etc.)	6	4 (or 5)
5. Mystic virtuosi	10	5
II. Total	18 (or 19)	10 (or 13)
TOTAL	34 (or 36)	18 (or 21)

a. Permanent exiles are also included among the dead.

The similarity of the underlined totals of affiliated and unaffiliated Sufis in column A confirms my statement regarding the importance of "unaffiliated" Sufis even before the suppression of the orders.
84. This is clearly shown in the following table:

TABLE 4N.2

	A	B
	d. 900–930 1494–1524	d. 931–980s 1525–1570s
I. Shaykhs of Sufi orders	16 (or 17)	2[a]
II. Prominent "unattached" Sufis: craftsmen, "dispossessed" local *sayyids*,[b] literati and virtuosi.	18 (or 19)	16 (or 19)

a. This is an underestimate as the shaykhs of the then surviving Niʿmatullahi order are not represented.
b. Such as the family of the author, the Laleh *sayyids*. In period B, those Sufis who are affiliated to local *sayyids* (represented by the figure in row 1, column B) becomes "unattached" in the second period after the "disestablishment" or suppression of the local orders.

85. T. Hq. 3:158–59, 162; S. J. Ashtiyani, ed., *Anthologie des philosophes iraniens depuis le XVII e siecle jusqu'a nos jours* (Tehran, 1972), I, French introduction (H. Corbin), p. 31.

86. T. A. Ab. 2:851.

87. J. M. 3, pt. 1:506–10.

88. Q. Kh.: 160ff. Twenty-five men of learning and ninety-nine poets are mentioned in the other categories of the eminent men of the period.

89. Glassen, "Schah Ismaᶜil I und die theologen," p. 262.

90. N. Falsafī, *Zindigānī-ye Shāh ᶜAbbās-e Avval* (Tehran, 1960/1339), 1:26.

91. Ah. T.:583.

92. M. B. Dickson, "Shāh Ṭahmāsp and the Uzbeks," Ph.D. dissertation, Princeton (1958), pp. 192–93.

93. J. N. Hollister, *The Shiᶜa of India* (London, 1953), p. 130.

94. H. S. 4:603–18.

95. C. A. Storey, *Persian Literature: A Bio-bibliographical Survey* (London, 1927–39), 1:111.

96. Tk. N.:207–8.

97. T. Bạlbi, "Relazione di Persia, del clarissimo messer teodoro Balbi console veneto nella Siria dell'anno 1578 al 1582," in G. Berchet, *La Republica de Venezia e la Persia* (Torino, 1965), p. 282.

98. Falsafī 1:27–28. Among the sources, the best account—and one may add a highly analytical one—of Ismāᶜīl II's religious policy is to be found in T.A. Ab. 1:213–17.

99. W. Hinz, "Schah Esmāᶜīl II: Ein Beitrag zur Geschichte der Safaviden," *Mitteilungen des Seminars fur Orientalische Sprachen* 26 (Berlin, 1933):77.

100. Kh. T.:339; T. A. Ab. 1:214–16.

101. Kh. 6.:269a; Ah.T.:491–92.

102. T. A. Ab. 1:388.

103. J. Aubin, "Les Sunnites du Lareston et la chute des Safavids," *REI 33* (1965):152.

104. Falsafī 3:36–39. Falsafī also mentioned the massacre of a Kurdish Sunni tribe, the Mukrī tribe, and a number of instances of use of violence against other Sunni communities, but there is no evidence that these were carried out as *religious persecutions*.

105. A. Ḥaqīqat, "Daw farmān-e tārīkhī az dawrān-e ṣafaviyyeh dar masjid-e jāmiᶜ-e simnān," *Vaḥīd* 7, no. 1 (1970):73–74; and H. Modarresi Tabatabaʾi's comments, *Vaḥīd* 7, no. 2 (1970):122–23.

Chapter 5

1. Aubin, "Notables," pp. 37–81.

2. For the reign of Ṭahmāsp, the evidence is compactly gathered in a chapter of T. A. Ab. (T. A. Ab. 1:143–53). For the subsequent period, the information is drawn from Kh. T. and T. A. Ab., especially the obituary notices.

3. H.-R. Roemer, *Staatsschreiben der Timuridenzeit* (Wiesbaden, 1952), fasc. ff. 4b, 7a.

4. Ibid., commentary, pp. 143–46.

5. T. Akh. III: under years 915, 917, 919; *Ross Anon.*: 152a, 208b. See also K. M. Röhrborn, *Provinzen und Zentralgewalt Persiens im 16 und 17. Jahrhundert* (Berlin, 1966), pp. 72–73.

6. In Khurasan, where the military threat of the Uzbeks continued, however, Mīr Muḥammad ibn Mīr Yūsuf held the offices of *imārat* and *ṣadārat* jointly from 921 to 927 (1515–21) (*Ross Anon.*: 292a; H. S. 4:553–54; T. Akh., III).

7. This is clear from Ṭahmāsp's brief description of the functions of the office of the *ṣadr* in his autobiography (T. Sh. Tp.: 3; see also T. A. Ab. 1:144), attesting to the continuity in the Safavid institutional framework with the previous period. Over a century later Du Mans emphasizes the distribution of *awqāf* revenue to the needy and the deserving among the functions of the *ṣadr* (Du Mans: 160). Therefore, Savory's facile but generally accepted assertion that the "prime task [of the *ṣadr*] was to impose doctrinal unity on Persia by the energetic propagation of Twelver Shiᶜism," which was achieved under Ismāᶜīl I, and that its importance declined thereafter (*Cambridge History of Islam* 1:402), is both misleading and untenable. It is misleading insofar as it presents religious propaganda and assurance of doctrinal conformity as the main function of this office. It is true that this function was discharged by Ismāᶜīl's *ṣadr*s on occasion (*Ross Anon.*: 271a; T. J. A.: 278). But the sources in no way support the contention that imposition of doctrinal uniformity was the *ṣadr*'s primary function, nor that it was entrusted to him alone. We have already mentioned that the *ṣadr*s were not typically Shiᶜite theologians, and that they include at least one Sunni. In addition, what should be stressed is the continuity in the functions of the office with the Timurid and Aqqūyūnlū period: management of the religious endowments and the distribution of their revenue among the *sayyid*s and the religious functionaries.

Furthermore, the assertion is completely untenable as regards the alleged decline of the importance of the office. Though there were naturally ups and downs, both the early and the late Safavid sources clearly attest to the continued importance of the office, which in fact was enhanced in the seventeenth century with the steady increase in the volume of religious endowment over a prolonged period of economic prosperity. At the close of the Safavid era, Mīrzā Abū Ṭālib, the *ṣadr* of Suleymān, still ranks as the second, or at worst the third, most highly paid official of the realm (Tk. M.: tr. 86).

8. R. M. Savory, "The Principal Offices of the Safavid State During the Reign of Ismāᶜīl I (907–30/1501–24)," *BSOAS* 23 (1960): 79–83.

9. In 1563–64/971 Mīr Sayyid ᶜAlī Raḍavī Qumī is appointed the administrator of the shrine of Mashhad, *and* the vizier of the realm (Kh. T.: 209). The lack of differentiation of political/administrative and religious/financial functions was especially pronounced in Ardabīl. This is clearly shown by a *farmān* of Shāh Ṭahmāsp cited by "Röhrborn (p. 72). Furthermore, in 1637, the *mutavallī* of Ardabīl is said to have "both spiritual and temporal jurisdiction" (Olearius: 307). Finally, the ten *farmāns* issued by Ṭahmāsp II after the fall of Isfahan (between 1722/1135 and 1726–27/1139) and published by Fragner, clearly show the military (raising of troops), administrative, and fiscal duties of the *mutavallī* of Ardabīl (*Turcica*, 6 [1975]: 177–225).

10. M. Rāvandī, *Tārīkh-e Ijtimāᶜī-ye Īrān*, 2nd ed. (Tehran, 1977), 3:480.

11. Tk. H. L.

12. Chardin 5, chap. 2.

13. This is emphasized by Chardin, who compares the great mosque's administrator (*mutavallī*) to a factory overseer. See Chardin 6:65; also Gemelli: 166. The less important religious functionaries connected with the mosques—the preachers (sing. *vāᶜiẓ*), reciters of the Qurʾan (*qārī*) and of *adhān* (*muʾdhdhin*)—as well as "freelance" *mullā*s are excluded from my account of religious institutions.

14. Asnad Q., p. 26.

15. H. A. R. Gibb and H. Bowen, *Islamic Society and the West* 1, pt. 2, (Oxford, 1957), chaps. 8–12.

16. Sanson: 13, Tk. M. commentary: 111; Chardin 6:49.

17. H. Modarresi Tabataba'i, *Mithālhā-ye Ṣudūr-e Ṣafavī* (Qum, 1974/1353), pp. 21–23.

18. Du Mans: 81.

19. Rāvandī 3:485.

20. Chardin 6:298.

21. See above, p. 120.

22. H.S. 4:603–18; J.M. 3, pt. 1:298–379, 382–90.

23. Astrology, numerology, medicine, and architecture appear as professionalized branches of learning and not so much as the ingredients of the general culture of the literati.

24. Of the thirty-seven persons extracted from H.S., two appear as exclusively religious scholars, and two to have religious expertise in the religious sciences and at least one other branch of learning. The number of the exclusively religious specialists can be put at seven out of a total of some 100 persons mentioned in J.M. In both cases, no specialization is specified for a substantial number of the persons mentioned. It does not seem unreasonable to assume that the outlook of this last group, with no evident specialization, conforms to the general diversified pattern.

25. Q.U.: 204–352.

26. Q.U., R. Ad. and R.J. have been consulted for this purpose.

27. The obituary notices in Ah. T., Kh. T., and T. A. Ab. These are of course less detailed than the previous sources, and relate only to the most eminent of the *ʿulamāʾ*.

28. Column 6 of table 5.4 shows the emergence of a Shiʿite scholarly community in Mecca in the seventeenth century. This community consisted mainly of scholars from Jabal ʿĀmil and Iran (notably Astarābād), and it was there that the Akhbārī movement was launched by Muḥammad Amīn Astarābādī, though not without encountering the opposition of the *ʿulamāʾ* of Jabal ʿĀmil.

29. After becoming the capital of ʿAbbāsʾ's empire, roughly one-half of the total number of the important *ʿulamāʾ* residing in Iran inhabited it (table 5N.1 below). After an initial disproportionately large influx with the founding of the *madrasa*s (see row II of table 5N.1), about the same proportion of immigrants was absorbed by it.

30. Al-Karakī was given supervisory primary over the *shaykh al-Islām*s. The other eminent *mujtahid* of Ismāʿīl's time, Shaykh Zayn al-Dīn, the second martyr (d. 1557–58/965), was *Shaykh al-Islām* of Harat for some two years (from 928 to 930) before returning to Syria (H.S. 4:610). Mīr Sayyid Ḥusayn, the "mujtahid of the age" was the *Shaykh al-Islām* of Ardabīl under Ṭahmāsp (Kh. T.: 224a; T. A. Ab. 1:145). Shaykh ʿAlī Munshār Karakī (d. 1576–77/984) was the *Shaykh al-Islām* of Isfahan (Kh. T.: 249). Mīr ʿAbd al-Ṣamad Ḥusayn al-ʿĀmilī (d. 1576–77/984) was appointed *Shaykh al-Islām* of Harat and of Khurasan (T. A. Ab. 1:156), and his renowned son Bahāʾ al-Dīn ʿĀmilī became the *Shaykh al-Islām* of Isfahan in 1597–98/1006 (T. A. Ab. 1:156; Nafisī, pp. 20–45). Finally, al-Ḥurr alʿĀmilī, arriving in Iran in the last quarter of the seventeenth century, was appointed *Shaykh al-Islām* of Mashhad (*EI*[2]: al-Ḥurr al-ʿĀmlī).

TABLE 5N.1

Date of death	Main residence			
		Resident of Isfahan		
	Iran	Total	from Iran	first-gen. immigrants
I. 907–79	6	1		
1501–72			—	1
II. 980–1050	19	9		
1573–1640			4	5
III. 1051–1100	18	8		
1641–89			7	1
IV. 1101–51	18	9		
1689–1738			7	2

NOTE: this table is a further breaking down of the data of table 5.4.

31. T. A. Ab. 1:157–58; Kh. T.:97, 201.

32. J. M. 3, pt. 1:310–15.

33. Kh. T.:177; J. M. 3, pt. 1:360, 375–76. On the other hand, as evidence of assimilation of the *shaykh al-Islāms* into the hierocracy, the following references may be cited: J. M. 3, pt. 1:307–8, 310–15, 361–63.

34. *Mujtahids* and *pīsh-namāz* of the most important mosques or of the royal household.

35. The above, plus the "clerical estate"—scholars, qadis, *ṣadrs*, administrators of important holy shrines, and powerful provincial *sayyids*.

36. Glassen, "Ismāʿīl und Theologen," esp. pp. 262–63.

37. Cited from a manuscript of T. J. A. in Rāvandī 3:483.

38. *Ross Anon.*: 113(a).

39. Kh. T.: 102(a); *Ross Anon.*: 198(a); *ʿĀlam Ārā-ye Shāh Ismāʿīl*, A. Muntaẓir-Ṣāhib, ed. (Tehran, 1971/1349), pp. 479–81.

40. Kh. T.: 104(a); V.S.A.: 461. The *farmān* restricts religio-legal authority in the provinces to the deputies (*vukalaʾ*) of al-Karakī as the foremost religious authority of the realm. Later anachronistic versions of the *farmān* given in R.J. and reproduced in R. Ad., 5:246, are unreliable.

41. Khj.: 35, 42. On this point, see further section 5.3.2 below.

42. Khj.: 15, 27, 35, 42.

43. Algar, *Religion and State*, p. 23, n. 88.

44. T. Sh. Tp.: 12–13; T.J.A.: 285.

45. See the list of his publications in R. Ad. 5:247.

46. Kh. T.: 136; Ah. T.: 303–4; R. Ad. 4:258–60.

47. T. Akh. III: under year 938.

48. T. Sh. Tp.: 14. This crucial encounter is also reported in other major sources (T. Akh. III; Kh. T.: 135–36; Ah. T.: 304). Emphasis on the word "they" added.

49. T. Akh. III: year 938.

50. Ah. T.: 398.

51. T.J.A.:303; Kh. T.:183a–184.
52. Khj.:96.
53. Q.U.:349.
54. Khj.:102, 144, 146ff, 155–57.
55. Kh. T.:103–103a.
56. R. Ad., 5:247.
57. Khj.:169ff; Q. U.:235.
58. Kh. T.:342a–43; R. Ad. 5:248–49.
59. While stating that all the *ʿulamāʾ* acknowledged his *ijtihād*, the author of T. A. Ab. nevertheless consider Mīr Ḥusayn's self-designation as the "Seal of the Mujtahids" excessive (T. A. Ab. 1:458).
60. Because of the writings on Safavid institutions rely heavily on Tk. M., which was written after the eclipse of the office of *Shaykh al-Islām* resulting from the creation of the office of *Mullā-bāshī*, this fact is not appreciated in the literature. But see Chardin 9:515.
61. R. S. N. 8:439; Chardin 9:481ff; Gemelli:147–48; L. Lockhart, *The Fall of the Safavi Dynasty and the Afghan Occupation of Persia* (Cambridge, 1958), p. 72.
62. See section 5.3.4 below.
63. Troeltsch 2:517–21.
64. Ibn Babūya was said to have been born into this world through a prayer of the Hidden Imam (Corbin, *Islam Iranien* 4:126); and the Imam is said to have written a eulogy in praise of al-Mufīd (Ay. H.:577; M. M. 1:477).
65. T. Hq. 1:273ff. and the references given in the following notes below.
66. Hm. Th.:chap. 2.
67. Q.U.:205ff., 230–31, 233, 236–37, 244ff., 298–99, 303–4.
68. Khj.:1:276.
69. Q.U.:304–5.
70. Z.B.:344. Earlier, the Muqqadas had apparently held the extreme view that *taqlīd* is permissible even in the "Principles of Religion" (*Uṣūl al-Dīn*); V.S.A.:494–95.
71. Z.U.: pages unnumbered; part 4 "*fi'l-ijtihād wa'l-taqlīd*."
72. M.U.:232.
73. U. Kafi 1:68–69.
74. McDermott, *Theology of al-Mufīd*, pp. 257–60.
75. Dh. U. Sh.:797–98.
76. Dh. U. Sh.:801.
77. Dh. U. Sh.:655.
78. Dh. U. Sh.:656.
79. *ʿUddat al-Uṣūl*, a treatise on principles of jurisprudence written by al-Ṭūsī, the last of the three great Shiʿite theologians of Baghdad, contains no discussion of *taqlīd* and the juristic authority of the *ʿulamāʾ*. See its abridged translation and summary by A. Gorjī, in A. Davvānī, ed., *Hizāreh-ye Shaykh-e Ṭūsī* (Tehran, 1970/1349), vol. 2.
80. M. W.:247; T. W.: pt. 12, chap. 3, discussion 2 (pages unnumbered), chap. 4, discussions 2 and 3.
81. Brunsvig, "UṢŪL AL-FIQH imamite," pp. 204, 210.
82. In *Minhāj al-Karāma*, presumably written before his works on the *Uṣūl al-Fiqh*, al-Ḥillī categorically states that the Shiʿites do not accept *raʾy* (personal opinion) and *ijtihād*

(Persian trans. by S. A. Ḥusaynī Chālūsī under the title *Jadhaba-ye Vilāyat*, 2d ed. [Tehran, 1967/1346], p. 25.)

83. T.W.: pt. 12, discussion 1: استفراغ الوسع من الفقيه لتحصيل ظن بحكم شرعي

84. T.W.: pt. 12, chap. 4.

85. M.W.: 243; T.W.: pt. 12, discussion 1.

86. ʿAbduh, p. 205.

87. M. Nw.: IV, no. 20. In fact, they continued down to the present century.

88. Z.U.: pt. 4: الاجتهاد ملكة يقتدر بها على استنباط الحكم الشرعي الفرعي من الاصل

89. M. Din: 236–37.

90. M. Din: 232–33.

91. Z.B.: 343–47.

92. *Mukhtaṣar*: 272–73.

93. Shar. Is., chapter on *Khums*, 1:184. It is only in the sixteenth century that the gloss on the above phrase by ʿAli ibn Zayn al-Dīn, the second martyr, identifies the referent of the phrase as "the just jurist . . . as he is the *nāʾib* of the Imam and His appointee" (*Masālik al-Afham ila Sharḥ Sharāyiʿ al-Islām* [Beirut, 1957], 1:57).

94. Calder, pp. 163–64.

95. See above, p. 000.

96. Calder, pp. 169, 164.

97. Ibid., p. 165.

98. N.B.R.: 94a, 119b–120a.

99. M. Nw.: IV, subsections 19 and 20.

100. N.B.R.: 92a.

101. Modesty is not a characteristic of Mīr Dāmād, of whom it is said that "the spirit of God was his spirit" (*rūḥ allāh rūḥuh*). In his poetry, Mīr Dāmād would state, "I am the king of the realm of knowledge by heavenly armies" (Tk. N.: 149–50), and in his philosophical works he would deign to consider Fārābī and Ibn Sīnā (Avicenna) his partners in instruction of leadership in philosophy. In view of these extravagant claims, his interest in philosophy, and his vague but unusually ambitious interpretation of general vicegerency, in retrospect, it is easy to see him as a forerunner of Rūḥullāh Khumaynī.

102. Cited in the biography of Mīr Dāmād by Ishkivarī in Mīr Dāmād, *Kitāb al-Qabasāt*, M. Muḥaqqiq, ed. (Tehran, 1977/1356), p. 39: فالسلطان العادل و هو الامام المعصوم او من يكون منصوباً من قبله صلوات الله عليه على الخصوص او من له استحقاق ان ينوب عنه سلام الله عليه على العموم

103. Ibid., p. 41.

104. Chardin 5: 194–95.

105. N.B.R.: 94a.

106. و اما الحوادث الواقعة فارجعوا الى رواة حديثنا فانهم حجتي عليكم و انا حجة الله عليكم

107. Hm. Th.: chap. 1.

108. N.B.R.: 119b–120b; M. Nw.: 4, no. 20.

109. Chardin 5: 210.

110. Hm. Th.: esp. chap. 1.

111. Weber, *Religion of China*, p. 142.

112. S. Nafīsī, *Aḥvāl va Ashʿār-e Shaykh-e Bahāʾī*, pp. 19–28.

113. Ibid., pp. 51, 68.

114. S. J. Ashtiyani, ed., *Anthologie des philosophes iraniens depuis le XVIIe siècle jusqu'à nos jours* (Tehran, 1972), 1 (Persian introduction, vii).

115. R. J. (*Tatmim*), 7:120.

116. Madelung, "AKHBĀRIYYA," *EI*[2] *Supplement.*

117. Mullā Muḥsin [Fayḍ] Kāshānī, *Safīnat al-Najāt*, ed. and trans. M. R. Tafrashī Naqūsānī (?, 1976–77/1397), pp. 36–39. Elsewhere Fayḍ accordingly defines the function of the *nā'ib ʿāmm*, who should be virtuous and familiar with the ways of the Imams, as simply directing the layman's attention to the relevant traditions of the Imams (K. Mk.: 104–5).

118. An interesting letter from Shāh Ṭāhir Dakanī to Shāh Ṭahmāsp written at the end of the *Ghuluww* period illustrates the importance of the charisma of lineage in the early Safavid period. He refers to the "harem of imamate" (*ḥaramsarā-ye imāmat*) (Asnad Tp: 74, 76). Writing about the eminent *sayyid*s and *naqīb*s, Qāḍī Aḥmad Qumī adduces a famous *ḥadīth* to refer to them as the assets left by the Prophet among mankind (Kh. T.:366a, text corrupt).

119. *ʿĀlam-ārā-ye Shāh Ismāʿīl*, p. 480.

120. *Faḍā'il al-Sādāt* (Tehran, 1896–97/1314), pp. 113, 359, 428–29.

121. Ec. & S.: 1009.

122. T. Hq. 3:164–65.

123. T. A. Ab. 2:851–52.

124. Hm. Th., written in 1634–35/1044.

125. T. Hq. 3:163–64.

126. Q. Kh.:52.

127. Q. Kh.:156–59.

128. Tk. N.:152. Khwānsārī was also a student of Majlisī the Elder, and of Sulṭān al-ʿulamā' himself (T. Hq. 1:267, 269; 3:164).

129. Ab. N.:256, 321.

130. Ab. N.:254–55, 321; Tk. N.:209–10.

131. Röhrborn, p. 33.

132. Chardin 9:515–18.

133. J.M. 3, pt. 1:506–10. It should be pointed out that both reclusiveness (*gusheh-gīrī*, *ʿuzlat*) and asceticism (*zuhd*, *riyāḍat*) were highly valued, albeit not easily realizable, ideals; that they find incidence not only among the mystics, but also among the learned and the pious in general (J.M. 3, pt. 1:319, 332–33, 342–43, 351–52; T. A. Ab. 2:805).

134. J.M. 3, pt. 1:315–17, 327, 336, 343–51.

135. R.T.S.: 12–28.

136. Q.U.:334–35.

137. F. Rahman, *The Philosophy of Molla Sadra* (Albany, 1975), pp. 224, 236–44.

138. Seh Asl:74, 84–86.

139. Seh Asl:5–7.

140. Seh Asl:7, 36–45. Chardin was to note that the Sufis firmly deny (physical) resurrection (Chardin 4, chap. 11).

141. Seh Asl:6–7, 20, 36, 68; K.A.J.:79, 83, Rahman, pp. 254–62; H. Corbin, *En Islam Iranien* (Paris, 1972), 4:95–105, esp. 96–97.

142. *Kilid-e Bihisht*, S. M. Mishkāt, ed. (Tehran, 1936/1315).

143. Corbin, *Islam Iranien* 4:20.

144. Mullā ʿAbd al-Razzāq Lāhījī, *Gawhar-e Murād* (Tehran 1958/1377, H. Q.).
145. W. Madelung, "ʿABD-al-RAZZĀQ LĀHĪJĪ," *Encyclopedia Iranica*, (forthcoming).
146. Muḥsin ibn Murtaḍā Fayḍ Kāshānī, *Rafʿ al-Fitna*, Central Library of Tehran University, MS no. 3303, ff. 1, 2, 6–7.
147. Du Mans: 60–61.
148. Arb.: 2b, 4a–4b.
149. Arb.: 3b–4a.
150. This is borne out by the inscriptions on his earlier coins. See Kaempfer: 51.
151. R. Ad. 5: 239.
152. Shaykh Jaʿfar is the author of a book entitled *Tuḥfa-ye Sulṭānī dar Ḥikmat-e Ṭabīʿī va Ḥikmat-e Ilāhī* (printed in Tehran, 1960–1/1339), where he attempts to integrate "natural" and "divine philosophy" (comprising the five "principles of religion"). According to Ḥazīn Lāhījī, he had been promised the grand vizierate, but his opponents changed the shah's mind (Tk. H. L.: 33). In his instance, the philosophical outlook can be seen in direct conjunction with the administrative bent.
153. Tk. N.: 168.
154. Sayyid Muḥammad Mahdi Ṭabāṭabāʾī, Baḥr al-ʿUlūm, *Rijāl* (Najaf, 1965/1385), 3: 225–26.
155. Tk. N.: 157.
156. T. Hq. 1: 177–78.
157. R.S.J.: 5. Majlisī also refers the reader to the last volume of the *Biḥār*.
158. F.D.: 767 (serial folio no.).
159. F.D.: 768–69.
160. T. Hq. 1: 178–80, 257–58, 285.
161. Ibid., 1: 280–84.
162. Ay. H.: 233–36, 575–82.
163. Q.U.: 300.
164. T. Hq. 1: 176; Ay. H.: 237.
165. Rāvandī 3: 517. The components of this stereotype include the incorrectly guttural pronunciation of Persian common words, and an exaggerated propensity for the use of *fatḥa* instead of the more congenial *kasra* among the vowels.
166. R.S.N. 8: 493. Both "innovators" (*mubtadiʿ*) and "inventors" (*mukhtariʿ*) are pejorative terms. See also B. Si.: 51–52.
167. Tk. H.L.: 85–86, 189–90, 192.
168. V.S.A.: 540.
169. Ibid., p. 566.
170. S. A. Arjomand, "The Office of *Mullā-bāshī* in Shiʿite Iran, "*SI* 57 (1983): 137–38.
171. Seh Asl: 27, 64, 91. The mulla does not hesitate to use strong words. In one passage, he refers to the worldly orthodox or official *ʿulamāʾ* as those "apes, swine and worshipers of the Worldly Idol [*ṭāghūt*] in the robe of piety and propriety" (Seh Asl: 48).
172. K.A.J.: 110.
173. Ec. & S.: 1175.
174. K.A.J.: 3.
175. Du Mans: 221; Chardin 4: chap. 10.

176. K. Mk.: 9–10.
177. Seh Asl: 84.
178. Ay. H.: 234. Majlisi, like so many other Shiᶜite *ᶜulamāʾ* after him, uses the phrase *ᶜawāmm kaʾl-anᶜām* (masses who are like cattle). Occasionally, the phrase *bal hum aḍallu* (nay, rather they are further astray; Qurʾan, 7: 179) is also added.
179. Ay. H.: 251, 407.
180. R.S.J.: 4; Browne, *Literary History*, 4: 904.
181. F.D.: 721–23, 775–76.
182. Muḥammad Bāqir Majlisī, *Ikhtiyārāt* (?, 1910/1328 Q), pp. 117–18.
183. Lockhart, p. 76; Carmelites 1: 474.
184. Tk. H. L.: 53; B. Si.: 51–52.
185. See also J. Ashtiyani's introduction to Mullā Ṣadrā's *Shawāhid al-Rubūbiyya* (Mashhad, 19667/1347), pp. 117–25.
186. M. Mudarris Chahārdihī, "Āqā Muḥammad Riḍā Saḥbā Qumsheh-ī," *Yādigār* 1 (1946/1325): 77.

Chapter 6

1. Sachedina, pp. 150–51, 168, 171.
2. S. Ṣadr, *Kitāb al-Mahdī* (Tarjuma-ye), Persian trans. by M. J. Najafi (Tehran, 1965/1344), p. 14.
3. A description of these events, i.e., the reign of total chaos and tyranny, the appearance of the *Dajjāl* (Antichrist) and of Sufyānī, the return of Imām Ḥusayn and Jesus Christ, and so on, is given in H. Yq.: 333–68.
4. Chardin 7: 456–57. See also Gemelli: 154.
5. Chardin 9: 144. An indication of the prevalence of mildly apocalyptic expectations is found in Du Mans: 59. Corruption of judges and disobedience of children are interpreted as signs of the approaching end of time.
6. K. Gh.: 261–62; Sachedina: 156.
7. K. Nq.: 500.
8. Ay. H.: 152. It should also be noted that book 6 of *Ḥaqq al-Yaqīn* on Resurrection (*Maᶜād*) follows immediately upon the section on the return of the Mahdi, beginning with "physical resurrection," "the suffering of the people of cruelty and mischief by the physical fire," and the entry of "the people of faith" into "physical paradise" (pp. 368–83). Just over a century later, the return of the Mahdi was to be termed the "Lesser Resurrection" as distinct from the "Greater Resurrection" in the other world. See below, p. 000.
9. Du Mans: 57.
10. K. Gh.: 277.
11. Concluding section of book 1 of H. Yq.: 334–35; Ṣadr, pp. 270–74.
12. M.M. 1: 78–79.
13. H. Yq.: 331ff.
14. Ht. Q.: 5–6.
15. H. Yq.: 301–2.
16. Du Mans: 58; Q.U.: 106, 299, 322; R. Ad. 4: 480.
17. H. Corbin, "Pour une morphologie de la spiritualité shiᶜite," *Eranos Jahrbuch* 29 (1960): 82. Potential *ghuluww* is thus sublimated; gnostic Shiᶜism obviates the need for chiliasm.

18. H. Modarresi Tabataba'i, "Dō risāla dar Sayr va sulūk: Āqā Muḥammad Bīdābādī," *Vaḥīd* 11, no. 4 (1973/1352): 14.
19. Ec. & S.: 490–92.
20. Ec. & S.: 1175–76.
21. E. G. Browne's translation. The phrase "friends of God" has been substituted for Browne's "saints" in the second verse (*Literary History*, 4: 175–77; Persian text ibid., pp. 173–75).
22. V.S.A.: 448.
23. N.B.R.: 104(b)–105(a), 125(b), 126(b).
24. M.M. 1: 78–79.
25. Hm. Th.: chaps. 1 and 5; pages unnumbered.
26. Laoust, "Critique du Sunnisme," pp. 40ff.
27. Hq. Y.: 154–278.
28. Mrt. A.: 22a.
29. Olearius: 244–46, 322; Chardin 6: 302: "On voit des imamzadés partout," Kaempfer: 132–35.
30. Chardin 5: 2.
31. Du Mans: 73.
32. Mullā Muḥammad Ṭāhir Qumī, *Shish Risāla-ye Fārsī*, ed. M. J. Ḥusaynī Urmavī (Tehran, 1960–61/1339), pp. 3–15, 48–73, 318–19.
33. Ibid., p. 316.
34. In *Ḥaqq al-Yaqīn*, prophecy also receives little attention. Even then we are told not so much about the function and necessity of prophecy (as in al-Ḥillī's *Bāb*) as about the miracles of Muhammad: that he was shadowless, that no bird flew over his head and no fly or mosquito sat upon him, that he could see ahead and behind, that "the seal of prophecy was placed upon his august back, and the light radiating from it was greater than the light of the sun" (pp. 26–27), etc.
35. H. Yq.: 154–278, 368–534.
36. Ay. H.: 152.
37. Ay. H.: 403.
38. Ay. H.: 403–23; Zd. M.
39. The editions used for the above tables 6.1 and 6.2 are as follows: Kulaynī, *al-Kafī, Furūʿ* (Tehran, 1957/1377Q), 4: 184–380 on Ḥajj, 4: 548–89 on Ziyārāt; Ibn Babūya, *Man la yaḥḍuruhu 'l-faqīh* (Tehran 1970/1390 Q), 2: 196–344 on Ḥajj, 2: 345–83 on Ziyārāt; al-Ṭūsī, *al-Istibṣār* (Najaf, 1956/1375Q), 2: 139–336 on Ḥajj; al-Ṭūsī *Tahdhīb al-Aḥkām* (Najaf 1960/1380Q), 5: entire on Ḥajj, 5: 2–119 on Ziyārāt; al-Ṭūsī, *al-Nihāya* (Beirut, 1970/1390Q), pp. 202–68 on Ḥajj; Majlisī, *Biḥār al-Anwār* (Tehran, 1968/1388Q), 99: entire on Ḥajj, 100: 101–455, 101 and 102: entire on Ziyārāt; al-Ḥurr al-ʿĀmilī, *Wasāʾil al-Shīʿa* (Beirut, 1971/1391Q), 8 and 9: entire on Ḥajj, 10: 1–234 on Ḥajj, 10: 235–470 on Ziyārāt.
40. This direct substitution is confirmed by a series of revealing rhetorical questions Majlisī addresses to the Sufis in Ay. H. when he asks the hypothetical Sufi whether in the hereafter he would make the Mullā-ye Rūmī (Jalāl al-Dīn) the intercessor (*Shafīʿ*), or whether he would take a refuge with Muḥy al-Dīn (Ibn ʿArabī). See Ay. H.: 578.
41. Ht. Q.: 38; cf. D. M. Donaldson's translation in *The Shiʿite Religion* (London, 1933).
42. Tk. N.: 66, 114, 117.

Chapter 7

1. H.Q.:22, 184–86. In the transmission of the sacred lore, very little is actually discarded but the relative salience of propositions is constantly altered through accretions and commentaries. In the (unfinished) volume 3 of *Ḥayāt al-Qulūb* on imamate, Majlisī does reiterate al-Ḥillī's statement quoted above (p. 38) in a brief section, but the tenor of the book as a whole in no way suggests a political conception of imamate. It is significant that in the section devoted to interpretation of the verses of the Qurʾan "entrusting knowledge, charity and the meteing out of justice [*qisṭ va mīzān*] to the rule [*vilāyat*] of the Imams"—which would clearly have political implications—the otherworldly connotations are unmistakable: the Imams administer justice in the other world.

2. Zd. M.:480, 497. The believer will be brought out of his grave and resuscitated for that purpose when necessary.

3. Falsafī, pp. 17–20.

4. Q.U.:270.

5. Asnad Q.:87–88.

6. Lambton, "Nineteenth-Century View of *Jihād*," p. 185; Algar, *Religion and State*, p. 22.

7. Arjomand, "Religion, Political Action and Legitimate Domination in Shiʿite Iran," pp. 96–97.

8. Muḥammad ibn ʿAbdul-Ḥusayn al-Ḥusaynī, *Faḍāʾil al-Sādāt* (Tehran, 1896–97/1314 [1691–92/1103], p. 96. The publisher wrongly attributes the authorship of the book to Mīr-Dāmād.

9. *Faḍāʾil al-Sādāt*, p. 96; cf. Q.U.:235.

10. Ay. H.:503.

11. Chardin 5:2, 219–20.

12. The use of the term "esoteric," chosen by Corbin, to refer to the Shiʿite *ʿirfān* of this period is unsatisfactory; and I have therefore employed the term "gnostic Shiʿism." The term "esoteric" seems best reserved for mystery religions of the Ḥurūfī type, esoteric Ismāʿīlī cosmologies and the like. Shiʿite *ʿirfān* of the seventeenth century is a different type of phenomenon.

Let us take a book with an apparently esoteric title: Mullā Muḥsin Fayḍ's *Kalamāt-e Maknūneh* ("The Hidden Words"), whose title, to concede even more, has a numerological value corresponding to the year of its composition (K. Mk.:221). It certainly is an eloquent hymn to pantheism, but it uses no "esoteric" symbology. The words are used unambiguously, and the arguments constructed as rationally as possible, even though the mystical experience of pantheistic unity is attempts to evoke is neither attainable nor fully apprehensible by means of discursive reason alone. As for the numerological/astrological references contained in the book, it should be pointed out that these do not distinguish *Kalamāt-e Maknūneh* from other literary and philosophical works of the period, as they permeate the world view and culture of premodern Iran.

A fortiori, the term is much less applicable to the rational philosophical system of Mullā Ṣadrā, which is no more "esoteric" than those of, say, Hegel or Heidegger. In fact, in his attack on popular mysticism, Mullā Ṣadrā firmly rejects the *shaṭḥiyyāt* (the ecstatic utterances of the Sufi shaykhs, often compiled by their disciples) on grounds of their cryptic ambiguity (especially in K.A.J.).

13. H. Corbin, "Imamologie et philosophie," in *Shiʿisme*, p. 165. Emphasis added.

14. Ibid., p. 167.

15. Mullā Muḥsin Fayḍ, *Risālāt: Tarjumāt al-Ṣalāt, Ulfat-nāmeh, Āʾineh-ye Shāhī* (Shiraz, 1941/1320), p. 5 (pages numbered separately for each tract).

16. Troeltsch, p. 810.

17. Ibid., p. 563. However, the differences between Shiᶜite and Lutheran mysticism are equally interesting. For Lutheranism, mystical love pours itself into existing forms of human life, including the state (ibid., pp. 525, 529). By contrast, *social* arrangements, including the state, are nowhere endowed with a comparably strong accent of ontological reality. Rather, the accent of ontological reality is placed on the entire cosmos whose most significant termini are the macrocosm—constellation of astral bodies and the subject of the science of astronomy—and the microcosm—the constitution of the self and the subject of the science of psychology. In Fayḍ's *Mirror*, the social order is typically *not* endowed with much significance. For gnostic Shiᶜism, psychology and astronomy in particular and rational philosophy in general are the means for the cognitive penetration of the cosmos and attainment of inner light, after which religious texts could be hermeneutically comprehended. Thus, the attitude of gnostic Shiᶜism to religious texts invites another comparison, this time to the Jewish mysticism of the cabala, where Rabbi Simeon of the *Zohar* prototypically *opens* the verses of the Scripture and where the words of sacred texts "must be infinite, or, to put it in a different way, the absolute word is as such meaningless, but it is *pregnant* with meaning" (G. Scholem, *On the Kabbalah and Its Symbolism* [New York, 1965], p. 12; see also p. 30). For gnostic Shiᶜism, it is the gnosis of origin and destination (*mabdaᶜ* and *maᶜād*) that guarantees the correct hermeneutical comprehension, and therefore opening, of the sacred texts.

18. M. T. Dānish-pajūh, "Dāvarī miyān-e pārsā va dānishmand," *Nashriyeh-ye Dānīshkadeh-ye Adabiyyāt-e Tabrīz* 9 (1957/Summer 1336): 127–28.

19. Tk. N.: 156.

20. J. Ab.: 137–38.

21. Du Mans: 79. Chardin bases his account of the Shiᶜite religion on extensive translations from the *Jāmiᶜ* (Chardin 6:326–496, 7:1–246).

22. J. Ab.: 161–62.

23. Ibid., pp. 150–61.

24. A. Munzavī, *Fihrist-e Kitābhā-ye Fārsī* (Tehran, 1970/1349), 2:18.

25. Ay. H.: 499–501.

26. Ay. H.: 489–92. In his emphasis on justice, his reference to paternal benignity, and in stating that "the kingdom may even last with infidelity [*kufr*], but it will not last with injustice [*ẓulm*]," Majlisī is drawing extensively on the patrimonial theories of kingship.

27. Ay. H.: 505–6.

28. Cited by Lambton, *State and Government in Medieval Islam*, p. 283.

29. Nq. A.: 41, Kh. T.: 255a–256, 304a. According to the latter source, Mīr Sayyid ᶜAlī on both occasions.

30. See note 70 to chapter 5 above, p. 304.

31. Cited by Lambton, *State and Government*, pp. 279–80.

32. Chardin 9:483–91. On this occasion, the *shaykh al-Islām* was Mīrza ᶜAlī Riḍā. The second coronation, when Suleymān actually took that name instead of his original name of Ṣafī II, took place some two years later in 1668/1079. Muḥammad Bāqir Sabzavārī delivered the *khuṭba* and gave the king the new name of Suleymān (Chardin 10:92–95).

33. Ravandi 3:485.

34. L. Lockhart, *Nādir Shāh* (London, 1938), pp. 107–8.

35. See appendix 3 to H. Modarresi Tabataba'i, "*Kharāj* in Shī'ī Law," D. Phil. thesis, University of Oxford, 1982.

36. Sourdel, p. 196.

37. See above p. 97, and Woods, p. 151 and note, p. 264.

38. *Mihmān-nāmeh-ye Bukhārā*, M. Sotoudeh, ed. (Tehran, 1962/1341), see esp. the conclusion, pp. 354–56.

39. Röhrborn, p. 24.

40. Quoted in Minorsky, introduction to *Tadhkirat al-Mulūk*, p. 13. It should be pointed out, however, that the claims to legitimacy put forward to the sedentary majority were different (and much more moderate). In a *farmān* issued by Ismā'īl in 1521/917, two Qur'anic verses (2:118 and 38:25) are adduced to prove the legitimacy of his reign, and his descent from the "house of *vilāyat*" (God-ordained sovereignty [of 'Alī]) and imamate is emphasized. A *farmān* issued on the following year bears the seal "sufī-ye kāmil" (the perfect Sufi). Scarcia-Amoretti has noted the change of emphasis on the type of charismatic legitimation of Ismā'īl's leadership reflected in the later references to him as a *sayyid-e ḥusaynī* (descendant of the Prophet through Ḥusayn) rather than as a *shaykh-oghlū* (son of the [Sufi] shaykh; Scarcia-Amoretti, pp. 82–83). This change also corresponds to the extension of his domination over the sedentary population of Iran.

41. *Memoirs of Shāh Ṭahmāsp* (Calcutta, 1912).

42. N.B.R.:99–100; M. Nw., section 4, subsection 15; Nq. A.:522.

43. See R. M. Savory, "The Safavid State and Polity," *IS* 7 (1974):179–212.

44. Kh. T.:304a.

45. Chardin 9:474–77.

46. T. A. Ab. 2:1077–79.

47. Olearius:402.

48. Cited by Lambton, "A 19th-Century View of *Jihād*," *SI* 32 (1970):184.

49. Lambton, "Justice," p. 118.

50. T. Akh. III; Kh. T.:187a; Nq. A.:283.

51. Nq. A.:387.

52. Ah. T.:236; Kh. T.:93a, 259: مخالفة الملوک عار فی العاجل و نار فی الآجل

53. Kh. T.:108b, 366–366a.

54. T. A. Ab. 2:1099–116.

55. T. Akh.; E. Glassen, *Die Fruhen Safaviden*, pp. 126–27.

56. Brown, *Literary History* 4:354.

57. T. Akh., Ṣahīfa III, first f.

58. *Ross Anon.*:19(b), 64(b).

59. T. Akh. III, fourteenth f.: سلطنت آخرالزمان بآن اعلی حضرت مخصوص است

60. T. J. A.:281; Kh. T.:66a.

61. Arb.: 12a, 27b, 177b.

62. E.g., T. A. Ab. 1:379 and 2:762, 916, 919; A. Sh.:1.

63. The epithet al-Mūsawī (i.e., descendant of Mūsā al-Kāẓim) was deployed after al-Ṣafavī throughout the Safavid period (Kasravī, *Shaykh Ṣafī va Tabārash*).

64. Z. T. A. Ab.:60

65. Asnād Q.: 52–53.

66. N.B.R.:120b: بل تعظمونه غاية التعظيم حتى تعتقدوه مرشداً كاملاً وقطباً واصلاً .

67. According to Sanson, the king claims to be the "Head of their Religion." The Persians believe "he can neither be Damn'd or Judg'd whatever crimes he commits . . . because they believe he can never Sin" (p. 11). In another passage, Sanson again stresses that the Persians are "prepossessed and bigoted with the Infallibility of the Prince" (p. 97). Kaempfer confirms this general belief in the infallibility of the ruler, pointing out that it is defended by some of the *mullās* (Kaempfer: 15–16).

68. Chardin 5:215–16.

69. See p. 186 below.

70. Chardin 5:216. On this point Chardin is fully corroborated by Du Mans's slightly earlier account (Du Mans: 162) and by Kaempfer, a decade or so later (Kaempfer: 125–28).

71. Cited by H. Enayat in *Modern Islamic Political Thought* (London, 1982), p. 173.

72. Du Mans: 162.

73. Arb.: 9b–10a.

74. R. J. Perry, "The Last Safavids, 1722–1773," *IRAN* 9 (1971): 67.

Chapter 8

1. E.g., Asnad Tp.: 508–9; Nq. A.: 460–61, 502.

2. Asnad Tp.: 508–12.

3. A. Sh. Tp.: 136–37.

4. Ṭahmāsp decided to give up wine drinking despite the insistence of his entourage that it was one of the necessities of kingship (T. Sh. Tp.: 29–30).

5. Kh. T.: 98a; see also T.J.A.: 302 and Rohrborn, p. 70.

6. Asnad Tp.: 513–14.

7. T. Akh. III, twenty-second f.

8. Kh. T.: 329.

9. Asnād Ab. 1: 118–19.

10. Röhrborn, p. 70; Asnād Ab. 1: 118–19.

11. Ah. T.: 396.

12. Kh. T.: 225.

13. Ab. N.: 218–19.

14. Ec. & S.: 1010–15.

15. Nq. A.: 151.

16. Falsafī 4: 21–25. In T. A. Ab. 2: 760–62, the value of ʿAbbās's property is estimated at 100,000 *tūmāns*, producing an equal revenue of 7,000.

17. T. A. Ab. 2: 1004–5.

18. Ab. N.: 80–81, 94.

19. Her will is reproduced in Kh. T.: 202–3.

20. Asnad Tp.: 343–49.

21. Lockhart, p. 48. The *madrasa* is at present known as Madrasa-ye Chahār Bāgh.

22. Kh. T.: 146; Ah. T.: 313.

23. Ab. N.: 71–72.

24. Lockhart, pp. 38–39.

25. Hm. Th.: esp. chap. 5.

26. Aubin, "Les Sunnites de Larestan," p. 156.

27. Lockhart, pp. 70–79.

28. Q. U.: 205; *A Chronicle of the Carmelites in Persia and the Papal Mission of the XVIIth and XVIIIth Centuries*, anonymously edited (London, 1939), Carmelites, 2: 473–74. It is important to note that, with the establishment of the Shiʿite hierocracy, the initiator of a major religious policy is for the first time not the monarch guided mainly by "reason of state," but the hierocracy in pursuit of its doctrinal interests. That the weak Shāh Sulṭān-Ḥusayn did not initiate this religious policy, is borne out by the evidence of his lenient and more favorable disposition toward religious minorities after Majlisī's death (ibid.: 522, 558).

29. V.S.A.: 531–32.

30. Muḥammad Mahdī Iṣfahānī, *Niṣf-e Jahān fi Taʿrīf al-Iṣfahān*, M. Sotudeh, ed. (Tehran, 1961/1340 [1891/1308 H.Q.]), pp. 185–86; Lockhart, pp. 70–79.

31. T. Hq. 1: 179.

32. Chardin 4: 11.

33. Q.U.: 205, 323; Lockhart, *The Fall of the Safavi Dynasty*, p. 38. The details of this suppression are obscure and need further research.

34. Mj. T.: 25: Shaykh Bahāʾ al-Dīn, a plaintiff against early Afghan depredation from Khurasan was expelled from Isfahan, accused of Sufism; similar accusations were leveled against a number of literati (Tk. H. L.: 52–53).

35. Mj. T.: 49–50.

36. Narrative: 206.

37. *Ross Anon.*: 69b, 231a, 232a.

38. Falsafī 2: 125–26, n. 3 (source *Rawḍat al-Ṣafaviyya*).

39. E.g., in Ah. T.: 352, in connection with the third Georgian *ghaza* of 1552/958 we read: و اهل و عیال و اموال و اسباب بارث شرعی از مقتولان به قاتلان انتقال نمود. Emphasis added.

40. M. Nw. IV: no. 16.

41. J. Ab.: 161. While it is explicitly stated that the wives and children of those against whom *jihād* is waged because they rebel against the Imam cannot be appropriated, no similar explicit statement is made regarding the sons and wives of the People of the Book, but their appropriation is justified by clear implication of the more general statements (ibid., pp. 153–55, 159–61).

42. Kh. T.: 330, 331; Nq. A.: 152.

43. Nq. A.: 151. See also T. A. Ab. I: 291.

44. T. A. Ab. 2: 1106.

45. Chardin 5: 261–62.

46. T. Mk.: 3.

47. H. Inalcik, "Land Problems in the Ottoman Empire," *Muslim World* 45 (1955): 221–28.

48. Khj.: 19–20, 32.

49. Khj.: 32; emphasis added.

50. Khj.: 33–34: ولا يجوز لمن عليه الخراج ... سرقته ولا جحوده

51. Khj.: 176.

52. Khj.: 180, 185.

53. N.B.R.: 120b–121b. A fuller discussion of the tracts on *kharāj* is now available in W. Madelung, "Shiʿite Discussions on the Legality of the *Kharāj*," in *Proceedings of the*

Ninth Congress of the Union Européennes des Arabisants et Islamisants, R. Peters, ed. (Leiden, 1981), pp. 193–202.

54. In addition to Khj., this rate is given in a *farmān* of 1526/932 (Asnad Tp.: 509) and referred to in N.B.R.: 120b.

55. Asnad Tp.: 22–23.

56. Kh. T.: 242–242a.

57. Rāvandī 3: 159.

58. Chardin 6: 54–55.

59. Röhrborn p. 63.

60. Du Mans: 89, 124; Chardin 6: 82–84.

61. Chardin 6: 93.

62. Du Mans: 38.

63. Chardin 5: 280, 6: 75, 96; Röhrborn, p. 63.

64. Ec. & S.: 843–45.

65. E.g., Röhrborn, p. 63, n. 380.

66. Ec. & S.: 843–44, 856.

67. A. Sh. Tp.: 138 (18).

68. Chardin 5: 265, 281–82.

69. Röhrborn, p. 67, no. 405 (source T. A. Ab.); Chardin 5: 273–80.

70. J. Ab.: 360–65.

71. Röhrborn, p. 69.

72. Chardin 6: 98.

73. Röhrborn, p. 62.

74. Chardin 6: 107, 117–18.

75. Sanson: 16.

76. Asnad Q.: 54–56.

77. Nq. A.: 113–16.

78. Nq. A.: 119.

79. Nq. A.: 118–20; Kh. T.: 301, 309, 317a; T. A. Ab. 1: 261, 272–74.

80. T. A. Ab. 1: 275.

81. T. A. Ab. 2: 952–53; Falsafī 3: 52–53.

82. Z. T. A. Ab.: 83–84; Olearius: 324. Some eight years later, an unfortunate baker who, "on account of his resemblance to Darvīsh Riḍā had become his successor," and had gathered a following was hanged by the order of Shāh Ṣafī (Z. T. A. Ab.: 241).

83. T. Hq. 3: 157–58 (based on *Tārīkh-e Firishteh*).

84. S. Kiyā, *Nuqṭaviyān ya Pasīkhāniyān*, *Irān kūdeh*, 13 (Tehran, n.d.), esp. pp. 74–75.

85. Nq. A.: 515.

86. Kiyā, p. 36 (source *Tārīkh-e Alfī*); Falsafī 3: 43–45.

87. Nq. A.: 516–17; T. A. Ab. 1: 474.

88. See the testimony of a Nuqṭavī "trustee" who had migrated to India to the author of the *Dabistān al-Madhāhib* (reproduced in Falsafī 2: 48) as well as the account of ʿAbbās I's astrologer (reproduced in Kiyā, p. 42).

89. Falsafī 3: 48–49.

90. Nq. A.: 518–22; Falsafī 2: 340–342.

91. T. A. Ab. 1:476; Falsafī 3:47; Nq. A.:523–24; Kiyā, pp. 40–41.
92. Nq. A.:565–66.
93. Du Mans:47–88.
94. Ec. & S.:1161.
95. S. Runciman, *The Byzantine Theocracy* (Cambridge, 1977), p. 145; the little-studied *faki* movement in the Ottoman Empire.
96. Sanson:16.
97. Ab. N.:131.
98. Ab. N.:249–50.
99. Chardin 6:58–84.
100. Chardin 5:216–18.
101. See note 95 above.
102. Nq. A.:192–193. These men were chanters of the iniquities of ᶜAlī's enemies (and, presumably, also ᶜAlī's virtues): *tabarrāʾī*.
103. Rāvandī 3:488.

Chapter 9

1. Troeltsch 1:100.
2. Frankfort, p. 342.
3. Parker, pp. 20–21.
4. C. J. Friedrich, *The Philosophy of Law in Historical Perspective*, 2nd ed. (Chicago, 1963), p. 36.
5. Runciman, p. 27.
6. *Essays*:327; Ec. & S.:1168–70.
7. Tellenbach, p. 164.
8. Madelung, "The Assumption of the Title of Shāhanshāh," p. 84.
9. U. Kafi 3:405–7.
10. Cited by S. D. Goitein, *Studies in Islamic History and Institutions* (Leiden, 1966), p. 206.
11. Ibid., pp. 206–7; *Iḥyāʾ ᶜUlūm al-Dīn* (Cairo, 1967/1387 Q.), 2:181–94.
12. *Iḥyāʾ* 2:438: افضل الجهاد كلمة حق امام سلطان جائر
13. *Tibyān* 2:236–37; Mj. B. 5:202–3.
14. Z. B.:685.
15. Ibid., p. 686.
16. Ibid., p. 687.
17. H. Sh.:18. The entire treatise is on imamate and the vilification of the rightly guided caliphs. It illustrates the use made of the doctrine of imamate, particularly in the form of ᶜAlid legitimism, as a utopian substitute for a theory of authority.
18. Q.U.:260, 281.
19. Ay. H.:502–4.
20. V.S.A.:554.
21. Ibid., pp. 555, 565.
22. Ibid., p. 536.
23. H. S.:609–10.
24. J. M. 3, pt. 1:310, 333–34.

25. R. Ad. 8:77.
26. J. Ab.:348. The term used is *ḥākim ẓālim* and not *sulṭān jā'ir*.
27. Ibid., pp. 353–54, 357, 360–64, 370, 373.
28. Ibid., pp. 351–52.
29. M. Nw.: IV, no. 20.
30. Tk. N.:145.
31. Chardin 6: 91–92. *Guh mīkhurī* (you eat shit) is said to be his typical manner of swearing.
32. Du Mans:172–75.
33. Ec. & S.:813.
34. Du Mans:16–18, 21.
35. Chardin 6:71–73.

Conclusion to Part 2

1. See Gibb and Bowen, *Islamic Society and the West* 1, pt. 1, pp. 26–38.

Introduction to Part 3

1. R. Shaᶜbānī, "Siyāsat-e Madhhabi-ye Nādir," *Vaḥīd* 7, no. 9 (1970):1137.
2. Lockhart, *Nādir Shāh*, p. 278.
3. J. Hanway, *An Historical Account of the British Trade over the Caspian Sea* (London, 1753), 4:218–19.
4. Malcolm 2:50–51; A. K. S. Lambton, *Landlord and Peasant in Persia* (Oxford, 1953), pp. 131–32.
5. Iṣfahānī, pp. 256–57.
6. Hanway, p. 127.
7. A. Iqbāl, "Vathīqa-ye ittiḥād-e islām-e nādirī," *Yādigār* 4, no. 6 (1947):43.
8. Lockhart, p. 151; Shaᶜbānī, p. 1153 (source: Mj. T.). According to contemporary Dutch sources which are being edited by Dr. Willem Floor, Nādir had forbidden the Muharram ceremonies by May 1734, and issued an order that the names of the rightly guided caliphs be pronounced in the *khutba*. I am grateful to Dr. Floor for this information.
9. Iqbāl, "*Vathīqa*," pp. 44–45.
10. Ibid., pp. 45–53; ᶜAbdullāh ibn al-Ḥusayn al-Suwaydī, *Mu'tamir al-Najaf* (Cairo, 1973–4/1393).
11. Iqbāl, "Vathīqa," pp. 53–56.
12. Al-Suwaydī:50ff.
13. Iqbāl, "ᶜĀqibat-e kār-e Nādir Shāh," *Yādigār* 2, no. 2 (1945):41, 43.
14. J. Hanway, *The Revolutions of Persia* (London, 1753), 2:130–31.
15. J. R. Perry, *Karīm Khān Zand: A History of Iran 1747–1779* (Chicago, 1979), pp. 220–22.
16. Algar, *Religion and State*, p. 33.
17. S. Nafīsī, *Tārīkh-e Ijtimāᶜī va Siyāsī-ye Īrān* (Teheran, 1956/1335), 1:51.
18. Mrt. A.:31ff.
19. Algar, *Religion and State*, pp. 33ff, 45, 47, 51, 63.
20. A. Iqbāl, "Muḥammad Ḥusayn Khān Marvī," *Yādigār* 2, no. 6 (1946):74–80.

21. Rāvandī 3:510.
22. Algar, *Religion and State*, pp. 52–53.
23. A useful summary of the above-described trends is provided by table I.1.
24. Browne, *Literary History* 4:391–401.
25. Gibb and Bowen, chaps. 9, 13.
26. Malcolm 2:316.
27. For a description of the parasite social position of the *sayyid*s in the Qājār period, see Rāvandī 3:511–12.

Chapter 10

1. For a discussion of these principles of legitimacy, see Woods, p. 182.
2. Nādir's letters to the Ottoman caliph and other authorities were published in Turkey under the title of *Sūret Nāmei Humāyūn* (n.d.).
3. Al-Suwaydī, p. 53.
4. Perry, *Karīm Khān Zand*, pp. 215–17.
5. Ibid., pp. 1–8; Mj. T.:90–97, 114–38. The view that legitimate rulership belongs to the religious doctors irrespective of Safavid descent also appears to have gained currency.
6. Ec. & S.:1147.
7. A. K. S. Lambton, "Some New Trends in Islamic Political Thought in Late 18th and Early 19th Century Persia," *SI* 40 (1974):116–18, 128.
8. Mrt. A.:52a; emphasis added. The crucial phrase is the following: اجراء اوامر و نواهی بعلاوه تفویض الحق از جانب پادشاه دین پناه بایشان مفوض شد
9. Lambton, "*Jihād*," p. 189; J. Langeh-rūdī, *Tārīkh-e Ḥuqūq-e Īrān*, (Tehran, n.d.), p. 22, n. 1.
10. ʿAbd al-Razzāq Dunbulī, *Maʾāthir-e Sulṭānīyya* (Tabriz, 1825–26/1241), p. 145-bis.
11. *Kitāb al-Jihādiyya* (Tabriz, 1818/1233), pages unnumbered: (20), i.e. twentieth page.
12. Ibid., (53).
13. *Munshaʾāt-e Qāʾim Maqām-e Farāhānī* (Tehran, n.d.), pp. 199–200. Note that the phrase "the *shāhanshāh* of the world *and of religion*" implies an overlap of religious and political authority in favor of the king. The fact underlying this overlap was that no conceptual distinction could be made between Islam as religion or culture and the Islamic community as society or an independent social order. For implications of this lack of differentiation, see pp. 251–252 below.
14. For the biography of Sayyid Jaʿfar Kashfī see R. Ad. 5:60–62.
15. The *Tuḥfat al-Mulūk* commissioned by Prince Muḥammad Taqī Mīrzā and dedicated to Fatḥ ʿAlī Shāh is a comprehensive treatise on "reason and ignorance" or a compendium of all branches of knowledge and includes a chapter on political theory (*siyāsat-e mudun*). I have used a sumptuous illustrated edition of the book published in 1857/1273 in Tehran. The pages were unnumbered in this edition, but have been given numbers below.
16. Th. M.:123a.

TABLE I.1 Geographical Distribution of the Prominent Shiʿite *ʿUlamāʾ* of the Post-Safavid Period[a]

	Main residence							
Date of death	Iran	of whom: Isfahan	Tehran	Other	Arab Iraq	Bahrain	India	Total[b]
Afshār period	2				—	—	—	2 (2)
1738–57		1	—	1				
Zand period	1				—	1	—	2 (2)
1757–76[c]		—	—	1				
Zand/Qājār	2				2	—	—	4 (4)
1776–95		1	—	1				
Qājār period								
1796–1816	1				5	—	—	6 (6)
		1	—	—				
1816–35	9				7	1	2	19 (16)
		5	2	2				
1835–54	7				3	—	—	10 (9)
		2	1	4				
(1855–74)	7				3	—	3	13 (12)
		3	2	2				

a. SOURCES: R. J. and its "supplement" (*tatim*), the *Aḥsan al-Wadīʿa* by Muḥammad Mahdī al-Kāẓimī, Najaf, 1968/1388 [1929/1348].

b. A total of five cases of double entry have had to be made. The figures in parentheses indicate the absolute number of persons.

c. The apparent overlap of the period is due to the fact that the Christian and not the *hijrī* dates are given.

17. Ibid.

18. Ibid., f. 123b.

19. R. Ad. 5:60.

20. Th. M.: 122a.

21. In this case *niyābat* is said to be *ʿāmma* because the *ḥadīth* is issued *bar vajh-e ghaybat* (Th. M.: 126b). *Niyābat-e ʿĀmma* is general *only* in the sense that it does not devolve on a special (*khāṣṣ*) person specifically designated by the Hidden Imam himself; "public" or "collective" would be a more accurate rendering of *ʿāmma*.

22. Because the instructions are issued to him *bar vajh-e khiṭāb* (ibid.).

23. Th. M.: 126b.

24. In an earlier passage too, Kashfī substantiates his argument in favor of the necessity of sovereignty by citing ʿAlī's words to this effect addressed to the dissident Kharijites (Th. M.: 122a).

25. Th. M.: 124a–26a.

26. Hollister, *The Shiʿa of India*, p. 130.

27. R.-Q. Hidāyat, *Rawḍat al-Ṣafā-ye Nāṣirī* (Tehran, 1960–61/1339), 9:318–19, 379.

28. Afshār, ed., *Rūznāmeh-ye Khāṭirāt-e Iʿtimād al-Salṭana*, p. 596.

29. I. Taymūrī, *ʿAṣr-e Bīkhabarī yā Tārīkh-e Imtiyāzāt dar Īrān* (Tehran, 1953–54/1332), p. 124.

30. Faḍl Allāh Nūrī, ed. *Suʾāl va Javāb* (Bombay, 1893), pp. 61–62. For a more elaborate statement of the theory of the two powers with the explicit derivation of the authority of the ruler from Imamate, see *Kitab-e Huquq-e Duval va Milal*, Tehran, 1895/1312 Q., pp. 49–59.

31. See Gobineau's letter for 20 September 1857 to Tocqueville. A. de Tocqueville, *The European Revolution and Correspondence with Gobineau*, J. Lukacs, ed. and trans. (New York, 1959), pp. 314–17.

32. M. H. Iʿtimād al-Salṭana, *al-Maʾāthir waʾl-Āthār* (Tehran, 1888), p. 137.

33. Ay. H.: 499–501.

34. I. Ṣafāʾī, ed., *Asnād-i Nō-yāfteh* (Tehran, 1971/1349), pp. 39–46, 142–43, 209.

35. Arjomand, "Office of *Mullā-bāshī*," pp. 144–45.

36. *Jihādiyya*, p. (46).

37. Lambton, *Landlord and Peasant*, pp. 139–40.

38. *Jihādiyya*, pp. (49–50).

39. Lambton, *State and Government*, pp. 247–48, 287; J. Ab.: 102; *Wasāʾil al-Shīʿa* 6:337–64; Q.U.: 193.

40. M. U. II; esp. section "fi bayān jawāz al-taqlīd va ʿadam wujūb al-ijtihād ʿaynan"; pages unnumbered; Q. Usul: 355ff.

41. Q. Usul: 392–412, 429–30; M. U. II.

42. A.-Q. Gorjī, "Nigāhī be taḥavvul-e ʿilm-e uṣūl," *Maqālāt va Bar-rasī-hā* 13–16 (1973–74/1352); published separately by the faculty of divinity, University of Tehran as pamphlet 10; idem, "Taḥqīqī dar qiyās-e istinbāṭ," *Maqālāt va Bar-rasī-hā* 21–22 (1975/1354): 24. The topic does not even appear in Anṣārī's practical *risāla*, published in Tehran in 1875–76/1292. The topic was occasionally treated in the later books on *uṣūl*, but chiefly reappears in the *Risālāt ʿAmaliyya* (collection of practical rulings) of the *mujtahids*.

43. Scarcis, "Intorno . . ." p. 237.

44. Mullā Aḥmad Narāqī, *ʿAwāʾid al-Ayyām* (? Tehran, 1903/1321), pp. 151, 185ff.
45. Shaykh Muḥammad Ḥasan Najafī, *Jawāhir al-Kalām*, 6th ed. (Najaf, 1956–80/1377–1401), 21:394–99.
46. Gorji, "Taḥqīqī . . ." p. 19.
47. A. Iqbāl, "Ḥujjat al-Islām Ḥajj Muḥammad Bāqir Shaftī (1180–1260 Q.)," in *Yādigār* 5, no. 10 (1949):41; Q.U.: 145.
48. Malcolm 2:315–16; A. Sepsis, "Quelques Mots sur l'État Religieux Actuel de la Perse," *Revue de l'Orient* 3 (1844): 100.
49. Malcolm 2:429–30. Other trends were already setting in the 1840s. With the incipient modernization of Qājār state, Sepsis notes that Hājjī Mīrzā Āqāsī was seeking to curb the power of the religious courts (Sepsis, pp. 105–6).
50. Madelung, "Authority in Twelver Shiʿism," pp. 165, 172, n. 9; Strothmann, *Zwölfer-Schiʿa*, p. 93.
51. General introduction, section I.2.
52. Lambton, "Some New Trends in Political Thought," p. 103.
53. G. H. Mueller, "The Notion of Rationality in the Work of Max Weber," *European Journal of Sociology* 20, no. 1 (1979): 149–71.
54. Ec. & S.: 810, 813, 822–23.
55. Gorjī, "Nigāhī."
56. N. J. Coulson, *Conflicts and Tensions in Islamic Jurisprudence* (Chicago, 1969), pp. 58–60.
57. *Jawāhir al-Kalām* 11:178; cited by Sachedina, p. 107.
58. M. ʿAbduh Burūjirdī, *Mabānī-ye Ḥuqūq-e Islāmī* (Tehran, 1962/1341), pp. 223–25.
59. M. Anṣārī, *Zindigānī va Shakhṣiyyat-e Shaykh Murtaḍā Anṣārī* (Ahwaz, 1960–61/1380), pp. 39–40.
60. Shaykh Murtaḍā Anṣārī, *Farāʾid al-Uṣūl* (Tehran, n.d.), pp. 2, 193–444.
61. H. Löschner, *Die dogmatischen grundlagen des Schiʿitschen Rechts* (C. Hammans Verlag, 1971), p. 195.
62. S. A. Fāṭimī, *Tajrīd al-Uṣūl* (Mashhad, 1974), p. 169.
63. A. Mamaqānī, *Dīn va Shuʾūn* (Tehran, 1956–57/1335 [Istanbul, 1918]), p. 48; Anṣārī's *al-Makāsib* (1881–28/1299), pp. 71–72.

Chapter 11

1. See pp. 5–6 above.
2. M. A. Muʿallim Ḥabīb-ābādī, *Makārim al-Āthār* (Isfahan, n.d.), 5:1616.
3. Q.U.: 143–45.
4. Algar, *Religious and State*, pp. 52–53; N. Tkh. 1:159–60, 168, 311, 329, 345–46.
5. Algar, *Religion and State*, pp. 46ff.
6. Olearius: 263–64.
7. J. Calmard, "Le Mécénat de representation de *Taʿziye*, I," *Le Monde iranien et l'Islam* 2 (1974):74.
8. Ibid., pp. 76–79, 88, 95, 106–13. H. Massé, "Poèmes consacrés aux Imams," *Shiʿisme*, pp. 271–279. As Calmard points out in the sequel to this article ("Le Mécénat,

II," *Le Monde iranien et l'Islam* 4 [1976–77]: 133–62), Amīr Kabīr, the first grand vizier of Nāṣir al-Dīn Shāh, opposed the *ta*ᶜ*zieh*, but by that time it had struck deep roots in popular religiosity.

9. Calmard "Mécéat," pp. 84, 93, 110, 113–14, 119–20.

10. Algar, Religious and State, pp. 87–89, 116, n. 70, 153–55.

11. H. Lasswell, following Merriam, defines "miranda" in contradistinction to "credenda" as "symbols of sentiment and identification in the political myth." See "The Language of Power," H. Lasswell, N. Leites, et al., eds., *Studies in Quantitative Semantics* (Cambridge, 1949), p. 5.

12. *Jihādiyya*: (22–23, 64).

13. A famous eighteenth-century *ᶜālim*, Shaykh Yūsuf Baḥrānī states that when composing his book *Ḥadāʾiq*, "I evaded [the writing of] the book on *jihād*, and whatever pertains to *jihād*, as little benefit results from [the consideration of] such matters in this age" (Q.U.: 273).

14. *Jihādiyya*: (17), (25).

15. Malcolm 2: 315–17.

16. Sepsis, p. 100.

17. ᶜAbduh, pp. 172–74.

18. M.U. II: section on *taqlīd*.

19. ᶜAbdullāh Mostawfī, *Sharḥ-e Zindigānī-ye Man* (Tehran, n.d.), 1: 100; Rāvandī 3: 526–27.

20. Q.U.: 145–46.

21. See section 11.2.2 below.

22. Algar, *Religion and State*, p. 109. This of course created a tremendous security problem in Isfahn. The *lūṭīs* were given sanctuary (*bast*) by Shaftī in exchange for their services. At night they would engage in murder, robbery, and rape with impunity. "The next day, they would wash their swords, which were red with the blood of Muslims, in the water-tanks or the mosques" (translated from *Nāsikh al-Tavārīkh*, ibid., p. 112).

23. Malcolm 2: 266ff, 274.

24. Algar, *Religion and State*, p. 39; Nafīsī, *Tārīkh-e Ijtimāᶜī* 2: 42–48.

25. Mrt. A.: 26.

26. Nafisi, *Tārīkh-e Ijtimāᶜī* 2: 40–41.

27. This is how Stuart explained the "circumstances": "This long fast of Ramazan creates a great deal of religious ferment. The Soofis are frightened" (cited in Algar, *Religion and State*, pp. 118–19).

28. Ibid., pp. 138–43, 147.

29. Chardin 4: 194–95.

30. Malcolm 2: 315.

31. Muḥammad Ḥasan Khān Iᶜtimād al-Salṭana, *al-Maʾāthir va'l-Āthār* (Tehran, 1888), pp. 135–86.

32. R. Ad. 1: 41.

33. Muᶜallim Ḥabīb-ābādī 2: 555.

34. Lambton, "Persian *ᶜulamāʾ*," in *Shīᶜisme*, pp. 259–60.

35. Ibid., p. 261; M. J. Khurmūjī, *Ḥaqayiq al-Akhbār-e Nāṣirī*, H. Khadīv Jam, ed. (Tehran, 1965/1344), p. 137; *Khāṭirāt-e Iᶜtimād al-Salṭana*, p. 403.

36. *Khāṭirāt-e Iʿtimād al-Salṭana*, pp. 63, 478, 538–39, 551, 694–98.
37. F. Adamiyyat and H. Nāṭiq, *Afkār-e Ijtimāʿī va Siyāsī dar Āthār-e Muntashir-nashuda-ye Dawrān-e Qājār* (Tehran, 1977), pp. 11–19.
38. Iqbāl, "Shaftī."
39. *Maʾāthir waʾl-Āthār*, p. 137.
40. Lambton, "Persian *ʿulamāʾ*," p. 254.
41. Khurmūjī, pp. 146–47, 158, 191; R.S.N. 10:700–701.
42. Munzavī 2:1712.
43. Modarresi Tabatabaʾi, "*Kharāj* in Shīʿī Law," appendix 3.
44. In his letter of 15 January 1856 to Tocqueville, Gobineau writes that all somewhat literate people are prone to Sufism (Tocqueville, *Oeuvres complètes* 9:250). Gobineau, however, was writing at a time when the Shiʿite hierocracy was slowly recovering from the shock of Shaykhī and Bābī schisms, and when philosophy, buttressing gnostic Shiʿism of the type represented by Aḥsāʾī, was still being fairly widely taught (A. de Gobineau, *Les Religions et les philosophie dans l'Asie centrale*, [Paris, 1957 (1865)], pp. 64–107). As the Shiʿite hierocracy recovered and the second phase of the *Uṣūlī* movement prevailed, the situation of "high" Sufism, together with the teaching of philosophy, became more precarious. It appeared that, as the *Uṣūlī* jurist Shaykh Muḥammad Ḥasan Najafī had remarked, "it was but to abolish philosophy [*ḥikmat*] that God chose Muḥammad ibn ʿAbdullāh [as his Prophet]" (Q.U.: 105).
45. See the fragment of his autobiography in Ṣafī-ʿAlī Shāh, *Zubdat al-Asrār* (Tehran, 1963/1341), p. 6.
46. Mīrzā Muḥammad Dhuʾl-Riyāsatayn, *Risala-ye Vujūb-e Duʿā-ye Pādishāh* (Tehran, n.d. [ca. 1890]).
47. A. A. Vazīrī, *Tārīkh-e Kirmān*, H. Farmānfarmāʾiān, ed. (Tehran, 1962/1340), pp. 349–50.
48. Algar, *Religion and State*, p. 39; Perry, *Karīm Khān Zand*, p. 221.
49. N. Tkh. 1:269.
50. Algar, *Religion and State*, pp. 55–56, 119; Ravandi 3:518.
51. Sepsis, p. 106.
52. H. Saʿādat-Nūrī, *Ẓill al-Sulṭān* (Tehran, 1968/1347) 1:61; cf. Algar, *Religion and State*, pp. 100, 121, 126, and the erroneous editorial note by I. Afshar, *Rūznāmeh-ye Khāṭirat-e Iʿtimād al-Salṭana*, p. 56.
53. R.S.N. 10:708–9. The terms *pādishāh-e Islām* and *ahl-e Islām* are used in the text by Hidāyat.
54. T. Parsons, "Christianity and Modern Industrial Society," in E. A. Tiryakian, ed., *Sociological Theory, Values and Sociocultural Change* (New York, 1963), p. 40.
55. The situation was identical in medieval Christianity where "each of the two powers [the Church and the state] can and must in case of necessity (*casualiter* and *per accidens*) assume for the weal of the whole body, functions which in themselves are not its proper functions" (O. Gierke, *Political Theories of the Middle Ages* [Boston, 1958], p. 18).
56. Faḍl Allāh Nuri, ed., *Suʾāl va Javāb* (Bombay, 1893), pp. 61–62.
57. Algar, *Religion and State*, p. 116.
58. Taymuri, pp. 43–47, 124–26.
59. Algar, *Religion and State*, pp. 68–69.

60. H. Corbin, "L'École Shaykhie en Théologie Shiᶜite," *Annuaire de l'École Pratique des Hautes Etudes: Section des Sciences Religieuses* (1960–61), pp. 1–60.
61. Niᶜmatullāh Raḍavī, *Tadhkirat al-Awliyā*ᵓ (Kirman, n.d. [1894–95/1312]).
62. Corbin, "L'École Shaykhie," pp. 52–57.
63. Ḥājj Muḥammad Karīm Khān Kirmānī, *Risāla-ye Ḥuqūq-e Ikhvān* (Kirman, 1976/1355), p. 18.
64. A. Amanat, "The Early Years of the Babi Movement: Background and Development," D. Phil. thesis, Oxford University, 1981; E. G. Browne "The Bābīs of Persia I: Sketches of Their History and Personal Experiences among Them," *JARS* (1889); also his *A Traveller's Narrative of the Bab* (Amsterdam, 1975/Cambridge, 1891); *Materials for the Study of the Babi Religion* (London, 1918); and E. G. Browne, ed., *The New History of Mirza ᶜAli Muhammad the Bab*, (Cambridge, 1893).
65. E. G. Browne, ed., *Kitāb-i Nuqṭatᵓl-Kāf*, E. J. W. Gibb Memorial Series, vol. 15 (1910), p. 135.
66. Browne, *Traveller's Narrative*, pp. 222ff. From the beginning the Bāb was convinced that "externally" he was the gate to the Imam but "internally" the Imam himself (Amanat, p. 194). The author of the *Nuqṭatuᵓl-Kāf* quotes the Bāb as saying that he manifested his knowledge (*ᶜilm*) in four languages: "The first, the language of the signs [*āyāt*], the second, the language of inner dialogue [*munājāt*], the third the language of addresses [*khutub*], and the fourth the language of visitations [*ziyārāt*] and of commentaries of the verses [of the Qurᵓan] and of the traditions of the Immaculate Imams; because the language of Signs belongs to my heart [*fuᵓād*], which is the manifestation of God and is called the language of God, and the language of inner dialogue belongs to servanthood [of God], love and annihilation. It is attributed to the Prophet of God, and its manifestation is conceivable in the mirror of the mind [*ᶜaql*]. The language of addresses is attributed to the principle of Friendship of God [*vilāyat*], and is manifested in the mirror of the soul [*nafs*]. The language of commentaries belongs to the station of Babhood, and is associated with the body [*jism*]" (p. 107).
67. Browne, *Traveller's Narrative*, p. 310.
68. Personal communication with Dr. Abbas Amanat. I am grateful to Dr. Amanat for this point, and for reading and commenting on an earlier draft of this section.
69. Browne, *Traveller's Narrative*, pp. 222–24.
70. Amanat, esp. pp. 47, 188.
71. Browne, *Traveller's Narrative*, esp. p. 214, Accounts of Babism in R.S.N. and N. Tk. The "traveller" maintains that the *majority* of the Babi involved in the Māzandarān uprising were clerics (*Traveller's Narrative*, Persian text, p. 47); Amanat, pp. 298, 360.
72. V. Minorsky, review of M. S. Ivanov, "*The Bābī Risings in Iran in 1848–1852*," BSOAS 11 (1943–46):879–80; Amanat, pp. 114–24.
73. Amanat, pp. 306ff.
74. Ibid., pp. 188, 272–87, 301–5, 318, 327–29.
75. Ibid., p. 421.
76. Browne, ed., *Nuqṭatuᵓl-Kāf*, pp. 92–93.
77. Browne's translation, *The New History*, pp. 357–58 (source: *Nuqṭatuᵓl-Kāf*), em-

phasis added to bring out Qurrat al-ʿAyn's opposition to the advocates of rigorous ethical regulation of life.

78. Browne, *Traveller's Narrative*, p. 177. According to the Safavid historian Qāḍī Nūrullāh Shūshtarī, the Green Isle (*Jazīrat al-Khaḍrāʾ*) was the abode of the Mahdi. See above, pp. 161–62.

79. Browne's translation, *Materials for the Study of the Babi Religion*, p. 350; original, p. 349.

80. Amanat, p. 331 and supplement to p. 331.

Conclusion to Part 3

1. V. Murvar, "Integrative and Revolutionary Capabilities of Religion," in H. M. Johnson, ed., *Religious Change and Continuity* (San Francisco, 1979), p. 79.

Chapter 12

1. A possibility alluded to only in passing by Weber (Ec. & S.: 550).

2. Troeltsch 1: 113.

3. S. N. Eisenstadt, "Religious Organizations and Political Process," in *Tradition, Change and Modernity* (New York, 1973), p. 191.

4. R.S.N., 9:379.

5. Ullmann, *Medieval Papalism*, pp. 148, 197.

Epilogue

1. Gregory VII's argument for the freedom of the Church already contained the principle of theocratic monism: "The Son of God had given Peter and his successors the power to bind and loose souls, a power, that is to say, which is spiritual and heavenly; *how much more*, then, can Peter dispose of what is purely earthly and secular?" (Tellenbach, p. 153; emphasis added). An argument analogous to Gregory's that the limitation of the power of the keys to the soul alone is unreasonable can be made in other religious traditions as well.

2. Ullmann, *Medieval Papalism*, p. 120: "the papalist claim to world monarchy was the direct result of the stimulus afforded by the crusades."

3. Mullā Aḥmad Narāqī, *ʿAwāyid al-Ayyām* ([?] Tehran, 1903/1321 Q.), pp. 185–205. The *ʿAwāyid* is the only legal work referred to by Khumaynī in support of his theory of the sovereignty of the jurist. However, the primary objective of Narāqī's discussion of vicegerency is to strengthen the *juristic* authority of the *mujtahid*s. The bulk of the discussion is devoted to the "delimitation" of the scope of the authority of the jurists as the vicegerents of the Imam, and their collective authority is delimited to the exclusion of temporal rule. (For Khumaynī's reference to Narāqī as his forerunner, see R. Khumaynī, *Ḥukūmat-e Islāmī* [Najaf, 1971], pp. 98, 142.)

4. Parsons, p. 46.

5. *Khāṭirāt-e Iʿtimād al-Salṭana*, pp. 765–66, 783, 785.

6. Ec. & S.: 1177.

7. S. A. Arjomand, "Shiʿite Islam and the Revolution in Iran," *Government and Opposition: A Journal of Comparative Politics* 16 (1981):297–98.

8. S. A. Arjomand, "The *ʿUlamāʾ*'s Traditionalist Opposition to Parliamentarianism: 1907–1909," *Middle Eastern Studies* 17, no. 2 pp. 177–84.

9. Khumayni, *Ḥukūmat-e Islāmī*; A. Tihrani, *Madīna-ye Faḍila dar Islām* (Tehran, 1975–76/1354). Some century and a half earlier, Narāqī had ended his discussion of the authority of the jurist by saying that it was for the jurists to look upon the functions of the Imam, and to search for instances similar to intervention in public endowments and in certain testamentary cases, where the function could be performed by jurists (*ʿAwāʾid al-Ayyām*, p. 205). Khumaynī finally undertook such a search, and decided that rulership was a similar instance to those Narāqī had enumerated.

10. S. A. Arjomand "The State and Khomeini's Islamic Order," *Iranian Studies* 13, n.s. 1–4 (1980):147–64.

11. See p. 163 above.

12. I am grateful to Dr. Ahmad Ashraf for this information.

13. See pp. 182–83 and p. 312, n. 59.

14. "Ittiṣāl-e Dō Nahḍat" (The Connectedness of the Two Movements), *Sorūsh* 167 (November 1982/Ābān 1361): 28–33.

References

Primary Published and Unpublished Sources

Anonymous. *ʿĀlam Ārā-ye Shāh Ismāʿīl*. Edited by A. Muntaẓir-Ṣāḥib. Tehran, 1971/1349.

———. *History of Shāh Ismāʿīl*. British Library, MS Or 3248 (*Ross Anonymous*).

———. *Muʿtaqad al-Imāmiyya*. Edited by M. T. Dānish-pajūh. Tehran, 1961/1339.

———. *A Narrative of Italian Travels in Persia in the Fifteenth and Sixteenth Centuries*. Hakluyt Society, vol. 49, pt. 2. London, 1873.

———. *Rasāʾil-e Javān-mardān*. Edited by M. Ṣarrāfī. Tehran, 1973/1352.

———. *Tadhkirat al-Mulūk*. Edited by V. Minorsky. London: E. J. W. Gibb Memorial Series, n.s., 16, 1943.

Afūshteh-ye Naṭanzī, Maḥmūd. *Nuqāwat al-Āthār fī Dhikr al-Akhyar*. Edited by E. Ishrāqī. Tehran, 1971/1350.

ʿĀmilī, Bahā al-Dīn. *Jāmʿ ʿAbbāsī*. Bombay, 1901–2/1319 Q. Reissued by Intishārāt-e Farāhānī in Tehran, n.d.

———. *Kuliyyat-e Shaykh-e Bahāʾī*. Edited by G. Javāhirī. Tehran: Maḥmūdī, n.d.

———. *Zubdat al-Uṣūl*. n.p., 1851/1267.

Amīnī, ʿAbd al-Ḥusayn Aḥmad. *Shahīdān-e Rāh-e Faḍilat*. Tehran, n.d.

Anṣārī, Shaykh Murtaḍā. *Farāʾid al-Uṣūl*. Tehran, n.d.

———. *al-Makāsib*. n.p. 1881–82/1299.

———. *Risāla ʿAmaliyya*. Tehran, 1875–76/1292.

Ardabīlī, Mullā Aḥmad Muqqaddas. *Ḥadīqat al-Shīʿa*. Tehran: ʿIlmiyya Islāmiyya, n.d.

———. *Zubdat al-Bayān fī Aḥkām al-Qurʾān*. Tehran, 1966/7/1386 Q.

al-Ashʿarī, Saʿd ibn ʿAbdullāh. *Kitāb al-Maqālāt va'l-Firaq*. Edited by M. J. Mashkūr. Tehran, 1963.

Ibn Bābūya, Abū Jaʿfar Muḥammad. *Iʿtiqadat (Kitāb al-Iʿtiqād)*. Tehran: Shams, 1959/1379 Q.

———. *Man la yaḥḍuruhu'l-faqīh*. Tehran, 1970/1390 Q.

Bahbahānī, Aḥmad. *Mirʾātu-l-Aḥwāl Jahān Numa*. British Library Or MS Add. 24052.

Balbi, T. "Relazione di Persia, del Clarissimo messer Teodoro Balbi console veneto nella Siria dell'anno 1578 al 1582." In G. Berchet, *La Republica de Venezia e la Persia*. Torino, 1865.

Chardin, J. *Les Voyages du Chevalier Chardin en Perse*. 10 vols. Edited by L. Langlès. Paris, 1811.

A Chronicle of the Carmelites in Persia and the Papal Mission of the XVIIth and XVIIIth Centuries. 2 vols. London, 1939.

[Darvīsh Muḥammad.] *Ṣifat-nāma-ye Darvīsh Muḥammad Khān-e Ghāzī*. Edited by G. Scarcia. Rome, 1965.

Du Mans, Rafael. *Estat de la Perse en 1660*. Edited by Schefer. Paris, 1890.

Dunbulī, ʿAbd al-Razzāq. *Maʾāthir-e Sulṭāniyya*. Tabriz, 1825–6/1241.

Fayḍ Kāshānī, Mullā Muḥsin. *Kalamāt-e Maknuneh*. Tehran, 1898–99/1316 Q.

———. *Rafʿ al-Fitna*. Central Library of Tehran University, MS no. 3303.

———. *Risālāt: Tarjumat al-Ṣalāt, Ulfat-nāmeh, Āʾīneh-ye Shāhī*. Shiraz, 1941/1320.

———. *Safīnat al-Najāt*. Edited and translated by M. R. Tafrishī. N.p. 1976–77/1397.

Gemelli/Careri, J. F. "A Voyage Round the World." (Visited Iran in 1694.) In J. Churchill, ed., *A Collection of Voyages*, vol. 4. London, 1704.

Ghaffārī, Qāḍī Aḥmad. *Tārīkh-e Jahān-ārā*. Tehran: Hafiz, n.d.

al-Ghazālī, Abū Ḥāmid Muḥammad. *Iḥyāʾ ʿUlūm al-Dīn*. Cairo, 1967/1387 Q.

Ghazali's Book of Counsel for Kings. [*Naṣīḥat al-Mulūk*.] Translated by F. R. C. Bagley. London: Oxford University Press, 1964.

Gobineau, A. de. *Religions et philosophies dans l'Asie centrale*. Paris, 1957 [1865].

Hanway, J. *An Historical Account of the British Trade over the Caspian Sea*. London, 1753.

———. *The Revolutions of Persia*. London, 1753.

Ḥasan ibn Zayn al-Dīn, Shaykh. *Maʿālim al-Dīn wa Malādh al-Mujtahidīn*. Tehran: ʿIlmiyya Islāmiyya, 1958/1378 Q.

Ḥazīn, Shaykh Muḥammad ʿAlī. *Tadhkira-ye Ḥazīn-e Lāhījī*, published as *The Life of Sheikh Mohammed Ali Hazin*. Edited by F. C. Belfour. London, 1831.

Hidāyat, Riḍā Qulī Khān. *Rawḍat al-Ṣafā-ye Nāṣirī*. 10 vols. Tehran, 1960–61/1339.

al-Ḥillī, Ibn al-Muṭahhar. *al-Babu'l-Hadi Ashar*. Translated by W. M. Miller. London: Royal Asiatic Society, 1928.

———. *Sharāyiʿ al-Islām*. Persian trans. Edited by M. T. Dānish-pajūh. 4 vols. Tehran: Tehran University Press, 1967–74/1346–53.

al-Ḥillī, Ibn al-Muṭahhar. *al-Babuʾl-Hadi Ashar*. Translated by W. M. Miller. London: Royal Asiatic Society, 1928.

———. *Jadhaba-ye Vilāyat*. Persian translation of *Minhāj al-Karāma* by S. A. Ḥusaynī Chālūsī. 2nd ed. Tehran, 1967/1346.

———. *Mabādī al-Wusūl ilā ʿilm al-Uṣūl*. Najaf, 1970.

———. *Tahdhīb al-Wusūl ila ʿIlm al-Uṣūl*. Tehran, 1890–91/1308 Q.

al-Ḥurr al ʿĀmilī, Muḥammad ibn al-Ḥasan. *Amal al-Āmil*. Baghdad, 1965–66/1385.

———. *Wasāʾil al-Shīʿa*. 18 vols. 1971/1391 Q.

Iṣfahānī, Muḥammad Mahdī. *Niṣf-e Jahān fī Taʿrīf al-Iṣfahān*. Edited by M. Sotūdeh. Tehran, 1961/1340 [1891/1308 H.Q.].

Ibn Isfandiyār. *Nāmeh-ye Tansar*. Edited by M. Minavī. Tehran, 1932–33/1311.

Iskandar Beg Turkamān, Munshī. *Tārīkh-e ʿĀlam-ārā-ye ʿAbbāsī*. 2 vols. Tehran, 1971/1350.

Iskandar Beg Turkamān and Muḥammad ibn Yūsuf. *Dhayl-e Tārīkh-e Ālam-ārā-ye ʿAbbāsī*. Edited by Suheylī Khwānsārī. Tehran: Islāmiyya, 1938–39/1317.
Iʿtimād al-Salṭana, Muḥammad Ḥasan Khān. *al-Maʾāthir waʾl-Āthār.* Tehran, 1888.
———. *Rūznāmeh-ye Khāṭirāt-e Iʿtimād al-Salṭana*. Edited by E. Afshār. Tehran, 1971/1350.
Kaempfer, Engelbert. *Dar Darbar-e Shahanshahan-e Iran*. Translated by K. Jahāndārī. Tehran, 1971/1350. Being the Persian translation of *Amoenitatum exoticarum politico-physico-medicarum Fasciculi V*. Lemgo, 1712.
Kamareh-ī, Shaykh Jaʿfar. *Tuḥfa-ye Sulṭānī dar Ḥikmat-e Ṭabīʿī va Ḥikmat-e Ilāhī*. Tehran, 1960–61/1339.
al-Karakī, Shaykh ʿAlī, et al. *al-Riḍaʾiyyāt wa'l-Kharājiyyāt*. Tehran, 1895–96/1313 Q.
Karbalāʾī Tabrīzī, Ḥāfiẓ Ḥusayn. *Rawḍāt al-Jinān va Jannāt al-Janān*. 2 vols. Edited by J. Sulṭān al-Qurrāʾī. Tehran, 1965/1344.
Kashfī, Sayyid Jaʿfar. *Tuḥfat al-Mulūk*. Tehran, 1857/1273 Q.
Kāshifī, Ḥusayn Vāʾiẓ. *Futuwwat-nāmeh-ye Sulṭānī*. Edited by M. J. Maḥjūb. Tehran, 1971/1350.
Khātūnābādī, Sayyid ʿAbd al-Ḥusayn. *Vaqāyiʿ al-Sanīn wa'l-Aʿwām*. Tehran: Islamiyya, 1973/1352.
Khunjī, Faḍl Allāh Rūzbihān. *Mihmān-nāmeh-ye Bukhārā*. Edited by M. Sotūdeh. Tehran, 1962/1341.
———. *Persia in* A.D. *1478–1490: An Abridged Translation of Faḍlullāh B. Rūzbihān Khunjī's Tārīkh-i Ālām-ārā-yi Amīnī*. Edited by V. Minorsky. London: Royal Asiatic Society, 1957.
Khūrmūjī, M. J. *Ḥaqāyiq al-Akhbār-e Nāṣirī*. Edited by H. Khadīv Jam. Tehran, 1965/1344.
Khwānd Amīr (Ghiyāth al-Dīn ibn Humām al- Dīn al-Ḥusaynī). *Ḥabīb al Siyar.* 4 vols. J. Homāʾī. Tehran: Khayyām, 1954.
Khwansārī, Muḥammad Bāqir. *Rawḍāt al-Jannāt fī Aḥwāl al-ʿUlamāʾ wa'l Sādāt*. Edited by M. A. Rawḍātī. Tehran, 1947/1367 Q.
Krusinski, J. T. *The History of the Late Revolutions of Persia*. London, 1740.
Kulaynī al-Rāzī, Muḥammad ibn Yaʿqūb. *Furūʿ al-Kāfī*. Tehran, 1957/1377.
———. *Uṣūl al-Kāfī*. With Persian translation and commentary by J. Muṣṭafavī. Tehran, n.d.
Lāhījī, Mullā ʿAbd al-Razzāq. *Gawhar-e Murād*. Tehran, 1958/1377 Q.
Majlisī, Muḥammad Bāqir. *ʿAyn al-Ḥayāt*. Tehran: ʿIlmī, 1954/1333.
———. *Biḥār al-Anwār.* 110 vols. Tehran, 1948–68/1327–47.
———. *Ḥaqq al-Yaqīn*. Tehran, 1968/1347.
———. *Ḥayāt al-Qulūb, III: dar Imāmat*. Tehran, 1955/1374 Q.
———. *Ikhtiyārāt*. Press of Ḥajj Mīrzā Aḥmad, 1910/1328 Q.
———. *Risāla-ye Suʾāl va Javāb*. Printed together with *Tadhkirat al-Awliyā'* et al. Tabriz, 1953/1332.
———. *Zād al-Maʿād*. Tehran, 1902/1320 Q.
Majlisī, Muḥammad Taqī. *Risāla-ye Tashvīq-e Sālikīn*. Printed together with *Risāla-ye Suʾāl va Javāb* et al. Tabriz, 1953/1332.
Malcolm, Sir John. *History of Persia*. 2 vols. London, 1829.

Marᶜashī Ṣafavī, Mīrzā Muḥammad Khalīl. *Majmaᶜ al-Tawārīkh*. Edited by A. Iqbāl. Tehran, 1949/1328.

Marᶜashī, Mīr Ẓahīr al-Dīn. *Tārīkh-e Ṭabaristān va Rūyān va Māzandarān*. Edited by M. H. Tasbīḥī. Tehran, 1966/1345.

Maᶜṣūm ᶜAlī Shāh. *Ṭarāʾiq al-Ḥaqāʾiq*. 3 vols. Edited by M. J. Maḥjūb. Tehran, 1960/1339.

Mīrkhwānd. *Rawḍat al-Ṣafā*. Vol. 4. Tehran: Khayyām, 1960/1339.

Mīr Dāmād, Muḥammad Bāqir. *Kitāb al-Qabasāt*. Edited by M. Muḥaqqiq. Tehran, 1977.

Mīr Makhdūm Shīrāzī. *al-Nawāqiḍ li-Bunyān al-Rawāfiḍ*. British Library MS, Or 7991.

Mīr Muḥammad Ḥusaynī (Mīr Lawḥī). *Arbaᶜīn*. Central Library of Tehran University, MS no. 1154 (Mishkāt Collection, no. 619).

Mudarris, M. A. *Rayḥānat al-Adab*. 8 vols. Tabriz, 1967.

Mufīd, Muḥammad. *Jāmiᶜ Mufīdī*. 3 vols. Edited by I. Afshār. Tehran, 1961/1340.

Muḥammad Ashraf ibn ᶜAbdul-Ḥusayn al-Ḥusaynī. *Faḍāʾil al-Sādāt*. Tehran, 1896–97/1314.

al-Murtaḍā, Sayyid. *al-Dharīᶜa ilā Uṣūl al-Sharīᶜa*. Edited by A. Q. Gorjī. Tehran: Tehran University Press, 1969–70/1348.

Naṣrābādī, Mīrzā Muḥammad Ṭāhir. *Tadhkira-ye Naṣrābādī*. Edited by V. Dastgirdī. Tehran: Furūghī, 1973/1352.

Nawbakhtī. *Tarjuma-ye Firaq al-Shīᶜa-ye Nawbakhtī*. Edited and translated by M. J. Mashkūr. Tehran, 1974/1353.

Niẓām al-Mulk Ṭūsī. *Siyar al-Mulūk*. Edited by H. Darke. Tehran, 1976.

[Nūrbakhsh, Muḥammad.] The Writings of Sayyid Muḥammad Nūrbakhsh. Published in J. Ṣadaqiyānlū, *Taḥqīq dar Aḥvāl va Āthār-e Sayyid Muḥammad Nūrbakhsh Uvaysī Quhistānī*. Tehran, 1972/1351.

Olearius, Adam. *Relation du voyage en Moscovie et en Perse*. Paris, 1656.

Procopius. *The Secret History*. English translation. Harmondsworth: Penguin, 1966.

Qāʾim-Maqām, Abul'l-Qāsim. *Munshaʾāt-e Qāʾim Maqām-e Farahānī*. Tehran: Intishārāt-e Āpādānā va Arasṭū, n.d.

Qāʾim-Maqām, ᶜĪsā. *Kitāb al-Jihādiyya*. Tabriz, 1818/1233.

al-Qāshānī, ᶜAbdullāh ibn Muḥammad. *Tārīkh-e Öljeitü*. Edited by M. Hambaly. Tehran, 1969–70/1348.

al-Qazvīnī al-Rāzī, ᶜAbd al-Jalīl. *Kitāb al-Naqḍ*. Edited by S. J. Ḥusaynī Urmavī. Tehran, 1952/1331.

Qumī, Abu'l-Qāsim. *Qawānīn al-Uṣūl*. Tehran, n.d.

[Qumī,] Muḥammad Ṭāhir ibn Muḥammad Ḥusayn. *al-Fawāʾid al-Dīniyya*. Central Library of Tehran University, NS no. 2479.

Qumī, Mullā Muḥammad Ṭāhir. *Shish Risāla-ye Fārsī*. Edited by M. J. Ḥusaynī Urmavī. Tehran, 1960–61/1339.

———. *Tuḥfat al-Akhyār*. Qum, 1973/1393 Q.

Qumī, Qāḍī Aḥmad. *Khulāṣat al-Tawārīkh*. Preussiche (now Deutsche) Staatsbibliothek, Berlin, MS Orient. fol. 2202.

Qumī, Qāḍī Saᶜīd, *Kilīd-e Bihisht*. Edited by S. M. Mishkāt. Tehran, 1936/1315.

Rashīd al-Dīn Faḍl Allāh. *Jāmiᶜ al-Tawārīkh*. Edited by B. Karīmī. Tehran: Iqbāl, n.d.

Rāvandī. *Rāḥat al-Ṣudūr.* Edited by Muḥammad Iqbāl. London: Luzac, 1921.

Rūmlū, Ḥasan. *Aḥsan al-Tawārīkh.* Edited by C. N. Seddon. Baroda: Oriental Institute, 1931.

Sanson [missionary]. *The Present State of Persia.* London, 1695.

[Shāh Ṭahmāsp Ṣafavī.] *Āʾīn-e Shāh Ṭahmāsp-e Ṣafavī dar Qānūn-e Salṭanat.* Published by M. T. Dānish-pajūh in *Barrasīha-ye Tārīkhī* 7, no. 1, 1972/1351.

[———]. *Memoirs of Shah Tahmasp.* Calcutta, 1912.

Shahristānī, Abu'l-Fatḥ Muḥammad ibn ʿAbd al-Karīm. *al Milal va-l-Niḥal.* Edited by M. R. Jalālī Nāʾīnī. Tehran, 1971/1350.

Shāmlū, Valī Qulī, *Qiṣaṣ al-Khāqānī.* British Library, Add. MS 7656.

[Shīrāzī, Muḥammd Ḥasan.] *Suʾāl va Javāb.* Edited by Nūrī, Faḍl Allāh. Bombay, 1893.

Shīrāzī, Ṣadr al-Dīn Muḥammad (Mullā Ṣadrā), *Kasr Aṣnām al-Jāhiliyya.* Edited by M. T. Dānish-pajūh. (Tehran, 1962/1340).

———. *Risāla-ye Seh Aṣl.* Edited by S. H. Nasr. Tehran: Tehran University Press, 1961/1340.

———. *Shawāhid al-Rubūbiyya.* Edited by S. J. Āshtiyānī. Mashhad, 1967/1347.

Shīrvānī, Zayn al-ʿĀbidīn. *Bustān al-Siyāḥa.* Shiraz, 1923–24/1342 Q.

Shūshtarī, Qāḍī Nūrullāh. *Majālis al-Muʾminīn.* 2 vols. Tehran: Islamiyya, 1975–76/1354.

[———.] *Maṣāʾib al-Nawāṣib.* Library of Majlis (Tehran), MS 2036.

Sipihr, Mīrzā Muḥammad Taqī. *Nasikh al-Tawārīkh.* 4 vols. Edited by M. B. Bihbūdī. Tehran: Islamiyya, 1965–66/1344.

al-Suwaydī, ʿAbdullāh ibn al-Ḥusayn. *Muʾtamir al-Najaf.* Cario, 1973–47/1393.

Ṭabāṭabāʾī, Sayyid Muḥammad. *Mafātīḥ al-Uṣūl.* Tehran, n.d.

Ṭabāṭabāʾī, Sayyid Muḥammad Mahdī [Baḥr al-ʿulūm]. *Rijāl.* Najaf, 1965/1385.

al-Tabrisī, Faḍl ibn Ḥasan. *Tafsīr Majmaʿ al-Bayān.* Translated by Aḥmad Bihishtī. Qum, 1970–71/1349.

Textes persan relatifs a la secte des Hourufis. Edited by C. Huart. London: E. J. W. Gibb Memorial Series, vol. 9, 1909.

Tocqueville, Alexis de. *Oeuvres complètes, IX: Correspondence d'Alexis de Tocqueville et d'Arthur de Gobineau.* Edited by J. P. Mayer. 2nd ed., Paris: Gallimard, 1959. In part translated into English as the following.

———. *The European Revolution and Correspondence with Gobineau.* Edited and translated by Lukacs. New York, 1959.

Tunikābunī, Muḥammad. *Qiṣaṣ al-ʿUlamāʾ.* Tehran: ʿIlmiyya Islāmiyya, n.d. 1878.

al-Ṭūsī, Muḥammad ibn Ḥasan. *al-Istibṣār fima'Khtulifa min al-Akhbār.* Najaf, 1956/1375 Q.

———. *Kitāb al-Ghayba.* Edited by Tihrānī, Āqā Buzurg. Najaf, 1965–66/1385 Q.

———. *al-Nihāya fī Mujarrad al-Fiqh wa'l Fatāwā.* Tehran, 1963/1342.

———. *Tafsīr al-Tibyān.* Najaf, 1957.

———. *Tahdhīb al-Aḥkām.* 10 vols. Najaf, 1960/1380 Q.

Vaḥīd Qazvīnī, Mīrzā Muḥammad Ṭāhir. *ʿAbbās-nāmeh.* Edited by I. Dihgān. Tehran, 1951/1329.

al-Yaʿqūbī, Aḥmad ibn Wāḍiḥ. *Tārīkh* [*Historiae*]. Edited by M. Th. Houtsma. Leiden, 1883.

Zayn al-Dīn ʿAlī ibn ʿAbdulmuʾmin. *Takmilat al-Akhbār.* University of Tehran Microfilm no. 1981. Copied 1571/979.

Zayn al-Dīn, Shaykh, al-Shahīd al-Thānī. *Masālik al-Afhām ila Sharḥ Sharāyiʿ al-Islām.* Beirut, 1957.

Other Books

ʿAbduh Burūjirdī, M. *Mabāni-ye Ḥuqūq-e Islāmī.* Tehran, 1962/1341.

Ādamiyyat, F. and H. Nāṭiq. *Afkār-e Ijtimāʿī va Siyāsī va Iqtiṣādī dar Āthār-e Muntashir-nashudeh-ye Dawrān-e Qājār.* Tehran: Amīr Kabīr, 1977.

Algar, H. *Religion and the State in Iran: 1785–1906.* Berkeley: University of California Press, 1969.

Andrae, T. *Muhammad: the Man and His Faith.* New York: C. Scribner's Sons, 1936.

Anṣārī, M. *Zindigānī va shakhṣiyyat-e Shaykh Murtaḍā Anṣārī.* Ahwaz, 1960–61/1380.

Āshtiyānī, S. J., ed. *Anthologie des philosophes iraniens depuis le XVIIIe siècle jusqu'à nos jours.* Tehran, 1972.

Bailey, H. W. *Zoroastrian Problems in the Ninth-Century Books.* Oxford: Clarendon Press, 1971.

Barker, E. *From Alexander to Constantine.* Oxford, 1956.

Bausani, A. *Persia religiosa.* Milan: Il Saggiatore, 1959.

Baynes, N. H. "Eusebius and the Christian Empire." In *Byzantine Studies and Other Essays.* London: London University Press, 1955.

Baynes, N. H. and H. St. L. B. Moss, *Byzantium: An Introduction to East Roman Civilization.* Oxford, 1961.

Bendix, R. *Kings or People: Power and the Mandate to Rule.* California, 1978.

Benveniste, E. *Le Vocabulaire des institutions indo-européenes.* Vol. 2: *Pouvoir, droit, religion.* Paris, 1969.

Binder, L. "The Proof of Islam: Religion and Politics in Iran." In *Arabic and Islamic Studies in Honor of Hamilton A. R. Gibb.* Leiden. 1966.

Boyce, M. *The Letter of Tansar.* Rome Is. M.E.D., 1980.

Boyle, J. A., ed. *The Cambridge History of Iran.* Volume 5: *The Saljuq and Mongol Periods.* Cambridge: Cambridge University Press, 1968.

Browne, E. G. *Literary History of Persia.* 4 vols. Cambridge: University Press, 1924.

———. *A Traveller's Narrative of the Bab.* Amsterdam: Philo Press, 1975 [Cambridge, 1891].

———, ed. *The Tārīkh-i Jadīd or New History of Mirza Ali Muhammad the Bab.* Cambridge, 1893.

———, ed. *Kitāb-i Nuqṭatuʾl-Kāf: Being the Earliest History of the Babis Compiled by Ḥājjī Mīrzā Jānī of Kāshān Between the Years* A.D. *1850 and 1852.* E. J. W. Gibb Memorial Series, vol. 15, 1910.

———, ed. *Materials for the Study of the Babi Religion.* London: Cambridge University Press, 1918.

Brunschvig, R. and von Grunebaum, G., eds. *Classicisme et declin culturel dans l'histoire de l'Islam.* Paris: Besson, Chantemerle, 1957.

Busse, Herbert. "The Revival of Persian Kingship Under the Buyids." In *Islamic Civilization 950–1150.* Edited by D. S. Richards. Oxford: Cassirer, 1973.

Cahen, P. C. "The Body Politic." In G. E. von Grunebaum, ed., *Unity and Diversity in Muslim Civilization*. Chicago, 1955.
Christensen, A. *Les Kayanids*. Copenhagen, 1931.
Corbin, H. *En Islam iranien, aspects spirituels et philosophiques*. 4 vols. Paris: Gallimard, 1971–72.
———. *Histoire de la philosophie islamique*. Paris: Gallimard, 1964.
Coulson, N. J. *A History of Islamic Law*. Edinburgh: The University Press, 1964.
———. *Conflicts and Tensions in Islamic Jurisprudence*, Chicago: University of Chicago Press, 1969.
Davvānī, A., ed. *Hizāreh-ye Shaykh-e Ṭūsī*. Vol. 2. Tehran, 1970/1349.
Donaldson, D. M. *The Shiʿite Religion*. London, 1933.
Duchesne-Guillemin, J. *Zoroastrianism: Symbols and Values*. New York: Harper and Row, 1966.
Dumont, L. *Religion, Politics and History in India*. The Hague/Paris: Mouton, 1970.
Efendiev, O. A. *Obrazovanie Azerbaidzhanskogo gosudarstva Sefevidov*. Baku, 1961.
Eisenstadt, S. N. *Tradition, Change and Modernity*. New York, 1973.
Enayat, H. *Modern Islamic Political Thought*. London: Macmillan, 1982.
Ensslin, W., "The Government and Administration of the Byzantine Empire." Chapter 20 of *The Cambridge Medieval History*, vol. 4: *The Byzantine Empire*. Cambridge, 1967.
Falsafī, N. *Zindigānī-ye Shāh ʿAbbās-e Avval*. 4 vols. Tehran, 1960/1339.
Farzam, H. *Shāh-e Valī va Daʿ vī-ye Mahdaviyyat*. Isfahan: University Press, 1969/1348.
Fātimī, S. A. *Tajrīd al-Uṣūl*. Mashhad, 1974.
Frankfort, H. *Kingship and the Gods*. Chicago: University of Chicago Press, 1948.
Friedrich, C. J. *The Philosophy of Law in Historical Perspective*. 2nd ed. Chicago: University of Chicago Press, 1963.
Gibb, H. A. R. *Studies on the Civilization of Islam*. Edited by Shaw, S. J. and Polk, W. R. Boston: Beacon Press, 1962.
Gibb, H. A. R. and Bowen, H. *Islamic Society and the West*. Vol. 1, pt. 2. Oxford: Oxford University Press, 1957.
Gierke, O. *Political Theories of the Middle Age*. Translated by Maitland, F. W. Boston: Beacon Press, 1958.
Glassen, E. *Die fruhen Safawiden nach Qadi Ahmad Qumi*. Freiburg, 1968.
Goitein, S. D. *Studies in Islamic History and Institutions*. Leiden: Brill, 1966.
Goldziher, I. *Muslim Studies*. London, 1971 [1889–90].
Grunebaum, G. E. von. *Medieval Islam*. Chicago: University of Chicago Press, 1954.
———, ed. *Unity and Diversity in Muslim Civilization*. Chicago: University of Chicago Press, 1955.
Hocart, A. M. *Kings and Councillors: An Essay in Comparative Anatomy of Human Society*. Edited by Needham, R. Chicago: University of Chicago Press, 1970.
Hodgson, M. G. S. *The Order of Assassins: The Struggle of Early Nizari Ismaʾilis Against the Islamic World*. The Hague: Mouton, 1955.
———. *The Venture of Islam*. 3 vols. Chicago: University of Chicago Press, 1974.
Hollister, J. N. *The Shiʿa of India*. London: Luzac, 1953.
Holt, P. M., A. K. S. Lambton, and B. Lewis, eds. *Cambridge History of Islam*. 2 vols. Cambridge: Cambridge University Press, 1970.
Iqbāl Āshtiyānī, A. *Tārīkh-e Mughul*. 4th impression. Tehran 1977–78/1356.

———. *Khāndān-e Nawbakhtī*. Tehran 1932/1311.
Jafri, S. H. M. *Origins and Early Development of Shiᶜa Islam*. London: Langman, 1979.
Johnson, A. R. *Sacral Kingship in Ancient Israel*. Cardiff, 1955.
———. "Hebrew Conception of Kingship." In *Myth, Ritual and Kingship*. Edited by S. H. Hooke. Oxford, 1958.
Kasravī, A. *Shaykh Ṣafī va Tabārash*. Tehran, 1977[1944]/1356 [1323].
———. *Tārīkh-e Pānṣad Sāleh-ye Khūzistān*. 3rd ed. Tehran, 1951/1330.
Keddie, N. R., ed. *Scholars, Saints and Sufis: Muslim Institutions since 1500*. Berkeley: University of California Press, 1972.
Kern, F. *Kingship and Law in the Middle Ages*. Translated by S. B. Chrimes. Oxford: Basil Blackwell, 1968.
Khadduri, M. and S. Liebesney, eds. *Law in the Middle East*. Washington: Middle East Institute, 1955.
Khumaynī, R. *Ḥukūmat-e Islāmī*. Tehran, n.d. [1970].
Kiyā, S. *Nuqṭaviyān ya Pasīkhāniyān*. *Irān Kūdeh*. 13. Tehran, n.d.
Lambton, A. K. S. *Landlord and Peasant in Persia*. Oxford: Oxford University Press, 1953.
———. *State and Government in Medieval Islam*. Oxford, 1981.
Langeh-rūdī, J. *Tārīkh-e Ḥuqūq-e Irān*. Tehran: Ma rifat, n.d.
Laoust, H. *Les Schismes dans l'Islam*. Paris, 1965.
Lasswell, H. "The Language of Power." In *Studies in Quantitative Semantics*. Edited by Lasswell, H., Leites, N. et al. Cambridge: MIT Press, 1949.
Lockhart, L. *The Fall of the Safavi Dynasty and the Afghan Occupation of Persia*. Cambridge: Cambridge University Press, 1958.
———. *Nadir Shah*. London: Luzac, 1938.
Löschner, H. *Die dogmatischen grundlagen des Schiᶜitschen Rechts*. Koln: C. Heymann Verlag, 1971.
McDermott, M. J. *The Theology of al-Shaykh al-Mufid*. Beirut, 1970.
Madelung, W., "Authority in Twelver Shiᶜism in the Absence of the Imam." In Makdisi, G. et al., *La Notion d'Autorité au Moyen Age: Islam, Byzance, Occident. Colloques internationaux de la Napoule, 1978*. Paris: Presses Universitaires de France, 1982.
———. "New Documents Concerning al-Maʾmūn, al-Faḍl b. Sahl and ᶜAlī al-Riḍā." In Wadad al- Qadi, ed., *Studia Arabica et Islamica*. Beirut, 1981.
Mamaqānī, A. *Dīn va Shuʾūn*. Tehran, 1956–57/1335 (Istanbul, 1918).
Martin, B. G. "A Short History of the Khalwati Order of Dervishes." In N. R. Keddie, ed., *Scholars, Saints and Sufis*. Berkeley, Los Angeles, 1972.
Mashkūr, M. J. *Tārīkh-e Tabrīz tā Pāyān-e Qarn-e Nuhum-e Hijrī*. Tehran, 1973–74/1352.
Massignon, L. *La Passion de Husayn Ibn Mansur Hallaj*. New ed. Paris: Callimard, 1975.
Mazzaoui, M. M. *The Origins of the Safavids: Shiᶜism, Sufism, and the Gulat*. Weisbaden, 1972.
Modarresī Ṭabāṭabāʾī, H. *Mithālha-ye Ṣudūr-e Ṣafavī*. Qum, 1974/1353.
Mostawfī, ᶜAbdullāh. *Tārīkh-e Zindigānī-ye Man*. Tehran, Zavvār, n.d.
Mottahedeh, R. *Loyalty and Leadership in an Early Islamic Society*. Princeton, 1980.
Munzavī, A. *Fihrist-e Kitābha-ye Fārsī*. Vol. 2. Tehran, 1976/1349.

Murtazavī, M. *Taḥqīq dar bāreh-ye Dawreh-ye Īl-Khānān-e Īrān*. Tehran, 1963/1341.
Murvar, V. "Integrative and Revolutionary Capabilities of Religion." In Johnson, H. M., ed. *Religious Change and Continuity*. San Francisco: Jossey-Bass, 1979.
Muẓaffar, Shaykh M. R. *ʿAqaʾ id va Taʿālīm-e Shīʿa*. Persian translation by M. Mujtahidī Shabistarī. Tehran, 1958/1347.
Nafīsī, S. *Aḥvāl va Ashʿār-e Shaykh-e Bahāʾī*. Tehran, 1937/1316.
———. *Tārīkh-e Ijtimāʿī va Siyāsī-ye Īrān*. Tehran, 1956/1335.
Navāʾī, A. H., ed. *Asnād va Mukātibāt-e Tārīkhī: Shāh ʿAbbās Avval*. Tehran, 1973/1352.
———, ed. *Shāh Ṭahmāsp-e Ṣafavī: Majmūʿa-ye Asnād va Mukātibāt-e Tārīkhī*. Tehran, 1970/1350.
Niebuhr, H. R. *The Social Sources of Denominationism*. New York: H. Holt, 1929.
Parker, T. M. *Christianity and the State in Light of History*. New York: Harper, 1955.
Parsons, T. "Christianity and Modern Industrial Society," In *Sociological Theory, Values and Sociocultural Change*. Edited by E. A. Tiryakian. New York: Free Press, 1963.
Perry, J. R. *Karim Khan Zand: A History of Iran 1747–1779*. Chicago: University of Chicago Press, 1979.
Petrushevsky, I. P. *Islām dar Īrān*. Persian translation by Kishāvarz, K. Tehran, 1971–72/1350.
———. *Kishāvarzī va Munāsibāt-e Arḍī dar Īrān-e ʿAhd-e Mughul*. Persian translation of *Zemledelie i agrarnie otnosheniya v Irane XIII–XIV vekov* by K. Kishāvarz. Tehran 1976–77/1355.
Qāʾim-maqāmī, J., ed. *Yikṣad va Panjāh Sanad-e Tārīkhī*. Tehran, 1969/1348.
Rahman, F. *The Philosophy of Molla Sadra*. Albany: State University of New York Press, 1975.
Rāvandī, M. *Tārīkh-e Ijtimāʿī-ye Īrān*. 2nd ed. 3 vols. Tehran, 1977.
La Regalita Sacra. The Sacral Kingship: Contributions to the Central Theme of the VIIIth International Congress of the History of Religions (Rome, April 1955). Leiden: E. J. Brill, 1959.
Röhrborn, K. M. *Provinzen und Zentralgewalt Persiens im 16. und 17. Jahrhundert*. Berlin: de Gruyter, 1966.
Roemer, H. R. *Der Niedergang Irans nach dem Tode Ismaʾils des Grausamen 1577–1581*. Wurzburg: K. Triltsch, 1939.
———. *Staatsschreiben der Timuridenzeit*. Wiesbaden: 1952.
Rosenthal, E. I. J. *Political Thought in Medieval Islam*. Cambridge, 1958.
Runciman, S. *The Byzantine Theocracy*. Cambridge: Cambridge University Press, 1977.
Sachedina, A. A. *Islamic Messianism: The Idea of Mahdi in Twelver Shiʿism*. New York: SUNY Press, 1981.
Ṣadr, S. *Kitāb al-Mahdī (Tarjuma-ye)*. Persian translation by M. J. Najafī. Tehran 1965/1344.
Ṣafāʾī, I., ed. *Asnād-e Nō-yāfteh*. Tehran, 1971/1349.
Sarwar, G. *History of Shah Ismaʿil Safawi*. Aligarh, 1939.
Savory, R. M. "A 15th Century Safavid Propagandist at Harat." In D. Sinor, ed. *American Oriental Society, Middle West Branch*. Semi-Centennial Volume. Bloomington: Indiana University Press, 1969.
Schacht, J. *The Origins of Muhammadan Jurisprudence*. Oxford: Oxford University Press, 1950.

———. *An Introduction to Islamic Law.* Oxford: University Press, 1964.
Schimmel, A. M. *Mystical Dimensions of Islam.* Chapel Hill: University of North Carolina Press, 1975.
Schluchter, W. *The Rise of Western Rationalism: Max Weber's Developmental History.* California University Press, 1981.
Shaban, M. A. *Islamic History: A New Interpretation.* 2 vols. Cambridge: Cambridge University Press, 1971 and 1976.
Le Shiʿisme imâmite [Colloque de Strasbourg]. Paris: Presses Universitaires de France, 1970.
Smith, J. M., Jr. *The History of the Sarbidar Dynasty, 1336–1381* A.D.*, and Its Sources.* The Hague/Paris: Mouton, 1970.
Sourdel, D. "Les Conceptions Imâmites au debut du XI Siècle d'après le Shaykh al-Mufīd." In D. S. Richards, ed., *Islamic Civilization 950–1150.* Oxford, 1973.
Storey, C. A. *Persian Literature: A Bio-bibliographical Survey.* London: Luzac, 1927–39.
Strothmann, R. *Die Zwölferschīʿa.* Leipzig: O. Harrassowitz, 1926.
Tarn, W. W. *Hellenistic Civilization.* 3rd edition. New York, 1961.
Tellenbach, G. *Church, State and Christian Society at the Time of the Investiture Contest.* Translated by R. F. Bennett. New York: Harper, 1970 [Leipzig, 1936].
Taymūrī, I. *ʿAṣr-e Bīkhabarī ya Tārīkh-e Imtiyāzāt dar Īrān.* Tehran, 1953–54/1332.
Tevfiq, R. "Etude sur la religion des Hourufis." In *Textes persans relatifs à la secte des Hourufis.* Edited by C. Huart. London, 1909.
Tierney, B. *The Crisis of Church and State 1050–1300.* Englewood, N.J.: Prentice Hall, 1964.
Tihrānī, A. *Madīna-ye Fāḍila dar Islām.* Tehran, 1975–76/1354.
Troeltsch, E. *The Social Teachings of the Christian Churches.* 2 vols. Translated by O. Wyon. London: Macmillan, 1931.
Ullmann, W. *Medieval Papalism: The Political Theories of the Medieval Canonists.* London: Methuen, 1949.
———. *A Short History of the Papacy in the Middle Ages.* London, 1972.
Vazīrī, A. A. *Tārīkh-e Kirmān.* Edited by H. Farmānfarmāʾiān. Tehran, 1962/1340.
Wallace-Hadrill, J. M. *Early Germanic Kingship in England and on the Continent.* Oxford, 1971.
Weber, M. *Ancient Judaism.* Glencoe: Free Press, 1952.
———. *Economy and Society.* Edited by G. Roth and C. Wittich. Berkeley and Los Angeles: University of California Press, 1978.
———. *From Max Weber: Essays in Sociology.* Edited by H. H. Gerth and C. Wright Mills. New York: Oxford University Press, 1946.
———. *Religion of India.* Glencoe: Free Press, 1958.
———. *Religion of China.* Glencoe: Free Press, 1951.
Wittek, P. *The Rise of the Ottoman Empire.* London: Royal Asiatic Society, 1938.
Woods, J. E. *The Aqquyunlu: Clan, Confederation, Empire.* Minneapolis and Chicago: Bibliotheca Islamica, 1976.
Zaehner, R. C. *The Dawn and Twilight of Zoroastrianism.* New York: Oxford University Press, 1961.

———. *The Teachings of the Magi: A Compendium of Zoroastrian Beliefs*. New York: Oxford University Press, 1976.

Articles

Algar, H. "The Naqshbandī Order: A Preliminary Survey of Its History and Significance." *SI* 44 (1976).

———. "ASTARĀBĀDĪ, Fazlollāh." *Encyclopedia Iranica* (forthcoming).

Arjomand, S. A. "Religion, Political Action and Legitimate Domination in Shiᶜite Iran: 14th to 18th Centuries A.D." *Archives européennes de sociologie* 20 (1979).

———. "The Shiᶜite Hierocracy and the State in Pre-Modern Iran: 1785–1890." *Archives européennes de sociologie* 22 (1981).

———. "Religious Extremism (*Ghuluww*), Sufism and Sunnism in Safavid Iran: 1501–1722." *Journal of Asian History* 15 (1981).

———. "The State and Khomeini's Islamic Order." *Iranian Studies* 13 (1980).

———. "The *ᶜUlamaʾs* Traditionalist Opposition to Parliamentarianism: 1907–1909." *Middle Eastern Studies* 17 (1981).

———. "Shiᶜite Islam and the Revolution in Iran." *Government and Opposition: A Journal of Comparative Politics* 16 (1981).

———. "The Office of *Mulla-bashi* in Shiᶜite Iran." *SI* 57 (1983).

Aubin, J. "Šāh Ismāᶜīl et les notables de l'Iraq persan." *JESHO* 2 (1959).

———. "Les Sunnites du Lārestān et la chute des Safavids." *REI* 33 (1965).

Bausani, A. "ḤURŪFIYYA," *EI*[2]

Browne, E. G. "The Bābīs of Persia I. Sketches of Their History and Personal Experiences Among Them." *JRAS* (1889).

———. "Further Notes on the Literature of the Ḥurūfīs and their Connection with the Bektāshī Order of Dervishes." *JRAS* (1907).

Calder, N. "Accommodation and Revolution in Imāmī Shīᶜī Jurisprudence: Khymayni and the Classical Tradition," *Middle Eastern Studies* 18 (1982).

Calmard, J. "Le Chiᶜism imâmite en Iran a l'époque seldjoukide d'après le *Kitāb al-Naqḍ*." *Le Monde iranien et l'Islam* 1 (1971).

———. "Le Mécénat de representation de Ta'ziye." *Le Monde Iranien et l'Islam* 6 (1974).

Corbin, H. "Pour une morphologie de la spiritualité shiᶜite." *Eranos Jahrbuch* 29 (1960).

———. "l'Ecole shaykhie en Théologie shiᶜite." *Annuaire de l'Ecole Pratique des Hautes Etudes, Section des Sciences Religieuses* 1960–61.

Dānish-Pajūh, M. T. "Dāvarī Miyān-e Pārsā va dānishmand." *Nashriyeh-ye Dānishkadeh-ye Adabiyyāt-e Tabrīz* (1957/Summer 1336).

Eliash, J. "The Ithna ᶜAsharī Shīᶜī Juristic Theory of Political and Legal Authority." *SI* 29 (1969).

———. "Some Misconceptions Regarding the Juridical Status of the Iranian *ᶜulamāᶜ*." IJMES 10 (1979).

Farzām, H. "Ikhtilāf-e Jāmī ba Shāh-e Valī." *Nashriyeh-ye Dānish-kadeh-ye Ababiyyāt-e Iṣfahān* 1 (1964/1343).

Fragner, B. "Ardabil zwischen Sultan und Schah: Zehn Urkunden Schah Ṭahmāsps II." *Turcica* 6 (1975).

Frye, R. N. "The Charisma of Kingship in Ancient Iran." *Iranica Antiqua* 4 (1964).

Glassen, E. "Schah Ismāᶜīl, ein Mahdi der Anatolischen Turkmenen?" *ZDMG* 121 (1971).

———. "Schah Ismāᶜīl I und die theologen seiner Zeit." *Der Islam* 48 (1971–72).

Gorjī, A. Q. "Taḥqiqī dar qiyās-e istinbāṭ." *Maqālāt va Barrasī-ha* 21–22 (1975/1354).

———. "Nigāhī bi taḥavvul-e ᶜilm-e uṣūl." *Maqālāt va Barrasī-ha* 13–16 (1973–74/1352).

Gringnaschi, M. "Quelques spécimens de la littérature sassanide conservés dans les bibliothèques d'Istanbul." *Journal Asiatique* 254 (1966).

Ḥaqīqat, A. "Dō farmān-e tārīkhī az dawrān-e ṣafaviyyeh dar masjid-e jāmiᶜ -e simnān." *Vaḥīd* 7, no. 1 (1970).

Hinz, W. "Schah Esmaᶜil II: Ein Beitrag zur Geschichte der Safaviden." *Mitteilungen des Seminars fur Orientalische Sprachen* 26 (Berlin, 1933).

Hodgson, M. G. S. "How Did the Early Shiᶜa Become Sectarian?" *Journal of the American Oriental Society* 75 (1955).

Inalcik, H. "Land Problems in the Ottoman Empire." *Muslim World* 45 (1955).

Iqbāl, A. "Muḥammad Ḥusayn Khān Marvī." *Yādigār* 2, no. 6 (1946).

———. "ᶜĀqibat-e Kār-e Nādir Shāh." *Yādigār* 2, no. 2 (1945).

———. "Vathīqa-ye ittiḥād-e Islām-e nādirī," *Yādigār* 4, no. 6 (1947).

———. "Ḥujjat al-Islām Ḥajj Muḥammad Bāqir Shaftī (1180–1260 Q.)." *Yādigār* 5, no. 0 (1949).

Ivanow, W. "A Forgotten Branch of the Ismāᶜīlīs." *JRAS* 14 (1938).

Kalberg, S. "Max Weber's Types of Rationality: Cornerstones for the Analysis of Rationalization Processes in History." *American Journal of Sociology* 85, no. 5 (1980).

Keddie, N. R. "Religion and Irreligion in Early Iranian Nationalism." *Comparative Studies in Society and History* 4 (1962).

Kohlberg, E. "The Development of the Imami Shiᶜi Doctrine of *Jihad*." *ZDMG* 126 (1976).

———. "From Imamiyya to Ithna–ᶜAshariyya." *BSOAS* 39 (1976).

Lambton, A. K. S. "The Theory of Kingship in the *Naṣiḥat al-Mulūk* of Ghazali." *Islamic Quarterly* 1 (1954).

———. "*Quis Custodiet Custodes*. Some Reflections on the Persian Theory of Government." *SI* 5–6 (1956).

———. "Justice in the Medieval Persian Theory of Kingship." *SI* 17 (1962).

———. "A Reconsideration of the Position of the *Marjaᶜ al-Taqlid* and the Religious Institution." *SI* 20 (1964).

———. "A Nineteenth-Century View of *Jihād*." *SI* 32 (1970).

———. "Some New Trends in Islamic Political Thought in Late Eighteenth and Early Nineteenth Century Persia." *SI* 40 (1974).

Lapidus, M. "The Separation of State and Religion in the Development of Early Islamic Society." *IJMES* 6 (1975).

Madelung, W. "The Assumption of the Title of *Shāhanshāh* by the Buyids and the Reign of the Daylam (*Dawlat al-Daylam*)." *Journal of Near Eastern Studies* 29 (1969).

———. "HISHĀM b. al-ḤAKAM." *EI*² 3.
———. "IMĀMA." *EI*² 3.
———. "ʿIṢMA." *EI*² 4.
———. "AKHBĀRIYYA." *EI*². supplement.
———. "A Treatise of the Sharīf al-Murtaḍā on the Legality of Working for the Government (*Masʾala fi'l-ʿamal maʿ'l-sulṭān*)." *BSOAS* 43 (1980).
———. "Shiʿite Discussions on the legality of the *Kharāj*." *Proceedings of the Ninth Congress of the Union Europeennes des Arabisants et Islamisants*. R. Peters, ed. Leiden, 1981.
———. "ʿABD -al-RAZZĀQ LĀHĪJĪ." *Encyclopedia Iranica.*
Melikoff, I. "Le problème Kizilbaš." Turcica 6 (1975).
Minorsky, V. "The Poetry of Shāh Ismāʿīl I." *BSOAS* 10 (1942).
———. Review of M. S. Ivanov, "The Babi Risings in Iran in 1848–1852." *BSOAS* 11 (1943–64).
———. "MUSHAʿSHAʿ." *EI Supplement* (1937).
Modarresī Ṭabāṭabāʾī, H. "Dhayl-e Chand athar va katība-ye tārīkhī-ye dīgar." *Vaḥīd* 5 (1969/1348).
———. "Dō risāla dar sayr va sulūk. Āqā Muḥammad Bīdābādī." *Vaḥīd* II, no. 4 (1973/1352).
Molé, M. "Les Kubrawiya entre Sunnisme et Shiisme aux huitième et neuvième siècles de l'Hégire." *REI* 29 (1961).
Mudarris Chahārdihī, M. "Āqā Muḥammad Riḍā Ṣahbā Qumsheh-ī." *Yādigār* 1 (1946/1325).
Mueller, G. H. "The Notion of Rationality in the Work of Max Weber." *Archives européennes de sociologie* 20, no. 1 (1979).
Nafīsī, S. "Saʿd al-Dīn Ḥamūya." *Yādigār* 2, no. 10 (1945).
Perry, R. J. "The Last Safavids, 1722–1773." *Iran* 9 (1971).
al-Qadi, W. "An Early Fatimid Political Document," *SI* 48 (1978).
Ritter, H. "Die Anfange der Ḥurūfīsekte." *Oriens*, 7 (1954).
Roemer, H. "Problèmes de l'histoire safavide avant la stabilisation de la dynastie sous Šāh ʿAbbās." *Actes. Vᵉ Congrès international d'Arabisants et d'Islamisants* (1970).
Savory, R. M. "The Principal Offices of the Safavid State During the Reign of Ismāʿīl I." *BSOAS* 23 (1960).
———. "The Provisional Administration of the Early Safavid Empire." *BSOAS* 27 (1964).
———. "The Office of *Khalīfat al-Khulafāʾ* under the Safavids." *Journal of American Oriental Society* 85 (1965).
———. "The Safavid State and Polity." *IS* 7 (1974).
Schacht, J. "Zur soziologischen Betrachtung des islamischen Rechts." *Der Islam* 22 (1935).
Scarcia, G. "A proposito del problema della sovranita presso gli Imamiti." *AION* 7 (1957).
———. "Intorno alle controversie tra *Uṣūlī* e *Akhbārī* presso gli Imamiti." *Rivista deglia Studi Orientali* 33 (1958).
———. "Dal ms., Egerton 1104 del 'British museum,' etc." *Aion* 14, no. 2 (1964).

———. "AL-ḤURR AL- ʿĀMILĪ." *EI*²3.

Scarcia-Amoretti, B. "L'Islam in Persia fra Timūr e Nādir." *Annali della Facolta di Lingue e Letterature Straniere Di Ca'Foscari* 13, no. 3 (1974).

Sepsis, A. "Quelques Mots sur l'Etat Religieux Actuel de la Perse." *Revue de l'Orient* 3 (1844).

Shaʿbānī, R. "Siyāsat-e Madhhabi-ye Nādir." *Vaḥīd* 7, no. 9 (1970).

Sperl, S. "Islamic Kingship and Arabic Panegyric Poetry in the Early 9th Century." *Journal of Arabic Literature* 8 (1977).

Tambiah, S. J. "Buddhism and This-Worldly Activity." *Modern Asian Studies* 7, no. 1 (1973).

Yazici, T. "GULSHANĪ." *EI*²2.

Zarrinkoob, A. H. "Persian Sufism in Historical Perspective." *IS* 3 (1970).

Unpublished Studies and Ph.D. Dissertations

Amanat, A. "The Early Years of the Babi Movement: Background and Development." D. Phil. thesis, Oxford University, 1981.

Calder, N. "The Structure of Authority in Imami Shiʿi Jurisprudence." Ph.D. thesis, University of London, 1980.

Dawood, A. H. H. O. M. "A Comparative Study of Arabic and Persian Mirrors for Princes from the Second to the Sixth Century A.H." Ph.D. thesis, University of London, 1965.

Dickson, M. A. "Shah Tahmasp and the Uzbeks." Ph.D. dissertation, Princeton University, 1958.

Madelung, W. "Lectures on History of Shīʿism." University of Chicago, 1976.

Modarresi Tabatabaʾi, H. "*Kharāj* in Shiʿi Law." D. Phil. thesis, Oxford University, 1982.

Index

ᶜAbbās I, the Great, 109, 175, 200, 206, 296n.18; and clerical notables, 123, 125; and kingship, 172, 180, 181; military actions of, 111, 192–93; rebellions under, 197, 198–99; and Sufism, 111, 114, 116–17, 119, 147, 211; and Sunnism, 120–21
ᶜAbbās II, 114, 116, 119, 124, 173, 190; conversion of Jews by, 189; and Sufism, 147–51, 152, 184–86, 191, 211, 212
ᶜAbbās III, 251
ᶜAbbasid caliphate, 27, 28, 29, 38, 40, 42, 49, 123; beginnings of, 33–34; and Imāmiyya, 57; and kingship, 93–94, 98, 99, 233–34; overthrown, 96
ᶜAbbās Mīrzā, 224
ᶜAbd al-ᶜĀlī, Shaykh, 137, 178
ᶜAbd al-Bāqī, Mīr Niẓām al-Dīn, 116
ᶜAbd al-Ḥusayn Mujtahid, Shaykh, 245
ᶜAbd al-Jabbār, Qāḍī, 283n.32
ᶜAbd al-Jalīl, Qāḍī, 30, 57, 65, 289n.168
ᶜAbd al-Laṭīf, 120
ᶜAbd al-Laṭīf Jāmī, 77
ᶜAbd al-Raḥīm Damāvandī, 116
ᶜAbd al-Razzāq Lāhījī, Mullā, 148, 150, 156, 175
ᶜAbdullāh Mujtahid, Mullā, 250
ᶜAbdullāh Tunī, Mullā, 172
Abraham, 176
Abū Bakr, 112
Abū Dharr, 204
Abū Ḥanīfa, 46, 48, 147, 166, 216, 285n.73
Abū Isḥaq Kāzirūnī, 112
Abū Jaᶜfar al-ᶜAmrī, 40–41
Abū Khadīja, 51, 232, 141–42
Abū'l Qāsim Amrī, 198
Abu'l-Qāsim al-Ḥusayn ibn ᶜAli al-Maghribī, 63
Abu'l-Suᶜūd, 193
Abū Naṣr Sābūr, 57
Abū Sahl Ismāᶜīl ibn ᶜAlī al-Nawbakhtī, 40–43, 284n.50
Abū Salama, 34
ᶜAdil Shāh, 216–17
Affectual action, 2–3
Afghānī, Jamāl ad-Dīn, 247
Afghan invasion, 154, 186, 191, 215, 216
Afshār family, 215–17, 262–63
Aḥmad Aḥsāʾī, Shaykh, 153, 219, 252–53
Aḥmad Ghaffārī, Qāḍī, 133
Aḥmad Pasha, 216
Aḥmad Qumī, 120
Aḥmad Tunī, Mullā, 153
Ahura Mazdā, 90
Aʾineh-ye Shāhī ("The Mirror for the

Jalayirids, 99
Jāmi ᶜAbbāsī, 175, 192, 196, 207–8, 231, 232
Jāmi ᶜal-Maqāṣid (al-Karakī), 142
Jāmi ᶜMufīdī, 117, 119, 127, 149
Jāvidān-nāmeh (Book of Eternity) (Faḍl Allāh Astarābādī), 72
Jawāhir al-Kalām (Najafī), 232
Jazīra-ye Akhḍar, 161–62
Jevdet Pasha, 267
Jews, 45, 86, 189, 250. *See also* Judaism
Jihād, 204, 230, 232, 241–42; in *Jāmi ᶜAbbāsī*, 175, 192; and political ethos of Islam, 33; restrictions on, 61–64, 142; against Russia, 224–25. See also *Ghazā*
John VIII, Pope, 88
Judaism, 86, 203, 311n.17. *See also* Jews
Junayd, 70, 79, 80, 82
Juristic principle, 14, 269–70
Justice: administration of, *see* Shiᶜite law; concept of, 85, 94–98, 203, 205, 222, 223, 227

Kalām al-Mahdī (Mushaᶜshaᶜ), 77
Kalamāt-e Maknūneh (Fayḍ), 301n.12
Kalimāt al-ᶜulyā, 74
Kamāl al-Dīn, 68
Kanī, Mullā ᶜAlī, 159, 228, 252
al-Karakī, Mīr Sayyid Ḥusayn, 136–37, 144
al-Karakī al-ᶜĀmili, Shaykh ᶜAlī, 14, 55, 145, 177, 178, 179, 183, 190, 302n.30, 303n.40; on juristic authority of *ᶜulamā*ᵓ, 140, 141–42; on *laᶜn*, 165; and Shiᶜite hierocracy, 107, 125, 133–37, 144, 159, 166, 206, 222; on taxation, 193–94, 230
Karbalā, 27, 73, 164, 190, 240, 241, 252
Karbalāᶜī, 114, 117, 118
Karīm Khān Zand, 186, 217, 221, 244, 250
Kārnāmāk, 92
al-Kashāf (Zamakhsharī), 205
Kashan, 106, 113, 188–89, 198, 201, 218, 246
Kashfī, Āqā Sayyid Jaᶜfar ibn Abī Isḥāq, 225–29, 232, 235, 236, 237
Kasravī, A., 183
Kautilya, 89, 100, 101
Kavi Vištāspi, 90
Kawthar pond, 166, 171–72
Kāzim Rashtī, Sayyid, 253, 254
Khabūshānī, Shaykh Ḥājī Muḥammad, 114
Khaksar, 244
Khalīfa, Shaykh, 69
Khalīfas, 110–11, 114, 163
*Khalifat-al-khulafa*ᵓ, 110–11
Khalīl Qazvīnī, Mullā, 152
Khalīlullāh, Shāh, 116–17, 250
Khalvatiyya, 112, 113
Khāniqāhs, 30, 66–67, 119, 149
Kharāj, 134, 136, 137, 142, 193–94, 230, 231
Khiḍr, Shaykh, 119, 158
Khumaynī, Āyatullah Rūḥullāh, 268–70, 305n.101, 325n.3
Khums, 127, 193, 230–31
Khunjī, Faḍl Allāh Ruzbihān, 79, 80, 83, 179
Khurasan, 69, 106, 116, 256
Khurasanians, 33–34
Khuzistan, 76–77
Khwāja ᶜAlī, Shaykh, 78
Khwāja ᶜAlī Akbar, 119
Khwāja Isḥaqkhatlānī, 75
Khwānsarī, Āqā Ḥusayn, 148, 151
Kilīd-e Bihisht (Qumī), 150
Kingship, 22; in dualistic theory of power, 225–29; and Fatḥ ᶜAlī Shāh, 222, 223–24; al-Murtaḍā on, 63–64; and Nādir Shāh, 216, 221; sacral, 5–9, 12, 85–89, 105, 200–204; under Safavids, 163–64, 171–201, 205–6, 221–22, 223, 227, 228; Susanian (patrimonial), 89–100, 176, 188, 211, 222; al-Ṭūsī on, 64
Kitāb al-Ghayba (al-Ṭūsī), 44
Kitāb al-Jihādiyya (Qāᵓim Maqām the Elder), 225
Kitāb al-Khilāf, (al-Ṭūsī), 54